Oxford Essential Arabic Dictionary

ENGLISH–ARABIC

ARABIC–ENGLISH

OXFORD
UNIVERSITY PRESS

Great Clarendon Street, Oxford OX2 6DP

Oxford University Press is a department of the University of Oxford.
It furthers the University's objective of excellence in research, scholarship, and education by publishing worldwide in

Oxford New York

Auckland Cape Town Dar es Salaam Hong Kong Karachi
Kuala Lumpur Madrid Melbourne Mexico City Nairobi
New Delhi Shanghai Taipei Toronto

With offices in

Argentina Austria Brazil Chile Czech Republic France Greece
Guatemala Hungary Italy Japan Poland Portugal Singapore
South Korea Switzerland Thailand Turkey Ukraine Vietnam

Published in the United States
by Oxford University Press Inc., New York

First edition published 2010

British Library Cataloguing in Publication Data

Data available

Library of Congress Cataloging in Publication Data

Data available

ISBN 978-0-19-956115-5

11

Typeset by Datagrafix, Inc.
Printed in China by Golden Cup

Preface

This dictionary is intended to help learners of Arabic and English. It contains a basic vocabulary in each language and highlights some of the difficulties of each of them. Pronunciation of English is given in IPA and Arabic headwords are given in alphabetical order with their vowels. Proper names of countries, cities, religions, etc are given in the alphabetical listing of headwords. Thanks are due to Mai Zaki and Muhammad Habib Bewley for their contributions and comments.

Raed Al-Jabari
Editor

تم إعداد هذا القاموس من أجل مساعدة دارسي اللغتين العربية والإنجليزية. يضم هذا القاموس المفردات الرئيسية في كلا اللغتين مع شرح كيفية استعمال بعض هذه المفردات. لتسهيل استخدام هذا القاموس، ولتحسين اللفظ عند دارسي اللغة العربية، تم ترتيب المفردات في الجزء العربي ترتيباً أبجدياً وتم تشكيلها بشكل دقيق وواضح. أما بالنسبة للجزء الإنجليزي، فقد تم اتباع الترتيب الأبجدي المتعارف عليه عالمياً للغة الأنجليزية. بالنسبة لأسماء الدول وأسماء الديانات والمدن الرئيسية في العالم، فقد تم ترتيبها ترتيباً أبجدياً في كِلا الجزئين.

تتقدم أسرة مُعدي هذا القاموس بجزيل بالشكر لمحمد حبيب بيولي ومي زكي على مشاركتهم القيِّمة وتقديم النُصح.

دكتور رائد يحيى الجَعبري
المحرر

Note on trademarks and proprietary status

This dictionary includes some words which have, or are asserted to have, proprietary status as trademarks or otherwise. Their inclusion does not imply that they have acquired for legal purposes a non-proprietary or general significance, nor any other judgement concerning their legal status. In cases where the editorial staff have some evidence that a word has proprietary status this is indicated by the label ®, but no judgement concerning the legal status of such words is made or implied thereby.

Abbreviations

adj	adjective	صِفة
adv	adverb	ظَرف
art	article	أداة تَعريف
aux v	auxiliary verb	فِعل مُساعِد
conj	conjunction	حَرف عَطف
contr	contracted form	صيغة مُختَصَرة
excl	exclamation	تَعَجُّب
interj	interjection	تَعَجُّب
modal v	modal verb	فعل مُساعِد
n	noun	اسم
num	numeral	عَدَد
phv	phrasal verb	عِبارة فِعل
pl	plural	جَمْع
prep	preposition	حَرف جَر
pron	pronoun	ضَمير
UK	British English	إنجليزِيَّة بَريطانيَّة
US	American English	إنجليزِيَّة أمريكِيَّة
v	verb	فِعل

الاختصارات ♦

demonstrative	أداة إشارة	أ إش
particle of comparison	أداة تَشبيه	أ تش
question forms	أداة استِفهام	أ إس
possessive	أداة مِلكِيَّة	أ م
negative	أداة نَفي	أ ن
conditional	أداة شَرط	أ شر
plural	جَمْع	ج
adverb	حال	ح
preposition	حَرف جَر	حج
verb	فِعل	ف
noun	اسْم	س
adjective	صِفة	ص
pronoun	ضَمير	ض
adverb	ظَرف	ظ
number	عَدَد	عد
feminine	مُؤَنَّث	م
masculine	مُذَكَّر	مذ
singular	مُفرَد	مف

Guide to the dictionary

Arabic-English

part of speech نوع الكَلا م

ذَهَبَ ف to go

irregular plural جَمع التكسير

طابِع س ج /طَوابِعُ/ (مُلْصَق) stamp

ج /طِباع/ (صِفَة في الإنْسان) character

discriminator شَرح المَعنى

أَبْقى ف (حافَظَ عَلى اسْتِمْرارِيَّة شَيْء)

to maintain

to keep (احْتَفَظ ب)

أَبْكَمُ ص م بَكْماءُ ج /بُكْم/ dumb

irregular feminine form المؤنث

Note on Arabic verbs
Arabic verbs in the English-Arabic section of the dictionary are given in their simple present form. In the Arabic-English section they are given in the simple past.
Note on Arabic nouns and adjectives in both sections
A dammah on the last letter of a word indicates it is a diptote. (م) after a noun means it is feminine, although it does not have a feminine ending. ج م indicates the irregular feminine plural of an adjective.

English-Arabic

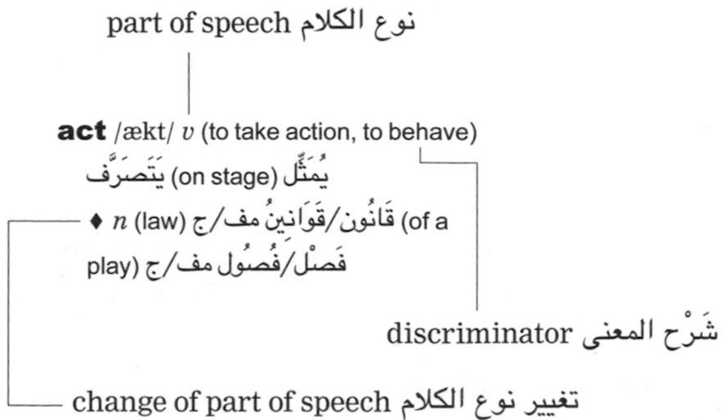

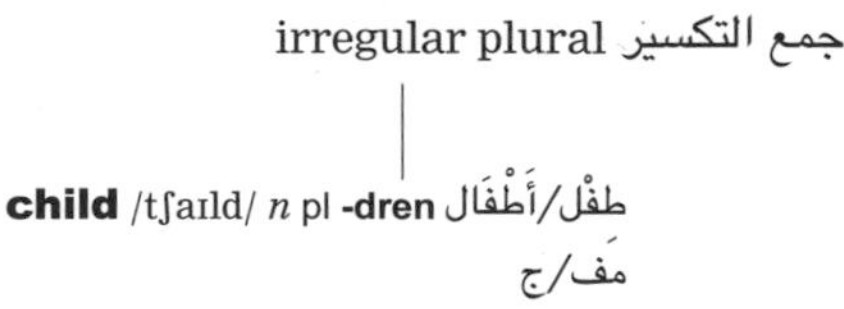

irregular parts of verb تصريف غير منتظم للفعل

know /nəʊ/ *v* **knew, known** (the answer, a fact) يَعْلَم

purse /pɜːs/ *n* (for money) مِحْفَظَة/مَحَافِظُ مف/ج (US: handbag) حَقِيبَة يَد نِسَائِيَّة

US English إنجليزية أمريكية

The Arabic Alphabet

Pronunciation guide	*Roman equivalent*
as the *a* in *act*	a
as the *b* in *boy*	b
as the *t* in *tap*	t
as the *th* in *thousand*	th
as the *j* in *jet*	j
strongly aspirated *h*	ẖ
as the *ch* in Scottish *loch*	kh
as the *d* in *dome*	d
as the *th* in *this*	dh
rolled *r* as in Spanish	r
as the *z* in *zebra*	z
as the *s* in *sun*	s
as the *sh* in *shut*	sh
strongly articulated *s* as the *s* in *somber*	s̱
strongly articulated *d* as in *duh*	ḏ
strongly articulated *t* as in *talk*	ṯ
strongly articulated, like the *th* in *though*	ẕ
a guttural 'ah'	'
a sound similar to a French *r*	gh
as the *f* in *fun*	f
strongly articulated *k* as in *Qatar*	q
as the *k* in *Kabul*	k
as the *l* in *London*	l
as the *m* in *man*	m
as the *n* in *noon*	n
as the *h* in *house*	h
as the *w* in *wife* or *oo* in *ooze*	w
as the *y* in *yacht* or *ee* in *meet*	y

Name of letter	*Final*	*Medial*	*Initial*	*Arabic letter*
ألف	ـا	ـاـ	اـ	ا
بَاء	ـب	ـبـ	بـ	ب
تاء	ـت	ـتـ	تـ	ت
ثاء	ـث	ـثـ	ثـ	ث
جيم	ـج	ـجـ	جـ	ج
حاء	ـح	ـحـ	حـ	ح
خاء	ـخ	ـخـ	خـ	خ
دال	ـد	ـدـ	دـ	د
ذال	ـذ	ـذـ	ذـ	ذ
راء	ـر	ـرـ	رـ	ر
زاي	ـز	ـزـ	زـ	ز
سين	ـس	ـسـ	سـ	س
شين	ـش	ـشـ	شـ	ش
صاد	ـص	ـصـ	صـ	ص
ضاد	ـض	ـضـ	ضـ	ض
طاء	ـط	ـطـ	طـ	ط
ظاء	ـظ	ـظـ	ظـ	ظ
عَيْن	ـع	ـعـ	عـ	ع
غَيْن	ـغ	ـغـ	غـ	غ
فاء	ـف	ـفـ	فـ	ف
قاف	ـق	ـقـ	قـ	ق
كاف	ـك	ـكـ	كـ	ك
لام	ـل	ـلـ	لـ	ل
ميم	ـم	ـمـ	مـ	م
نون	ـن	ـنـ	نـ	ن
هاء	ـه	ـهـ	هـ	ه
واو	ـو	ـوـ	وـ	و
ياء	ـي	ـيـ	يـ	ي

Arabic diacritics used in this dictionary

Pronunciation guide	*place*	*Diacritic*	
as *i* in *fit* فِعْل، مَرِض، سَمِعَ	رِ	kasrah	كَسْرَة
as *u* in *sun* ذَهَبَ، أَخَذَ، سَمَك	رَ	fat<u>h</u>ah	فَتْحَة
as *u* in *put* فُسْتُق، أَنْتُم، قُبول	رُ	<u>d</u>ammah	ضَمَّة
indicates the absence of a vowel as *n* in *sand* انْتِهاء، أَكْل، مَفْتوح	رْ	suk<u>u</u>n	سُكون
indicates that each letter must be stressed as the medial /n/ sounds in *unknown* شَغَّلَ، مُحَدِّث، تَسَوُّل	رّ	shaddah	شَدَّة

Note on diacritics

In the English–Arabic part of the dictionary, long vowels are vocalized, so a kasrah and a y<u>a</u>' together form a long *ee*. In the Arabic–English part the diacritics are not given for long vowels.

An alif without a hamza at the beginning of a word is an alif with a hamzat al-wa<u>s</u>l. If no vowel precedes this hamzat al-wa<u>s</u>l, it is pronounced *i*.

English pronunciation guide

1. Consonants الحُروف الساكِنة

p	pen	/pen/	s	see	/siː/
b	bad	/bæd/	z	zoo	/zuː/
t	tea	/tiː/	ʃ	shoe	/ʃuː/
d	did	/dɪd/	ʒ	vision	/'vɪʒn/
k	cat	/kæt/	h	hat	/hæt/
g	get	/get/	m	man	/mæn/
tʃ	chain	/tʃem/	n	now	/naʊ/
dʒ	jam	/dʒæm/	ŋ	sing	/sɪŋ/
f	fall	/fɔːl/	l	leg	/leg/
v	van	/væn/	r	red	/red/
θ	thin	/θm/	j	yes	/jes/
ð	this	/ðɪs/	w	wet	/wet/

2. The symbol (r) indicates that British pronunciation will have /r/ only if a vowel sound follows directly at the beginning of the next word, as in far away; otherwise the /r/ is omitted.

الرَمز (r) يُظهِر بأنه إذا جاء الحَرف /r/ في نِهاية الكَلمة فإنه لا يُلفَظ في اللهجة البريطانية إلا اذا بَدأت الكلمة التي تَالية بِحرف علة كما هو الحال في far away. أمّا في اللهجة الأمريكيَّة فإن الحَرف (r) يَلفَظ في جَميع الأحوال.

2. Vowels and diphthongs

حُروف العِلَّة ورُموز اللَفظ

iː	see	/siː/
i	happy	/ˈhæpi/
ɪ	sit	/sɪt/
e	ten	/ten/
æ	cat	/kæt/
ɑː	father	/ˈfɑːðə(r)/
ɒ	got	/gɒt/
ɔː	saw	/sɔː/
ʊ	put	/pʊt/
u	actual	/ˈæktʃuəl/
uː	too	/tuː/
ʌ	cup	/kʌp/

ɜː	fur	/fɜː(r)/
ə	about	/əˈbaʊt/
eɪ	say	/seɪ/
əʊ	go	/gəʊ/
oʊ	go	/goʊ/
aɪ	my	/maɪ/
ɔɪ	boy	/bɔɪ/
aʊ	now	/naʊ/
ɪə	near	/nɪə(r)/
eə	hair	/heə(r)/
ʊə	pure	/pjʊə(r)/

3. Stress

تَشديد الحُروف

Primary stress is shown by /ˈ/
Secondary stress is shown by /ˌ/

الرَمز /ˈ/ يُدَلل على تَشديد رَئيسي للحرف والرَمز /ˌ/ يُدلل على تَشديد خَفيف.

A

a /ə, eɪ/ *art* (see also: the) (أَدَاة نَكِرَة) ("a", "an" have no equivalent in Arabic)
I saw a tall man رَأَيْتُ رَجُلاً طَوِيلاً

abandon /ə'bændən/ *v* يَهْجُر

abduction /æb'dʌkʃn/ *n* اخْتِطَاف

ability /ə'bɪləti/ *n* pl **-ties** قُدْرَة

able /'eɪbl/ *adj* (skilled) مُتَمَكِّن (capable) قَادِر

abnormal /æb'nɔːml/ *adj* غَيْر عَادِيّ

abnormality /æbnɔː'mæləti/ *n* pl **-ties** عِلَّة/عِلَل مف/ج

abolish /ə'bɒlɪʃ/ *v* يُلْغِي

abortion /ə'bɔːʃn/ *n* إِجْهَاض

about /ə'baʊt/ *prep* فِي، عَن

above /ə'bʌv/ *prep* فَوْقَ
It's above the fire place. إِنَّهَا فَوْقَ المِدْفَأَة
It is above 20 degrees.
إِنَّهَا فَوْقَ 20 دَرَجَة مِئَوِيَّة

abroad /ə'brɔːd/ *adv* (to) لِلخَارِج (in) بِالخَارِج

absence /'æbsəns/ *n* غِيَاب

absent /'æbsənt/ *adj* غَائِب

absolute /'æbsəluːt/ *adj* مُطْلَق

abstract /'æbstrækt/ *adj* تَجْرِيدِيّ

Abu Dhabi /ˌabuː 'dɑːbi/ *n* أَبُو ظَبِيّ

abundant /ə'bʌndənt/ *adj* وَفِير

abuse /ə'bjuːz/ *v* يُسِيئ مُعَامَلَة
♦ /ə'bjuːs/ *n* إِسَاءَة مُعَامَلَة

academic /ækə'demɪk/ *adj* أَكَادِيمِيّ

academy /ə'kædəmi/ *n* pl **-mies** أَكَادِيمِيَّة

accelerate /ək'seləreɪt/ *v* يُسَرِّع

accent /'æksent/ *n* (in speaking) لَهْجَة (in writing) نَبْرَة

accept /ək'sept/ *v* يَقْبَل

access /'ækses/ *n* مَدْخَل/مَدَاخِلُ مف/ج

accessible /ək'sesəbl/ *adj* مُتَيَسِّر

accident /'æksɪdənt/ *n* (in car, etc) حَادِث/حَوَادِثُ مف/ج (coincidence) مُصَادَفَة

accidental /æksɪ'dentl/ *adj* عَارِض

accidentally /æksɪ'dentəli/ *adv* بِالصُدْفَة

accommodate /ə'kɒmədeɪt/ *v* يُوَفِّر سَكَناً

accommodation /əkɒmə'deɪʃn/ *n* US **-tions pl** مَسْكَن/مَسَاكِنُ مف/ج

A

accompany /əˈkʌmpəni/ *v* يَصْطَحِب

accomplishment /əˈkʌmplɪʃmənt/ *n* إِنْجَاز/إِنْجَازَات مف/ج

account /əˈkaʊnt/ *n* (in a bank) حِسَاب/حِسَابَات مف/ج (story) رِوَايَة

accountable /əˈkaʊntəbl/ *adj* مَسْئُول

accountant /əˈkaʊntənt/ *n* مُحَاسِب

accuracy /ˈækjərəsi/ *n* دِقَّة

accurate /ˈækjərət/ *adj* دَقِيق

accurately /ˈækjərətli/ *adv* بِدِقَّة

accusation /ækjuˈzeɪʃn/ *n* اتِّهَام/اتِّهَامَات مف/ج

accuse /əˈkjuːz/ *v* يَتَّهِم

accused /əˈkjuːzd/ *n* مُتَّهَم

accustom /əˈkʌstəm/ *v* يُعَوِّد

ache /eɪk/ *v* يُؤْلِم

achieve /əˈtʃiːv/ *v* يُنْجِز

achievement /əˈtʃiːvmənt/ *n* إِنْجَاز/إِنْجَازَات مف/ج

acid /ˈæsɪd/ *n* حِمْض/أَحْمَاض مف/ج

acknowledge /əkˈnɒlɪdʒ/ *v* (a mistake) يَعْتَرِف بِـ (a letter) يُؤَكِّد

acquaintance /əˈkweɪntəns/ *n* مَعْرِفَة/مَعَارِف مف/ج

acquire /əˈkwaɪə(r)/ *v* يَكْتَسِب

acre /ˈeɪkə(r)/ *n* أَكْر

across /əˈkrɒs/ *prep* (a road, river) عَبْرَ
♦ *adv* (to run, walk) مِن جَانِب لِآخَر

act /ækt/ *v* (to take action, to behave) يَتَصَرَّف (on stage) يُمَثِّل
♦ *n* (law) قَانُون/قَوَانِين مف/ج (of a play) فَصْل/فُصُول مف/ج

action /ˈækʃn/ *n* تَأْثِير/تَأْثِيرَات مف/ج

activate /ˈæktɪveɪt/ *v* يُشَغِّل

active /ˈæktɪv/ *adj* نَشِيط

activist /ˈæktɪvɪst/ *n* نَاشِط

activity /ækˈtɪvəti/ *n* pl **-ties** نَشَاط/أَنْشِطَة مف/ج

actor /ˈæktə(r)/ *n* مُمَثِّل

actress /ˈæktrəs/ *n* مُمَثِّلَة

actual /ˈæktʃuəl/ *adj* (words) حَقِيقِيّ (cost) فِعْلِيّ

actually /ˈæktʃuəli/ *adv* فِي الوَاقِع

acute /əˈkjuːt/ *adj* شَدِيد

adapt /əˈdæpt/ *v* يُكَيِّف

add /æd/ *v* يُضِيف

add up *v* يَجْمَع

addict /ˈædɪkt/ *n* مُدْمِن

addiction /əˈdɪkʃn/ *n* إِدْمَان

addition /əˈdɪʃn/ *n* (process) جَمْع

additional /əˈdɪʃənl/ *adj* إِضَافِيّ

address /əˈdres/ *n* عُنْوَان/عَنَاوِين مف/ج
♦ *v* (a letter) يُعَنْوِن (a meeting) يُخَاطِب

adequate /ˈædɪkwət/ *adj* كَافٍ

adequately /ˈædɪkwətli/ *adv* عَلَى نَحْوٍ كَافٍ

adhere /əd'hɪə(r)/ *v* يَتَقَيَّد بِـ

adjust /ə'dʒʌst/ *v* يُعَدِّل

adjustment /ə'dʒʌstmənt/ *n* تَعْديل/ تَعْديلات مف/ج

administration /ədmɪnɪ'streɪʃn/ *n* إدَارَة

administrative /əd'mɪnɪstrətɪv/ *adj* إدَاريّ

administrator /əd'mɪnɪstreɪtə(r)/ *n* مُدير

admiral /'ædmərəl/ *n* أَميرَال

admiration /ædmə'reɪʃn/ *n* إِعْجَاب

admire /əd'maɪə(r)/ *v* يُعْجَب بِـ

admission /əd'mɪʃn/ *n* قُبول

admit /əd'mɪt/ *v* (an accusation) يُقِرّ (to allow in) يُدْخِل

adolescent /ædə'lesnt/ *adj* مُرَاهِق

adopt /ə'dɒpt/ *v* يَتَبَنَّى

adoption /ə'dɒpʃn/ *n* تَبَنٍّ

adore /ə'dɔ:(r)/ *v* يُتَيَّم بِـ

adult /'ædʌlt/ *adj* بَالِغ
♦ *n* رَاشِد

advance /əd'vɑ:ns/ *v* (to go forward) يَتَقَدَّم (to progress) يَتَطَوَّر
♦ *n* (progress) تَقَدُّم (payment) دُفْعَة مُقَدَّمَة

advanced /əd'vɑ:nst/ *adj* مُتَقَدِّم

advantage /əd'vɑ:ntɪdʒ/ *n* ميزَة

adverse /'ædvɜ:s/ *adj* مُعَاكِس

advertise /'ædvətaɪz/ *v* يُعْلِن

advertisement /əd'vɜ:tɪsmənt/ *n* إِعْلَان/إِعْلَانَات مف/ج

advertising /'ædvətaɪzɪŋ/ *n* الإِعْلَان

advice /əd'vaɪs/ *n* نَصيحَة/نَصَائِح مف/ج

advise /əd'vaɪz/ *v* (to give advice to) يُرْشِد (caution) يَنْصَح

adviser /əd'vaɪzə(r)/ *n* **-sor** مُسْتَشَار , مُرْشِد

advocate /'ædvəkeɪt/ *n* مُحَامٍ

affair /ə'feə(r)/ *n* (scandal) فَضيحَة/ عَلَاقَة (relationship) فَضَائِح مف/ج

affect /ə'fekt/ *v* يُؤْثِر عَلَى

affection /ə'fekʃn/ *n* عَاطِفَة/عَوَاطِف مف/ج

affirm /ə'fɜ:m/ *v* يُؤَكِّد عَلَى

affirmative /ə'fɜ:mətɪv/ *adj* تَأْكيديّ

afford /ə'fɔ:d/ *v* يَسْتَطيع الضُفُوع

afraid /ə'freɪd/ *adj* خَائف

Africa /'afrɪkə/ *n* أَفْريقيَا

African /'æfrɪkən/ *adj, n* أَفْريقيّ/أَفَارِقَة ص/س/ج

after /'ɑ:ftə(r)/ *prep* بَعْد

aftermath /'ɑ:ftəmæθ/ *n* عَاقِبَة/عَوَاقِب مف/ج

afternoon /ɑ:ftə'nu:n/ *n* ظُهْر

afterward /'ɑ:ftəwəd(s)/ *adv* **-ds** فيمَا بَعْد

again /ə'gen/ *adv* ثَانيَة

A

against /ə'genst/ *prep* ضِدَّ

age /eɪʤ/ *n* عُمْر/أَعْمَار مف/ج

aged /'eɪʤd/ *adj* (old) مُسِنّ /'eɪʤɪd/ (of a certain age) مِن سِنّ

agency /'eɪʤənsi/ *n* pl **-cies** (business) وِكَالَة (of government) هَيْئَة

agenda /ə'ʤendə/ *n* جَدْوَل الأَعْمَال

agent /'eɪʤənt/ *n* (of an organization) عَمِيل/ (franchisee) وَكِيل/وُكَلَاءُ مف/ج عُمَلَاءُ مف/ج

aggression /ə'greʃn/ *n* عُدْوَان

aggressive /ə'gresɪv/ *adj* عُدْوَانِيّ

ago /ə'gəʊ/ *adv* فِي المَاضِي
not long ago مُنْذُ فَتْرَة لَيْسَت بَعِيدَة
It happened five days ago. حَدَثَت قَبْلَ خَمْسَة أَيَّام

agony /'ægəni/ *n* pl **-nies** أَلَم/آلَام مف/ج

agree /ə'gri:/ *v* (with sb) يَتَّفِق عَلَى (to do sth) يَقْبَل بِـ

agreement /ə'gri:mənt/ *n* (same opinion) تَوَافُق (document) اتِّفَاقِيَّة

agricultural /ægrɪ'kʌltʃərəl/ *adj* زِرَاعِيّ

agriculture /'ægrɪkʌltʃə(r)/ *n* زِرَاعَة

ahead /ə'hed/ *adv* قُدُماً

aid /eɪd/ *v* يُسَاعِد
♦ *n* مُسَاعَدَة

aim /eɪm/ *n* هَدَف/أَهْدَاف مف/ج

air /eə(r)/ *n* هَوَاء
♦ *v* يُهَوِّي

airline /'eəlaɪn/ *n* شَرِكَة طَيَرَان

airplane /'eəpleɪn/ *n* طَائِرَة

airport /'eəpɔ:t/ *n* مَطَار/مَطَارَات مف/ج

aisle /aɪl/ *n* مَمْشَى/مَمَاشٍ مف/ج

alarm /ə'lɑ:m/ *n* جِهَاز مُنَبِّه
♦ *v* يُخِيف

album /'ælbəm/ *n* أَلْبُوم/أَلَابِيمُ مف/ج

alcohol /'ælkəhɒl/ *n* كُحُول

alcoholic /ælkə'hɒlɪk/ *adj, n* مُدْمِن كُحُولِيَّات

Alexandria /,alɪg'zɑ:ndrɪə/ *n* الإِسْكَنْدَرِيَّة

Algeria /al'dʒɪərɪə/ *n* الجَزَائِر

Algerian /al'ʤɪərɪən/ *adj, n* جَزَائِرِيّ ص/س

Algiers /al'dʒɪəz/ *n* الجَزَائِر

alien /'eɪliən/ *n* أَجْنَبِيّ

alignment /ə'laɪnmənt/ *n* تَرْتِيب

alike /ə'laɪk/ *adv* بِنَفْس الطَرِيقَة

alive /ə'laɪv/ *adj* عَلَى قَيْد الحَيَاة

all /ɔ:l/ *adj* (with pl) جَمِيع ، كُلّ
all the banks جَمِيع البُنُوك
They're all here. جَمِيعُهُم هُنَا
all the money كُلّ الأَمْوَال
not all of them لَيْسَ كُلَّهُم
(with sing) كُلّ
It's all here. كُلُّهَا هُنَا
That's all I want. ذَلِكَ كُلُّ مَا أُرِيد
(temp) طِوَالَ
all summer طِوَالَ الصَيْف

♦ *adv* تَماماً

It's all dirty. إنَّهَا مُتَّسِخَة تَماماً

allegation /ælə'geɪʃn/ *n* ادِّعَاء/ادِّعَاءات مف/ج

allege /ə'ledʒ/ *v* يَدَّعِي

allegiance /ə'li:dʒəns/ *n* وَلاَء

allergic /ə'lɜ:dʒɪk/ *adj* حَسَّاس لِـ

allergy /'ælədʒi/ *n* pl **-gies** حَسَّاسيَّة

alleviate /ə'li:vieɪt/ *v* يُخَفِّف

alley /'æli/ *n* زُقَاق

alliance /ə'laɪəns/ *n* تَحَالُف

allow /ə'laʊ/ *v* (sb to do sth) يَسْمَح (smoking) يُجِيز (children) يَأْذَن

allowance /ə'laʊəns/ *n* إعَانَة

all right /ɔ:l'rʌɪt/ *interj* حَسَناً

almond /'ɑ:mənd/ *n* لَوْز

almost /'ɔ:lməʊst/ *adv* (fifty, etc) تَقْرِيباً (ready, etc) عَلَى الأَغْلَب

alone /ə'ləʊn/ *adv* وَحِيداً

along /ə'lɒŋ/ *prep* بِطُول

aloud /ə'laʊd/ *adv* بِصَوْت عالٍ

already /ɔ:l'redi/ *adv* بِالفِعْل

also /'ɔ:lsəʊ/ *adv* أَيْضاً

altar /'ɔ:ltə(r)/ *n* مَذْبَح/مَذَابِحُ مف/ج

alter /'ɔ:ltə(r)/ *v* يُغَيِّر

alteration /ɔ:ltə'reɪʃn/ *n* تَغْيِير/تَغْيِيرات مف/ج

alternate /ɔ:l'tɜ:nət/ *adj* (in series) مُتَنَاوِب (US: optional) خِيَارِيّ

alternative /ɔ:l'tɜ:nətɪv/ *adj* خِيَارِيّ/ ♦ *n* بَدِيل/بَدَائِلُ مف/ج

although /ɔ:l'ðəʊ/ *conj* مَعَ أَنَّ

Although he worked hard, he failed.

مَعَ أَنَّهُ اجْتَهَدَ فَقَدْ رَسَبَ

altitude /'æltɪtju:d/ *n* الارْتِفَاع العَامُودِيّ

altogether /ɔ:ltə'geðə(r)/ *adv* كَامِلَةً

always /'ɔ:lweɪz/ *adv* دَوْماً

I always leave at 5.

أُغَادِر دَوْماً فِي السَاعَة الخَامِسَة

I have always lived here.

لَقَد عِشْتُ هُنَا دَوْماً

amateur /'æmətə(r)/ *n* هَاوٍ

amaze /ə'meɪz/ *v* يُدْهِش

amazing /ə'meɪzɪŋ/ *adj* مُدْهِش

ambassador /æm'bæsədə(r)/ *n* سَفِير

amber /'æmbə(r)/ *n* كَهْرَمَان

ambiguous /æm'bɪgjuəs/ *adj* غَامِض

ambition /æm'bɪʃn/ *n* طُمُوح

ambitious /æm'bɪʃəs/ *adj* طَمُوح

ambulance /'æmbjələns/ *n* سَيَّارَة الإسْعَاف

amendment /ə'mendmənt/ *n* تَعْدِيل/ تَعْدِيلاَت مف/ج

America /ə'merɪkə/ *n* (the USA) أَمْرِيكَا (continent) القَارَّة الأَمْرِيكِيَّة

American /ə'merɪkən/ *adj, n* أَمْرِيكِيّ ص/س

Amman /ə'mɑ:n/ *n* عَمَّان

A

A

ammunition /æmju'nɪʃn/ *n* ذَخِيرَة

among /ə'mʌŋ/ *prep* وَسْطَ

amount /ə'maʊnt/ *n* (owing) مَبْلَغ (of people, etc) مِقْدَار/مَقَادِيرُ مف/ج

amplify /'æmplɪfaɪ/ *v* يُضَخِّم

amuse /ə'mju:z/ *v* (the children) يُسَلِّي (cartoons) يُضْحِك

amusement /ə'mju:zmənt/ *n* (quality) تَسْلِيَة (entertainment) وَسِيلَة تَسْلِيَة

an /ən, æn/ *art* (أَدَاة تَنْكِير)

analyse /'ænəlaɪz/ *v* US **-lyze** يُحَلِّل

analysis /ə'næləsɪs/ *n* pl **-lyses** تَحْلِيل/ تَحْلِيلاَت مف/ج

analyst /'ænəlɪst/ *n* مُحَلِّل

ancestor /'ænsestə(r)/ *n* سَلَف/أَسْلاَف مف/ج

ancestral /æn'sestrəl/ *adj* سَلَفِيّ

anchor /'æŋkə(r)/ *n* مِرْسَاة

ancient /'eɪnʃənt/ *adj* قَدِيم

and /ənd, ænd/ *conj* وَ

anecdote /'ænɪkdəʊt/ *n* حِكَايَة

angel /'eɪndʒl/ *n* مَلَك/مَلاَئِكَة مف/ج

anger /'æŋgə(r)/ *n* غَضَب

angle /'æŋgl/ *n* زَاوِيَة/زَوَايَا مف/ج

angry /'æŋgri/ *adj* غَاضِب

animal /'ænɪml/ *n* حَيَوَان/حَيَوَانَات مف/ج

ankle /'æŋkl/ *n* كَاحِل/كَوَاحِلُ مف/ج

anniversary /ænɪ'vɜ:səri/ *n* pl **-ries** ذِكْرَى سَنَوِيَّة

announce /ə'naʊns/ *v* يُعْلِن

announcement /ə'naʊnsmənt/ *n* إِعْلاَن

annoy /ə'nɔɪ/ *v* يُغْضِب

annoyance /ə'nɔɪəns/ *n* إِزْعَاج

annoying /ə'nɔɪɪŋ/ *adj* مُزْعِج

annual /'ænjuəl/ *adj* سَنَوِيّ
♦ *n* نَشْرَة سَنَوِيَّة

annually /'ænjuəli/ *adv* سَنَوِيّاً

anonymous /ə'nɒnɪməs/ *adj* مَجْهُول المَصْدَر

another /ə'nʌðə(r)/ *adj, pron* آخَرُ/ أُخْرَى مذ/م

answer /'ɑ:nsə(r)/ *v* (to reply) يَرُدّ (the question) يُجِيب
♦ *n* إِجَابَة

ant /ænt/ *n* نَمْلَة/نَمْل مف/ج

antenna /æn'tenə/ *n* هَوَائِيّ/هَوَائِيَّات مف/ج

antibiotic /æntibaɪ'ɒtɪk/ *n* مُضَادّ حَيَوِيّ

antisocial /ænti'səʊʃl/ *adj* غَيْر اجْتِمَاعِيّ

anxiety /æŋ'zaɪəti/ *n* pl **-ties** قَلَق

anxious /'æŋkʃəs/ *adj* قَلِق

any /'eni/ *adj* (in questions, negatives) أَيّ
Is there any milk?
هَل يُوجَد أَيّ مِن الحَلِيب؟

Did you buy any cigarettes? هَل اِشْتَرَيْتَ أَيّاً مِن السَجَائِر؟
I haven't got any money. لاَ أَمْلُك أَيّاً مِن المَال
We didn't see any soldiers. لَم نَرَ أَيّ جُنْدِيّ
Use any card you want. اسْتَخْدِم أَيّ بِطَاقَة تُرِيد
♦ *pron* (in questions, negatives) أَيّ
Have you got any left? هَل تَبَقَّى لَدَيْكَ أَيّ شَيْء؟
We didn't see any of them. لَم نَرَ أَيّاً مِنْهُم
♦ *adv* (expressing degree) أَيّ حَدّ أَو مَدَى
It can't get any worse. لاَ يُمْكِن أَن تَسُوء أَكْثَر

anybody /'enibɒdi/ *pron* (see anyone)

anyhow /'enihaʊ/ *adv* عَلَى أَيّ حَال

anyone /'eniwʌn/ *pron* أَيّ شَخْص
Anyone can do that. أَيّ شَخْص يَسْتَطِيع عَمَل ذَلِكَ
I can't see anyone there. لاَ أَسْتَطِيع رُؤْيَة أَيّ شَخْص هُنَاكَ
Did anyone phone? هَل هَاتَفَ أَيّ شَخْص؟

anything /'eniθɪŋ/ *pron* أَيّ شَيْء

anyway /'eniweɪ/ *adv* عَلَى أَيّ حَال

anywhere /'eniweə(r)/ *adv* فِي أَيّ مَكَان

apart /ə'pɑːt/ *adv* بَعِيداً عَن البَعْض

apartment /ə'pɑːtmənt/ *n* شَقَّة/شِقَق مف/ج

apologize /ə'pɒlədʒaɪz/ *v* يَعْتَذِر

apology /ə'pɒlədʒi/ *n* pl **-gies** اعْتِذَار/اعْتِذَارَات مف/ج

apparatus /æpə'reɪtəs/ *n* جِهَاز/أَجْهِزَة مف/ج

apparent /ə'pærənt/ *adj* وَاضِح

apparently /ə'pærəntli/ *adv* مِن الوَاضِح

appeal /ə'piːl/ *n* طَلَب/طَلَبَات مف/ج

appear /ə'pɪə(r)/ *v* (to come into view) يَظْهَر (to seem) يَبْدُو

appearance /ə'pɪərəns/ *n* (of a person) هَيْئَة (of a place) مَظْهَر/مَظَاهِر مف/ج

appetite /'æpɪtaɪt/ *n* شَهِيَّة

applaud /ə'plɔːd/ *v* يُصَفِّق (لإِظْهَار الإِعْجَاب)

applause /ə'plɔːz/ *n* التَصْفِيق (لإِظْهَار الإِعْجَاب)

apple /'æpl/ *n* تُفَّاحَة/تُفَّاح مف/ج

appliance /ə'plaɪəns/ *n* أَدَاة/أَدَوَات مف/ج

application /æplɪ'keɪʃn/ *n* (for a job, etc) التَقَدُّم بِطَلَب (of the rules) تَطْبِيق

apply /ə'plaɪ/ *v* (ointment, etc) يَدْهَن (عَلَى الجِلْد) (force) يُطَبِّق (for a job) يَتَقَدَّم بِطَلَب

appoint /ə'pɔɪnt/ *v* يُعَيِّن

appointment /ə'pɔɪntmənt/ *n* (engagement) مَوْعِد/مَوَاعِيد مف/ج

A

(of a member, etc) تَعْيِين

appreciate /ə'pri:ʃieɪt/ *v* يُقَدِّر

approach /ə'prəʊtʃ/ *v* يَقْتَرِب مِن
♦ *n* نَهْج

appropriate /ə'prəʊpriət/ *adj* (clothes) مُلَائِم (behaviour) لَائِق

approval /ə'pru:vl/ *n* تَصْدِيق

approve /ə'pru:v/ *v* (accounts, etc) يُصَدِّق (to agree) يُوَافِق عَلَى

approximately /ə'prɒksɪmətli/ *adv* تَقْرِيباً

apricot /'eɪprɪkɒt/ *n* مِشْمِش

April /'eɪprəl/ *n* (see August) شَهْر نِيسَان

Arab /'ærəb/ *adj, n* عَرَبِيّ/عَرَب ص/س/ج

Arabian /ə'reɪbiən/ *adj, n* عَرَبِيّ/عَرَب ص/س/ج

Arabic /'ærəbɪk/ *adj* عَرَبِيّ
♦ *n* اللُغَة العَرَبِيَّة
to learn Arabic يَتَعَلَّم اللُغَة العَرَبِيَّة
to answer in Arabic يَجِيب بِالعَرَبِيَّة

arch /ɑ:tʃ/ *n* قَوْس/أَقْوَاس مف/ج

architect /'ɑ:kɪtekt/ *n* مُهَنْدِس مِعْمَارِيّ

architecture /'ɑ:kɪtektʃə(r)/ *n* فَنّ العِمَارَة

archives /'ɑ:kaɪvz/ *n* مَحْفُوظَات

area /'eəriə/ *n* (of room, etc) مِنْطَقَة/مَنَاطِق مف/ج (region) إِقْلِيم/أَقَالِيم مف/ج

arena /ə'ri:nə/ *n* مَيْدَان/مَيَادِين مف/ج

Argentina /ˌɑ:dʒən'ti:nə/ *n* الأَرْجَنْتِين

Argentinian /ˌɑ:dʒən'tɪniən/ *adj, n* أَرْجَنْتِينِيّ ص/س

aren't /ɑ:nt/ *contr* (= are not: see be)

argue /'ɑ:gju:/ *v* (to quarrel) يَتَجَادَل (the case) يُحَاوِل بَرْهَنَة

argument /'ɑ:gjumənt/ *n* (with conflict) جِدَال (reasoning debate) مُنَاظَرَة

arm /ɑ:m/ *n* ذِرَاع/أَذْرُع (م) مف/ج

arms /ɑ:mz/ *n* سِلَاح/أَسْلِحَة مف/ج

arm /ɑ:m/ *v* يُسَلِّح

armed /ɑ:md/ *adj* مُسَلَّح

army /'ɑ:mi/ *n* pl **-mies** جَيْش/جُيُوش مف/ج

around /ə'raʊnd/ *adv* فِي مَكَان قَرِيب
♦ *prep* (the house, etc) حَوْلَ (fifty, etc) حَوَالَي

arrange /ə'reɪndʒ/ *v* (a meeting) يُرَتِّب (flowers, etc) يُنَسِّق

arrangement /ə'reɪndʒmənt/ *n* تَرْتِيب/تَرْتِيبَات مف/ج

arrest /ə'rest/ *v* يَعْتَقِل
♦ *n* اعْتِقَال/اعْتِقَالَات مف/ج

arrival /ə'raɪvl/ *n* وُصُول

arrive /ə'raɪv/ *v* يَصِل

arrogance /'ærəgəns/ *n* تَكَبُّر

arrogant /'ærəgənt/ *adj* مُتَكَبِّر

arrow /'ærəʊ/ *n* سَهْم/سِهَام مف/ج

art /ɑːt/ *n* (of a culture) فَنّ/فُنُون (skill) مَهَارَة

artery /'ɑːtəri/ *n* pl **-ries** شِرْيَان/شَرَايِين مف/ج

arthritis /ɑː'θraɪtɪs/ *n* اِلْتِهَاب المَفَاصِل

artichoke /'ɑːtɪtʃəʊk/ *n* خُرْشُوف

article /'ɑːtɪkl/ *n* (text) مَقَال/مَقَالاَت (item) قِطْعَة/قِطَع مف/ج مف/ج

artificial /ɑːtɪ'fɪʃl/ *adj* اِصْطِنَاعِيّ

artist /'ɑːtɪst/ *n* فَنَّان

as /əz, æz/ *conj* (when, while) بَيْنَمَا *as we left* بَيْنَمَا غَادَرْنَا (in the way that) مِثْلَمَا *As you know, ...* مِثْلَمَا تَعْلَم (because) لِأَنَّ *As there were no trains, we got the bus.* لِأَنَّهُ لَم يَكُن هُنَاكَ قِطَارَات أَخَذْنَا البَاص (in contrasts) كَأَنَّ *as if ...: We talked on as if nothing had happened.* تَابَعْنَا الحَدِيث وَكَأَنَّهُ لَم يَحْدُث شَيْء (in comparisons) مِثْل *as ... as: He's as strong as I am.* قُوَّتُهُ مِثْلَ قُوَّتِي

ash /æʃ/ *n* رَمَاد

ashamed /ə'ʃeɪmd/ *adj* خَجُول

Asia /'eɪʃə/ *n* آسِيَا

Asian /'eɪʃn/ *adj, n* آسْيَوِيّ ص/س

aside /ə'saɪd/ *adv* جَانِباً

ask /ɑːsk/ *v* (about sth) يَسْأَل (the price, sb's name) يَطْلُب (sb to do sth) يَدْعُو

asleep /ə'sliːp/ *adj* نَائِم

aspect /'æspekt/ *n* مَظْهَر/مَظَاهِر مف/ج

ass /æs/ *n* حِمَار/حَمِير مف/ج

assassin /ə'sæsɪn/ *n* قَاتِل

assassination /əsæsɪ'neɪʃn/ *n* اِغْتِيَال/اِغْتِيَالاَت مف/ج

assault /ə'sɔːlt/ *v* (with violence) يَغْتَصِب (sexually) يَعْتَدِي عَلَى

assemble /ə'sembl/ *v* (people) يُجَمِّع (a kit) يَتَجَمَّع

assembly /ə'sembli/ *n* تَجَمُّع/تَجَمُّعَات مف/ج

assert /ə'sɜːt/ *v* يُؤَكِّد

assess /ə'ses/ *v* يُقَيِّم

assessment /ə'sesmənt/ *n* تَقْيِيم/تَقْيِيمَات مف/ج

asset /'æset/ *n* شَيْء نَافِع

assignment /ə'saɪnmənt/ *n* (task) مَهَمَّة/مَهَام مف/ج (in education) وَاجِب/وَاجِبَات مف/ج

assist /ə'sɪst/ *v* يُسَاعِد

assistance /ə'sɪstəns/ *n* مُسَاعَدَة

assistant /ə'sɪstənt/ *n* مُسَاعِد

associate /ə'səʊsieɪt/ *v* يَرْبِط
♦ /ə'səʊsiət/ *n* شَرِيك

A

associated /ə'səʊsieɪtɪd/ *adj* مُتَرَابِط

association /əsəʊsi'eɪʃn/ *n* /اتِّحَاد اتِّحَادَات مف/ج

assume /ə'sjuːm/ *v* يَفْتَرِض

assumption /ə'sʌmpʃn/ *n* /افْتِرَاض افْتِرَاضَات مف/ج

assurance /ə'ʃʊərəns/ *n* /ضَمَان ضَمَانَات مف/ج

assure /ə'ʃʊə(r)/ *v* يَضْمَن

asthma /'æsmə/ *n* رَبْو

astonish /ə'stɒnɪʃ/ *v* يُدْهِش

asylum /ə'saɪləm/ *n* (political) لُجُوء (institution) مُسْتَشْفَى الأَمْرَاض العَقْلِيَّة

at /ət, æt/ *prep* (time) فِي
at 4.30 p.m.
فِي السَاعَة الرَابِعَة وَالنصْف مَسَاءً
(place) عِنْدَ
we meet at the station نَلْتَقِي عِنْدَ المَحَطَّة
to wait at the door يَنْتَظِر عِنْدَ البَاب
(with speeds, etc) عَلَى
at 800 km per hour
عَلَى سُرْعَة 800 كم فِي السَاعَة
at boiling point عَلَى دَرَجَة الغَلَيَان
(in the home of) فِي
I'm staying at Jack's.
أَمْكُثُ فِي مَنْزِل جَاك (in email: @) عَلَى

Athens /'aθɪnz/ *n* أَثِينَا

athlete /'æθliːt/ *n* رِيَاضِيّ

athletic /æθ'letɪk/ *adj* رِيَاضِيّ

Atlantic Ocean /ət'læntɪk/ *n* المُحِيط الأَطْلَسِيّ

atmosphere /'ætməsfɪə(r)/ *n* (earth's) الغِلَاف الجَوِّيّ (in office, etc) جَوّ/أَجْوَاء مف/ج

atom /'ætəm/ *n* ذَرَّة

atomic /ə'tɒmɪk/ *adj* (of atoms) ذَرِّيّ (energy) نَوَوِيّ

atrocity /ə'trɒsəti/ *n* pl **-ties** وَحْشِيَّة

attach /ə'tætʃ/ *v* (a cable) يُوَصِّل (a letter) يُرْفِق

attack /ə'tæk/ *n* هُجُوم/هَجَمَات مف/ج
♦ *v* يُهَاجِم

attempt /ə'tempt/ *n* (try) مُحَاوَلَة
♦ *v* (to try to do sth) يُحَاوِل

attend /ə'tend/ *v* يَحْضُر

attendance /ə'tendəns/ *n* حُضُور

attendant /ə'tendənt/ *n* مُرَاقِب

attention /ə'tenʃn/ *n* انْتِبَاه

attitude /'ætɪtjuːd/ *n* مَوْقِف/مَوَاقِف مف/ج

attorney /ə'tɜːni/ *n* مُحَامٍ

attract /ə'trækt/ *v* يَجْذِب

attraction /ə'trækʃn/ *n* (feature) جَذْب (of opposites) تَجَاذُب

attractive /ə'træktɪv/ *adj* جَذَّاب

aubergine /'əʊbəʒiːn/ *n* /بَاذِنْجَانَة بَاذِنْجَان مف/ج

auction /'ɔːkʃn/ *n* مَزَاد

audience /'ɔːdiəns/ *n* حُضُور

audio /'ɔːdiəʊ/ *adj* سَمْعِيّ

A

audit /'ɔːdɪt/ *n* مُرَاجَعَة حِسَابَات

auditor /'ɔːdɪtə(r)/ *n* مُرَاجِع حِسَابَات

August /'ɔːgəst/ *n* شَهْر آب

every August كُلّ شَهْر آب

in August فِي شَهْر آب

next August شَهْر آب القَادِم

last August شَهْر آب المَاضِي

aunt /ɑːnt/ *n* (mother's sister) خَالَة (father's sister) عَمَّة (mother's brother's wife) زَوْجَة خَال (father's brother's wife) زَوْجَة عَمّ

Australia /ɒ'streɪlɪə/ *n* أُسْتُرَالِيَا

Australian /ɒ'streɪliən/ *adj, n* أُسْتُرَالِيّ ص/س

Austria /'ɒstrɪə/ *n* النِمْسَا

Austrian /'ɒstrɪən/ *adj, n* نِمْسَاوِيّ ص/س

authentic /ɔː'θentɪk/ *adj* أَصْلِيّ

author /'ɔːθə(r)/ *n* مُؤَلِّف

authorize /'ɔːθəraɪz/ *v* يُفَوِّض

authority /ɔː'θɒrəti/ *n* pl **-ties** سُلْطَة

autobiography /ɔːtəbaɪ'ɒgrəfi/ *n* pl **-phies** سِيرَة ذَاتِيَّة

automatic /ɔːtə'mætɪk/ *adj* تِلْقَائِيّ

automatically /ɔːtə'mætɪkli/ *adv* تِلْقَائِيّاً

autumn /'ɔːtəm/ *n* خَرِيف

available /ə'veɪləbl/ *adj* مُتَوَفِّر

avenue /'ævənjuː/ *n* طَرِيق مُشَجَّر

average /'ævərɪʤ/ *adj* مُتَوَسِّط

avocado /ævə'kɑːdəʊ/ *n* أَفُوكَادُو

avoid /ə'vɔɪd/ *v* يَتَجَنَّب

await /ə'weɪt/ *v* يَنْتَظِر

awake /ə'weɪk/ *adj* مُسْتَيْقِظ

award /ə'wɔːd/ *n* جَائِزَة/جَوَائِزُ مف/ج ♦ *v* يَمْنَح

aware /ə'weə(r)/ *adj* مُدْرِك

away /ə'weɪ/ *adv* بَعِيد

awe /ɔː/ *n* رَهْبَة

awesome /'ɔːsəm/ *adj* مُدْهِش

awful /'ɔːfl/ *adj* رَدِيء

awkward /'ɔːkwəd/ *adj* (question) أَخْرَق/خَرْقَاءُ مذ/م (clumsy) مُحْرِج

axe /æks/ *n* US **ax** بَلْطَة/بَلَطَات مف/ج

B

baby /ˈbeɪbi/ *n* pl **-bies** طِفْل/أَطْفَال مف/ج

bachelor /ˈbætʃələ(r)/ *n* أَعْزَب/عُزَّاب مف/ج

back /bæk/ *adv* إِلَى الخَلْف
♦ *n* ظَهْر

backbone /ˈbækbəʊn/ *n* العَمُود الفَقَرِيّ

background /ˈbækgraʊnd/ *n* (of a picture) خَلْفِيَّة (social, etc) خِبْرَة

backward /ˈbækwəd/ *adj* مُتَخَلِّف
♦ *adv* **-ds** إِلَى الوَرَاء

bacon /ˈbeɪkən/ *n* لَحْم الخِنْزِير

bacteria /bækˈtɪəriə/ *n pl* جَرَاثِيم

bad /bæd/ *adj* (not good) فَاسِد
a bad meal وَجْبَة فَاسِدَة
(teacher, dancer) سَيِّئ
(accident, injuries) خَطِير
It was a bad accident. كَانَ حَادِثاً خَطِيراً
(evil) شِرِّير
He was a bad man. كَانَ رَجُلاً شِرِّيراً
(harmful) ضَارّ
Cigarettes are bad for you.
السَجَائِر مُضِرَّة لَكَ

badge /bædʒ/ *n* شَارَة

badly /ˈbædli/ *adv* عَلَى نَحْو سَيِّئ

bag /bæg/ *n* (for shopping) حَقِيبَة/حَقَائِب
(for rubbish) كِيس/أَكْيَاس مف/ج مف/ج

baggage /ˈbægɪdʒ/ *n* أَمْتِعَة

Baghdad /bagˈdad/ *n* بَغْدَاد

Bahrain /bɑːˈreɪn/ *n* البَحْرَيْن

Bahraini /bɑːˈreɪni/ *adj, n*
بَحْرَيْنِيّ ص/س

bail /beɪl/ *n* كَفَالَة

bait /beɪt/ *n* طُعْم

bake /beɪk/ *v* يَخْبِز

baker /ˈbeɪkə(r)/ *n* خَبَّاز

balance /ˈbæləns/ *n* (equilibrium) تَوَازُن (on account) رَصِيد/أَرْصِدَة مف/ج

balcony /ˈbælkəni/ *n* pl **-nies** شُرْفَة

ball /bɔːl/ *n* (for games) كُرَة (dance) رَقْص

ballet /ˈbæleɪ/ *n* رَقْصَة البَالِيه

balloon /bəˈluːn/ *n* بَالُون/بَالُونَات مف/ج

ballot /ˈbælət/ *n* اقْتِرَاع/اقْتِرَاعَات مف/ج

ban /bæn/ *v* (smoking) يَحْظُر
♦ *n* حَظْر

band /bænd/ *n* (of musicians) فِرْقَة مُوسِيقِيَّة (for a parcel, box) شَرِيط/شَرَائِط مف/ج

bang /bæŋ/ *n* دَوِيّ

bank /bæŋk/ *n* (financial) مَصْرِف/مَصَارِفُ مف/ج (of a river) ضَفَّة/ضِفَاف مف/ج
♦ *v* يُودِع

banker /ˈbæŋkə(r)/ *n* مَصْرِفِيّ

bankrupt /ˈbæŋkrʌpt/ *adj, n* مُفْلِس

bankruptcy /ˈbæŋkrʌptsi/ *n* pl **-cies** إِفْلَاس

banner /ˈbænə(r)/ *n* رَايَة

bar /bɑː(r)/ *n* (of metal or wood) قَضِيب حَدِيدِيّ أَو خَشَبِيّ (of a hotel, etc) حَانَة

bare /beə(r)/ *adj* (feet, etc) عَارٍ (empty) فَارِغ

barely /ˈbeəli/ *adv* بِالكَاد

bargain /ˈbɑːgən/ *n* صَفْقَة

bark /bɑːk/ *v* يَنْبَح

barley /ˈbɑːli/ *n* شَعِير

barman /ˈbɑːmən/ *n* pl **-men** سَاقٍ

barmaid /ˈbɑːmeɪd/ *n* سَاقِيَة

barn /bɑːn/ *n* حَظِيرَة

barrel /ˈbærəl/ *n* بِرْمِيل/بَرَامِيلُ مف/ج

barrier /ˈbæriə(r)/ *n* حَاجِز/حَوَاجِزُ مف/ج

base /beɪs/ *n* قَاعِدَة/قَوَاعِدُ مف/ج
♦ *v* يَبْنِي عَلَى أَسَاس

baseball /ˈbeɪsbɔːl/ *n* لَعْبَة البِيسْبُول

basement /ˈbeɪsmənt/ *n* قَبْو/أَقْبَاء مف/ج

basic /ˈbeɪsɪk/ *adj* رَئِيسِيّ

basin /ˈbeɪsn/ *n* حَوْض/أَحْوَاض مف/ج

basis /ˈbeɪsɪs/ *n* pl **-ses** أَسَاس/أُسُس مف/ج

basket /ˈbɑːskɪt/ *n* سَلَّة/سِلَال مف/ج

basketball /ˈbɑːskɪtbɔːl/ *n* كُرَة السَّلَّة

bass /beɪs/ *n* (in singing) جَهُور (in music) أَخْفَض صَوْت في العَزْف /bæs/ pl (fish) سَمَك القَارُوس

bat /bæt/ *n* (in sports) مَضْرَب/مَضَارِبُ مف/ج (mammal) خُفَّاش/خَفَافِيشُ مف/ج

batch /bætʃ/ *n* مَجْمُوعَة

bath /bɑːθ/ *n* حَوْض اسْتِحْمَام

bathroom /ˈbɑːθrʊm/ *n* (for washing, etc) حَمَّام/حَمَّامَات مف/ج (with only a toilet) مِرْحَاض/مَرَاحِيضُ مف/ج

battery /ˈbætəri/ *n* pl **-ries** بَطَّارِيَّة

battle /ˈbætl/ *n* (between armies) مَعْرَكَة/مَعَارِكُ مف/ج (struggle) كِفَاح
♦ *v* يُصَارِع

bay /beɪ/ *n* خَلِيج/خُلْجَان مف/ج

be /bi, bi/ *aux v* **is, are, was, were, been** (continuous tenses) يَكُون (فِعْل مُسَاعِد يَدُلّ عَلَى الاسْتِمْرَارِيَّة)
She is sleeping. هِيَ نَائِمَة
He was writing. كَانَ يَكْتُب (in passives) يَكُون
He was killed in an accident. قُتِلَ فِي حَادِث
They were taught by Professor Stein. تَعَلَّمُوا عَلَى يَد الأُسْتَاذ سْتَيْن
(descriptions) يَكُون

B

She is blonde. هِيَ شَقْرَاء
He is alive. هُوَ حَيّ
They are angry. هُم غَاضِبُون
I am hungry/thirsty. أَنَا جَائِع/عَطْشَان
We're hot/cold. نَشْعُر بِالحَرّ/بِالبَرْد
It's in Saudi Arabia. هُوَ فِي السَعُودِيَّة
(with quantities) يَكُون
There is one mistake. يُوجَد خَطَأ وَاحِد
There are many people in the square.
يُوجَد العَدِيد مِن النَاس فِي السَاحَة
(time) يَكُون
It is/it's 12 o'clock.
السَاعَة هِيَ الثَانِيَة عَشْرَة

beach /biːtʃ/ *n* شَاطِئ/شَوَاطِئ مف/ج

bead /biːd/ *n* خَرَزَة/خَرَز مف/ج

beam /biːm/ *n* (of light) شُعَاع/أَشِعَّة
(in house) عَارِضَة/عَوَارِض مف/ج

bean /biːn/ *n* حَبَّة/حُبُوب مف/ج

bear /beə(r)/ *n* دُبّ/دِبَبَة مف/ج
♦ *v* **bore, borne** يَتَحَمَّل

beard /bɪəd/ *n* لِحْيَة/لِحَى مف/ج

beat /biːt/ *v* **beat, beaten** (to defeat) يَهْزِم
(to hit) يَضْرِب

beautiful /ˈbjuːtɪfl/ *adj* جَمِيل

beauty /ˈbjuːti/ *n* جَمَال

because /bɪˈkɒz/ *conj* بِسَبَب

become /bɪˈkʌm/ *v* **became, become** يُصْبِح

bed /bed/ *n* سَرِير/أَسِرَّة مف/ج

bedroom /ˈbedrʊm/ *n* غُرْفَة النَوْم

bee /biː/ *n* نَحْلَة/نَحْل مف/ج

beef /biːf/ *n* لَحْم البَقَر

beer /bɪə(r)/ *n* بِيرَة

beetroot /ˈbiːtruːt/ *n* شَمَنْدَر، بَنْجَر

before /bɪˈfɔː(r)/ *prep* (earlier than) قَبْلَ
(in front of) أَمَامَ

beg /beg/ *v* (for money) يَتَسَوَّل (to plead with) يَتَوَسَّل إِلَى

begin /bɪˈgɪn/ *v* **began, begun** (terms, classes, etc) يَبْدَأ (a lesson, a speech) يَسْتَهِلّ

beginner /bɪˈgɪnə(r)/ *n* مُبْتَدِئ

beginning /bɪˈgɪnɪŋ/ *n* بِدَايَة

behave /bɪˈheɪv/ *v* يَتَصَرَّف

behaviour /bɪˈheɪvjə(r)/ *n* US **-vior** سُلُوك

behind /bɪˈhaɪnd/ *prep* (at the back of) خَلْفَ
behind the sofa خَلْفَ الأَرِيكَة (in order) وَرَاء
♦ *adv* فِي الخَلْف
to stay behind يَتَخَلَّف
to leave sth behind يَتْرُك شَيْئاً مَا خَلْفه

Beijing /beɪˈʒɪŋ/ *n* بِكِين

Beirut /beɪˈruːt/ *n* بَيْرُوت

belief /bɪˈliːf/ *n* مُعْتَقَد/مُعْتَقَدَات مف/ج

believe /bɪˈliːv/ *v* يُصَدِّق

bell /bel/ *n* جَرَس/أَجْرَاس مف/ج

belong /bɪˈlɒŋ/ *v* يَنْتَسِب إِلَى

below /bɪˈləʊ/ *prep* (lower than) تَحْتَ

below the table تَحْتَ الطَاوِلَة

(with numbers, etc)

below zero تَحْتَ الصفر

♦ *adv* أَسْفَل

the apartment below الشقَّة السُفْلَى

belt /belt/ *n* حِزَام/أَحْزِمَة مف/ج

bench /bentʃ/ *n* مَقْعَد/مَقَاعِدُ مف/ج

bend /bend/ *v* **bent** يَلْتَوِي

♦ *n* مُنْعَطَف

beneath /bɪ'ni:θ/ *prep* تَحْتَ

benefit /'benɪfɪt/ *n* (advantage) فَائِدَة (social subsidy) إِعَانَة مَالِيَّة

♦ *v* يُفِيد

Berlin /bə:'lɪn/ *n* بِرْلِين

berry /'beri/ *n* pl **-ries** تُوت

beside /bɪ'saɪd/ *prep* بِجَانِب

beside the house بِجَانِب البَيْت

She sat beside me. جلَسَت بِجَانِبِي

best /best/ *adj* أَفْضَلُ

the best song أَفْضَل أُغْنِيَة

♦ *adv* الأَفْضَل

Who played (the) best? مَن لَعِبَ الأَفْضَلَ؟

bet /bet/ *n* (act of betting) رِهَان (stake) مَال الرِهَان

♦ *v* **bet, bet** يُرَاهِن

Bethlehem /'bɛθlɪhɛm/ *n* بَيْت لَحْم

betray /bɪ'treɪ/ *v* يَخُون

better /'betə(r)/ *adj* (price, hotel) أَفْضَلُ

It's better than the old one. هُوَ أَفْضَل مِن القَدِيم (improving) أَحْسَنُ

My French is getting better. لُغَتِي الفَرَنْسِيَّة تَتَحَسَّن (in health)

I'm better now. أَنَا أَحْسَن الآن

♦ *adv* (to work, drive) أَفْضَلُ

You did better today. كَانَ عَمَلُكَ أَفْضَل اليَوْم (in health) أَفْضَلُ صِحِّياً

I am feeling better today أَشْعُرُ بِأَنَّنِي أَحْسَن اليَوْم

between /bɪ'twi:n/ *prep* بَيْنَ

beyond /bɪ'jɒnd/ *prep* وَرَاءَ

Bible, the /'baɪbl/ *n* الإِنْجِيل/الأَنَاجِيل مف/ج

bicycle /'baɪsɪkl/ *n* دَرَّاجَة هَوَائِيَّة

bid /bɪd/ *n* عَطَاء/عَطَاءَات مف/ج

big /bɪg/ *adj* (large) كَبِير/كِبَار مف/ج ضَخْم/ضِخَام مف/ج

It's too big for me. هُوَ كَبِير عَلَيَّ

(important) كَبِير/كِبَار مف/ج

a big problem مُشْكِلَة كَبِيرَة

bike /baɪk/ *n* (bicycle) دَرَّاجَة هَوَائِيَّة (motorbike) دَرَّاجَة نَارِيَّة

bill /bɪl/ *n* فَاتُورَة/فَوَاتِيرُ مف/ج

bin /bɪn/ *n* سَلَّة المُهْمَلاَت

biography /baɪ'ɒgrəfi/ *n* pl **-phies** سِيرَة

biologist /baɪ'ɒlədʒɪst/ *n* عَالِم الأَحْيَاء

biology /baɪ'ɒlədʒi/ *n* عِلْم الأَحْيَاء

bird /bɜ:d/ *n* طَائِر/طُيُور مف/ج

birth /bɜ:θ/ *n* وِلاَدَة

B

birthday /ˈbɜːθdeɪ/ *n* عيد ميلاد

biscuit /ˈbɪskɪt/ *n* بَسْكَويت

bishop /ˈbɪʃəp/ *n* أُسْقُف/أَساقِفَة مف/ج

bit /bɪt/ *n* (of cloth, of wood) قِطْعَة/قِطَع مف/ج (of salt, sugar, oil) مِقْدَار ضَئِيل

bitch /bɪtʃ/ *n* كَلْبَة

bite /baɪt/ *n* (mouthful) قَضْمَة
(wound) لَدْغَة
♦ *v* **bit, bitten** يَقْضَم

bitter /ˈbɪtə(r)/ *adj* (taste) مُرّ (criticism) لاذِع

bitterness /ˈbɪtənəs/ *n* مَرارَة

black /blæk/ *adj* أَسْوَد/سَوْداء/سُود مذ/م/ج
black coffee قَهْوَة سَوْداء
the Black community مُجْتَمَع السُود
to go black أَصْبَحَ أَسْوَد، يَسْوَدّ
to wear black يَرْتَدِي السَوَاد

bladder /ˈblædə(r)/ *n* المَثانَة البَوْلِيَّة

blade /bleɪd/ *n* نَصْل/نِصَال مف/ج

blame /bleɪm/ *n* لَوْم
♦ *v* يَلُوم

blank /blæŋk/ *adj* فارِغ

blanket /ˈblæŋkɪt/ *n* بَطَّانِيَّة

blast /blɑːst/ *n* اِنْفِجَار/اِنْفِجَارَات مف/ج

bleak /bliːk/ *adj* قاتِم

bleed /bliːd/ *v* **bled, bled** يَنْزِف

blend /blend/ *n* (of ingredients) خَلِيط/خَلائِط مف/ج
♦ *v* (the ingredients) يَخْلِط

bless /bles/ *v* يُبارِك

blessing /ˈblesɪŋ/ *n* نِعْمَة/نِعَم مف/ج

blind /blaɪnd/ *adj* أَعْمَى/عَمْيَاء/عُمْي مذ/م/ج
♦ *v* يُعْمِي

blink /blɪŋk/ *v* يُطْرِف بِعَيْنِه

block /blɒk/ *n* (of wood) كُتْلَة/كُتَل مف/ج
(in building) لَبِنَة
♦ *v* (the way) يُعِيق (sb's progress, etc) يُعَرْقِل

blond /blɒnd/ *adj* أَشْقَر/شَقْرَاء/شُقْر مذ/م/ج

blood /blʌd/ *n* دَم

bloody /ˈblʌdi/ *adj* دَمَوِيّ

blot /blɒt/ *n* بُقْعَة/بُقَع مف/ج

blow /bləʊ/ *n* ضَرْبَة
♦ *v* **blew, blown** (in breathing) يَنْفُخ
(of winds, gales) يَهُبّ

blue /bluː/ *adj* أَزْرَق/زَرْقَاء/زُرْق مذ/م/ج
to feel blue يَشْعُر بِالكَآبَة
♦ *n* اللَوْن الأَزْرَق
to be dressed in blue يَلْبَس اللَوْن الأَزْرَق

blues /bluːz/ *n* مُوسِيقَى البْلُوز

board /bɔːd/ *n* لَوْح/أَلْوَاح مف/ج
♦ *v* يَسْتَقِلّ

boast /bəʊst/ *v* يَتَبَاهَى

boat /bəʊt/ *n* مَرْكِب/مَرَاكِب مف/ج

body /ˈbɒdi/ *n* pl **-dies** (live) جِسْم/أَجْسَام مف/ج (dead) جُثَّة/جُثَث مف/ج

boil /bɔɪl/ *v* يَغْلِي

bold /bəʊld/ *adj* (idea) جَرِيء (explorer, etc) جَسُور

bolt /bəʊlt/ *n* (for door) رِتَاج/رِتَاجَات مِسْمَار/مَسَامِيرُ مف/ج (for nut) مف/ج

bomb /bɒm/ *n* قُنْبُلَة/قَنَابِلُ مف/ج
♦ *v* يَقْصِف بِالقَنَابِل

bond /bɒnd/ *n* سَنَد/سَنَدَات مف/ج

bone /bəʊn/ *n* عَظْم/عِظَام مف/ج

bony /ˈbəʊni/ *adj* عَظْمِيّ

bonus /ˈbəʊnəs/ *n* زِيَادَة

book /bʊk/ *n* كِتَاب/كُتُب مف/ج
♦ *v* (a room, a table) يَحْجِز
(a player) يُدَوِّن

booking /ˈbʊkɪŋ/ *n* حَجْز

boom /buːm/ *n* (noise) دَوِيّ (economic) ازْدِهَار

boot /buːt/ *n* (footwear) جَزْمَة/جِزَم صُنْدُوق السَّيَّارَة (of a car) مف/ج

border /ˈbɔːdə(r)/ *n* (with countries) حَافَّة/حَوَافُّ مف/ج (for cloth) حَدّ/حُدُود

bore /bɔː(r)/ *v* (an audience) يُمَلِّل (a hole) يَثْقُب

boring /ˈbɔːrɪŋ/ *adj* مُمِلّ

born /bɔːn/ *adj* مَوْلُود

borrow /ˈbɒrəʊ/ *v* يَقْتَرِض، يَسْتَعِير
He borrowed $25 from me.
اقْتَرَضَ مِنِّي خَمْسَةَ وَعِشْرِين دُولاَراً
Can I borrow your car?
هَل بِإِمْكَانِي اسْتِعَارَة سَيَّارَتِكِ؟

boss /bɒs/ *n* رَئِيس/رُؤَسَاءُ مف/ج

both /bəʊθ/ *adj* كِلا/كِلْتَا مذ/م
Both sisters were there.
كِلْتَا الأُخْتَيْن كَانَتَا هُنَاكَ
♦ *pron* كِلَا/كِلْتَا مذ/م
Both are excellent players.
كِلَاهُمَا لَاعِبَان جَيِّدَان
I know both of them. أَعْرِف كِلْتَاهُمَا

bother /ˈbɒðə(r)/ *v* يُزْعِج

bottle /ˈbɒtl/ *n* زُجَاجَة

bottom /ˈbɒtəm/ *n* (of a hill, list) قَاع
(buttocks) رَدْف/أَرْدَاف مف/ج
♦ *adj* أَسْفَلُ

bounce /baʊns/ *v* يَرْتَدّ

boundary /ˈbaʊndri/ *n* pl **-ries** حَدّ/حُدُود مف/ج

bout /baʊt/ *n* نَوْبَة

bow /baʊ/ *v* (from respect) يَنْحَنِي
♦ *n* /baʊ/ (weapon) قَوْس/أَقْوَاس مف/ج

bowl /bəʊl/ *n* سُلْطَانِيَّة

bowling /ˈbəʊlɪŋ/ *n* بُولِينْج

box /bɒks/ *n* صُنْدُوق/صَنَادِيقُ مف/ج
♦ *v* يَلْكُم

boxer /ˈbɒksə(r)/ *n* مُلَاكِم

boy /bɔɪ/ *n* وَلَد/أَوْلَاد مف/ج

boyfriend /ˈbɔɪfrend/ *n* خَلِيل/خُلَّان مف/ج

bra /brɑː/ *n* صَدْرِيَّة

bracket /ˈbrækɪt/ *n* كَتِيفَة/كَتَائِفُ مف/ج

brackets /ˈbrækɪts/ *n pl* قَوْس مَعْقُوف

B

brain /breɪn/ *n* دمَاغ/أَدْمِغَة مف/ج

brake /breɪk/ *n* مِكْبَح/مَكَابِحُ مف/ج

branch /brɑːntʃ/ *n* فَرْع/فُرُوع مف/ج

brand /brænd/ *n* مَارْكَة

brass /brɑːs/ *n* نُحَاس أَصْفَر

brave /breɪv/ *adj* شُجَاع

breach /briːtʃ/ *n* ثَغْرَة

bread /bred/ *n* خُبْز

break /breɪk/ *n* (in a bone) كَسْر/كُسُور مف/ج (pause) اسْتِرَاحَة
♦ *v* **broke, broken** (a plate, etc) يَكْسِر (machines, objects) يَتَعَطَّل (to fall apart) يَتَكَسَّر

breakdown /ˈbreɪkdaʊn/ *n* (of a car, machine, of negotiations) تَعَطُّل (nervous) انْهِيَار عَصَبِيّ

breakfast /ˈbrekfəst/ *n* إِفْطَار

breakthrough /ˈbreɪkθruː/ *n* تَقَدُّم

breast /brest/ *n* ثَدْي

breath /breθ/ *n* نَفَس

breathe /briːð/ *v* يَتَنَفَّس

breathtaking /ˈbreθteɪkɪŋ/ *adj* مُثِير

breed /briːd/ *n* سُلاَلَة
♦ *v* **bred, bred** (birds, animals) يَتَنَاسَل (in farming) يُرَبِّي

breeze /briːz/ *n* نَسِيم/نَسَائِمُ مف/ج

brick /brɪk/ *n* لَبِنَة

bride /braɪd/ *n* عَرُوس/عَرَائِسُ مف/ج

bridge /brɪdʒ/ *n* (structure) جِسْر/جُسُور مف/ج (card game) لَعْبَة البْرِيدْج

brief /briːf/ *adj* مُخْتَصَر

briefing /ˈbriːfɪŋ/ *n* مُوجَز

bright /braɪt/ *adj* (light) سَاطِع (clever) ذَكِيّ

brilliant /ˈbrɪliənt/ *adj* بَارِع

bring /brɪŋ/ *v* **brought, brought** يَجْلِب

British /ˈbrɪtɪʃ/ *adj* بَرِيطَانِيّ

Briton /ˈbrɪtn/ *n* بَرِيطَانِيّ

broad /brɔːd/ *adj* وَاسِع

broadband /ˈbrɔːdbænd/ *n* الرَبْط بِشَبَكَة الإِنْتِرْنِت

broadcast /ˈbrɔːdkɑːst/ *n* بَثّ
♦ *v* **-cast, -cast** يَبُثّ

broccoli /ˈbrɒkəli/ *n* بْرُوكُلِي

brochure /ˈbrəʊʃə(r)/ *n* كُتَيِّب

broke /brəʊk/ *adj* مُفْلِس

broken /ˈbrəʊkən/ *adj* (plate, limb) مَكْسُور (machine, clock) مُعَطَّل

broker /ˈbrəʊkə(r)/ *n* سِمْسَار/سَمَاسِرَة مف/ج

bronze /brɒnz/ *adj* بْرُونْزِيّ

brother /ˈbrʌðə(r)/ *n* أَخ/إِخْوَة مف/ج

brown /braʊn/ *adj* بُنِّيّ
to turn brown يُصْبِح بُنِّيّاً
♦ *n* اللَوْن البُنِّيّ

browser /ˈbraʊzə(r)/ *n* مُسْتَعْرِض

bruise /bruːz/ *n* كَدْمَة

brush /brʌʃ/ *n* فُرْشَاة/فُرَش مف/ج
♦ *v* يُصَفِّف

Brussels /'brʌs(ə)lz/ *n* مَدِينَة بْرُوكْسِل

Brussels sprout /brʌslz'spraʊt/ *n* كُرُنُب بْرُوكْسِل

brutal /'bru:tl/ *adj* وَحْشِيّ

bubble /'bʌbl/ *n* فُقَّاعَة

bucket /'bʌkɪt/ *n* دَلْو/دِلَاء مف/ج

bud /bʌd/ *n* بُرْعُم/بَرَاعِم مف/ج

Buddhism /'bʊdɪzəm/ *n* البُوذِيَّة

budget /'bʌdʒɪt/ *n* مِيزَانِيَّة

bug /bʌg/ *n* (insect) حَشَرَة (disease) عِلَّة/عِلَل مف/ج

build /bɪld/ *v* **built, built** يَبْنِي

builder /'bɪldə(r)/ *n* بَنَّاء

building /'bɪldɪŋ/ *n* بِنَايَة

bulb /bʌlb/ *n* (for lighting) الجُزْء الزُّجَاجِيّ مِن المِصْبَاح (plant) بَصَلَة/بَصَل مف/ج

bull /bʊl/ *n* ثَوْر/ثِيرَان مف/ج

bullet /'bʊlɪt/ *n* رَصَاصَة

bulletin /'bʊlətɪn/ *n* بَيَان

bully /'bʊli/ *v* يُعَرْبِد

bump /bʌmp/ *n* تَوَرُّم
♦ *v* يَصْدُم

bunch /bʌntʃ/ *n* (of keys, etc) حِزْمَة/حِزَم مف/ج (of people) مَجْمُوعَة

bundle /'bʌndl/ *n* رُزْمَة/رُزَم مف/ج

burden /'bɜ:dn/ *n* حِمْل/أَحْمَال

bureaucracy /bjʊə'rɒkrəsi/ *n* pl -**cies** بِيرُوقْرَاطِيَّة

bureaucrat /'bjʊərəkræt/ *n* بِيرُوقْرَاطِيّ

burglary /'bɜ:gləri/ *n* pl -**ries** سَطْو

burial /'beriəl/ *n* دَفْن

burn /bɜ:n/ *n* حَرْق/حُرُوق مف/ج
♦ *v* **burned, burnt** (be on fire) يَحْرِق (a letter, etc) يَحْتَرِق (a CD) يَنْسَخ

burst /bɜ:st/ *v* يُفَجِّر

bury /'beri/ *v* يَدْفِن

bus /bʌs/ *n* حَافِلَة رُكَّاب

bush /bʊʃ/ *n* شُجَيْرَة

business /'bɪznəs/ *n* (company) مُؤَسَّسَة تِجَارِيَّة (trade) عَمَل تِجَارِيّ

businessman /'bɪznəsmæn/ *n* pl -**men** رَجُل أَعْمَال

businesswoman /'bɪznəswʊmən/ *n* pl -**women** سَيِّدَة أَعْمَال

bust /bʌst/ *n* صَدْر/صُدُور مف/ج

busy /'bɪzi/ *adj* (market) مُزْدَحِم (occupied) مَشْغُول

but /bʌt/ *conj* لَكِنَّ

butter /'bʌtə(r)/ *n* زُبْدَة

butterfly /'bʌtəflaɪ/ *n* pl -**flies** فَرَاشَة

button /'bʌtn/ *n* زِرّ/أَزْرَار مف/ج

buy /baɪ/ *v* **bought** يَشْتَرِي

buyer /'baɪə(r)/ *n* مُشْتَرٍ

by /baɪ/ *prep* (method) بِوَاسِطَة

by bus بِوَاسِطَة البَاص
by e-mail بِوَاسِطَة البَرِيد الإِلكْتْرُونِيّ
(time) فِي مَوْعِد لاَ يَتَجَاوَز كَذَا
by Friday فِي مَوْعِد لاَ يَتَجَاوَز الجُمْعَة
by 9 o'clock فِي مَوْعِد لاَ يَتَجَاوَز التَاسِعَة
(close to) بِجَانِب
The bus stop is by the garage.
مَوْقِف البَاصَات بِجَانِب المَرْأَب (in
passives) مِن قِبَل
He was helped by a passer-by.
سُوعِدَ مِن قِبَل عَابِر طَرِيق (showing
difference) بِ
to win by 20 points يَفُوز بِعِشْرِين نُقْطَة
♦ *adv* (to walk, etc) يَمُرّ عَن
to walk by sb يَمُرّ عَن شَخْص مَا

bypass /ˈbaɪpɑːs/ *n* طَرِيق جَانِبِيّ

C

cab /kæb/ *n* سَيَّارَة أُجْرَة

cabbage /ˈkæbɪʤ/ *n* مَلْفُوف

cabin /ˈkæbɪn/ *n* (in a plane) غُرْفَة قِيَادَة الطَّائِرَة (on a ship) حُجْرَة نَوْم فِي سَفِينَة

cabinet /ˈkæbɪnət/ *n* خِزَانَة

cable /ˈkeɪbl/ *n* سِلْك/أَسْلَاك مف/ج

cafeteria /kæfəˈtɪəriə/ *n* مِقْصَف

cage /keɪʤ/ *n* قَفَص/أَقْفَاص مف/ج

cake /keɪk/ *n* كَعْكَة/كَعْك مف/ج

Cairo /ˈkʌɪərəʊ/ *n* القَاهِرَة

calcium /ˈkælsiəm/ *n* كَالْسِيُوم

calculate /ˈkælkjuleɪt/ *v* (the ratio) يَحْسِب (the risks) يُقَيِّم

calculation /kælkjuˈleɪʃn/ *n* حِسَاب

calendar /ˈkælɪndə(r)/ *n* رُزْنَامَة

calf /kɑːf/ *n* pl **-lves** (animal) عِجْل/عُجُول مف/ج (part of leg) رَبْلَة سَاق

call /kɔːl/ *n* (sound) نِدَاء (visit) زِيَارَة (by telephone) مُكَالَمَة
♦ *v* (a person) يُنَادِي (to phone) يُهَاتِف

call centre *n* مَرْكَز الاتِّصَال

caller /ˈkɔːlə(r)/ *n* المُهَاتِف

calm /kɑːm/ *adj* (sea, wind) سَاكِن (expression, speaker) هَادِئ

calorie /ˈkæləri/ *n* سُعْر/سُعْرَات مف/ج

camera /ˈkæmərə/ *n* آلَة تَصْوِير

camp /kæmp/ *n* مُخَيَّم/مُخَيَّمَات مف/ج
♦ *v* يُخَيِّم

campaign /kæmˈpeɪn/ *n* حَمْلَة

camper /ˈkæmpə(r)/ *n* مُخَيِّم

can /kən, kæn/ *modal v* يَسْتَطِيع
(ability) يَقْدِر
I can hear you. أَسْتَطِيع سَمَاعَك
She can't see you. لَا تَسْتَطِيع رُؤْيَتَك
He can't drive. لَا يَسْتَطِيع السِيَاقَة
(permission) يُمْكِن
You can park there.
يُمْكِنُكَ إِيقَاف السَيَّارَة هُنَاك
You can't stay here. لَا يُمْكِنُكَ المُكُوث هُنَا
(possibility)
Anything can happen.
أَيّ شَيْء مُمْكِن حُدُوثُه (in requests, offers) يُمْكِن (تُسْتَعْمَل لِلسُؤَال)
Can I help you? هَل يُمْكِنُنِي مُسَاعَدَتُكَ؟
Can you tell me the time?
هَل يُمْكِنُكَ أَنْ تُخْبِرَنِي كَم السَاعَة؟

canal /kəˈnæl/ *n* قَنَاة/قَنَوَات
the Suez Canal قَنَاة السُوِيس

cancel /ˈkænsl/ *v* يُلْغِي

cancer /ˈkænsə(r)/ *n* مَرَض السَرَطَان

C

Canada /'kanədə/ *n* كَنَدَا

Canadian /kə'neɪdiən/ *adj, n* كَنَدِيّ ص/س

candidate /'kændɪdət/ *n* مُرَشَّح

candle /'kændl/ *n* شَمْعَة

candy /'kændi/ *n* pl **-dies** حَلْوَى

cane /keɪn/ *n* قَصَب، خَيْزُرَان

cannot /'kænɒt/ *modal v* (see can)

can't /kɑːnt/ *contr* (= cannot: see can)

canvas /'kænvəs/ *n* قِنَّب

cap /kæp/ *n* قُبَّعَة

capability /keɪpə'bɪləti/ *n* pl **-ties** قُدْرَة

capable /'keɪpəbl/ *adj* قَادِر

capable of قَادِر عَلَى

capacity /kə'pæsəti/ *n* pl **-ties** سِعَة

cape /keɪp/ *n* رَأْس

capital /'kæpɪtl/ *n* (city) عَاصِمَة/عَوَاصِمُ مف/ج (in economics) رَأْس المَال

capitalism /'kæpɪtəlɪzəm/ *n* رَأْسْمَالِيَّة

capitalist /'kæpɪtəlɪst/ *n* رَأْسْمَالِيّ

captain /'kæptɪn/ *n* (of a team) قَائِد (in the army, navy) نَقِيب

capture /'kæptʃə(r)/ *n* الأَسْر ♦ *v* يَأْسِر

car /kɑː(r)/ *n* سَيَّارَة

caraway /'kærəweɪ/ *n* كَرَاوْيَا

carbohydrate /kɑːbəʊ'haɪdreɪt/ *n* كَارْبُوهَيْدْرَات

carbon /'kɑːbən/ *n* كَرْبُون

card /kɑːd/ *n* بِطَاقَة

cardamom /'kɑːdəməm/ *n* هَيْل، حَبّ الهَيْل

cardboard /'kɑːdbɔːd/ *n* كَرْتُون

care /keə(r)/ *n* (of the sick, etc) رِعَايَة (worry) اهْتِمَام

career /kə'rɪə(r)/ *n* مِهْنَة/مِهَن مف/ج

careful /'keəfl/ *adj* حَذِر

carefully /'keəfəli/ *adv* بِعِنَايَة

carer /'keərə(r)/ *n* مُوَظَّف رِعَايَة

cargo /'kɑːgəʊ/ *n* حُمُولَة

carnival /'kɑːnɪvl/ *n* كَرْنَفَال/كَرْنَفَالَات مف/ج

carob /'kærəb/ *n* خَرُّوب

carol /'kærəl/ *n* تَرْنِيمَة/تَرَانِيمُ مف/ج

car park *n* مَوْقِف سَيَّارَات

carpenter /'kɑːpəntə(r)/ *n* نَجَّار

carpet /'kɑːpɪt/ *n* سَجَّادَة/سَجَّادَات وَسَجَاجِيدُ مف/ج

car rental /'rentəl/ *n* تَأْجِير سَيَّارَات

carriage /'kærɪdʒ/ *n* عَرَبَة

carrier /'kæriə(r)/ *n* شَرِكَة النَقْل

carrot /'kærət/ *n* جَزَر

carry /'kæri/ *v* (a baby, bags) يَحْمِل (a cargo) يَنْقِل

cart /kɑːt/ *n* كَارَّة

cartoon /kɑː'tuːn/ *n* فِيلْم كَرْتُون

cartridge /'kɑːtrɪdʒ/ *n* /خَرْطُوشَة
خَرَاطِيش مف/ج

carve /kɑːv/ *v* (a statue) يَنْحَت
(meat) يُقَطِّع

case /keɪs/ *n* (for clothes)
حَقِيبَة سَفَر (for bottles) عُلْبَة/عُلَب
مف/ج (instance) حَالَة

cash /kæʃ/ *n* مَال نَقْداً
♦ *v* يَصْرِف شِيكاً

cashew /'kæʃuː/ *n* كَاجُو

cashier /kæ'ʃɪə(r)/ *n* مُوَظَّف كَاش

casino /kə'siːnəʊ/ *n* نَادِي قِمَار

cast /kɑːst/ *n* فَرِيق المُمَثِّلِين

castle /'kɑːsl/ *n* قَلْعَة/قِلَاع مف/ج

casual /'kæʒuəl/ *adj* غَيْر رَسْمِيّ

casualty /'kæʒuəlti/ *n* pl **-ties**
ضَحِيَّة/ضَحَايَا مف/ج

cat /kæt/ *n* قِطَّة/قِطَط مف/ج

catalogue /'kætəlɒg/ *n* US **-log**
دَلِيل مُصَوَّر

catalyst /'kætəlɪst/ *n* عَامِل مُسَاعِد

catastrophe /kə'tæstrəfi/ *n* /كَارِثَة
كَوَارِث مف/ج

catastrophic /kætə'strɒfɪk/ *adj*
كَارِثِيّ

catch /kætʃ/ *v* **caught** (a cat, etc)
يُمْسِك بِـ (a prisoner) يَقْبِض عَلَى
(a cold) يَأْخُذ العَدْوَى

category /'kætəgəri/ *n* pl **-ries** فِئَة

cater /'keɪtə(r)/ *v* يُقَدِّم الطَعَام

cathedral /kə'θiːdrəl/ *n* كَاتِدْرَائِيَّة

cauliflower /'kɒliflaʊə(r)/ *n* قَرْنَبِيط

cause /kɔːz/ *n* (of the fire, etc) قَضِيَّة
♦ *v* (an accident, etc) يُسَبِّب

caution /'kɔːʃn/ *n* تَحْذِير

cautious /'kɔːʃəs/ *adj* حَذِر

cave /keɪv/ *n* كَهْف/كُهُوف مف/ج

cavity /'kævəti/ *n* pl **-ties** فَجْوَة

cayenne /keɪ'en/ *n* فِلْفِل أَحْمَر

ceiling /'siːlɪŋ/ *n* سَقْف/أَسْقُف مف/ج

celebrate /'selɪbreɪt/ *v* يَحْتَفِل بِـ

celebration /selɪ'breɪʃn/ *n* احْتِفَال

celebrity /sə'lebrəti/ *n* شَخْص مَشْهُور

cell /sel/ *n* زِنْزَانَة/زَنَازِينُ مف/ج

cell phone *n* هَاتِف خَلَوِيّ

cement /sɪ'ment/ *n* إِسْمَنْت

cemetery /'semətri/ *n* pl **-ries**
مَقْبَرَة/مَقَابِرُ مف/ج

censorship /'sensəʃɪp/ *n* الرِقَابَة

cent /sent/ *n* سِنْت

centimetre /'sentɪmiːtə(r)/ *n* US **-ter**
سَنْتِمِيتْر

centigrade /'sentɪgreɪd/ *n* مِئَوِيّ

central /'sentrəl/ *adj* مَرْكَزِيّ

centre /'sentə(r)/ *n* US **-ter** /مَرْكَز
مَرَاكِزُ مف/ج

C

centre back *n* دِفَاع مُتَأَخِّر

centre forward *n* دِفَاع مُتَقَدِّم

centre half *n* دِفَاع وَسَط

century /'sentʃəri/ *n* pl **-ries** /قَرْن قُرُون مف/ج

cereal /'sɪəriəl/ *n* حُبُوب

ceremony /'serəməni/ *n* pl **-nies** احْتِفَال/احْتِفَالَات مف/ج

certain /'sɜːtn/ *adj* مُتَأَكِّد

certainly /'sɜːtnli/ *adv* بِالتَأْكِيد

certificate /sə'tɪfɪkət/ *n* شَهَادَة

certify /'sɜːtɪfaɪ/ *v* يُصَادِق عَلَى

CD /siː'diː/ *n* قُرْص التَسْجِيل

CDROM /siːdiː'rɑm/ *n* قُرْص التَسْجِيل

chain /tʃeɪn/ *n* سِلْسِلَة/سَلَاسِلُ مف/ج

chair /tʃeə(r)/ *n* كُرْسِيّ/كَرَاسِيُّ مف/ج

chairman /'tʃeəmən/ *n* pl **-men** رَئِيس/رُؤَسَاءُ مف/ج

chairwoman /'tʃeəwʊmən/ *n* pl **-men** مُدِيرَة

challenge /'tʃæləndʒ/ *n* /تَحَدٍّ تَحَدِّيَات مف/ج

♦ *v* يَتَحَدَّى

challenger /'tʃælɪndʒə(r)/ *n* مُتَحَدٍّ

challenging /'tʃælɪndʒɪŋ/ *adj* عَسِير

chamber /'tʃeɪmbə(r)/ *n* غُرْفَة/غُرَف مف/ج

champagne /ʃæm'peɪn/ *n* شَامْبَانْيَا

champion /'tʃæmpiən/ *n* /بَطَل أَبْطَال مف/ج

championship /'tʃæmpiənʃɪp/ *n* بُطُولَة

chance /tʃɑːns/ *n* (opportunity) فُرْصَة/فُرَص مف/ج (possibility) إِمْكَانِيَّة

change /tʃeɪndʒ/ *n* (alteration) تَعْدِيل/تَعْدِيلَات مف/ج (as concept) تَغْيِير (coins) فَكَّة النُقُود

♦ *v* (become different) يُغَيِّر (the rules, etc) يُعَدِّل

channel /'tʃænl/ *n* قَنَاة/قَنَوَات مف/ج

chaos /'keɪɒs/ *n* فَوْضَى

chaotic /keɪ'ɒtɪk/ *adj* فَوْضَوِيّ

chap /tʃæp/ *n* رَجُل/رِجَال مف/ج

chapter /'tʃæptə(r)/ *n* فَصْل

character /'kærəktə(r)/ *n* شَخْصِيَّة

characterize /'kærəktəraɪz/ *v* يَصِف

characteristic /kærəktə'rɪstɪk/ *adj* مُمَيَّز

♦ *n* سِمَة

charge /tʃɑːdʒ/ *n* (fee) رَسْم دَفْع (accusation) تُهْمَة/تُهَم مف/ج (of electricity) شُحْنَة

♦ *v* (a customer) يَفْرِض رَسْماً (a suspect) يَتَّهِم (batteries) يَشْحَن

charitable /'tʃærətəbl/ *adj* خَيْرِيّ

charity /'tʃærəti/ *n* pl **-ties** جَمْعِيَّة خَيْرِيَّة

charm /tʃɑːm/ *n* (quality) جَاذِبِيَّة (for luck) سِحْر

charming /ˈtʃɑːmɪŋ/ *adj* جَذَّاب

chart /tʃɑːt/ *n* (with statistics) رَسْم بَيَانِيّ (map) خَرِيطَة/خَرَائِطُ مف/ج

chase /tʃeɪs/ *n* مُطَارَدَة
♦ *v* يُطَارِد

chat /tʃæt/ *n* مُحَادَثَة
♦ *v* يَتَحَدَّث

cheap /tʃiːp/ *adj* رَخِيص

cheat /tʃiːt/ *v* (in exams, etc) يَغُشّ (a person) يَخْدَع

check /tʃek/ *n* (pattern) تَقْلِيمَة القِمَاش (US: in banking) شِيك/شِيكَات مف/ج
♦ *v* يَتَفَحَّص

checkers /ˈtʃekəz/ *n* US لَعْبَة الضَامَا

cheek /tʃiːk/ *n* خَدّ/خُدُود مف/ج

cheer /tʃɪə(r)/ *v* يُبْهِج
♦ *n* تَشْجِيع

cheerful /ˈtʃɪəfl/ *adj* مُبْتَهِج

cheese /tʃiːz/ *n* جُبْنَة

chef /ʃef/ *n* طَاهٍ/طُهَاة مف/ج

chemical /ˈkemɪkl/ *adj* كِيمَاوِيّ

chemist /ˈkemɪst/ *n* كِيمْيَائِيّ

chemistry /ˈkemɪstri/ *n* كِيمْيَاء

cheque /tʃek/ *n* شِيك/شِيكَات مف/ج

cherry /ˈtʃeri/ *n* pl **-ries** كَرَز

chess /tʃes/ *n* شَطْرَنْج

chest /tʃest/ *n* (part of body) صَدْر/صُدُور مف/ج (trunk) صُنْدُوق/صَنَادِيقُ مف/ج

chestnut /ˈtʃesnʌt/ *n* كَسْتَنَاء

chew /tʃuː/ *v* يَمْضُغ

chick /tʃɪk/ *n* صُوص/صِيصَان مف/ج

chicken /ˈtʃɪkɪn/ *n* دَجَاجَة/دَجَاج مف/ج

chickpea /ˈtʃɪkpiː/ *n* حُمُّص

chief /tʃiːf/ *adj* رَئِيسِيّ
♦ *n* رَئِيس/رُؤَسَاءُ مف/ج

child /tʃaɪld/ *n* pl **-dren** طِفْل/أَطْفَال مف/ج

childhood /ˈtʃaɪldhʊd/ *n* طُفُولَة

chill /tʃɪl/ *v* يُبَرِّد
♦ *n* بَرْد

chilli /ˈtʃɪli/ *n* فِلْفِل حَارّ

chin /tʃɪn/ *n* ذَقْن

china /ˈtʃaɪnə/ *n* خَزَف صِينِيّ

China /ˈtʃʌɪnə/ *n* الصِين

Chinese /tʃaɪˈniːz/ *adj* صِينِيّ
♦ *n* (language) اللُغَة الصِينِيَّة (people) صِينِيّ

chip /tʃɪp/ *n* (on a plate, cup) كَسْر/كُسُور مف/ج (of wood) قِطْعَة/قِطَع مف/ج (in computing) شَرِيحَة/شَرَائِحُ مف/ج (in bag) رَقَائِق بَطَاطَا (UK: French fries) إِصْبَع بَطَاطَا مَقْلِيّ

chocolate /ˈtʃɒklət/ *n* شُوكُولَاتَة

choice /tʃɔɪs/ *n* خَيَار/خَيَارات مف/ج

C

choir /'kwaɪə(r)/ *n* فَرِيق مِن المُنْشِدِين

choke /tʃəʊk/ *v* يَتَشَرْدَق

cholesterol /kə'lestərɒl/ *n* كُولِسْتُرُول

choose /tʃuːz/ *v* **chose, chosen** يَخْتَار

chop /tʃɒp/ *v* يُقَطِّع

chore /tʃɔː(r)/ *n* عَمَل رُوتِينِيّ

chorus /'kɔːrəs/ *n* pl **-ses** أَعْضَاء فِرْقَة مُوسِيقِيَّة

Christ /kraɪst/ *n* عِيسَى المَسِيح

Christian /'krɪstʃən/ *adj, n* مَسِيحِيّ ص/س

Christianity /krɪsti'ænəti/ *n* مَسِيحِيَّة

Christmas /'krɪsməs/ *n* عِيد المِيلَاد المَجِيد

chronic /'krɒnɪk/ *adj* مُزْمِن

chuckle /'tʃʌkl/ *v* يَضْحَك

chunk /tʃʌŋk/ *n* قِطْعَة كَبِيرَة/قِطَع مف/ج

church /tʃɜːtʃ/ *n* كَنِيسَة/كَنَائِسُ مف/ج

cigarette /sɪgə'ret/ *n* سِيجَارَة/سَجَائِرُ مف/ج

cinema /'sɪnəmə/ *n* (place) دَار السِينَمَا (industry) صِنَاعَة السِينَمَا

cinnamon /'sɪnəmən/ *n* قِرْفَة

circle /'sɜːkl/ *n* دَائِرَة/دَوَائِرُ مف/ج
♦ *v* يَدُور

circuit /'sɜːkɪt/ *n* دَائِرَة كَهْرَبِيَّة

circular /'sɜːkjələ(r)/ *adj* مُسْتَدِير

circulate /'sɜːkjəleɪt/ *v* يُوَزِّع

circulation /sɜːkjə'leɪʃn/ *n* (of newspapers, etc) نَشْرَة (of blood) الدَوْرَة الدَمَوِيَّة

circumstance /'sɜːkəmstæns/ *n* حَالَة

circus /'sɜːkəs/ *n* سِيرْك

citizen /'sɪtɪzn/ *n* مُوَاطِن

citizenship /'sɪtɪzənʃɪp/ *n* مُوَاطَنَة

city /'sɪti/ *n* pl **-ties** مَدِينَة/مُدُن مف/ج

civil /'sɪvl/ *adj* (rights) حُكُومِيّ (answer) مُهَذَّب

civil servant *n* مُوَظَّف مَدَنِيّ

civilian /sə'vɪliən/ *adj, n* مَدَنِيّ

claim /kleɪm/ *v* (to allege) يَدَّعِي (damages) يُطَالِب
♦ *n* (allegation) ادِّعَاء/ادِّعَاءَات مف/ج (in insurance) دَعْوَى/دَعَاوَى مف/ج

clap /klæp/ *v* يُصَفِّق

clarity /'klærəti/ *n* وُضُوح

clash /klæʃ/ *n* اشْتِبَاك/اشْتِبَاكَات مف/ج
♦ *v* يَتَنَازَع

class /klɑːs/ *n* فِئَة

classic /'klæsɪk/ *adj* فَاخِر
♦ *n* أَثَر كْلَاسِيكِيّ

classical /'klæsɪkl/ *adj* قَدِيم

classification /klæsɪfɪ'keɪʃn/ *n* تَصْنِيف/تَصْنِيفَات مف/ج

classify /ˈklæsɪfaɪ/ *v* يُصَنِّف

classmate /ˈklɑːsmeɪt/ *n* زَمِيل الدِرَاسَة

classroom /ˈklɑːsrʊm/ *n* غُرْفَة الصَفّ

clause /klɔːz/ *n* بَنْد/بُنُود مف/ج

claw /klɔː/ *n* مَخْلَب/مَخَالِبُ مف/ج

clay /kleɪ/ *n* طِين

clean /kliːn/ *adj* نَظِيف
♦ *v* يُنَظِّف

cleaner /ˈkliːnə(r)/ *n* عَامِل نَظَافَة

cleaner's /ˈkliːnəz/ *n* مَغْسَلَة

clear /klɪə(r)/ *adj* فَارِغ
♦ *v* يُزِيل

clearly /ˈklɪəli/ *adv* بِوُضُوح

clementine /ˈkleməntiːn/ *n* كَلَمَنْتِينَا

clench /klentʃ/ *v* يَقْبِض

clergy /ˈklɜːdʒi/ *n* رِجَال الدين

clerk /klɑːk/ *n* مُوَظَّف

clever /ˈklevə(r)/ *adj* ذَكِيّ

click on /klɪk ɑn/ *v* يَنْقُر عَلَى

client /ˈklaɪənt/ *n* زَبُون/زَبَائِنُ مف/ج

cliff /klɪf/ *n* جُرُف/أَجْرَاف مف/ج

climate /ˈklaɪmət/ *n* مُنَاخ

climax /ˈklaɪmæks/ *n* ذُرْوَة

climb /klaɪm/ *n* تَسَلُّق
♦ *v* (a hill, etc) يَتَسَلَّق (planes, etc) يَصْعَد

clinical /ˈklɪnɪkl/ *adj* سَرِيرِيّ

cloak /kləʊk/ *n* شَال

clock /klɒk/ *n* سَاعَة

close /kləʊz/ *v* (doors, etc) يَنْغَلِق (a door, etc) يُغْلِق
♦ *adj* /kləʊs/ قَرِيب
♦ *adv* /kləʊs/ عَلَى مَقْرِبَة

closed /kləʊzd/ *adj* مُغْلَق

closet /ˈklɒzɪt/ *n* خِزَانَة

cloth /klɒθ/ *n* (for clothing) قُمَاش/أَقْمِشَة مف/ج (for cleaning, etc) خِرْقَة/خِرَق مف/ج

clothe /kləʊð/ *v* يُلْبِس

clothing /ˈkləʊðɪŋ/ *n* مَلَابِسُ

cloud /klaʊd/ *n* غَيْمَة/غُيُوم مف/ج

clove /kləʊv/ *n* (garlic) فَصّ (spice) قَرَنْفُل

clown /klaʊn/ *n* مُهَرِّج

club /klʌb/ *n* (place) نَادٍ/نَوَادٍ مف/ج (of swimmers, etc) جَمْعِيَّة (for golf, etc) مِضْرَب/مَضَارِبُ مف/ج

clue /kluː/ *n* (in crime) مِفْتَاح حَلّ اللُّغْز (in crosswords) مِفْتَاح الحَلّ

cluster /ˈklʌstə(r)/ *n* مَجْمُوعَة

clutch /klʌtʃ/ *n* قَابِض/قَوَابِضُ مف/ج

coach /kəʊtʃ/ *n* (of a train) عَرَبَة قِطَار (bus) حَافِلَة رُكَّاب (in sports) مُدَرِّب

coal /kəʊl/ *n* فَحْم

coalition /kəʊəˈlɪʃn/ *n* ائْتِلَاف/ائْتِلَافَات مف/ج

coast /kəʊst/ *n* سَاحِل

C

coastal /ˈkəʊstl/ *adj* سَاحِلِيّ

coat /kəʊt/ *n* مِعْطَف/مَعَاطِفُ

cocaine /kəʊˈkeɪn/ *n* الكُوكَايِين

cocktail /ˈkɒkteɪl/ *n* كُوكْتِيل

cocoa /ˈkəʊkəʊ/ *n* كَاكَاو

coconut /ˈkəʊkənʌt/ *n* جَوْز الهِنْد

cod /kɒd/ *n* سَمَك القُد

code /kəʊd/ *n* رَمْز سِرّيّ

coffee /ˈkɒfi/ *n* قَهْوَة

coffin /ˈkɒfɪn/ *n* تَابُوت/تَوَابِيتُ مف/ج

coin /kɔɪn/ *n* عُمْلَة مَعْدِنِيَّة

coincide /kəʊɪnˈsaɪd/ *v* يَتَزَامَن

coincidence /kəʊˈɪnsɪdəns/ *n* مُصَادَفَة

cold /kəʊld/ *adj* (weather, etc) بَارِد
a cold drink مَشْرُوب بَارِد
I'm cold. أَشْعُر بِالبَرْد
It's cold today. هَذَا اليَوْم بَارِد
♦ *n* (low temperature) بُرُودَة (illness) زُكَام

collaborate /kəˈlæbəreɪt/ *v* يَتَعَاوَن

collaboration /kəlæbəˈreɪʃn/ *n* تَعَاوُن

collapse /kəˈlæps/ *v* (roofs, walls) يَتَحَطَّم (stock market) يَنْهَار

collar /ˈkɒlə(r)/ *n* (of a shirt, etc) قَبَّة (for a pet) طَوْق الرَقَبَة

colleague /ˈkɒliːg/ *n* زَمِيل/زُمَلَاءُ مف/ج

collect /kəˈlekt/ *v* (stamps, etc) يَجْمَع (for charity) يَجْبِي (a person from a place) يَأْخُذ

collection /kəˈlekʃn/ *n* (of stamps, etc) مَجْمُوعَة (of rubbish, etc) تَجْمِيع

collector /kəˈlektə(r)/ *n* مُجَمِّع

college /ˈkɒlɪdʒ/ *n* كُلِّيَّة

collide /kəˈlaɪd/ *v* يَتَصَادَم

collision /kəˈlɪʒn/ *n* تَصَادُم

colonel /ˈkɜːnl/ *n* عَقِيد

colony /ˈkɒləni/ *n* pl **-nies** مُسْتَعْمَرَة

colour /ˈkʌlə(r)/ *n* US **-lor** لَوْن/أَلْوَان مف/ج

colour *v* US **-lor** يُلَوِّن

colourful /ˈkʌləfl/ *adj* US **-lorful** غَنِيّ بِالأَلْوَان

column /ˈkɒləm/ *n* (of building) عَمُود/أَعْمِدَة مف/ج (of vehicles, etc) طَابُور/طَوَابِيرُ مف/ج

columnist /ˈkɒləmnɪst/ *n* كَاتِب مَقَال

combat /ˈkɒmbæt/ *n* مَعْرَكَة/مَعَارِكُ مف/ج
♦ *v* يُحَارِب

combination /kɒmbɪˈneɪʃn/ *n* خَلِيط

combine /kəmˈbaɪnd/ *v* يَخْلِط

combined /kəmˈbaɪn/ *adj* مُشْتَرَك

combo player /ˈkɑmbəʊ/ *n* مُشَغِّل دِي فِي دِي وَفِيدْيُو

come /kʌm/ *v* **came, come** (to speaker) يَأْتِي
Come here! تَعالَ هُنَا
The bus is coming البَاص آتٍ (to reach) يَصِل
The water came to my knees. وَصَلَت المِيَاه إِلَى رُكْبَتَيَّ
The party came to an end. وَصَلَت الحَفْلَة إِلَى نِهَايَتِهَا (goods) يَأْتِي
These shoes also come in black. هَذَا الحِذَاء يَأْتِي أَيْضاً بِاللَّوْن الأَسْوَد (in order) يَأْتِي
She came last. جاءَت بِالأَخِير

come back *phv* يَعُود
She's coming back later. سَتَعُود فِيمَا بَعْد

come down *phv* يَهْبِط
The prices have come down. هَبَطَت الأَسْعَار

come from *phv* يَأْتِي مِن
I come from Birmingham. أَنَا مِن بِيرْمِنْجْهَام

come in *phv* يَدْخُل
He came in quietly. دَخَلَ بِهُدُوء
Come in! اُدْخُل

come off *phv* يَسْقُط
The lid came off. سَقَطَ الغِطَاء

come on *phv* يَبْدَأ
The lights came on. أُنِيرَت الأَضْوَاء

come out *phv* (to emerge) يَظْهَر
The sun came out. ظَهَرَت الشَّمْس
They came out of the house. خَرَجُوا مِن المَنْزِل (films, etc) يُعْرَض
The movie is coming out next week. سَيَبْدَأ عَرْض الفِيلْم فِي الأُسْبُوع القَادِم

come up *phv* يَبْرُز
It came up in the conversation. بَرَزَت خِلَالَ المُنَاقَشَة

comedian /kə'mi:diən/ *n* مُمَثِّل هَزْلِيّ

comedy /'kɒmədi/ *n* pl **-dies** هَزْل

comfort /'kʌmfət/ *n* (of a hotel, etc) رَاحَة
♦ *v* يُوَاسِي

comfortable /'kʌmftəbl/ *adj* مُرِيح

comic /'kɒmɪk/ *adj* هَزْلِيّ

coming /'kʌmɪŋ/ *n* مَجِيء

command /kə'mɑ:nd/ *v* يَأْمُر
♦ *n* أَمْر/أَوَامِرُ مف/ج

commander /kə'mɑ:ndə(r)/ *n* قَائِد

commemorate /kə'meməreɪt/ *v* يُحْيِي ذِكْرَى

comment /'kɒment/ *n* تَعْلِيق/تَعْلِيقَات مف/ج
♦ *v* يُعَلِّق عَلَى

commentary /'kɒməntri/ *n* pl **-ries** تَعْلِيق/تَعْلِيقَات مف/ج

commentator /'kɒmənteɪtə(r)/ *n* مُعَلِّق

commerce /'kɒmɜ:s/ *n* تِجَارَة

commercial /kə'mɜ:ʃl/ *adj* تِجَارِيّ

commercially /kə'mɜ:ʃəli/ *adv* تِجَارِياً

C

C

commission /kə'mɪʃn/ *n* /لَجْنَة
لِجَان مف/ج

commit /kə'mɪt/ *v* (a crime) يَرْتَكِب
(time, funds) يُخَصِّص

commitment /kə'mɪtmənt/ *n*
الْتِزَام/الْتِزَامَات مف/ج

committee /kə'mɪti/ *n* لَجْنَة/لِجَان
مف/ج

commodity /kə'mɒdəti/ *n* pl **-ties**
مَادَّة أَوَّلِيَّة

common /'kɒmən/ *adj* (frequent)
عَامّ (shared) مُنْتَشِر

commonly /'kɒmənli/ *adv* عَادَةً

communal /kə'mju:n/ *adj* مُشْتَرَك

communicate /kə'mju:nɪkeɪt/ *v*
يَتَّصِل بِـ

communication /kəmju:nɪ'keɪʃn/
n اتِّصَال/اتِّصَالَات مف/ج

communications
/kəmju:nɪ'keɪʃnz/ *n* مُوَاصَلَات

communism /'kɒmjunɪzəm/ *n*
شُيُوعِيَّة

communist /'kɒmjənɪst/ *n* شُيُوعِيّ

community /kə'mju:nəti/ *n* pl
-ties مُجْتَمَع/مُجْتَمَعَات مف/ج

commuter /kə'mju:tə(r)/ *n* مُتَنَقِّل
بَيْنَ العَمَل وَالبَيْت

compact /kəm'pækt/ *adj* مُكْتَنِز

companion /kəm'pæniən/ *n* /رَفِيق
رُفَقَاءُ مف/ج

company /'kʌmpəni/ *n* pl **-nies** (in
business) شَرِكَة (of people) رِفْقَة

comparable /'kɒmpərəbl/ *adj* مُمَاثِل

comparative /kəm'pærətɪv/ *adj*
مُقَارَن

compare /kəm'peə(r)/ *v* يُقَارِن

comparison /kəm'pærɪsn/ *n* مُقَارَنَة

compartment /kəm'pɑ:tmənt/
n مَقْصُورَة

compassion /kəm'pæʃn/ *n* شَفَقَة

compatible /kəm'pætəbl/ *adj*
مُتَوَافِق

compel /kəm'pel/ *v* يُجْبِر

compensate /'kɒmpenseɪt/ *v* يُعَوِّض

compensation /kɒmpen'seɪʃn/ *n*
تَعْوِيض/تَعْوِيضَات مف/ج

compete /kəm'pi:t/ *v* يُنَافِس

competence /'kɒmpɪtəns/ *n* كَفَاءَة

competent /'kɒmpɪtənt/ *adj* كُفْء

competition /kɒmpə'tɪʃn/ *n*
(event) مُسَابَقَة (in commerce) مُنَافَسَة

competitive /kəm'petətɪv/ *adj*
تَنَافُسِيّ

competitiveness /
kəm'petətɪvnəs/ *n* تَنَافُس

competitor /kəm'petɪtə(r)/ *n* مُنَافِس

complain /kəm'pleɪn/ *v* يَتَذَمَّر

complaint /kəm'pleɪnt/ *n* /شَكْوَى
شَكَاوَى مف/ج

complete /kəm'pli:t/ *adj* مُكْتَمِل
♦ *v* يُكْمِل

completely /kəm'pli:tli/ *adv* تَمَاماً

completion /kəm'pli:ʃn/ *n* إِكْمَال

complex /'kɒmpleks/ *adj* مُعَقَّد
♦ *n* مُجَمَّع/مُجَمَّعَات مف/ج

complexity /kəm'pleksəti/ *n* pl -ties تَعْقِيد/تَعْقِيدَات مف/ج

complicate /'kɒmplɪkeɪt/ *v* يُعَقِّد

complicated /'kɒmplɪkeɪtɪd/ *adj* مُعَقَّد

complication /kɒmplɪ'keɪʃn/ *n* تَعْقِيد/تَعْقِيدَات مف/ج

compliment /'kɒmplɪmənt/ *n* مُجَامَلَة

comply /kəm'plaɪ/ *v* يُطِيع

component /kəm'pəʊnənt/ *n* مُكَوِّن/مُكَوِّنَات مف/ج

compose /kəm'pəʊz/ *v* (to make) يُشَكِّل (music, a symphony) يُؤَلِّف

composer /kəm'pəʊzə(r)/ *n* مُلَحِّن

composition /kɒmpə'zɪʃn/ *n* تَرْكِيب

compound /'kɒmpaʊnd/ *n* مُجَمَّع/ مُجَمَّعَات مف/ج

comprehensive /kɒmprɪ'hensɪv/ *adj* شَامِل

compromise /'kɒmprəmaɪz/ *n* تَسْوِيَة

compulsory /kəm'pʌlsəri/ *adj* إِلْزَامِيّ

computer /kəm'pju:tə(r)/ *n* حَاسُوب

comrade /'kɒmreɪd/ *n* رَفِيق/رِفَاق مف/ج

conceal /kən'si:l/ *v* يُخْفِي

conceive /kən'si:v/ *v* (an idea) يَعْتَقِد (become pregnant) تَحْبَل

concentrate /'kɒnsntreɪt/ *v* يُرَكِّز فِي

concentration /kɒnsn'treɪʃn/ *n* تَرْكِيز

concept /'kɒnsept/ *n* مَفْهُوم/مَفَاهِيمُ مف/ج

conception /kən'sepʃn/ *n* حَمْل

conceptual /kən'septʃuəl/ *adj* مَفَاهِيمِيّ

concern /kən'sɜ:n/ *v* يَخُصّ
♦ *n* (worry) قَلَق (responsibility) شَأْن/ شُؤُون مف/ج

concerned /kən'sɜ:nd/ *adj* (worried) قَلِق (involved in) مُتَوَرِّط

concerning /kən'sɜ:nɪŋ/ *prep* فِيمَا يَتَعَلَّق بِـ

concert /'kɒnsət/ *n* حَفْلَة مُوسِيقِيَّة

concession /kən'seʃn/ *n* تَنَازُل/ تَنَازُلَات مف/ج

conclude /kən'klu:d/ *v* يَسْتَنْتِج

conclusion /kən'klu:ʒn/ *n* خَاتِمَة

concrete /'kɒŋkri:t/ *adj* وَاقِعِيّ
♦ *n* إِسْمَنْت

condemn /kən'dem/ *v* يُدِين

C

C

condition /kən'dɪʃn/ *n* (state) حَالَة (of a contract) شَرْط/شُرُوط مف/ج

conditions *npl* ظُرُوف

condom /'kɒndɒm/ *n* وَاقٍ جِنْسِيّ

conduct /'kɒndʌkt/ *n* (behaviour) سُلُوك/سُلُوكِيَّات مف/ج

♦ *v* (an experiment, etc) يُجْرِي (a party, etc) يُرْشِد

conductor /kən'dʌktə(r)/ *n* (of orchestra) قَائِد مُوسِيقِيّ (of bus) مُرَاقِب التَذَاكِر

confer /kən'fɜ:(r)/ *v* يَتَشَاوَر

conference /'kɒnfərəns/ *n* مُؤْتَمَر / مُؤْتَمَرَات مف/ج

confess /kən'fes/ *v* يَعْتَرِف

confession /kən'feʃn/ *n* اعْتِرَاف/ اعْتِرَافَات مف/ج

confidence /'kɒnfɪdəns/ *n* ثِقَة

confident /'kɒnfɪdənt/ *adj* وَاثِق

confidential /kɒnfɪ'denʃl/ *adj* سِرِّيّ

configuration /kənfɪgə'reɪʃn/ *n* هَيْئَة

confirm /kən'fɜ:m/ *v* يُؤَكِّد

confirmation /kɒnfə'meɪʃn/ *n* تَأْكِيد/تَأْكِيدَات مف/ج

conflict /'kɒnflɪkt/ *n* صِرَاع/صِرَاعَات مف/ج

conform /kən'fɔ:m/ *v* يَتَطَابَق

confrontation /kɒnfrʌn'teɪʃn/ *n* مُوَاجَهَة

confuse /kən'fju:z/ *v* يُرْبِك

confused /kən'fju:zd/ *adj* مُرْتَبِك

confusion /kən'fju:ʒn/ *n* حَيْرَة

congestion /kən'dʒestʃən/ *n* ازْدِحَام

congratulate /kən'grætʃuleɪt/ *v* يُهَنِّئ

congratulations / kən'grætʃuleɪʃnz/ *n pl* (to winners, a team) تَهْنِئَة/تَهَانِئ مف/ج *Congratulations!* مَبْرُوك

congregation /kɒŋgrɪ'geɪʃn/ *n* رَعَايَا

congress /'kɒŋgres/ *n* مُؤْتَمَر / مُؤْتَمَرَات مف/ج

connect /kə'nekt/ *v* يُوصِل

connection /kə'nekʃn/ *n* (in transport) مُوَاصَلَة (conceptual) رَبْط (electrical) وَصْلَة

conquer /'kɒŋkə(r)/ *v* (a country, etc) يَفْتَح بَلَداً (a mountain, etc) يَتَغَلَّب عَلَى

conquest /'kɒŋkwest/ *n* غَزْو

conscience /'kɒnʃəns/ *n* ضَمِير / ضَمَائِرُ مف/ج

conscious /'kɒnʃəs/ *adj* وَاعٍ

consciousness /'kɒnʃəsnəs/ *n* وَعْي

consecutive /kən'sekjətɪv/ *adj* مُتَعَاقِب

consensus /kən'sensəs/ *n* إِجْمَاع

consent /kən'sent/ *n* مُوَافَقَة ♦ *v* يُوَافِق

consequence /'kɒnsɪkwəns/ *n* عَاقِبَة/عَوَاقِبُ مف/ج

consequently /'kɒnsɪkwəntli/ *adv* تَبْعاً لِذَلِك

conservation /kɒnsə'veɪʃn/ *n* مُحَافَظَة

conservative /kən'sɜːvətɪv/ *adj* (policy) مُحَافِظ (estimate) مُعْتَدِل

conserve /kən'sɜːv/ *v* يُحَافِظ عَلَى

consider /kən'sɪdə(r)/ *v* (a decision, etc) يُفَكِّر فِي (to bear in mind) يَعْتَبِر

considerable /kən'sɪdərəbl/ *adj* ضَخْم

considerably /kən'sɪdərəbli/ *adv* إِلَى حَدّ بَعِيد

consideration /kənsɪdə'reɪʃn/ *n* اعْتِبَار/اعْتِبَارَات مف/ج

considering /kən'sɪdərɪŋ/ *prep* إِذَا أَخَذْنَا بِعَيْن الاعْتِبَار

consistent /kən'sɪstənt/ *adj* مُتَوَافِق

consolation /kɒnsə'leɪʃn/ *n* مُوَاسَاة

console /kən'səʊ/ *n* وَحْدَة التَحَكُّم

consolidate /kən'sɒlɪdeɪt/ *v* يُعَزِّز

consolidation /kənsɒlɪ'deɪʃn/ *n* تَعْزِيز/تَعْزِيزَات مف/ج

conspiracy /kən'spɪrəsi/ *n* pl -cies مُؤَامَرَة

constant /'kɒnstənt/ *adj* دَائِم

constantly /'kɒnstəntli/ *adv* بِشَكْل دَائِم

C

constituency /kən'stɪtjuənsi/ *n* pl -cies دَائِرَة انْتِخَابِيَّة

constitute /'kɒnstɪtjuːt/ *v* يُشَكِّل

constitution /kɒnstɪ'tjuːʃn/ *n* دُسْتُور

constraint /kən'streɪnt/ *n* قَيْد/قُيُود مف/ج

construct /kən'strʌkt/ *v* يُشَيِّد

construction /kən'strʌkʃn/ *n* (of a city, etc) إِنْشَاء/إِنْشَاءَات مف/ج (building) بِنَايَة (in grammar) تَرْكِيب/تَرَاكِيبُ مف/ج

constructive /kən'strʌktɪv/ *adj* بَنَّاء

consult /kən'sʌlt/ *v* يَسْتَشِير

consultant /kən'sʌltənt/ *n* (advisor) مُسْتَشَار (UK: in medicine) طَبِيب اسْتِشَارِيّ

consultation /kɒnsl'teɪʃn/ *n* (doctors, patients) اسْتِشَارَة (of members) مُشَاوَرَة

consume /kən'sjuːm/ *v* يَسْتَهْلِك

consumer /kən'sjuːmə(r)/ *n* مُسْتَهْلِك

contact /'kɒntækt/ *n* شَخْص مَعْرِفَة ♦ *v* يَتَّصِل

contain /kən'teɪn/ *v* (buildings) يَسْتَوْعِب (books, reports) يَحْتَوِي

container /kən'teɪnə(r)/ *n* (for

small items) صُنْدُوق/صَنَادِيقُ مف/ج
(for goods) حَاوِيَة

C

contaminate /kən'tæmɪneɪt/ *v* يُلَوِّث

contamination /kəntæmɪ'neɪʃn/ *n* تَلَوُّث

contemporary /kən'temprəri/ *n* pl **-ries** مُعَاصِر
♦ *adj* حَدِيث

contempt /kən'tempt/ *n* ازْدِرَاء

content /'kɒntent/ *n* مُحْتَوَى

contest /'kɒntest/ *n* مُسَابَقَة

contestant /kən'testənt/ *n* مُتَسَابِق

context /'kɒntekst/ *n* سِيَاق

continent /'kɒntɪnənt/ *n* قَارَّة

continental /kɒntɪ'nentl/ *adj* قَارِّيّ

continually /kən'tɪnjuəli/ *adv* بِاسْتِمْرَار

continue /kən'tɪnju:/ *v* (to go on with) يَسْتَمِرّ (to go on) يُوَاصِل

continuing /kən'tɪnjuɪŋ/ *adj* مُسْتَمِرّ

continuity /kɒntɪ'nju:əti/ *n* اسْتِمْرَارِيَّة

contract /'kɒntrækt/ *n* عَقْد/عُقُود مف/ج

contractor /kən'træktə(r)/ *n* مُتَعَهِّد

contradict /kɒntrə'dɪkt/ *v* يُنَاقِض

contradiction /kɒntrə'dɪkʃn/ *n* تَنَاقُض/تَنَاقُضَات مف/ج

contradictory /kɒntrə'dɪktəri/ *adj* مُتَنَاقِض

contrary /'kɒntrəri/ *adj* مُنَاقِض

contrast /'kɒntrɑ:st/ *n* (difference) تَبَايُن (on TV, etc) تَبَايُن/تَبَايُنَات مف/ج

contribute /kən'trɪbju:t/ *v* يُسَاهِم

contribution /kɒntrɪ'bju:ʃn/ *n* مُسَاهَمَة

contributor /kən'trɪbjətə(r)/ *n* مُسَاهِم

control /kən'trəʊl/ *n* تَحَكُّم/تَحَكُّمَات مف/ج
♦ *v* يَتَحَكَّم

controlled /kən'trəʊld/ *adj* مَضْبُوط

controversial /kɒntrə'vɜ:ʃl/ *adj* مُثِير لِلجَدَل

controversy /'kɒntrəvɜ:si/ *n* pl **-sies** جِدَال

convenience /kən'vi:niəns/ *n* مُلَاءَمَة

convenient /kən'vi:niənt/ *adj* مُلَائِم

convention /kən'venʃn/ *n* (congress) اجْتِمَاع/اجْتِمَاعَات مف/ج (norm) تَقْلِيد/تَقَالِيدُ مف/ج (treaty) اتِّفَاقِيَّة

conventional /kən'venʃənl/ *adj* تَقْلِيدِيّ

conversation /kɒnvə'seɪʃn/ *n* مُحَادَثَة

conversion /kən'vɜ:ʃn/ *n* تَحْوِيل

convert /kən'vɜːt/ *v* (in a process) يُحَوِّل (to a religion) يُبَدِّل
♦ *n* مُعْتَنِق دِيَانَة أُخْرَى

convey /kən'veɪ/ *v* يَنْقُل

convict /'kɒnvɪkt/ *v* يُدِين

convicted /'kɒnvɪktəd/ *adj* مُدَان

conviction /kən'vɪkʃn/ *n* (belief) إِيمَان (by a court) إِدَانَة

convince /kən'vɪns/ *v* يُقْنِع

cook /kʊk/ *n* طَاهٍ/طُهَاة مف/ج
♦ *v* يَطْهُو

cool /kuːl/ *adj* بَارِد
a cool drink مَشْرُوب بَارِد
a cool day يَوْم بَارِد
a cool summer صَيْف بَارِد (informal: good) جَيِّد جِدّاً
That's cool! هَذَا جَيِّد جِدّاً

cooperate /kəʊ'ɒpəreɪt/ *v* يَتَعَاوَن

cooperation /kəʊɒpə'reɪʃn/ *n* تَعَاوُن

cooperative /kəʊ'ɒpərətɪv/ *adj* (colleague) مُتَعَاوِن (farm, etc) تَعَاوُنِيّ

coordinate /kəʊ'ɔːdɪneɪt/ *v* يُنَسِّق

coordination /kəʊɔːdɪ'neɪʃn/ *n* تَنْسِيق/تَنْسِيقَات مف/ج

cope /kəʊp/ *v* يَتَغَلَّب عَلَى

copper /'kɒpə(r)/ *n* نُحَاس

copy /'kɒpi/ *n* pl **-pies** نُسْخَة/نُسَخ مف/ج
♦ *v* (a document, etc) يَنْسَخ (a person) يُقَلِّد

copyright /'kɒpiraɪt/ *n* حَقّ الطَبْع

coral /'kɒrəl/ *n* مَرْجَان

cord /kɔːd/ *n* حَبْل/أَحْبَال مف/ج

core /kɔː(r)/ *n* لُبّ

coriander /kɒri'ændə(r)/ *n* كُزْبَرَة

cork /kɔːk/ *n* فِلِّينَة

corn /kɔːn/ *n* (cereals) حَبَّة الذُرَة أَو القَمْح (in US: maize) ذُرَة (on the foot) مِسْمَار قَدَم

corner /'kɔːnə(r)/ *n* (of a room) زَاوِيَة/زَوَايَا مف/ج (of two streets) زَاوِيَة الطَرِيق

corporation /kɔːpə'reɪʃn/ *n* شَرِكَة

corpse /kɔːps/ *n* جُثَّة/جُثَث مف/ج

correct /kə'rekt/ *adj* صَحِيح
♦ *v* يُصَحِّح

correction /kə'rekʃn/ *n* تَصْحِيح/تَصْحِيحَات مف/ج

correctly /kə'rektli/ *adv* عَلَى نَحْو صَحِيح

correspond /kɒrə'spɒnd/ *v* (by letter, email) يَتَرَاسَل (figures) يَتَوَافَق

correspondence /kɒrə'spɒndəns/ *n* مُرَاسَلَة

correspondent /kɒrə'spɒndənt/ *n* مُرَاسِل

corridor /'kɒrɪdɔː(r)/ *n* رُوَاق/أَرْوِقَة مف/ج

C

corrode /kə'rəʊd/ *v* يُصْدِئ

corrupt /kə'rʌpt/ *adj* فَاسِد

corruption /kə'rʌpʃn/ *n* فَسَاد

cost /kɒst/ *n* تَكْلِفَة/تَكَالِيفُ مف/ج
♦ *v* **cost** يُكَلِّف

costly /'kɒstli/ *adj* مُكْلِف

costume /'kɒstju:m/ *n* زِيّ

cottage /'kɒtɪʤ/ *n* كُوخ/أَكْوَاخ مف/ج

cotton /'kɒtn/ *n* قُطْن

couch /kaʊtʃ/ *n* أَرِيكَة/أَرَائِكُ مف/ج

cough /kɒf/ *n* سُعَال
♦ *v* يَسْعُل

could /kʊd/ *modal v* (ability) يَسْتَطِيع
I could hear the radio.
اسْتَطَعْتُ سَمَاع المِذْيَاع
She couldn't see you. لَم تَسْتَطِع رُؤْيَتَكَ
He couldn't drive then.
لَم يَسْتَطِع السِيَاقَة إذاً
He couldn't understand.
لَم يَسْتَطِع فَهْم ذَلِكَ (permission) يُمْكِن
He told me I couldn't have it.
أَخْبَرَنِي أَنَّهُ لاَ يُمْكِنُنِي أَخْذُهَا (possibility) يُمْكِن
We could still go there.
لاَ يَزَال بِإِمْكَانِنَا الذَهَاب إِلَى هُنَاكَ (in requests) هَل بِإِمْكَانِكَ
Could you tell me the cost?
هَل بِإِمْكَانِكَ أَنْ تُخْبِرَنِي عَن التَكْلِفَة؟
Could you carry my case?
هَل بِإِمْكَانِكَ حِمْلَان حَقِيبَتِي؟

couldn't /'kʊdnt/ *contr* (= could not: see could)

council /'kaʊnsl/ *n* مَجْلِس/مَجَالِسُ مف/ج

councillor /'kaʊnsələ(r)/ *n* عُضْو مَجْلِس

count /kaʊnt/ *v* (to say numbers) يَعُدّ (the votes) يَعُدّ (be valid) يُحْسَب

counter /'kaʊntə(r)/ *n* (in a shop) طَاوِلَة (in a bank) شُبَّاك الزَبَائِن

country /'kʌntri/ *n* pl **-ties** (political unit) دَوْلَة/دُوَل مف/ج (non-urban area) الرِيف

countryside /'kʌntrisaɪd/ *n* رِيف/أَرْيَاف مف/ج

county /'kaʊnti/ *n* pl **-ties** إِقْلِيم/أَقَالِيمُ مف/ج

couple /'kʌpl/ *n* زَوْج، رَجُل وَامْرَأَة

courage /'kʌrɪʤ/ *n* شَجَاعَة

courgette /kʊə'ʒet/ *n* كُوسَا

courier /'kʊriə(r)/ *n* عَامِل أَو شَرِكَة النَقْل

course /kɔ:s/ *n* (of lessons) فَصْل دِرَاسِيّ (of a meal) لَوْن الطَعَام

court /kɔ:t/ *n* مَحْكَمَة/مَحَاكِمُ مف/ج

courtesy /'kɜ:təsi/ *n* pl **-sies** لَطَافَة

courtroom /'kɔ:trʊm/ *n* قَاعَة المَحْكَمَة

couscous /'ku:sku:s/ *n* كُسْكُسِيّ

cousin /'kʌzn/ *n* ابْن أَو بِنْت عَمّ أَو خَال أَو عَمَّة أَو خَالَة

cover /'kʌvə(r)/ *n* (shelter) غِطَاء/ أَغْطِيَة مف/ج (of books, etc) غِلَاف/ أَغْلِفَة مف/ج (in insurance) تَغْطِيَة (for furniture) غِطَاء/أَغْطِيَة مف/ج
♦ *v* يُغَطِّي ♦

cow /kaʊ/ *n* بَقَرَة/بَقَر مف/ج

cowboy /'kaʊbɔɪ/ *n* رَاعِي البَقَر

crab /kræb/ *n* سَرَطَان

crack /kræk/ *n* شَقّ/شُقُوق مف/ج
♦ *v* يَتَصَدَّع ♦

craft /krɑ:ft/ *n* حِرْفَة/حِرَف مف/ج

craftsman /'krɑ:ftsmən/ *n* pl **-men** حِرَفِيّ

crash /kræʃ/ *n* حَادِث تَصَادُم

crash *v* (a vehicle) يَصْطَدِم بِـ (planes, etc) يَتَحَطَّم

crawl /krɔ:l/ *v* يَزْحَف

crazy /'kreɪzi/ *adj* مَجْنُون

cream /kri:m/ *n* (on milk) قِشْطَة (cosmetic, etc) مَرْهَم/مَرَاهِمُ مف/ج

create /kri'eɪt/ *v* يَخْلُق

creation /kri'eɪʃn/ *n* ابْتِكَار/ابْتِكَارَات مف/ج

creative /kri'eɪtɪv/ *adj* إِبْدَاعِيّ

creator /kri'eɪtə(r)/ *n* مُبْدِع

creature /'kri:tʃə(r)/ *n* مَخْلُوق/ مَخْلُوقَات مف/ج

credible /'kredəbl/ *adj* مُمْكِن تَصْدِيقُهُ

credit /'kredɪt/ *n* ائْتِمَان
♦ *v* يُضِيف مَالاً لِلحِسَاب ♦

creditor /'kredɪtə(r)/ *n* دَائِن

credit rating /'reɪtɪŋ/ *n* التَّقْيِيم الائْتِمَانِيّ

creek /kri:k/ *n* (inlet) جَدْوَل/جَدَاوِلُ مف/ج (US: stream) نَهْر صَغِير

creep /kri:p/ *v* **crept** يَزْحَف

creepy /'kri:pi/ *adj* مُرَوِّع

crew /kru:/ *n* طَاقِم/أَطْقُم مف/ج

cricket /'krɪkɪt/ *n* (insect) صَرَّار اللَيْل (game) الكْرِيكِت

crime /kraɪm/ *n* جَرِيمَة/جَرَائِمُ مف/ج

criminal /'krɪmɪnl/ *adj* إِجْرَامِيّ
♦ *n* مُجْرِم

crisis /'kraɪsɪs/ *n* pl **-ses** أَزْمَة

crisp /krɪsp/ *adj* هَشّ
♦ *n* UK (in packet) رَقَائِق بَطَاطَا

critic /'krɪtɪk/ *n* نَاقِد

critical /'krɪtɪkl/ *adj* (comment) نَاقِد (illness) حَرِج

criticize /'krɪtɪsaɪz/ *v* يَنْتَقِد، يَنْقُد

criticism /'krɪtɪsɪzəm/ *n* نَقْد، انْتِقَاد

crop /krɒp/ *n* مَحْصُول/مَحَاصِيلُ مف/ج

cross /krɒs/ *adj* غَاضِب
♦ *n* صَلِيب/صُلْبَان مف/ج
♦ *v* يَعْبُر

crossbar /'krɒsbɑ:(r)/ *n* عَارِضَة المَرْمَى

C

crossing /'krɒsɪŋ/ *n* (act) عُبُور (for pedestrians) مَعْبَرمُشَاة (for trains) نُقْطَة عُبُور

crosswalk /'krɒswɔːk/ *n* US مَمَرّ لِلمُشَاة

crowd /kraʊd/ *n* حَشْد/حُشُود مف/ج

crowded /'kraʊdɪd/ *adj* مُزْدَحِم

crown /kraʊn/ *n* تَاج/تِيجَان مف/ج

crude /kruːd/ *adj* (oil) خَام (joke) فَجّ

cruel /kruːəl/ *adj* وَحْشِيّ

cruelty /'kruːəlti/ *n* وَحْشِيَّة

cruise /kruːz/ *n* رِحْلَة بَحْرِيَّة مِن أَجْل المُتْعَة

crumble /'krʌmbl/ *v* يَتَفَتَّت

crush /krʌʃ/ *v* يَسْحَق

cry /kraɪ/ *n* (shout) صَيْحَة (for help, etc) صَرْخَة

♦ *v* (to shed tears) يَبْكِي

crystal /'krɪstl/ *n* بَلُّور

cucumber /'kjuːkʌmbə(r)/ *n* خِيَار

cumin /'kʌmɪn/ *n* كَمُّون

culprit /'kʌlprɪt/ *n* المُتَّهَم

cult /kʌlt/ *n* طَائِفَة/طَوَائِفُ مف/ج

cultivate /'kʌltɪveɪt/ *v* (the land) يَحْرُث (crops) يَزْرَع (friendship) يَسْعَى إِلَى

culture /'kʌltʃə(r)/ *n* ثَقَافَة

cup /kʌp/ *n* (for drinking) كُوب/أَكْوَاب (م) مف/ج (trophy) كَأْس/كُؤُوس مف/ج

cupboard /'kʌbəd/ *n* خِزَانَة

curb /kɜːb/ *v* يَضْبِط

curd /kɜːd/ *n* خُثَارَة اللَبَن

cure /kjʊə(r)/ *n* (remedy) دَوَاء/أَدْوِيَة مف/ج (process) عِلَاج

♦ *v* يُعَالِج

curiosity /kjʊəri'ɒsəti/ *n* فُضُول

curious /'kjʊəriəs/ *adj* (fact) غَرِيب (to know) فُضُولِيّ

curl /kɜːl/ *n* تَجْعِيدَة/تَجَاعِيدُ مف/ج

currency /'kʌrənsi/ *n* pl **-cies** عُمْلَة

current /'kʌrənt/ *adj* حَالِيّ

♦ *n* (of water, air) تَدَفُّق (electricity) تَيَّار

curriculum /kə'rɪkjələm/ *n* مِنْهَاج/مَنَاهِجُ مف/ج

curriculum vitae *n* سِيرَة ذَاتِيَّة

curse /kɜːs/ *n* لَعْنَة

♦ *v* (to express anger) يَلْعَن (to condemn) يَشْتُم

curtain /'kɜːtn/ *n* سِتَارَة/سَتَائِرُ مف/ج

curve /kɜːv/ *n* (line) مُنْحَنَى/مُنْحَنَيَات مف/ج (in a road) مُنْعَطَف/مُنْعَطَفَات مف/ج

cushion /'kʊʃn/ *n* وِسَادَة

custard /'kʌstəd/ *n* كَسْتَر

custom /'kʌstəm/ *n* (national) عُرْف/أَعْرَاف مف/ج (sth you do regularly) عَادَة

customary /'kʌstəməri/ *adj* مُعْتَاد

customer /ˈkʌstəmə(r)/ *n* /زَبُون
زَبَائِنُ مف/ج

customs /ˈkʌstəmz/ *n pl* دَائِرَة
الجَمَارِك

cut /kʌt/ *v* **cut** (bread, grass) يَقْطَع
(spending, etc) يُخَفِّض
♦ *n* (with a knife) جُرْح (in wages)
تَخْفِيض/تَخْفِيضَات مف/ج

cute /kjuːt/ *adj* جَذَّاب

cycle /ˈsaɪkl/ *n* حَلَقَة

cyclist /ˈsaɪklɪst/ *n* رَاكِب الدَرَّاجَة

cylinder /ˈsɪlɪndə(r)/ *n* أُسْطُوَانَة

Cyprus /ˈsʌɪprəs/ *n* قُبْرُص

D

dad /dæd/ *n* أَب/آبَاء مف/ج

daddy /'dædi/ *n* pl **-dies** أَب/آبَاء مف/ج

dagger /'dægə(r)/ *n* خَنْجَر/خَنَاجِرُ مف/ج

daily /'deɪli/ *adj* يَوْمِيّ

dam /dæm/ *n* سَدّ/سُدُود مف/ج

damage /'dæmɪʤ/ *n* ضَرَر/أَضْرَار مف/ج

♦ *v* يُتْلِف

damaged /'dæmɪʤd/ *adj* تَالِف

Damascus /də'mæskəs/ *n* دِمَشْق

dance /dɑ:ns/ *n* رَقْص

♦ *v* يَرْقُص

dancer /'dɑ:nsə(r)/ *n* رَاقِص

dancing /'dɑ:nsɪŋ/ *n* رَقْص

danger /'deɪnʤə(r)/ *n* خَطَر/أَخْطَار مف/ج

dangerous /'deɪnʤərəs/ *adj* خَطِر

dare /deə(r)/ *v* (be brave enough) يَجْرُؤ (sb to do sth) يَتَحَدَّى

dark *adj* (house, street) مُظْلِم

a dark room غُرْفَة مُظْلِمَة

It's getting dark. بَدَأَ الظَلَام يَحَلّ

(colour, shade) غَامِق/غَوَامِقُ مف/ج

her dark brown hair شَعْرُهَا البُنِّيّ الغَامِق

♦ *n* ظَلَام

darkness /'dɑ:knəs/ *n* ظُلْمَة

darling /'dɑ:lɪŋ/ *n* حَبِيب

dash /dæʃ/ *n* شَرْطَة

♦ *v* يَتَدَافَع

database /'deɪtəbeɪs/ *n* قَاعِدَة بَيَانَات

date /deɪt/ *n* (in time) تَارِيخ

What's the date today?

مَا هُوَ تَارِيخ اليَوْم؟

The date is the 23rd of August.

التَارِيخ هُوَ الثَالِث وَالعِشْرُون مِن آب

(social) لِقَاء (fruit) تَمْرَة/تَمْر مف/ج

daughter /'dɔ:tə(r)/ *n* بِنْت/بَنَات (م) مف/ج

dawn /dɔ:n/ *n* (early morning) فَجْر

(beginning) مَهْد

day /deɪ/ *n* يَوْم/أَيَّام مف/ج

daylight /'deɪlaɪt/ *n* ضَوْء النَهَار

daytime /'deɪtaɪm/ *n* وَقْت النَهَار

dead /ded/ *adj* مَيِّت

deaf /def/ *adj* أَطْرَش/طَرْشَاء/طُرْش مذ/م/ج

deal /di:l/ *n* صَفْقَة

♦ *v* **dealt** (cards) يُوَزِّع وَرَق اللَعِب

dealer /'di:lə(r)/ *n* تَاجِر/تُجَّار مف/ج

dear /dɪə(r)/ *adj* (in letters) عَزِيزِي/ غَالٍ/غَوَالٍ (beloved) عَزِيزَتِي مذ/م مف/ج

death /deθ/ *n* مَوْت

debate /dɪ'beɪt/ *n* مُنَاقَشَة

debris /'debri:/ *n* حُطَام

debt /det/ *n* دَيْن/دُيُون مف/ج

decade /'dekeɪd/ *n* عَقْد/عُقُود مف/ج

decaffeinated /di:'kæfɪneɪtɪd/ *adj* خَالِي الكَفِيِين

decay /dɪ'keɪ/ *n* اهْتِرَاء
♦ *v* يَتَحَلَّل

deceive /dɪ'si:v/ *v* يَخْدَع

December /dɪ'sembə(r)/ *n* (see August) دِيسَمْبِر

decent /'di:snt/ *adj* مُهَذَّب

decide /dɪ'saɪd/ *v* (to take a decision) يُقَرِّر (the result, the issue) يَحْسِم

decision /dɪ'sɪʒn/ *n* قَرَار/قَرَارَات مف/ج

decisive /dɪ'saɪsɪv/ *adj* حَاسِم

deck /dek/ *n* ظَهْر السَفِينَة

declaration /deklə'reɪʃn/ *n* تَصْرِيح/ تَصْرِيحَات مف/ج

declare /dɪ'kleə(r)/ *v* (innocent, guilty) يُعْلِن (one's income) يُصَرِّح

decline /dɪ'klaɪn/ *n* تَرَاجُع
♦ *v* يَتَدَهْوَر

decorate /'dekəreɪt/ *v* يُزَخْرِف

decoration /dekə'reɪʃn/ *n* (item) تَزْيِين (act) زَخْرَفَة

decrease /'di:kri:s/ *n* نَقْص
♦ /dɪ'kri:s/ *v* يَنْخَفِض

dedicate /'dedɪkeɪt/ *v* يُخَصِّص

dedicated /'dedɪkeɪtɪd/ *adj* مُخْلِص

deduction /dɪ'dʌkʃn/ *n* اسْتِنْتَاج/ اسْتِنْتَاجَات مف/ج

deed /di:d/ *n* عَمَل/أَعْمَال مف/ج

deep /di:p/ *adj* عَمِيق

deepen /'di:pən/ *v* يُعَمِّق

deer /dɪə(r)/ *n* pl **deer** أَيِّل

defeat /dɪ'fi:t/ *n* هَزِيمَة/هَزَائِمُ مف/ج
♦ *v* يَنْهَزِم

defect /'di:fekt/ *n* خَلَل

defence /dɪ'fens/ *n* US **-ense** (of country) دِفَاع (in sport) خَطّ الدِفَاع

defend /dɪ'fend/ *v* يَحْمِي

deficiency /dɪ'fɪʃnsi/ *n* pl **-cies** نَقْص

deficit /'defɪsɪt/ *n* عَجْز

define /dɪ'faɪn/ *v* يُعَرِّف

definite /'defɪnət/ *adj* (answer) وَاضِح (plan) مُحَدَّد

definitely /'defɪnətli/ *adv* بِالتَأْكِيد

definition /defɪ'nɪʃn/ *n* (of a word) تَعْرِيف/تَعْرِيفَات مف/ج (of an image) إِيضَاح/إِيضَاحَات مف/ج

defy /dɪ'faɪ/ *v* يَعْصِي

D

D

degrade /dɪ'greɪd/ *v* يَتَحَلَّل

degree /dɪ'griː/ *n* (in scale) دَرَجَة (in education) دَرَجَة عِلْمِيَّة

delay /dɪ'leɪ/ *n* تَأْخِير/تَأْخِيرَات مف/ج ♦ *v* (a departure) يُؤَخِّر (a ceremony) يُؤَجِّل

delegate /'delɪgət/ *n* مَنْدُوب

delegation /delɪ'geɪʃn/ *n* وَفْد/وُفُود مف/ج

delete /dɪ'liːt/ *v* يَحْذِف

deletion /dɪ'liːʃn/ *n* حَذْف

deliberate /dɪ'lɪbərət/ *adj* مُتَعَمَّد

delicate /'delɪkət/ *adj* (jewellery, etc) رَقِيق (health) ضَعِيف/ضُعَفَاءُ مف/ج

delicious /dɪ'lɪʃəs/ *adj* لَذِيذ

delight /dɪ'laɪt/ *n* بَهْجَة ♦ *v* يُسْعِد

delightful /dɪ'laɪtfl/ *adj* بَهِيج

delinquent /dɪ'lɪŋkwənt/ *n* خَارِج عَلَى القَانُون

deliver /dɪ'lɪvə(r)/ *v* يُوَصِّل

delivery /dɪ'lɪvəri/ *n* pl **-ries** تَوْصِيل

delivery man *n* مُوَظَّف تَوْصِيل

demand /dɪ'mɑːnd/ *n* (for goods) طَلَب (order) أَمْر/أَوَامِرُ مف/ج ♦ *v* (high quality) يَتَطَلَّب (a refund) يُطَالِب

demanding /dɪ'mɑːndɪŋ/ *adj* كَثِير المَطَالِب

democracy /dɪ'mɒkrəsi/ *n* pl **-cies** دِيمُوقْرَاطِيَّة

democratic /demə'krætɪk/ *adj* دِيمُقْرَاطِيّ

demolish /dɪ'mɒlɪʃ/ *v* يُدَمِّر

demolition /demə'lɪʃn/ *n* تَدْمِير

demon /'diːmən/ *n* شَيْطَان/شَيَاطِينُ مف/ج

demonstrate /'demənstreɪt/ *v* (a process, new product) يُوَضِّح (politically) يَتَظَاهَر

demonstration /demən'streɪʃn/ *n* (of a process, product) إِيضَاح (protest) مُظَاهَرَة

den /den/ *n* عَرِين/عَرَائِنُ مف/ج

denial /dɪ'naɪəl/ *n* إِنْكَار

denounce /dɪ'naʊns/ *v* يَشْجُب

dense /dens/ *adj* كَثِيف

density /'densəti/ *n* كَثَافَة

dental /'dentl/ *adj* مُتَعَلِّق بِالأَسْنَان

dentist /'dentɪst/ *n* طَبِيب أَسْنَان

deny /dɪ'naɪ/ *v* (a charge) يُنْكِر (to deprive) يَرْفُض مَنْحاً

depart /dɪ'pɑːt/ *v* يُغَادِر

department /dɪ'pɑːtmənt/ *n* (section) قِسْم/أَقْسَام مف/ج (ministry) وِزَارَة

departure /dɪ'pɑːtʃə(r)/ *n* (from a place) مُغَادَرَة

dependence /dɪ'pendəns/ *n* تَبَعِيَّة

dependent /dɪ'pendənt/ *adj* مُعْتَمِد عَلَى غَيْرِه

deploy /dɪ'plɔɪ/ *v* يَنْشُر

deposit /dɪ'pɒzɪt/ *n* (down payment) عَرْبُون (sediment) تَرَسُّب/تَرَسُّبَات مف/ج
♦ *v* (a load) يَضَع (money) يُودِع (فِي البَنْك)

depress /dɪ'pres/ *v* يُحْزِن

depressed /dɪ'prest/ *adj* مُكْتَئِب

depression /dɪ'preʃn/ *n* (psychological) اِكْتِئَاب (economic) كَسَاد

deprivation /deprɪ'veɪʃn/ *n* حِرْمَان

depth /depθ/ *n* عُمْق/أَعْمَاق مف/ج

deputy /'depjuti/ *n* pl **-ties** نَائِب

descendant /dɪ'sendənt/ *n* سَلِيل

descent /dɪ'sent/ *n* هُبُوط

describe /dɪ'skraɪb/ *v* يُوصِف

description /dɪ'skrɪpʃn/ *n* وَصْف

desert /'dezət/ *n* صَحْرَاء/صَحَارٍ مف/ج
♦ *v* /dɪ'zɜːt/ (one's family) يَهْجُر (from army) يَفِرّ مِن الخِدْمَة

deserve /dɪ'zɜːv/ *v* يَسْتَحِقّ

design /dɪ'zaɪn/ *v* (a traffic system, restaurant, a book jacket) يُصَمِّم
♦ *n* (on paper) تَصْمِيم

designer /dɪ'zaɪnə(r)/ *n* مُصَمِّم

desirable /dɪ'zaɪərəbl/ *adj* مَرْغُوب

desire /dɪ'zaɪə(r)/ *n* أُمْنِيَّة/أَمَانِيّ مف/ج
♦ *v* يَرْغَب

desk /desk/ *n* مَكْتَب/مَكَاتِب مف/ج

desktop computer /'desktɑp/ *n* حَاسُوب مَكْتَبِيّ

despair /dɪ'speə(r)/ *n* يَأْس

desperate /'despərət/ *adj* مُتَلَهِّف

despise /dɪ'spaɪz/ *v* يَحْتَقِر

despite /dɪ'spaɪt/ *prep* بِالرَغْم مِن

dessert /dɪ'zɜːt/ *n* حَلْوَى تُقَدَّم بَعْدَ وَجْبَة الطَعَام

destination /destɪ'neɪʃn/ *n* المَكَان المَقْصُود

destiny /'destəni/ *n* قَدَر

destroy /dɪ'strɔɪ/ *v* يُدَمِّر

destruction /dɪ'strʌkʃn/ *n* تَدْمِير

detached /dɪ'tætʃt/ *adj* مَفْصُول

detail /'diːteɪl/ *n* تَفْصِيل/تَفَاصِيلُ مف/ج

detailed /'diːteɪld/ *adj* مُفَصَّل

detain /dɪ'teɪn/ *v* يَحْجِز

detect /dɪ'tekt/ *v* يَكْتَشِف

detective /dɪ'tektɪv/ *n* مُحَقِّق

detention /dɪ'tenʃn/ *n* تَوْقِيف

deter /dɪ'tɜː(r)/ *v* يَرْدَع

deteriorate /dɪ'tɪəriəreɪt/ *v* يَتَقَهْقَر

determination /dɪtɜːmɪ'neɪʃn/ *n* التَصْمِيم عَلَى عَمَل شَيْء

determined /dɪ'tɜːmɪnd/ *adj* مُصَمِّم عَلَى رَأْيِه

D

D

detest /dɪ'test/ *v* (sb) يَمْقُت (cheese) يَبْغَض

devastate /'devəsteɪt/ *v* يُدَمِّر

devastating /'devəsteɪtɪŋ/ *adj* مُدَمِّر

develop /dɪ'veləp/ *v* (a property) يُطَوِّر (to increase) يَتَطَوَّر

development /dɪ'veləpmənt/ *n* تَطَوُّر

device /dɪ'vaɪs/ *n* جِهَاز/أَجْهِزَة مف/ج

devil /'devl/ *n* شَيْطَان/شَيَاطِينُ مف/ج

devise /dɪ'vaɪz/ *v* يَبْتَكِر

devote /dɪ'vəʊt/ *v* يُكَرِّس

devotion /dɪ'vəʊʃn/ *n* إِخْلَاص

diabetes /daɪə'biːtiːz/ *n* دَاء السُكَّرِيّ

diagnose /daɪəg'nəʊz/ *v* يُشَخِّص

diagnosis /daɪəg'nəʊsɪs/ *n* pl **-ses** تَشْخِيص

diagram /'daɪəgræm/ *n* مُخَطَّط بَيَانِيّ

dial /'daɪəl/ *v* يُدِير قُرْص الهَاتِف

dialogue /'daɪəlɒg/ *n* US **-log** حِوَار

diameter /daɪ'æmɪtə(r)/ *n* قُطْر الدَائِرَة

diamond /'daɪəmənd/ *n* مَاسَة

diary /'daɪəri/ *n* pl **-ries** (personal record) مُفَكِّرَة يَوْمِيَّة (for future events) مُذَكِّرَات

dictate /dɪk'teɪt/ *v* يُمْلِي

dictator /dɪk'teɪtə(r)/ *n* دِكْتَاتُور

dictatorship /dɪk'teɪtəʃɪp/ *n* دِكْتَاتُورِيَّة

dictionary /'dɪkʃənri/ *n* pl **-ries** قَامُوس/قَوَامِيسُ مف/ج

didn't /'dɪdnt/ *contr* (= did not: see do)

die /daɪ/ *v* يَمُوت

diesel /'diːzl/ *n* دِيزِل

diet /'daɪət/ *n* (limited intake) حِمْيَة (food eaten) غِذَاء

differ /'dɪfə(r)/ *v* يَخْتَلِف

difference /'dɪfrəns/ *n* اخْتِلَاف/ اخْتِلَافَات مف/ج

different /'dɪfrənt/ *adj* مُخْتَلِف

difficult /'dɪfɪkəlt/ *adj* صَعْب

difficulty /'dɪfɪkəlti/ *n* pl **-ties** صُعُوبَة

dig /dɪg/ *v* **dug** يَحْفُر

digest /'daɪdʒest/ *v* يَهْضُم

digit /'dɪdʒɪt/ *n* رَقَم

digital /'dɪdʒɪtl/ *adj* رَقْمِيّ

digital camera *n* كَامِيرَا رَقْمِيَّة

digital TV *n* تِلْفَاز رَقْمِيّ

digital radio *n* رَادْيُو رَقْمِيّ

dignity /'dɪgnəti/ *n* كَرَامَة

dilemma /daɪ'lemə/ *n* مُعْضِلَة

dilute /daɪ'luːt/ *v* يُخَفِّف

dim /dɪm/ *adj* ضَوْء خَافِت

diminish /dɪ'mɪnɪʃ/ *v* يُقَلِّل

dinar /'diːnɑː(r)/ *n* دِينَار/دَنَانِيرُ مف/ج

dine /daɪn/ *v* يَتَعَشَّى

dinner /'dɪnə(r)/ *n* (in evening) عَشَاء (at midday) غَدَاء

diplomacy /dɪ'pləʊməsi/ *n* دِبْلُومَاسِيَّة

diplomat /'dɪpləmæt/ *n* دِبْلُومَاسِيّ

direct /daɪ'rekt/ *adj* مُبَاشِر ♦ *v* (a movie) يُخْرِج (an orchestra) يُوَجِّه (an operation) يُدِير

direction /daɪ'rekʃn/ *n* (course) اتِّجَاه (of a movie, play) إِخْرَاج

directions /daɪ'rekʃns/ *n pl* تَوْجِيه

directive /daɪ'rektɪv/ *n* قَرَار/قَرَارَات مف/ج

directly /daɪ'rektli/ *adv* مُبَاشَرَةً

director /daɪ'rektə(r)/ *n* (of an institute, etc) مُدِير (of a movie, etc) مُخْرِج

dirham /'dɪərhəm/ *n* دِرْهَم/دَرَاهِم مف/ج

dirt /dɜːt/ *n* وَحْل

dirty /'dɜːti/ *adj* (clothes, street) مُتَّسِخ (joke) بَذِيء

disability /dɪsə'bɪləti/ *n* pl **-ties** إِعَاقَة

disabled /dɪs'eɪbld/ *adj* (person) مُعَاق (access, parking) لِلْمُعَاقِين

disadvantage /dɪsəd'vɑːntɪdʒ/ *n* سَيِّئَة

disagree /dɪsə'griː/ *v* يُخَالِف

disagreement /dɪsə'griːmənt/ *n* خِلَاف/خِلَافَات مف/ج

disappear /dɪsə'pɪə(r)/ *v* يَخْتَفِي

disappearance /dɪsə'pɪərəns/ *n* اخْتِفَاء

disappoint /dɪsə'pɔɪnt/ *v* يُخَيِّب آمَالاً

disappointment /dɪsə'pɔɪntmənt/ *n* خَيْبَة أَمَل

disaster /dɪ'zɑːstə(r)/ *n* كَارِثَة/كَوَارِث مف/ج

disastrous /dɪ'zɑːstrəs/ *adj* كَارِثِيّ

disc /dɪsk/ *n* **disk** قُرْص/أَقْرَاص مف/ج

discard /dɪs'kɑːd/ *v* يَتَخَلَّص

discharge /dɪs'tʃɑːdʒ/ *v* (smoke, gas) يُطْلِق (a patient) يُخْرِج (from the army) يُسَرِّح

disciple /dɪ'saɪpl/ *n* حَوَارِيّ

discipline /'dɪsəplɪn/ *n* انْضِبَاط

disclose /dɪs'kləʊz/ *v* يَكْشِف (عَن)

disclosure /dɪs'kləʊʒə(r)/ *n* الكَشْف عَن

disco /'dɪskəʊ/ *n* حَانَة رَقْص

discomfort /dɪs'kʌmfət/ *n* ضِيق

disconnect /dɪskə'nekt/ *v* يَفْصِل

discount /'dɪskaʊnt/ *n* خَصْم/خُصُومَات مف/ج

discourage /dɪs'kʌrɪdʒ/ *v* يُثَبِّط الهِمَّة

discover /dɪ'skʌvə(r)/ *v* يَكْتَشِف

discovery /dɪ'skʌvəri/ *n* pl **-ries** اكْتِشَاف/اكْتِشَافَات مف/ج

discrepancy /dɪs'krepənsi/ *n* pl **-cies** تَعَارُض/تَعَارُضَات مف/ج

discretion /dɪ'skreʃn/ *n* فِطْنَة

D

D

discrimination /dɪskrɪmɪ'neɪʃn/ *n* تَمْيِيز

discuss /dɪ'skʌs/ *v* يُنَاقِش

discussion /dɪ'skʌʃn/ *n* مُنَاقَشَة

disease /dɪ'zi:z/ *n* مَرَض/أَمْرَاض مف/ج

disguise /dɪs'gaɪz/ *v* يَتَنَكَّر

disgust /dɪs'gʌst/ *n* اشْمِئْزَاز
♦ *v* يُقَرِّف

dish /dɪʃ/ *n* (plate) صَحْن/صُحُون طَبَق/أَطْبَاق مف/ج (food) مف/ج

disk /dɪsk/ *n* قُرْص/أَقْرَاص مف/ج

dislike /dɪs'laɪk/ *n* (of a person) اسْتِيَاء
my dislike of his brother
اسْتِيَائِي لِأَخِيهِ (of a place, etc) كُرْه
I have a dislike of air travel.
لَدَيَّ كُرْه لِلسَفَر جَوّاً
♦ *v* (a person) يَسْتَاء
I dislike her. أَسْتَاء مِنْهَا (air travel, pop music) يَكْرَه
I dislike flying. أَكْرَه الطَيَرَان (garlic) يَشْمَئِزّ (من)
I dislike mussels. أَشْمَئِزّ مِن بَلَح البَحْر

dismiss /dɪs'mɪs/ *v* (a class, etc) يَطْرُد (an employee) يَفْصِل

disorder /dɪs'ɔ:də(r)/ *n* فَوْضَى

dispatch /dɪ'spætʃ/ *v* يُرْسِل

dispense /dɪ'spens/ *v* يَصْرِف

disperse /dɪ'spɜ:s/ *v* يَتَفَرَّق

display /dɪ'spleɪ/ *v* (items for sale, a work of art) يَعْرِض
♦ *n* (of temper, anger) إِظْهَار (public event) عَرْض/عُرُوض مف/ج

disposal /dɪ'spəʊzl/ *n* التَخَلُّص مِن

dispute /dɪ'spju:t/ *n* (about money, a boundary) نِزَاع/نِزَاعَات مف/ج
♦ *v* (the bill, an invoice, an account) يُجَادِل

disrupt /dɪs'rʌpt/ *v* يُعَطِّل

dissolve /dɪ'zɒlv/ *v* (a solid) يُذِيب (a partnership) يَفُضّ

distance /'dɪstəns/ *n* مَسَافَة

distant /'dɪstənt/ *adj* بَعِيد

distinct /dɪ'stɪŋkt/ *adj* وَاضِح

distinction /dɪ'stɪŋkʃn/ *n* (difference) فَارِق/فَوَارِق مف/ج (excellence) امْتِيَاز/امْتِيَازَات مف/ج

distinctive /dɪ'stɪŋktɪv/ *adj* مُمَيَّز

distinguish /dɪ'stɪŋgwɪʃ/ *v* يُمَيِّز بَيْنَ

distort /dɪ'stɔ:t/ *v* يُحَرِّف

distortion /dɪ'stɔ:ʃn/ *n* تَحْرِيف

distract /dɪ'strækt/ *v* يُلْهِي

distraction /dɪ'strækʃn/ *n* لَهْو

distress /dɪ'stres/ *n* كَرْب/كُرُوب مف/ج

distribute /dɪ'strɪbju:t/ *v* يُوَزِّع

distribution /dɪstrɪ'bju:ʃn/ *n* (of food) تَوْزِيع/تَوْزِيعَات مف/ج (supply system) تَوْزِيع

distributor /dɪ'strɪbjətə(r)/ *n* مُوَزِّع

district /ˈdɪstrɪkt/ *n* مُقَاطَعَة

disturb /dɪˈstɜːb/ *v* يُزْعِج

disturbance /dɪˈstɜːbəns/ *n* اضْطِرَاب/اضْطِرَابَات مف/ج

dive /daɪv/ *v* يَغْطُس

diver /ˈdaɪvə(r)/ *n* غَوَّاص

diverse /daɪˈvɜːs/ *adj* مُتَنَوِّع

divert /daɪˈvɜːt/ *v* يُحَوِّل اتِّجَاه

divide /dɪˈvaɪd/ *v* يُقَسِّم

dividend /ˈdɪvɪdend/ *n* أَرْبَاح

divine /dɪˈvaɪn/ *adj* سَمَاوِيّ

division /dɪˈvɪʒn/ *n* (of land) تَقْسِيم (in maths) قِسْمَة

divorce /dɪˈvɔːs/ *n* طَلَاق
♦ *v* يُطَلِّق

do /duː/ *aux v* **does, did, done** (in questions) هَل
Do you take sugar? هَل تَسْتَخْدِم السُكَّر؟
(in negative) أَدَاة تُسْتَخْدَم لِلنَفْي
He doesn't want to come.
لَا يُرِيدُ أَنْ يَأْتِي (referring to sth said already) تُسْتَخْدَم لِتَجَنُّب إِعَادَة الفِعْل
I like it here. So do I. أُحِبُّ هُنَا. وَأَنَا كَذَلِك
We came by bus, but Hassan didn't.
جِئْنَا بِالحَافِلَة، لَكِن لَم يَأْتِ بِهَا حَسَن
♦ *v* (to carry out) يَعْمَل
Do it now! اعْمَلْهُ الآن
I've done the calculations.
عَمِلْتُ الحِسَابَات
What do you do? مَاذَا تَعْمَل؟ (to affect) يَفْعَل
The rain did a lot of good.
فَعَلَ المَطر عِدَّة أَشْيَاء حَسَنَة
What did he do to you? مَاذَا فَعَلَ لَك؟

do without *phv* يَسْتَغْنِي عَن

dock /dɒk/ *n* رَصِيف المِينَاء/أَرْصِفَة مف/ج

doctor /ˈdɒktə(r)/ *n* (in medicine) طَبِيب/أَطِبَّاء مف/ج (academic) دُكْتُور/دكَاتِرَة مف/ج

doctrine /ˈdɒktrɪn/ *n* عَقِيدَة/عَقَائِد مف/ج

document /ˈdɒkjument/ *n* (on paper) وَثِيقَة/وَثَائِق مف/ج (electronic) مُسْتَنَد/مُسْتَنَدَات مف/ج

documentary /dɒkjuˈmentri/ *n* pl -ries وَثَائِقِيّ

documentation /dɒkjumenˈteɪʃn/ *n* تَوْثِيق

dodge /dɒʤ/ *v* يَتَفَادَى

doesn't /ˈdʌznt/ *contr* (= does not: see do)

dog /dɒg/ *n* كَلْب/كِلَاب مف/ج

Doha /ˈdəʊhɑː/ *n* الدُوحَة

doll /dɒl/ *n* دُمْيَة/دُمَى مف/ج

dollar /ˈdɒlə(r)/ *n* دُولَار

domain /dəˈmeɪn/ *n* (of knowledge) حَقْل/حُقُول مف/ج، نِطَاق/نِطَاقَات مف/ج

domestic /dəˈmestɪk/ *adj* (work, violence) مَنْزِلِيّ (flight, policy) مَحَلِّيّ

dominant /ˈdɒmɪnənt/ *adj* مُهَيْمِن

D

D

dominate /'dɒmɪneɪt/ *v* يُهَيْمِن عَلَى

domination /dɒmɪ'neɪʃn/ *n* هَيْمَنَة

donate /dəʊ'neɪt/ *v* يَتَبَرَّع

donation /dəʊ'neɪʃn/ *n* تَبَرُّع/ تَبَرُّعَات مف/ج

donor /'dəʊnə(r)/ *n* مُتَبَرِّع

don't /dəʊnt/ *contr* (= do not: see do)

door /dɔ:(r)/ *n* بَاب/أَبْوَاب مف/ج

dosage /'dəʊsɪʤ/ *n* جُرْعَة

dose /dəʊs/ *n* جُرْعَة

dot /dɒt/ *n* نُقْطَة/نِقَاط مف/ج

double /'dʌbl/ *adj* مُزْدَوَج

doubt /daʊt/ *n* شَكّ/شُكُوك مف/ج
♦ *v* (a story, the truth) يَشُكّ فِي (if sth will happen) يَشُكّ

doubtful /'daʊtfl/ *adj* غَيْر مُتَأَكِّد

down /daʊn/ *adv* (at or to a lower point) إِلَى الأَسْفَل
They are down in the basement. هُم أَسْفَل فِي القَبْو
I walked down into the town. مَشَيْتُ إِلَى مَرْكَز المَدِينَة
Please sit down. اجْلِس رَجَاءً
(decreasing) مُتَدَنٍّ
Sales are down. المَبِيعَات مُتَدَنِّيَة
♦ *prep* (a hill, the stairs, etc) نُزُولاً
I walked down the steps. نَزَلْتُ الدَرَج
(a page) أَسْفَلُ (the coast, a river, a street) إِلَى نِهَايَة
Go down the street, until اذْهَب إِلَى نِهَايَة الشَارِع حَتَّى ...
♦ *adj* (depressed) مُكْتَئِب (not working) مُغْلَق

download /daʊn'ləʊd/ *v* يُحَمِّل

downstairs /daʊn'steəz/ *adv* (situated) الطَابِق الأَسْفَل (moving down) إِلَى أَسْفَل

downturn /'daʊntɜ:n/ *n* رُكُود

dozen /'dʌzn/ *n* دَزِّينَة

draft /drɑ:ft/ *n* (of a letter) مُسْوَدَّة (banker's) حُوَالَة (US: air current) تَيَّار هَوَائِيّ
♦ *v* يُصِيغ مُسْوَدَّة

drag /dræg/ *v* يَسْحَب

dragon /'drægən/ *n* تِنِّين

drain /dreɪn/ *n* مَصْرَف/مَصَارِفُ مف/ج
♦ *v* (a tank) يُجَفِّف (water, oil) يَنْضَح

drama /'drɑ:mə/ *n* (genre) الأَدَب المَسْرَحِيّ (of an event) حَدَث مُؤَثِّر

dramatic /drə'mætɪk/ *adj* (change) مُفَاجِئ (events) مُثِير

draught /drɑ:ft/ *n* تَيَّار هَوَائِيّ

draughts /'drɑ:fts/ *n* لُعْبَة الضَامَا

draw /drɔ:/ *n* (in scores) تَعَادُل/تَعَادُلاَت (in a raffle, etc) سَحْب قُرْعَة مف/ج
♦ *v* **drew, drawn** (a picture) يَرْسُم (in games) يَتَعَادَل

drawer /'drɔ:ə(r)/ *n* دُرْج/أَدْرَاج مف/ج

drawing /'drɔ:ɪŋ/ *n* (picture) رَسْم/ رُسُومَات مف/ج (action) رَسْم

drawing pin *n* دَبُّوس لإِلْصَاق الوَرَق عَلَى لَوْحَة الحَائِط

dreadful /'dredfl/ *adj* بَغِيض

dream /dri:m/ *n* حُلْم/أَحْلَام مف/ج
♦ *n* **dreamed or dreamt** يَحْلَم

dress /dres/ *n* فُسْتَان/فَسَاتِينُ مف/ج
♦ *v* (oneself) يَلْبِس (a baby) يُلْبِس (a wound) يُضَمِّد

drift /drɪft/ *v* يَنْجَرِف

drill /drɪl/ *n* مِثْقَاب كَهْرَبَائِيّ
♦ *v* (a hole) يَثْقُب (students) يُدَرِّب

drink /drɪŋk/ *n* (water, etc) مَشْرُوب/ مَشْرُوبَات مف/ج (alcoholic) مُسْكِر
♦ *v* **drank, drunk** (water) يَشْرَب

drip /drɪp/ *v* (liquids) يُنَقِّط
♦ *n* (in medicine) مِحْقَن تَنْقِيط فِي الوَرِيد دَوَاء/أَدْوِيَة مف/ج (in medicine) مف/ج

drum /drʌm/ *n* طَبْلَة

drunken /'drʌŋkən/ *adj* سَكْرَان

dry /draɪ/ *adj* جَافّ
♦ *v* **dries, dried** (to become dry) يَجِفّ (to make dry) يُجَفِّف

Dublin /'dʌblɪn/ *n* دَبْلِن

duck /dʌk/ *n* بَطَّة/بَطّ مف/ج

due /dju:/ *adj* (scheduled) مُفْتَرَض (payable) مُسْتَحَقّ

duke /dju:k/ *n* نَبِيل/نُبَلَاءُ مف/ج

dull /dʌl/ *adj* (day) غَائِم (lecture) مُمِلّ (pain) خَفِيف

dumb /dʌm/ *adj* (unable to speak) أَبْكَم/بَكْمَاء/بُكْم مذ/م/ج (stupid) غَبِيّ

dump /dʌmp/ *n* مَزْبَلَة/مَزَابِلُ مف/ج
♦ *v* (cases, rubbish, etc) يَرْمِي

duration /dju'reɪʃn/ *n* فَتْرَة

during /'djʊərɪŋ/ *prep* خِلَالَ

dust /dʌst/ *n* غُبَار/أَغْبِرَة مف/ج

dustman /'dʌstmən/ *n* pl **-men** رَجُل نَظَافَة

dusty /'dʌsti/ *adj* مُغَبَّر

Dutch /dʌtʃ/ *adj* هُولَنْدِيّ
♦ *n* (language) اللُغَة الهُولَنْدِيَّة (people) هُولَنْدِيُّون

duty /'dju:ti/ *n* pl **-ties** (obligation) وَاجِب/وَاجِبَات مف/ج (at work) مُهِمَّة (tax) ضَرِيبَة/ضَرَائِبُ مف/ج

drive /draɪv/ *v* **drove, driven** (a car, truck) يَقُود (to go by car) يَنْتَقِل بِعَرَبَة (a passenger) يُوَصِّل (sb to despair) يَجْعَل
♦ *n* (for vehicle access) طَرِيق خَاصّ (short journey) نُزْهَة بِالسَّيَّارَة

driver /'draɪvə(r)/ *n* سَائِق

driving /'draɪvɪŋ/ *n* سِيَاقَة

drop /drɒp/ *n* قَطْرَة
♦ *v* يُسْقِط

drought /draʊt/ *n* جَفَاف

drown /draʊn/ *v* يَغْرَق

drug /drʌg/ *n* (narcotic) مُخَدِّر/مُخَدِّرَات

DVD /diːviːˈdiː/ *n* قُرْص دِي فِي دِي

DVD player *n* مُشَغِّل دِي فِي دِي

DVD recorder *n* مُسَجِّل دِي فِي دِي

dye /daɪ/ *n* صِبْغَة

dynamic /daɪˈnæmɪk/ *adj* فَعَّال

E

each /iːtʃ/ *pron* كُلّ

eager /'iːgə(r)/ *adj* مُتَلَهِّف

eagle /'iːgl/ *n* نِسْر/نُسُور مف/ج

ear /ɪə(r)/ *n* أُذُن/آذَان مف/ج

earl /ɜːl/ *n* الإِيرْل

early /'ɜːli/ *adj* مُبَكِّر

the early train القِطَار المُبَكِّر

We were early. كُنَّا مُبَكِّرين

♦ *adv* بَاكِراً، مُبَكِّراً

She woke early. اسْتَيْقَظَت بَاكِراً

Please arrive 15 minutes early. الرَجَاء كُن مُبَكِّراً بِخَمْس عَشْرَة دَقِيقَة

earn /ɜːn/ *v* يَجْنِي

earth /ɜːθ/ *n* (soil) تُرْبَة (the Earth) الأَرْض

earthquake /'ɜːθkweɪk/ *n* زِلْزَال/زَلَازِل مف/ج

easily /'iːzəli/ *adv* بِسُهُولَة

east /iːst/ *n* (point of the compass) شَرْق

The sun rises in the east. تُشْرِق الشَمْس مِن الشَرْق

(of a country) *to live in the east* يَعِيش في شَرْقِيّ البِلَاد

(eastern hemisphere) *the East* الشَرْق

♦ *adj* شَرْقِيّ

♦ *adv* (location) فِي الشَرْق (to drive) إِلَى الشَرْق

eastern /'iːstən/ *adj* شَرْقِيّ

easy /'iːzi/ *adj* (exam) سَهْل (life) مُرْتَاح

eat /iːt/ *v* **ate, eaten** (meat, a meal) يَأْكُل (to have a meal) يَأْكُل

echo /'ekəʊ/ *n* pl **-oes** صَدَى/أَصْدَاء مف/ج

ecology /i'kɒlədʒi/ *n* عِلْم البِيئَة

economic /iːkə'nɒmɪk/ *adj* اقْتِصَادِيّ

economics /iːkə'nɒmɪks/ *n* عِلْم الاقْتِصَاد

economist /ɪ'kɒnəmɪst/ *n* عَالِم اقْتِصَاد

economy /ɪ'kɒnəmi/ *n* pl **-mies** اقْتِصَاد

edge /edʒ/ *n* (of a table) حَافَّة/حَوَافّ (of a knife, etc) نَصْل مف/ج

edit /'edɪt/ *v* يُحَرِّر (خَبَراً)

edition /ɪ'dɪʃn/ *n* طَبْعَة

editor /'edɪtə(r)/ *n* مُحَرِّر

E

editorial /edɪ'tɔ:riəl/ *n* كَلِمَة المُحَرِّر

educate /'edʒukeɪt/ *v* (children) يُعَلِّم (the public) يُثَقِّف

education /edʒu'keɪʃn/ *n* تَعْلِيم

educational /edʒu'keɪʃənl/ *adj* تَعْلِيمِيّ

educator /'edʒukeɪtə(r)/ *n* مُعَلِّم

effect /ɪ'fekt/ *n* (result) تَأْثِير/تَأْثِيرَات (impression) أَثَر/آثَار مف/ج مف/ج
♦ *v* يُحْدِث

effective /ɪ'fektɪv/ *adj* فَعَّال

effectively /ɪ'fektɪvli/ *adv* بِفَعَّالِيَّة

effectiveness /ɪ'fektɪvnəs/ *n* فَعَّالِيَّة

efficiency /ɪ'fɪʃnsi/ *n* فَعَّالِيَّة

efficient /ɪ'fɪʃnt/ *adj* فَعَّال

effort /'efət/ *n* مَجْهُود/مَجْهُودَات مف/ج

egg /eg/ *n* بَيْضَة/بَيْض مف/ج

eggplant /'egplɑ:nt/ *n* بَاذِنْجَان

Egypt /'i:dʒɪpt/ *n* مِصْر

Egyptian /ɪ'dʒɪpʃ(ə)n/ *adj, n* مِصْرِيّ ص/س

Eid al-Adha /i:dæl'ædhə/ *n* عِيد الأَضْحَى

Eid al-Fitr /i:dæl'fi:tr/ *n* عِيد الفِطْر

eight /eɪt/ *num* ثَمَانِيَة

eighth /eɪtθ/ *adj* ثَامِن
♦ *adv* ثَامِناً
♦ *n* (see tenth) الثَّامِن

eighty /'eɪti/ *num* ثَمَانُون

eighteen /eɪ'ti:n/ *num* ثَمَانِيَة عَشَر

either /'aɪðə(r)/ *adj* (one of two) أَيّ

Take either one of the cars.
خُذ أَيّ مِن السَيَّارَتَيْن (both) كِلاَ
Either suggestion is good.
كِلَا الاقْتِرَاحَان جَيِّدَان
♦ *pron* (one of two) أَحَد الأَمْرَيْن
(both) كِلاَ
♦ *adv* أَيْضاً
They didn't go either.
هُم لَم يَذْهَبُوا أَيْضاً
♦ *conj* إِمَّا...أَو
You can go either by car or by train.
يُمْكِنُكَ أَنْ تَذْهَب إِمَّا بِالسَيَّارَة أَو بِالقِطَار

elbow /'elbəʊ/ *n* مِرْفَق/مَرَافِقُ مف/ج

elderly /'eldəli/ *adj* مُسِنّ

elect /ɪ'lekt/ *v* يَنْتَخِب

elected /ɪ'lektəd/ *adj* مُنْتَخَب

election /ɪ'lekʃn/ *n* انْتِخَاب/انْتِخَابَات مف/ج

electric /ɪ'lektrɪk/ *adj* كَهْرَبَائِيّ

electrical /ɪ'lektrɪkl/ *adj* كَهْرَبَائِيّ

electricity /ɪlek'trɪsəti/ *n* كَهْرَبَاء

electronic /ɪlek'trɒnɪk/ *adj* إِلِكْتْرُونِيّ

elegant /'elɪgənt/ *adj* أَنِيق

element /'elɪmənt/ *n* (in a plan) عَامِل/عَوَامِلُ مف/ج (in chemistry) عُنْصُر/عَنَاصِرُ مف/ج

elementary /elɪ'mentri/ *adj* أَسَاسِيّ

elephant /'elɪfənt/ *n* فيل/أَفْيَال وَفِيلَة مف/ج

elevator /'elɪveɪtə(r)/ *n* **US** مصْعَد/ مَصَاعِدُ مف/ج

eleven /ɪ'levn/ *num* أَحَد عَشَر

eligible /'elɪʤəbl/ *adj* مُؤَهَّل

eliminate /ɪ'lɪmɪneɪt/ *v* يُزِيل

elimination /ɪlɪmɪ'neɪʃn/ *n* إِزَالَة

email /'i:meɪl/ *n* (system) بَرِيد إِلِكْتِرُونِيّ (message) رِسَالَة إِلِكْتِرُونِيَّة
♦ *v* يُرْسِل رِسَالَة إِلِكْتِرُونِيَّة

embark /ɪm'bɑ:k/ *v* (on a ship) يَرْكَب (on a project) يَبْدَأ

embarrass /ɪm'bærəs/ *v* يُحْرِج

embarrassment /ɪm'bærəsmənt/ *n* إِحْرَاج

embassy /'embəsi/ *n* pl **-sies** سِفَارَة

embrace /ɪm'breɪs/ *n* عِنَاق
♦ *v* (sb) يُعَانِق

emerge /i'mɜ:ʤ/ *v* يَظْهَر

emergency /i'mɜ:ʤənsi/ *n* pl **-cies** طَارِئَة/طَوَارِئُ مف/ج

emoticon /ɪ'məʊtɪkɒn/ *n* أَيْقُونَة عَاطِفَة

emotion /ɪ'məʊʃn/ *n* عَاطِفَة/عَوَاطِفُ مف/ج

emotional /ɪ'məʊʃənl/ *adj* عَاطِفِيّ

emperor /'empərə(r)/ *n* إِمْبِرَاطُور

emphasis /'emfəsɪs/ *n* تَأْكِيد/ تَأْكِيدَات مف/ج

emphasize /'emfəsaɪz/ *v* يُؤَكِّد

empire /'empaɪə(r)/ *n* إِمْبِرَاطُورِيَّة

employ /ɪm'plɔɪ/ *v* (a worker) يُوَظِّف (a tactic) يَسْتَخْدِم

employee /ɪm'plɔɪi:/ *n* مُوَظَّف

employer /ɪm'plɔɪə(r)/ *n* صَاحِب العَمَل

employment /ɪm'plɔɪmənt/ *n* وَظِيفَة/وَظَائِفُ مف/ج

empty /'empti/ *adj* فَارِغ
an empty stadium مُدَرَّج فَارِغ
♦ *v* يُفْرِغ

enable /ɪ'neɪbl/ *v* يُمَكِّن

enclose /ɪn'kləʊz/ *v* (an invoice) يُرفِق (with a wall, etc.) يُطَوِّق

encounter /ɪn'kaʊntə(r)/ *v* يُوَاجِه

encourage /ɪn'kʌrɪʤ/ *v* يُشَجِّع

encouragement /ɪn'kʌrɪʤmənt/ *n* تَشْجِيع

encouraging /ɪn'kʌrɪʤɪŋ/ *adj* مُشَجِّع

end /end/ *n* (of a book, road) نِهَايَة (aim) غَايَة
♦ *v* (roads, stories) يَنْتَهِي (a performance) يُنْهِي

endeavour /ɪn'devə(r)/ *n* US **-vor** مُحَاوَلَة

E

E

ending /'endɪŋ/ *n* نِهَايَة

endive /'endaɪv/ *n* نَبْتَة الهِنْدِبَاء

endless /'endləs/ *adj* مُتَوَاصِل

endorse /ɪn'dɔːs/ *v* (a candidate) يُقِرّ (a document) يُضِيف مُلَاحَظَة عَلَى وَثِيقَة

endorsement /ɪn'dɔːsmənt/ *n* إِقْرَار

endure /ɪn'djʊə(r)/ *v* يَحْتَمِل

enemy /'enəmi/ *n* pl **-mies** /عَدُوّ أَعْدَاء مف/ج

energetic /enə'dʒetɪk/ *adj* نَشِيط

energy /'enədʒi/ *n* طَاقَة

enforce /ɪn'fɔːs/ *v* (قانوناً) يُطَبِّق

engage /ɪn'geɪdʒ/ *v* يَجْذِب

engaged /ɪn'geɪdʒd/ *adj* (to be married) مَخْطُوب (busy) مَشْغُول

engagement /ɪn'geɪdʒmənt/ *n* (to be married) خِطْبَة (appointment) تَرْتِيب/تَرْتِيبَات مف/ج

engine /'endʒɪn/ *n* مُحَرِّك/مُحَرِّكَات مف/ج

engineer /endʒɪ'nɪə(r)/ *n* مُهَنْدِس

England /'ɪŋglənd/ *n* إِنْجِلْتِرَا

English /'ɪŋglɪʃ/ *adj* إِنْجِلِيزِيّ
♦ *n* (language) اللُّغَة الإِنْجِلِيزِيَّة
to teach English يُدَرِّس اللُّغَة الإِنْجِلِيزِيَّة
to answer in English يُجِيب بِالإِنْجِلِيزِيَّة (people) إِنْجِلِيز

enhance /ɪn'hɑːns/ *v* يُعَزِّز

enhancement /ɪn'hɑːnsmənt/ *n* تَعْزِيز/تَعْزِيزَات مف/ج

enjoyable /ɪn'dʒɔɪəbl/ *adj* مُمْتِع

enjoyment /ɪn'dʒɔɪmənt/ *n* /مُتْعَة مُتَع مف/ج

enlarge /ɪn'lɑːdʒ/ *v* يُكَبِّر

enlist /ɪn'lɪst/ *v* يَتَطَوَّع

enormous /ɪ'nɔːməs/ *adj* (success, sum) هَائِل (ship, building) /ضَخْم ضِخَام مف/ج
an enormous statue
نُصْب تِذْكَارِيّ ضَخْم

enough /ɪ'nʌf/ *adj* (money, sand) وَافٍ (problems, cars) كَافٍ
Two shirts will be enough.
قَمِيصَان سَوْفَ يَكُونَان كِفَايَة
♦ *adv* إِلَى حَدّ كَافٍ
There weren't enough people.
لَم يَكُن هُنَاكَ عَدَد وَافٍ مِن النَاس
♦ *pron* (in number) كِفَايَة (in quantity) كَافٍ

enquiry /ɪn'kwaɪəri/ *n* pl **-ries** (investigation) تَحْقِيق/تَحْقِيقَات مف/ج (question) اسْتِفْسَار/اسْتِفْسَارَات مف/ج

enrich /ɪn'rɪtʃ/ *v* يُخَصِّب

enter /'entə(r)/ *v* (a place, etc) يَدْخُل (data) يُدْخِل

enterprise /'entəpraɪz/ *n* رُوح الإِبْدَاع

entertain /entə'teɪn/ *v* يُسَلِّي

entertaining /entə'teɪnɪŋ/ *adj* مُسَلٍّ

entertainment /entə'teɪnmənt/ *n* تَسْلِيَة

enthusiasm /ɪn'θju:ziæzəm/ *n* حَمَاس

enthusiast /ɪn'θju:ziæst/ *n* مُتَحَمِّس

enthusiastic /ɪnθju:zi'æstɪk/ *adj* مُتَحَمِّس

entire /ɪn'taɪə(r)/ *adj* كَامِل

entirely /ɪn'taɪəli/ *adv* تَمَاماً

entity /'entəti/ *n* pl **-ties** كِيَان/كِيَانَات مف/ج

entrance /'entrəns/ *n* مَدْخَل/مَدَاخِلُ مف/ج

entrepreneur /ɒntrəprə'nɜ:(r)/ *n* مُقَاوِل

entry /'entri/ *n* pl **-ries** (act) دُخُول (in a list, etc) مَادَّة/مَوَادُّ مف/ج

envelope /'envələʊp/ *n* مَظْرُوف/مَظَارِيفُ

environment /ɪn'vaɪrənmənt/ *n* بِيئَة

envisage /ɪn'vɪzɪʤ/ *v* يَتَخَيَّل

envision /ɪn'vɪʒn/ *v* يَتَخَيَّل

epic /'epɪk/ *adj* مَلْحَمِيّ
♦ *n* مَلْحَمَة/مَلَاحِمُ مف/ج

epidemic /epɪ'demɪk/ *n* وَبَاء/أَوْبِئَة مف/ج

episode /'epɪsəʊd/ *n* مَرْحَلَة/مَرَاحِلُ مف/ج

equal /'i:kwəl/ *adj* مُسَاوٍ
♦ *v* يُسَاوِي

equality /i'kwɒləti/ *n* مُسَاوَاة

equally /'i:kwəli/ *adv* بِالتَّسَاوِي

equip /ɪ'kwɪp/ *v* (an expedition) يُزَوِّد (with knowledge) يُجَهِّز

equipment /ɪ'kwɪpmənt/ *n* مُعَدَّات

equivalent /ɪ'kwɪvələnt/ *adj* مُسَاوٍ

era /'ɪərə/ *n* عَهْد/عُهُود مف/ج

eradicate /ɪ'rædɪkeɪt/ *v* يَسْتَأْصِل

erase /ɪ'reɪz/ *v* يَمْحُو

eraser /ɪ'reɪzə(r)/ *n* مِمْحَاة/مَمَاحٍ مف/ج

erect /ɪ'rekt/ *v* (a monument) يُشَيِّد (a tent) يَنْصُب

erode /ɪ'rəʊd/ *v* يَتَآكَل

erosion /ɪ'rəʊʒn/ *n* تَآكُل

error /'erə(r)/ *n* خَطَأ/أَخْطَاء مف/ج

erupt /ɪ'rʌpt/ *v* يَتَفَجَّر

escalate /'eskəleɪt/ *v* يَتَصَاعَد

escape /ɪ'skeɪp/ *n* هُرُوب
♦ *v* (from danger) يَهْرُب

escort /'eskɔ:t/ *v* يُرَافِق

especially /ɪ'speʃəli/ *adv* (to like) خُصُوصاً (cold, difficult) بِشَكْل اسْتِثْنَائِيّ

essay /e'seɪ/ *n* مَقَالَة

essence /'esns/ *n* (quality) جَوْهَر (liquid) عِطْر/عُطُور مف/ج

essential /ɪ'senʃl/ *adj* (necessary)

E

أَسَاسِيّ (difference) ضَرُورِيّ

establish /ɪ'stæblɪʃ/ *v* (a business, a school) يُؤَسِّس

established /ɪ'stæblɪʃt/ *adj* مُثْبَت

E

establishment /ɪ'stæblɪʃmənt/ *n* مُؤَسَّسَة

estate /ɪ'steɪt/ *n* عِزْبَة/عِزَب مف/ج

estimate /'estɪmeɪt/ *v* يُقَدِّر
♦ *n* تَقْدِير/تَقْدِيرَات مف/ج

estimated /'estɪmeɪtəd/ *adj* مُخَمَّن

estimation /estɪ'meɪʃn/ *n* رَأْي/ آرَاء مف/ج

eternal /ɪ'tɜːnl/ *adj* أَبَدِيّ

eternity /ɪ'tɜːnəti/ *n* أَبَدِيَّة

ethical /'eθɪkl/ *adj* أَخْلَاقِيّ

ethnic /'eθnɪk/ *adj* عِرْقِيّ

euro /'jʊərəʊ/ *n* يُورُو (عُمْلَة النَقْد الأُورُوبِّيَّة)

Europe /'jʊərəp/ *n* أُورُوبَّا

European /jʊərə'piːən/ *adj, n* أُورُوبِّيّ، ص/س

European Union *n* الاِتِّحَاد الأُورُوبِّيّ

eurozone /'jʊərə(ʊ)zəʊn/ *n* دُوَل اليُورُو

evacuate /ɪ'vækjueɪt/ *v* يُخْلِي

evaluate /ɪ'væljueɪt/ *v* يُقَيِّم

evaluation /ɪvælju'eɪʃn/ *n* تَقْيِيم

even /'iːvn/ *adv* حَتَّى
♦ *adj* سَهْل/سُهُول مف/ج

evening /'iːvnɪŋ/ *n* مَسَاء

event /ɪ'vent/ *n* حَدَث/أَحْدَاث مف/ج

eventual /ɪ'ventʃuəl/ *adj* نِهَائِيّ

eventually /ɪ'ventʃuəli/ *adv* فِي نِهَايَة الأَمْر

ever /'evə(r)/ *adv* مِن قَبْل
Have you ever been to Beirut?
هَل ذَهَبْتَ إِلَى بَيْرُوت مِن قَبْل؟
(in negatives) أَبَداً
No one ever thinks of that.
لاَ أَحَد يُفَكِّر فِي ذَلِك أَبَداً
(in time) فِي أَيّ وَقْت مَضَى
the biggest car I've ever seen
أَكْبَر سَيَّارَة رَأَيْتُهَا فِي أَيّ وَقْت مَضَى

every /'evri/ *adj* كُلّ
every child كُلّ طِفْل
every tree كُلّ شَجَرَة
every month كُلّ شَهْر

everybody /'evribɒdi/ *pron* (see everyone)

everyday /'evrideɪ/ *adj* يَوْمِيّ

everyone /'evriwʌn/ *pron* كُلّ شَخْص
Everyone knows that.
كُلّ شَخْص يَعْرِف ذَلِكَ
He gave everyone a gift.
أَعْطَى كُلّ شَخْص هَدِيَّة

everything /'evriθɪŋ/ *pron* كُلّ شَيْء
everything you do كُلّ شَيْء تَفْعَلُهُ
I know everything. أَعْلَم كُلّ شَيْء

everywhere /'evriweə(r)/ *adv* فِي

كُلّ مَكَان
They are everywhere. هُم فِي كُلّ مَكَان

evidence /'evɪdəns/ *n* دَلِيل/أَدِلَّة مف/ج

evident /'evɪdənt/ *adj* وَاضِح

evidently /'evɪdəntli/ *adv* مِن الوَاضِح

evil /'i:vl/ *adj* شِرِّير

evolution /i:və'lu:ʃn/ *n* تَطَوُّر

evolve /i'vɒlv/ *v* يَتَطَوَّر

exact /ɪg'zækt/ *adj* دَقِيق

exactly /ɪg'zæktli/ *adv* تَمَاماً

exaggerate /ɪg'zædʒəreɪt/ *v* يُبَالِغ

examination /ɪgzæmɪ'neɪʃn/ *n* (in school, etc) اخْتِبَار/اخْتِبَارَات مف/ج (by doctor) فَحْص/فُحُوصَات مف/ج (of accounts) مُرَاجَعَة

examine /ɪg'zæmɪn/ *v* يَتَفَحَّص

example /ɪg'zɑ:mpl/ *n* مِثَال/أَمْثِلَة مَف/ج

exceed /ɪk'si:d/ *v* يَتَجَاوَز

excellence /'eksələns/ *n* بَرَاعَة

excellent /'eksələnt/ *adj* رَائِع

except /ɪk'sept/ *prep* مَا عَدَا

exception /ɪk'sepʃn/ *n* اسْتِثْنَاء

exceptional /ɪk'sepʃənl/ *adj* (student) مُمْتَاز (case) اسْتِثْنَائِيّ

exceptionally /ɪk'sepʃənəli/ *adv* بِشَكْل اسْتِثْنَائِيّ

excerpt /'eksɜ:pt/ *n* مُقْتَطَف/ مُقْتَطَفَات مف/ج

excess /'ekses/ *n* زِيَادَة

excessive /ɪk'sesɪv/ *adj* مُفْرِط

exchange /ɪks'tʃeɪndʒ/ *n* (of gifts, etc) تَبَادُل (cultural) تَبَادُل الزِيَارَات
♦ *v* (gifts) يَتَبَادَل (in shop) يَسْتَبْدِل

excite /ɪk'saɪt/ *v* يُثِير

excitement /ɪk'saɪtmənt/ *n* إِثَارَة

exciting /ɪk'saɪtɪŋ/ *adj* مُثِير

exclaim /ɪk'skleɪm/ *v* يَصْرُخ

exclude /ɪk'sklu:d/ *v* يَسْتَثْنِي

exclusive /ɪk'sklu:sɪv/ *adj* حَصْرِيّ

exclusively /ɪk'sklu:sɪvli/ *adv* حَصْرِيّاً

excuse /ɪk'skju:s/ *n* عُذْر/أَعْذَار مف/ج
♦ /ɪk'skju:s/ *v* يَعْذُر
Excuse me, (please)!
أُعْذُرْنِي مِن فَضْلِك

execute /'eksɪkju:t/ *v* (to kill) يَعْدِم (to carry out) يُنَفِّذ

execution /eksɪ'kju:ʃn/ *n* إِعْدَام

executive /ɪg'zekjətɪv/ *n* (person) مَسْئُول تَنْفِيذِيّ (administration) هَيْئَة تَنْفِيذِيَّة

exemption /ɪg'zempʃn/ *n* إِعْفَاء

exercise /'eksəsaɪz/ *n* (physical activity) تَمْرِين/تَمْرِينَات مف/ج (in education) تَدْرِيب/تَدْرِيبَات مف/ج

E

♦ *v* (for fitness) يَتَدَرَّب (a right) يُمَارِس

exhaust /ɪg'zɔːst/ *v* يَسْتَنْفِد

exhibit /ɪg'zɪbɪt/ *v* يَعْرِض

exhibition /eksɪ'bɪʃn/ *n* مَعْرَض/مَعَارِضُ مف/ج

exile /'eksaɪl/ *n* (situation) مَنْفَى/ (person) مَنْفِيّ مَنَافٍ مف/ج

exist /ɪg'zɪst/ *v* (to be) يُوجَد (to be alive) يَحْيَا

existence /ɪg'zɪstəns/ *n* وُجُود

exit /'eksɪt/ *n* (way out) مَخْرَج/مَخَارِجُ مف/ج

exotic /ɪg'zɒtɪk/ *adj* غَرِيب/غُرَبَاءُ مف/ج

expand /ɪk'spænd/ *v* (to make bigger) يُوَسِّع (to become bigger) يَتَوَسَّع

expansion /ɪk'spænʃn/ *n* تَوَسُّع

expect /ɪk'spekt/ *v* يَتَوَقَّع

expectation /ekspek'teɪʃn/ *n* تَوَقُّع/تَوَقُّعَات مف/ج

expedition /ekspə'dɪʃn/ *n* بِعْثَة

expel /ɪk'spel/ *v* يَطْرُد

expenditure /ɪk'spendɪtʃə(r)/ *n* (spending money) إِنْفَاق (money spent) مَصْرُوف/مَصْرُوفَات مف/ج

expense /ɪk'spens/ *n* تَكْلِفَة/تَكَالِيفُ مف/ج

expensive /ɪk'spensɪv/ *adj* مُكْلِف

experience /ɪk'spɪəriəns/ *n* خِبْرَة

♦ *v* يُجَرِّب

experienced /ɪk'spɪəriənst/ *adj* خَبِير

experiment /ɪk'sperɪmənt/ *n* تَجْرِبَة/تَجَارِبُ مف/ج

♦ *v* يُجْرِي تَجْرِبَة

experimental /ɪksperɪ'mentl/ *adj* تَجْرِيبِيّ

expert /'ekspɜːt/ *adj* مُتَخَصِّص

♦ *n* خَبِير

expertise /ekspɜː'tiːz/ *n* خِبْرَة

expiration date /ɪkspaɪə'reɪʃn/ *n* US تَارِيخ الاِنْتِهَاء

expire *v* يَنْتَهِي

expiry date /ɪk'spaɪəri/ *n* تَارِيخ الاِنْتِهَاء

explain /ɪk'spleɪn/ *v* (a process) يُوَضِّح (an absence) يُعَلِّل

explanation /eksplə'neɪʃn/ *n* (of process) تَوْضِيح/تَوْضِيحَات مف/ج (for absence) تَفْسِير/تَفْسِيرَات مف/ج

explicit /ɪk'splɪsɪt/ *adj* (instructions) وَاضِح (image) غَيْر مُتَحَفِّظ

explode /ɪk'spləʊd/ *v* يَنْفَجِر

exploit /ɪk'splɔɪt/ *v* (workers) يَسْتَغِلّ (resources) يَسْتَغِلّ

exploitation /eksplɔɪ'teɪʃn/ *n* اِسْتِغْلَال

exploration /eksplə'reɪʃn/ *n*

اسْتِكْشَاف

explosion /ɪk'spləʊʒn/ *n* انْفِجَار/ انْفِجَارَات مف/ج

explosive /ɪk'spləʊsɪv/ *adj* مُتَفَجِّر
♦ *n* مَادَّة مُتَفَجِّرَة

export /'ekspɔːt/ *v* يُصَدِّر
♦ /eks'pɔːt/ *n* صَادِرَات

expose /ɪk'spəʊz/ *v* يَفْضَح

exposure /ɪk'spəʊʒə(r)/ *n* (to danger) تَعَرُّض

express /ɪk'spres/ *v* يُعَبِّر عَن

expression /ɪk'spreʃn/ *n* تَعْبِير/ تَعْبِيرَات مف/ج

extend /ɪk'stend/ *v* يُمَدِّد

extension /ɪk'stenʃn/ *n* (to a visa) تَمْدِيد (to a building) مُلْحَق/مُلْحَقَات (telephone) هَاتِف دَاخِلِيّ مف/ج

extent /ɪk'stent/ *n* مَدَى

external /ɪk'stɜːnl/ *adj* خَارِجِيّ

extinction /ɪk'stɪŋkʃn/ *n* انْقِرَاض

extra /'ekstrə/ *adj* إِضَافِيّ

extraordinary /ɪk'strɔːdnri/ *adj* غَرِيب

extreme /ɪk'striːm/ *adj* (danger) مُفْرِط (opinions) مُتَطَرِّف

extremely /ɪk'striːmli/ *adv* إِلَى أَبْعَد حَدّ

eye /aɪ/ *n* عَيْن/أَعْيُن (م) مف/ج

eyebrow /'aɪbraʊ/ *n* حَاجِب/حَوَاجِب مف/ج

E

F

fabric /'fæbrɪk/ *n* قُمَاش/أَقْمِشَة مف/ج
fabulous /'fæbjələs/ *adj* رَائِع
face /feɪs/ *n* وَجْه/وُجُوه مف/ج
♦ *v* يُوَاجِه
facility /fə'sɪləti/ *n* pl **-ties** مُنْشَأَة
fact /fækt/ *n* حَقِيقَة/حَقَائِقُ مف/ج
faction /'fækʃn/ *n* فَصِيل/فَصَائِلُ مف/ج
factor /'fæktə(r)/ *n* عَامِل/عَوَامِلُ مف/ج
factory /'fæktri/ *n* pl **-ries** مَصْنَع/مَصَانِعُ مف/ج
factual /'fæktʃuəl/ *adj* وَاقِعِيّ
faculty /'fæklti/ *n* pl **-ties** (natural ability) حَاسَّة/حَوَاسّ مف/ج (in university) كُلِّيَّة (professors) هَيْئَة التَدْرِيس
fade /feɪd/ *v* يَبْهَت لَوْنُهُ
fail /feɪl/ *v* (in exams) يَرْسُب فِي امْتِحَان (to win, to help) يَفْشَل (brakes) يَتَعَطَّل
failure /'feɪljə(r)/ *n* (in exams) فَشَل (person, plan) فَاشِل
faint /feɪnt/ *adj* بَاهِت
fair /feə(r)/ *adj* (rule) عَادِل (hair, skin) أَشْقَر/شَقْرَاء/شُقْر مذ/م/ج (weather) صَافٍ
♦ *n* مَعْرَض/مَعَارِضُ مف/ج
fairly /'feəli/ *adv* (tall, hot) إِلَى حَدّ مَا (justly) بِشَكْل عَادِل
fairy /'feəri/ *n* pl **-ries** جِنِّيّ
faith /feɪθ/ *n* (in sb, sth) إِيمَان (religious) دِيَانَة
faithful /'feɪθfl/ *adj* مُخْلِص
fake /feɪk/ *n* مُزَيَّف
falafel /fə'læfl/ *n* فَلَافِل
fall /fɔːl/ *n* (in prices, etc) انْخِفَاض/انْخِفَاضَات مف/ج (on steps, etc) سُقُوط (US: season) خَرِيف
♦ *v* **fell, fallen** (leaves, etc) يَسْقُط (prices, etc) يَنْخَفِض
false /fɔːls/ *adj* (accusation) خَاطِئ (hair, etc) زَائِف
fame /feɪm/ *n* شُهْرَة

familiar /fə'mɪliə(r)/ *adj* مَألُوف

family /'fæməli/ *n* pl **-lies** (all ages) أُسْرَة/أُسَر مف/ج (children) عَائِلَة

famous /'feɪməs/ *adj* مَشْهُور

fan /fæn/ *n* (for cooling) مِرْوَحَة/مَرَاوِحُ مف/ج (in sport) مُشَجِّع (of a star, etc) مُعْجَب

fancy /'fænsi/ *adj* فَاخِر

fantastic /fæn'tæstɪk/ *adj* رَائِع

fantasy /'fæntəsi/ *n* pl **-sies** وَهْم/أَوْهَام مف/ج

far /fɑː(r)/ *adv* (in distances) بَعِيد

She went far into the countryside.

ذَهَبَت بَعِيداً فِي الرِيف

It's very far away/far off.

هِيَ بَعِيدَة جِداً

fare /feə(r)/ *n* أُجْرَة السَفَر

Far East *n* الشَرْق الأَدْنَى

farm /fɑːm/ *n* مَزْرَعَة/مَزَارِعُ مف/ج

farmer /'fɑːmə(r)/ *n* مُزَارِع

farming /'fɑːmɪŋ/ *n* زِرَاعَة

fascinate /'fæsɪneɪt/ *v* يَفْتِن

fascinating /'fæsɪneɪtɪŋ/ *adj* فَاتِن

fashion /'fæʃn/ *n* مُوضَة

fashionable /'fæʃnəbl/ *adj* عَصْرِيّ

fast /fɑːst/ *adj* (car, etc) سَرِيع (of clocks) مُتَقَدِّم فِي الوَقْت (colours) ثَابِت

♦ *v* يَصُوم

to fast from sunrise to sunset

يَصُوم مِن بُزُوغ الشَمْس حَتَّى مَغِيبِهَا

fat /fæt/ *adj* سَمِين

♦ *n* دُهْن

fatal /'feɪtl/ *adj* (accident, etc) مُمِيت (mistake) فَادِح

fate /feɪt/ *n* القَدَر

fat-free /'fæt'friː/ *adj* خَالِي الدُهْن

father /'fɑːðə(r)/ *n* (parent) أَب/آبَاء مف/ج (priest) كَاهِن/كَهَنَة مف/ج

fatigue /fə'tiːg/ *n* إِجْهَاد

fatty /'fæti/ *adj* مُدْهِن

faucet /'fɔːsɪt/ *n* US حَنَفِيَّة

fault /fɔːlt/ *n* (responsibility) غَلْطَة (in a product, design) خَلَل

favour /'feɪvə(r)/ *n* US **-vor** مَعْرُوف

♦ *v* US **-vor** يُفَضِّل

favourable /'feɪvərəbl/ *adj* US **-vorable** إِيجَابِيّ

favourite /'feɪvərɪt/ *adj, n* US **-vorite** مُفَضَّل

fax /fæks/ *n* pl **-xes** فَاكْس/فَاكْسَات مف/ج

fear /fɪə(r)/ *n* خَوْف

♦ *v* يَخَاف

feasible /'fiːzəbl/ *adj* مَعْقُول

F

feast /fiːst/ *n* وَلِيمَة/وَلائِم مف/ج

feast day *n* *feast day* يَوْم العِيد

feat /fiːt/ *n* عَمَل بُطُولِيّ

feather /ˈfeðə(r)/ *n* رِيشَة/رِيش مف/ج

feature /ˈfiːtʃə(r)/ *n* مِيزَة

February /ˈfebruəri/ *n* (see August) شَهْر شُبَاط

federal /ˈfedərəl/ *adj* فِدْرَالِيّ

federation /fedəˈreɪʃn/ *n* (of states) حُكُومَة فِدْرَالِيَّة (in sport, etc) اتِّحَاد/اتِّحَادَات مف/ج

fee /fiː/ *n* رَسْم/رُسُوم مف/ج

feed /fiːd/ *v* **fed** يُطْعِم

feedback /ˈfiːdbæk/ *n* تَعْقِيب عَلَى عَمَل

feel /fiːl/ *v* **felt** يَشْعُر

feeling /ˈfiːlɪŋ/ *n* إِحْسَاس/أَحَاسِيس مف/ج

female /ˈfiːmeɪl/ *adj* أُنْثَى

feminine /ˈfemənɪn/ *adj* أُنْثَوِيّ

feminism /ˈfemənɪzəm/ *n* حَرَكَة نِسَائِيَّة

feminist /ˈfemənɪst/ *n* مُؤَيِّد لِلمُسَاوَاة بَيْنَ الجِنْسَيْن

fence /fens/ *n* سِيَاج/أَسْيِجَة مف/ج

fennel /ˈfenl/ *n* نَبْتَة الشُمْرَة

ferry /ˈferi/ *n* pl **-ries** عَبَّارَة

fertile /ˈfɜːtaɪl/ *adj* (land) خَصْب (of females) مِخْصَاب، خَصْب

fertilize /ˈfɜːtəlaɪz/ *v* يُسَمِّد

festival /ˈfestɪvl/ *n* (secular) مَهْرَجَان/مَهْرَجَانَات مف/ج احْتِفَال/احْتِفَالات مف/ج (religious) احْتِفَال/احْتِفَالاَت مف/ج

feta /ˈfɛtə/ *n* جُبْنَة يُونَانِيَّة

fetch /fetʃ/ *v* يَجْلِب

fever /ˈfiːvə(r)/ *n* حُمَّى

few /fjuː/ *adj* (a few) قَلِيل، بَعْض

A few people know that. بَعْض النَاس يَعْلَمُون ذَلِك

They have a few ideas. لَدَيْهِم بَعْض الأَفْكَار

a few weeks ago قَبْلَ أَسَابِيع قَلِيلَة

(not many) قَلِيل

few men رِجَال قَلِيلُون

♦ *pron* قَلِيل

Few know about it. قَلِيلُون يَعْلَمُون ذَلِك

Few of them try. قَلِيلُون مِنْهُم يُحَاوِلُون

fewer /ˈfjuːər/ *adj* أَقَلّ

fewer accidents than before حَوَادِث أَقَلّ مِن السَابِق

fewer and fewer people نَاس أَقَلّ وَأَقَلّ

♦ *pron* أَقَلّ

fewer than ten cars أَقَلّ مِن عَشْر سَيَّارَات

fewest /'fju:est/ *adj* الأَقَلّ

the fewest accidents for ten years

عَدَد الحَوَادِث الأَقَلّ مُنْذُ عَشْر سَنَوَات

Who made fewest mistakes?

مَن عَمِلَ أَقَلّ الأَخْطَاء؟

fibre /'faɪbə(r)/ *n* US **-ber** أَلْيَاف

fiction /'fɪkʃn/ *n* الأَدَب الخَيَالِيّ

field /fi:ld/ *n* (on a farm) حَقْل/حُقُول
مَلْعَب/مَلَاعِبُ مف/ج (for sport) مف/ج
(of study) مَجَال/مَجَالَات مف/ج

fierce /fɪəs/ *adj* (animal, person)
عَنِيف (heat, wind) شَدِيد (competition)
قَوِيّ

fifteen /fɪf'ti:n/ *num* خَمْسَةَ عَشَرَ

fifth /fɪfθ/ *adj* خَامِس/خَوَامِسُ مف/ج
♦ *adv* خَامِساً
♦ *n* (see tenth) الخَامِس

fiftieth /'fɪftiəθ/ *adj* الخَمْسُون

fifty /'fɪfti/ *num* خَمْسُون

fig /fɪg/ *n* تِين

fight /faɪt/ *n* (physical) /شِجَار
شِجَارَات مف/ج (against injustice, etc)
مُكَافَحَة
♦ *v* **fought** (physically) يَتَشَاجَر
(injustice) يُكَافِح

figure /'fɪgə(r)/ *n* (number) /عَدَد
شَخْصِيَّة بَارِزَة (person) أَعْدَاد مف/ج
(body shape) شَكْل/أَشْكَال مف/ج

file /faɪl/ *n* (tool) مِبْرَد/مَبَارِدُ مف/ج
(for letters, etc) مِلَفّ/مِلَفَّات مف/ج
♦ *v* يَحْفَظ مَعْلُومَات فِي مِلَفّ

Filipina /ˌfɪlɪ'pi:nə/ *n* فِلِبِّينِيَّة

Filipino /fɪlɪ'pi:nəʊ/ *adj* فِلِبِّينِيّ

fill /fɪl/ *v* (a hole) يَمْلَأ (a tank, etc) يَمْتَلِئ

film /fɪlm/ *n* فِيلْم/أَفْلَام مف/ج
♦ *v* يُصَوِّر

filter /'fɪltə(r)/ *n* مِصْفَاة/مَصَافٍ مف/ج

final /'faɪnl/ *adj* أَخِير

finally /'faɪnəli/ *adv* أَخِيراً

finance /faɪ'næns/ *v* يُمَوِّل

financial /faɪ'nænʃ/ *adj* مَالِيّ

find /faɪnd/ *v* **found** يَجِد

fine /faɪn/ *adj* (weather) صَافٍ (well)
عَالِي الجَوْدَة (silks, etc) بِصِحَّة جَيِّدَة
(performer) بَارِع
♦ *n* غَرَامَة

finger /'fɪŋgə(r)/ *n* إِصْبَع/أَصَابِعُ مف/ج

finish /'fɪnɪʃ/ *n* (of a race) نِهَايَة (on a
product) لَمْسَة نِهَائِيَّة
♦ *v* (to get to the end of) يُنْهِي (to use
up) يَسْتَنْفِد (to end) يَنْتَهِي

finished /'fɪnɪʃt/ *adj* مُنْجَز

fire /'faɪə(r)/ *n* (for warmth) نَار (م)
(causing damage) حَرِيق/حَرَائِقُ مف/ج
♦ *v* (a gun) يُطْلِق النَار (an employee)
يَفْصِل (مِن العَمَل)

F

F

firearm /'faɪərɑːm/ *n* سِلاَح يَدَوِيّ

fireplace /'faɪəpleɪs/ *n* مُسْتَوْقَد

firm /fɜːm/ *adj* (ground) صُلْب (grip, etc) صَارِم

♦ *n* شَرِكَة

first /fɜːst/ *adj* (in a series) أَوَّل/أَوَائِلُ مف/ج

our first child طِفْلُنَا الأَوَّل (time) أَوَّل

first prize الجَائِزَة الأُولَى

♦ *adv* أَوَّلاً

First, let's eat. أَوَّلاً، دَعْنَا نَأْكُل

to come first in a race يَأْتِي أَوَّلاً فِي مُسَابَقَة

when I first came to this country أَوَّل مَرَّة جِئْتُ فِيهَا لِهَذِهِ الدَوْلَة

♦ *n* الأَوَّل

the first of March, March the first الأَوَّل مِن آذَار

fish /fɪʃ/ *n* pl **fish, fishes** (live) سَمَكَة/سَمَك وَأَسْمَاك مف/ج pl (as food) سَمَك

♦ *v* يَصْطَاد سَمَكاً

fisherman /'fɪʃəmən/ *n* **-men** صَيَّاد سَمَك

fishing /'fɪʃɪŋ/ *n* صَيْد السَمَك

fit /fɪt/ *adj* مُتَمَتِّع بِاللِيَاقَة

♦ *n* نَوْبَة

fitness /'fɪtnəs/ *n* لِيَاقَة

five /faɪv/ *num* خَمْسَة

fix /fɪks/ *v* (to attach) يُثَبِّت (to repair) يُصْلِح

fixed /fɪkst/ *adj* ثَابِت

flag /flæg/ *n* عَلَم/أَعْلاَم مف/ج

flame /fleɪm/ *n* لَهَب

flan /flæn/ *n* كَعْكَة بَيْض مَعَ جُبْنَة

flash /flæʃ/ *n* وَمِيض/أَوْمِضَة مف/ج

♦ *v* يُوْمِض

flash stick *n* قَلَم الذَاكِرَة

flashlight *n* مِشْعَل كَهْرَبَائِيّ

flat /flæt/ *adj* (surface) سَهْل/سُهُول مف/ج (shoes) مُسْتَوٍ

♦ *n* UK شِقَّة/شِقَق مف/ج

flat screen *n* شَاشَة مُسَطَّحَة

flavour /'fleɪvə(r)/ *n* US **-vor** مَذَاق/مَذَاقَات مف/ج

flaw /flɔː/ *n* عَيْب/عُيُوب مف/ج

flee /fliː/ *v* **fled** يَهْرُب

fleet /fliːt/ *n* أُسْطُول/أَسَاطِيلُ مف/ج

flesh /fleʃ/ *n* لَحْم

flexible /'fleksəbl/ *adj* مَرِن

flight /flaɪt/ *n* رِحْلَة جَوِّيَّة

flight attendant *n* (female) مُضِيفَة جَوِّيَّة

flirt /flɜːt/ *v* يُغَازِل

float /fləʊt/ *v* يَطْفُو
 ♦ *n* عَرَبَة مُزَخْرَفَة

flock /flɒk/ *n* (of sheep) قَطِيع/قُطْعَان
 (of birds) سِرْب/أَسْرَاب مف/ج مف/ج

flood /flʌd/ *n* (of river, etc) فَيَضَان/
 فَيَضَانَات مف/ج (of protests, etc)
 سَيْل/سُيُول مف/ج
 ♦ *v* يَغْمُر

floor /flɔː(r)/ *n* (of a room) أَرْضِيَّة
 (in building) طَابِق/طَوَابِقُ مف/ج

flour /ˈflaʊə(r)/ *n* دَقِيق

flow /fləʊ/ *v* (liquids) يَتَدَفَّق (ideas)
 يَنْسَاب

flower /ˈflaʊə(r)/ *n* زَهْرَة/أَزْهَار
 وزُهُور مف/ج
 ♦ *v* يُزْهِر

flu /fluː/ *n* إِنْفْلُونْزَا

fluid /ˈfluːɪd/ *n* سَائِل/سَوَائِلُ مف/ج
 ♦ *adj* مَائِع

fly /flaɪ/ *v* **flies, flew, flown** (birds,
 aeroplanes) يَطِير
 ♦ *n* pl **flies** (insects) ذُبَابَة/ذُبَاب
 فُتْحَة السِرْوَال (in trousers) مف/ج

focus /ˈfəʊkəs/ *n* بُؤْرَة/بُؤَر مف/ج

fog /fɒg/ *n* ضَبَاب

fold /fəʊld/ *v* يَطْوِي
 ♦ *n* طَوْيَة

folder /ˈfəʊldə(r)/ *n* (for letters)
 حَافِظَة مِلَفَّات (in word processing)
 مُجَلَّد/مُجَلَّدَات مف/ج

folk /fəʊk/ *n* نَاس

follow /ˈfɒləʊ/ *v* يَتْبَع

follower /ˈfɒləʊə(r)/ *n* تَابِع/أَتْبَاع
 مف/ج

following /ˈfɒləʊɪŋ/ *adj* تَالٍ

font /fɒnt/ *n* خَطّ/خُطُوط مف/ج

food /fuːd/ *n* (what one eats) طَعَام

fool /fuːl/ *n* أَحْمَق/حَمْقَاء/حُمْق
 مذ/م/ج
 ♦ *v* يَسْتَغْفِل

foolish /ˈfuːlɪʃ/ *adj* أَحْمَق/حَمْقَاء/
 حُمْق مذ/م/ج

foot /fʊt/ *n* pl **feet** قَدَم/أَقْدَام (م)
 مف/ج

football /ˈfʊtbɔːl/ *n* (soccer) لُعْبَة كُرَة
 القَدَم (in US) لُعْبَة كُرَة القَدَم الأَمْرِيكِيَّة
 (ball) كُرَة قَدَم

for /fə(r), fɔː(r)/ *prep* (with
 destination, recipient) إِلَى
 a letter for Mrs Andrews
 رِسَالَة إِلَى السَّيِّدَة أَنْدْرُوز
 Is this the train for London?
 هَل هَذَا هُوَ القِطَار الذَاهِب إِلَى لُنْدُن؟
 (showing purpose) مِن أَجْل

F

It's for sending messages. هِيَ مِن أَجْل إِرْسَال الرَسَائِل
He came for his letters. جَاءَ مِن أَجْل رَسَائِلِه (as an employee of) لِصَالِح
We all work for RevCon. جَمِيعُنَا نَعْمَل لِصَالِح "رِفْكُون" (in time) لِ، مِن
for five minutes لِخَمْسَة دَقَائِق
I waited for a month. انْتَظَرْتُ لِشَهْر
the first time for weeks المَرَّة الأُولَى مِن أَسَابِيع (with distance) لِمَسَافَة
We drove for miles. قُدْنَا السَيَّارَة لِمَسَافَة أَمْيَال
(giving the reason) تَكْرِيماً لِ
a medal for bravery مِيدَالِيَة تَكْرِيماً لِلشَجَاعَة (with prices) مُقَابِل
to buy/sell a rug for $100 يَشْتَرِي/يَبِيع سِجَّادَة مُقَابِل 100 دُولَار
(in support of) دِفَاعاً عَن
a campaign for equality حَمْلَة دِفَاعاً عَن المُسَاوَاة

forbid /fə'bɪd/ *v* **forbade, forbidden** يَحْظُر

force /fɔːs/ *n* (violence) عُنْف (of the wind) قُوَّة مف/ج
♦ *v* (to oblige) يُجْبِر (a door, etc) يَدْفَع بِالقُوَّة

ford /fɔːd/ *n* مَخَاضَة

forecast /'fɔːkɑːst/ *n* تَنَبُّؤ/تَنَبُّؤَات مف/ج
♦ *v* **-cast or -casted** يَتَنَبَّأ

forefront /'fɔːfrʌnt/ *n* طَلِيعَة

forehead /'fɔːhed/ *n* جَبِين/جُبُن مف/ج

foreign /'fɒrən/ *adj* (language) أَجْنَبِيّ (policy) خَارِجِيّ

foreigner /'fɒrənə(r)/ *n* أَجْنَبِيّ

forensic /fə'renzɪk/ *adj* قَضَائِيّ

forest /'fɒrɪst/ *n* غَابَة

forge /fɔːdʒ/ *v* يُزَوِّر

forget /fə'get/ *v* **-get, -gotten** يَنْسَى

forgive /fə'gɪv/ *v* **-gave, -given** يَعْفُو عَن

fork /fɔːk/ *n* (for eating) شَوْكَة/شوك مف/ج (in road) تَفَرُّع/تَفَرُّعَات مف/ج

form /fɔːm/ *n* (shape) شَكْل/أَشْكَال مف/ج (paper) نَمُوذَج/نَمَاذِج مف/ج (version) نَوْع/أَنْوَاع مف/ج
♦ *v* يُشَكِّل

formal /'fɔːml/ *adj* رَسْمِيّ

formality /fɔː'mæləti/ *n* إِجْرَاء شَكْلِيّ

format /'fɔːmæt/ *n* تَرْتِيب
♦ *v* يُنَسِّق

formation /fɔː'meɪʃn/ *n* تَشْكِيل

former /'fɔːmə(r)/ *adj* سَابِق

formerly /'fɔːməli/ *adv* سَابِقاً

formula /'fɔːmjələ/ *n* (in maths) صِيغَة/صِيَغ مف/ج (for success) طَرِيقَة/طُرُق مف/ج

formulate /'fɔːmjuleɪt/ *v* يَصُوغ

fort /fɔːt/ *n* حِصْن/حُصُون مف/ج

forthcoming /fɔːθ'kʌmɪŋ/ *adj* قَادِم

fortnight /'fɔːtnaɪt/ *n* UK أُسْبُوعَان

fortunate /'fɔːtʃənət/ *adj* مَحْظُوظ

fortunately /'fɔːtʃənətli/ *adv* لِحُسْن الحَظّ

fortune /'fɔːtʃuːn/ *n* ثَرْوَة

forty /'fɔːti/ *num* أَرْبَعُون

forum /'fɔːrəm/ *n* مُنْتَدَى/مُنْتَدَيَات مف/ج

forward /'fɔːwəd/ *adv* -**ds** إِلَى الأَمَام
♦ *v* يُرْسِل

fossil /'fɒsl/ *n* حَفْرِيَّة

foul /faʊl/ *adj* كَرِيه
♦ *n* عَرْقَلَة
♦ *v* يُعَرْقِل

found /faʊnd/ *v* يُؤَسِّس

foundation *n* (institution) مُؤَسَّسَة
foundations *n pl* أَسَاس/أَسَاسَات وَأُسُس مف/ج

fountain /'faʊntən/ *n* نَافُورَة/نَوَافِيرُ مف/ج

four /fɔː(r)/ *num* أَرْبَعَة

fourteen /fɔː'tiːn/ *num* أَرْبَعَة عَشَر

fourth /fɔːθ/ *adj* رَابِع/رَوَابِعُ
♦ *adv* رَابِعاً
♦ *n* (see tenth) الرَابِع

fox /fɒks/ *n* ثَعْلَب/ثَعَالِبُ مف/ج

fraction /'frækʃn/ *n* كَسْر/كُسُور مف/ج

fracture /'fræktʃə(r)/ *n* كَسْر/كُسُور مف/ج

fragile /'frædʒaɪl/ *adj* هَشّ

fragment /'frægmənt/ *n* جُزْء/أَجْزَاء مف/ج

frame /freɪm/ *n* (of a picture, etc) إِطَار/إِطَارَات مف/ج (of buildings, etc) هَيْكَل/هَيَاكِلُ مف/ج

framework /'freɪmwɜːk/ *n* هَيْكَل/هَيَاكِلُ مف/ج

France /frɑːns/ *n* فَرَنْسَا

franchise /'fræntʃaɪz/ *n* امْتِيَاز/امْتِيَازَات مف/ج

franchisee /fræntʃaɪ'ziː/ *n* صَاحِب الامْتِيَاز

fraud /frɔːd/ *n* احْتِيَال

freak /friːk/ *n* شَخْص مُولَع بِشَيْء مَا

free /friː/ *adj* حُرّ
free kick *n* ضَرْبَة حُرَّة

F

freedom /'fri:dəm/ *n* حُرِّيَّة

freeway /'fri:weɪ/ *n* US طَرِيق سَرِيع

freeze /fri:z/ *v* **froze, frozen** (food) يَتَجَمَّد (lakes, etc) يُجَمِّد

French /frentʃ/ *adj* فَرَنْسِيّ
♦ *n* (language) اللُغَة الفَرَنْسِيَّة
(people) فَرَنْسِيُّون

French fries /fraɪz/ *n* رَقَائِق بَطَاطَا مَقْلِيَّة

frequent /'fri:kwənt/ *adj* مُتَكَرِّر

frequently /'fri:kwəntli/ *adv* كَثِيراً

fresh /freʃ/ *adj* (fruit, etc) طَازِج
(start) جَدِيد

fresher /'freʃə(r)/ *n* طَالِب جَامِعِيّ فِي السَنَة الأُولَى

freshman /'freʃmən/ *n* US pl **-men** طَالِب جَامِعِيّ فِي السَنَة الأُولَى

Friday /'fraɪdeɪ/ *n* (see Wednesday) يَوْم الجُمْعَة

fridge /frɪdʒ/ *n* ثَلاَّجَة

friend /frend/ *n* صَدِيق/أَصْدِقَاءُ مف/ج

friendly /'frendli/ *adj* (people) وَدُود
(atmosphere) لَطِيف

friendship /'frendʃɪp/ *n* صَدَاقَة

frighten /'fraɪtn/ *v* يُخِيف

fringe /frɪndʒ/ *n* غُرَّة

fritter /'frɪtə(r)/ *n* فَطِيرَة مَقْلِيَّة

frog /frɒg/ *n* ضِفْدَع/ضَفَادِعُ مف/ج

from /frɒm/ *prep* (showing start point) مِن
the bus from London البَاص مِن لَنْدَن
two kilometres from here
كِيلُومِتْرَيْن مِن هُنَا (showing origin) مِن
people from India النَاس مِن الهِنْد
an email from my father
رِسَالَة إِلِكْتْرُونِيَّة مِن وَالِدِي
made from the best ingredients
مَصْنُوع مِن أَفْضَل المُكَوِّنَات (in time) مِن
from 10 o'clock to 11.30 مِن السَاعَة العَاشِرَة إِلَى السَاعَة الحَادِيَة عَشْرَة وَالنِصْف
from now on مِن الآن فَصَاعِد
(showing extent) مِن
from 0 to 60 mph
مِن صِفْر إِلَى 60 مِيل فِي السَاعَة
from birth to death
مِن المِيلاَد إِلَى المَمَات

front /frʌnt/ *n* (of a house, car) مُقَدِّمَة
in front of the house فِي مُقَدِّمَة المَنْزِل
at the front of the procession
فِي مُقَدِّمَة المَوْكِب

frontier /'frʌntɪə(r)/ *n* حَدّ/حُدُود مف/ج

frown /fraʊn/ *n* عُبُوس
♦ *v* يَعْبَس

frozen /'frəʊzn/ *adj* مُتَجَمِّد

fruit /fru:t/ *n* ثَمَرَة/ثِمَار مف/ج

frustrate /frʌ'streɪt/ *v* يُحْبِط

frustration /frʌ'streɪʃn/ *n* إِحْبَاط

fry /fraɪ/ *v* يَقْلِي

fuel /'fju:əl/ *n* وَقُود

fulfil /fʊl'fɪl/ *v* US **-fill** يُنْجِز

full /fʊl/ *adj* (bottle) كَامِل
the full story القِصَّة الكَامِلَة
The glass was full. كَانَ الكُوب مُمْتَلِئاً
(after eating) شَبْعَان
I am full أَنَا شَبْعَان

fully /'fʊli/ *adv* تَمَاماً

fun /fʌn/ *n* مَرَح

function /'fʌŋkʃn/ *n* وَظِيفَة/وَظَائِف مف/ج

fund /fʌnd/ *n* تَمْوِيل
♦ *v* يُمَوِّل

fundamental /fʌndə'mentl/ *adj* أَسَاسِيّ

funeral /'fju:nərəl/ *n* جَنَازَة

fungus /'fʌŋgəs/ *n* pl **fungi** /فُطْر فُطْرِيَّات مف/ج

funny /'fʌni/ *adj* (humorous) مُضْحِك
(strange) غَرِيب

fur /fɜ:(r)/ *n* فَرْو

furious /'fjʊəriəs/ *adj* ثَائِر

furniture /'fɜ:nɪtʃə(r)/ *n* أَثَاث

fury /'fjʊəri/ *n* ثَوْرَة غَضَب

fusion /'fju:ʒn/ *n* دَمْج

future /'fju:tʃə(r)/ *adj* مُسْتَقْبَلِيّ
♦ *n* مُسْتَقْبَل

F

G

G

gain /geɪn/ *n* رِبْح/أَرْبَاح مف/ج ♦ *v* يَزْدَاد

gallery /ˈgæləri/ *n* pl **-ries** مَعْرَض فُنُون

Galilee /ˈgalɪliː/ *n* مَدِينَة الجَلِيل

gamble /ˈgæmbl/ *v* يُقَامِر

game /geɪm/ *n* لُعْبَة/أَلْعَاب مف/ج

gamer /ˈgeɪmə(r)/ *n* لَاعِب

gaming /ˈgeɪmɪŋ/ *n* لَعْب

gang /gæŋ/ *n* عِصَابَة

gap /gæp/ *n* فَجْوَة

garage /ˈgærɑːʒ/ *n* مَرْأَب/مَرَائِبُ مف/ج

garbage /ˈgɑːbɪʤ/ *n* قُمَامَة

garbage collector *n* US رَجُل نَظَافَة

garden /ˈgɑːdn/ *n* حَدِيقَة/حَدَائِقُ مف/ج

gardener /ˈgɑːdnə(r)/ *n* بُسْتَانِيّ

garlic /ˈgɑːlɪk/ *n* ثوم

garment /ˈgɑːmənt/ *n* عَبَاءَة

gas /gæs/ *n* (in physics) غَاز/غَازَات مف/ج (US: for cars) بَنْزِين

gasp /gɑːsp/ *v* يَشْهَق

gasoline /ˈgæsəliːn/ *n* US بَنْزِين

gate /geɪt/ *n* (into a garden) بَوَّابَة (at an airport) مَدْخَل/مَدَاخِلُ مف/ج

gather /ˈgæðə(r)/ *v* (to meet) يَتَجَمَّع (to bring together) يَجْمَع

gathering /ˈgæðərɪŋ/ *n* تَجَمُّع/تَجَمُّعَات مف/ج

gay /geɪ/ *adj* شَاذّ جِنْسِيّاً

Gaza City /ˈgɑːʒə/ *n* غَزَّة

gears /gɪəʒ/ *n pl* نَاقِل الحَرَكَة

gem /ʤem/ *n* حَجَر كَرِيم

gender /ˈʤendə(r)/ *n* جِنْس

general /ˈʤenrəl/ *adj* عَامّ ♦ *n* لِوَاء/أَلْوِيَة مف/ج

generally /ˈʤenrəli/ *adv* عُمُوماً

generate /ˈʤenəreɪt/ *v* يُوَلِّد

generation /ʤenəˈreɪʃn/ *n* جِيل/أَجْيَال مف/ج

generator /ˈʤenəreɪtə(r)/ *n* مُوَلِّد كَهْرَبَائِيّ/مُوَلِّدَات مف/ج

generic /ʤəˈnerɪk/ *adj* عَامّ

generosity /ʤenəˈrɒsəti/ *n* كَرَم

generous /ˈʤenərəs/ *adj* (person)

وَفِير (helping) كَرِيم

genetic /dʒəˈnetɪk/ *adj* جِينِيّ

genius /ˈdʒiːniəs/ *n* (person) عَبْقَرِيّ (intelligence) عَبْقَرِيَّة

genocide /ˈdʒenəsaɪd/ *n* إِبَادَة جَمَاعِيَّة

gentle /ˈdʒentl/ *adj* (person) لَطِيف/ لُطَفَاء مف/ج (exercise) خَفِيف

gentleman /ˈdʒentlmən/ *n* pl **-men** رَجُل لَطِيف

gently /ˈdʒentli/ *adv* بِلُطْف

genuine /ˈdʒenjuɪn/ *adj* حَقِيقِيّ

geography /dʒiˈɒgrəfi/ *n* جُغْرَافْيَا

geometry /dʒiˈɒmətri/ *n* عِلْم الهَنْدَسَة

German /ˈdʒɜːmən/ *adj* أَلْمَانِيّ ♦ *n* (language) اللُغَة الأَلْمَانِيَّة (citizen) أَلْمَانِيّ/أَلْمَان مف/ج

Germany /ˈdʒɜːməni/ *n* أَلْمَانِيَا

gesture /ˈdʒestʃə(r)/ *n* إِيمَاءَة

get /get/ *v* **got,** (US: past participle) **gotten** (to obtain) يَحْصُلُ عَلَى
John got the job.
حَصَلَ جون عَلَى الوَظِيفَة
I got some eggs.
حَصَلْتُ عَلَى بَعْض البَيْض
(to bring) يَجْلِب
Get me that knife. اجْلِب لِي تِلْكَ السِكِّين
(to receive) يَسْتَلِم
She got your letter. اسْتَلَمَت رِسَالَتَك
(a cold) يُصَاب (بِمَرَض)
I'm getting a cold. أُصِبْتُ بِالرَشْح
(to become) يُصْبِح
She's got taller. أَصْبَحَت أَطْوَل
It's getting easier. تُصْبِح أَسْهَل
You'll get wet. سَوْفَ تَتَبَلَّل (to bring about a result) يُحْضِر، يَجْعَل
Can you get it to work?
هَل بِاسْتِطَاعَتِكَ أَنْ تَجْعَلَهَا تَعْمَل؟
I got the car washed. غَسَلْتُ السَيَّارَة
Get James to help you.
احْضِر جِيمْس لِمُسَاعَدَتِكَ (to arrive) يَصِل
We got there at two o'clock.
وَصَلْنَا هُنَاكَ السَاعَة الثَانِيَة

get away *phv* (from work, etc) يَذْهَب (to escape) يَهْرُب

get back *phv* (to return) يَعُود
They get back tomorrow.
سَيَعُودُون غَداً (a possession) يَسْتَعِيد، يَسْتَرِدّ
Did you get your watch back?
هَل اسْتَعَدْتَ سَاعَتَك؟

get in *phv* (to arrive) يَصِل
He got in late last night.
وَصَلَ مُتَأَخِّراً اللَيْلَة المَاضِيَة
The last bus gets in at midnight.
يَصِل البَاص الأَخِير فِي مُنْتَصَف اللَيْل

get out *phv* (of a room) يَخْرُج

G

Get out! اُخْرُج (to remove) يُخْرِج

I'll get the car out of the garage.

سَوْفَ أُخْرِج السَيَّارَة مِن المَرْأَب

get over *phv* (an illness) يَتَعَافَى

ghost /gəʊst/ *n* شَبَح/أَشْبَاح مف/ج

giant /ˈdʒaɪənt/ *n* مَارِد

G

gift /gɪft/ *n* (present) هَدِيَّة/هَدَايَا

(ability) مَوْهِبَة/مَوَاهِب مف/ج مف/ج

gigabyte /ˈgɪgəbaɪt/ *n* جِيجَابَايْت (مِقْيَاس حَجْم السعَة فِي الحَاسِوب وَيُعَادِل 1024 مِيجَابَايْت)

gigantic /dʒaɪˈgæntɪk/ *adj* ضَخْم/ضِخَام مف/ج

giggle /ˈgɪgl/ *v* يُقَهْقِه

ginger /ˈdʒɪndʒə(r)/ *n* زَنْجَبِيل

gill /gɪl/ *n* خَيْشُوم/خَيَاشِيمُ مف/ج

girl /gɜːl/ *n* بِنْت/بَنَات (م) مف/ج

girlfriend /ˈgɜːlfrend/ *n* خَلِيلَة

give /gɪv/ *v* **gave, given** (a present, etc) يُعْطِي (a talk) يُدْلِي

give up *phv* يُقْلِع عَن

glad /glæd/ *adj* سَعِيد

glance /glɑːns/ *n* لَمْحَة

♦ *v* يَلْمَح

gland /glænd/ *n* غُدَّة/غُدَد مف/ج

glare /gleə(r)/ *n* ضَوْء سَاطِع

glass /glɑːs/ *n* (material) زُجَاج (for water, etc) كَأْس/كُؤُوس (م) مف/ج

glimpse /glɪmps/ *n* لَمْحَة

global /ˈgləʊbl/ *adj* عَالَمِيّ

globalization /gləʊbəlaɪˈzeɪʃn/ *n* عَوْلَمَة

globe /gləʊb/ *n* الكُرَة الأَرْضِيَّة

gloom /gluːm/ *n* ظَلَام

gloomy /ˈgluːmi/ *adj* كَئِيب

glory /ˈglɔːri/ *n* مَجْد/أَمْجَاد مف/ج

glove /glʌv/ *n* قُفَّاز/قُفَّازَات مف/ج

glow /gləʊ/ *n* تَوَهُّج

♦ *v* يَتَوَهَّج

go /gəʊ/ *v* **goes, went, gone** (on foot, by car, etc) يَذْهَب

He went by bus/by train.

ذَهَبَ بِالبَاص/القِطَار

We're going to town.

إِنَّنَا ذَاهِبُون إِلَى مَركَز المَدِينَة

They went to Egypt for their holidays.

ذَهَبُوا إِلَى مِصْر لِقَضَاء إِجَازَتِهِم

(to leave) يُغَادِر

I must go now. يَجِب أَنْ أُغَادِر الآن

(to be kept: plates, etc) يُوضَع

Where do these tools go?

أَيْنَ تُوضَع هَذِه الأَدوَات

(to do sth specific) يَذْهَب

to go for a walk يَذْهَب لِلتَمَشّي
Shall we go for a coffee?
هَلاَّ ذَهَبْنَا لاحْتِسَاء القَهْوَة؟ (to work: machines) يَعْمَل
The AC is going again.
المُكَيِّف يَعْمَل ثَانِيَةً (to form the future) سَوْفَ
We're going to leave tomorrow.
سَوْفَ نُغَادِر غَداً
He's going to study medicine.
سَوْفَ يَدْرُس الطِبّ

go away *phv* (to leave) يُغَادِر
to go away for a week
يُغَادِر لِمُدَّة أُسْبُوع

go back *phv* (to return) يَعُود
to go back home يَعُود إِلَى البَيْت
He went back to the beginning.
عَادَ إِلَى البِدَايَة

go down *phv* (prices, the tide) يَهْبِط (the sun) يَغْرُب

go in *phv* (to a house, room) يَدْخُل
They went in at two o'clock.
دَخَلُوا البَيْت فِي السَاعَة الثَانِيَة (the sun) يَتَوَارَى (خَلْفَ الغُيُوم)
The sun's gone in. تَوَارَت الشَمْس

go off *phv* (alarm) يَنْطَلِق (bombs, guns) يَنْفَجِر (to cut out: electricity) يَنْقَطِع

go on *phv* (to happen) يَحْدُث
What's going on? مَاذَا يَحْدُث؟
(talking, eating, etc) يَسْتَمِرّ
He went on speaking for two hours.
اسْتَمَرَّ فِي الحَدِيث لِسَاعَتَيْن

goal /gəʊl/ *n* هَدَف/أَهْدَاف مف/ج

goalkeeper /'gəʊlki:pə(r)/ *n* حَارِس المَرْمَى

goat /gəʊt/ *n* مَاعِز

god /gɒd/ *n* إِلَه/آلِهَة مف/ج

gold /gəʊld/ *n* ذَهَب

golden /'gəʊldən/ *adj* ذَهَبِيّ

golf /gɒlf/ *n* لُعْبَة الجُولْف

golf club *n* (place) نَادِي جُولْف
(instrument) مِضْرَب الجُولْف

good /gʊd/ *adj* (of high quality) جَيِّد
a good doctor طَبِيب جَيِّد (enjoyable) مُمْتِع
We had a good time. قَضَيْنَا وَقْتاً مُمْتِعاً
(news) سَارّ (children) مُؤَدَّب (healthy: diet) مُفِيد
Vegetables are good for you.
الخُضْرَوَات مُفِيدَة لَكَ (in greetings) سَعِيد
good afternoon! مَسَاء الخَيْر
good evening! مَسَاء الخَيْر
good morning! صَبَاح الخَيْر
good night! لَيْلَة سَعِيدَة (well, fine) بِصِحَّة جَيِّدَة

G

goodbye /gʊd'baɪ/ *interj* وَدَاعاً

goodwill /gʊd'wɪl/ *n* سُمْعَة حَسَنَة

goose /gu:s/ *n* وَزَّة/وَزّ مف/ج

gospel /'gɒspl/ *n* الإِنْجِيل

gossip /'gɒsɪp/ *n* نَمِيمَة، قِيل وَقَال

govern /'gʌvn/ *v* يَحْكُم

government /'gʌvənmənt/ *n* حُكُومَة

governor /'gʌvənə(r)/ *n* حَاكِم/حُكَّام مف/ج

grab /græb/ *v* يَخْطِف

grade /greɪd/ *n* (mark, score) دَرَجَة (school year group) الصَفّ/الصُفُوف مف/ج

♦ *v* (eggs, fruit, students) يُصَنِّف

grade school *n* US مَدْرَسَة ابْتِدَائِيَّة

gradient /'greɪdiənt/ *n* انْحِدَار

gradual /'grædʒuəl/ *adj* تَدْرِيجِيّ

gradually /'grædʒuəli/ *adv* تَدْرِيجِيّاً

graduate /'grædʒueɪt/ *v* يَتَخَرَّج

♦ *n* خِرِّيج جَامِعَة

graduation /grædʒu'eɪʃn/ *n* حَفْلَة التَخَرُّج

grain /greɪn/ *n* (seeds) حُبُوب (of sand, salt) حَبَّة/حُبُوب مف/ج

gram /græm/ *n* غْرَام/غْرَامَات مف/ج

grammar /'græmə(r)/ *n* عِلْم النَحْو

grand /grænd/ *adj* فَاخِر

grandfather /'grænfɑ:ðə(r)/ *n* جَدّ/أَجْدَاد مف/ج

grandmother /'grænmʌðə(r)/ *n* جَدَّة

grandparent /'grænpeərənt/ *n* جَدّ أَو جَدَّة

grant /grɑ:nt/ *n* مِنْحَة/مِنَح مف/ج

♦ *v* يَمْنَح

grape /greɪp/ *n* عِنَب/أَعْنَاب مف/ج

graph /grɑ:f/ *n* رَسْم بَيَانِيّ

graphic /'græfɪk/ *adj* مُتَعَلِّق بِالرَسْم البَيَانِيّ

grass /grɑ:s/ *n* عُشْب

grateful /'greɪtfl/ *adj* شَاكِر

gratitude /'grætɪtju:d/ *n* العِرْفَان بِالجَمِيل

grave /greɪv/ *adj* (consequences, news, situation) خَطِير

♦ *n* قَبْر/قُبُور مف/ج

gravity /'grævəti/ *n* الجَاذِبِيَّة

graze /greɪz/ *v* (cows, sheep) يَأْكُل العُشْب (one's knee) يَجْلُط

great /greɪt/ *adj* (difficulty, success, pleasure) كَبِير (very good) عَظِيم

greed /gri:d/ *n* جَشَع

Greek /gri:k/ *adj* يُونَانِيّ
♦ *n* (language) اللُغَة اليُونَانِيَّة (citizen) يُونَانِيّ/يُونَان مف/ج

green /gri:n/ *adj* (grass, leaves) أَخْضَر/ خَضْرَاء/خُضْر مذ/م/ج
to turn green يُصْبِح أَخْضَر/يَخْضَرّ
(fruit) غَيْر نَاضِج (issues) حِزْب الخُضُر
♦ *n* اللَوْن الأَخْضَر
to be dressed in green يَلْبِس الأَخْضَر
(in a village) مِنْطَقَة خَضْرَاء

green card *n* (for car insurance) بِطَاقَة تَأْمِين لِلقِيَادَة خَارِج بْرِيطَانِيَا
(for US residence) وَثِيقَة إِقَامَة فِي أَمْرِيكَا

green pepper *n* فِلْفِل أَخْضَر

greet /gri:t/ *v* يُحَيِّي

greeting /'gri:tɪŋ/ *n* تَحِيَّة

grey /greɪ/ *adj* رَمَادِيّ
♦ *n* اللَوْن الرَمَادِيّ

grief /gri:f/ *n* حُزْن

grievance /'gri:vəns/ *n* مَظْلَمَة/ مَظَالِمُ مف/ج

grim /grɪm/ *adj* مُزْعِج

grin /grɪn/ *n* ابْتِسَامَة
♦ *v* يَبْتَسِم

grind /graɪnd/ *v* **ground** يَطْحَن

grip /grɪp/ *n* قَبْضَة
♦ *v* يُمْسِك بِإِحْكَام

groan /grəʊn/ *v* يَئِنّ

grocery /'grəʊsəri/ *n* pl **-ries** بِقَالَة

groove /gru:v/ *n* أُخْدُود/أَخَادِيدُ مف/ج

gross /grəʊs/ *adj* (earnings) إِجْمَالِيّ
(negligence) فَادِح (manners) فَظّ

ground /graʊnd/ *n* سَطْح الأَرْض

grounds /graʊndz/ *n pl* (of a building) سَاحَات (motive) دَوَافِعُ

group /gru:p/ *n* مَجْمُوعَة

grow /grəʊ/ *v* **grew, grown** (person, business) يَكْبُر (grass, crops) يَنْمُو
(cultivate) يَزْرَع (your hair) يُرَبِّي

growl /graʊl/ *v* يُهَمِّر

growth /grəʊθ/ *n* (process) نُمُوّ
(lump) وَرَم/أَوْرَام مف/ج

grumble /'grʌmbl/ *v* يَتَذَمَّر

guarantee /gærən'ti:/ *n* ضَمَان/ ضَمَانَات مف/ج
♦ *v* يَضْمَن

guard /gɑ:d/ *n* حَارِس/حُرَّاس مف/ج
♦ *v* يَحْرُس

guardian /'gɑ:diən/ *n* وَصِيّ/أَوْصِيَاءُ مف/ج

guess /ges/ *n* pl **-sses** تَخْمِين
♦ *v* (to reply without facts) يُخَمِّن (to

G

suppose) يَظُنّ

guest /gest/ *n* (in sb's home) /ضَيْف
نَزِيل/نُزَلَاءُ (at a hotel) ضُيُوف مف/ج
مف/ج

guidance /ˈgaɪdns/ *n* تَوْجِيه

guide /gaɪd/ *n* دَلِيل
♦ *v* يُرْشِد

guilt /gɪlt/ *n* شُعُور بِالذَنْب

guilty /ˈgɪlti/ *adj* مُذْنِب

guitar /gɪˈtɑː(r)/ *n* القِيثَارَة

gulf /gʌlf/ *n* خَلِيج/خِلْجَان مف/ج
the Arabian Gulf الخَلِيج العَرَبِيّ

gum /gʌm/ *n* (in mouth) لِثَة الفَم (glue)
صَمْغ (for chewing) عِلْكَة

gun /gʌn/ *n* سِلَاح/أَسْلِحَة مف/ج

gut /gʌt/ *n* أَمْعَاء

gutter /ˈgʌtə(r)/ *n* مِزْرَاب/مَزَارِيبُ
مف/ج

guy /gaɪ/ *n* شَابّ/شَبَاب مف/ج

gym /dʒɪm/ *n* مَرْكَز لِيَاقَة

H

habit /'hæbɪt/ *n* عَادَة

hadn't /'hædnt/ *contr* (= had not: see have)

haddock /'hædək/ *n* سَمَك قُد أَصْفَر

hail /heɪl/ *v* (ice) تُمْطِر السَمَاء بَرَداً (an announcement) يُشِيد بِـ

hair /heə(r)/ *n* (one strand) شَعْرَة (many) شَعْر

hairdresser /'heədresə(r)/ *n* حَلاَّق

half /hɑːf/ *adj* نِصْف/أَنْصَاف مف/ج

for half price بِنِصْف الثَمَن

He gave me half an apple.

أَعْطَانِي نِصْف تُفَّاحَة

♦ *adv* (closed, full, finished) نِصْف

It's half empty. هُوَ نِصْف فَارِغ

The door was half open.

كَانَ البَاب نِصْف مَفْتُوح

♦ *pron* نِصْف *half of the money*

نِصْف المَال

♦ *n* (of a book, cake) مُنْتَصَف

half way through فِي مُنْتَصَف الطَرِيق

the second half of the movie

النِصْف الثَانِي مِن الفِلْم

(in telling time) نِصْف

half past three/ (US) after three

الثَالِثَة وَالنِصْف (in sports) شَوْط/

أَشْوَاط مف/ج

halfway /hɑːf'weɪ/ *adv* فِي مُنْتَصَف المَسَافَة

hall /hɔːl/ *n* (in a house) رُدْهَة (for meetings, etc) قَاعَة

halt /hɒlt/ *v* يَتَوَقَّف

ham /hæm/ *n* فَخْذ الخِنْزِير

hammer /'hæmə(r)/ *n* مِطْرَقَة/مَطَارِقُ مف/ج

hand /hænd/ *n* مف/ج (م) يَد/أَيْدٍ وَأَيَادٍ

♦ *v* يُسَلِّم

handbag /'hændbæg/ *n* حَقِيبَة يَد

handful /'hændfʊl/ *n* حَفْنَة/حَفَنَات مف/ج

handicap /'hændikæp/ *n* إِعَاقَة

handle /'hændl/ *n* مِقْبَض/مَقَابِضُ مف/ج

♦ *v* يُمْسِك

handy /'hændi/ *adj* مُلاَئِم

hang /hæŋ/ *v* **hung, hung** يُعَلِّق

H

happen /ˈhæpən/ *v* يَحْدُث

happening /ˈhæpənɪŋ/ *n* حُدُوث

happily /ˈhæpɪli/ *adv* بِسَعَادَة

happiness /ˈhæpinəs/ *n* سَعَادَة

happy /ˈhæpi/ *adj* (person) سَعِيد (memory) سَارّ

harass /həˈræs/ *v* يُضَايِق

harassment /ˈhærəsmənt/ *n* مُضَايَقَة

harbour /ˈhɑːbə(r)/ *n* US **-bor** مِينَاء/مَوَانِئُ مف/ج

hard /hɑːd/ *adj* (not soft) صُلْب (difficult) صَعْب

hardly /ˈhɑːdli/ *adv* بِالكَاد

hardship /ˈhɑːdʃɪp/ *n* ضَائِقَة

hardware /ˈhɑːdweə(r)/ *n* (computers) أَجْهِزَة (tools, etc) مُعِدَّات

harm /hɑːm/ *n* ضَرَر/أَضْرَار مف/ج ♦ *v* يُؤْذِي

harmful /ˈhɑːmfl/ *adj* ضَارّ

harmless /ˈhɑːmləs/ *adj* غَيْر ضَارّ

harsh /hɑːʃ/ *adj* (criticism) قَاسٍ (environment) مُزْعِج

harvest /ˈhɑːvɪst/ *n* حَصَاد

hasn't /ˈhæznt/ *contr* (= has not: see have)

hat /hæt/ *n* قُبَّعَة

hate /heɪt/ *n* بُغْض ♦ *v* يَكْرَه

hatred /ˈheɪtrɪd/ *n* بَغْضَاء

haul /hɔːl/ *v* يَسْحَب

haunt /hɔːnt/ *v* يُلَازِم

have /həv, hæv/ *v* **has, had, had** (a car, mobile, brother, flat) يَمْلِك

We have a cat. نَمْلِك هِرّاً

We had a letter from him.

تَلَقَّيْنَا مِنْهُ رِسَالَة (to form the perfect tenses) (تُسْتَعْمَل لِلدَّلَالَة عَلَى انْتِهَاء الفِعْل وَتُفِيد (لَقَد))

We have eaten already. لَقَد أَكَلْنَا

I have just seen him. لَقَد رَأَيْتُهُ الآن

Has anyone seen Amina today?

هَل مِنْكُم مَن رَأَى أَمِينَة اليَوْم؟

We had said goodbye.

لَقَد وَدَّعْنَا بَعْضَنَا البَعْض (homework, a class, things to do) لَدَى

I have chemistry three times a week.

لَدَيَّ ثَلَاث حِصَص كِيمِيَاء كُلّ أُسْبُوع

(an idea, a feeling) لَدَى

I have a plan. لَدَيَّ خِطَّة

have to *v* (obligation) يَقْتَضِي

I have to leave now.

يَقْتَضِي أَنْ أُغَادِر الآن

haven't /ˈhævnt/ *contr* (= have not: see have)

hawk /hɔːk/ *n* صَقْر/صُقُور مف/ج

hay /heɪ/ *n* تِبْن

he /hiː/ *pron* هُوَ

He went shopping. هُوَ ذَهَبَ لِلتَسَوُّق

head /hed/ *n* رَأْس/رُؤُوس مف/ج

♦ *v* يَتَوَجَّه إِلَى

headache /'hedeɪk/ *n* صُدَاع

header /'hedə(r)/ *n* ضَرْبَة رَأْس

heading /'hedɪŋ/ *n* عُنْوَان/عَنَاوِينُ مف/ج

head teacher *n* مُدِير مَدْرَسَة

heal /hiːl/ *v* يَشْفَى

health /helθ/ *n* صِحَّة

healthy /'helθi/ *adj* سَلِيم

hear /hɪə(r)/ *v* **heard** يَسْمَع

hearing /'hɪərɪŋ/ *n* سَمْع

heart /hɑːt/ *n* قَلْب/قُلُوب مف/ج

heat /hiːt/ *n* حَرّ

♦ *v* يُسَخِّن

heaven /'hevn/ *n* الجَنَّة

heavy /'hevi/ *adj* ثَقِيل

hectare /'hekteə(r)/ *n* هِكْتَار (عَشَرَة دُونَمَات)

Hebron /'hɛbrɒn/ *n* مَدِينَة الخَلِيل

he'd /hiːd/ *contr* (= he had, he would: see have, would)

hedge /hedʒ/ *n* سِيَاج مِن شُجَيْرَات

heel /hiːl/ *n* كَعْب/أَكْعَاب مف/ج

height /haɪt/ *n* (of a tree, etc) ارْتِفَاع/ارْتِفَاعَات مف/ج (person's) طُول/أَطْوَال مف/ج (off the ground) عُلُوّ مف/ج

heir /eə(r)/ *n* وَرِيث

helicopter /'helɪkɒptə(r)/ *n* طَائِرَة عَامُودِيَّة

hell /hel/ *n* جَهَنَّم

hello /hə'ləʊ/ *interj* (in conversation) مَرْحَباً (on telephone) أَلُو

he'll /hiːl/ *contr* (= he will: see will)

helmet /'helmɪt/ *n* خُوذَة/خُوَذ مف/ج

help /help/ *n* مُسَاعَدَة

♦ *v* يُسَاعِد

helpful /'helpfl/ *adj* مُفِيد

helpless /'helpləs/ *adj* عَاجِز

her /hɜː(r)/ *adj* (صِيغَة المُلْكِيَّة لِلمُؤَنَّث الغَائِب (لَهَا))

her book كِتَابُهَا

♦ *pron* (direct object) (ضَمِير المُؤَنَّث المُفْرَد الغَائِب لِلمَفْعُول بِهِ المُبَاشِر(هَا))

He saw her. رَآهَا (indirect object) (ضَمِير المُؤَنَّث المُفْرَد الغَائِب لِلمَفْعُول بِهِ غَيْر المُبَاشِر (هَا))

He passed her a plate. أَعْطَاهَا صَحْناً

They gave the job to her. أَعْطُوا الوَظِيفَة لَهَا

H

(after prep, in comparisons)

We weren't with her. لَم نَكُن مَعَهَا

I'm taller than her. أَنَا أَطْوَل مِنْهَا

herb /hɜːb/ *n* عُشْب/أَعْشَاب مف/ج

herd /hɜːd/ *n* قَطِيع/قُطْعَان مف/ج

here /hɪə(r)/ *adv* (in this place) هُنَا

We eat here often. نَأْكُل هُنَا كَثِيراً

(to this place) هُنَا

Come here! تَعَالَ هُنَا (in expressions)

Here you are! تَفَضَّل

Here they come. هَاهُم يَأْتُون

heritage /ˈherɪtɪdʒ/ *n* تُرَاث

hero /ˈhɪərəʊ/ *n* بَطَل

heroin /ˈherəʊɪn/ *n* مَادَّة الهِيرُوِين

heroine /ˈherəʊɪn/ *n* بَطَلَة

hers /hɜːz/ *poss pron* لَهَا

Both dresses are hers. كِلَا الثَّوْبَان لَهَا

herself /hɜːˈself/ *pron* نَفْسَهَا

She hurt herself. جَرَحَت نَفْسَهَا

(for emphasis) بِنَفْسِهَا

She repaired it herself.

أَصْلَحَتْهُ بِنَفْسِهَا

She was by herself. كَانَت لِوَحْدِهَا

he's /hiːz/ *contr* (= he is, he has: see be, have)

hesitate /ˈhezɪteɪt/ *v* يَتَرَدَّد

heterosexual /hetərəˈsekʃuəl/ *adj* مُحِبّ لِلجِنْس الآخَر

hi /haɪ/ *interj* مَرْحَباً

Hi, Hassan!, Hi Amina!

مَرْحَباً يَا حَسَن! مَرْحَباً يَا أَمِينَة

hidden /ˈhɪdn/ *adj* مَخْفِيّ

hide /haɪd/ *v* **hid, hidden** (the cash, etc) يُخْفِي (the truth) يَكْتُم (children, animals) يَخْتَبِئ

high /haɪ/ *adj* (mountain) عَالٍ

The wall is very high.

الحائط عالٍ جِدّاً

(in number, price) مُرْتَفِع

a high number of cases

عَدَد مُرْتَفِع مِن القَضَايَا

Food prices are high.

أَسْعَار المَأْكُولَات مُرْتَفِعَة

highlight /ˈhaɪlaɪt/ *n* أَبْرَز الأَحْدَاث

♦ *v* يُسَلِّط الأَضْوَاء عَلَى

high-resolution /haɪˈrezəluʃn/ *adj* عَالِي الدِقَّة

highway /ˈhaɪweɪ/ *n* طَرِيق رَئِيسِيّ

hill /hɪl/ *n* تَلَّة/تِلَال مف/ج

him /hɪm/ *pron* (direct object) (ضَمِير المُفْرَد المُذَكَّر الغَائِب (ه))

She saw him. هِيَ رَأَتْهُ (indirect object) (ضَمِير المُفْرَد المُذَكَّر الغَائِب (ه))

I gave him a present. أَعْطَيْتُهُ هَدِيَّة

She threw it to him. رَمَتْهَا لَهُ

(after prep, in comparisons)

We went with him. ذَهَبْنَا معَهُ

I'm younger than him. أَنَا أَصْغَر مِنْهُ

himself /hɪm'self/ *pron* (reflexive) نَفْسَهُ

He hurt himself. جَرَحَ نَفْسَهُ

(for emphasis) بِنَفْسِهِ

He built it himself. بَنَاهُ بِنَفْسِهِ

He was by himself. كَانَ بِمفْرَدِهِ

hinder /'hɪndə(r)/ *v* يُعِيق

Hindu /hɪn'du:/ *n* هِنْدُوسِيّ/هِنْدُوس مف/ج

hint /hɪnt/ *n* تَلْمِيح

♦ *v* (sth) يُلَمِّح

hip /hɪp/ *n* وِرْك/أَوْرَاك (م) مف/ج

hire /'haɪə(r)/ *v* (a bike, etc) يُؤَجِّر (an employee) يُوَظِّف

hire car *n* سَيَّارَة أُجْرَة

his /hɪz/ *adj* (صِيغَة المُلْكِيَّة لِلمُذَكَّر الغَائِب (لَهُ))

his books كُتُبُهُ

♦ *poss pron* لَهُ

That was his. كَانَ ذَلِكَ لَهُ

hiss /hɪs/ *v* يُهَسْهِس

historian /hɪ'stɔ:riən/ *n* مُؤَرِّخ

historic /hɪ'stɒrɪk/ *adj* تَارِيخِيّ

historical /hɪ'stɒrɪkl/ *adj* تَارِيخِيّ

history /'hɪstri/ *n* تَارِيخ

hit /hɪt/ *v* **hit** (a ball) يَضْرِب (your head, etc) يَرْتَطِم (a tree, a wall) يَصْدُم

♦ *n* (song) عَمَل نَاجِح (on Internet) نَتِيجَة البَحْث

hobby /'hɒbi/ *n* pl **bies** هِوَايَة

hockey /'hɒki/ *n* لُعْبَة الهُوكِي

hold /həʊld/ *v* **held** (in your hands) يَمْسِك (in your arms) يَحْمِل

♦ *n* (of a ship, plane) مَخْزَن/مَخَازِنُ مف/ج

hole /həʊl/ *n* (in the ground, shoe) ثُقْب/ثُقُوب مف/ج (animal's) جُحْر/ جُحُور مف/ج

holiday /'hɒlədeɪ/ *n* (from work, school) عُطْلَة (public) عِيد/أَعْيَاد مف/ج

hollow /'hɒləʊ/ *adj* فَارِغ

holy /'həʊli/ *adj* مُقَدَّس

home /həʊm/ *n* (where you live) مَنْزِل/مَنَازِلُ مف/ج (house and family) بَيْت/بُيُوت مف/ج (for children, the old) مَلْجَأ/مَلَاجِئُ مف/ج

home page *n* الصَفْحَة الرَئِيسِيَّة

homeland /'həʊmlænd/ *n* وَطَن/ أَوْطَان مف/ج

homeless /'həʊmləs/ *adj* مُتَشَرِّد

homemade /həʊ'meɪd/ *adj* مُعَدّ فِي البَيْت

H

homosexual /həʊmə'sekʃuəl/ *adj* شَاذّ جِنْسِياً

honest /'ɒnɪst/ *adj* صَادِق

honesty /'ɒnəsti/ *n* صِدْق

honey /'hʌni/ *n* عَسَل

honour /'ɒnə(r)/ *n* US **-nor** شَرَف
♦ *v* (an agreement) يُنَفِّذ (the dead) يُشَرِّف

hood /hʊd/ *n* قَلَنْسُوَة

hook /hʊk/ *n* خُطَّاف

hop /hɒp/ *v* يَثِب

hope /həʊp/ *n* أَمَل/آمَال مف/ج
♦ *v* يَأْمَل

hopeless /'həʊpləs/ *adj* مَيْئُوس مِنْهُ

horizon /hə'raɪzn/ *n* أُفُق/آفَاق مف/ج

horizontal /hɒrɪ'zɒntl/ *adj* أُفُقِيّ

horn /hɔːn/ *n* (of a bull) قَرْن/قُرُون
بُوق/أَبْوَاق مف/ج (in music) مف/ج
مُنَبِّه/مُنَبِّهَات مف/ج (car's)

horrible /'hɒrəbl/ *adj* (picture) كَرِيه
(weather) فَظِيع (murder, etc) مُرَوِّع

horrify /'hɒrɪfaɪ/ *v* يُرَوِّع

horror /'hɒrə(r)/ *n* رُعْب

horse /hɔːs/ *n* حِصان/حُصُن وَأَحْصِنَة مف/ج

hospital /'hɒspɪtl/ *n* مُسْتَشْفَى/ مُسْتَشْفَيَات مف/ج

hospitality /hɒspɪ'tæləti/ *n* حُسْن الضِيَافَة

host /həʊst/ *n* مُسْتَضِيف

hostage /'hɒstɪdʒ/ *n* رَهِينَة/رَهَائِنُ مف/ج

hostile /'hɒstaɪl/ *adj* عَدَائِيّ

hostility /hɒ'stɪləti/ *n* pl **-ties** عَدَاء/ عَدَاءَات مف/ج

hot /hɒt/ *adj* (soup, day, pan)
سَاخِن، حَارّ
a hot drink مَشْرُوب سَاخِن
I'm hot. أَشْعُر بِالحَرّ
It's hot today. هَذَا اليَوْم حَارّ

hotel /həʊ'tel/ *n* فُنْدُق/فَنَادِقُ مف/ج

hour /'aʊə(r)/ *n* سَاعَة/سَاعَات مف/ج
two hours later بَعْدَ سَاعَتَيْن
in four hours بَعْدَ أَرْبَع سَاعَات
every hour كُلّ سَاعَة
It will take an hour.
سَوْفَ تَسْتَغْرِق سَاعَة

house /haʊs/ *n* مَنْزِل/مَنَازِلُ مف/ج

housing /'haʊzɪŋ/ *n* إِسْكَان

how /haʊ/ *adv* كَيْفَ
How do you do it? كَيْفَ تَفْعَل ذَلِكَ؟
How are you? (I'm) Fine!
كَيْفَ حَالُكَ؟ أَنَا جَيِّد!
How do you do! كَيْفَ حَالُكَ؟
(with adj, adv) كَم

H

How much does it cost? كَم يُكَلِّف ذَلِكَ؟
How many miles have you walked? كَم مِيلاً مَشَيْتَ؟
How long is it? كَم مُدَّتُهَا؟
How old are you? كَم عُمْرُكَ؟

however /haʊ'evə(r)/ *conj* (but) وَمَعَ ذَلِكَ
I understand, however I have a few questions. أَنَا أَفْهَم، وَمَعَ ذَلِكَ فَلَدَيَّ بَعْض الأَسْئِلَة
(any way) كَيْفَمَا *You can decorate them however you want.* تَسْتَطِيع تَزْيِينَهَا كَيْفَمَا تَشَاء
♦ *adv* (good, cold) مَهْمَا
however long it takes مَهْمَا طَالَ الوَقْت

hub /hʌb/ *n* مِحْوَر/مَحَاوِرُ مف/ج

hug /hʌg/ *n* عِنَاق
♦ *v* يُعَانِق

huge /hju:ʤ/ *adj* ضَخْم

human /'hju:mən/ *adj* إِنْسَانِيّ

humanitarian /hju:mænɪ'teəriən/ *adj* إِنْسَانِيّ

humanity /hju:'mænəti/ *n* البَشَرِيَّة

humble /'hʌmbl/ *adj* مُتَوَاضِع

humiliate /hju:'mɪlieɪt/ *v* يُذِلّ

humiliation /hju:mɪli'eɪʃn/ *n* إِذْلَال

humorous /'hju:mərəs/ *adj* هَزَلِيّ

hummus /'hʊməs/ *n* حُمُّص

humour /'hju:mə(r)/ *n* US **-mor** حِسّ الدُعَابَة

hundred /'hʌndrəd/ *num* مِائَة

hunger /'hʌŋgə(r)/ *n* جُوع

hungry /'hʌŋgri/ *adj* جَائِع/جُوَّع مف/ج

hunt /hʌnt/ *n* صَيْد
♦ *v* يَصْطَاد

hunter /'hʌntə(r)/ *n* صَيَّاد

hurdle /'hɜ:dl/ *n* حَاجِز/حَوَاجِزُ مف/ج

hurl /hɜ:l/ *v* يَقْذِف

hurricane /'hʌrɪkən/ *n* إِعْصَار/أَعَاصِيرُ مف/ج

hurry /'hʌri/ *n* عَجَلَة
♦ *v* يُسْرِع

hurt /hɜ:t/ *v* **hurt** (head, teeth) يُؤْلِم (one's leg, etc) يُؤْذِي (to upset) يَجْرَح شُعُوراً

husband /'hʌzbənd/ *n* زَوْج/أَزْوَاج مف/ج

hut /hʌt/ *n* كُوخ/أَكْوَاخ مف/ج

hydrogen /'haɪdrəʤən/ *n* هَيْدْرُوجِين

H

I

I /aɪ/ *pron* أَنَا
I'm English. أَنَا إِنْجْلِيزِيّ
James and I went shopping. ذَهَبْتُ أَنَا وَجِيمْس لِلتَّسَوُّق

ice /aɪs/ *n* جَلِيد

icing /'aɪsɪŋ/ *n* خَلِيط مِن السُّكَّر وَالحَلِيب وَالزُّبْدَة لِتَزْيِين الكَعْك

icon /'aɪkɒn/ *n* أَيْقُونَة

icy /'aɪsi/ *adj* جَلِيدِيّ

I'd /ʌɪd/ *contr* (= I had, I would: see have, would)

idea /aɪ'dɪə/ *n* (thought) فِكْرَة/أَفْكَار مف/ج (aim) هَدَف/أَهْدَاف مف/ج

ideal /aɪ'di:əl/ *adj* (wife, holiday) مِثَالِيّ ♦ *n* طُمُوح/طُمُوحَات مف/ج

identical /aɪ'dentɪkl/ *adj* مُتَشَابِه

identification /aɪdentɪfɪ'keɪʃn/ *n* تَعْرِيف

identify /aɪ'dentɪfaɪ/ *v* يُعَرِّف

identity /aɪ'dentəti/ *n* pl **-ties** هُوِيَّة

idiot /'ɪdiət/ *n* أَحْمَق/حَمْقَاء/حُمْق مذ/م/ج

idol /'aɪdl/ *n* (star) مَعْبُود (false god) صَنَم/أَصْنَام مف/ج

if /ɪf/ *conj* (in conditionals) إِنْ
If you refuse, you will be sorry. إِنْ تَرْفُض سَوْفَ تَنْدَم
(unreal conditional) لَوْ
If I knew the answer, I would tell you. لَوْ عَلِمْتُ الجَوَاب لَقُلْتُ لَكَ (in indirect speech) إِذَا
Ask him if he can play. اسْأَلْهُ إِذَا كَانَ يَسْتَطِيع اللَّعْب

ignorant /'ɪgnərənt/ *adj* جَاهِل

ignore /ɪg'nɔ:(r)/ *v* يَتَجَاهَل

ill /ɪl/ *adj* مَرِيض/مَرْضَى مف/ج

I'll /ʌɪl/ *contr* (= I will, I shall: see will, shall)

illegal /ɪ'li:gl/ *adj* غَيْر قَانُونِيّ

illness /'ɪlnəs/ *n* مَرَض/أَمْرَاض مف/ج

illuminate /ɪ'lu:mɪneɪt/ *v* يُنِير

illusion /ɪ'lu:ʒn/ *n* وَهْم/أَوْهَام مف/ج

illustrate /'ɪləstreɪt/ *v* يُوَضِّح

illustration /ɪlə'streɪʃn/ *n* تَوْضِيح

I'm /ʌɪm/ *contr* (= I am: see be)

image /ˈɪmɪdʒ/ *n* (picture) صُورَة/صُوَر (organization's, etc) تَصَوُّر مف/ج

imaginary /ɪˈmædʒɪnəri/ *adj* خَيَالِيّ

imagination /ɪmædʒɪˈneɪʃn/ *n* تَخَيُّل/تَخَيُّلَات مف/ج

imaginative /ɪˈmædʒɪnətɪv/ *adj* إِبْدَاعِيّ

imagine /ɪˈmædʒɪn/ *v* يَتَخَيَّل

imam /ɪˈmɑːm/ *n* إِمَام/أَئِمَّة مف/ج

imitate /ˈɪmɪteɪt/ *v* يُقَلِّد

immediate /ɪˈmiːdiət/ *adj* فَوْرِيّ

immediately /ɪˈmiːdiətli/ *adv* مُبَاشَرَةً

immense /ɪˈmens/ *adj* ضَخْم

immigrant /ˈɪmɪgrənt/ *n* مُهَاجِر

immigration /ɪmɪˈgreɪʃn/ *n* هِجْرَة

imminent /ˈɪmɪnənt/ *adj* وَشِيك

immune /ɪˈmjuːn/ *adj* مَنِيع

immunity /ɪˈmjuːnəti/ *n* مَنَاعَة

impact /ˈɪmpækt/ *n* تَأْثِير/تَأْثِيرَات مف/ج

impair /ɪmˈpeə(r)/ *v* يُعِيق

imperial /ɪmˈpɪəriəl/ *adj* إِمْبِرَاطُورِيّ

implement /ˈɪmplɪmənt/ *v* يُنَفِّذ

implementation /ɪmplɪmenˈteɪʃn/ *n* تَطْبِيق/تَطْبِيقَات مف/ج

implicate /ˈɪmplɪkeɪt/ *v* يُوَرِّط

implication /ɪmplɪˈkeɪʃn/ *n* أَثَر/آثَار مف/ج

imply /ɪmˈplaɪ/ *v* يَتَضَمَّن

import /ɪmˈpɔːt/ *v* يَسْتَوْرِد ♦ /ˈɪmpɔːt/ *n* (act) اسْتِيرَاد

importance /ɪmˈpɔːtns/ *n* أَهَمِّيَّة

important /ɪmˈpɔːtnt/ *adj* هَامّ

imports /ˈɪmpɔːts/ *n pl* وَارِدَات

impose /ɪmˈpəʊz/ *v* يَفْرِض

impossible /ɪmˈpɒsəbl/ *adj* مُسْتَحِيل

impress /ɪmˈpres/ *v* يُبْهِر

impression /ɪmˈpreʃn/ *n* /انْطِبَاع انْطِبَاعَات مف/ج

impressive /ɪmˈpresɪv/ *adj* مُؤَثِّر

imprison /ɪmˈprɪzn/ *v* يَسْجِن

imprisonment /ɪmˈprɪznmənt/ *n* اعْتِقَال

improve /ɪmˈpruːv/ *v* يُحَسِّن

improvement /ɪmˈpruːvmənt/ *n* تَحْسِين/تَحْسِينَات مف/ج

in /ɪn/ *prep* (a box, house) دَاخِلَ
in a brown envelope دَاخِلَ ظَرْف بُنِّيّ
(a city, a state, etc) فِي
the best in the world الأَفْضَل فِي العَالَم

I fell in the river. سَقَطْتُ فِي النَهْر

Put it in the bag. ضَعْهَا فِي الحَقِيبَة

to be in debt يَكُون مَدْيُوناً

You are in danger. أَنْتَ فِي خَطَر

(during time) فِي

in June 2007 فِي حُزَيْرَان 2007

in the morning فِي الصَبَاح

(within time) خِلاَلَ

the first time in years
المَرَّة الأُولَى خِلاَلَ عِدَّة سَنَوَات

(expressing manner) بِ

to pay in euros يَدْفَع بِاليُورُو

in groups of five
بِمَجْمُوعَات مُشَكَّلَة من خَمْسَة أَفْرَاد

♦ *adv* (indicating movement) إِلَى الدَاخِل

to walk in يَدْخُل

Come in! !اُدْخُل

(at home, work) فِي البَيْت

Is anybody in? هَل أَحَد مَا فِي البَيْت؟

He's not in today.
هُوَ لَيْسَ فِي البَيْت اليَوْم

inability /ɪnə'bɪləti/ *n* عَجْز

inaccurate /ɪn'ækjərət/ *adj* غَيْر دَقِيق

inadequate /ɪn'ædɪkwət/ *adj* غَيْر كَافٍ

inappropriate /ɪnə'prəʊpriət/ *adj* غَيْر مُلاَئِم

incentive /ɪn'sentɪv/ *n* مُحَفِّز/ مُحَفِّزَات مف/ج

inch /ɪntʃ/ *n* إِنْش: وَحْدَة قِيَاس تُسَاوِي 2.45 سم

incident /'ɪnsɪdənt/ *n* حَادِث/حَوَادِثُ مف/ج

include /ɪn'klu:d/ *v* يَشْمَل

included /ɪn'klu:dɪd/ *adj* مَشْمُول

inclusive /ɪn'klu:sɪv/ *adj* شَامِل

income /'ɪnkʌm/ *n* دَخْل

incomplete /ɪnkəm'pli:t/ *adj* نَاقِص

incorporate /ɪn'kɔ:pəreɪt/ *v* يَدْمِج

incorrect /ɪnkə'rekt/ *adj* خَاطِئ

increase /ɪn'kri:s/ *v* (to become greater) يَزْدَاد (to make sth greater) يُزِيد

♦ /'ɪŋkri:s/ *n* زِيَادَة

increasing /'ɪŋkrisɪŋ/ *adj* مُتَزَايِد

incredible /ɪn'kredəbl/ *adj* لاَ يُصَدَّق

incur /ɪn'kɜ:(r)/ *v* يَجْلِب لِنَفْسِهِ

indeed /ɪn'di:d/ *adv* بِالفِعْل

independence /ɪndɪ'pendəns/ *n* اسْتِقْلاَل

independent /ɪndɪ'pendənt/ *adj* مُسْتَقِلّ

index /'ɪndeks/ *n* pl **-dexes, -dicies** (of in a book) فِهْرِسْت/فَهَارِسُ مف/ج

prices, etc) مُؤَشِّر/مُؤَشِّرَات مف/ج

India /'ɪndɪə/ *n* الهِنْد

Indian /'ɪndiən/ *adj, n* /هِنْدِيّ هُنُود ص/س/مف/ج

indicate /'ɪndɪkeɪt/ *v* (to point to) يُشِير إلَى (in driving) يُعْطِي إشَارَة

indication /ɪndɪ'keɪʃn/ *n* إشَارَة

indicator /'ɪndɪkeɪtə(r)/ *n* /مُؤَشِّر مُؤَشِّرَات مف/ج

indictment /ɪn'daɪtmənt/ *n* لاَئِحَة إتِّهَام/لَوَائِحُ مف/ج

indirect /ɪndaɪ'rekt/ *adj* غَيْر مُبَاشِر

individual /ɪndɪ'vɪʤuəl/ *adj* (for one person) شَخْصِيّ

individually /ɪndɪ'vɪʤuəli/ *adv* عَلَى انْفِرَاد

indoor /'ɪndɔ:(r)/ *adj* دَاخِلِيّ

inducement /ɪn'dju:smənt/ *n* رَشْوَة/رَشَاوَى مف/ج

induction /ɪn'dʌkʃn/ *n* تَنْصِيب العَمَل

indulge /ɪn'dʌlʤ/ *v* يُشْبِع رَغَبَات

industrial /ɪn'dʌstriəl/ *adj* صِنَاعِيّ

industry /'ɪndəstri/ *n* pl **-ries** صِنَاعَة

ineffective /ɪnɪ'fektɪv/ *adj* غَيْر فَعَّال

inevitable /ɪn'evɪtəbl/ *adj* حَتْمِيّ

inexpensive /ɪnɪk'spensɪv/ *adj* رَخِيص

infamous /'ɪnfəməs/ *adj* سَيِّئ السُّمْعَة

infant /'ɪnfənt/ *n* رَضِيع

infantry /'ɪnfəntri/ *n* سِلاَح المُشَاة

infect /ɪn'fekt/ *v* يُعْدِي

infection /ɪn'fekʃn/ *n* عَدْوَى

infectious /ɪn'fekʃəs/ *adj* مُعْدٍ

inference /'ɪnfərəns/ *n* /اسْتِنْتَاج اسْتِنْتَاجَات مف/ج

I

infertility /ɪnfɜ:'tɪləti/ *n* عُقْم

inferior /ɪn'fɪəriə(r)/ *adj* (rank) أَدْنَى (quality) رَدِيء دَرَجَة

infinite /'ɪnfɪnət/ *adj* غَيْر مَحْدُود

inflammation /ɪnflə'meɪʃn/ *n* الْتِهَاب/الْتِهَابَات مف/ج

inflation /ɪn'fleɪʃn/ *n* /تَضَخُّم تَضَخُّمَات مف/ج

inflexible /ɪn'fleksəbl/ *adj* صُلْب

inflict /ɪn'flɪkt/ *v* يَفْرِض

influence /'ɪnfluəns/ *n* /تَأْثِير تَأْثِيرَات مف/ج

♦ *v* يُؤَثِّر عَلَى

influential /ɪnflu'enʃl/ *adj* مُؤَثِّر

inform /ɪn'fɔ:m/ *v* يُعْلِم

informal /ɪn'fɔ:ml/ *adj* غَيْر رَسْمِيّ

information /ɪnfə'meɪʃn/ *n* (about a country, etc) مَعْلُومَات (for telephone numbers) (in US) اسْتِعْلَامَات مف/ج

informative /ɪn'fɔːmətɪv/ *adj* مَعْلُومَاتِيّ

ingredient /ɪn'griːdiənt/ *n* مُكَوِّن/ مُكَوِّنَات مف/ج

inhabit /ɪn'hæbɪt/ *v* يَسْكُن

inhabitant /ɪn'hæbɪtənt/ *n* مُقِيم

inhale /ɪn'heɪl/ *v* يَسْتَنْشِق

inherit /ɪn'herɪt/ *v* يَرِث

inheritance /ɪn'herɪtəns/ *n* إِرْث

inhibit /ɪn'hɪbɪt/ *v* يُثَبِّط

inhibition /ɪnhɪ'bɪʃn/ *n* كَبْت

initial /ɪ'nɪʃl/ *adj* أَوَّلِيّ

initials /ɪ'nɪʃlʒ/ *n pl* الحُرُوف الأُولَى مِن الأَسْمَاء

initiation /ɪnɪʃi'eɪʃn/ *n* مَرَاسِم إِدْخَال شَخْص فِي عُضْوِيَّة جَمْعِيَّة

initiative /ɪ'nɪʃətɪv/ *n* مُبَادَرَة

inject /ɪn'ʤekt/ *v* يَحْقِن

injection /ɪn'ʤekʃn/ *n* حَقْن

injure /'ɪnʤə(r)/ *v* يَجْرَح

injury /'ɪnʤəri/ *n* pl **-ries** إِصَابَة

injury time *n* الوَقْت بَدَل الضَائِع

injustice /ɪn'ʤʌstɪs/ *n* ظُلْم

ink /ɪŋk/ *n* حِبْر

inmate /'ɪnmeɪt/ *n* مَسْجُون/مَسَاجِين مف/ج

inn /ɪn/ *n* خَان

inner /'ɪnə(r)/ *adj* دَاخِلِيّ

innocence /'ɪnəsns/ *n* بَرَاءَة

innocent /'ɪnəsnt/ *adj* بَرِيء

inquire /ɪn'kwʌɪə/ *v* يَسْتَفْسِر

inquiry /ɪn'kwʌɪri/ *n* pl **-ries** (question) اسْتِفْسَار/اسْتِفْسَارَات مف/ج (investigation) تَحْقِيق/تَحْقِيقَات مف/ج

insect /'ɪnsekt/ *n* حَشَرَة

insecurity /ɪnsɪ'kjʊərəti/ *n* pl **-ties** فُقْدَان الأَمَان

insert /ɪn'sɜːt/ *v* يُدْخِل

inside /ɪn'saɪd/ *prep* (a city, a house) دَاخِل

♦ *n* (of a house, etc) دَاخِل

insight /'ɪnsaɪt/ *n* إِدْرَاك

insist /ɪn'sɪst/ *v* يُصِرّ عَلَى

insistence /ɪn'sɪstəns/ *n* إِصْرَار

inspect /ɪn'spekt/ *v* يُفَتِّش

inspection /ɪn'spekʃn/ *n* تَفْتِيش/ تَفْتِيشَات مف/ج

inspector /ɪn'spektə(r)/ *n* مُفَتِّش

inspiration /ɪnspə'reɪʃn/ *n* إِلْهَام

inspire /ɪn'spaɪə(r)/ *v* يُلْهِم

install /ɪn'stɔːl/ *v* يُرَكِّب

installation /ɪnstə'leɪʃn/ *n* تَرْكِيب

instance /'ɪnstəns/ *n* مِثَال/أَمْثِلَة مف/ج

instant /'ɪnstənt/ *adj* فَوْرِيّ

instead /ɪn'sted/ *adv* بَدَلاً مِن

instinct /'ɪnstɪŋkt/ *n* غَرِيزَة/غَرَائِز مف/ج

institute /'ɪnstɪtjuːt/ *n* مَعْهَد/مَعَاهِد مف/ج

♦ *v* يُؤَسِّس

institution /ɪnstɪ'tjuːʃn/ *n* مُؤَسَّسَة

instruct /ɪn'strʌkts/ *v* يُوَجِّه

instructions /ɪn'strʌktʃnʒ/ *n pl* (information) تَعْلِيمَات (orders) أَوَامِر

instructor /ɪn'strʌktə(r)/ *n* مُعَلِّم

instrument /'ɪnstrəmənt/ *n* أَدَاة/أَدَوَات مف/ج

insufficient /ɪnsə'fɪʃnt/ *adj* غَيْر كَافٍ

insult /ɪn'sʌlt/ *v* يُهِين

♦ /'ɪnsʌlt/ *n* إِهَانَة

insurance /ɪn'ʃʊərəns/ *n* تَأْمِين/تَأْمِينَات مف/ج

insure /ɪn'ʃʊə(r)/ *v* يُؤَمِّن

intact /ɪn'tækt/ *adj* سَلِيم

integral /'ɪntɪgrəl/ *adj* مُكَمِّل

integrate /'ɪntɪgreɪt/ *v* يَنْدَمِج

integrated /'ɪntɪgreɪtɪd/ *adj* مُتَآلِف

integration /ɪntɪ'greɪʃn/ *n* انْدِمَاج

integrity /ɪn'tegrəti/ *n* نَزَاهَة

intellectual /ɪntə'lektʃuəl/ *adj* فِكْرِيّ

intelligence /ɪn'telɪdʒəns/ *n* ذَكَاء

intelligent /ɪn'telɪdʒənt/ *adj* ذَكِيّ/أَذْكِيَاءُ مف/ج

intense /ɪn'tens/ *adj* شَدِيد

intensely /ɪn'tensli/ *adv* بِشِدَّة

intensify /ɪn'tensɪfaɪ/ *v* يُكَثِّف

intensity /ɪn'tensəti/ *n* كَثَافَة

intention /ɪn'tenʃn/ *n* نِيَّة/نَوَايَا مف/ج

intercourse /'ɪntəkɔːs/ *n* جِمَاع

interest /'ɪntrest/ *n* (in a subject) اهْتِمَام/اهْتِمَامَات مف/ج (on loan) فَائِدَة/فَوَائِدُ مف/ج

♦ *v* يُرَغِّب

interested /'ɪntrəstɪd/ *adj* مُهْتَمّ

interesting /'ɪntrestɪŋ/ *adj* مُشَيِّق

interference /ɪntə'fɪərəns/ *n* (in sb's affairs) تَدَخُّل/تَدَخُّلَات مف/ج (in broadcasting) تَدَاخُل/تَدَاخُلَات مف/ج

interior /ɪn'tɪəriə(r)/ *n* دَاخِل

intermediate /ɪntə'miːdiət/ *adj* مُتَوَسِّط

internal /ɪn'tɜ:nl/ *adj* دَاخِلِيّ

international /ɪntə'næʃnəl/ *adj* دُوَلِيّ

Internet /'ɪntənet/ *n* شَبَكَة الرَبْط الدُوَلِيّ (إِنْتَرنِت)

Internet café *n* مَقْهَى إِنْتَرْنِت

interpret /ɪn'tɜ:prɪt/ *v* (into a language) يُتَرْجِم فَوْرِيّاً (figures, a dream) يُفَسِّر

I

interpretation /ɪntɜ:prɪ'teɪʃn/ *n* تَفْسِير/تَفْسِيرَات مف/ج

interrogation /ɪnterə'geɪʃn/ *n* اسْتِجْوَاب

interrupt /ɪntə'rʌpt/ *v* يُقَاطِع

interruption /ɪntə'rʌpʃn/ *n* تَعْطِيل

intersection /ɪntə'sekʃn/ *n* تَقَاطُع/تَقَاطُعَات مف/ج

interval /'ɪntəvl/ *n* فَاصِل/فَوَاصِل مف/ج

intervene /ɪntə'vi:n/ *v* يَتَدَخَّل

intervention /ɪntə'venʃn/ *n* تَدَخُّل/تَدَخُّلَات مف/ج

interview /'ɪntəvju:/ *n* (for a job, etc) مُقَابَلَة (with a celebrity) مُقَابَلَة صَحَفِيَّة

♦ *v* (sb for a job) يُجْرِي مُقَابَلَة (a politician, an actor, etc) يُقَابِل

interviewer /'ɪntəvju:ə(r)/ *n* مُجْرِي المُقَابَلَة

intimate /'ɪntɪmeɪt/ *adj* حَمِيم

intimidate /ɪn'tɪmɪdeɪt/ *v* يُخَوِّف بِالتَهْدِيد

into /'ɪntu:/ *prep* (expressing movement) إِلَى دَاخِل

We went into the building. ذَهَبْنَا إِلَى دَاخِل البِنَايَة

He got into bed. اسْتَلْقَى فِي فِرَاشِه

(movement ending in impact) بِ

The car crashed into the wall. اصْطَدَمَت السَيَّارَة بِالحَائِط (showing change) إِلَى

The meeting turned into a celebration. تَحَوَّلَ الاِجْتِمَاع إِلَى احْتِفَال

introduce /ɪntrə'dju:s/ *v* (a person) يُعَرِّف عَلَى (a new product, a change, a law) يُدْخِل

introduction /ɪntrə'dʌkʃn/ *n* (of sb to sb) تَعَارُف (of a law, product) إِدْخَال

invade /ɪn'veɪd/ *v* يَغْزُو

invasion /ɪn'veɪʒn/ *n* غَزْو

invent /ɪn'vent/ *v* (a machine) يَخْتَرِع (a story) يَخْتَلِق

invention /ɪn'venʃn/ *n* اخْتِرَاع/اخْتِرَاعَات مف/ج

inventory /'ɪnvəntri/ *n* pl **-ries** (of a house to rent) قَائِمَة جَرْد (stocks) مَخْزُون/مَخْزُونَات مف/ج

invest /ɪn'vest/ *v* يَسْتَثْمِر

investigate /ɪn'vestɪgeɪt/ *v* يُحَقِّق

investigation /ɪnvestɪ'geɪʃn/ *n* تَحْقِيق/تَحْقِيقَات مف/ج

investigative /ɪn'vestɪgətɪv/ *adj* تَحْقِيقِيّ

investment /ɪn'vestmənt/ *n* اسْتِثْمَار/اسْتِثْمَارَات مف/ج

investor /ɪn'vestə(r)/ *n* مُسْتَثْمِر

invisible /ɪn'vɪzəbl/ *adj* خَفِيّ

invitation /ɪnvɪ'teɪʃn/ *n* دَعْوَة

invite /ɪn'vaɪt/ *v* (sb to do sth) يَدْعُو (comments, questions) يَطْلُب

invoke /ɪn'vəʊk/ *v* يَسْتَشْهِد

involve /ɪn'vɒlv/ *v* يَتَطَلَّب

involvement /ɪn'vɒlvmənt/ *n* تَوَرُّط

Iran /ɪ'rɑːn/ *n* إِيرَان

Iranian /ɪ'reɪnɪən/ *adj, n* إِيرَانِيّ ص/س

Iraq /ɪ'rɑːk/ *n* العِرَاق

Iraqi /ɪ'rɑːki/ *adj, n* عِرَاقِيّ ص/س

Ireland /'aɪələnd/ *n* إِيرْلَنْدَا

Irish /'aɪrɪʃ/ *adj* إِيرْلَنْدِيّ ♦ *n* (language) إِيرْلَنْدِيّ (people) إِيرْلَنْدِيُّون

iron /'aɪən/ *n* (metal) حَدِيد (implement) مِكْوَاة/مَكَاوٍ مف/ج

ironic /aɪ'rɒnɪk/ *adj* سَاخِر

irony /'aɪrəni/ *n* سُخْرِيَّة

irrational /ɪ'ræʃənl/ *adj* غَيْر عَقْلَانِيّ

irregular /ɪ'regjələ(r)/ *adj* غَيْر مُنْتَظِم

irrelevant /ɪ'reləvənt/ *adj* غَيْر مُرْتَبِط بِالمَوْضُوع

irresponsible /ɪrɪ'spɒnsəbl/ *adj* غَيْر مَسْؤُول

irrigate /'ɪrɪgeɪt/ *v* يَرْوِي (الأَرْض)

irrigation /ɪrɪ'geɪʃn/ *n* رَيّ

irritate /'ɪrɪteɪt/ *v* (a person) يُغْضِب (one's throat, skin) يُهَيِّج

Islam /'ɪzlɑːm/ *n* الإِسْلَام

Islamabad /ɪz'lɑːməbad/ *n* إِسْلَام أَبَاد

Islamic /ɪz'lamɪk/ *adj* إِسْلَامِيّ

island /'aɪlənd/ *n* جَزِيرَة/جُزُر مف/ج

isn't /'ɪznt/ *contr* (= is not: see be)

isolate /'aɪsəleɪt/ *v* يَعْزِل

isolated /'aɪsəleɪtɪd/ *adj* مَعْزُول

isolation /aɪsə'leɪʃn/ *n* عُزْلَة

ISP /aɪes'piː/ *n* مُزَوِّد خِدْمَة الإِنْتَرْنِت

Israel /'ɪzreɪəl/ *n* إِسْرَائِيل

Israeli /ɪz'reɪli/ *adj, n* إِسْرَائِيلِيّ ص/س

issue /'ɪsjuː/ *n* (topic) مَوْضُوع/

I

مُشْكِلَة/ مَوَاضِيعُ مف/ج (problem) مَشَاكِلُ مف/ج (of a magazine, etc) إِصْدَار/إِصْدَارَات مف/ج

♦ *v* (a visa, permit) يُصْدِر

Istanbul /ˌɪstanˈbʊl/ *n* إِسْطَنْبُول

it /ɪt/ *pron* (subject) (ضَمِير الغَائِب المُفْرَد لِجَمَاد أَو حَيَوَان أَو لِلمَجْهُول (هُوَ، هِيَ))

It's me. إِنَّهُ أَنَا (direct object: thing, animal) (ضَمِير المَفْعُول بِهِ المُبَاشِر لِجَمَاد أَو حَيَوَان)

I can see it. أَسْتَطِيع رُؤْيَتَهَا

Leave it there. ضَعْهَا هُنَاكَ (indirect object: thing, animal) (ضَمِير المَفْعُول بِهِ غَيْر المُبَاشِر لِجَمَاد أَو حَيَوَان)

I gave it a bone. أَعْطَيْتُهَا عَظْمَة (after prep, in comparisons) ه/ها مذ/م

What shall I do with it?
مَاذَا أَفْعَل بِهَا؟

Italian /ɪˈtaljən/ *adj* إِيطَالِيّ

♦ *n* (language) اللُّغَة الإِيطَالِيَّة (citizen) إِيطَالِيّ

Italy /ˈɪtəli/ *n* إِيطَالِيَا

item /ˈaɪtəm/ *n* مَادَّة/مَوَادّ

its /ɪts/ *adj* it صِيغَة المُلْكِيَّة مِن

The river overflowed its banks.
غَمَرَ النَهْر ضِفَّتَيْه

it'll /ˈɪtl/ *contr* (= it will: see will)

it's /ɪts/ *contr* (= it is, it has: see be, have)

itself /ɪtˈself/ *pron* (reflexive) نَفْسَهُ/ نَفْسَهَا مذ/م

It starts itself automatically.
تُشَغِّل نَفْسَهَا تِلْقَائِيّاً

I've /ʌɪv/ *contr* (= I have: see have)

I

J

jack /ʤæk/ *n* رَافِعَة

jacket /'ʤækɪt/ *n* جَاكِيت

jade /ʤeɪd/ *n* يَشْم

jail /ʤeɪl/ *n* سِجْن/سُجُون مف/ج

jam /ʤæm/ *n* (for bread) مُرَبَّى (of cars, etc) ازْدِحَام

January /'ʤænjuəri/ *n* (see August) كَانُون الثَانِي

Japan /dʒə'pan/ *n* اليَابَان

Japanese /ʤapə'ni:z/ *adj* يَابَانِيّ ♦ *n* (language) اللُغَة اليَابَانِيَّة (people) يَابَانِيُّون

jar /ʤɑ:(r)/ *n* مَرْطَبَان

jaw /ʤɔ:/ *n* فَكّ

jealous /'ʤeləs/ *adj* غَيُور

jealousy /'ʤeləsi/ *n* غَيْرَة

Jeddah /'dʒedə/ *n* جَدَّة

jerk /ʤɜ:k/ *v* يَهُزّ بِعُنْف

jersey /'ʤɜ:zi/ *n* سُتْرَة

Jerusalem /dʒə'ru:sələm/ *n* القُدْس

Jerusalem artichoke *n* القُلْقَاس الرُومِيّ

jet /ʤet/ *n* (plane) طَائِرَة نَفَّاثَة (of water, gas) تَنْفِيث

Jew /ʤu:/ *n* يَهُودِيّ/يَهُود مف/ج

jewel /'ʤu:əl/ *n* جَوْهَرَة/جَوَاهِرُ مف/ج

jewellery /'ʤu:əlri/ *n* US **jewelry** مُجَوْهَرَات

Jewish /'ʤu:ɪʃ/ *adj* يَهُودِيّ

job /ʤɒb/ *n* (employment) وَظِيفَة/ عَمَل/أَعْمَال مف/ج (task) وَظَائِفُ مف/ج

jockey /'ʤɒki/ *n* خَيَّال

jogging /'ʤɒgɪŋ/ *n* هَرْوَلَة

join /ʤɔɪn/ *v* (one thing to another) يُلْصِق (a club, an organization) يَلْتَحِق بِـ (a party, a queue) يَنْضَمّ إِلَى

joint /ʤɔɪnt/ *adj* (decision, effort, venture) مُشْتَرَك ♦ *n* (between bones) مفْصَل/مَفَاصِلُ مف/ج (between components) وَصْلَة

jointly /ʤɔɪntli/ *adv* بِالاِشْتِرَاك

joke /ʤəʊk/ *n* (funny story, etc) نُكْتَة (prank) مَزْحَة

Jordan /'dʒɔ:d(ə)n/ *n* الأُرْدُنّ

Jordanian /ʤɔː'deɪnɪən/ *adj, n* أُرْدُنِّيّ ص/س

journal /'ʤɜːnl/ *n* مَجَلَّة

journalism /'ʤɜːnəlɪzəm/ *n* صَحَافَة

journalist /'ʤɜːnəlɪst/ *n* صُحُفِيّ

journey /'ʤɜːni/ *n* رِحْلَة

joy /ʤɔɪ/ *n* ابْتِهَاج

judge /ʤʌʤ/ *n* قَاضٍ/قُضَاة مف/ج
♦ *v* (a competition) يَحْكُم

J

judgment /'ʤʌʤmənt/ *n* (in law) حُكْم/أَحْكَام مف/ج (ability) تَقْدِير

jug /ʤʌg/ *n* إِبْرِيق/أَبَارِيقُ مف/ج

juice /ʤuːs/ *n* عَصِير/عَصَائِرُ مف/ج

July /ʤu'laɪ/ *n* (see August) شَهْر تَمُّوز

jump /ʤʌmp/ *n* (leap) قَفْزَة (increase) ارْتِفَاع مُفَاجِئ
♦ *v* يَقْفِز

junction /'ʤʌŋkʃn/ *n* مُلْتَقَى طُرُق

June /ʤuːn/ *n* (see August) شَهْر حُزَيْرَان

jungle /'ʤʌŋgl/ *n* دَغَل/أَدْغَال مف/ج

junior /'ʤuːniə(r)/ *adj* نَاشِئ

junk /ʤʌŋk/ *n* خُرْدَة

jury /'ʤʊəri/ *n* pl **-ries** هَيْئَة المُحَلَّفِين

just /ʤʌst/ *adj* عَادِل
♦ *adv* (exactly) بِالضَبْط (hardly) بِالكَاد (only) مُجَرَّد

justice /'ʤʌstɪs/ *n* عَدَالَة

justification /ʤʌstɪfɪ'keɪʃn/ *n* تَبْرِير/تَبْرِيرَات مف/ج

justify /'ʤʌstɪfaɪ/ *v* يُبَرِّر

juvenile /'ʤuːvənaɪl/ *adj* صِبْيَانِيّ

K

kebab /kɪ'bæb/ *n* شَاوِيرْمَا

Karachi /kə'rɑːtʃi/ *n* كَرَاتْشِي

keen /kiːn/ *adj* (to do sth) مُتَحَمِّس لِ
(hearing) حَادّ

keep /kiːp/ *v* **kept** (a receipt, etc) يَحْتَفِظ بِ (still, warm, etct) يُوَاصِل
(closed, dry) يُبْقِي

kennels /'kenəlz/ *n* pl مَرْكَز حَضَانَة لِلكِلاَب

key /kiː/ *n* مِفْتَاح/مَفَاتِيح مف/ج

keyboard /'kiːbɔːd/ *n* لَوْحَة مَفَاتِيح

Khartoum /kɑː'tuːm/ *n* الخَرْطوم

kick /kɪk/ *v* يَرْكُل
♦ *n* رَكْلَة
kick-off *n* انْطِلاَق الكُرَة

kid /kɪd/ *n* (child) طِفْل/أَطْفَال مف/ج
(young goat) جَدْي، سَخْلَة
♦ *v* يُمَازِح

kidnap /'kɪdnæp/ *v* يَخْطِف

kidney /'kɪdni/ *n* كِلْيَة/كِلَى مف/ج

kill /kɪl/ *v* يَقْتُل

killer /'kɪlə(r)/ *n* قَاتِل

kilo /'kiːləʊ/ *n* كِيلُو

kilometre /'kɪləmiːtə(r)/ *n* US **meter** كِيلُومِتْر

kind /kaɪnd/ *adj* لَطِيف
♦ *n* نَوْع/أَنْوَاع مف/ج

kindness /'kaɪndnəs/ *n* لُطْف

king /kɪŋ/ *n* مَلِك/مُلُوك مف/ج

kingdom /'kɪŋdəm/ *n* مَمْلَكَة/مَمَالِكُ مف/ج

kiss /kɪs/ *n* قُبْلَة/قُبَل مف/ج
♦ *v* يُقَبِّل

kit /kɪt/ *n* طَقْم/أَطْقُم مف/ج

kitchen /'kɪtʃɪn/ *n* مَطْبَخ/مَطَابِخُ مف/ج

knee /niː/ *n* رُكْبَة/رُكَب مف/ج

kneel /niːl/ *v* **kneeled or knelt** يَرْكَع

knife /naɪf/ *n* pl **knives** سِكِّين/سَكَاكِينُ مف/ج

knock /nɒk/ *n* طَرْقَة
♦ *v* يَطْرُق

knot /nɒt/ *n* عُقْدَة/عُقَد مف/ج

know /nəʊ/ *v* **knew, known** (the answer, a fact) يَعْلَم

I know the answer. أَعْلَم الإِجَابَة.

I don't know her address.
لاَ أَعْلَم عُنْوَانَهَا (a person, a city) يَعْرِف

I know Kate. أَعْرِف كِيت

I know how this TV works.
أَعْرِف كَيْفَ يَعْمَل هَذَا التِلْفَاز

knowledge /ˈnɒlɪʤ/ *n* مَعْرِفَة/ مَعَارِفُ مف/ج

Koran, the /kəˈrɑːn/ *n* القُرْآن

Kuwait /kʊˈweɪt/ *n* الكُوَيْت

Kuwaiti /kʊˈweɪti/ *adj, n* كُوَيْتِيّ ص/س

K

L

label /ˈleɪbl/ *n* مُلْصَق/مُلْصَقَات مف/ج
♦ *v* يَضَع مُلْصَقاً

laboratory /ləˈbɒrətri/ *n* pl **-ries**
مُخْتَبَر/مُخْتَبَرَات مف/ج

labour /ˈleɪbə(r)/ *n* US **-bor** (work)
عَمَل/أَعْمَال مف/ج (workers) عُمَّال
(in birth) مَخَاض

labourer /ˈleɪbərə(r)/ *n* US **-borer**
عَامِل/عُمَّال مف/ج

lack /læk/ *n* نَقْص
♦ *v* يَفْتَقِر إِلَى

ladder /ˈlædə(r)/ *n* سُلَّم/سَلَالِمُ مف/ج

lady /ˈleɪdi/ *n* pl **-dies** سَيِّدَة

lake /leɪk/ *n* بُحَيْرَة

lamb /læm/ *n* (animal) حَمْل (meat)
لَحْم الحَمْل

lame /leɪm/ *adj* أَعْرَج/عَرْجَاء/عُرْج
مذ/م/ج

lamp /læmp/ *n* مِصْبَاح/مَصَابِيحُ مف/ج

land /lænd/ *n* (not sea) يَابِسَة (for building, etc) أَرْض/أَرَاضٍ (م) مف/ج
♦ *v* (planes, etc) يَحُطّ (from ships) يَنْزِل

landlady /ˈlændleɪdi/ *n* pl **-dies**
صَاحِبَة المِلْك

landlord /ˈlændlɔːd/ *n* (of a house)
مَالِك/مُلَّاك مف/ج (of a pub) صَاحِب
الحَانَة

landmark /ˈlændmɑːk/ *n* مَعْلَم/
مَعَالِمُ مف/ج

landscape /ˈlændskeɪp/ *n* مَنْظَر
طَبِيعِيّ

lane /leɪn/ *n* (narrow road) زُقَاق/أَزِقَّة
مف/ج (in major road) مَسْرَب/مَسَارِبُ
مف/ج

language /ˈlæŋgwɪʤ/ *n* لُغَة

laptop /ˈlæptɒp/ *n* حَاسُوب مَحْمُول

large /lɑːʤ/ *adj* كَبِير
a large quantity of food
كَمِّيَّة كَبِيرَة مِن الطَعَام
a large crowd of people
حَشْد كَبِير مِن النَاس

last /lɑːst/ *adj* (in a series) أَخِير
the last day of the month
اليَوْم الأَخِير مِن الشَهْر
our last child طِفْلُنَا الأَخِير

L

♦ *adv* أَخيراً

to come last يَأْتِي أَخيراً

♦ *v* (continue) يَسْتَمِرّ

The storm lasted for hours.

اسْتَمَرَّت العَاصِفَة لِعدَّة سَاعَات

(hold out) يَكْفِي

This will last us until Monday.

هٰذَا سَيَكْفِينَا حَتَّى يَوْم الاِثْنَيْن

lasting /ˈlɑːstɪŋ/ *adj* دَائِم

late /leɪt/ *adj* (arrival) مُتَأَخِّر

a late start بِدَايَة مُتَأَخِّرَة

It's late, I'd better go.

الوَقْت مُتَأَخِّر، مِن الأَفْضَل أَنْ أَذْهَب

(at the end of)

in his late forties

فِي أَوَاخِر الأَرْبَعِين مِن عُمْرِه

in the late 20th century

فِي أَوَاخِر القَرْن العِشْرِين

♦ *adv* (to arrive, etc) مُتَأَخِّراً

The train left late. غَادَرَ القِطَار مُتَأَخِّراً

(at the end of a period) مُتَأَخِّراً

late in the evening مُتَأَخِّراً فِي المَسَاء

lately /ˈleɪtli/ *adv* حَدِيثاً

laugh /lɑːf/ *n* ضِحْكَة

♦ *v* يَضْحَك

launch /lɔːntʃ/ *v*

(an investigation) يَبْدَأ (a product) يَطْرَح

♦ *n* (of a product) طَرْح بِالأَسْوَاق

(of a ship, etc) إِنْزَال السَفِينَة إِلَى المَاء

(motor boat) زَوْرَق/زَوَارِقُ مف/ج

laundry /ˈlɔːndri/ *n* pl **-ries**

(business) مَصْبَغَة/مَصَابِغُ مف/ج

(clothes) غَسِيل (مَلَابِس مَغْسُولَة أَو مُعَدَّة لِلغَسِيل)

law /lɔː/ *n* قَانُون/قَوَانِينُ مف/ج

lawn /lɔːn/ *n* عُشْب الإِنْجِيل

lawyer /ˈlɔːjə(r)/ *n* مُحَامٍ

lay /leɪ/ *v* **laid** (to put down) يَضَع (an egg) تَبِيض (the table) يُهَيِّئ

layer /ˈleɪə(r)/ *n* طَبَقَة

layout /ˈleɪaʊt/ *n* تَصْمِيم/تَصْمِيمَات مف/ج

lazy /ˈleɪzi/ *adj* كَسُول

lead /liːd/ *v* **led** (in a race, competition) يَتَصَدَّر

♦ *n* (for a dog) مِقْوَد الحَيَوَان

/led/(metal) رَصَاص

leader /ˈliːdə(r)/ *n* قَائِد

leadership /ˈliːdəʃɪp/ *n* قِيَادَة

leaf /liːf/ *n* وَرَقَة/أَوْرَاق مف/ج

leaflet /ˈliːflət/ *n* نَشْرَة/نَشَرَات مف/ج

league /liːg/ *n* دَوْرِيّ

leak /liːk/ *n* (hole, crack) شَقّ/شُقُوق مف/ج (lost gas, etc) تَسَرُّب/تَسَرُّبَات مف/ج

♦ *v* يَتَسَرَّب

lean /liːn/ *adj* قَلِيل الدَهْن

♦ *v* **leaned or leant** يَنْحَنِي

leap /liːp/ *v* **leaped or leapt** يَقْفِز

learn /lɜːn/ *v* **learned or learnt** يَتَعَلَّم

learner /ˈlɜːnə(r)/ *n* مُتَعَلِّم

learning /ˈlɜːnɪŋ/ *n* تَعَلُّم

lease /liːs/ *n* عَقْد إِيجَار

least /liːst/ *adj* الأَقَلّ

I have (the) least money. أَمْلُك المَال الأَقَلّ

♦ *pron* الأَدْنَى

the least we can do الحَدّ الأَدْنَى مِمَّا نَسْتَطِيع عَمَلَهُ

♦ *adv* الأَقَلّ

Who works least? مَن الأَقَلّ عَمَلاً؟

at least ten people عَشَرَة أَشْخَاص عَلَى الأَقَلّ

leather /ˈleðə(r)/ *n* جِلْد/جُلُود مف/ج

leave /liːv/ *n* إِجَازَة

♦ *v* **left** (to depart) يُغَادِر (the airport, one's village, country) يَرْحَل (open, closed, on, etc.) يَتْرُك

Lebanon /ˈlɛbənən/ *n* لُبْنَان

Lebanese /lɛbəˈniːz/ *adj, n* لُبْنَانِيّ ص/س

lecture /ˈlektʃə(r)/ *n* مُحَاضَرَة

lecturer /ˈlektʃərə(r)/ *n* مُحَاضِر

leek /liːk/ *n* بَصَل الكُرَاث

left /left/ *adj* (hand, side) أَيْسَر/يُسْرَى مذ/م

my left foot قَدَمِي اليُسْرَى

♦ *adv* (in directions) يَسَاراً

Turn left here. تَوَجَّه يَسَاراً هُنَا

♦ *n* (side, direction) يَسَار

It's on your left. هُوَ عَلَى يَسَارِك

Turn to the left. تَوَجَّه إِلَى اليَسَار

left click *n* نَقْرَة بِزِرّ الفَأْرَة الأَيْسَر

left click *v* (folder, icon) يَنْقُر بِزِرّ الفَأْرَة الأَيْسَر

leg /leg/ *n* سَاق/سِيقَان (م) مف/ج

legacy /ˈlegəsi/ *n* pl **-cies** مِيرَاث

legal /ˈliːgl/ *adj* (to do with the law) قَانُونِيّ (allowed by law) قَانُونِيّ

legally /ˈliːgəli/ *adv* قَانُونِيّاً

legislation /ledʒɪsˈleɪʃn/ *n* قَوَانِين

legislator /ˈledʒɪsleɪtə(r)/ *n* مُشَرِّع

legislature /ˈledʒɪsleɪtʃə(r)/ *n* هَيْئَة تَشْرِيعِيَّة

legitimate /lɪˈdʒɪtɪmət/ *adj* شَرْعِيّ

leisure /ˈleʒə(r)/ *n* وَقْت فَرَاغ

lemon /ˈlemən/ *n* لَيْمُونَة/لَيْمُون مف/ج

lemonade /leməˈneɪd/ *n* لِيمُونَادَة

lend /lend/ *v* **lent** (sth to sb) يُعِير

L

He lent me his car. أَعَارَنِي سَيَّارَتَه

Could you lend me $25? هَل بِإِمْكَانِكَ أَنْ تُقْرِضَنِي خَمْسَة وَعِشْرِين دُولَاراً؟

lender /ˈlendə(r)/ *n* مُقْرِض

length /leŋθ/ *n* طُول/أَطْوَال مف/ج

lengthy /ˈleŋθi/ *adj* مُطَوَّل

lens /lenz/ *n* عَدَسَة

lentil /ˈlentl/ *n* عَدَس

less /les/ *adj* (money, water) أَقَلّ

less cement إِسْمَنْت أَقَلّ

♦ *pron* (not as much) أَقَلّ

less than a kilo أَقَلّ مِن كِيلُوغْرَام

They need less than we do. يَحْتَاجُون أَقَلّ مِمَّا نَحْتَاج

♦ *adv* (to eat, to sleep less) أَقَلّ

I sleep less these days. أَنَام أَقَلّ مِن المُعْتَاد هَذِهِ الأَيَّام

lessen /ˈlesn/ *v* (to become less) يَقِلّ (to make less) يُقَلِّل

lesson /ˈlesn/ *n* حِصَّة دِرَاسِيَّة

let /let/ *v* (sth happen) يَدَع (to rent out) يُؤَجِّر (to rent from) يَسْتَأْجِر

lethal /ˈliːθl/ *adj* مُمِيت

letter /ˈletə(r)/ *n* (of alphabet) حَرْف/حُرُوف مف/ج (message) رِسَالَة/رَسَائِل مف/ج

lettuce /ˈletɪs/ *n* خَسَّة/خَسّ مف/ج

level /ˈlevl/ *adj* (surface) مُسْتَوٍ (score) مُتَسَاوٍ

♦ *n* (of water) مُسْتَوَى/مُسْتَوَيَات مف/ج

♦ *v* (to flatten) يُسَوِّي (the score) يُعَادِل

liable /ˈlaɪəbl/ *adj* مَسْئُول قَانُونِيّاً

liar /ˈlaɪə(r)/ *n* كَذَّاب

liberal /ˈlɪbərəl/ *adj* (tolerant) مُتَسَامِح (in politics) تَحَرُّرِيّ (portion, dose) مُسْرِف

liberate /ˈlɪbəreɪt/ *v* يُحَرِّر

liberated /ˈlɪbəreɪtɪd/ *adj* مُتَحَرِّر

liberation /lɪbəˈreɪʃn/ *n* تَحْرِير

liberty /ˈlɪbəti/ *n* حُرِّيَّة

library /ˈlaɪbrəri/ *n* pl **-ries** مَكْتَبَة

Libya /ˈlɪbɪə/ *n* لِيبِيَا

Libyan /ˈlɪbɪən/ *adj, n* لِيبِيّ ص/س

licence /ˈlaɪsns/ *n* US **-cense** (to drive a car) رُخْصَة/رُخَص مف/ج (to software, etc) تَرْخِيص/تَرَاخِيص مف/ج

license /ˈlaɪsns/ *v* يُرَخِّص

lick /lɪk/ *v* يَلْعَق

lid /lɪd/ *n* غِطَاء/أَغْطِيَة مف/ج

lie /laɪ/ *n* كِذْبَة

♦ *v* **lied** (to be untruthful) يَكْذِب **lay, lain** (on a bed, on the floor) يَضْطَجِع

life /laɪf/ *n* الحَيَاة

lifelong /ˈlaɪflɒŋ/ *adj* مَدَى الحَيَاة

lift /lɪft/ *v* يَرْفَع
♦ *n* مِصْعَد/مَصَاعِدُ مف/ج

light /laɪt/ *adj* (colours) فَاتِح/فَوَاتِحُ مف/ج
her light brown hair
شَعْرُهَا البُنِّيّ الفَاتِح (not dark) مُنِير
a light room غُرْفَة مُنِيرَة (not heavy)
(rain, traffic) طَفِيف خَفِيف
♦ *n* (of day, etc) ضَوْء (lamp) نُور
♦ *v* **lighted, lit** يُشْعِل

lighting /'laɪtɪŋ/ *n* إِضَاءَة

lightning /'laɪtnɪŋ/ *n* بَرْق

like /laɪk/ *v* (a person) يَوَدّ
I like Matt. أَوَدّ مَات (a design) يُعْجِب
I like your shirt. يُعْجِبُنِي قَمِيصكَ
I like the red car best.
تُعْجِبُنِي السَيَّارَة الحَمْرَاء أَكْثَر مِن غَيْرِهَا
(an activity) يُحِبّ
I like water skiing. أُحِبّ التَزَلُّج عَلَى المَاء
(food) يَرْغَب
Do you like boiled eggs?
هَل تَرْغَب فِي بَيْض مَسْلُوق؟ (in statements) يُرِيد
I'd like this one, please.
أُرِيد هَذَا إِذَا سَمَحْتَ
I would like to ask a question.
أُرِيد أَنْ أَسْأَل سُؤَالاً (in questions) يَرْغَب
Would you like tea or coffee?
هَل تَرْغَب شَاي أَم قَهْوَة؟

likelihood /'laɪklihʊd/ *n* احْتِمَالِيَّة

likely /'laɪkli/ *adj* مُحْتَمَل

lily /'lɪli/ *n* pl **-lies** زَنْبَق

limb /lɪm/ *n* طَرَف/أَطْرَاف مف/ج

limit /'lɪmɪt/ *n* حَدّ/حُدُود مف/ج
♦ *v* يُقَيِّد

limitation /lɪmɪ'teɪʃn/ *n* تَقْيِيد/تَقْيِيدَات مف/ج

limited /'lɪmɪtɪd/ *adj* مَحْدُود

line /laɪn/ *n* (on paper) خَطّ/خُطُوط مف/ج (cord) حَبْل/حِبَال مف/ج (of trees, etc) صَفّ/صُفُوف مف/ج (queue) طَابُور/طَوَابِيرُ مف/ج

linesman /'laɪnzmən/ *n* pl **-men** حَكَم الرَايَة

line-up /laɪn/ *n* قَائِمَة/قَوَائِمُ مف/ج

linguistic /lɪŋ'gwɪstɪk/ *adj* لُغَوِيّ

link /lɪŋk/ *n* (connection) رَابِط/رَوَابِطُ مف/ج (of a chain) حَلَقَة
♦ *v* (people, things) يَرْبِط

lion /'laɪən/ *n* أَسَد/أُسُود مف/ج

lip /lɪp/ *n* شَفَة/شِفَاة مف/ج

liquid /'lɪkwɪd/ *adj* (fuels) سَائِل/سَوَائِلُ مف/ج
♦ *n* سَائِل/سَوَائِلُ مف/ج

liquor /'lɪkə(r)/ *n* كُحُول

Lisbon /'lɪzbən/ *n* لِشْبُونَة

L

list /lɪst/ *n* قائِمَة/قَوائِمُ مف/ج
♦ *v* يُسَجِّل (فِي قائِمَة)

listen /ˈlɪsn/ *v* يُصْغِي
listen to *phv* يَسْتَمِع

listener /ˈlɪsənə(r)/ *n* مُسْتَمِع

literal /ˈlɪtərəl/ *adj* حَرْفِيّ

literary /ˈlɪtərəri/ *adj* أَدَبِيّ

literature /ˈlɪtrətʃə(r)/ *n* الأَدَب

litigation /lɪtɪˈgeɪʃn/ *n* تَقاضٍ

litre /ˈliːtə(r)/ *n* US **liter** لِتْر/لِتْرات مف/ج

L

litter /ˈlɪtə(r)/ *n* (paper, etc) قُمامَة (of kittens, puppies) بَطْن/بُطُون مف/ج

little /ˈlɪtl/ *adj* (small) صَغِير/صِغار مف/ج
a little boy طِفْل صَغِير (amount) ضَئِيل
in a little while بَعْدَ فَتْرَة وَجِيزَة
♦ *pron* قَلِيل/قَلِيلُون مف/ج
to do little to help
يَعْمَل القَلِيل مِن أَجْل المُساعَدَة
to earn little يَجْنِي القَلِيل

live /lɪv/ *v* (to be alive) يَعِيش (in a place) يُقِيم
♦ *adj* /laɪv/(not dead) حَيّ (charged) مَشْحُون بِتَيّار كَهْرَبائِيّ

livelihood /ˈlaɪvlihʊd/ *n* وَسِيلَة الرِزْق

lively /ˈlaɪvli/ *adj* حَيَوِيّ

liver /ˈlɪvə(r)/ *n* كَبِد

load /ləʊd/ *n* حِمْل/أَحْمال مف/ج
♦ *v* يُحَمِّل

loaded /ˈləʊdɪd/ *adj* مُحَمَّل

loaf /ləʊf/ *n* رَغِيف خُبْز

loan /ləʊn/ *n* قَرْض/قُرُوض مف/ج

lobby /ˈlɒbi/ *n* pl **-bies** رُواق/أَرْوِقَة مف/ج

lobster /ˈlɒbstə(r)/ *n* سَرَطان البَحْر

local /ˈləʊkl/ *adj* (dish, custom, etc) مَوْضِعِيّ (anaesthetic) مَحَلِّيّ

localization /ləʊkəlaɪˈzeɪʃn/ *n* تَوْطِين

locality /ləʊˈkæləti/ *n* pl **-ties** مَرْكَز/مَراكِزُ مف/ج

locate /ləʊˈkeɪt/ *v* يُعَيِّن مَوْضِعاً

location /ləʊˈkeɪʃn/ *n* مَوْقِع/مَواقِعُ مف/ج

lock /lɒk/ *n* (on a door, etc) قِفْل/أَقْفال مف/ج (on a canal) هَوِيس/أَهْوِسَة مف/ج
♦ *v* (a door, window, box) يُقْفِل

log /lɒg/ *n* زِنْد (الخَشَب)

logic /ˈlɒdʒɪk/ *n* المَنْطِق

logical /ˈlɒdʒɪkl/ *adj* مَنْطِقِيّ

logo /ˈləʊgəʊ/ *n* شِعار/شِعارات مف/ج

London /ˈlʌndən/ *n* لَنْدَن

lone /ləʊn/ *adj* وَحِيد

lonely /ˈləʊnli/ *adj* مُوحِش

long /lɒŋ/ *adj* (in extent) طَوِيل/طِوَال مف/ج

long hair شَعْر طَوِيل

It's a long way. هُوَ طَرِيق طَوِيل

(in time) طَوِيل

a long conversation مُحَادَثَة طَوِيلَة

♦ *adv* (in time) طَوِيلاً

We didn't wait long. لَم نَنْتَظِر طَوِيلاً (تُسْتَعْمَل لِلسُّؤَال عَن الزَمَن)

How long did you live there? كَم عِشْتَ هُنَاك؟

look /lʊk/ *v* (at sb or sth) يَنْظُر (to seem) يَبْدُو

♦ *n* (appearance) مَظْهَر/مَظَاهِر

(at sb or sth) نَظْرَة مف/ج

loop /lu:p/ *n* عُقْدَة/عُقَد مف/ج

loose /lu:s/ *adj* (knot, stitch) رَخْو

(free) طَلِيق

loosen /ˈlu:sn/ *v* يُرَخِّي

lord /lɔ:d/ *n* نَبِيل/نُبَلاَء مف/ج

lorry /ˈlɒri/ *n* pl **-ries** شَاحِنَة

lose /lu:z/ *v* (glasses, etc) يُضِيع **lost**

(a match, game) يَخْسَر

loss /lɒs/ *n* خَسَارَة/خَسَائِرُ مف/ج

lost /lɒst/ *adj* (glasses, etc) مَفْقُود (in navigating) تَائِه (battle, game) خَاسِر

lot /lɒt/ *n* وَفْرَة

lottery /ˈlɒtəri/ *n* pl **-ries** يَانَصِيب

loud /laʊd/ *adj* عَالٍ

lounge /laʊndʒ/ *n* رَدْهَة

love /lʌv/ *n* (of family, etc) غَرَام

to be in love يَكُون فِي قِصَّة غَرَام

(of country) حُبّ (of literature) شَغَف

(of an activity) وَلَع

his love of sailing وَلَعُهُ بِالإِبْحَار

♦ *v* (one's family) يُحِبّ

(romantically) يَعْشَق (a hobby) يُولَع

(doing sth) يُحِبّ

I love to travel. أَنَا أُحِبّ السَفَر

She loves swimming. تُحِبّ السِبَاحَة

lovely /ˈlʌvli/ *adj* (weather, person) رَائِع (face) فَاتِن (poem, garden, etc) جَمِيل

lover /ˈlʌvə(r)/ *n* عَشِيق

loving /ˈlʌvɪŋ/ *adj* حَنُون

low /ləʊ/ *adj* (not high) هَابِط

a low table طَاوِلَة هَابِطَة (in number) قَلِيل

lower prices أَسْعَار أَقَلّ (voice, note) مُنْخَفِض

lower /ˈləʊə(r)/ *v* يُخَفِّض

loyal /ˈlɔɪəl/ *adj* مُخْلِص

loyalty /ˈlɔɪəlti/ *n* pl **-ties** إِخْلاَص

luck /lʌk/ *n* حَظّ

lucky /ˈlʌki/ *adj* مَحْظُوظ

luggage /ˈlʌgɪdʒ/ *n* أَمْتِعَة

lump /lʌmp/ *n* (of earth, etc) كُتْلَة/كُتَل (on one's body) نُتُوء/نُتُوءَات مف/ج (in breast) وَرَم/أَوْرَام مف/ج

lunch /lʌntʃ/ *n* غَدَاء

lunchtime /ˈlʌntʃtaɪm/ *n* وَقْت الغَدَاء

lung /lʌŋ/ *n* رِئَة

luxury /ˈlʌkʃəri/ *n* pl **-ries** رَفَاهِيَّة

L

M

mace /meɪs/ *n* قِشْرَة جَوْزَة الطِيب

machine /mə'ʃiːn/ *n* آلَة

machinery /mə'ʃiːnəri/ *n* مَجْمُوعَة آلَات

mackerel /'mækrəl/ *n* سَمَك الإسْقُمْرِيّ

mad /mæd/ *adj* (mentally ill) مَجْنُون/ مَجَانِينُ مف/ج (scheme) غَيْر مَنْطِقِيّ (angry) غَاضِب (about sth) مَهْوُوس

madness /'mædnəs/ *n* جُنُون

Madrid /mə'drɪd/ *n* مَدْرِيد

magazine /mægə'ziːn/ *n* مَجَلَّة

magic /'mædʒɪk/ *adj* سِحْرِيّ
♦ *n* سِحْر

magistrate /'mædʒɪstreɪt/ *n* قَاضٍ/قُضَاة مف/ج

magnetic /mæg'netɪk/ *adj* مِغْنَاطِيسِيّ

magnificent /mæg'nɪfɪsnt/ *adj* فَاتِن

maid /meɪd/ *n* خَادِمَة

mail /meɪl/ *v* يُرْسِل بِالبَرِيد
♦ *n* بَرِيد

mail man *n* US pl **-men** سَاعِي البَرِيد

main /meɪn/ *adj* رَئِيسِيّ

mainland /'meɪnlænd/ *n* البَرّ الرَئِيسِيّ

mainly /'meɪnli/ *adv* بِشَكْل رَئِيسِيّ

maintain /meɪn'teɪn/ *v* يُحَافِظ عَلَى

maintenance /'meɪntənəns/ *n* صِيَانَة

maize /meɪz/ *n* ذُرَة

major /'meɪdʒə(r)/ *adj* (road, town, problem, change) رَئِيسِيّ
♦ *n* (above captain, below colonel) رَائِد/رُوَّاد مف/ج

majority /mə'dʒɒrəti/ *n* pl **-ties** أَغْلَبِيَّة

make /meɪk/ *n* (product) مَارْكَة
♦ *v* made (to produce) يَعْمَل
I made an omelette. عَمِلْتُ بَيْضاً مَقْلِياً
They make computers. يَصْنَعُون الحَوَاسِيب (to cause change) يَجْعَل
It made me angry. جَعَلَنِي ذَلِكَ غَاضِباً
They have made a lot of changes. أَحْدَثُوا الكَثِير مِن التَغْيِيرَات
He made me wait. جَعَلَنِي أَنْتَظِر (to

M

change) يُحْدِث
That made it worse. جَعَلَهُ ذَلِكَ أَسْوَأ
(money) يَصْنَع
He makes a lot of money.
يَصْنَع مَالاً كَثِيراً

maker /'meɪkə(r)/ *n* صَانِع

makeup /'meɪkʌp/ *n* أَدَوَات تَجْمِيل

malaria /mə'leəriə/ *n* المَلَارْيَا

male /meɪl/ *adj* مُذَكَّر

mammal /'mæml/ *n* ثَدْيِيّ/ثَدْيِيَّات مف/ج

man /mæn/ *n* pl **-men** رَجُل/رِجَال مف/ج

M

manage /'mænɪʤ/ *v* (to do sth) يَتَدَبَّر (a business) يُدِير

management /'mænɪʤmənt/ *n* (control) إِدَارَة (in companies) الإِدَارَة

manager /'mænɪʤə(r)/ *n* (in a company) مُدِير/مُدَرَاءُ مف/ج
(of team) مُدِير فَرِيق رِيَاضِيّ

mandate /'mændeɪt/ *n* تَفْوِيض

mandatory /mæn'deɪtəri/ *adj* إِجْبَارِيّ

mango /'mæŋgəʊ/ *n* pl **-goes** مَانْجُو

manipulate /mə'nɪpjuleɪt/ *v* يَتَلَاعَب بِـ

mankind /mæn'kaɪnd/ *n* الجِنْس البَشَرِيّ

manner /'mænə(r)/ *n* (way) طَرِيقَة/طُرُق مف/ج (attitude) سُلُوك

mansion /'mænʃn/ *n* قَصْر/قُصُور مف/ج

manual /'mænjuəl/ *adj* يَدَوِيّ

manufacture /mænju'fæktʃə(r)/ *v* يُصَنِّع

manufacturer /mænju'fæktʃərə(r)/ *n* مُصَنِّع

many /'meni/ *adj* (people, ships, etc) عَدِيد
many friends أَصْدِقَاء عَدِيدُون
many questions أَسْئِلَة عَدِيدَة
many problems to solve
مَشَاكِل عَدِيدَة بِحَاجَة لِحَلّ
How many tables are there?
كَم عَدَد الطَاوِلَات هُنَاكَ؟
♦ *pron* (a large number) كَثِير
Many did not survive. لَم يَنْجُو الكَثِير
That's too many. ذَلِكَ كَثِير جِدّاً
How many are there? كَم يُوجَد هُنَاكَ؟

map /mæp/ *n* خَرِيطَة/خَرَائِطُ مف/ج

marble /'mɑːbl/ *n* (stone) رُخَام (in games) كِلَّة/كِلَال مف/ج

march /mɑːtʃ/ *n* مَسِيرَة
♦ *v* يَسِير

March /mɑːtʃ/ *n* (see August) شَهْر آذَار

mare /meə(r)/ *n* فَرَس/أَفْرَاس مف/ج

margarine /mɑːdʒəˈriːn/ *n* مَرْغَرِين

margin /ˈmɑːdʒɪn/ *n* هَامِش/هَوَامِشُ مف/ج

marine /məˈriːn/ *n* جُنْدِيّ البَحْرِيَّة

marjoram /ˈmɑːdʒərəm/ *n* سُمْسُق

mark /mɑːk/ *n* (spot) عَلَامَة (for school work) عَلَامَة

♦ *v* (for identification) يُعَلِّم (student's work) يُصَحِّح

market /ˈmɑːkɪt/ *n* سُوق/أَسْوَاق مف/ج

♦ *v* يُسَوِّق

marketing /ˈmɑːkɪtɪŋ/ *n* تَسْوِيق

marketplace /ˈmɑːkɪtpleɪs/ *n* سَاحَة السُوق

marriage /ˈmærɪdʒ/ *n* زَوَاج

married /ˈmærid/ *adj* مُتَزَوِّج

marrow /ˈmærəʊ/ *n* كُوسَا

marry /ˈmæri/ *v* يَتَزَوَّج

martyr /ˈmɑːtə(r)/ *n* شَهِيد/شُهَدَاءُ مف/ج

martyrdom /ˈmɑːtədəm/ *n* شَهَادَة

marvellous /ˈmɑːvələs/ *adj* رَائِع

mask /mɑːsk/ *n* قِنَاع/أَقْنِعَة مف/ج

mass /mæs/ *n* كُتْلَة كَبِيرَة

massacre /ˈmæsəkə(r)/ *n* مَجْزَرَة/مَجَازِرُ مف/ج

massage /ˈmæsɑːʒ/ *n* تَدْلِيك

massive /ˈmæsɪv/ *adj* هَائِل

mast /mɑːst/ *n* صَارٍ/صَوَارٍ مف/ج

master /ˈmɑːstə(r)/ *n* مُدَرِّس

♦ *v* يُتْقِن

masterpiece /ˈmɑːstəpiːs/ *n* تُحْفَة/تُحَف مف/ج

mat /mæt/ *n* حَصِيرَة/حُصْر مف/ج

match /mætʃ/ *n* (to light a fire) عُود ثِقَاب (in sports) مُبَارَاة/مُبَارَيَات مف/ج

♦ *v* يَتَنَاسَق

material /məˈtɪəriəl/ *n* قُمَاش/أَقْمِشَة مف/ج

mathematics /mæθəˈmætɪks/ *n* عِلْم الرِيَاضِيَّات

maths /mæθs/ *n* US **math** (see mathematics)

matter /ˈmætə(r)/ *v* يَهُمّ

♦ *n* (material) مَادَّة/مَوَادُّ مف/ج (problem) مُشْكِلَة/مَشَاكِلُ مف/ج

mature /məˈtjʊə(r)/ *adj* نَاضِج

maturity /məˈtjʊərəti/ *n* نُضْج

maximum /ˈmæksɪməm/ *adj* الحَدّ الأَقْصَى

may /meɪ/ *modal v* (possibility) رُبَّمَا، قَد

She may be ill. قَد تَكُون مَرِيضَة

M

You may know this already.
رُبَّمَا أَنَّكَ تَعْلَم هذَا
He may have missed the train.
رُبَّمَا فَاتَهُ القِطَار (permission) مُمْكِن
May I come in? هَل بِإمْكَانِي الدُخُول؟

May /meɪ/ *n* (see August) أَيَّار

maybe /'meɪbi/ *adv* رُبَّمَا

mayor /meə(r)/ *n* عُمْدَة/عُمَد مف/ج

me /mi:/ *pron* (direct object) (ضَمِير المُتَكَلِّم المَفْعُول بِهِ المُبَاشِر)
She knows me. تَعْرِفُنِي (indirect object) (ضَمِير المُتَكَلِّم المَفْعُول بِهِ غَيْر المُبَاشِر)
He gave it to me. أَعْطَاهَا لِي
He passed me the plate.
أَعْطَانِي الصَحْن (after prep, in comparisons)
They went without me. ذَهَبُوا بِدُونِي
She's older than me. هِيَ أَكْبَر مِنِّي

meal /mi:l/ *n* (food) أَكْلَة (occasion) وَلِيمَة/وَلَائِمُ مف/ج

mean /mi:n/ *adj* (with money) بَخِيل/بُخَلَاءُ مف/ج (unkind) خَسِيس/أَخِسَّاءُ مف/ج
♦ *v* meant (words, rules) يَعْنِي (to do sth)
يَقْصِد

meaning /'mi:nɪŋ/ *n* مَعْنَى/مَعَانٍ مف/ج

means /mi:nz/ *n pl* مَوَارِدُ مَالِيَّة

meanwhile /'mi:nwaɪl/ *adv* فِي غُضُون ذَلِكَ

measure /'meʒə(r)/ *v* يَقِيس
♦ *n* (of size, quantity) دَرَجَة (as remedy) إِجْرَاء

measurement /'meʒəmənt/ *n* مِقْيَاس/مَقَايِيسُ مف/ج

meat /mi:t/ *n* لَحْم

Mecca /'mekə/ *n* مَكَّة

mechanic /mə'kænɪk/ *n* مِيكَانِيكِيّ

mechanical /mə'kænɪkl/ *adj* مِيكَانِيكِيّ

mechanism /'mekənɪzəm/ *n* آلِيَّة

medal /'medl/ *n* مِيدَالْيَة

mediate /'mi:dieɪt/ *v* يَتَوَسَّط

medical /'medɪkl/ *adj* طِبِّيّ

medicine /'medsn/ *n* (cure) دَوَاء/أَدْوِيَة مف/ج (science) طِبّ

meditation /medɪ'teɪʃn/ *n* تَأَمُّل

Mediterranean /medɪtə'reɪniən/ *adj* بَحْر مُتَوَسِّطِيّ
♦ *n* البَحْر المُتَوَسِّط

medium /'mi:diəm/ *adj* مُتَوَسِّط

meet /mi:t/ *v* **met** (by arrangement) يُقَابِل (by chance) يَلْتَقِي

meeting /'mi:tɪŋ/ *n* (by

arrangement) اجْتِمَاع/اجْتِمَاعَات (by chance) لِقَاء مف/ج

melody /'melədi/ *n* pl **-dies** لَحْن/أَلْحَان مف/ج

melon /'melən/ *n* شَمَّام

melt /melt/ *v* يَذُوب

member /'membə(r)/ *n* عُضْو/أَعْضَاء مف/ج

memo /'meməʊ/ *n* مُذَكِّرَة

memorable /'memərəbl/ *adj* لَا يُنْسَى

memorandum /memə'rændəm/ *n* مُذَكِّرَة

memorial /mə'mɔ:riəl/ *n* نُصُب تِذْكَارِيّ

memory /'meməri/ *n* pl **-ries** (of events, etc) ذِكْرَى/ذِكْرَيَات مف/ج (person's) ذَاكِرَة

mental /'mentl/ *adj* عَقْلِيّ

mentality /men'tæləti/ *n* عَقْلِيَّة

mention /'menʃn/ *v* (by name) يَذْكُر ♦ *n* (by name) ذِكْر

menu /'menju:/ *n* (in restaurants) قَائِمَة طَعَام (in software) قَائِمَة/قَوَائِمُ مف/ج

merchant /'mɜ:tʃənt/ *n* تَاجِر/تُجَّار مف/ج

mercury /'mɜ:kjəri/ *n* زِئْبَق

mercy /'mɜ:si/ *n* رَحْمَة

merely /'mɪəli/ *adv* مُجَرَّد

merge /mɜ:ʤ/ *v* يَدْمِج

merger /'mɜ:ʤə(r)/ *n* انْدِمَاج

merit /'merɪt/ *n* مِيزَة

mess /mes/ *n* فَوْضَى

message /'mesɪʤ/ *n* رِسَالَة/رَسَائِلُ مف/ج

messenger /'mesɪnʤə(r)/ *n* رَسُول/رُسُل مف/ج

messy /'mesi/ *adj* فَوْضَوِيّ

metal /'metl/ *n* مَعْدِن/مَعَادِنُ مف/ج

metaphor /'metəfə(r)/ *n* اسْتِعَارَة

meter /'mi:tə(r)/ *n* عَدَّاد/عَدَّادَات مف/ج

method /'meθəd/ *n* طَرِيقَة/طُرُق مف/ج

metre /'mi:tə(r)/ *n* US **-ter** مِتْر/أَمْتَار مف/ج

Mexican /'meksɪkən/ *adj, n* مَكْسِيكِيّ ص/س

Mexico /'mɛksɪkəʊ/ *n* المَكْسِيك

microphone /'maɪkrəfəʊn/ *n* مُكَبِّر صَوْت

microscope /'maɪkrəskəʊp/ *n* مِجْهَر/مَجَاهِرُ مف/ج

microwave /'maɪkrəweɪv/ *n* مَايْكْرُوِيف

M

middle /ˈmɪdl/ *n* مُنْتَصَف

Middle East *n* الشَرْق الأَوْسَط

Middle Eastern *adj* شَرْق أَوْسَطِيّ

midnight /ˈmɪdnaɪt/ *n* مُنْتَصَف اللَيْل

midwife /ˈmɪdwaɪf/ *n* قَابِلَة

might /maɪt/ *modal v* رُبَّمَا

I might invite them. رُبَّمَا أَدْعُوهُم

He might not see it. رُبَّمَا لَا يَرَاهُ

They might have arrived by now. رُبَّمَا أَنَّهُم وَصَلُوا الآن

mighty /ˈmaɪti/ *adj* قَوِيّ

migrant /ˈmaɪgrənt/ *n* مُهَاجِر

migrate /maɪˈgreɪt/ *v* يُهَاجِر

M

migration /maɪˈgreɪʃn/ *n* هِجْرَة

mild /maɪld/ *adj* مُعْتَدِل

mile /maɪl/ *n* مِيل/أَمْيَال مف/ج

militant /ˈmɪlɪtənt/ *adj* مُسَلَّح

military /ˈmɪlətri/ *adj* عَسْكَرِيّ

milk /mɪlk/ *n* حَلِيب

mill /mɪl/ *n* (for cereals) مَطْحَنَة/مَطَاحِنُ مف/ج (for steel, etc) مَحْلَج/مَحَالِجُ مف/ج

millet /ˈmɪlɪt/ *n* حَبَّة الجَاوُوس

millimetre /ˈmɪlimiːtə(r)/ *n* US **meter** مِلِّمِيتر

million /ˈmɪljən/ *num* مِلْيُون/مَلَايِينُ مف/ج

millionaire /mɪljəˈneə(r)/ *n* مِلْيُونير

mind /maɪnd/ *n* عَقْل/عُقُول مف/ج

♦ *v* (to object) يُعَارِض (to be careful of) يَحْذَر

mine /maɪn/ *poss pron* لِي

Those pens are mine. تِلْكَ الأَقْلَام لِي

♦ *n* مَنْجَم/مَنَاجِمُ مف/ج

♦ *v* يُنَقِّب

miner /ˈmaɪnə(r)/ *n* مُنَقِّب

mineral /ˈmɪnərəl/ *n* مَعْدِنِيّ

minimal /ˈmɪnɪməl/ *adj* أَدْنَى/دُنْيَا مذ/م

minimize /ˈmɪnɪmaɪz/ *v* يُقَلِّل

minimum /ˈmɪnɪməm/ *n* الحَدّ الأَدْنَى

minister /ˈmɪnɪstə(r)/ *n* (in politics) وَزِير/وُزَرَاءُ مف/ج (in the church) كَاهِن/كَهَنَة مف/ج

ministry /ˈmɪnɪstri/ *n* pl **-ries** وِزَارَة

minor /ˈmaɪnə(r)/ *adj* ثَانَوِيّ

♦ *n* قَاصِر/قُصَّر مف/ج

minority /maɪˈnɒrəti/ *n* pl **-ties** أَقَلِّيَّة

mint /mɪnt/ *n* نَعْنَاع

minus /ˈmaɪnəs/ *prep* نَاقِص

minute /maɪˈnjuːt/ *adj* ضَئِيل جِدّاً

a minute percentage نِسْبَة ضَئِيلَة جِدّاً

♦ *n* /ˈmɪnɪt/ دَقِيقَة/دَقَائِقُ مف/ج

The time is one minute past three.
السَاعَة الثَالِثَة ودَقِيقَة وَاحِدَة
I'll see you in a minute.
سأَرَاكَ بَعْدَ دَقِيقَة
It's five minutes' walk from here.
يَبْعُد خَمْس دَقَائِق مَشْياً مِن هُنَا

miracle /'mɪrəkl/ *n* مُعْجِزَة

mirror /'mɪrə(r)/ *n* مِرْآة/مَرَايَا مف/ج

miserable /'mɪzrəbl/ *adj* (unhappy) بَائِس (salary, etc) هَزِيل

misery /'mɪzəri/ *n* pl **-ries** تَعَاسَة

mislead /mɪs'li:d/ *v* **-led** يُضَلِّل

miss /mɪs/ *v* (a bus, etc) يَفُوتُهُ (an absent person) يَفْتَقِد
♦ *n* آنِسَة

missile /'mɪsaɪl/ *n* صَارُوخ/صَوَارِيخ مف/ج

missing /'mɪsɪŋ/ *adj* مَفْقُود

mist /mɪst/ *n* ضَبَاب

mistake /mɪ'steɪk/ *n* (error) خَطَأ/أَخْطَاء مف/ج
♦ *v* **-took, -taken** يُخْطِئ

mistaken /mɪ'steɪkən/ *adj* خَاطِئ

misunderstand /mɪsʌndə'stænd/ *v* **-stood** يُسِيء الفَهْم

misunderstanding /mɪsʌndə'stændɪŋ/ *n* سُوء فَهْم

mix /mɪks/ *v* (to put together) يَخْلِط (to combine) يَمْزُج

mixed /mɪkst/ *adj* (ingredients) مُخْتَلَط (school, etc) مَمْزُوج

mixture /'mɪkstʃə(r)/ *n* مَزِيج/أَمْزِجَة مف/ج

mobile /'məʊbaɪl/ *adj* (phone) نَقَّال (library, home) مُتَنَقِّل

mobile phone *n* هَاتِف خَلَوِيّ

mobility /məʊ'bɪləti/ *n* حَرَكَة

mock /mɒk/ *v* يَسْخَر مِن

model /'mɒdl/ *n* (of a plane, etc) نَمُوذَج/نَمَاذِجُ مف/ج (person) عَارِضَة أَزْيَاء
♦ *v* (using clay, etc) يُشَكِّل (clothes) يَعْرِض أَزْيَاء

modem /'məʊdem/ *n* مُودِم

moderate /'mɒdərət/ *adj* (policy) مُعْتَدِل (price) مُتَوَسِّط

modern /'mɒdn/ *adj* عَصْرِيّ

modest /'mɒdɪst/ *adj* (person) مُتَوَاضِع (hotel, proposal) مُعْتَدِل

modification /mɒdɪfɪ'keɪʃn/ *n* تَعْدِيل/تَعْدِيلَات مف/ج

modify /'mɒdɪfaɪ/ *v* يُعَدِّل

moisture /'mɔɪstʃə(r)/ *n* رُطُوبَة

moment /'məʊmənt/ *n* لَحْظَة

M

momentarily /ˈməʊməntrəli/ *adv* لِلَحْظَة

monarchy /ˈmɒnəki/ *n* pl **-chies** (state) مَمْلَكَة (system) نِظَام مَلَكِيّ

Monday /ˈmʌndeɪ/ *n* (see Wednesday) الاِثْنَيْن

monetary /ˈmʌnɪtri/ *adj* مَالِيّ

money /ˈmʌni/ *n* مَال

monitor /ˈmɒnɪtə(r)/ *n* شَاشَة

monk /mʌŋk/ *n* رَاهِب/رُهْبَان مف/ج

monkey /ˈmʌŋki/ *n* قِرْد/قُرُود مف/ج

monopoly /məˈnɒpəli/ *n* pl **-lies** احْتِكَار

monster /ˈmɒnstə(r)/ *n* وَحْش/وُحُوش مف/ج

month /mʌnθ/ *n* شَهْر/شُهُور وَأَشْهُر مف/ج

monthly /ˈmʌnθli/ *adj* شَهْرِيّ

monument /ˈmɒnjumənt/ *n* أَثَر/آثَار مف/ج

mood /muːd/ *n* مِزَاج/أَمْزِجَة مف/ج

moon /muːn/ *n* قَمَر/أَقْمَار مف/ج

moral /ˈmɒrəl/ *adj* أَخْلَاقِيّ
♦ *n* مَغْزَى القِصَّة

morale /məˈrɑːl/ *n* مَعْنَوِيَّات

morality /məˈræləti/ *n* أَخْلَاق

more /mɔː(r)/ *adj* (additional) إِضَافِيّ
more questions أَسْئِلَة إِضَافِيَّة
We need more concrete. نَحْتَاج لِإِسْمَنْت إِضَافِيّ (in comparisons) أَكْثَرُ
He has more work than me. لَدَيْهِ عَمَل أَكْثَر مِنِّي
♦ *pron* (addition) أَكْثَرُ
We need more. نَحْتَاج إِلَى أَكْثَر (in comparisons) أَكْثَرُ
He has more than me. لَدَيْهِ أَكْثَر مِنِّي
♦ *adv* (to a greater degree) أَكْثَرُ
This book is more interesting. هَذَا الكِتَاب أَكْثَر إِمْتَاعاً
more efficiently أَكْثَر فَاعِلِيَّة

morning /ˈmɔːnɪŋ/ *n* صَبَاح

Moroccan /məˈrɒk(ə)n/ *adj, n* مَغْرِبِيّ/مَغَارِبَة ص/س/ج

Morocco /məˈrɒkəʊ/ *n* المَغْرِب

mortality /mɔːˈtæləti/ *n* فَنَائِيَّة

mortgage /ˈmɔːɡɪdʒ/ *n* رَهْن عَقَارِيّ

Moscow /ˈmɒskəʊ/ *n* مُوسْكُو

mosque /mɒsk/ *n* مَسْجِد/مَسَاجِدُ مف/ج
to attend a mosque يَذْهَب إِلَى المَسْجِد

mosquito /mɒsˈkiːtəʊ/ *n* بَعُوضَة/بَعُوض مف/ج

moss /mɒs/ *n* طُحْلُب/طَحَالِبُ مف/ج

most /məʊst/ *adj* (the majority of) الأَكْثَر
We have most points. لَدَيْنَا النِقَاط الأَكْثَر
(as superlative) الأَكْثَر
two days, at most يَوْمَان عَلَى الأَكْثَر
♦ *pron* (the majority) مُعْظَم
most of my friends مُعْظَم أَصْدِقَائِيّ
most of the time مُعْظَم الوَقْت (as superlative) الأَكْثَر
Who has (the) most? مَن لَدَيْهِ الأَكْثَر؟
Most of all they export oil. أَهَمّ شَيْء أَنَّهُم يَسْتَخْرِجُون النَفْط

mostly /ˈməʊstli/ *adv* غَالِباً مَا

mother /ˈmʌðə(r)/ *n* أُمّ/أُمَّهَات (م) مف/ج

motion /ˈməʊʃn/ *n* حَرَكَة

motivate /ˈməʊtɪveɪt/ *v* يُحَفِّز

motivation /məʊtɪˈveɪʃn/ *n* دَافِع/دَوَافِعُ مف/ج

motive /ˈməʊtɪv/ *n* دَافِع/دَوَافِعُ مف/ج

motor /ˈməʊtə(r)/ *n* مُحَرِّك/مُحَرِّكَات مف/ج

motorist /ˈməʊtərɪst/ *n* سَائِق

motorway /ˈməʊtəweɪ/ *n* طَرِيق سَرِيع

mound /maʊnd/ *n* كَوْمَة

mount /maʊnt/ *v* يَرْكَب

mountain /ˈmaʊntən/ *n* جَبَل/جِبَال مف/ج

mourn /mɔːn/ *v* يَتَفَجَّع عَلَى

mouse /maʊs/ *n* pl **mice** فَأْر/فِئْرَان مف/ج

mouth /maʊθ/ *n* (person's) فَم/أَفْوَاه مف/ج (of a cave, etc) فَتْحَة (of a river) مَصَبّ/مَصَبَّات مف/ج

move /muːv/ *n* (in chess, etc) نَقْلَة (to new address) انْتِقَال
♦ *v* (an object) يُحَرِّك (to new address) يَنْتَقِل إِلَى (emotionally) يُحَرِّك مَشَاعِر

movement /ˈmuːvmənt/ *n* حَرَكَة

movie /ˈmuːvi/ *n* فِيلْم/أَفْلَام مف/ج

MP3 player /empiːˈθriː/ *n* مُشَغِّل إِم بِي ثِرِي

Mr /ˈmɪstə(r)/ *n* سَيِّد/سَادَة مف/ج

Mrs /ˈmɪsɪz/ *n* سَيِّدَة

Ms /məz/ *n* سَيِّدَة

much /mʌtʃ/ *adj* كَثِير
♦ *adv* كَثِيراً

mud /mʌd/ *n* وَحْل

mug /mʌg/ *n* كُوب/أَكْوَاب مف/ج

multiply /ˈmʌltɪplaɪ/ *v* يُضَاعِف

municipal /mjuːˈnɪsɪpl/ *adj* بَلَدِيّ

murder /ˈmɜːdə(r)/ *v* يَقْتُل
♦ *n* جَرِيمَة قَتْل

murderer /ˈmɜːdərə(r)/ *n* قَاتِل

murmur /'mɜːmə(r)/ *v* يُتَمْتِم

Muscat /'mʌskat/ *n* مَسْقَط

muscle /'mʌsl/ *n* عَضَلَة

muscular /'mʌskjələ(r)/ *adj* عَضَلِيّ

museum /mju'ziːəm/ *n* مَتْحَف/ مَتَاحِفُ مف/ج

mushroom /'mʌʃruːm/ *n* فِطْر

music /'mjuːzɪk/ *n* مُوسِيقَى

musical /'mjuːzɪkl/ *adj* مُوسِيقِيّ
♦ *n* مَسْرَحِيَّة أَو فِيلْم غِنَائِيّ

musician /mju'zɪʃn/ *n* عَازِف مُوسِيقِيّ

M

Muslim /'mʊzlɪm/ *adj* مُسْلِم، إِسْلَامِيّ
♦ *n* مُسْلِم

mussel /'mʌsl/ *n* بَلَح البَحْر

must /mʌst/ *modal v* (obligation) يَجِب
You must be there at 2 o'clock. يَجِب أَنْ تَكُون هُنَاكَ فِي السَاعَة الثَانِيَة
You mustn't be late. يَجِب أَلَّا تَتَأَخَّر
Must I come? هَل يَجِب عَلَيَّ أَنْ آتِي؟
(supposition) مِن المُؤَكَّد
He must be tired. مِن المُؤَكَّد أَنَّهُ مُتْعَب

mustard /'mʌstəd/ *n* خَرْدَل

mustn't /'mʌsnt/ *contr* (= must not: see must)

mutter /'mʌtə(r)/ *v* يُدَمْدِم

mutton /'mʌtn/ *n* لَحْم الضَأْن

mutual /'mjuːtʃuəl/ *adj* مُتَبَادَل

mutual fund *n* مَشْرُوع اسْتِثْمَارِيّ

my /maɪ/ *adj* (ضَمِير المُتَكَلِّم المُضَاف إِلَيْهِ)
my book كِتَابِي
my friends صَدِيقِي

myself /maɪ'self/ *pron* (reflexive) نَفْسِي
I hurt myself. جَرَحْتُ نَفْسِي (for emphasis) بِنَفْسِي
I can do it myself. أَسْتَطِيع عَمَلَهَا بِنَفْسِي
I was by myself. كُنْتُ لِوَحْدِي

mysterious /mɪ'stɪəriəs/ *adj* غَامِض

mystery /'mɪstri/ *n* غُمُوض

myth /mɪθ/ *n* أُسْطُورَة/أَسَاطِيرُ مف/ج

N

Nablus /ˈnɑːbləs/ *n* نَابُلُس

nail /neɪl/ *n* (of finger, toe) ظُفْر/أَظَافِرُ مف/ج (in carpentry) مِسْمَار/مَسَامِيرُ مف/ج

naked /ˈneɪkɪd/ *adj* عارٍ/عُرَاة مف/ج

name /neɪm/ *n* اسْم/أَسْمَاء مف/ج
♦ *v* يُسَمِّي

namely /ˈneɪmli/ *adv* تَحْدِيداً

nap /næp/ *n* قَيْلُولَة

narrow /ˈnærəʊ/ *adj* ضَيِّق

nasty /ˈnɑːsti/ *adj* (remark) بَذِيء (fall, cut) خَطِير

nation /ˈneɪʃn/ *n* (country) أُمَّة/أُمَم مف/ج (population) شَعْب/شُعُوب مف/ج

national /ˈnæʃnəl/ *adj* وَطَنِيّ

nationality /næʃəˈnæləti/ *n* pl -ties جِنْسِيَّة

native /ˈneɪtɪv/ *adj* أَصْلِيّ
♦ *n* قَوْمِيّ

natural /ˈnætʃrəl/ *adj* (products, etc) طَبِيعِيّ (parent) فِطْرِيّ

naturally /ˈnætʃrəli/ *adv* (of course) طَبِيعِيّاً (to act) بِالطَّبْع

nature /ˈneɪtʃə(r)/ *n* (flora, fauna) الطَّبِيعَة (character) طَبِيعَة/طَبَائِعُ مف/ج

naval /ˈneɪvl/ *adj* بَحْرِيّ

navigate /ˈnævɪgeɪt/ *v* يَقُود

navigation /nævɪˈgeɪʃn/ *n* قِيَادَة

navy /ˈneɪvi/ *n* pl **-vies** سِلاَح البَحْرِيَّة

Nazareth /ˈnazərəθ/ *n* النَاصِرَة

near /nɪə(r)/ *adj* (in distance) قَرِيب
the nearest hospital المُسْتَشْفَى الأَقْرَب
The hotel is quite near. الفُنْدُق قَرِيب جِدّاً (in time) قَرِيب
the near future المُسْتَقْبَل القَرِيب
♦ *adv* (in distance) قَرِيب
Don't go too near! لاَ تَقْتَرِب كَثِيراً (in time) قَرِيب
Winter is getting near. الشِتَاء يَقْتَرِب
♦ *prep* (in distance) قَرِيب مِن
It's near the station. هُوَ قَرِيب مِن المَحَطَّة
I sat near them. جَلَسْتُ قَرِيب مِنْهُم (in time) عَلَى مَقْرَبَة مِن

near the beginning
عَلَى مَقْرَبَةٍ مِن البِدَايَة
We are getting near the holidays.
نَقْتَرِب مِن العُطْلَة

nearby /nɪəˈbaɪ/ *adj* مُجَاوِر
a nearby park مُنْتَزَه مُجَاوِر
♦ *adv* قَرِيب
They live nearby.
يَعِيشُون عَلَى مَقْرَبَة مِن هُنَا

nearly /ˈnɪəli/ *adv* تَقْرِيباً

neat /niːt/ *adj* مُرَتَّب

necessary /ˈnesəsəri/ *adj* ضَرُورِيّ

necessity /nəˈsesəti/ *n* pl **-ties**
ضَرُورَة

N

neck /nek/ *n* رَقَبَة/رِقَاب مف/ج

necklace /ˈnekləs/ *n* عِقْد/عُقُود مف/ج

nectarine /ˈnektəriːn/ *n* رَحِيقَانِي

need /niːd/ *v* (help, money) يَحْتَاج إِلَى
Do you need any help?
هَل تَحْتَاج لأَيّ مُسَاعَدَة؟
The soup needs more salt.
تَحْتَاج الشُرْبَة إِلَى مِلْح أَكْثَر (to do sth)
بِحَاجَة
I need to go now.
أَنَا بِحَاجَة لأَنْ أَذْهَب الآن
You need to see a doctor.
إِنَّك بِحَاجَة لِرُؤْيَة الطَبِيب

♦ *n* حَاجَة
Their greatest need is medicines.
حَاجَتُهُم العُظْمَى هِيَ الدَوَاء

needle /ˈniːdl/ *n* إِبْرَة/إِبَر مف/ج

needn't /ˈniːdnt/ *contr* (= need not: see need)

negative /ˈnegətɪv/ *adj* سَلْبِيّ
♦ *n* عِبَارَة نَافِيَة

neglect /nɪˈglekt/ *n* إِهْمَال
♦ *v* يُهْمِل

negligence /ˈneglɪdʒəns/ *n* إِهْمَال

negotiate /nɪˈgəʊʃieɪt/ *v* يُفَاوِض

negotiation /nɪgəʊʃiˈeɪʃn/ *n*
تَفَاوُض

neighbour /ˈneɪbə(r)/ *n* US **-bor**
جَار/جِيرَان مف/ج

neighbourhood /ˈneɪbəhʊd/ *n*
US **-borhood** حَيّ/أَحْيَاء مف/ج

neither /ˈnaɪðə(r)/ *pron* لاَ أَحَد مِنْهُمَا
Neither is any good. لاَ أَحَد مِنْهُمَا جَيِّد
(neither ... nor ...) لاَ ...وَلاَ
Neither you nor I understand the problem. لاَ أَنْتَ وَلاَ أَنَا نَفْهَم المُشْكِلَة

nephew /ˈnefjuː/ *n* ابْن الأَخ أَو الأُخْت

nerve /nɜːv/ *n* عَصَب/أَعْصَاب مف/ج

nervous /ˈnɜːvəs/ *adj* عَصَبِيّ

nest /nest/ *n* عُشّ/أَعْشَاش مف/ج

net /net/ *n* شَبَكَة

♦ *adj* (profit) صَافٍ

Netherlands, the /'neðələndz/ *n* هُولَنْدَا

network /'netwɜ:k/ *n* شَبَكَة

neutral /'nju:trəl/ *adj* مُحَايِد

never /'nevə(r)/ *adv* لاَ قَطّ

He's never been to Cairo.

لَم يَذْهَب إِلَى القَاهِرَة قَطّ

He never remembers his keys.

لاَ يَتَذَكَّر مَفَاتِيحَهُ عَلَى الإِطْلاَق

nevertheless /nevəðə'les/ *adv* وَبِرَغْمِ ذَلِكَ

new /nju:/ *adj* جَدِيد

newcomer /'nju:kʌmə(r)/ *n* قَادِم جَدِيد

New Delhi /'deli/ *n* نِيودِلْهِي

news /nju:z/ *n* أَخْبَار

newspaper /'nju:zpeɪpə(r)/ *n* صَحِيفَة/صُحُف مف/ج

New York /'jɔ:rk/ *n* نِيويُورْك

New Zealand /'zi:lənd/ *n* نْيُوزِيلاَنْدَا

New Zealander /'zi:ləndə/ *n* نْيُوزِيلاَنْدِيّ

next /nekst/ *adj* تَالٍ

next week الأُسْبُوع القَادِم

Take the next turning.

خُذ المُنْعَطَف التَالِي

♦ *adv* (time) بَعْدَ ذَلِك

Who's next? مَن بَعْدَهُ؟

What shall we do next?

مَاذَا سَوْفَ نَفْعَل بَعْدَ ذَلِك؟

next to بِجَانِب

I sat next to Amina.

جَلَسْتُ بِجَانِب أَمِينَة

nice /naɪs/ *adj* (person) لَطِيف/لُطَفَاء مف/ج (neighbourhood) جَمِيل (taste, soup) لَذِيذ

nickname /'nɪkneɪm/ *n* لَقَب/أَلْقَاب مف/ج

Nicosia /ˌnɪkə'sɪə/ *n* نِيقُوسِيَا

niece /ni:s/ *n* ابْنَة الأَخ أَو الأُخْت

night /naɪt/ *n* (time of darkness) لَيْل (evening) لَيْلَة/لَيَالٍ مف/ج

nightclub /'naɪtklʌb/ *n* مَلْهَى لَيْلِيّ

nine /naɪn/ *num* تِسْعَة

nineteen /naɪn'ti:n/ *num* تِسْعَةَ عَشَر

ninety /'naɪnti/ *num* تِسْعُون

ninth /naɪnθ/ *adj* تَاسِع/تَوَاسِعُ مف/ج

♦ *adv* تَاسِعاً

♦ *n* (see tenth) التَاسِع

nitrogen /'naɪtrədʒən/ *n* نَيْتْرُوجِين

N

no /nəʊ/ *interj* (negative reply) لاَ

I said no. قُلْتُ لاَ

No, thank you. شُكْراً، لاَ

♦ *adj* لاَ

There are no potatoes left.

لَم يَتَبَقَّ بَطَاطَا

I have no money and no job.

لاَ أَمْلُك مَالاً وَلاَ عَمَلاً

No smoking. مَمْنُوع التَدْخِين

♦ *adv* لَيْس

no more than $10

لَيْسَ أَكْثَر مِن عَشْرَة دُولَارَات

He's no fool. لَيْسَ أَحْمَق

noble /'nəʊbl/ *adj* نَبِيل/نُبَلاَءُ مف/ج

nobody /'nəʊbədi/ *pron* لاَ أَحَد

Nobody answered the door.

لَم يُجِب عَلَى البَاب أَحَد

nod /nɒd/ *n* إِيمَاءَة

♦ *v* يُومِئ

noise /nɔɪz/ *n* (sound) صَوْت/أَصْوَات

(too loud) ضَوْضَاء مف/ج

noisy /'nɔɪzi/ *adj* (street) ضَاجّ

(children) صَاخِب

nominate /'nɒmɪneɪt/ *v* يُرَشِّح

nomination /nɒmɪ'neɪʃn/ *n* تَرْشِيح

none /nʌn/ *pron* (with plural) لاَ أَحَد

None of us know him.

لاَ يَعْرِفُهُ أَحَد مِنَّا

None of the keys work.

لاَ يَعْمَل أَيّ مِن المَفَاتِيح (with uncountable) لاَ شَيْء

none of that لاَ شَيْء مِن ذَلِك

nonsense /'nɒnsns/ *n* هُرَاء

noon /nuːn/ *n* ظُهْر

no one /'nəʊwʌn/ *pron* (see: nobody)

normal /'nɔːml/ *adj* طَبِيعِيّ

normally /'nɔːməli/ *adv* عَادَةً

north /nɔːθ/ *n* شَمَال

♦ *adj* شَمَالِيّ

♦ *adv* نَحْوَ الشَمَال

northern /'nɔːðən/ *adj* شَمَالِيّ

nose /nəʊz/ *n* أَنْف/أُنُوف مف/ج

not /nɒt/ *adv* لاَ، غَيْر، لَم، لَيْس

not today لَيْسَ اليَوْم

She is not/isn't here. هِيَ غَيْر مَوْجُودَة

He did not stop. لَم يَتَوَقَّف

I asked you not to tell him.

طَلَبْتُ مِنْكَ أَلَّا تُخْبِرَهُ

notable /'nəʊtəbl/ *adj* بَارِز

note /nəʊt/ *n* (reminder) مُلاَحَظَة

(message) رِسَالَة

♦ *v* يُدَوِّن

notebook /'nəʊtbʊk/ *n* مُفَكِّرَة

noted /'nəʊtɪd/ *adj* شَهِير

not-for-profit /nɒtfə'prɒfɪt/ *adj* غَيْر رِبْحِيّ

nothing /'nʌθɪŋ/ *pron* لاَ شَيْء
nothing special لاَ شَيْء خَاصّ
There is nothing I can do.
لاَ يُوجَد شَيْء أَسْتَطِيع عَمَلَهُ

notice /'nəʊtɪs/ *n* (sign) إِخْطَار/ انْتِبَاه (attention) إِخْطَارَات مف/ج
♦ *v* يُلاَحِظ

noticeable /'nəʊtɪsəbl/ *adj* وَاضِح

notify /'nəʊtɪfaɪ/ *v* يُبَلِّغ

notion /'nəʊʃn/ *n* فِكْرَة/أَفْكَار مف/ج

novel /'nɒvl/ *n* رِوَايَة

novelist /'nɒvəlɪst/ *n* رِوَائِيّ

novelty /'nɒvlti/ *n* pl **-ties** حَدَاثَة

November /nəʊ'vembə(r)/ *n* (see August) شَهْر تِشْرِين الثَّانِي

novice /'nɒvɪs/ *n* مُبْتَدِئ

now /naʊ/ *adv* الآن

nowhere /'nəʊweə(r)/ *adv* لاَ مَكَان
There's nowhere to park.
لاَ يُوجَد مَكَان لإِيقَاف السَيَّارَة

nuclear /'nju:kliə(r)/ *adj* نَوَوِيّ

nucleus /'nju:kliəs/ *n* pl **nuclei** نُوَاة

nuisance /'nju:sns/ *n* إِزْعَاج

number /'nʌmbə(r)/ *n* (figure) رَقَم/ أَرْقَام مف/ج (amount) عَدَد/أَعْدَاد مف/ج

numerous /'nju:mərəs/ *adj* عَدِيد

nun /nʌn/ *n* رَاهِبَة

nurse /nɜ:s/ *n* مُمَرِّض
♦ *v* يَرْعَى

nursery /'nɜ:səri/ *n* pl **-ries** (for children) حَضَانَة (for plants) مَشْتَل/ مَشَاتِل مف/ج

nut /nʌt/ *n* (fruit) جَوْزَة/جَوْز مف/ج (metal fixing) صَمُولَة/صَوَامِيل مف/ج

nutmeg /'nʌtmeg/ *n* جَوْزَة الطِيب

nutrition /nju'trɪʃn/ *n* تَغْذِيَة

O

oak /əʊk/ *n* بَلُّوطَة/بَلُّوط مف/ج

oath /əʊθ/ *n* قَسَم

oats /əʊts/ *n pl* نَبْتَة الشُوفَان

obesity /əʊ'bi:səti/ *n* سُمْنَة

obey /ə'beɪ/ *v* يُطِيع

object /'ɒbdʒɪkt/ *n* (aim) هَدَف/أَهْدَاف مف/ج (thing) شَيْء/أَشْيَاء مف/ج
♦ *v* /əb'dʒekt/ يَعْتَرِض عَلَى

objection /əb'dʒekʃn/ *n* اعْتِرَاض

objective /əb'dʒektɪv/ *adj* مَوْضُوعِيّ
♦ *n* هَدَف/أَهْدَاف مف/ج

obligation /ɒblɪ'geɪʃn/ *n* الْتِزَام/الْتِزَامَات مف/ج

oblige /ə'blaɪdʒ/ *v* يُجْبِر

oblivious /ə'blɪviəs/ *adj* غَيْر وَاعٍ

obscure /əb'skjʊə(r)/ *adj* (allusion) غَامِض (hard to see) بَاهِت

observation /ɒbzə'veɪʃn/ *n* مُرَاقَبَة، مُلَاحَظَة

observe /əb'zɜ:v/ *v* (wildlife, etc) يُرَاقِب (the rules, etc) يُطِيع

observer /əb'zɜ:və(r)/ *n* مُرَاقِب

obsession /əb'seʃn/ *n* هَوَس

obstacle /'ɒbstəkl/ *n* عَائِق

obstruction /əb'strʌkʃn/ *n* عَائِق/عَوَائِق مف/ج

obtain /əb'teɪn/ *v* يَحْصُل عَلَى

obvious /'ɒbviəs/ *adj* وَاضِح

obviously /'ɒbviəsli/ *adv* بِوُضُوح

occasion /ə'keɪʒn/ *n* مُنَاسَبَة

occasional /ə'keɪʒənl/ *adj* عَارِض

occupant /'ɒkjəpənt/ *n* مُسْتَأْجِر

occupation /ɒkju'peɪʃn/ *n* (job) وَظِيفَة/وَظَائِف مف/ج (of a country) احْتِلَال

occupy /'ɒkjupaɪ/ *v* (sb's time, a space) يُشْغِل (a country) يَحْتَلّ

occur /ə'kɜ:(r)/ *v* يَحْدُث

occurrence /ə'kʌrəns/ *n* حَدَث/أَحْدَاث مف/ج

ocean /'əʊʃn/ *n* مُحِيط/مُحِيطَات مف/ج

o'clock /ə'klɒk/ *adv* السَاعَة
It's one/four o'clock.
السَاعَة الوَاحِدَة/الرَابِعَة

O

October /ɒk'təʊbə(r)/ *n* (see August) شَهْر تِشْرِين الأَوَّل

odd /ɒd/ *adj* (person, idea) غَرِيب (sock) مُفْرَد

of /əv, ɒv/ *prep* (connected to) (أَدَاة إِضَافَة)

the name of the road اسْم الشَارِع

a friend of Gordon صَدِيق جُورْدُن

the story of our people قِصَّة شَعْبِنَا

the first day of the month أَوَّل يَوْم فِي الشَهْر (with material) مِن

a bracelet made of silver إِسْوَار مَصْنُوع مِن الفِضَّة (containing) (أَدَاة دَلَالَة)

a glass of water كُوب مَاء (from a group, set) مِن

two of our team اثْنَان مِن فَرِيقِنَا (telling the time) قَبْلَ/إِلَّا

(US) *at five of ten* فِي العَاشِرَة إِلَّا خَمْس دَقَائِق (in dates) مِن

the 11th of December الحَادِي عَشَر مِن كَانُون الأَوَّل

off /ɒf/ *prep* (from) مِن

I cut a piece off the end. قَطَعْتُ قِطْعَة مِن النِهَايَة

He took it off my desk. أَخَذَهَا مِن مَكْتَبِي (in distances) (بَعِيد عَن

a metre off the ground أَعْلَى مِن الأَرْض بِمِتْر وَاحِد (absent) غَائِب

She's off work. هِيَ غَائِبَة عَن العَمَل ♦ *adv* (تَدُلّ عَلَى الاِبْتِعَاد عَن أَو تَرْك المَكَان)

I'll be off now. سَوْفَ أَذْهَب الآن

I got off at the bus station. نَزَلْتُ فِي مَحَطَّة البَاص (distant) بَعِيد

It's 5 miles off. تَبْعُد خَمْسَة أَمْيَال

July is a long way off. شَهْر تَمُّوز مَا زَالَ بَعِيداً (from school, work) فِي عُطْلَة

to take time off يَأْخُذ عُطْلَة (light, radio, etc) مُطْفَأ

All the lights were off. كَانَت جَمِيع الأَنْوَار مُطْفَأَة (race, show) مُلْغَى

Tomorrow's game is off. مُبَارَاة الغَد مُلْغَاة (with prices) خَصْم

He offered me 20% off. عَرَضَ عَلَيَّ 20% خَصْم

♦ *adj* فَاسِد

The fish is off. السَمَك فَاسِد

offence /ə'fens/ *n* US **-ense** (resentment) إِهَانَة (illegal act) جَرِيمَة/جَرَائِمُ مف/ج

offend /ə'fend/ *v* يُضَايِق

offender /ə'fendə(r)/ *n* مُعْتَدٍ

O

offensive /ə'fensɪv/ *adj* (remark) مُهِين (move, play) هُجُومِيّ
♦ *n* هَجْمَة

offer /'ɒfə(r)/ *n* (to do sth) عَرْض/عُرُوض مف/ج
♦ *v* (to do sth) يَعْرِض (a meal, lift) يُقَدِّم

office /'ɒfɪs/ *n* مَكْتَب/مَكَاتِبُ مف/ج

officer /'ɒfɪsə(r)/ *n* ضَابِط/ضُبَّاط مف/ج

official /ə'fɪʃl/ *adj* رَسْمِيّ

offshore /ɒf'ʃɔ:(r)/ *adj* فِي البَحْر بِالقُرْب مِن الشَاطِئ

often /'ɒfn/ *adv* كَثِيراً

oil /ɔɪl/ *n* (for cooking, lubrication) زَيْت/زُيُوت مف/ج (petroleum) نَفْط

ok /əʊ'keɪ/ *interj* **(okay)** حَسَناً

old /əʊld/ *adj* (not new) قَدِيم
old shoes حِذَاء قَدِيم
an old friend صَدِيق قَدِيم (not young) عَجُوز/عَجَائِزُ
an old man رَجُل عَجُوز (not current: edition) مَاضٍ (about age) (تُسْتَعْمَل لِلسُؤَال عَن العُمْر)
How old are you? كَم عُمْرُكَ؟
James is ten years old. يَبْلُغ عُمْر جِيمس عَشْر سَنَوَات

olive /'ɒlɪv/ *n* زَيْتُون

olive oil *n* زَيْت الزَيْتُون

Oman /əʊ'mɑ:n/ *n* عُمَان

Omani /əʊ'mɑ:ni/ *adj, n* عُمَانِيّ ص/س

omission /ə'mɪʃn/ *n* حَذْف

omit /ə'mɪt/ *v* يَحْذِف

on /ɒn/ *prep* (showing position) عَلَى
on the desk عَلَى المَكْتَب
the first turn on the right أَوَّل مُنْعَطَف عَلَى اليَمِين
on the front page عَلَى الصَفْحَة الرَئِيسِيَّة (with days, dates) فِي
on Tuesday فِي يَوْم الثُلَاثَاء
on the 25th of June فِي الخَامِس وَالعِشْرِين مِن آب (with means of transport) فِي
She came on the bus. جَاتَت فِي البَاص (being played, shown) عَلَى
She appeared on TV. ظَهَرَت عَلَى التِلْفَاز (about) عَن
his speech on the crisis حَدِيثُهُ عَن الأَزْمَة (holiday, a trip) فِي
I was there on business. كُنْتُ هُنَاكَ فِي عَمَل
♦ *adv* (showing continuity) قُدُماً
It went on for two hours. اسْتَمَرَّت لِمُدَّة سَاعَتَيْن (with clothes) (تَدُلّ عَلَى ارْتِدَاء مَلْبَس)

O

He didn't have a coat on.
عَلَى (in position) لَم يَرْتَدِ مِعْطَفاً الشَيْء
Is the cap on? هَل الغَطَاء مَوْجُود؟
(light, computer) مُشْعَل
The television's on. التِلْفَاز مُشْعَل

once /wʌns/ *adv* مَرَّة

one /wʌn/ *num* وَاحِد
♦ *pron* شَخْص/أَشْخَاص مف/ج

oneself /wʌn'self/ *pron* نَفْسَهُ

ongoing /'ɒngəʊɪŋ/ *adj* مُسْتَمِرّ

onion /'ʌnjən/ *n* بَصَل

online /ɒn'laɪn/ *adj, adv* عَبْرَ الإِنْتَرْنِت

only /'əʊnli/ *adv* فَقَط
♦ *adj* وَحِيد

onward /'ɒnwəd/ *adv* **-ds** لِلأَمَام

open /'əʊpən/ *adj* (door, shop, etc) مَفْتُوح
♦ *v* (a door, shop, etc) يَفْتَح

opera /'ɒpərə/ *n* أُوبِرا

operate /'ɒpəreɪt/ *v* (in medicine) يُجْرِي عَمَلِيَّة جِرَاحِيَّة (a machine) يُشَغِّل (machines, etc) يَشْتَغِل

operation /ɒpə'reɪʃn/ *n* (in medicine) عَمَلِيَّة جِرَاحِيَّة (of machines) تَشْغِيل (mission) عَمَلِيَّة

operator /'ɒpəreɪtə(r)/ *n* عَامِل الهَاتِف

opinion /ə'pɪnjən/ *n* رَأْي/آرَاء مف/ج

opponent /ə'pəʊnənt/ *n* خَصْم/خُصُوم مف/ج

opportunity /ɒpə'tju:nəti/ *n* pl **-ties** فُرْصَة/فُرَص مف/ج

oppose /ə'pəʊz/ *v* يُعَارِض

opposite /'ɒpəzɪt/ *adj* مُعَاكِس
♦ *prep* أَمَامَ

opposition /ɒpə'zɪʃn/ *n* مُعَارَضَة

oppression /ə'preʃn/ *n* اضْطِهَاد

optical /'ɒptɪkl/ *adj* بَصَرِيّ

optimism /'ɒptɪmɪzəm/ *n* تَفَاؤُل

optimistic /ɒptɪ'mɪstɪk/ *adj* مُتَفَائِل

optional /'ɒpʃənl/ *adj* اخْتِيَارِيّ

or /ɔ:(r)/ *conj* أَو

oral /'ɔ:rəl/ *adj* شَفَهِيّ

orange /'ɒrɪnʤ/ *adj* بُرْتُقَالِيّ
♦ *n* (fruit) بُرْتُقَال (colour) اللَوْن البُرْتُقَالِيّ

orbit /'ɔ:bɪt/ *n* فَلَك/أَفْلَاك مف/ج

orchestra /'ɔ:kɪstrə/ *n* فِرْقَة مُوسِيقِيَّة

ordeal /'ɔ:di:l/ *n* مِحْنَة/مِحَن مف/ج

order /'ɔ:də(r)/ *n* (for goods, a meal) طَلَبِيَّة (command) أَمْر/أَوَامِرُ مف/ج (sequence) تَرْتِيب
♦ *v* (goods, a meal) يَطْلُب (to give

O

instructions to) يَأْمر (to organize) يُرَتِّب

ordinary /'ɔːdnri/ *adj* (batteries, paper) عَادِيّ (procedure) مُعْتَاد

oregano /ɒrɪ'gɑːnəʊ/ *n* تَابِل

organ /'ɔːgən/ *n* (body part) عُضْو/أَعْضَاء مف/ج (in music) أُرْغُن

organic /ɔː'gænɪk/ *adj* عُضْوِيّ

organization /ɔːgənaɪ'zeɪʃn/ *n* مُنَظَّمَة

organize /'ɔːgənaɪz/ *v* يُنَظِّم

origin /'ɒrɪʤɪn/ *n* أَصْل/أُصُول مف/ج

original /ə'rɪʤənl/ *adj* (interesting) جَدِيد (earliest) أَصْلِيّ

originally /ə'rɪʤənəli/ *adv* فِي الأَصْل

originate /ə'rɪʤɪneɪt/ *v* يُنْشِئ

orthodox /'ɔːθədɒks/ *adj* تَقْلِيدِيّ

other /'ʌðə(r)/ *adj* آخَر/أُخْرَى مف/ج

Ottawa /'ɒtəwə/ *n* أُوتَاوَا

ought /ɔːt/ *modal v* (obligation: ought to) يَجِب

I ought to go now. يَجِب أَنْ أَذْهَب الآن

(with recommendations) يَحْسُن

You ought to give up smoking. يَحْسُن أَنْ تُقْلِع عَن التَدْخِين

They ought not to behave like that. لَا يَحْسُن أَنْ يَتَصرَّفُوا كَذَلِكَ

our /'aʊə(r)/ *adj* لَنَا

This is our house. هَذَا بَيْتُنَا

ourselves /aʊə'selvz/ *pron* (reflexive) أَنْفُسَنَا

We hurt ourselves. جَرَحْنَا أَنْفُسَنَا (for emphasis) بِأَنْفُسِنَا

We built it ourselves. بَنَيْنَاهَا بِأَنْفُسِنَا

We were by ourselves. كُنَّا بِمُفْرَدِنَا

out /aʊt/ *adv* (to the outside) إِلَى الخَارِج

to walk out يَمْشِي إِلَى الخَارِج

When do they come out? مَتَى سَيَخْرُجُون؟ (not in) بِالخَارِج

The boss is out. المُدِير فِي الخَارِج (for sale) لِلبَيْع

outbreak /'aʊtbreɪk/ *n* نُشُوب

outcome /'aʊtkʌm/ *n* نَتِيجَة/نَتَائِج مف/ج

outdoor /'aʊtdɔː(r)/ *adj* خَارِجِيّ

outer /'aʊtə(r)/ *adj* خَارِجِيّ

outfit /'aʊtfɪt/ *n* طَقْم/أَطْقُم مف/ج

outing /'aʊtɪŋ/ *n* نُزْهَة

outline /'aʊtlaɪn/ *n* حَدّ/حُدُود مف/ج ♦ *v* يُوجِز

outlook /'aʊtlʊk/ *n* (future) مُسْتَقْبَل (attitude) وِجْهَة نَظَر مُتَوَقَّع

output /'aʊtpʊt/ *n* إِنْتَاج

outrage /'aʊtreɪʤ/ *n* غَضَب

outside /aʊt'saɪd/ *adj* خَارِجِيّ

O

♦ *prep* خَارِجَ

♦ *n* خَارِج الشَيْء

outsider /aʊt'saɪdə(r)/ *n* /دَخِيل دُخَلَاءُ مف/ج

outstanding /aʊt'stændɪŋ/ *adj* بَارِز

oven /'ʌvn/ *n* فُرْن/أَفْرَان مف/ج

over /'əʊvə/ *prep* (above) فَوْقَ

over my bed فَوْقَ سَرِيرِي

to fly over the city يُحَلِّق فَوْقَ المَدِينَة

(more than) أَكْثَر مِن

over forty students

أَكْثَر مِن أَرْبَعِين طَالِباً

over half the population

أَكْثَر مِن نِصْف عَدَد السُكَّان (on or to the other side of) عَلَى/إِلَى الجَانِب الآخَر مِن

She jumped over the fence.

قَفَزَت إِلَى الجَانِب الآخَر مِن السِيَاج

(covering) عَلَى

Put a cloth over the bread.

ضَع خِرْقَة عَلَى الخُبْز

♦ *adv* (to a lower position) عَلَى الأَرْض

He fell over. سَقَطَ عَلَى الأَرْض (to the opposite side) عَلَى الوَجْه الآخَر

to turn the mattress over

يَقْلِب الفَرْشَة عَلَى الوَجْه الآخَر (to a place, person) نَحْوَ مَكَان مُعَيَّن

He came over for a chat.

جَاءَ إِلَى هُنَا مِن أَجْل الدَرْدَشَة (finished) مُنْتَهٍ

The show was over by 10.

كَانَ العَرْض مُنْتَهِياً عِنْدَ العَاشِرَة

Their marriage is over.

لَقَد انْتَهَى زَوَاجُهُمَا

overcome /əʊvə'kʌm/ *v* **-came, -come** يَتَغَلَّب عَلَى

overlook /əʊvə'lʊk/ *v* يَتَغَاضَى عَن

overnight /əʊvə'naɪt/ *adv* طِوَالَ اللَيْلَة

overseas /əʊvə'si:z/ *adj* عَبْرَ البِحَار

oversee /əʊvə'si:/ *v* **-saw, -seen** يُشْرِف عَلَى

oversight /'əʊvəsaɪt/ *n* سَهْو

overtake /əʊvə'teɪk/ *v* **-took, -taken** يَتَجَاوَز

overthrow /əʊvə'θrəʊ/ *v* **-threw, -thrown** يُطِيح

overturn /əʊvə'tɜ:n/ *v* يَقْلِب

overweight /əʊvə'weɪt/ *adj* وَزن زَائِد

owe /əʊ/ *v* يَدِين

own /əʊn/ *adj* خَاصّ بِه

♦ *v* يَمْلُك

owner /'əʊnə(r)/ *n* مَالِك/مُلَاَّك مف/ج

oxygen /'ɒksɪdʒən/ *n* أُكْسِجِين

P

Pacific Ocean /pə'sɪfɪk/ *n* المُحِيط الهَادِئ

pack /pæk/ *v* يَحْزِم

package /'pækɪʤ/ *n* طَرْد/طُرُود مف/ج

packet /'pækɪt/ *n* عُلْبَة/عُلَب مف/ج

pad /pæd/ *n* إِضْمَامَة

paediatrician /pi:diə'trɪʃn/ *n* طَبِيب أَطْفَال

page /peɪʤ/ *n* (in book) وَرَقَة/أَوْرَاق مف/ج (one side) صَفْحَة
 ♦ *v* يُرْسِل رِسَالَة

P

pager /'peɪʤə(r)/ *n* جِهَاز إِلِكْتْرُونِيّ مَحْمُول لِاسْتِقْبَال الرَسَائِل

pain /peɪn/ *n* أَلَم/آلَام مف/ج

painful /'peɪnfl/ *adj* مُؤْلِم

paint /peɪnt/ *n* طِلَاء
 ♦ *v* (a surface) يَدْهَن (a picture) يَرْسُم

painter /'peɪntə(r)/ *n* دَهَّان

painting /'peɪntɪŋ/ *n* لَوْحَة

pair /peə(r)/ *n* زَوْج/أَزْوَاج مف/ج

Pakistan /ˌpɑ:kɪ'stɑ:n/ *n* بَاكِسْتَان

palace /'pæləs/ *n* قَصْر/قُصُور مف/ج

pale /peɪl/ *adj* (almost white) شَاحِب (weak: colours) بَاهِت

Palestine /'palɪstaɪn/ *n* فِلِسْطِين

Palestinian /palə'stɪnɪən/ *adj, n* فِلِسْطِينِيّ ص/س

palm /pɑ:m/ *n* (of the hand) رَاحَة اليَد

 palm (tree) *n* (tree: producing coconuts) شَجَرَة جَوْز الهِنْد

 (: producing dates) نَخْلَة/نَخِيل مف/ج

pan /pæn/ *n* قِدْر/قُدُور مف/ج

pancake /'pænkeɪk/ *n* فَطِيرَة

panic /'pænɪk/ *n* هَلَع

paper /'peɪpə(r)/ *n* وَرَقَة/أَوْرَاق مف/ج

 papers *n pl* (documents) وَثِيقَة

paprika /'pæprɪkə/ *n* فِلْفِل حُلْو

parade /pə'reɪd/ *n* اسْتِعْرَاض

paragraph /'pærəgrɑ:f/ *n* فَقْرَة

parallel /'pærəlel/ *adj* مُتَوَازٍ

paramedic /pærə'medɪk/ *n* مُسْعِف

parcel /'pɑ:sl/ *n* طَرْد/طُرُود مف/ج

parent /'peərənt/ *n* أَب أَو أُمّ

parental /pə'rentl/ *adj* مُتَعَلِّق بِالأَبَوَيْن

Paris /'pærɪs/ *n* بَارِيس

park /pɑ:k/ *n* حَدِيقَة/حَدَائِقُ مف/ج

♦ *v* يُرْكِن سَيَّارَة

parking /ˈpɑːkɪŋ/ *n* إِرْكَان السَيَّارَة

parking lot *n* US مَوْقِف سَيَّارَات

parliament /ˈpɑːləmənt/ *n* مَجْلِس النُوَّاب

parliamentary /pɑːləˈmentri/ *adj* نِيَابِيّ

parsley /ˈpɑːsli/ *n* بَقْدُونِس

part /pɑːt/ *n* (piece) جُزْء/أَجْزَاء مف/ج (for a car, etc) قِطْعَة/قِطَع مف/ج
♦ *v* (company) يَفْصِل

partial /ˈpɑːʃl/ *adj* جُزْئِيّ

participant /pɑːˈtɪsɪpənt/ *n* مُشَارِك

participate /pɑːˈtɪsɪpeɪt/ *v* يُشَارِك

participation /pɑːtɪsɪˈpeɪʃn/ *n* مُشَارَكَة

particle /ˈpɑːtɪkl/ *n* جُسَيْم/جُسَيْمَات مف/ج

particular /pəˈtɪkjələ(r)/ *adj* (special) خَاصّ (specific) مُحَدَّد

partly /ˈpɑːtli/ *adv* جُزْئِيّاً

partner /ˈpɑːtnə(r)/ *n* (associate) زَمِيل/زُمَلَاءُ مف/ج (in games) شَرِيك

partnership /ˈpɑːtnəʃɪp/ *n* شَرَاكَة

party /ˈpɑːti/ *n* pl **-ties** (group of people) جَمَاعَة (in politics) حِزْب/أَحْزَاب مف/ج (occasion) حَفْلَة

pass /pɑːs/ *v* (people, cars) يَمُرّ عَن (days, hours) يَنْقَضِي (an exam) يَنْجَح (the salt, etc) يُعْطِي (in football, etc) يُمَرِّر (a car, etc) يَتَجَاوَز
♦ *n* (in exams) نَجَاح (in football, etc) تَمْرِيرَة

passage /ˈpæsɪdʒ/ *n* مَمَرّ/مَمَرَّات مف/ج

passenger /ˈpæsɪndʒə(r)/ *n* رَاكِب/رُكَّاب مف/ج

passion /ˈpæʃn/ *n* (emotion) عَاطِفَة/عَوَاطِفُ مف/ج

passion fruit *n* زَهْرَة الآلَام

passport /ˈpɑːspɔːt/ *n* جَوَاز سَفَر

password /ˈpɑːswɜːd/ *n* كَلِمَة المُرُور

past /pɑːst/ *adj* (events) مَاضٍ (week, year) مُنْصَرِم
♦ *n* المَاضِي
♦ *prep* بَعْدَ
♦ *adv* مَارّاً عَن

pasta /ˈpæstə/ *n* مَكَرُونَة

paste /peɪst/ *n* مَعْجُون/مَعَاجِينُ مف/ج

pastry /ˈpeɪstri/ *n* مُعَجَّنَات

pat /pæt/ *v* يُمَلِّس

path /pɑːθ/ *n* طَرِيق/طُرُق مف/ج

pathetic /pəˈθetɪk/ *adj* مُحْزِن

patience /ˈpeɪʃns/ *n* صَبْر

patient /ˈpeɪʃnt/ *adj* صَبُور
♦ *n* مَرِيض/مَرْضَى مف/ج

patriotic /pætriˈɒtɪk/ *adj* وَطَنِيّ

patrol /pəˈtrəʊl/ *n* دَوْرِيَّة

P

♦ *v* يَقُوم بِدَوْرِيَّة

patron /'peɪtrən/ *n* زَبُون دَائِم

pattern /'pætn/ *n* نَمُوذَج/نَمَاذِج مف/ج

pause /pɔ:z/ *v* يَتَوَقَّف لِبُرْهَة
♦ *n* تَوَقُّف قَصِير

pavement /'peɪvmənt/ *n* رَصِيف/أَرْصِفَة مف/ج

pawpaw /'pɔ:pɔ:/ *n* ثَمَرَة البَابُو

pay /peɪ/ *n* أَجْر/أُجُور مف/ج
♦ *v* **paid** يَدْفَع

payment /'peɪmənt/ *n* دُفْعَة

payroll /'peɪrəʊl/ *n* كَشْف الأُجُور

PC /pi:'si:/ *n* حَاسُوب شَخْصِيّ

pea /pi:/ *n* بَازِلَّا

peace /pi:s/ *n* سَلَام

peach /pi:tʃ/ *n* خَوْخ

peaceful /'pi:sfl/ *adj* سِلْمِيّ

peak /pi:k/ *n* (mountain) ذُرْوَة (high point) أَوْج

peanut /'pi:nʌt/ *n* فُسْتُق سُودَانِيّ

pearl /pɜ:l/ *n* لُؤْلُؤَة/لَآلِئ مف/ج

peasant /'peznt/ *n* فَلَّاح

peculiar /pɪ'kju:liə(r)/ *adj* غَرِيب/غُرَبَاء مف/ج

pedestrian /pə'destriən/ *n* مَاشٍ/مُشَاة مف/ج

pediatrician /pi:diə'trɪʃn/ *n* US طَبِيب أَطْفَال

peel /pi:l/ *v* يُقَشِّر

pen /pen/ *n* قَلَم

penalty /'penəlti/ *n* pl **-ties** (in law) عُقُوبَة (in sports, games) جَزَاء

penalty kick *n* ضَرْبَة جَزَاء

pencil /'pensl/ *n* قَلَم رَصَاص

penetrate /'penɪtreɪt/ *v* يَخْتَرِق

peninsula /pə'nɪnsjələ/ *n* شِبْه جَزِيرَة

penny /'peni/ *n* pl **-nies** بِنْس: 1/100 مِن الجُنَيْه الإِسْتَرْلِينِيّ

pension /'penʃn/ *n* مَعَاش التَقَاعُد

pensioner /'penʃənə(r)/ *n* مُتَقَاعِد

people /'pi:pl/ *n* (nation etc) شَعْب/شُعُوب مف/ج (humans) نَاس

pepper /'pepə(r)/ *n* فِلْفِل

peppermint /'pepəmɪnt/ *n* نَعْنَاع

percent /pə'sent/ *n* بِالمِائَة
ten percent عَشَرَة بِالمِائَة

percentage /pə'sentɪdʒ/ *n* نِسْبَة مِئَوِيَّة

perfect /'pɜ:fɪkt/ *adj* كَامِل

perfection /pə'fekʃn/ *n* كَمَال

perfectly /'pɜ:fɪktli/ *adv* بِالكَامِل

perform /pə'fɔ:m/ *v* (a task, an operation) يُنْجِز (actors, etc) يُؤَدِّي

performance /pə'fɔ:məns/ *n* أَدَاء

performer /pə'fɔ:mə(r)/ *n* مُؤَدٍّ

period /'pɪəriəd/ *n* (in history) عَصْر/عُصُور مف/ج (a time of) فَتْرَة (in sentence) نُقْطَة/نِقَاط مف/ج

P

(woman's) دَوْرَة شَهْرِيَّة

permanent /'pɜːmənənt/ *adj* دَائِم

permission /pə'mɪʃn/ *n* تَصْرِيح/تَصَارِيحُ مف/ج

permit /pə'mɪt/ *v* يَسْمَح ♦ *n* /'pɜːmɪt/ تَصْرِيح/تَصَارِيحُ مف/ج

persistent /pə'sɪstənt/ *adj* مُثَابِر

person /'pɜːsn/ *n* pl **people** شَخْص/أَشْخَاص مف/ج

personal /'pɜːsənl/ *adj* شَخْصِيّ

personality /pɜːsə'næləti/ *n* pl **-ties** شَخْصِيَّة

personnel /pɜːsə'nel/ *n* أَفْرَاد العَمَل

perspective /pə'spektɪv/ *n* وُجْهَة نَظَر

persuade /pə'sweɪd/ *v* يُقْنِع

pest /pest/ *n* حَشَرَة

pet /pet/ *n* حَيَوَان أَلِيف

petition /pə'tɪʃn/ *n* عَرِيضَة/عَرَائِضُ مف/ج

petrol /'petrəl/ *n* بَنْزِين

pharmacist /'fɑːməsɪst/ *n* صَيْدَلَانِيّ/صَيَادِلَة مف/ج

pharmacy /'fɑːməsi/ *n* pl **-cies** صَيْدَلِيَّة

phase /feɪz/ *n* مَرْحَلَة/مَرَاحِلُ مف/ج

phenomenal /fə'nɒmɪnl/ *adj* رَائِع

Philippines /'fɪlɪpiːnz/ *n pl* الفِلِبِّين

philosopher /fə'lɒsəfə(r)/ *n* فَيْلَسُوف/فَلَاسِفَة مف/ج

philosophy /fə'lɒsəfi/ *n* الفَلْسَفَة

phone /fəʊn/ *n* هَاتِف/هَوَاتِفُ مف/ج ♦ *v* يُهَاتِف

photo /'fəʊtəʊ/ *n* صُورَة فُوتُوغْرَافِيَّة/صُوَر مف/ج

photograph /'fəʊtəgrɑːf/ *v* يُصَوِّر

photographer /fə'tɒgrəfə(r)/ *n* مُصَوِّر فُوتُوغْرَافِيّ

photography /fə'tɒgrəfi/ *n* التَصْوِير الفُوتُوغْرَافِيّ

phrase /freɪz/ *n* عِبَارَة

physical /'fɪzɪkl/ *adj* بَدَنِيّ

physician /fɪ'zɪʃn/ *n* طَبِيب عَامّ

physicist /'fɪzɪsɪst/ *n* فِيزْيَائِيّ

physics /'fɪzɪks/ *n* الفِيزْيَاء

pianist /'pɪənɪst/ *n* عَازِف بِيَانُو

piano /pi'ænəʊ/ *n* بِيَانُو

pick /pɪk/ *n* مِعْوَل/مَعَاوِلُ مف/ج ♦ *v* (fruit, vegetables) يَقْطِف (to choose) يَخْتَار

pickle /'pɪkl/ *n* مُخَلَّل

picnic /'pɪknɪk/ *n* نُزْهَة

picture /'pɪktʃə(r)/ *n* (image) صُورَة/صُوَر مف/ج (painting) لَوْحَة

pie /paɪ/ *n* فَطِيرَة/فَطَائِرُ مف/ج

piece /piːs/ *n* (of wood, etc) قِطْعَة/قِطَع مف/ج (component) جُزْء/أَجْزَاء مف/ج (in chess, etc) قِطْعَة/قِطَع مف/ج

pierce /pɪəs/ *v* يَثْقُب

P

pig /pɪg/ *n* خِنْزِير/خَنَازِيرُ مف/ج

pile /paɪl/ *n* كُومَة/أَكْوَام مف/ج

pile up *phv* يُكَوِّم

pilgrim /ˈpɪlgrɪm/ *n* حَاجّ/حُجَّاج مف/ج

pilgrimage /ˈpɪlgrɪmɪʤ/ *n* حَجّ

to go on a pilgrimage يَذْهَب إِلَى الحَجّ

the pilgrimage to Mecca الحَجّ إِلَى مَكَّة

pill /pɪl/ *n* قُرْص/أَقْرَاص مف/ج

pillar /ˈpɪlə(r)/ *n* عَمُود/أَعْمِدَة مف/ج

pillow /ˈpɪləʊ/ *n* وِسَادَة

pilot /ˈpaɪlət/ *n* (of an aircraft) طَيَّار (of a ship) قُبْطَان السَفِينَة

pimento /pɪˈmentəʊ/ *n* فِلْفِل أَحْمَر حُلْو

pin /pɪn/ *n* دَبُّوس/دَبَابِيسُ مف/ج

♦ *v* (a curtain, dress) ثَبَّتَ بِدَبُّوس

P

pine /paɪn/ *n* صَنَوْبَر

pineapple /ˈpaɪnæpl/ *n* أَنَانَاس

pink /pɪŋk/ *adj* زَهْرِيّ

pioneer /paɪəˈnɪə(r)/ *n* رَائِد/رُوَّاد مف/ج

pipe /paɪp/ *n* (tube) أُنْبُوب/أَنَابِيبُ مف/ج (for smoking) غَلْيُون

pipeline /ˈpaɪplaɪn/ *n* خَطّ أَنَابِيب

pirate /ˈpaɪrət/ *n* قُرْصَان/قَرَاصِنَة مف/ج

pistol /ˈpɪstl/ *n* مُسَدَّس/مُسَدَّسَات مف/ج

pitcher /ˈpɪtʃə(r)/ *n* إِبْرِيق/أَبَارِيقُ مف/ج

pitta /ˈpiːtə/ *n* رَغِيف مُدَوَّر

pity /ˈpɪti/ *n* شَفَقَة

pizza /ˈpiːtsə/ *n* بِيتْزَا

place /pleɪs/ *n* مَكَان/أَمَاكِنُ مف/ج

plain /pleɪn/ *adj* صَافٍ

♦ *n* سَهْل/سُهُول مف/ج

plan /plæn/ *n* (for action) خُطَّة/خُطَط (drawing) تَصْمِيم/تَصْمِيمَات مف/ج مف/ج

♦ *v* يُخَطِّط

plane /pleɪn/ *n* طَائِرَة

planet /ˈplænɪt/ *n* كَوْكَب/كَوَاكِبُ مف/ج

plant /plɑːnt/ *n* نَبَات/نَبَاتَات مف/ج

♦ *v* يَزْرَع

plantation /plɑːnˈteɪʃn/ *n* مَزْرَعَة/ مَزَارِعُ مف/ج

plastic /ˈplæstɪk/ *adj* بِلَاسْتِيكِيّ

♦ *n* بِلَاسْتِيك

plate /pleɪt/ *n* (for food) طَبَق/أَطْبَاق (metal sheet) شَرِيحَة/شَرَائِحُ مف/ج مف/ج

platform /ˈplætfɔːm/ *n* رَصِيف/ أَرْصِفَة مف/ج

play /pleɪ/ *v* (children) يَلْعَب (the drums, guitar) يَعْزِف

♦ *n* (children's) لَعِب (drama) مَسْرَحِيَّة

player /ˈpleɪə(r)/ *n* لَاعِب

playful /ˈpleɪfl/ *adj* مُدَاعِب

playground /'pleɪgraʊnd/ *n* مَلْعَب/ مَلَاعِبُ مف/ج

playlist /'pleɪlɪst/ *n* قَائِمَة الأَغَانِي المُسَجَّلَة

play-off /'pleɪɒf/ *n* شَوْطَيْن إِضَافِيَّيْن

plead /pli:d/ *v* يَتَوَسَّل

pleasant /'pleznt/ *adj* (view, surprise) سَارّ (person) لَطِيف

please /pli:z/ *v* (one's parents, the audience) يُسْعِد (as request) مِن فَضْلِكَ *Two coffees, please!* فِنْجَانَيْن قَهْوَة مِن فَضْلِكَ (to an offer) *Yes, please!* نَعَم إِذَا سَمَحْتَ!

pleasure /'pleʒə(r)/ *n* (satisfaction) مُتْعَة/مُتَع (enjoyment) سُرُور

pledge /pledʒ/ *v* يَتَعَهَّد

plot /plɒt/ *n* (plan) مُؤَامَرَة (of a novel) حَبْكَة الرِوَايَة (of land) قِطْعَة أَرْض ♦ *v* يَتَآمَر

plug /plʌg/ *n* (for electricity) قَابِس/ قَوَابِسُ مف/ج (for sinks) سَدَّادَة

plum /plʌm/ *n* بَرْقُوق

plumber /'plʌmə(r)/ *n* سَمْكَرِيّ/ سَمَاكِرَة مف/ج

plunge /plʌndʒ/ *v* يَغْطُس

plus /plʌs/ *prep* إِضَافَةً إِلَى

pneumonia /nju:'məʊniə/ *n* الْتِهَاب رِئَوِيّ

pocket /'pɒkɪt/ *n* جَيْب/جُيُوب مف/ج

poem /'pəʊɪm/ *n* قَصِيدَة/قَصَائِدُ مف/ج

poet /'pəʊɪt/ *n* شَاعِر/شُعَرَاءُ

poetry /'pəʊətri/ *n* شِعْر

point /pɔɪnt/ *n* (sharp end) رَأْس/ رُؤُوس مف/ج (purpose) الفِكْرَة الرَئِيسِيَّة ♦ *v* يُشِير إِلَى

pointless /'pɔɪntləs/ *adj* عَدِيم الفَائِدَة

poison /'pɔɪzn/ *n* سَمّ/سُمُوم مف/ج ♦ *v* يُسَمِّم

Poland /'pəʊlənd/ *n* بُولَنْدَا

pole /pəʊl/ *n* عَمُود/أَعْمِدَة مف/ج

Pole /pəʊl/ *n* بُولَنْدِيّ

police /pə'li:s/ *n* شُرْطَة

policeman /pə'li:smən/ *n* pl **-men** شُرْطِيّ/رِجَال الشُرْطَة مف/ج

policewoman /pə'li:swʊmən/ *n* pl **-men** شُرْطِيَّة

policy /'pɒləsi/ *n* pl **-cies** (plan) سِيَاسَة (in insurance) شِهَادَة التَأْمِين

polish /'pɒlɪʃ/ *n* مَادَّة مُلَمِّعَة

Polish /'pəʊlɪʃ/ *adj* بُولَنْدِيّ ♦ *n* اللُغَة البُولَنْدِيَّة

polite /pə'laɪt/ *adj* مُهَذَّب

political /pə'lɪtɪkl/ *adj* سِيَاسِيّ

politician /pɒlə'tɪʃn/ *n* سِيَاسِيّ

pollution /pə'lu:ʃn/ *n* تَلَوُّث

pomegranate /'pɒmɪgrænɪt/ *n* رُمَّان

pond /pɒnd/ *n* مُسْتَنْقَع/مُسْتَنْقَعَات مف/ج

P

pool /puːl/ *n* بِرْكَة/بِرَك مف/ج

poor /pʊə(r)/ *adj* (country, person) فَقِير/فُقَرَاءُ مف/ج
This is a poor area. هٰذِهِ مِنْطَقَة فَقِيرَة
The family was poor. كَانَت العَائِلَة فَقِيرَة
(results, sales) ضَعِيف/ضُعَفَاءُ مف/ج
Prospects are poor. الِاحْتِمَالَات ضَعِيفَة
♦ *n* الفُقَرَاء

popcorn /'pɒpkɔːn/ *n* فُشَار، حَبّ الذُرَة مَشْوِيّ حَتَّى يَتَفَتَّح

pope /pəʊp/ *n* البَابَا

popular /'pɒpjələ(r)/ *adj* (well liked) مَحْبُوب (of the people) شَعْبِيّ

popularity /pɒpju'lærəti/ *n* شَعْبِيَّة

population /pɒpju'leɪʃn/ *n* سُكَّان

porch /pɔːtʃ/ *n* شُرْفَة/شُرَف مف/ج

pork /pɔːk/ *n* لَحْم الخِنْزِير

port /pɔːt/ *n* (harbour) مِينَاء/مَوَانٍ مف/ج (on a computer) مَخْرَج/مَخَارِجُ مف/ج

portable /'pɔːtəbl/ *adj* مَحْمُول

porter /'pɔːtə(r)/ *n* حَمَّال

portion /'pɔːʃn/ *n* (part of a whole) جُزْء/أَجْزَاء مف/ج (of food) حِصَّة/حِصَص مف/ج

portrait /'pɔːtreɪt/ *n* صُورَة/صُوَر مف/ج

Portugal /'pɔːtjʊg(ə)l/ *n* البُرْتُغَال

Portuguese /pɔːtjʊ'giːz/ *adj* بُرْتُغَالِيّ
♦ *n* (language) اللُغَة البُرْتُغَالِيَّة (people) بُرْتُغَالِيّ

pose /pəʊz/ *v* يَسْتَوْضِع

position /pə'zɪʃn/ *n* (place) مَكَان/مَوْقِع/مَوَاقِعُ مف/ج (job) أَمْكِنَة مف/ج

positive /'pɒzətɪv/ *adj* (reply) مُتَأَكِّد (attitude, result) إِيجَابِيّ

positively /'pɒzətɪvli/ *adv* بِشَكْل إِيجَابِيّ

possess /pə'zes/ *v* يَمْتَلِك

possession /pə'zeʃn/ *n* مُمْتَلَك/مُمْتَلَكَات مف/ج

possibility /pɒsə'bɪləti/ *n* pl **-ties** احْتِمَالِيَّة

possible /'pɒsəbl/ *adj* مُحْتَمَل

post /pəʊst/ *n* (for fence) عَمُود/أَعْمِدَة مف/ج (job) وَظِيفَة/وَظَائِفُ مف/ج (mail) بَرِيد
♦ *v* يُرْسِل بِالبَرِيد

poster /'pəʊstə(r)/ *n* (for advertising) إِعْلَان/إِعْلَانَات مف/ج (on the Internet) مُرْسِل

postman /'pəʊstmən/ *n* pl **-men** سَاعِي البَرِيد/سُعَاة مف/ج

postpone /pə'spəʊn/ *v* يُؤَجِّل

posture /'pɒstʃə(r)/ *n* وَضْع/أَوْضَاع مف/ج

pot /pɒt/ *n* قِدْر/قُدُور مف/ج

potato /pə'teɪtəʊ/ *n* بَطَاطَا

potential /pə'tenʃl/ *adj* مُحْتَمَل
♦ *n* إِمْكَانِيَّة

pound /paʊnd/ *n* جُنَيْه إِسْتَرْلِينِيّ

pour /pɔː(r)/ *v* (tea, water) يَسْكُب (to flow) يَصُبّ

poverty /ˈpɒvəti/ *n* فَقْر

powder /ˈpaʊdə(r)/ *n* مَسْحُوق/مَسَاحِيقُ مف/ج

power /ˈpaʊə(r)/ *n* (physical) قُوَّة/قُوَى مف/ج (political) سُلْطَة (electrical) طَاقَة

powerful /ˈpaʊəfl/ *adj* قَوِيّ

practical /ˈpræktɪkl/ *adj* عَمَلِيّ

practically /ˈpræktɪkli/ *adv* عَمَلِيّاً

practice /ˈpræktɪs/ *n* (for music, sport) تَمْرِين/تَمْرِينَات مف/ج (procedure) مُمَارَسَة

practise /ˈpræktɪs/ *v* US **-tice** يَتَدَرَّب

praise /preɪz/ *n* إِطْرَاء/إِطْرَاءَات مف/ج ♦ *v* يَمْدَح

prawn /prɔːn/ *n* سَمَك القُرَيْدِس

pray /preɪ/ *v* يُصَلِّي

prayer /preə(r)/ *n* صَلَاة/صَلَوَات مف/ج

preach /priːtʃ/ *v* يُوعِظ

precaution /prɪˈkɔːʃn/ *n* وِقَايَة

precede /prɪˈsiːd/ *v* يَسْبِق زَمَنِيّاً

precious /ˈpreʃəs/ *adj* غَالٍ

precise /prɪˈsaɪs/ *adj* دَقِيق

precisely /prɪˈsaɪsli/ *adv* بِدِقَّة

precision /prɪˈsɪʒn/ *n* دِقَّة

predecessor /ˈpriːdɪsesə(r)/ *n* سَلَف/أَسْلَاف مف/ج

predict /prɪˈdɪkt/ *v* يَتَنَبَّأ

predictable /prɪˈdɪktəbl/ *adj* مُمْكِن التَنَبُّؤ بِهِ

prediction /prɪˈdɪkʃn/ *n* تَنَبُّؤ

prefer /prɪˈfɜː(r)/ *v* يُفَضِّل

He prefers coffee to tea.

يُفَضِّل القَهْوَة عَلَى الشَاي

I prefer to stay at home.

أُفَضِّل البَقَاء فِي البَيْت

preference /ˈprefrəns/ *n* تَفْضِيل/تَفْضِيلَات مف/ج

pregnancy /ˈpregnənsi/ *n* pl **-cies** حَمْل

pregnant /ˈpregnənt/ *adj* حَامِل/حَوَامِلُ مف/ج

prejudice /ˈpredʒudɪs/ *n* تَحَيُّز

preliminary /prɪˈlɪmɪnəri/ *adj* تَمْهِيدِيّ

premature /ˈpremətʃə(r)/ *adj* خَدِيج/خُدَّج مف/ج

premium /ˈpriːmiəm/ *n* قِسْط/أَقْسَاط مف/ج

preparation /prepəˈreɪʃn/ *n* إِعْدَاد/إِعْدَادَات مف/ج

prepare /prɪˈpeə(r)/ *v* (a speech, a meal) يُعِدّ (oneself) يُجَهِّز

prescribe /prɪˈskraɪb/ *v* يُوصِف

prescription /prɪˈskrɪpʃn/ *n* وَصْفَة طِبِّيَّة

P

presence /'prezns/ *n* حُضُور

present /'preznt/ *adj* (being there) حَالِ (current) حَاضِر

♦ *n* /'preznt/ (gift) هَدِيَّة/هَدَايَا مف/ج (in time) الحَاضِر

♦ *v* /prɪ'zent/ (the prizes) يُقَدِّم (a plan) يَعْرِض

presentation /prezn'teɪʃn/ *n* تَقْدِيم

presently /'prezntli/ *adv* الآن

preservation /prezə'veɪʃn/ *n* حِفْظ

preservative /prɪ'zɜːvətɪv/ *n* مَوَادّ حَافِظَة

preserve /prɪ'zɜːv/ *v* (fruit, meat) يُحَافِظ عَلَى (our heritage) يَحْفَظ

president /'prezɪdənt/ *n* رَئِيس/رُؤَسَاءُ مف/ج

press /pres/ *n* صَحَافَة

♦ *v* (the button) يَضْغَط

P

pressure /'preʃə(r)/ *n* ضَغْط/ضُغُوط مف/ج

prestige /pre'stiːʒ/ *n* احْتِرَام

prestigious /pre'stɪdʒəs/ *adj* مَرْمُوق

presumably /prɪ'zjuːməbli/ *adv* من المُحْتَمَل

pretend /prɪ'tend/ *v* يَدَّعِي

pretty /'prɪti/ *adj* (dress, flower) جَمِيل

♦ *adv* إِلَى حَدّ مَا

prevent /prɪ'vent/ *v* (sb from doing sth) يَمْنَع (sth from happening) يَحُول دُونَ

prevention /prɪ'venʃn/ *n* مَنْع

previous /'priːviəs/ *adj* سَابِق

previously /'priːviəsli/ *adv* سَابِقاً

price /praɪs/ *n* سِعْر/أَسْعَار مف/ج

♦ *v* يُسَعِّر

pride /praɪd/ *n* فَخْر

priest /priːst/ *n* كَاهِن/كَهَنَة مف/ج

primarily /praɪ'merəli/ *adv* بِشَكْل رَئِيسِيّ

primary /'praɪməri/ *adj* (function) رَئِيسِيّ (education) ابْتِدَائِيّ

prime /praɪm/ *adj* رَئِيسِيّ

prince /prɪns/ *n* أَمِير/أُمَرَاءُ مف/ج

princess /prɪn'ses/ *n* أَمِيرَة

principal /'prɪnsəpl/ *adj* أَسَاسِيّ

♦ *n* (of a school) مُدِير/مُدَرَاءُ مف/ج (of a college, etc) رَئِيس/رُؤَسَاءُ مف/ج

principle /'prɪnsəpl/ *n* (theory) قَاعِدَة/قَوَاعِدُ مف/ج (moral rule) مَبْدَأ/مَبَادِئُ مف/ج

print /prɪnt/ *n* (reproduction) طِبَاعَة (of a photograph) صُورَة مَطْبُوعَة

♦ *v* يَطْبَع

printer /'prɪntə(r)/ *n* آلَة طَابِعَة

prior /'praɪə(r)/ *adj* سَابِق

priority /praɪ'ɒrəti/ *n* pl **-ties** أَوْلَوِيَّة

prison /'prɪzn/ *n* سِجْن/سُجُون مف/ج

prisoner /'prɪznə(r)/ *n* (in jail) سَجِين/سُجَنَاءُ مف/ج (of war) أَسِير/أَسْرَى مف/ج

privacy /'prɪvəsi/ *n* خُصُوصِيَّة

private /'praɪvət/ *adj* خَاصّ

privilege /'prɪvəlɪʤ/ *n* امْتِيَاز/ امْتِيَازَات مف/ج

privileged /'prɪvəlɪʤd/ *adj* مُمَيَّز

prize /praɪz/ *n* جَائِزَة/جَوَائِز

probability /prɒbə'bɪləti/ *n* احْتِمَالِيَّة

probably /'prɒbəbli/ *adv* مِن المُحْتَمَل

problem /'prɒbləm/ *n* (difficulty) مَسْأَلَة/مَسَائِلُ مف/ج (in maths) مُشْكِلَة

procedure /prə'siːʤə(r)/ *n* إِجْرَاء/ إِجْرَاءَات مف/ج

proceed /prə'siːd/ *v* يُوَاصِل

process /'prəʊses/ *n* عَمَلِيَّة

procession /prə'seʃn/ *n* مَوْكِب/ مَوَاكِبُ مف/ج

proclaim /prə'kleɪm/ *v* يُصَرِّح

produce /prə'djuːs/ *v* يُنْتِج
♦ /'prɒdjuːs/ *n* سِلْعَة/سِلَع مف/ج

producer /prə'djuːsə(r)/ *n* مُنْتِج

product /'prɒdʌkt/ *n* مُنْتَج/مُنْتَجَات مف/ج

production /prə'dʌkʃn/ *n* إِنْتَاج

productive /prə'dʌktɪv/ *adj* مُنْتِج

productivity /prɒdʌk'tɪvəti/ *n* إِنْتَاجِيَّة

profession /prə'feʃn/ *n* مِهْنَة/مِهَن مف/ج

professional /prə'feʃənl/ *adj* مُحْتَرِف

professor /prə'fesə(r)/ *n* أُسْتَاذ جَامِعِيّ

profit /'prɒfɪt/ *n* (money) رِبْح/أَرْبَاح مف/ج (advantage) فَائِدَة/فَوَائِدُ مف/ج
♦ *v* يَسْتَفِيد

profitable /'prɒfɪtəbl/ *adj* مُرْبِح

program /'prəʊgræm/ *n* (computing) بَرْنَامَج/بَرَامِجُ مف/ج

programme /'prəʊgræm/ *n* US -gram (schedule) بَرْنَامَج/بَرَامِجُ مف/ج

progress /prə'gres/ *v* يَتَقَدَّم
♦ /'prəʊgres/ *n* تَقَدُّم

progression /prə'greʃn/ *n* تَعَاقُب

progressive /prə'gresɪv/ *adj* (improvement) مُتَوَالٍ (reformer) تَقَدُّمِيّ

prohibit /prə'hɪbɪt/ *v* يَمْنَع

prohibition /prəʊɪ'bɪʃn/ *n* مَنْع

project /'prɒʤekt/ *n* مَشْرُوع/ مَشَارِيعُ مف/ج

prolong /prə'lɒŋ/ *v* يُطَوِّل

prominent /'prɒmɪnənt/ *adj* شَهِير

promise /'prɒmɪs/ *n* وَعْد/وُعُود مف/ج
♦ *v* يُوعِد

promote /prə'məʊt/ *v* (an officer, a civil servant) يُرَقِّي (a product, a theory) يُعَزِّز

promotion /prə'məʊʃn/ *n* (of

P

a soldier, employee) تَرْقِيَة (in marketing) تَرْوِيج

pronounce /prə'naʊns/ *v* يَنْطِق

proof /pru:f/ *n* دَلِيل/دَلَائِلُ وَأَدِلَّة مف/ج

propaganda /prɒpə'gændə/ *n* دِعَايَة

propel /prə'pel/ *v* يُسَيِّر

proper /'prɒpə(r)/ *adj* مُنَاسِب

properly /'prɒpəli/ *adv* بِشَكْل مُنَاسِب

property /'prɒpəti/ *n* pl **-ties** (characteristic) خَاصِّيَّة/خَصَائِصُ (land, possessions) مِلْكِيَّة مف/ج

prophet /'prɒfɪt/ *n* نَبِيّ/أَنْبِيَاءُ مف/ج *the Prophet Muhammad* النَبِيّ مُحَمَّد

proportion /prə'pɔ:ʃn/ *n* نِسْبَة/ نِسَب مف/ج

proportional /prə'pɔ:ʃənl/ *adj* تَنَاسُبِيّ

proposal /prə'pəʊzl/ *n* اقْتِرَاح/ اقْتِرَاحَات مف/ج

propose /prə'pəʊz/ *v* يَقْتَرِح

proposed /prə'pəʊzd/ *adj* مُقْتَرَح

prosecute /'prɒsɪkju:t/ *v* يُقَاضِي

prosecution /prɒsɪ'kju:ʃn/ *n* مُقَاضَاة

prosecutor /'prɒsɪkju:tə(r)/ *n* الْمُدَّعِي العَامّ

prospect /'prɒspekt/ *n* احْتِمَال/ احْتِمَالَات مف/ج

prosperity /prɒ'sperəti/ *n* ازْدِهَار

prostitute /'prɒstɪtju:t/ *n* عَاهِرَة

protect /prə'tekt/ *v* يَحْمِي

protection /prə'tekʃn/ *n* حِمَايَة

protein /'prəʊti:n/ *n* بْرُوتِين/بْرُوتِينَات مف/ج

protest /'prəʊtest/ *n* احْتِجَاج/ احْتِجَاجَات مف/ج
♦ /prə'test/ *v* يَحْتَجّ

proud /praʊd/ *adj* فَخُور

prove /pru:v/ *v* **proved, proved or proven** يُثْبِت

provide /prə'vaɪd/ *v* يُزَوِّد

province /'prɒvɪns/ *n* مُقَاطَعَة

provincial /prə'vɪnʃl/ *adj* مُتَعَلِّق بِالْمُقَاطَعَة

provision /prə'vɪʒn/ *n* تَوْفِير

provocative /prə'vɒkətɪv/ *adj* اسْتِفْزَازِيّ

provoke /prə'vəʊk/ *v* يَسْتَفِزّ

prune /pru:n/ *n* بَرْقُوق

psychiatrist /saɪ'kaɪətrɪst/ *n* طَبِيب نَفْسَانِيّ

psychological /saɪkə'lɒdʒɪkl/ *adj* نَفْسِيّ

psychologist /saɪ'kɒlədʒɪst/ *n* عَالِم نَفْسَانِيّ

psychology /saɪ'kɒlədʒi/ *n* عِلْم النَفْس

pub /pʌb/ *n* حَانَة

public /'pʌblɪk/ *adj* عَامّ

♦ *n* شَعْب/شُعُوب مف/ج

publication /pʌblɪ'keɪʃn/ *n* نَشْر

publicity /pʌb'lɪsəti/ *n* شَعْبِيَّة

publish /'pʌblɪʃ/ *v* يَنْشُر

publisher /'pʌblɪʃə(r)/ *n* نَاشِر

pudding /'pʊdɪŋ/ *n* حَلْوَى تُقَدَّم بَعْدَ الطَعَام

pull /pʊl/ *v* (a door, a string, a wire) يَسْحَب

pull out *phv* (a drawer) يَخْلَع

pull up *phv* يَرْفَع

pulse /pʌls/ *n* (heartbeat) نَبْض (food) حُبُوب

pump /pʌmp/ *n* مِضَخَّة
♦ *v* يَضُخّ

pumpkin /'pʌmpkɪn/ *n* يَقْطِين

punch /pʌntʃ/ *v* يَلْكِم
♦ *n* لَكْمَة

punish /'pʌnɪʃ/ *v* يُعَاقِب

punishment /'pʌnɪʃmənt/ *n* عِقَاب/عِقَابَات مف/ج

pupil /'pju:pl/ *n* تِلْمِيذ/تَلَامِيذُ مف/ج

puppy /'pʌpi/ *n* pl **-pies** جَرْو/جِرَاء مف/ج

purchase /'pɜ:tʃəs/ *n* (act) شِرَاء
♦ *v* يَشْتَرِي

pure /pjʊə(r)/ *adj* (gold, water) نَقِيّ (morally) طَاهِر

purity /'pjʊərəti/ *n* نَقَاء

purple /'pɜ:pl/ *adj* أُرْجُوَانِيّ
♦ *n* اللَوْن الأُرْجُوَانِيّ

purpose /'pɜ:pəs/ *n* هَدَف/أَهْدَاف مف/ج

purse /pɜ:s/ *n* (for money) مِحْفَظَة/مَحَافِظُ مف/ج (US: handbag) حَقِيبَة يَد نِسَائِيَّة

pursue /pə'sju:/ *v* (a thief) يُطَارِد (an aim) يَسْعَى

pursuit /pə'sju:t/ *n* مُطَارَدَة

push /pʊʃ/ *n* دَفْعَة
♦ *v* يَدْفَع

put /pʊt/ *v* **put** (to place) يَضَع
Put it in the cupboard.
ضَعْهَا فِي الخَزَانَة
I don't know where I've put it.
لَا أَعْلَم أَيْنَ وَضَعْتُهَا

put away *phv* (to store) يُسَتِّف
Put your things away. سَتِّف حَاجِيَّاتِكَ

put back *phv* (to return) يُعِيد
Put it back on the shelf.
أَعِدْهَا عَلَى الرَفّ
(a clock) يُرْجِع
You need to put your watch back one hour. أَرْجِع سَاعَتَكَ سَاعَة لِلخَلْف

put forward *phv* (a clock) يُقَدِّم

put off *phv* (a meeting, etc) يُؤَجِّل (causing dislike) يُنَفِّر
The smell put me off eating it.
نَفَّرَتْنِي الرَائِحَة مِن أَكْلِهَا (a light, etc) يُطْفِئ

P

put on *phv* (clothing) يَلْبَس *Put your shoes on.* الْبَس حِذَائَكَ

(a light, etc) يُشْعِل *I'll put the oven on.* سَوْفَ أُشْعِل الفُرْن

put out *phv* (a fire, etc) يُطْفِئ

put up *phv* (prices) يَزِيد (a person) يُسَكِّن

put up with *phv* (to tolerate) يَتَحَمَّل

puzzle /ˈpʌzl/ *n* (game) أُحْجِيَّة/ (mystery) لُغْز/أَلْغَاز

♦ *v* يُحَيِّر

Q

Qatar /ka'tɑː/ *n* قَطَر

Qatari /ka'tɑːri/ *adj, n* قَطَرِيّ ص/س

qualification /kwɒlɪfɪ'keɪʃn/ *n* مُؤَهِّل/مُؤَهِّلَات مف/ج

qualified /'kwɒlɪfaɪd/ *adj* مُؤَهَّل

qualify /'kwɒlɪfaɪ/ *v* يَتَأَهَّل

quality /'kwɒləti/ *n* جَوْدَة

quantity /'kwɒntəti/ *n* pl **-ties** كَمِّيَّة

quarter /'kwɔːtə(r)/ *n* (one fourth) رُبْع/أَرْبَاع مف/ج

a quarter of the class رُبْع الفَصْل

It is a quarter past seven. السَاعَة السَابِعَة وَالرُبْع (of year) فَصْل/فُصُول مف/ج

queen /kwiːn/ *n* مَلِكَة

question /'kwestʃən/ *n* سُؤَال/أَسْئِلَة مف/ج

♦ *v* (a person, suspect, witness) يَسْأَل

questionnaire /kwestʃə'neə(r)/ *n* اسْتِبْيَان/اسْتِبْيَانَات مف/ج

queue /kjuː/ *n* طَابُور/طَوَابِيرُ مف/ج

♦ *v* يَصْطَفّ

quick /kwɪk/ *adj* سَرِيع

quickly /'kwɪkli/ *adv* بِسُرْعَة

quiet /'kwaɪət/ *adj* هَادِئ

quince /kwɪns/ *n* سَفَرْجَل

quit /kwɪt/ *v* **quit or quitted** يَتْرُك

quite /kwaɪt/ *adv* (fairly: hot, good, etc) إِلَى حَدّ مَا (completely: right, etc) تَمَاماً

quiz /kwɪz/ *n* امْتِحَان/امْتِحَانَات مف/ج

quota /'kwəʊtə/ *n* حِصَّة/حِصَص مف/ج

quotation /kwəʊ'teɪʃn/ *n* اقْتِبَاس/اقْتِبَاسَات مف/ج

quote /kwəʊt/ *n* اقْتِبَاس/اقْتِبَاسَات مف/ج

♦ *v* يَقْتَبِس

Qur'an, the /kə'rɑːn/ *n* القُرْآن

R

Rabat /rə'bat/ *n* الرِبَاط

rabbi /'ræbaɪ/ *n* حَاخَام/حَاخَامَات مف/ج

rabbit /'ræbɪt/ *n* أَرْنَب/أَرَانِبُ مف/ج

race /reɪs/ *n* (competition) سِبَاق/سِبَاقَات مف/ج (ethnic group) عِرْق

racial /'reɪʃl/ *adj* عِرْقِيّ

radio /'reɪdiəʊ/ *n* مِذْيَاع/أَجْهِزَة المِذْيَاع مف/ج

radish /'rædɪʃ/ *n* فِجْل

radius /'reɪdiəs/ *n* pl **-ses** نِصْف القُطْر

raft /rɑːft/ *n* عَامَة

rag /ræg/ *n* خِرْقَة/خِرَق مف/ج

rage /reɪʤ/ *n* ثَوْرَة غَضَب

♦ *v* يَثُور

raid /reɪd/ *n* غَارَة

rail /reɪl/ *n* (barrier) دَرَبْزِين/دَرَبْزِينَات مف/ج (on a railway) سِكَّة/سِكَك مف/ج

railroad /'reɪlrəʊd/ *n* سِكَّة حَدِيد

railway /'reɪlweɪ/ *n* سِكَّة حَدِيد

rain /reɪn/ *n* مَطَر

♦ *v* يَمْطُرُ

rainbow /'reɪnbəʊ/ *n* قَوْس قُزَح

raise /reɪz/ *n* زِيَادَة

♦ *v* (a salary) يَرْفَع (a child) يُرَبِّي

raisin /'reɪzn/ *n* زَبِيب

rally /'ræli/ *n* pl **-lies** (public meeting) مَهْرَجَان/مَهْرَجَانَات مف/ج (car race) سِبَاق السَيَّارَات

Ramadan /'ræmədæn/ *n* شَهْر رَمَضَان

to observe Ramadan يُرَاعِي رَمَضَان

Ramallah /ræ'mæləh/ *n* رَام الله

ramp /ræmp/ *n* مُنْحَدَر/مُنْحَدَرَات مف/ج

random /'rændəm/ *adj* عَشْوَائِيّ

range /reɪnʤ/ *n* تَشْكِيلَة

rank /ræŋk/ *n* (in army, etc) رُتْبَة/رُتَب مف/ج (in a hierarchy) مَرْتَبَة/مَرَاتِبُ مف/ج

rape /reɪp/ *v* يَغْتَصِب

♦ *n* اغْتِصَاب

rapid /'ræpɪd/ *adj* سَرِيع

rapidly /'ræpɪdli/ *adv* بِسُرْعَة

rare /reə(r)/ *adj* (bird, antique, stamp) نَادِر (steak) غَيْر مُنْضَج جَيِّداً

R

raspberry /ˈrɑːzbəri/ *n* توت العُلَّيْق

rat /ræt/ *n* جُرْذ/جِرْذَان مف/ج

rate /reɪt/ *n* (tariff) نِسْبَة/نِسَب مف/ج (speed) مُعَدَّل/مُعَدَّلَات مف/ج

rather /ˈrɑːðə(r)/ *adv* (quite) إِلَى حَدّ مَا (very) لِلغَايَة

ratio /ˈreɪʃiəʊ/ *n* نِسْبَة/نِسَب مف/ج

rational /ˈræʃnəl/ *adj* عَقْلَانِيّ

rattle /ˈrætl/ *v* يُخَشْخِش

raven /ˈreɪvn/ *n* غُراب/غِرْبَان مف/ج

raw /rɔː/ *adj* نِيء

ray /reɪ/ *n* شُعَاع/أَشِعَّة مف/ج

reach /riːtʃ/ *v* (a place) يَصِل (by telephone) يَتَّصِل

reaction /riˈækʃn/ *n* تَفَاعُل/تَفَاعُلَات مف/ج

read /riːd/ *v* **read** يَقْرَأ

reading /ˈriːdɪŋ/ *n* قِرَاءَة

ready /ˈredi/ *adj* جَاهِز

real /rɪəl/ *adj* حَقِيقِيّ

realistic /rɪəˈlɪstɪk/ *adj* وَاقِعِيّ

reality /riˈæləti/ *n* وَاقِع

realize /ˈrɪəlaɪz/ *v* (the truth, a mistake) يُدْرِك (assets) يُحَوِّل إِلَى نَقْد

really /ˈrɪəli/ *adv* (in truth) حَقّاً (very: good, bad) لِلغَايَة

rear /rɪə(r)/ *v* يُرَبِّي

reason /ˈriːzn/ *n* مُبَرِّر

reasonable /ˈriːznəbl/ *adj* مَعْقُول

rebellion /rɪˈbeljən/ *n* ثَوْرَة

rebuild /riːˈbɪld/ *v* يُعِيد بِنَاء

receipt /rɪˈsiːt/ *n* إِيصَال/إِيصَالَات مف/ج

receive /rɪˈsiːv/ *v* يَسْتَلِم

receiver /rɪˈsiːvə(r)/ *n* سَمَّاعَة الهَاتِف

recent /ˈriːsnt/ *adj* حَدِيث

recently /ˈriːsntli/ *adv* حَدِيثاً

reception /rɪˈsepʃn/ *n* اسْتِقْبَال

receptionist /rɪˈsepʃənɪst/ *n* مُوَظَّف اسْتِقْبَال

recession /rɪˈseʃn/ *n* رُكُود اقْتِصَادِيّ

recharge /riːˈtʃɑːdʒ/ *v* يُعِيد الشَحْن

recipe /ˈresəpi/ *n* وَصْفَة

recite /rɪˈsaɪt/ *v* يُلْقِي

reckless /ˈrekləs/ *adj* مُهْمِل

reckon /ˈrekən/ *v* يُقَدِّر

recognition /rekəgˈnɪʃn/ *n* اعْتِرَاف

recognize /ˈrekəgnaɪz/ *v* (a person) يُمَيِّز (a government) يَعْتَرِف

recommend /rekəˈmend/ *v* (a hotel, plumber) يُزَكِّي (sb to do sth) يَنْصَح بِـ

R

recommendation /rekəmen'deɪʃn/ *n* تَوْصِيَة

reconcile /'rekənsaɪl/ *v* يُصْلِح

reconciliation /rekənsɪli'eɪʃn/ *n* مُصَالَحَة

reconsider /ri:kən'sɪdə(r)/ *v* يُعِيد النَظَر

reconstruct /ri:kən'strʌkt/ *v* يُعِيد بِنَاء

record /'rekɔ:d/ *n* (best/worst result) رَقَم قِيَاسِيّ (disc) أُسْطُوَانَة فُونُوغِرَافِيَّة ♦ /rɪ'kɔ:d/ *v* يُسَجِّل

recording /rɪ'kɔ:dɪŋ/ *n* تَسْجِيل/ تَسْجِيلَات مف/ج

recover /rɪ'kʌvə(r)/ *v* (from illness) يَشْفَى (sth lost) يَسْتَعِيد

recovery /rɪ'kʌvəri/ *n* (from illness) شِفَاء (of property) اسْتِرْجَاع

recreation /rekri'eɪʃn/ *n* اسْتِجْمَام

recruit /rɪ'kru:t/ *n* مُجَنَّد

recycle /ri:'saɪkl/ *v* يُعِيد التَصْنِيع

red /red/ *adj* (cloth, rose) أَحْمَر / حَمْرَاءُ / حُمْر مذ/م/ج
to go red أَصْبَحَ أَحْمَر/يَحْمَرّ
to have red hair يَكُون شَعْرُهُ أَحْمَر
♦ *n* اللَوْن الأَحْمَر
to be dressed in red يَرْتَدِي اللَوْن الأَحْمَر

red pepper *n* فِلْفِل أَحْمَر

reduce /rɪ'dju:s/ *v* يُخَفِّض

reduction /rɪ'dʌkʃn/ *n* انْخِفَاض/ انْخِفَاضَات مف/ج

redundancy /rɪ'dʌndənsi/ *n* pl -cies فَصْل الفَائِض مِن المُوَظَّفِين

redundant /rɪ'dʌndənt/ *adj* فَائِض عَن الحَاجَة

reed /ri:d/ *n* قَصَب

reef /ri:f/ *n* حَيْد بَحْرِيّ

referee /refə'ri:/ *n* حَكَم

reference /'refrəns/ *n* (mention) إِشَارَة (letter) رِسَالَة تَوْصِيَة

refine /rɪ'faɪn/ *v* يُكَرِّر

reflect /rɪ'flekt/ *v* يَعْكِس

reflection /rɪ'flekʃn/ *n* انْعِكَاس/ انْعِكَاسَات مف/ج

reform /rɪ'fɔ:m/ *v* يُعَدِّل

refresh /rɪ'freʃ/ *v* (a tired person) يُنْعِش (in computing) يُحَدِّث

refrigerator /rɪ'frɪdʒəreɪtə(r)/ *n* ثَلَّاجَة

refuge /'refju:dʒ/ *n* مَلْجَأ/مَلَاجِئُ مف/ج

refugee /refju'dʒi:/ *n* لَاجِئ

refusal /rɪ'fju:zl/ *n* رَفْض

refuse /rɪ'fju:z/ *v* يَرْفُض

R

regain /rɪ'geɪn/ *v* يَسْتَعِيد

regard /rɪ'gɑːd/ *v* يَعْتَبِر

regarding /rɪ'gɑːdɪŋ/ *prep* فِيمَا يَتَعَلَّق بِـ

region /'riːdʒən/ *n* مَنْطِقَة/مَنَاطِقُ مف/ج

regional /'riːdʒənl/ *adj* مَحَلِّيّ

register /'redʒɪstə(r)/ *v* يُسَجِّل
♦ *n* سِجِلّ/سِجِلَّات مف/ج

registration /redʒɪ'streɪʃn/ *n* تَسْجِيل

regret /rɪ'gret/ *n* نَدَم
♦ *v* يَنْدَم

regular /'regjələ(r)/ *adj* مُنْتَظَم

regularly /'regjələli/ *adv* بِانْتِظَام

regulate /'regjuleɪt/ *v* يُنَظِّم

regulation /regju'leɪʃn/ *n* (rule) قَانُون/قَوَانِينُ مف/ج (control) تَنْظِيم

rehabilitation /riːəbɪlɪ'teɪʃn/ *n* إِعَادَة تَأْهِيل

rehearsal /rɪ'hɜːsl/ *n* بْرُوفَة

reign /reɪn/ *n* فَتْرَة حُكْم

reinforce /riːɪn'fɔːs/ *v* يُدَعِّم

reject /rɪ'dʒekt/ *v* يَرْفُض

rejection /rɪ'dʒekʃn/ *n* رَفْض

relate /rɪ'leɪt/ *v* يَتَفَهَّم

related /rɪ'leɪtɪd/ *adj* قَرِيب

relation /rɪ'leɪʃn/ *n* قَرِيب/أَقَارِبُ مف/ج

relationship /rɪ'leɪʃnʃɪp/ *n* عَلَاقَة

relative /'relətɪv/ *adj* (advantage, comfort) مُرْتَبِط
♦ *n* (family member) قَرِيب/أَقَارِبُ مف/ج

relax /rɪ'læks/ *v* يَسْتَرْخِي

relaxation /riːlæk'seɪʃn/ *n* اسْتِرْخَاء

release /rɪ'liːs/ *v* يُحَرِّر

relevance /'reləvəns/ *n* صِلَة

relevant /'reləvənt/ *adj* ذُو صِلَة بِالمَوْضُوع

reliability /rɪlaɪə'bɪləti/ *n* الوُثُوق بِالشَيْء

reliable /rɪ'laɪəbl/ *adj* مَوْثُوق بِهِ

reliance /rɪ'laɪəns/ *n* اعْتِمَاد

relief /rɪ'liːf/ *n* (feeling) رَاحَة (assistance) مَعُونَة

relieve /rɪ'liːv/ *v* يُخَفِّف

religion /rɪ'lɪdʒən/ *n* دِين/أَدْيَان مف/ج

religious /rɪ'lɪdʒəs/ *adj* دِينِيّ

relocate /riːləʊ'keɪt/ *v* يَنْقُل

reluctance /rɪ'lʌktəns/ *n* تَرَدُّد

reluctant /rɪ'lʌktənt/ *adj* مُتَرَدِّد

remain /rɪ'meɪn/ *v* (in a position, place) يَظَلّ (in a job, post) يَبْقَى

remainder /rɪ'meɪndə(r)/ *n* بَاقٍ/بَوَاقٍ مف/ج

R

remark /rɪ'mɑːk/ *n* تَعْلِيق
♦ *v* يُعَلِّق

remarkable /rɪ'mɑːkəbl/ *adj* جَدِير بِالْمُلَاحَظَة

remedy /'remədi/ *n* pl **-dies** /عِلَاج عِلَاجَات مف/ج

remember /rɪ'membə(r)/ *v* يَتَذَكَّر

remind /rɪ'maɪnd/ *v* يُذَكِّر

remote /rɪ'məʊt/ *adj* (place) نَاءٍ (time, era) بَعِيد

remote control *n* جِهَاز التَحَكُّم عَن بُعْد

removal /rɪ'muːvl/ *n* إِزَالَة

remove /rɪ'muːv/ *v* يُزِيل

renew /rɪ'njuː/ *v* يُكَرِّر

renewal /rɪ'njuːəl/ *n* تَجْدِيد/تَجْدِيدَات مف/ج

renminbi /'renmɪnbi/ *n* رِنْمِنْبِي (العُمْلَة الصِينِيَّة)

rent /rent/ *n* إِيجَار/إِيجَارَات مف/ج
♦ *v* يَسْتَأْجِر

repair /rɪ'peə(r)/ *n* إِصْلَاح/إِصْلَاحَات مف/ج
♦ *v* يُصْلِح

repay /rɪ'peɪ/ *v* يُسَدِّد

repayment /rɪ'peɪmənt/ *n* تَسْدِيد

repeat /rɪ'piːt/ *v* يُعِيد

repellent /rɪ'pelənt/ *n* طارِد لِلحَشَرَات

repetition /repə'tɪʃn/ *n* إِعَادَة

replace /rɪ'pleɪs/ *v* يَسْتَبْدِل

replacement /rɪ'pleɪsmənt/ *n* اسْتِبْدَال

reply /rɪ'plaɪ/ *n* pl **-lies** رَدّ/رُدُود مف/ج
♦ *v* يَرُدّ

report /rɪ'pɔːt/ *n* تَقْرِير/تَقَارِيرُ مف/ج
♦ *v* (an accident, etc) يُبْلِغ (in journalism) يُرَاسِل

reporter /rɪ'pɔːtə(r)/ *n* مُرَاسِل

represent /reprɪ'zent/ *v* يُمَثِّل

representation /reprɪzen'teɪʃn/ *n* تَمْثِيل

representative /reprɪ'zentətɪv/ *adj* تَمْثِيلِيّ
♦ *n* مُمَثِّل

reproduce /riːprə'djuːs/ *v* يَنْسَخ

reproduction /riːprə'dʌkʃn/ *n* تَكَاثُر

republic /rɪ'pʌblɪk/ *n* جُمْهُورِيَّة

republican /rɪ'pʌblɪkən/ *adj* جُمْهُورِيّ

reputation /repju'teɪʃn/ *n* سُمْعَة

request /rɪ'kwest/ *n* (act) /مَطْلَب مَطَالِبُ مف/ج
♦ *v* يَطْلُب

R

require /rɪ'kwaɪə(r)/ *v* يَتَطَلَّب

requirement /rɪ'kwaɪəmənt/ *n* مُتَطَلَّب/مُتَطَلَّبَات مف/ج

rescue /'reskju:/ *n* إِنْقَاذ
♦ *v* يُنْقِذ

research /'ri:sɜ:tʃ/ *n* بَحْث/أَبْحَاث مف/ج

resemble /rɪ'zembl/ *v* يُشْبِه

resentment /rɪ'zentmənt/ *n* اسْتِيَاء

reservation /rezə'veɪʃn/ *n* حَجْز

reserve /rɪ'zɜ:v/ *n* احْتِيَاطِيّ/ احْتِيَاطِيَّات مف/ج
♦ *v* يَحْجِز

reservoir /'rezəvwɑ:(r)/ *n* خَزَّان/ خَزَّانَات مف/ج

residence /'rezɪdəns/ *n* مَسْكَن/ مَسَاكِنُ مف/ج

resident /'rezɪdənt/ *adj* مُقِيم
♦ *n* مُقِيم

residue /'rezɪdju:/ *n* فَضْلَة

resign /rɪ'zaɪn/ *v* يَسْتَقِيل

resignation /rezɪg'neɪʃn/ *n* اسْتِقَالَة

resist /rɪ'zɪst/ *v* يُقَاوِم

resistance /rɪ'zɪstəns/ *n* مُقَاوَمَة

resolve /rɪ'zɒlv/ *v* يَحِلّ

respect /rɪ'spekt/ *n* احْتِرَام
♦ *v* يَحْتَرِم

respectable /rɪ'spektəbl/ *adj* جَدِير بِالاِحْتِرَام

respective /rɪ'spektɪv/ *adj* شَخْصِيّ

response /rɪ'spɒns/ *n* إِجَابَة

responsibility /rɪspɒnsə'bɪləti/ *n* pl **-ties** مَسْئُولِيَّة

responsible /rɪ'spɒnsəbl/ *adj* مَسْئُول

rest /rest/ *n* (after exertion) رَاحَة (remainder) بَقِيَّة
♦ *v* يَرْتَاح

restaurant /'restrɒnt/ *n* مَطْعَم/ مَطَاعِمُ مف/ج

restrict /rɪ'strɪkt/ *v* يُحَدِّد

restriction /rɪ'strɪkʃn/ *n* تَحْدِيد

result /rɪ'zʌlt/ *n* (of a game, exam) نَتِيجَة/نَتَائِجُ مف/ج (of a storm) مُحَصِّلَة
♦ *result in v* يَنْتُج

resumé /'resju:meɪ/ *n* سِيرَة ذَاتِيَّة

retail /'ri:teɪl/ *v* يَبِيع بِالتَجْزِئَة

retailer /'ri:teɪlə(r)/ *n* بَائِع المُفَرَّق

retire /rɪ'taɪə(r)/ *v* يَتَقَاعَد

retired /rɪ'taɪəd/ *adj* مُتَقَاعِد

retreat /rɪ'tri:t/ *v* يَنْسَحِب

return /rɪ'tɜ:n/ *v* (to come back) يَعُود

R

(to give back) يُعيد

♦ *n* عَوْدَة

reunion /riːˈjuːniən/ *n* اجْتِماع الشَمْل

reunite /riːjuːˈnaɪt/ *v* يَجْمَع الشَمْل

reveal /rɪˈviːl/ *v* يَكْشِف

revelation /revəˈleɪʃn/ *n* إِفْشَاء

revenge /rɪˈvendʒ/ *n* انْتِقام

revenue /ˈrevənjuː/ *n* رَيْع

reverse /rɪˈvɜːs/ *v* يَتَحَرَّك لِلخَلْف

♦ *n* العَكْس

review /rɪˈvjuː/ *n* (article) نَقْد

(inspection) تَدْقِيق

reviewer /rɪˈvjuːə(r)/ *n* نَاقِد/نُقَّاد مف/ج

revise /rɪˈvaɪz/ *v* (an article) يُنَقِّح (for an exam) يُرَاجِع

revision /rɪˈvɪʒn/ *n* (for an exam) مُرَاجَعَة (of a text) تَنْقِيح

revive /rɪˈvaɪv/ *v* يُنْعِش

revolution /revəˈluːʃn/ *n* ثَوْرَة

revolutionary /revəˈluːʃənəri/ *adj* ثَوْرِيّ

reward /rɪˈwɔːd/ *n* مُكَافَأَة

♦ *v* يُكَافِئ

rhetoric /ˈretərɪk/ *n* بَلَاغَة

rhythm /ˈrɪðəm/ *n* إِيقَاع/إِيقَاعَات مف/ج

rial /ˈriːɑːl/ *n* رِيَال/رِيَالَات مف/ج

rib /rɪb/ *n* ضِلْع/أَضْلَاع مف/ج

ribbon /ˈrɪbən/ *n* شَرِيط/شَرَائِطُ مف/ج

rice /raɪs/ *n* أَرُزّ

rich /rɪtʃ/ *adj* (country, person) غَنِيّ/أَغْنِيَاءُ مف/ج

The family was rich. كَانَت العَائِلَة غَنِيَّة

ride /raɪd/ *n* نُزْهَة عَلَى دَابَّة أَو مَرْكَبَة

♦ *v* **rode, ridden** (in a vehicle) يَقُود

(on a horse, etc) يَمْتَطِي

rider /ˈraɪdə(r)/ *n* خَيَّال

ridge /rɪdʒ/ *n* قِمَّة الجَبَل

ridiculous /rɪˈdɪkjələs/ *adj* سَخِيف/سُخَفَاءُ مف/ج

rifle /ˈraɪfl/ *n* بُنْدُقِيَّة/بَنَادِقُ مف/ج

right /raɪt/ *adj* (way, answer) صَحِيح

the right answer الجَوَاب الصَحِيح

Is this the right address? هَل هَذَا هُوَ العُنْوَان الصَحِيح؟

You were right. كُنْتَ صَائِباً (not left) أَيْمَنُ/يُمْنَى مذ/م

my right hand يَدِي اليُمْنَى (fair, just) عَادِل

I won't do it because it is not right. لَن أَفْعَل ذَلِكَ لِأَنَّهُ غَيْر عَادِل

♦ *adv* (directly, completely) مُبَاشَرَةً

right in front of me أَمَامِي مُبَاشَرَةً

(well) جَيِّد

R

Everything is going right. كُلّ شَيْء يَسِير بِشَكْل جَيِّد (in directions) إِلَى اليَمِين

Turn right here. اتَّجِه هُنَا إِلَى اليَمِين

♦ *excl* (for emphasis) حَسَناً

Right, let's go! حَسَناً، دَعْنَا نَذْهَب

♦ *n* (side, direction) اليَمِين (م)

Turn to the right. اسْتَدِر إِلَى اليَمِين

It's on your right. هُوَ عَلَى يَمِينِكَ

(in law) حَقّ/حُقُوق مف/ج

women's rights حُقُوق المَرْأَة

You have the right to remain silent. لَكَ الحَقّ أَنْ تَبْقَى صَامِتاً (what is fair, just) الحَقّ

to know right from wrong يَعْرِف الحَقّ مِن البَاطِل

right click *v* يَنْقُر بِزِرّ الفَأْرَة الأَيْمَن

rightly /'raɪtli/ *adv* بِشَكْل صَحِيح

rigid /'rɪʤɪd/ *adj* صُلْب

ring /rɪŋ/ *n* (for finger) خَاتِم/خَوَاتِمُ (circular shape) دَائِرَة/دَوَائِرُ مف/ج (in boxing) حَلْقَة/ مف/ج حَلَقَات مف/ج

♦ *v* **rang, rung** يَرِنّ

ringtone /'rɪŋtəʊn/ *n* نَغْمَة

riot /'raɪət/ *n* شَغَب

rip /rɪp/ *v* يُمَزِّق

ripe /raɪp/ *adj* نَاضِج

rise /raɪz/ *n* (in prices) ارْتِفَاع/ ارْتِفَاعَات مف/ج (in productivity) زِيَادَة

♦ *v* **rose, risen** (prices) يَرْتَفِع (to get up) يَنْهَض

risk /rɪsk/ *n* خَطَر/أَخْطَار مف/ج

♦ *v* يُخَاطِر

risky /'rɪski/ *adj* خَطِر

ritual /'rɪtʃuəl/ *n* طَقْس/طُقُوس مف/ج

rival /'raɪvl/ *n* مُنَافِس

♦ *v* يُنَافِس

rivalry /'raɪvlri/ *n* pl **-ries** مُنَافَسَة

river /'rɪvə(r)/ *n* نَهْر/أَنْهَار مف/ج

the River Nile نَهْر النِيل

Riyadh /ri:'ɑ:d/ *n* الرِيَاض

riyal /'ri:jɑ:l/ *n* رِيَال/رِيَالَات مف/ج

road /rəʊd/ *n* (between towns) طَرِيق/طُرُق مف/ج (street) شَارِع/ شَوَارِعُ مف/ج

roar /rɔ:(r)/ *v* (animals) يَزْأَر (storm, crowd) يُصْدِر صَوْتاً عَالِياً

rob /rɒb/ *v* يَسْرِق

robbery /'rɒbəri/ *n* pl **-ries** سَرِقَة

robin /'rɒbɪn/ *n* أَبُو الحِنَّاء

rock /rɒk/ *n* صَخْرَة/صُخُور مف/ج

♦ *v* يَهُزّ

rocket /'rɒkɪt/ *n* صَارُوخ/صَوَارِيخُ مف/ج

R

rocky /'rɒki/ *adj* صَخْرِيّ

rod /rɒd/ *n* قَضِيب/قُضْبَان مف/ج

roe /rəʊ/ *n* بَطَارِخُ، بَيْض السمَك

roll /rəʊl/ *n* (of cloth, paper) لَفَّة
(bread) رَغِيف/أَرْغِفَة مف/ج
♦ *v* يُدَحْرِج

romance /rəʊ'mæns/ *n* غَرَام

romantic /rəʊ'mæntɪk/ *adj* غَرَامِيّ

Rome /rəʊm/ *n* رُومَا

roof /ru:f/ *n* pl **roofs, rooves** سَقْف/أَسْقُف مف/ج

room /rʊm/ *n* (in a house) غُرْفَة/غُرَف مف/ج (space) مُتَّسَع

root /ru:t/ *n* جَذْر/جُذُور مف/ج

rope /rəʊp/ *n* حَبْل/حِبَال مف/ج

rose /rəʊz/ *n* وَرْدَة/وُرُود مف/ج

rosemary /'rəʊzməri/ *n* إِكْلِيل الجَبَل

R

roster /'rɒstə(r)/ *n* جَدْوَل الْمُنَاوَبَات

rota /'rəʊtə/ *n* جَدْوَل الْمُنَاوَبَات

rotate /rəʊ'teɪt/ *v* يَدُور

rouble /'ru:bl/ *n* رُوبِل

rough /rʌf/ *adj* (surface) خَشِن
(weather) قَاسٍ

round /raʊnd/ *adj* مُسْتَدِير
♦ *n* جَوْلَة
♦ *prep* حَوْلَ

roundabout /'raʊndəbaʊt/ *n* دَوَّار/دَوَّارَات مف/ج

route /ru:t/ *n* مَسْلَك/مَسَالِكُ مف/ج

router /'raʊtə(r)/ *n* مُوَزِّع

routine /ru:'ti:n/ *n* نَفْس النِظَام

row *n* /raʊ/ (argument) مُشَادَّة كَلَامِيَّة
/rəʊ/ (of seats, trees) صَفّ/صُفُوف مف/ج

royal /'rɔɪəl/ *adj* مَلَكِيّ

rub /rʌb/ *v* يَفْرُك

rubber /'rʌbə(r)/ *n* (substance) مَطَّاط (eraser) مِمْحَاة/مَمَاحٍ مف/ج

rubbish /'rʌbɪʃ/ *n* (waste) نُفَايَة
(poor quality goods) هُرَاء

ruble /'ru:bl/ *n* US رُوبِل

ruby /'ru:bi/ *n* pl **-bies** يَاقُوت

rude /ru:d/ *adj* وَقِح

rugby /'rʌgbi/ *n* لُعْبَة الرَجْبِي

rugged /'rʌgɪd/ *adj* وَعِر

ruin /'ru:ɪn/ *n* حُطَام
♦ *v* يُدَمِّر

ruins /'ru:ɪnz/ *n pl* بَقَايَا

rule /ru:l/ *n* (of games, etc) قَاعِدَة/قَوَاعِدُ مف/ج (of a government) حُكْم
♦ *v* يَحْكُم

ruler /'ru:lə(r)/ *n* (for measuring)

(monarch) مِسْطَرَة/مَسَاطِرُ مف/ج
حَاكِم/حُكَّام مف/ج

ruling /ˈru:lɪŋ/ *n* حُكْم/أَحْكَام مف/ج

rumour /ˈru:mə(r)/ *n* US **-mor** إِشَاعَة

run /rʌn/ *v* **ran, run** يَجْرِي

run into *phv* يَصْدُم

runner /ˈrʌnə(r)/ *n* عَدَّاء

runway /ˈrʌnweɪ/ *n* مَدْرَج الطَّائِرَات

rural /ˈrʊərəl/ *adj* رِيفِيّ

rush /rʌʃ/ *n* عَجَلَة

♦ *v* يَنْدَفِع

Russia /ˈrʌʃə/ *n* رُوسْيَا

Russian /ˈrʌʃn/ *adj* رُوسِيّ

♦ *n* (language) اللُغَة الرُوسِيَّة (citizen)
رُوسِيّ/رُوس مف/ج

rye /raɪ/ *n* شَيْلَم

S

sack /sæk/ *n* كِيس/أَكْيَاس مف/ج
♦ *v* يَفْصِل مِن العَمَل

sacred /'seɪkrɪd/ *adj* مُقَدَّس

sacrifice /'sækrɪfaɪs/ *n* تَضْحِيَة
♦ *v* يُضَحِّي بِـ

sad /sæd/ *adj* (person) حَزِين (event) مُحْزِن

saddle /'sædl/ *n* سَرْج/سُرُوج مف/ج

sadly /'sædli/ *adv* بِحُزْن

sadness /'sædnəs/ *n* حُزْن

safe /seɪf/ *adj* آمِن
♦ *n* خَزْنَة

safely /'seɪfli/ *adv* بِسَلَامَة

safety /'seɪfti/ *n* أَمَان

saffron /'sæfrən/ *n* زَعْفَرَان

sage /seɪʤ/ *n* مَرْيَمِيَّة

sail /seɪl/ *n* شِرَاع/أَشْرِعَة مف/ج
♦ *v* يُبْحِر

sailor /'seɪlə(r)/ *n* بَحَّار

saint /seɪnt/ *n* قِدِّيس

salad /'sæləd/ *n* سَلَطَة

salami /sə'lɑːmi/ *n* سَلَامِي

salary /'sæləri/ *n* pl **-ries** /رَاتِب رَوَاتِبُ مف/ج

sale /seɪl/ *n* بَيْع

salmon /'sæmən/ *n* pl **salmon** سَمَك السَلَمُون

salt /sɒlt/ *n* مِلْح/أَمْلَاح مف/ج

salvation /sæl'veɪʃn/ *n* خَلَاص

same /seɪm/ *adj* نَفْسُهُ

sample /'sɑːmpl/ *n* عَيِّنَة

Sana'a /sa'nɑː/ *n* صَنْعَاء

sanctions /'sæŋktʃnʒ/ *n pl* مُقَاطَعَة

sand /sænd/ *n* رَمْل/رِمَال مف/ج

sandwich /'sænwɪʤ/ *n* /شَطِيرَة شَطَائِرُ مف/ج

San Francisco /ˌsan fran'sɪskəʊ/ *n* سَان فْرَانْسِيسْكُو

sardine /sɑː'diːn/ *n* سَارْدِين

satellite /'sætəlaɪt/ *n* قَمَر صِنَاعِيّ

satisfaction /sætɪs'fækʃn/ *n* رِضَى

satisfactory /sætɪs'fæktəri/ *adj* مُرْضٍ

satisfy /'sætɪsfaɪ/ *v* يُرْضِي

S

Saturday /'sætədeɪ/ *n* (see Wednesday) يَوْم السَبْت

sauce /sɔ:s/ *n* صَلْصَة

Saudi Arabia /'saʊdi ə'reɪbiə/ *n* السَعُودِيَّة

Saudi Arabian *adj, n* سَعُودِيّ ص/س

sausage /'sɒsɪʤ/ *n* نَقَانِق

save /seɪv/ *v* (from death, injury) يُنْقِذ (money) يَدَّخِر (a document) يَحْفَظ

saw /sɔ:/ *n* مِنْشَار/مَنَاشِيرُ مف/ج

say /seɪ/ *v* **said** يَقُول

She said it. قَالَتْهَا

They say (that) they can come.

يَقُولُون إِنَّهُ بِإِمْكَانِهِم المَجِيء

"I'm hungry," said Mollie.

قَالَت مُولِي "أَنَا جَائِعَة"

Did they say goodbye?

هَل قَالُوا وَدَاعاً؟

What does the sign say?

مَاذَا تَقُول اللَافِتَة؟

saying /'seɪɪŋ/ *n* مَثَل/أَمْثَال مف/ج

scale /skeɪl/ *n* مِقْيَاس/مَقَايِيسُ مف/ج

scan /skæn/ *v* يَفْحَص

scandal /'skændl/ *n* فَضِيحَة/فَضَائِحُ مف/ج

Scandinavia /skændɪ'neɪviə/ *n* اسْكَنْدِينَافِيَا

Scandinavian /skandɪ'neɪvɪən/ *adj, n* اسْكَنْدِينَافِيّ ص/س

scar /skɑ:(r)/ *n* شَطْبَة

scarce /skeəs/ *adj* نَادِر

scare /skeə(r)/ *v* يُرْعِب

♦ *n* رُعْب

scary /'skeəri/ *adj* مُرْعِب

scatter /'skætə(r)/ *v* يَنْثُر

scene /si:n/ *n* مَسْرَح الأَحْدَاث

scenery /'si:nəri/ *n* مَنْظَر/مَنَاظِرُ مف/ج

scent /sent/ *n* عِطْر/عُطُور مف/ج

schedule /'ʃedju:l/ *n* جَدْوَل/جَدَاوِلُ مف/ج

scheme /ski:m/ *n* مُخَطَّط/مُخَطَّطَات مف/ج

scholar /'skɒlə(r)/ *n* عَالِم/عُلَمَاءُ مف/ج

scholarship /'skɒləʃɪp/ *n* مِنْحَة دِرَاسِيَّة

school /sku:l/ *n* (for children) مَدْرَسَة/مَدَارِسُ مف/ج (US: university) جَامِعَة

science /'saɪəns/ *n* عِلْم/عُلُوم مف/ج

scientific /saɪən'tɪfɪk/ *adj* عِلْمِيّ

scientist /'saɪəntɪst/ *n* عَالِم/عُلَمَاءُ مف/ج

scope /skəʊp/ *n* نِطَاق/نِطَاقَات مف/ج

score /skɔ:(r)/ *n* النِقَاط المُحْرَزَة فِي مُبَارَاة
♦ *v* يُحْرِز

Scot /skɒt/ *n* إسْكُتْلَنْدِيّ

Scotland /'skɒtlənd/ *n* إسْكُتْلَنْدَة

Scottish /'skɒtɪʃ/ *adj* إسْكُتْلَنْدِيّ
♦ *n* (people) إسْكُتْلَنْدِيُّون

scout /skaʊt/ *n* كَشَّافَة

scowl /skaʊl/ *v* يَعْبَس

scrap /skræp/ *n* قِطْعَة

scrape /skreɪp/ *v* يَكْشُط

scratch /skrætʃ/ *n* خَدْش/خُدُوش مف/ج
♦ *v* (the paintwork, etc) يَخْدِش (one's head, etc) يَحُكّ

scream /skri:m/ *n* صَرْخَة
♦ *v* يَصْرَخ

screen /skri:n/ *n* شَاشَة

screw /skru:/ *n* بُرْغِيّ/بَرَاغِيُّ مف/ج

sculpture /'skʌlptʃə(r)/ *n* قِطْعَة فَنِّيَّة مَنْحُوتَة

sea /si:/ *n* بَحْر/بِحَار مف/ج
the Red Sea البَحْر الأَحْمَر

seal /si:l/ *n* فُقْمَة
♦ *v* يُغْلِق

search /sɜ:tʃ/ *n* بَحْث/أَبْحَاث مف/ج
♦ *v* (a house, an area) يَبْحَث

search engine *n* بَرْنَامَج البَحْث

season /'si:zn/ *n* (of the year) فَصْل/فُصُول مف/ج (in sport, etc) مَوْسِم/مَوَاسِمُ مف/ج

seasonal /'si:zənl/ *adj* مَوْسِمِيّ

seat /si:t/ *n* مَقْعَد/مَقَاعِدُ مف/ج

second /'sekənd/ *adj* ثَانٍ
♦ *adv* ثَانياً
to come second يَأْتِي ثَانِياً
♦ *n* (in a series) الثَانِي
the second of August, August the second الثَانِي مِن آب (of minute) ثَانِيَة/ثَوَانٍ مف/ج (short time) لَحْظَة
Let's stop for a second. دَعْنَا نَتَوَقَّف لِلَحْظَة

secondary /'sekəndri/ *adj* ثَانَوِيّ

secrecy /'si:krəsi/ *n* سِرِّيَّة

secret /'si:krət/ *adj* (payment, treaty, letter) سِرِّيّ
♦ *n* سِرّ/أَسْرَار مف/ج

secretary /'sekrətri/ *n* pl **-ries** (in an office) سِكْرِتِير (to committee) أَمِين سِرّ/أُمَنَاءُ مف/ج

section /'sekʃn/ *n* قِسْم/أَقْسَام مف/ج

secure /sɪ'kjʊə(r)/ *adj* (building, door) آمِن
♦ *v* (an agreement, consensus) يُؤَمِّن

security /sɪ'kjʊərəti/ *n* (protective

S

measures) أَمْن

security guard *n* حَارِس/حُرَّاس

see /siː/ *v* **saw, seen** (the screen, a person, a game) يَرَى (to understand) يَفْهَم (the danger, etc) يُدْرِك

seed /siːd/ *n* بِذْرَة/بُذُور مف/ج

seem /siːm/ *v* يَبْدُو

He seems happy/sad.
يَبْدُو سَعِيداً/حَزِيناً

They seem to be working.
يَبْدُو أَنَّهُم يَعْمَلُون

It seems as though they can come.
يَبْدُو حَسَب الاعْتِقَاد أَنَّهُ بِإِمْكَانِهِم المَجِيء

seize /siːz/ *v* يُمْسِك بِـ

seizure /ˈsiːʒə(r)/ *n* مُصَادَرَة

select /sɪˈlekt/ *v* (the members of a team, a candidate) يَخْتَار

♦ *adj* (resort, circle) فَاخِر

selection /sɪˈlekʃn/ *n* (of products) اخْتِيَار/ (of the team) مَجْمُوعَة مُخْتَارَة اخْتِيَارَات مف/ج

self /self/ *n* ذَات

selfish /ˈselfɪʃ/ *adj* أَنَانِيّ

sell /sel/ *v* **sold** يَبِيع

semi-final /semɪˈfaɪn(ə)l/ *n* قَبْلَ النِهَائِيّ

senate /ˈsenət/ *n* مَجْلِس الشُيُوخ

senator /ˈsenətə(r)/ *n* عُضْو مَجْلِس الشُيُوخ

send /send/ *v* **sent** يُرْسِل

send off *phv* (a footballer) يَطْرُد

sensation /senˈseɪʃn/ *n* (in a limb) إِحْسَاس (stir) اهْتِيَاج

sense /sens/ *n* (judgement) حِسّ (meaning) مَعْنَى/مَعَانٍ مف/ج (of smell, etc) حَاسَّة/حَوَاسّ مف/ج

♦ *v* يُدْرِك

sensible /ˈsensəbl/ *adj* مَعْقُول

sensitive /ˈsensətɪv/ *adj* حَسَّاس

sensor /ˈsensə(r)/ *n* جِهَاز اسْتِشْعَار

sentence /ˈsentəns/ *n* (in grammar) جُمْلَة/جُمَل مف/ج (in law) حُكْم/أَحْكَام مف/ج

separate /ˈseprət/ *adj* مُخْتَلِف

♦ /ˈsepəreɪt/ *v* يُفَرِّق

separately /ˈseprətli/ *adv* عَلَى انْفِرَاد

S

September /sepˈtembə(r)/ *n* (see August) شَهْر أَيْلُول

sequence /ˈsiːkwəns/ *n* تَسَلْسُل

Serbia /ˈsɜːbɪə/ *n* الصِرْب

Serbian /ˈsɜːbɪən/ *adj, n* صِرْبِيّ ص/س

series /ˈsɪəriːz/ *n* سِلْسِلَة/سَلَاسِل مف/ج

serious /ˈsɪəriəs/ *adj* (accident) خَطِير (suggestion) هَامّ

seriously /ˈsɪəriəsli/ *adv* بِصُورَة خَطِيرَة

seriousness /ˈsɪəriəsnəs/ *n* خُطُورَة

sermon /ˈsɜːmən/ *n* خُطْبَة دِينِيَّة/خُطَب مف/ج

servant /ˈsɜːvənt/ *n* خَادِم

serve /sɜːv/ *v* (food, drinks) يُقَدِّم (in a shop) يَخْدِم

service /ˈsɜːvɪs/ *n* (to the public) خِدْمَة (of a vehicle) صِيَانَة (in tennis) إِرْسَال

sesame seed /ˈsesəmi/ *n* سِمْسِم

session /ˈseʃn/ *n* جَلْسَة

set /set/ *n* مَجْمُوعَة

♦ *v* (cement) يَتَصَلَّب

setting /ˈsetɪŋ/ *n* مَكَان وَزَمَان المَشْهَد

settle /ˈsetl/ *v* (a dispute) يُسَوِّي (a debt, bill) يُسَدِّد

seven /ˈsevn/ *num* سَبْعَة

seventeen /sevnˈtiːn/ *num* سَبْعَة عَشَر

seventh /ˈsevnθ/ *adj* سَابِع/سَوَابِعُ مف/ج

♦ *adv* سَابِعاً

♦ *n* (see tenth) السَابِع

seventy /ˈsevnti/ *num* سَبْعُون

several /ˈsevrəl/ *adj* عِدَّة

severe /sɪˈvɪə(r)/ *adj* (criticism) صَارِم (injury) بَالِغ

sew /səʊ/ *v* **sewed, sewed or sown** يُخَيِّط

sex /seks/ *n* (gender) جِنْس (activity) جِمَاع

sexual /ˈsekʃuəl/ *adj* جِنْسِيّ

sexuality /sekʃuˈæləti/ *n* جِنْسَانِيَّة

shade /ʃeɪd/ *n* ظِلّ/ظِلَال مف/ج

shadow /ˈʃædəʊ/ *n* ظِلّ/ظِلَال

shake /ʃeɪk/ *v* **shook, shaken** يَخُضّ

shaky /ˈʃeɪki/ *adj* مُرْتَعِش

shall /ʃəl, ʃæl/ *modal v* (in future tenses) سَوْفَ

I shall invite them. سَوْفَ أَدْعُوهُم

I shan't be long. لَن أَتَأَخَّر (in suggestions) هَلَّا

Shall we go by bus? هَل سَنَذْهَب بِالبَاص؟

Shall I come with you? هَل آتِي مَعَك؟

(showing determination) سَوْفَ

We shall defeat them. سَوْفَ نَهْزِمُهُم

shallow /ˈʃæləʊ/ *adj* ضَحْل

shame /ʃeɪm/ *n* عَار

shan't /ʃɑːnt/ *contr* (= shall not: see shall)

S

shape /ʃeɪp/ *n* شَكْل/أَشْكَال مف/ج
♦ *v* يُشَكِّل

share /ʃeə(r)/ *n* (part of sth) /حِصَّة حِصَص مف/ج (in a company) /سَهْم أَسْهُم مف/ج
♦ *v* يُوَزِّع

shark /ʃɑ:k/ *n* سَمَك القِرْش

sharp /ʃɑ:p/ *adj* حَادّ

shatter /ˈʃætə(r)/ *v* يُكَسِّر

shave /ʃeɪv/ *v* يَحْلِق

she /ʃi:/ *pron* هِيَ
She is from France. هِيَ مِن فَرَنْسَا

shed /ʃed/ *n* سَقِيفَة

she'd /ʃi:d/ *contr* (= he had, he would: see have, would)

sheep /ʃi:p/ *n* pl **sheep** /خَرُوف خِرَاف وَخِرْفَان مف/ج

sheet /ʃi:t/ *n* (on bed) مُلاءَة (of metal, glass) لَوْح/أَلْوَاح مف/ج

shelf /ʃelf/ *n* رَفّ/رُفُوف مف/ج

shell /ʃel/ *n* (of egg) قِشْرَة/قُشُور (for gun) قَذِيفَة/قَذَائِفُ مف/ج مف/ج

she'll /ʃi:l/ *contr* (= she will: see will)

shellfish /ˈʃelfɪʃ/ *n* مَحَار

shelter /ˈʃeltə(r)/ *n* مَلْجَأ/مَلَاجِئُ مف/ج

shepherd /ˈʃepəd/ *n* رَاعٍ/رُعَاة مف/ج

she's /ʃi:z/ *contr* (= she is, she has: see be, have)

shield /ʃi:ld/ *v* يَقِي

shift /ʃɪft/ *n* مُنَاوَبَة

shine /ʃaɪn/ *v* **shined** or **shone** يُضِيء

shiny /ˈʃaɪni/ *adj* لَامِع

ship /ʃɪp/ *n* سَفِينَة/سُفُن مف/ج
♦ *v* يَشْحَن

shipment /ˈʃɪpmənt/ *n* شُحْنَة

shirt /ʃɜ:t/ *n* قَمِيص/قُمْصَان مف/ج

shiver /ˈʃɪvə(r)/ *v* يَرْتَعِش

shock /ʃɒk/ *n* صَدْمَة
♦ *v* يَصْدُم

shoe /ʃu:/ *n* حِذَاء/أَحْذِيَة مف/ج

shoot /ʃu:t/ *v* **shot** (to fire a gun) يُطْلِق النَار (to fire a gun at sb) يُطْلِق الرَصَاص

shooting /ˈʃu:tɪŋ/ *n* إِطْلَاق النَار

shop /ʃɒp/ *n* مَتْجَر/مَتَاجِرُ مف/ج
♦ *v* يَتَسَوَّق

shopper /ˈʃɒpə(r)/ *n* مُتَسَوِّق

shopping /ˈʃɒpɪŋ/ *n* (activity) تَسَوُّق (items) مُشْتَرَيَات

shore /ʃɔ:(r)/ *n* شَاطِئ/شَوَاطِئُ مف/ج

short /ʃɔ:t/ *adj* (story, interview) قَصِير/قِصَار مف/ج
short hair شَعْر قَصِير
It's a short distance.
إِنَّهَا مَسَافَة قَصِيرَة

S

She is quite short. هِيَ قَصِيرَة جِدّاً

shortage /'ʃɔːtɪʤ/ *n* نَقْص

shorten /'ʃɔːtn/ *v* يُقَصِّر

shot /ʃɒt/ *n* (from gun) طَلْقَة نَار (attempt) مُحَاوَلَة

shotgun /'ʃɒtgʌn/ *n* بُنْدُقِيَّة/بَنَادِقُ مف/ج

should /ʃʊd/ *modal v* (in recommendations) يَجِب

You should be careful.
يَجِب أَنْ تَكُون حَذِراً

You shouldn't watch it.
يَجِب أَنْ لَا تُشَاهِدَهُ (in suggestions) هَلَّا

Should I phone them?
هَل يَجِب أَنْ أُهَاتِفَهُم؟

shouldn't /'ʃʊdnt/ *contr* (= should not: see should)

shoulder /'ʃəʊldə(r)/ *n* كَتِف/ أَكْتَاف (م) مف/ج

S

shout /ʃaʊt/ *n* صَيْحَة
♦ *v* يَصِيح

show /ʃəʊ/ *v* **showed, showed or shown** (to reveal: emotions, facts) يُرِي (a report, an office) يُبَيِّن
♦ *n* عَرْض/عُرُوض مف/ج

shower /'ʃaʊə(r)/ *n* (of rain) زَخَّة (for washing) دُشّ

shrimp /ʃrɪmp/ *n* جَمْبَرِيّ

shrine /ʃraɪn/ *n* مَقَام/مَقَامَات مف/ج

shrink /ʃrɪŋk/ *v* **shrank, shrunk** يَنْكَمِش

shrub /ʃrʌb/ *n* شُجَيْرَة

shrug /ʃrʌg/ *v* يَهُزّ كَتِفَيْهِ

shuffle /'ʃʌfl/ *v* يُجَرْجِر قَدَمَيْهِ

shut /ʃʌt/ *v* **shut** (a window, case) يُغْلِق (doors, windows) يَنْغَلِق

shy /ʃaɪ/ *adj* خَجُول

sick /sɪk/ *adj* مَرِيض/مَرْضَى مف/ج

sickness /'sɪknəs/ *n* مَرَض/أَمْرَاض مف/ج

side /saɪd/ *n* (of a box, house) جَانِب/ جَوَانِبُ مف/ج (in sport) فَرِيق/أَفْرِقَة مف/ج

sidewalk /'saɪdwɔːk/ *n* US رَصِيف/ أَرْصِفَة مف/ج

siege /siːʤ/ *n* حِصَار

sigh /saɪ/ *v* يَتَنَهَّد

sight /saɪt/ *n* (ability) بَصَر (thing seen) مَشْهَد/مَشَاهِدُ مف/ج

sign /saɪn/ *n* (on a roadl) لَافِتَة (gesture) إِشَارَة (indication) مُؤَشِّر/ مُؤَشِّرَات مف/ج
♦ *v* يُوَقِّع

signal /'sɪgnəl/ *n* (to do sth) إِشَارَة (for radio, etc) إِشَارَة الإِرْسَال

signature /'sɪgnətʃə(r)/ *n* تَوْقِيع/ تَوْقِيعَات مف/ج

significant /sɪg'nɪfɪkənt/ *adj* هَامّ

silence /'saɪləns/ *n* صَمْت

♦ *v* يُسْكِت

silent /'saɪlənt/ *adj* (street) سَاكِن (not speaking) صَامِت

silk /sɪlk/ *n* حَرِير

silly /'sɪli/ *adj* سَاذِج

silver /'sɪlvə(r)/ *n* فِضَّة

SIM card /sɪm/ *n* شَرِيحَة التَعْرِيف

similar /'sɪmələ(r)/ *adj* مُمَاثِل

similarity /sɪmə'lærəti/ *n* pl **-ties** تَشَابُه/تَشَابُهَات مف/ج

simple /'sɪmpl/ *adj* (solution) بَسِيط (food) عَادِيّ

simplify /'sɪmplɪfaɪ/ *v* يُبَسِّط

simply /'sɪmpli/ *adv* بِبَسَاطَة

simultaneous /sɪml'teɪniəs/ *adj* مُتَزَامِن

sin /sɪn/ *n* خَطِيئَة

since /sɪns/ *prep* (because) بِمَا أَنَّ

Since you didn't enrol, you cannot take the exam. بِمَا أَنَّكَ لَم تُسَجِّل فَلَا يُمْكِنُكَ التَقَدُّم لِلإِمْتِحَان

(in time expressions) مُنْذُ

since last August مُنْذُ آب المَاضِي

I've been here since Saturday. أَنَا هُنَا مُنْذُ السَبْت

♦ *adv* (in time expressions) مُنْذُ ذَلِكَ الحِين

He has never been back since. لَم يَأْتِ مُنْذُ ذَلِكَ الحِين

sincere /sɪn'sɪə(r)/ *adj* صَادِق

sing /sɪŋ/ *v* **sang, sung** يُغَنِّي

singer /'sɪŋə(r)/ *n* مُغَنٍّ

single /'sɪŋgl/ *adj* (one only) وَحِيد (not married) عَازِب/عُزَّاب مف/ج (room, bed) فَرْدِيّ

sink /sɪŋk/ *v* **sank, sunk** يَغْطُس

♦ *n* حَوْض/أَحْوَاض مف/ج

sip /sɪp/ *n* رَشْفَة

sir /sɜː(r)/ *n* سَيِّد/سَادَة مف/ج

sister /'sɪstə(r)/ *n* أُخْت/أَخَوَات (م) مف/ج

sit /sɪt/ *v* **sat** يَجْلِس

site /saɪt/ *n* مَوْقِع/مَوَاقِعُ مف/ج

situation /sɪtʃu'eɪʃn/ *n* (condition) وَضْع/أَوْضَاع مف/ج (location) مَوْقِع/ مَوَاقِعُ مف/ج

six /sɪks/ *num* سِتَّة

sixteen /sɪks'tiːn/ *num* سِتَّة عَشَر

sixth /sɪksθ/ *adj* سَادِس/سَوَادِسُ مف/ج

♦ *adv* سَادِساً

S

♦ *n* (see tenth) السَادِس

sixty /'sɪksti/ *num* سِتُّون

size /saɪz/ *n* (of building) حَجْم/أَحْجَام (for clothes) مَقَاس/مَقَاسَات مف/ج (of paper, screws, etc) مِقْيَاس/ مَقَايِيسُ مف/ج

skate /skeɪt/ *n* مِزْلَجَة/مَزَالِجُ مف/ج
♦ *v* يَتَزَلَّج

skeleton /'skelɪtn/ *n* هَيْكَل عَظْمِيّ

sketch /sketʃ/ *n* مِسْوَدَّة رَسْمَة

ski /ski:/ *n* زَلاَّجَة

skill /skɪl/ *n* مَهَارَة

skilled /skɪld/ *adj* مَاهِر

skin /skɪn/ *n* (person's) جِلْد/جُلُود (of fruit, etc) قِشْرَة/قُشُور مف/ج

skinny /'skɪni/ *adj* نَحِيف

skip /skɪp/ *v* (with a rope) يَثِب (a meal, stage) يُفَوِّت

skirt /skɜ:t/ *n* تَنُّورَة/تَنَانِيرُ مف/ج

skull /skʌl/ *n* جُمْجُمَة/جَمَاجِمُ مف/ج

sky /skaɪ/ *n* pl **skies** سَمَاء/سَمَاوَات مف/ج

slab /slæb/ *n* لَوْح/أَلْوَاح مف/ج

slack /slæk/ *adj* رَخْو

slam /slæm/ *v* يَغْلِق بِقُوَّة

slap /slæp/ *v* يَصْفَع

slash /slæʃ/ *v* يَشْرُط

slate /sleɪt/ *n* لَوْح قِرْمِيد

slave /sleɪv/ *n* عَبْد/عِبَاد مف/ج

slavery /'sleɪvəri/ *n* عُبُودِيَّة

sleep /sli:p/ *n* نَوْم
♦ *v* **slept** يَنَام

sleeve /sli:v/ *n* كُمّ/أَكْمَام مف/ج

slice /slaɪs/ *n* شَرِيحَة/شَرَائِحُ مف/ج

slide /slaɪd/ *n* (in a playground) مَزْلَقَة/مَزَالِقُ مف/ج (photographic) شَرِيحَة/شَرَائِحُ مف/ج
♦ *v* **slid** يَنْزَلِق

slight /slaɪt/ *adj* طَفِيف

slightly /'slaɪtli/ *adv* بِشَكْل طَفِيف

slim /slɪm/ *adj* نَحِيف

slip /slɪp/ *n* (mistake) زَلَّة (underskirt) شَلْحَة
♦ *v* يَنْزَلِق

slogan /'sləʊgən/ *n* شِعَار/شِعَارَات مف/ج

slope /sləʊp/ *n* مُنْحَدَر/مُنْحَدَرَات مف/ج

slot /slɒt/ *n* فَتْحَة

Slovenia /slə'vi:nɪə/ *n* سْلُوفَانْيَا

Slovenian /slə'vi:nɪən/ *adj, n* سْلُوفِينِيّ ص/س

slow /sləʊ/ *adj* (train) بَطِيء (learner) غَبِيّ/أَغْبِيَاءُ مف/ج

S

smack /smæk/ *v* يَصْفَع

small /smɔːl/ *adj* (man, school) صَغِير/صِغَار مف/ج

a small loan قِرْض صَغِير

It's too small for me.

تَافِه (mistake) هُوَ صَغِير جِدّاً عَلَيَّ

smart /smɑːt/ *adj* (elegant) أَنِيق (clever) ذَكِيّ/أَذْكِيَاءُ مف/ج

smash /smæʃ/ *v* يُحَطِّم

smell /smel/ *v* **smelled or smelt** (the flowers) يَشُمّ (roses, coffee) يَفُوح مِنْهُ رَائِحَة

♦ *n* رَائِحَة/رَوَائِحُ مف/ج

smile /smaɪl/ *n* ابْتِسَامَة

♦ *v* يَبْتَسِم

smoke /sməʊk/ *n* دُخَّان

♦ *v* يُدَخِّن

smoker /'sməʊkə(r)/ *n* مُدَخِّن

smooth /smuːð/ *adj* نَاعِم

smuggle /'smʌgl/ *v* يُهَرِّب

snack /snæk/ *n* وَجْبَة خَفِيفَة

snake /sneɪk/ *n* ثُعْبَان/ثَعَابِينُ مف/ج

snatch /snætʃ/ *v* يَخْطِف

sniff /snɪf/ *v* يَتَنَشَّق

sniper /'snaɪpə(r)/ *n* قَنَّاص

snow /snəʊ/ *n* ثَلْج/ثُلُوج مف/ج

so /səʊ/ *adv* (very) جِدّاً

He's so handsome. هُوَ وَسِيم جِدّاً

(showing result) وَبِالتَّالِي

He's so lazy that he's lost his job.

هُوَ كَسُول وَبِالتَّالِي فَقَد خَسِرَ وَظِيفَتَهُ

(for emphasis) إِذاً

So, what's next? إِذاً مَاذَا بَعْد؟

♦ *conj* (as a result) وَبِالتَّالِي

He woke up late so

he missed the bus.

اسْتَيْقَظَ مُتَأَخِّراً وَبِالتَّالِي فَقَد فَاتَهُ البَاص

(in order that) لِكَي

so as to save water لِكَي نُوَفِّر المَاء

I spoke slowly so (that) he would

understand me.

تَكَلَّمْتُ بِبُطْء لِكَي يَفْهَمَنِي

soak /səʊk/ *v* (clothes) يَنْقَع (a person) يُبَلِّل

soap /səʊp/ *n* صَابُونَة/صَوَابِينُ مف/ج

sob /sɒb/ *v* يَنْشِج

soccer /'sɒkə(r)/ *n* لُعْبَة كُرَة القَدَم

social /'səʊʃl/ *adj* اجْتِمَاعِيّ

socialism /'səʊʃəlɪzəm/ *n* اشْتِرَاكِيَّة

socialist /'səʊʃəlɪst/ *adj*, *n* اشْتِرَاكِيّ ص/س

society /sə'saɪəti/ *n* pl **-ties** (club, etc) جَمْعِيَّة (in sociology) مُجْتَمَع/مُجْتَمَعَات مف/ج

sock /sɒk/ *n* جَوْرَب/جَوَارِبُ مف/ج

S

sofa /'səʊfə/ *n* أَرِيكَة/أَرَائِكُ مف/ج

soft /sɒft/ *adj* نَاعِم

soften /'sɒfn/ *v* (to become soft) يُطَرِّي (to make soft) يَطْرَى

software /'sɒftweə(r)/ *n* بَرَامِج الحَاسُوب

soil /sɔɪl/ *n* تُرْبَة/أَتْرِبَة مف/ج

soldier /'səʊldʒə(r)/ *n* جُنْدِيّ/جُنُود مف/ج

solicitor /sə'lɪsɪtə(r)/ *n* (in UK) مُحَامٍ

solid /'sɒlɪd/ *adj* (walls) صُلْب (gold, silver) خَام
♦ *n* مَادَّة صُلْبَة

solution /sə'lu:ʃn/ *n* حَلّ/حُلُول مف/ج

solve /sɒlv/ *v* يَحُلّ

Somali /sə'mɑ:li/ *n* (language) اللُغَةالصُومَالِيَّة
♦ *n* (person) صُومَالِيّ

Somalia /sə'mɑ:lɪə/ *n* الصُومَال

S

Somalian /sə'mɑ:lɪən/ *adj* صُومَالِيّ

some /sʌm/ *adj* (unspecified) بَعْض
some money بَعْض المَال (with plural nouns) بَعْض
some ideas بَعْض الأَفْكَار
Some people think he's wrong.
يَعْتَقِد بَعْض النَاس أَنَّهُ عَلَى خَطَأ
♦ *pron* (a number of sth) بِضْع
Some miles بِضْعَة كِيلُومِتْرَات (a quantity of sth) بَعْض
Try some, you'll like it.
تَذَوَّق بَعْضاً مِنْهَا فَسَوْفَ تُحِبُّهَا

somebody /'sʌmbədi/ *pron* شَخْص مَا
Somebody will find it.
شَخْص مَا سَيَجِدُهَا
Call somebody to fix it.
اتَّصِل بِشَخْص مَا لِيُصَلِّحَهَا

somehow /'sʌmhaʊ/ *adv* بِطَرِيقَة مَا

someone /'sʌmwʌn/ *pron* (see somebody)

something /'sʌmθɪŋ/ *pron* شَيْء مَا

sometimes /'sʌmtaɪmz/ *adv* أَحْيَاناً
I sometimes go by train.
أَذْهَب أَحْيَاناً بِالقِطَار

somewhat /'sʌmwɒt/ *adv* إِلَى حَدّ مَا

somewhere /'sʌmweə(r)/ *adv* فِي مَكَان مَا

son /sʌn/ *n* ابْن/أَبْنَاء مف/ج

song /sɒŋ/ *n* أُغْنِيَة/أَغَانٍ مف/ج

soon /su:n/ *adv* (in a short time) سَرِيعاً، حَالاً
She soon finished her homework.
أَنْجَزَت وَاجِبَهَا بِشَكْل سَرِيع
I'll see you soon. سَوْفَ أَرَاكَ حَالاً
as soon as حَالَمَا *Call me as soon as you land.* اتَّصِل بِي حَالَمَا تَحُطّ الطَائِرَة

sophisticated /sə'fɪstɪkeɪtɪd/ *adj*

(tastes) مُتَطَوِّر (software) رَفِيع الْمُسْتَوَى

sore /sɔ:(r)/ *adj* مُؤْلِم

sorghum /'sɔ:gəm/ *n* ذُرَة الْمَكَانِس

sorrow /'sɒrəʊ/ *n* أَسَف

sorry /'sɒri/ *adj* آسِف

sort /sɔ:t/ *n* نَوْع/أَنْوَاع مف/ج
♦ *v* يَفْرِز

soul /səʊl/ *n* رُوح/أَرْوَاح مف/ج

sound /saʊnd/ *adj* مَتِين
♦ *n* صَوْت/أَصْوَات مف/ج

soup /su:p/ *n* حِسَاء

sour /'saʊə(r)/ *adj* حَامِض/حَوَامِضُ مف/ج

source /sɔ:s/ *n* مَصْدَر/مَصَادِرُ مف/ج

south /saʊθ/ *n* جَنُوب
to live in the south يَعِيش فِي الجَنُوب
♦ *adj* فِي الجَنُوب
♦ *adv* نَحْوَ الجَنُوب

South Africa *n* جَنُوب إِفْرِيقِيَا

South African *adj, n* جَنُوب إِفْرِيقِيّ ص/س

South America *n* جَنُوب أَمْرِيكَا

South American *adj, n* جَنُوب أَمْرِيكِيّ ص/س

southern /'sʌðən/ *adj* جَنُوبِيّ

soybean /'sɔɪbi:n/ *n* فُول الصُّويَا

space /speɪs/ *n* (distance) مَسَافَة (in the universe) فَضَاء

spacecraft /'speɪskrɑ:ft/ *n* سَفِينَة فَضَاء

Spain /speɪn/ *n* إِسْبَانِيَا

spam /spæm/ *n* بَرِيد عَشْوَائِيّ

Spaniard /'spanjəd/ *n* إِسْبَانِيّ/إِسْبَان مف/ج

Spanish /'spænɪʃ/ *adj* إِسْبَانِيّ
♦ *n* (language) اللُّغَة الإِسْبَانِيَّة (people) إِسْبَان

spare /speə(r)/ *adj* احْتِيَاطِيّ
♦ *v* يُوَفِّر

spark /spɑ:k/ *n* شَرَارَة/شَرَار مف/ج

speak /spi:k/ *v* **spoke, spoken** (to talk) يَتَكَلَّم (a language) يَتَحَدَّث

speaker /'spi:kə(r)/ *n* مُكَبِّر الصَّوْت

special /'speʃl/ *adj* (equipment) خَاصّ (occasion) اسْتِثْنَائِيّ

specialist /'speʃəlɪst/ *n* أَخِصَّائِيّ

specialize /'speʃəlaɪz/ *v* يَتَخَصَّص

specially /'speʃəli/ *adv* بِشَكْل خَاصّ

specialty /'speʃəlti/ *n* pl **-ties** تَخَصُّص/تَخَصُّصَات مف/ج

species /'spi:ʃi:z/ *n* صِنْف/أَصْنَاف مف/ج

specific /spə'sɪfɪk/ *adj* مُحَدَّد

S

specify /'spesɪfaɪ/ *v* يُحَدِّد

specimen /'spesɪmən/ *n* (of a plant) عَيِّنَة (of blood) نَمُوذَج/نَمَاذِجُ مف/ج

spectacular /spek'tækjələ(r)/ *adj* مُذْهِل

spectator /spek'teɪtə(r)/ *n* مُتَفَرِّج

speculate /'spekjuleɪt/ *v* يُضَارِب

speech /spi:tʃ/ *n* (to meeting) خِطَاب/خِطَابَات مف/ج (way of speaking) لَهْجَة

speed /spi:d/ *n* سُرْعَة **sped** ♦ *v* يُسْرِع

speed camera *n* كَامِيرَة السُرْعَة

speedy /'spi:di/ *adj* سَرِيع

spell /spel/ *v* **spelled or spelt** يُهَجِّي

spend /spend/ *v* **spent** (money) يُنْفِق (time) يُمْضِي

sphere /sfɪə(r)/ *n* جِسْم كُرَوِيّ

spice /spaɪs/ *n* تَابِل/تَوَابِلُ مف/ج

S

spider /'spaɪdə(r)/ *n* عَنْكَبُوت/عَنَاكِبُ مف/ج

spill /spɪl/ *v* يَدْلُق

spin /spɪn/ *v* **span, spun** (wool, etc) يَغْزِل (turn in circles) يَدُور بِسُرْعَة

spinach /'spɪnɪʤ/ *n* سَبَانخ

spine /spaɪn/ *n* العَمُود الفِقْرِيّ

spirit /'spɪrɪt/ *n* (soul) رُوح/أَرْوَاح (morale) الرُوح المَعْنَوِيَّة مف/ج

spiritual /'spɪrɪtʃuəl/ *adj* رُوحَانِيّ

spit /spɪt/ *v* **spat** يَبْصُق

splash /splæʃ/ *v* يَرُشّ

splendid /'splendɪd/ *adj* رَائِع

split /splɪt/ *v* **split** يَتَمَزَّق

spoil /spɔɪl/ *v* **spoiled, spoilt** يُفْسِد

spoke /spəʊk/ *n* بَرْمَق/بَرَامِقُ مف/ج

spoon /spu:n/ *n* مِلْعَقَة/مَلَاعِقُ مف/ج

sport /spɔ:t/ *n* رِيَاضَة

spot /spɒt/ *n* (dot) رُقْعَة/رُقَع مف/ج (place) مَكَان/أَمَاكِنُ مف/ج (dirty mark) بُقْعَة/بُقَع مف/ج (pimple) بَثْرَة/بُثُور مف/ج

spotlight /'spɒtlaɪt/ *n* ضَوْء كَشَّاف

spouse /spaʊz/ *n* زَوْج

spray /spreɪ/ *n* رَذَاذ

spread /spred/ *v* **spread** (the jam, flour) يَكْسُو (news, fires) يَنْتَشِر

spring /sprɪŋ/ *n* (see summer) رَبِيع (in mattress, etc) زَنْبَرَك/زَنْبَرَكَات مف/ج (for water) نَبْع/نُبُوع مف/ج

spy /spaɪ/ *n* pl **spies** جَاسُوس/جَوَاسِيسُ مف/ج

squadron /'skwɒdrən/ *n* سِرْب/أَسْرَاب مف/ج

square /skweə(r)/ *adj* مُرَبَّع
♦ *n* (shape) مُرَبَّع/مُرَبَّعَات مف/ج (in towns) مَيْدَان/مَيَادِينُ مف/ج

squash /skwɒʃ/ *n* (crush) شَيْء (vegetable) قَرْعِيَّات، قَرْع مَهْرُوس (drink) عَصِير/عَصَائِرُ مف/ج وكُوسَا
♦ *v* يَسْحَق

squeeze /skwi:z/ *v* يَعْصُر

squid /skwɪd/ *n* سَمَك الحَبَّار

stab /stæb/ *v* يَطْعَن

stable /'steɪbl/ *adj* مُسْتَقِرّ
♦ *n* إِسْطَبْل/إِسْطَبْلَات مف/ج

stadium /'steɪdiəm/ *n* مَلْعَب مُدَرَّج

staff /stɑ:f/ *n* طَاقِم المُوَظَّفِين

stage /steɪʤ/ *n* (in development) مَرْحَلَة/مَرَاحِلُ مف/ج (in theatre) خَشَبَة المَسْرَح

stain /steɪn/ *n* (from liquid) بُقْعَة/بُقَع مف/ج
♦ *v* يُلَطِّخ

stair /steə(r)/ *n* دَرَج

staircase /'steəkeɪs/ *n* بَيْت الدَرَج

stall /stɔ:l/ *n* بَسْطَة

stamp /stæmp/ *n* طَابِع/طَوَابِعُ مف/ج
♦ *v* (a document) يَخْتِم

stand /stænd/ *n* حَمَّالَة عَرْض
♦ *v* **stood** يَقِف

standard /'stændəd/ *n* مِعْيَار/مَعَايِيرُ مف/ج
♦ *adj* عَادِيّ

star /stɑ:(r)/ *n* (in space) نَجْم/نُجُوم (celebrity) نَجْمَة/نَجمَات مف/ج

stare /steə(r)/ *v* يُحَدِّق

start /stɑ:t/ *n* بِدَايَة
♦ *v* يَبْدَأ

starve /stɑ:v/ *v* يَتَجَوَّع

state /steɪt/ *n* (condition) حَالَة (of a country) وِلاَيَة (nation) دَوْلَة/دُوَل
♦ *v* يُعَبِّر عَن

statement /'steɪtmənt/ *n* إِفَادَة

station /'steɪʃn/ *n* مَحَطَّة

statistic /stə'tɪstɪk/ *n* بَنْد إِحْصَائِيّ

statue /'stætʃu:/ *n* نُصْب تِذْكَارِيّ

stay /steɪ/ *n* إِقَامَة
♦ *v* (to remain) يَبْقَى (in a hotel, etc) يَمْكُث

steady /'stedi/ *adj* ثَابِت

steak /steɪk/ *n* شَرِيحَة لَحْم

steal /sti:l/ *v* **stole, stolen** يَسْرِق

steam /sti:m/ *n* بُخَار/أَبْخِرَة مف/ج

steel /sti:l/ *n* فُولاَذ

steep /sti:p/ *adj* (hill) شَدِيد الاِنْحِدَار (increase) حَادّ

steer /stɪə(r)/ *v* يَقُود

S

stem /stem/ *n* سَاق/سِيقَان (م) مف/ج

step /step/ *n* (in walking) خُطْوَة (on stairs) دَرَجَة
♦ *v* (عَلَى) يَدُوس

stereo /'steriəʊ/ *n* (sound quality) سْتِيرِيُو (player) مُسَجِّل سْتِيرِيُو

sterile /'steraɪl/ *adj* مُعَقَّم

stick /stɪk/ *n* عَصًا/عِصِيّ (م) مف/ج
♦ *v* يُلْصِق

sticky /'stɪki/ *adj* دَبِق

stiff /stɪf/ *adj* صُلْب

still /stɪl/ *adj* (unmoving) ثَابِت *to sit still* يَجْلِس بِشَكْل ثَابِت (water) بِدُون كَرْبُون
♦ *adv* لاَ يَزَال
He's still at the office.
لاَ يَزَال فِي المَكْتَب
He still works at the post office.
لاَ يَزَال يَعْمَل فِي مَكْتَب البَرِيد

S

sting /stɪŋ/ *v* **stung** يَلْسَع

stir /stɜː(r)/ *v* (in sleep) يَتَقَلَّب (the soup) يُحَرِّك

stock /stɒk/ *n* (supply) مَخْزُون/مَخْزُونَات مف/ج
♦ *v* يُخَزِّن

stolen /'stəʊlən/ *adj* مَسْرُوق

stomach /'stʌmək/ *n* مَعِدَة/مِعَد مف/ج

stone /stəʊn/ *n* (small rock) حَجَر/ حِجَارَة مف/ج (of a fruit) نَوَاة/نَوًى مف/ج

stool /stuːl/ *n* كُرْسِيّ بِلاَ ظَهْر أَو ذِرَاعَيْن

stop /stɒp/ *v* (a machine, car) يُوقِف (cars, engines) يَتَوَقَّف
♦ *n* (for bus, tram, etc) مَوْقِف/مَوَاقِف مف/ج

storage /'stɔːrɪdʒ/ *n* تَخْزِين

store /stɔː(r)/ *n* (supply) مَخْزَن/ مَخَازِن مف/ج (shop) دُكَّان/دَكَاكِين
♦ *v* يُخَزِّن

storm /stɔːm/ *n* عَاصِفَة/عَوَاصِف مف/ج

story /'stɔːri/ *n* pl **-ries** قِصَّة/قِصَص مف/ج

straight /streɪt/ *adj* مُسْتَقِيم
♦ *adv* مُبَاشَرَة

straightforward /streɪt'fɔːwəd/ *adj* سَهْل

strain /streɪn/ *n* ضَغْط/ضُغُوط مف/ج
♦ *v* (a muscle) يُجْهِد (vegetables) يُصَفِّي

strange /streɪndʒ/ *adj* غَرِيب/غُرَبَاء مف/ج

stranger /'streɪndʒə(r)/ *n* غَرِيب/ غُرَبَاء مف/ج

strap /stræp/ *n* رِبَاط/أَرْبِطَة مف/ج

strategy /'strætədʒi/ *n* pl **-gies** إسْتِرَاتِيجِيَّة

straw /strɔː/ *n* (dry stalks) قَشَّة/قَشّ (for drinking) قَصَبَة مَصّ مف/ج

strawberry /'strɔːbəri/ *n* pl **-ries** فَرَاوْلَة

stream /striːm/ *n* جَدْوَل/جَدَاوِلُ مف/ج

street /striːt/ *n* شَارِع/شَوَارِعُ مف/ج

strength /streŋθ/ *n* قُوَّة/قُوَى مف/ج

strengthen /'streŋθn/ *v* يُقَوِّي

stress /stres/ *n* (emotional) ضَغْط/ضُغُوط مف/ج (in grammar) تَشْدِيد
♦ *v* (an advantage) يُؤَكِّد

stressful /'stresfl/ *adj* مُرْهِق

stretch /stretʃ/ *n* امْتِدَاد/امْتِدَادَات مف/ج
♦ *v* يَمْتَدّ

strict /strɪkt/ *adj* صَارِم

strike /straɪk/ *n* إضْرَاب/إضْرَابَات مف/ج
♦ *v* **struck** (to hit) يَضْرِب (workers) يُضْرِب

striker /'straɪkə(r)/ *n* (worker) مُضْرِب عَن العَمَل (in football) رَأْس حَرْبَة

string /strɪŋ/ *n* خَيْط/خُيُوط مف/ج

strip /strɪp/ *n* قِطْعَة رَفِيعَة وَطَوِيلَة مِن أَرْض، قُمَاش، إلخ

stripe /straɪp/ *n* تَقْلِيمَة

stroke /strəʊk/ *n* (medical) جُلْطَة دِمَاغِيَّة
♦ *v* (a cat) يُمَسِّد

stroll /strəʊl/ *v* يَتَمَشَّى

strong /strɒŋ/ *adj* قَوِيّ

structure /'strʌktʃə(r)/ *n* تَرْكِيب

struggle /'strʌgl/ *n* كِفَاح
♦ *v* (to do sth) يُكَافِح (to fight) يُصَارِع

student /'stjuːdnt/ *n* طَالِب/طُلاَّب مف/ج

study /'stʌdi/ *n* pl **-dies** دِرَاسَة
♦ *v* يَدْرُس

stuff /stʌf/ *n* أَشْيَاءُ

stumble /'stʌmbl/ *v* يَتَعَثَّر

stupid /'stjuːpɪd/ *adj* غَبِيّ/أَغْبِيَاءُ مف/ج

style /staɪl/ *n* أُسْلُوب/أَسَالِيبُ مف/ج

stylish /'staɪlɪʃ/ *adj* أَنِيق

subject /'sʌbdʒekt/ *n* (of conversation) مَوْضُوع/مَوَاضِيعُ مف/ج (in education) مَادَّة دِرَاسِيَّة

submit /səb'mɪt/ *v* يَخْضَع لِ

subscriber /səb'skraɪbə(r)/ *n* مُشْتَرِك

subscription /səb'skrɪpʃn/ *n* اشْتِرَاك/اشْتِرَاكَات مف/ج

subsidiary /səb'sɪdiəri/ *n* pl **-ries** فَرْع/فُرُوع مف/ج

subsidy /'sʌbsədi/ *n* pl **-dies** دَعْم

substance /'sʌbstəns/ *n* مَادَّة/مَوَادّ مف/ج

substantial /səb'stænʃl/ *adj* كَبِير

substitute /'sʌbstɪtju:t/ *n* بَدِيل/بَدَائِلُ مف/ج

♦ *v* يَسْتَبْدِل

subtle /'sʌtl/ *adj* بَاهِت

suburb /'sʌbɜ:b/ *n* ضَاحِيَة/ضَوَاحٍ مف/ج

suburban /sə'bɜ:bən/ *adj* من الضَوَاحِي

subway /'sʌbweɪ/ *n* (in US: city transport) قِطَار أَنْفَاق (under road) نَفَق مُشَاة

succeed /sək'si:d/ *v* يَنْجَح

success /sək'ses/ *n* نَجَاح

S

successful /sək'sesfl/ *adj* نَاجِح

succession /sək'seʃn/ *n* تَعَاقُب

successor /sək'sesə(r)/ *n* خَلِيفَة/خُلَفَاءُ مف/ج

such /sʌtʃ/ *adj* مِثْل

suck /sʌk/ *v* يَمُصّ

Sudan /su:'dɑ:n/ *n* السُودَان

Sudanese /su:də'ni:z/ *adj, n* سُودَانِيّ ص/س

sudden /'sʌdn/ *adj* مُفَاجِئ

suddenly /'sʌdənli/ *adv* فَجْأَةً

sue /su:/ *v* يَرْفَع دَعْوَى عَلَى

suffer /'sʌfə(r)/ *v* يُعَانِي

suffering /'sʌfərɪŋ/ *n* مُعَانَاة

sufficient /sə'fɪʃnt/ *adj* كَافٍ

sugar /'ʃʊgə(r)/ *n* سُكَّر

suggest /sə'dʒest/ *v* يَقْتَرِح

suggestion /sə'dʒestʃən/ *n* اقْتِرَاح/اقْتِرَاحَات مف/ج

suicide /'su:ɪsaɪd/ *n* انْتِحَار

suit /su:t/ *n* بَدْلَة/بَدَلَات مف/ج

♦ *v* (to be convenient) يُنَاسِب (clothes, colour) يُلَائِم

suitable /'su:təbl/ *adj* مُلَائِم

suitcase /'su:tkeɪs/ *n* حَقِيبَة سَفَر

suite /swi:t/ *n* جَنَاح/أَجْنِحَة مف/ج

sum /sʌm/ *n* (of money) مَبْلَغ (addition) عَمَلِيَّة حِسَابِيَّة

summary /'sʌməri/ *n* pl **-ries** مُلَخَّص/مُلَخَّصَات مف/ج

summer /'sʌmə(r)/ *n* صَيْف

in summer فِي الصَيْف

last summer الصَيْف المَاضِي

next summer الصَيْف القَادِم

during the summer خِلَالَ الصَيْف

summit /'sʌmɪt/ *n* قِمَّة/قِمَم مف/ج

sun /sʌn/ *n* (م) شَمْس

Sunday /'sʌndeɪ/ *n* (see Wednesday) الأَحَد

sunlight /'sʌnlaɪt/ *n* ضَوْء الشَمْس

sunny /'sʌni/ *adj* مُشْمِس

sunset /'sʌnset/ *n* غُرُوب

sunshine /'sʌnʃaɪn/ *n* أَشِعَّة الشَمْس

superior /suː'pɪəriə(r)/ *adj* (quality, materials) أَفْضَل مِن (officer, rank) أَعْلَى مَنْزِلَة

superiority /suːpɪəri'ɒrəti/ *n* تَفَوُّق

supermarket /'suːpəmɑːkɪt/ *n* مَتْجَر كَبِير

supervise /'suːpəvaɪz/ *v* يُشْرِف

supervision /suːpə'vɪʒn/ *n* إِشْرَاف

supervisor /'suːpəvaɪzə(r)/ *n* مُشْرِف

supper /'sʌpə(r)/ *n* عَشَاء

supplement /'sʌplɪmənt/ *n* إِضَافَة

supply /sə'plaɪ/ *n* pl **lies** مَخْزُون
♦ *v* يُزَوِّد بِـ

support /sə'pɔːt/ *n* (physical) دِعَامَة (psychological) دَعْم
♦ *v* (a roof, etc) يَسْنِد (a team) يُسَانِد (financially) يَدْعَم

supporter /sə'pɔːtə(r)/ *n* مُشَجِّع

suppose /sə'pəʊz/ *v* يَفْتَرِض

sure /ʃʊə(r)/ *adj* مُتَأَكِّد

surely /'ʃʊəli/ *adv* بِالتَأْكِيد

surface /'sɜːfɪs/ *n* سَطْح/أَسْطُح مف/ج

surgeon /'sɜːdʒən/ *n* جَرَّاح

surgery /'sɜːdʒəri/ *n* pl **-ries** (premises) عِيَادَة (operation) جِرَاحَة

surplus /'sɜːpləs/ *n* فَائِض

surprise /sə'praɪz/ *n* مُفَاجَأَة
♦ *v* يُفَاجِئ

surrender /sə'rendə(r)/ *v* يَسْتَسْلِم

surround /sə'raʊnd/ *v* يُطَوِّق

survey /'sɜːveɪ/ *n* اسْتِبْيَان/اسْتِبْيَانَات مف/ج

survival /sə'vaɪvl/ *n* بَقَاء

survive /sə'vaɪv/ *v* يَنْجُو

survivor /sə'vaɪvə(r)/ *n* نَاجٍ

suspect *v* /sə'spekt/ (sth) يَشُكّ فِي
♦ *n* /'sʌspekt/ المُشْتَبَه بِهِ

suspend /sə'spend/ *v* يُعَلِّق

suspicion /sə'spɪʃn/ *n* شَكّ/شُكُوك مف/ج

suspicious /sə'spɪʃəs/ *adj* مَشْبُوه

swallow /'swɒləʊ/ *v* يَبْلَع

swap /swɒp/ *v* يَتَبَادَل

sway /sweɪ/ *v* يَتَمَايَل

swear /sweə(r)/ *v* **swore, sworn** (to promise) يُقْسِم (to say oaths) يَسُبّ

sweat /swet/ *n* عَرَق
♦ *v* يَعْرَق

sweater /'swetə(r)/ *n* سُتْرَة

sweep /swi:p/ *v* **swept** يَكْنُس

sweet /swi:t/ *adj* حُلْو

sweetbread /'swi:tbred/ *n* بَنْكِرْيَاس العِجْل أو الحَمَل

sweetcorn /'swi:tkɔ:n/ *n* ذُرَة سُكَّرِيَّة

sweetener /'swi:tnə(r)/ *n* مُحَلٍّ

sweet potato *n* بَطَاطَا حُلْوَة

swell /swel/ *v* **swelled, swollen or swelled** يَنْتَفِخ

swim /swɪm/ *v* **swam, swum** يَسْبَح

swimmer /'swɪmə(r)/ *n* سَبَّاح

swing /swɪŋ/ *n* أُرْجُوحَة/أَرَاجِيحُ مف/ج
♦ *v* **swung** يَتَأَرْجَح

swipe card /swaɪp/ *n* بِطَاقَة مُرُور إِلِكْتْرُونِيَّة

Swiss /swɪs/ *adj* سْوِيسْرِيّ
♦ *n* pl **Swiss** (citizen) سْوِيسْرِيّ

switch /swɪtʃ/ *n* مِفْتَاح الكَهْرَبَاء

sword /sɔ:d/ *n* سَيْف/سُيُوف مف/ج

Sydney /'sɪdni/ *n* سِدْنِي

symbol /'sɪmbl/ *n* رَمْز/رُمُوز مف/ج

symbolic /sɪm'bɒlɪk/ *adj* رَمْزِيّ

sympathetic /sɪmpə'θetɪk/ *adj* مُتَعَاطِف

sympathy /'sɪmpəθi/ *n* عَطْف

symptom /'sɪmptəm/ *n* عَرْض/ أَعْرَاض مف/ج

synagogue /'sɪnəgɒg/ *n* كَنِيس/ كَنَس مف/ج

Syria /'sɪrɪə/ *n* سُورِيَا

Syrian /'sɪrɪən/ *adj, n* سُورِيّ ص/س

system /'sɪstəm/ *n* نِظَام/نُظُم مف/ج

systematic /sɪstə'mætɪk/ *adj* مُنْتَظَم

S

T

tabbouleh /ˈtæbuːleɪ/ *n* تَبُّولَة

table /ˈteɪbl/ *n* (furniture) طَاوِلَة (of data) جَدْوَل/جَدَاوِلُ مف/ج

tackle /ˈtækl/ *n* (in sport) عَرْقَلَة لَاعِب الخَصْم لِأَخْذ الكُرَة مِنْهُ
♦ *v* (a problem) يُعَالِج (in sport) يُهَاجِم الخَصْم فِي سَاحَة المَلْعَب

tactic /ˈtæktɪk/ *n* وَسِيلَة/وَسَائِلُ مف/ج

tag /tæg/ *n* بِطَاقَة

tahini /təˈhiːni/ *n* طَحِينَة

tail /teɪl/ *n* ذَيْل/أَذْيَال مف/ج

tailor /ˈteɪlə(r)/ *n* خَيَّاط

take /teɪk/ *v* **took, taken** (to move, carry) يَأْخُذ
Take this to your mother. خُذ هَذَا لِأُمِّكَ (to accompany) يُرَافِق
He took me to the station. رَافَقَنِي إِلَى المَحَطَّة (to remove) يَأْخُذ
They've taken my bag. أَخَذُوا حَقِيبَتِي
Take some money from my purse. خُذ بَعْض النُقُود مِن مِحْفَظَتِي (a bus) يَأْخُذ
I took a taxi to get here. أَخَذْتُ سَيَّارَة أُجْرَة لِلمَجِيء هُنَا
Take the first exit. خُذ المَخْرَج الأَوَّل
(a photograph) يَلْتَقِط
They took a lot of photos. اِلْتَقَطُوا صُوَراً كَثِيرَة (medicine) يَبْتَلِع
Do you take milk? هَل تَسْتَعْمِل الحَلِيب
She doesn't take enough exercise. لَا تُمَارِس الرِيَاضَة بِمَا يَكْفِي (to last) يَحْتَاج
How long will it take? كَم مِن الوَقْت يَحْتَاج ذَلِكَ؟
It takes us four hours to get there. نَحتَاج إِلَى أَرْبَع سَاعَات لِلوُصُول هُنَاكَ

take away *phv* (to confiscate) يُصَادِر
They took his licence away. صَادَرُوا رُخْصَتَهُ (to lead off) يَنْقُل

take back *phv* (a purchase) يُرْجِع
I had to take the camera back. اُضْطُرِرْتُ لِإِرْجَاع آلَة التَصْوِير
(an accusation) يَتَرَاجَع عَن

take off *phv* (clothing) يَخْلَع *Take your coat off.* اخْلَع مِعْطَفَكَ
(time from work) يُعَطِّل (aircraft) يُقْلِع

take out *phv* يَدْعُو لِوَجْبَة خَارِجَ المَنْزِل

take over *phv* (to take control) يَتَوَلَّى

T

He's taken over as manager. لَقَد تولَّى مَنْصِب المُدِير

take up *phv* (space) يَمْلَأ (time) يَشْغَل

talent /'tælənt/ *n* مَوْهِبَة/مَوَاهِبُ مف/ج

talk /tɔ:k/ *n* (conversation) حَدِيث (lecture) مُحَاضَرَة
♦ *v* يَتَحَدَّث

tall /tɔ:l/ *adj* (person) طَوِيل (building, tree) عَالٍ

Talmud, the /'tælmʊd/ *n* التَلْمُود

tangerine /tændʒə'ri:n/ *n* مَنْدَرِين

tank /tæŋk/ *n* (military) دَبَّابَة (storage) خَزَّان/خَزَّانَات مف/ج

tanker /'tæŋkə(r)/ *n* نَاقِلَة نَفْط

tap /tæp/ *n* (for water) حَنَفِيَّة (light blow) نَقْرَة
♦ *v* يَنْقُر

tape /teɪp/ *n* (adhesive) شَرِيط لَاصِق (for recording) شَرِيط/أَشْرِطَة مف/ج

target /'tɑ:gɪt/ *n* هَدَف/أَهْدَاف مف/ج

tarragon /'tærəgən/ *n* نَبْتَة الطَرْخُون

T

tariff /'tærɪf/ *n* تَعْرِيفَة

task /tɑ:sk/ *n* مَهَمَّة/مَهَامٌّ مف/ج

taste /teɪst/ *n* (of food, etc) مَذَاق/مَذَاقَات مف/ج (liking) ذَوْق/أَذْوَاق مف/ج
♦ *v* يَذُوق

tasteless /'teɪstləs/ *adj* عَدِيم المَذَاق

tax /tæks/ *n* ضَرِيبَة/ضَرَائِبُ مف/ج
♦ *v* (goods) يَفْرِض ضَرِيبَة (people) يُدَفِّع ضَرِيبَة

taxation /tæk'seɪʃn/ *n* نِظَام الضَرِيبَة

taxi /'tæksi/ *n* سَيَّارَة أُجْرَة

taxi driver *n* سَائِق تَاكْسِي

tea /ti:/ *n* شَاي

teach /ti:tʃ/ *v* **taught** (physics) يُعَلِّم (a class) يُدَرِّس

teacher /'ti:tʃə(r)/ *n* مُعَلِّم

team /ti:m/ *n* فَرِيق/أَفْرِقَة مف/ج

teamster /'ti:mstə(r)/ *n* US سَائِق شَاحِنَة

tear /tɪə(r)/ *n* (from the eye) دَمْعَة/دُمُوع مف/ج /teə(r)/(in fabric) تَمَزُّق
♦ *v* /teə(r)/ **tore, torn** يُمَزِّق

tease /ti:z/ *v* يَسْتَفِزّ (عَلَى سَبِيل المِزَاح)

technical /'teknɪkl/ *adj* تَقْنِيّ

technician /tek'nɪʃn/ *n* فَنِّيّ

technique /tek'ni:k/ *n* أُسْلُوب/أَسَالِيبُ مف/ج

technology /tek'nɒlədʒi/ *n* pl **-gies** (equipment) عِلْم التَقْنِيَة (knowledge) عِلْم الصِنَاعَة

technological /teknə'lɒdʒɪkl/ *n* تَقْنِيّ

teenager /'ti:neɪdʒə(r)/ *n* مُرَاهِق

Tehran /tɛ:'rɑ:n/ *n* طَهْرَان

telephone /ˈtelɪfəʊn/ *n* /هَاتِف هَوَاتِفُ مف/ج
♦ *v* يُهَاتِف

television /ˈtelɪvɪʒn/ *n* تِلْفَاز/أَجْهِزَة التِلْفَاز مف/ج

tell /tel/ *v* **told** (to inform) يُخْبِر
Tell them to come. أَخْبِرْهُم بِأَنْ يَأْتُوا
Can you tell me how far it is? هَلَّا أَخْبَرْتَنِي كَم تَبْعُد؟
He told you not to do that. قَالَ لَكَ أَلَّا تَفْعَل ذَلِكَ (a story, etc) يَحْكِي، يَرْوِي
to tell a lie/the truth يَقُول الكَذِب/الحَقِيقَة
She told them a joke. رَوَت لَهُم نُكْتَة
Tell me what you saw. اروِي لِي مَا رَأَيْتَ (to tell apart) يُمَيِّز
Can you tell the difference between them? هَل بِإِمْكَانِكَ التَمْيِيز بَيْنَهُم؟
(the time) يَحْسِب
Learn to tell the time تَعَلَّم كَيْفَ تَحسِب الوَقْت

temper /ˈtempə(r)/ *n* مِزَاج

temperature /ˈtemprətʃə(r)/ *n* دَرَجَة الحَرَارَة

temple /ˈtempl/ *n* مَعْبَد/مَعَابِدُ مف/ج

temporary /ˈtemprəri/ *adj* مُؤَقَّت

tempt /tempt/ *v* يُغْرِي

ten /ten/ *num* عَشْرَة

tenancy /ˈtenənsi/ *n* فَتْرَة الإيجَار

tenant /ˈtenənt/ *n* مُسْتَأْجِر

tendency /ˈtendənsi/ *n* pl **-cies** مَيْل

tender /ˈtendə(r)/ *adj* طَرِيّ

tennis /ˈtenɪs/ *n* كُرَة المِضْرَب

tense /tens/ *adj* مُتَوَتِّر

tension /ˈtenʃn/ *n* تَوَتُّر

tent /tent/ *n* خَيْمَة/خِيَم مف/ج

tenth /tenθ/ *adj* عَاشِر/عَوَاشِرُ مف/ج
♦ *adv* عَاشِراً
to come tenth يَأْتِي عَاشِراً
♦ *n* العَاشِر
the tenth of May, May the tenth العَاشِر مِن أَيَّار

term /tɜːm/ *n* (word) مُصْطَلَح/مُصْطَلَحَات مف/ج (period of time) فَتْرَة (in education) فَصْل دِرَاسِيّ

terrace /ˈterəs/ *n* مَصْطَبَة/مَصَاطِبُ مف/ج

terrible /ˈterəbl/ *adj* مُفْزِع

terrific /təˈrɪfɪk/ *adj* رَائِع

terrify /ˈterɪfaɪ/ *v* يُرْعِب

territory /ˈterətri/ *n* pl **-ries** مِنْطَقَة/مَنَاطِقُ مف/ج

terror /ˈterə(r)/ *n* رُعْب

terrorism /ˈterərɪzəm/ *n* إِرْهَاب

terrorist /ˈterərɪst/ *n* إِرْهَابِيّ

test /test/ *n* (medical) فَحْص/فُحُوصَات مف/ج (at school) اخْتِبَار/اخْتِبَارَات مف/ج

♦ *v* (sth new) يَخْتَبِر (students) يَمْتَحِن

text /tekst/ *n* (printed matter) نَصّ
(text message) رِسَالَة نَصِّيَّة
♦ *v* يُرْسِل رِسَالَة نَصِّيَّة

textbook /'tekstbʊk/ *n* كِتَاب تَعْلِيمِيّ

text message *n* رِسَالَة نَصِّيَّة

than /ðæn/ *conj* مِمَّا
It's bigger than I thought it would be. هُوَ أَكْبَر مِمَّا اعْتَقَدْتُ
♦ *prep* مِن
less than thirty years أَقَلّ مِن ثَلَاثِين عَاماً
His house is bigger than ours. بَيْتُهُ أَكْبَر مِن بَيْتِنَا

thank /θæŋk/ *v* (a person) يَشْكُر
Thank you! أَشْكُرُكَ
Thank you very much! أَشْكُرُكَ جِدّاً
Thank you for the meal. أَشْكُرُكَ مِن أَجْل الطَعَام
No, thank you! لَا، شُكْراً

thankful /'θæŋkfl/ *adj* شَاكِر

that /ðæt/ *adj* ذَلِكَ/تِلْكَ مذ/م
We're staying at that hotel. نَنْزِل فِي ذَلِكَ الفُنْدُق
I don't like that lady. لَا أُحِبّ تِلْكَ المَرْأَة
♦ *conj* أَن
I hope that you will be able to come. آمُل أَن تَتَمَكَّن مِن المَجِيء
♦ *pron* (demonstrative) ذَلِكَ/تِلْكَ مذ/م
That belongs to her. ذَلِكَ مِلْك لَهَا
(relative) الَّذِي/الَّتِي مذ/م
The song that we learned at school. الأُغْنِيَة الَّتِي تَعَلَّمْنَاهَا فِي المَدْرَسَة (see those)

the /ðə, ðiː/ *art* ال

theatre /'θɪətə(r)/ *n* US **-ter**
(building) مَسْرَح/مَسَارِحُ مف/ج
(genre) الأَدَب المَسْرَحِيّ

theft /θeft/ *n* سَرِقَة

their /ðeə(r)/ *adj* لَهُم/لَهُنَّ
That is their house. ذَلِكَ بَيْتُهُم

them /ðem/ *pron* (direct object) هُم/هُنَّ/هَا ض/مذ/م
I haven't met them. لَم أُقَابِلْهُم
(indirect object) هُم/هُنَّ/هَا
Talk to them. تَحَدَّث مَعَهُنَّ
Give them the camera. أَعْطِهِم آلَة التَصْوِير (after prep, in comparisons) هُم/هُنَّ/هَا
Can you go with them? هَل تَسْتَطِيع الذَهَاب مَعَهُم؟

theme /θiːm/ *n* مَوْضُوع/مَوْضُوعَات مف/ج

theme park *n* مَدِينَة مَلَاهٍ

themselves /ðəm'selvz/ *pron*
(reflexive) أَنْفُسَهُم/أَنْفُسَهُنَّ ض/مذ/م
They hurt themselves. جَرَحُوا أَنْفُسَهُم
(for emphasis) بِأَنْفُسِهِم/بِأَنْفُسِهِنَّ ض/مذ/م
The boys can do it themselves. يَسْتَطِيع الأَوْلَاد عَمَلَهَا بِأَنْفُسِهِم
The children are by themselves. الأَطْفَال بِمُفْرَدِهِم

T

then /ðen/ *adv* (next) ثُمَّ (formerly) آنَذَاكَ

theology /θi'ɒlədʒi/ *n* عِلْم الأَدْيَان

theory /'θɪəri/ *n* pl **-ries** نَظَرِيَّة

therapy /'θerəpi/ *n* pl **-pies** عِلَاج

there /ðeə(r)/ *adv* (to a place) هُنَاكَ

I went there as a child.
ذَهَبْتُ هُنَاكَ عِنْدَمَا كُنْتُ طِفْلاً

(at a place) هُنَاكَ

When I was there I really enjoyed it.
اسْتَمْتَعْتُ بِهَا حَقّاً عِنْدَمَا كُنْتُ هُنَاكَ

She's over there هِيَ هُنَاكَ (there is, there are) *There's a hole in the door.*
هُنَاكَ ثُقْب فِي البَاب

There were five of us.
كَانَ هُنَاكَ خَمْسَة مِنَّا

therefore /'ðeəfɔ:(r)/ *conj* نَتِيجَةً لِذَلِكَ

there're /ðeərər/ *contr* (= there are: see be, there)

there's /ðeəz/ *contr* (= there is: see be, there)

these /ði:z/ *adj* (plural of this) هَؤُلَاءِ

These boys are nice.
هَؤُلَاءِ الأَوْلَاد لُطَفَاء

♦ *pron* (plural of this) هَؤُلَاءِ

These are my favourites.
هَؤُلَاءِ هُم المُفَضَّلُون لَدَيَّ (see this)

thesis /'θi:sɪs/ *n* pl **-ses** أُطْرُوحَة

they /ðeɪ/ *pron* هُم/هُنَّ ض/مذ/م

They are our best friends.
هُم أَفْضَل أَصْدِقَائِنَا

they'd /ðeɪd/ *contr* (= they had, they would: see have, would)

they'll /ðeɪl/ *contr* (= they will: see will; = they shall: see shall)

they're /ðeə(r)/ *contr* (= they are: see be)

they've /ðeɪv/ *contr* (= they have: see have)

thick /θɪk/ *adj* (wall) سَمِيك (sauce) كَثِيف (vegetation) سَمِيك

thickness /'θɪknəs/ *n* سَمَاكَة

thief /θi:f/ *n* لِصّ/لُصُوص مف/ج

thigh /θaɪ/ *n* فَخْذ/أَفْخَاذ (م) مف/ج

thin /θɪn/ *adj* (not fat) نَحِيف (not thick) رَفِيع (sauce) قَلِيل الكَثَافَة

thing /θɪŋ/ *n* شَيْء/أَشْيَاءُ مف/ج

think /θɪŋk/ *v* **thought** (to consider) يَعْتَقِد (giving opinion) يُفَكِّر

third /θɜ:d/ *adj* ثَالِث/ثَوَالِثُ

♦ *adv* ثَالِثاً

♦ *n* (see tenth) الثَّالِث

thirsty /'θɜ:sti/ *adj* ظَمْآن، عَطْشَان

thirteen /θɜ:'ti:n/ *num* ثَلَاثَة عَشَر

thirty /'θɜ:ti/ *num* ثَلَاثُون

this /ðɪs/ *adj* هَذَا/هَذِهِ مذ/م

This fruit is delicious.
هَذِهِ الفَاكِهَة لَذِيذَة

I like this car. أُحِبّ هَذِهِ السَّيَّارَة.

♦ *pron* هَذَا/هَذِهِ مذ/م

This is my house. هَذَا بَيْتِي (see these)

thorough /ˈθʌrə/ *adj* (analysis, report) مُفَصَّل (examination) كَامِل

thoroughly /ˈθʌrəli/ *adv* بِشَكْلٍ تَامّ

those /ðəʊz/ *adj* (plural of that) أُولَئِكَ

Those men are tall. أُولَئِكَ الرِجَال طِوَال

♦ *pron* (plural) أُولَئِكَ

Those are the best. أُولَئِكَ الأَفْضَل (see that)

though /ðəʊ/ *conj* (in spite of the fact that) مَعَ أَنَّ

Though he tried his best, he didn't succeed. مَعَ أَنَّهُ حَاوَلَ كُلّ مَا بِوُسْعِهِ لَم يَنْجَح (however) لَكِنَّ

She was exhausted though she wouldn't admit it. كَانَت مُنْهَكَة لَكِنَّهَا لَم تُقِرّ بِذَلِكَ

I went in the end though. لَكِنَّنِي ذَهَبْتُ فِي النِهَايَة

thought /θɔːt/ *n* فِكْرَة/أَفْكَار مف/ج

thousand /ˈθaʊznd/ *num* أَلْف

thread /θred/ *n* خَيْط/خُيُوط مف/ج

threat /θret/ *n* تَهْدِيد/تَهْدِيدَات مف/ج

threaten /ˈθretn/ *v* يُهَدِّد

three /θriː/ *num* ثَلاثَة

thrill /θrɪl/ *v* يُثِير

throat /θrəʊt/ *n* حَنْجَرَة/حَنَاجِرُ مف/ج

throne /θrəʊn/ *n* عَرْش/عُرُوش مف/ج

through /θruː/ *prep* (from end to end) خِلَالَ

a path through the forest طَرِيق خِلَالَ الغَابَة

The rain came in through the window. دَخَلَ المَطَر مِن خِلَال النَافِذَة

We talked through the night. تَحَدَّثْنَا طِيلَةَ اللَيْل (showing agency) بِوَاسِطَة

to achieve sth through hard work يُحَقِّق شَيْئاً مَا مِن خِلَال العَمَل الشَاقّ

♦ *adv* (from end to end) يَعْبُر مِن خِلَال شَيْءٍ مِن بِدَايَتِهِ وَحَتَّى نِهَايَتِهِ

Let him through, please. دَعْهُ يَدْخُل مِن فَضْلِكَ

It went straight through. مَرَّت بِشَكْل مُسْتَقِيم (start to finish) اجْتِيَاز شَيْءٍ مِن بِدَايَتِهِ وَحَتَّى نِهَايَتِهِ

I read my notes through again. قَرَأْتُ جَمِيع مُلَاحَظَاتِي ثَانِيَةً (on the phone) تَوْصِيل شَخْص عَبْرَ الهَاتِف بِشَخْص آخَر

Can you put me through to Mr Ahmed? هَل بِإِمْكَانِكَ تَوْصِيلِي بِالسَيِّد أَحْمَد؟ (finished) مُنْتَهٍ

throw /θrəʊ/ *v* **threw, thrown** يَرْمِي

thumb /θʌm/ *n* إِبْهَام

thumbtack /ˈθʌmtæk/ *n* US دَبُّوس لإِلْصَاق الوَرَق عَلَى لَوْحَة الحَائِط

Thursday /ˈθɜːzdeɪ/ *n* (see Wednesday) الخَمِيس

T

thyme /taɪm/ *n* نَبْتَة الزَعْتَر

ticket /ˈtɪkɪt/ *n* تَذْكَرَة/تَذَاكِرُ مف/ج

tide /taɪd/ *n* المَدّ وَالجَذْر

tie /taɪ/ *n* (clothing) رَبْطَة عُنُق (in contests) تَعَادُل/تَعَادُلَات مف/ج
♦ *v* (a knot) يَعْقِد (sth to sth) يَرْبِط

tie up *phv* (a captive) يُقَيِّد (a parcel) يَرْبِط

tiger /ˈtaɪgə(r)/ *n* نَمِر/نُمُور مف/ج

tight /taɪt/ *adj* (knot) مَشْدُود (clothes) ضَيِّق

tighten /ˈtaɪtn/ *v* يَشُدّ

tile /taɪl/ *n* (on a floor) بَلَاطَة/بَلَاط (on a roof) قِرْمِيد/قَرَامِيدُ مف/ج مف/ج

till /tɪl/ *prep* حَتَّى
♦ *n* دُرْج النُقُود

timber /ˈtɪmbə(r)/ *n* خَشَب البِنَاء

time /taɪm/ *n* (period) زَمَن/أَزْمَان مف/ج

a long/short time زَمَن طَوِيل/قَصِير

in record time فِي زَمَن قِيَاسِيّ

in two days' time فِي مُدَّة يَوْمَيْن

to spend a lot of time on sth يَقْضِي وَقْتاً طَوِيلاً عَلَى شَيْء مَا (on clock, etc) وَقْت/أَوْقَات مف/ج

at this time of night فِي هَذَا الوَقْت مِن اللَيْل

to tell the time يَقُول الوَقْت

What's the time? كَم السَاعَة؟

The time is six o'clock. السَاعَة السَادِسَة (occasion) مَرَّة

He came back four times. رَجَعَ أَرْبَع مَرَّات (experience) وَقْت

to have a good/bad time يَقْضِي وَقْتاً جَيِّداً/سَيِّئاً (in history) عَصْر/عُصُور مف/ج

in the time of Ptolemy IX فِي عَصْر بَطْلَيْمُوس التَاسِع

timetable /ˈtaɪmteɪbl/ *n* جَدْوَل زَمَنِيّ

tin /tɪn/ *n* (metal) قَصْدِير (container) عُلْبَة طَعَام

tiny /ˈtaɪni/ *adj* صَغِير جِدّاً

tip /tɪp/ *n* (of finger) رَأْس أَو قِمَّة الشَيْء (for a waiter) بَقْشِيش مف/ج

tire /ˈtaɪə(r)/ *v* يُتْعِب
♦ *n* US إِطَار/إِطَارَات مف/ج

tired /ˈtaɪəd/ *adj* مُتْعَب

tissue /ˈtɪsju:/ *n* (in anatomy) نَسِيج/أَنْسِجَة مف/ج (handkerchief) مَنْدِيل وَرَقِيّ

title /ˈtaɪtl/ *n* عُنْوَان/عَنَاوِينُ مف/ج

to /tə, tu:/ *prep* (destination) إِلَى

from beginning to end مِن البِدَايَة إِلَى النِهَايَة

She took me to the shop. أَخَذَتْنِي إِلَى المَتْجَر (with indirect object) لِ

Give the book to Emily. أَعْطِي الكِتَاب لإِمِلِي (showing purpose) كَي

To save time we went by car.

T

ذَهَبْنَا بِالسَّيَّارَةِ كَي نُوَفِّرَ الوَقْتَ (as far as) إِلَى
from Monday to Friday
مِن الاِثْنَيْنِ إِلَى الجُمْعَةِ
I got to page 50. وَصلْتُ إِلَى صَفْحَةِ 50
(in proportions) لِكُلّ
20 miles to the gallon
عِشْرُون مِيلاً لِكُلّ جَالُون (telling the time) إِلَّا
at ten to five
فِي السَاعَةِ الخَامِسَةِ إِلَّا عَشْرَ دَقَائِق

toast /təʊst/ *n* خُبْز مُحَمَّص

tobacco /tə'bækəʊ/ *n* تِبْغ

today /tə'deɪ/ *adv* (on this day) اليَوْم
She arrives today. سَتَصِل اليَوْم (in this age) اليَوْم
Today we have computers to do these jobs. اليَوْم لَدَيْنَا أَجْهِزَة حَاسُوب لِعَمَل هَذِهِ الوَظَائِف
♦ *n* (this day) اليَوْم
Today is my birthday.
اليَوْم هُوَ عِيد مِيلَادِي (this age) اليَوْم
today's young people شَبَاب اليَوْم

toe /təʊ/ *n* إِصْبَع القَدَم

T

together /tə'geðə(r)/ *adv* مَعاً

toilet /'tɔɪlət/ *n* مِرْحَاض/مَرَاحِيضُ مف/ج

Tokyo /'təʊkɪəʊ/ *n* طُوكِيُو

tolerance /'tɒlərəns/ *n* القُدْرَة عَلَى الاِحْتِمَال

tolerate /'tɒləreɪt/ *v* يَحْتَمِل

toll /təʊl/ *n* رَسْم/رُسُوم مف/ج

tomato /tə'mɑːtəʊ/ *n* بَنَدُورَة

tomb /tuːm/ *n* قَبْر/قُبُور مف/ج

tomorrow /tə'mɒrəʊ/ *adv* غَداً

ton /tʌn/ *n* طُنّ/أَطْنَان مف/ج

tone /təʊn/ *n* نَغَمَة

tongue /tʌŋ/ *n* لِسَان/أَلْسِنَة مف/ج

tonic /'tɒnɪk/ *n* دَوَاء مُقَوٍّ

tonic water *n* مَشْرُوب التُونِك

tonight /tə'naɪt/ *adv* اللَيْلَة

too /tuː/ *adv* (excessively) جِدّاً (also) أَيْضاً

tool /tuːl/ *n* أَدَاة/أَدَوَات مف/ج

tooth /tuːθ/ *n* pl **teeth** سِنّ/أَسْنَان مف/ج

top /tɒp/ *n* (of a tree, etc) قِمَّة/قِمَم مف/ج (for a jar) غِطَاء/أَغْطِيَة مف/ج
♦ *adj* رَفِيع المُسْتَوَى

top up *phv* يُضِيف رَصِيداً

topic /'tɒpɪk/ *n* مَوْضُوع/مَوَاضِيعُ مف/ج

torch /tɔːtʃ/ *n* مِشْعَل كَهْرَبَائِيّ

torture /'tɔːtʃə(r)/ *n* عَذَاب
♦ *v* يُعَذِّب

total /'təʊtl/ *adj* إِجْمَالِيّ
♦ *n* المَجْمُوع

totally /'təʊtəli/ *adv* تَمَاماً

touch /tʌtʃ/ *v* يَلْمِس
♦ *n* لَمْس

touchline /'tʌtʃlaɪn/ *n* خَطّ المَلْعَب

tough /tʌf/ *adj* مَتِين

tour /tʊə(r)/ *n* جَوْلَة

tourism /'tʊərɪzəm/ *n* سِيَاحَة

tourist /'tʊərɪst/ *n* (visitor) سَائِح/سُيَّاح مف/ج

tourist guide *n* دَلِيل سِيَاحِيّ

tournament /'tʊənəmənt/ *n* مُسَابَقَة

toward /tə'wɔ:d/ *prep* **-ds** نَحْوَ

towel /'taʊəl/ *n* فُوطَة/فُوَط مف/ج

tower /'taʊə(r)/ *n* بُرْج/أَبْرَاج مف/ج

town /taʊn/ *n* مَدِينَة/مُدُن مف/ج

toxic /'tɒksɪk/ *adj* سَامّ

toy /tɔɪ/ *n* لُعْبَة أَطْفَال

trace /treɪs/ *v* (on paper) يَنْسَخ رَسْماً عَلَى وَرَق شَفَّاف (origins of sth) يَتَتَبَّع

track /træk/ *n* (path) مَسَار/مَسَارَات (of railway) خَطّ/خُطُوط مف/ج مف/ج

trade /treɪd/ *n* تِجَارَة
♦ *v* يُتَاجِر

trademark /'treɪdmɑ:k/ *n* عَلَامَة تِجَارِيَّة

trader /'treɪdə(r)/ *n* تَاجِر/تُجَّار مف/ج

tradition /trə'dɪʃn/ *n* تَقْلِيد/تَقَالِيدُ مف/ج

traditional /trə'dɪʃənl/ *adj* تَقْلِيدِيّ

traffic /'træfɪk/ *n* حَرَكَة المُرُور

traffic circle *n* US دَوَّار

tragedy /'trædʒədi/ *n* pl **-dies** مَأْسَاة/مَآسٍ مف/ج

tragic /'trædʒɪk/ *adj* مُفْجِع

trailer /'treɪlə(r)/ *n* (for vehicle) مَقْطُورَة (for a film) مُقْتَطَفَات

train /treɪn/ *n* قِطَار/قِطَارَات مف/ج
♦ *v* يُدَرِّب

trainer /'treɪnə(r)/ *n* (coach) مُدَرِّب (shoe) حِذَاء رِيَاضِيّ

training /'treɪnɪŋ/ *n* تَدْرِيب

transaction /træn'zækʃn/ *n* صَفْقَة

transfer /træns'fɜ:(r)/ *v* يَنْقُل

transform /træns'fɔ:m/ *v* يُحَوِّل

transformation /trænsfə'meɪʃn/ *n* تَحْوِيل

transition /træn'zɪʃn/ *n* تَحَوُّل

translate /trænz'leɪt/ *v* يُتَرْجِم

translation /træns'leɪʃn/ *n* تَرْجَمَة

translator /træns'leɪtə(r)/ *n* مُتَرْجِم

transmit /træns'mɪt/ *v* يَبُثّ

transparent /træns'pærənt/ *adj* شَفَّاف

transplant /træns'plɑ:nt/ *v* يَزْرَع
♦ *n* زِرَاعَة

transport /træn'spɔ:t/ *v* يَنْقُل
♦ *n* نَقْل

trap /træp/ *n* مِصْيَدَة/مَصَائِدُ مف/ج

trash /træʃ/ *n* قُمَامَة

traumatic /trɔ:'mætɪk/ *adj* فَاجِع

travel /'trævl/ *v* يُسَافِر

traveller /'trævələ(r)/ *n* مُسَافِر

tray /treɪ/ *n* صِينِيَّة/صَوَانٍ مف/ج

treacle /'tri:kl/ *n* دِبْس السُكَّر

treasure /'treʒə(r)/ *n* كَنْز/كُنُوز مف/ج

treasury /'treʒəri/ *n* pl **-ries** خَزِينَة الدَوْلَة (وِزَارَة المَالِيَّة)

treat /tri:t/ *v* (well, badly) يُعَامِل (a patient) يُعَالِج

treatment /'tri:tmənt/ *n* عِلَاج

treaty /'tri:ti/ *n* pl **-ties** مُعَاهَدَة

tree /tri:/ *n* شَجَرَة/شَجَر مف/ج

tremble /'trembl/ *v* يَرْجُف

tremendous /trə'mendəs/ *adj* كَبِير

trench /trentʃ/ *n* خَنْدَق/خَنَادِقُ مف/ج

trend /trend/ *n* مَيْل

trial /'traɪəl/ *n* مُحَاكَمَة

triangle /'traɪæŋgl/ *n* مُثَلَّث/مُثَلَّثَات مف/ج

tribal /'traɪbl/ *adj* قَبَلِيّ

tribe /traɪb/ *n* قَبِيلَة/قَبَائِلُ مف/ج

tribute /'trɪbju:t/ *n* تَقْدِير

trick /trɪk/ *n* حِيلَة/حِيَل مف/ج

trigger /'trɪgə(r)/ *n* زِنَاد/أَزْنِدَة مف/ج

trim /trɪm/ *v* يُقَلِّم

trip /trɪp/ *n* رِحْلَة
♦ *v* يَتَعَثَّر

triple /'trɪpl/ *adj* ثُلَاثِيّ

Tripoli /'trɪpəli/ *n* طَرَابُلُس

triumph /'traɪʌmf/ *n* انْتِصَار/ انْتِصَارَات مف/ج

trivial /'trɪviəl/ *adj* تَافِه

trophy /'trəʊfi/ *n* pl **-phies** جَائِزَة/ جَوَائِزُ مف/ج

tropical /'trɒpɪkl/ *adj* اسْتِوَائِيّ

trouble /'trʌbl/ *n* (problems) مُشْكِلَة (extra effort) عَنَاء

trout /traʊt/ *n* pl **trout** سَمَك السَلْمُون المُرَقَّط

truck /trʌk/ *n* شَاحِنَة

truck driver *n* سَائِق شَاحِنَة

true /tru:/ *adj* (correct) حَقِيقِيّ (loyal) مُخْلِص

trunk /trʌŋk/ *n* (for belongings) صُنْدُوق/صَنَادِيقُ مف/ج (of tree) جِذْع/جُذُوع مف/ج (US: of car) صُنْدُوق السَيَّارَة

trust /trʌst/ *n* ثِقَة
♦ *v* يَثِق بِـ

truth /tru:θ/ *n* حَقِيقَة

try /traɪ/ *v* **tried** (to test) يُجَرِّب (to attempt to) يُحَاوِل (to taste) يَتَذَوَّق
♦ *n* pl **tries** مُحَاوَلَة

tub /tʌb/ *n* حَوْض/أَحْوَاض مف/ج

tube /tju:b/ *n* أُنْبُوب/أَنَابِيبُ مف/ج

Tuesday /'tju:zdeɪ/ *n* (see Wednesday) الثُلَاثَاء

T

tuition /tju'ɪʃn/ *n* تَعْلِيم

tumour /'tju:mə(r)/ *n* US **-mor** /وَرَم أَوْرَام مف/ج

tuna /'tju:nə/ *n* سَمَك التُّن

tune /tju:n/ *n* لَحْن/أَلْحَان مف/ج

Tunis /'tju:nɪs/ *n* مَدِينَة تُونِس

Tunisia /tju:'nɪzɪə/ *n* جُمْهُورِيَّة تُونِس

Tunisian /tju:'nɪzɪən/ *adj, n* تُونِسِيّ ص/س

tunnel /'tʌnl/ *n* نَفَق/أَنْفَاق مف/ج

turban /'tɜ:bən/ *n* عِمَامَة

Turk /tə:k/ *n* تُرْكِيّ/أَتْرَاك مف/ج

turkey /'tɜ:ki/ دِيك الحَبَش

Turkey /'tə:ki/ *n* تُرْكِيَا

Turkish /'tə:kɪʃ/ *adj* تُرْكِيّ
♦ *n* اللُّغَة التُّرْكِيَّة

turn /tɜ:n/ *n* (to left, right) انْعِطَاف (in a game) دَوْر/أَدْوَار مف/ج
♦ *v* (a key, etc) يَلُفّ (to left, right) يَلْتَفِت

turning /'tɜ:nɪŋ/ *n* مُنْعَطَف/مُنْعَطَفَات مف/ج

turtle /'tɜ:tl/ *n* سُلَحْفَاة/سَلَاحِفُ مف/ج

tutor /'tju:tə(r)/ *n* مُدَرِّس خَاصّ

twelve /twelv/ *num* اثْنَا عَشَرَ

twenty /'twenti/ *num* عِشْرُون

twice /twaɪs/ *adv* مَرَّتَيْن

twist /twɪst/ *n* الْتِوَاء

two /tu:/ *num* اثْنَان

type /taɪp/ *v* يَطْبَع (عَلَى الكُمْبْيُوتَر أَو الآلَة الكَاتِبَة)
♦ *n* نَوْع/أَنْوَاع مف/ج

typical /'tɪpɪkl/ *adj* (town, case) مُتَوَقَّع (generosity) نَفْس النَمُوذَج

typist /'taɪpɪst/ *n* كَاتِب آلَة

tyre /'taɪə(r)/ *n* إِطَار/إِطَارَات مف/ج

U

ugly /'ʌgli/ *adj* قَبِيح

ulcer /'ʌlsə(r)/ *n* قُرْحَة

umbrella /ʌm'brelə/ *n* مِظَلَّة

unable /ʌn'eɪbl/ *adj* غَيْر قَادِر

unacceptable /ʌnək'septəbl/ *adj* مَرْفُوض

unaware /ʌnə'weə(r)/ *adj* غَيْر مُدْرِك

uncle /'ʌŋkl/ *n* عَمّ أَو خَال أَو زَوْج عَمَّة أَو زَوْج خَالَة

uncomfortable /ʌn'kʌmftəbl/ *adj* غَيْر مُرِيح

uncommon /ʌn'kɒmən/ *adj* غَيْر مَأْلُوف

unconscious /ʌn'kɒnʃəs/ *adj* فَاقِد الوَعْي

uncover /ʌn'kʌvə(r)/ *v* يَكْشِف عَن

U

under /'ʌndə(r)/ *prep* (below) تَحْتَ

under the sofa تَحْتَ الأَرِيكَة

to go under the bridge

يَذْهَب تَحْتَ الجِسْر (less or fewer than)

أَقَلّ مِن

under twenty people

أَقَلّ مِن عِشْرِين شَخْصاً

She's under 18. هِيَ أَقَلّ مِن 18

It will be ready in under three weeks.

سَتَكُون جَاهِزَة فِي أَقَلّ مِن ثَلَاثَة أَسَابِيع

♦ *adv* (below an age, weight, etc) أَقَلّ

those aged 18 and under

الَّذِين أَعْمَارُهُم 18 وَأَقَلّ

undergo /ʌndə'gəʊ/ *v* **-goes, -went, -gone** يَخْضَع لِ

undergraduate /ʌndə'grædʒuət/ *n* طَالِب بَكَالُورِيُوس

underground /'ʌndəgraʊnd/ *adj* تَحْتَ الأَرْض

underline /ʌndə'laɪn/ *v* يَرْسُم خَطّاً تَحْتَ

understand /ʌndə'stænd/ *v* **-stood** يَفْهَم

understanding /ʌndə'stændɪŋ/ *n* فَهْم

undertake /ʌndə'teɪk/ *v* **-took, -taken** يَشْرَع فِي

underwater /ʌndə'wɔːtə(r)/ *adj* تَحْتَ المَاء

undo /ʌn'du:/ *v* **-does, -did, -done** يَفُكّ

unemployed /ʌnɪm'plɔɪd/ *adj* عَاطِل عَن العَمَل

unemployment /ʌnɪm'plɔɪmənt/ *n* بَطَالَة

unexpected /ʌnɪk'spektɪd/ *adj* غَيْر مُتَوَقَّع

unfair /ʌn'feə(r)/ *adj* (competition) ظَالِم (decision) غَيْر مُنْصِف

unfamiliar /ʌnfə'mɪliə(r)/ *adj* غَرِيب/غُرَبَاءُ مف/ج

unfortunate /ʌn'fɔ:tʃənət/ *adj* مَشْؤُوم

unfortunately /ʌn'fɔ:tʃənətli/ *adv* لِسُوءِ الحَظّ

unhappy /ʌn'hæpi/ *adj* حَزِين

uniform /'ju:nɪfɔ:m/ *n* زِيّ مُوَحَّد ♦ *adj* مُوَحَّد

union /'ju:niən/ *n* (fusion) تَوْحِيد (of workers) اتِّحَاد/اتِّحَادَات

unique /ju'ni:k/ *adj* فَرِيد

unit /'ju:nɪt/ *n* وَحْدَة

unite /ju'naɪt/ *v* يُوَحِّد

United Arab Emirates /'emɪrəts/ *n* الإمَارَات العَرَبِيَّة المُتَّحِدَة

United Kingdom *n* المَمْلَكَة المُتَّحِدَة

United States of America *n* الوِلَايَات المُتَّحِدَة الأمْرِيكِيَّة

unity /'ju:nəti/ *n* وَحْدَة

universal /ju:nɪ'vɜ:sl/ *adj* عَالَمِيّ

universe /'ju:nɪvɜ:s/ *n* كَوْن

university /ju:nɪ'vɜ:səti/ *n* pl **-ties** جَامِعَة

unknown /ʌn'nəʊn/ *adj* غَيْر مَعْرُوف

unless /ən'les/ *conj* مَا لَم

unlikely /ʌn'laɪkli/ *adj* غَيْر مُحْتَمَل

unlimited /ʌn'lɪmɪtɪd/ *adj* غَيْر مَحْدُود

unlock /ʌn'lɒk/ *v* يَفْتَح

unlucky /ʌn'lʌki/ *adj* غَيْر مَحْظُوظ

unnecessary /ʌn'nesəsəri/ *adj* غَيْر ضَرُورِيّ

unpaid /ʌn'peɪd/ *adj* غَيْر مَدْفُوع

unpleasant /ʌn'pleznt/ *adj* (task) وَقِح (person) كَرِيه (taste) بَغِيض

unpopular /ʌn'pɒpjələ(r)/ *adj* غَيْر شَعْبِيّ

unpredictable /ʌnprɪ'dɪktəbl/ *adj* لا يُمْكِن التَنَبُّؤ بِهِ

unreasonable /ʌn'ri:znəbl/ *adj* غَيْر مَعْقُول

unsuccessful /ʌnsək'sesfl/ *adj* فَاشِل

U

unsure /ʌn'ʃʊə(r)/ *adj* غَيْر مُتَيَقِّن

until /ən'tɪl/ *prep* حَتَّى

unusual /ʌn'ju:ʒuəl/ *adj* غَيْر عَادِيّ

unwilling /ʌn'wɪlɪŋ/ *adj* مُكْرَه

unwind /ʌn'waɪnd/ *v* **-wound** يَحُلّ

up /ʌp/ *adv* (going higher) لِلأَعْلَى
Please stand up. قِف رَجَاءً
Sales are up by 10%.
المَبِيعَات مُرْتَفِعَة بِنِسْبَة 10% (not in bed)
نَاهِض
Amina is up. أَمِينَة نَاهِضَة (as far as)
إِلَى حَدّ مُعَيَّن
up to fifty people حَتَّى خَمْسِين شَخْصاً
♦ *prep* (a hill, the stairs) إِلَى الأَعْلَى
We walked up the escalator.
مَشَيْنَا إِلَى أَعْلَى الدَرَج الكَهْرَبَائِيّ
(along) إِلَى النِهَايَة
They strolled up the road.
تَمَشُّوا إِلَى نِهَايَة الطَرِيق

update /ʌp'deɪt/ *v* يُزَوِّد بِآخِر الأَخْبَار

upgrade /ʌp'greɪd/ *v* يُحَدِّث

upper /'ʌpə(r)/ *adj* عُلْوِيّ

U

uprising /'ʌpraɪzɪŋ/ *n* اِنْتِفَاضَة

upset /ʌp'set/ *v* **-set** يُضَايِق

upstairs /ʌp'steəz/ *adv* (moving up)
الطَابِق العُلْوِيّ (situated) لِلطَابِق العُلْوِيّ

upward /'ʌpwəd/ *adv* **-ds** إِلَى أَعْلَى

urban /'ɜ:bən/ *adj* حَضَرِيّ

urge /ɜ:ʤ/ *n* دَافِع/دَوَافِع مف/ج
♦ *v* يَحُثّ

urgency /'ɜ:ʤənsi/ *n* إِلْحَاح

urgent /'ɜ:ʤənt/ *adj* طَارِئ

urine /'jʊərɪn/ *n* بَوْل

us /ʌs, əs / *pron* (direct object) (ضَمِير المُتَكَلِّم الجَمْع لِلمَفْعُول بِهِم المُبَاشِر) نَا
She knows us. تَعْرِفُنَا (indirect object)
(ضَمِير المُتَكَلِّم الجَمْع لِلمَفْعُول بِهِم غَيْر المُبَاشِر) نَا
She sent us a letter. أَرْسَلَت لَنَا رِسَالَة
(after prep) (ضَمِير المُتَكَلِّم الجَمْع) نَا
She's older than us. هِيَ أَكْبَر مِنَّا سِنّاً
They left without us. غَادَرُوا مِن دُونِنَا

USB port /ju:es'bi: pɔ:t/ *n* مَنْفَذ الحَاسُوب

use /ju:z/ *v* يَسْتَخْدِم
♦ *n* /ju:s/(purpose) /اسْتِخْدَام
(of chemicals) اسْتِخْدَامَات مف/ج
اسْتِخْدَام

used to /'ju:st tu, tə/ *modal v* كَانَ
I used to live in Beirut.
كُنْتُ أَعِيش فِي بَيْرُوت
We used to go there every year.
كُنَّا نَذْهَب إِلَى هُنَاكَ كُلّ عَام
They used not to sell it.
تَعَوَّدُوا أَلَّا يَبِيعُوه

useful /ˈjuːsfl/ *adj* مُفِيد

useless /ˈjuːsləs/ *adj* عَدِيم الفَائِدَة

user /ˈjuːzə(r)/ *n* مُسْتَخْدِم

usual /ˈjuːʒəl/ *adj* مُعْتَاد

usually /ˈjuʒəli/ *adv* عَادَةً

V

vacancy /ˈveɪkənsi/ *n* pl **-cies** وَظِيفَة شَاغِرَة

vacant /ˈveɪkənt/ *adj* شَاغِر/شَوَاغِر مف/ج

vacation /vəˈkeɪʃn/ *n* عُطْلَة

vaccination /væksɪˈneɪʃn/ *n* تَطْعِيم

vaccine /ˈvæksiːn/ *n* لِقَاح/لِقَاحَات مف/ج

vacuum /ˈvækjuəm/ *n* فَرَاغ هَوَائِيّ

vague /veɪg/ *adj* غَامِض

valid /ˈvælɪd/ *adj* سَارِي المَفْعُول

validate /ˈvælɪdeɪt/ *v* يُصَادِق عَلَى

validity /vəˈlɪdəti/ *n* شَرْعِيَّة

valley /ˈvæli/ *n* وَادٍ/وِدْيَان مف/ج

valuable /ˈvæljuəbl/ *adj* ثَمِين

value /ˈvælju:/ *n* قِيمَة/قِيَم مف/ج

♦ *v* (sb's advice) يُقَدِّر (a jewel) يُقَيِّم

valve /vælv/ *n* صَمَّام/صَمَّامَات مف/ج

van /væn/ *n* شَاحِنَة صَغِيرَة

vanilla /vəˈnɪlə/ *n* فَانِيلَة

vanish /ˈvænɪʃ/ *v* يَخْتَفِي

vanity /ˈvænəti/ *n* غُرُور

variation /veəriˈeɪʃn/ *n* تَبَايُن

varied /ˈveərid/ *adj* مُتَنَوِّع

variety /vəˈraɪəti/ *n* pl **-ties** تَنَوُّع

various /ˈveəriəs/ *adj* مُتَعَدِّد

vary /ˈveəri/ *v* يَخْتَلِف

vast /vɑːst/ *adj* كَبِير/كِبَار مف/ج

veal /viːl/ *n* لَحْم العِجْل

vegetable /ˈvedʒtəbl/ *n* خُضَار/خُضْرَوَات مف/ج

vegetation /vedʒə'teɪʃn/ *n* النَبَاتَات

vehicle /'viːəkl/ *n* مَرْكَبَة

vein /veɪn/ *n* وَرِيد/أَوْرِدَة مف/ج

vendor /'vendə(r)/ *n* بَائِع

ventilation /ventɪ'leɪʃn/ *n* تَهْوِيَة

verdict /'vɜːdɪkt/ *n* حُكْم/أَحْكَام مف/ج

verify /'verɪfaɪ/ *v* يَتَحقَّق مِن

verse /vɜːs/ *n* مَقْطَع شِعْرِيّ

version /'vɜːʃn/ *n* إِصْدَار/إِصْدَارَات مف/ج

vertical /'vɜːtɪkl/ *adj* عَامُودِيّ

very /'veri/ *adv* جِدّاً

vet /vet/ *n* بَيْطَرِيّ/بَيَاطِرَة مف/ج

viable /'vaɪəbl/ *adj* قَابِل لِلنَجَاح

vice /vaɪs/ *n* رَذِيلَة/رَذَائِلُ مف/ج

vicious /'vɪʃəs/ *adj* وَحْشِيّ

victim /'vɪktɪm/ *n* ضَحِيَّة/ضَحَايَا مف/ج

victor /'vɪktə(r)/ *n* مُنْتَصِر

victory /'vɪktəri/ *n* pl **-ries** انْتِصَار/انْتِصَارَات مف/ج

V

Vienna /vɪ'ɛnə/ *n* فِيينَا

view /vjuː/ *n* (from window) مَنْظَر/مَنَاظِرُ مف/ج (of situation) رُؤْيَة/رُؤًى مف/ج
♦ *v* يُعَايِن

viewpoint /'vjuːpɔɪnt/ *n* وُجْهَة نَظَر

vigorous /'vɪgərəs/ *adj* قَوِيّ

village /'vɪlɪdʒ/ *n* قَرْيَة/قُرَى مف/ج

vine /vaɪn/ *n* شَجَرَة العِنَب

vinegar /'vɪnɪgə(r)/ *n* خَلّ

violation /vaɪə'leɪʃn/ *n* انْتِهَاك/انْتِهَاكَات مف/ج

violence /'vaɪələns/ *n* عُنْف

violent /'vaɪələnt/ *adj* (attack) عَنِيف (storm) شَدِيد

violently /'vaɪələntli/ *adv* بِعُنْف

violin /vaɪə'lɪn/ *n* كَمَان

virgin /'vɜːdʒɪn/ *n* عَذْرَاء/عَذَارَى مف/ج

virtual /'vɜːtʃuəl/ *adj* فِعْلِيّ

virtue /'vɜːtʃuː/ *n* فَضِيلَة/فَضَائِلُ مف/ج

visa /'viːzə/ *n* تَأْشِيرَة دُخُول

visibility /vɪzə'bɪləti/ *n* رُؤْيَة

visible /'vɪzəbl/ *adj* مَرْئِيّ

vision /'vɪʒn/ *n* رُؤْيَا

visit /'vɪzɪt/ *n* زِيَارَة
♦ *v* يَزُور

visitor /'vɪzɪtə(r)/ *n* زَائِر

vital /'vaɪtl/ *adj* حَيَوِيّ

vitamin /'vɪtəmɪn/ *n* فِيتَامِين/فِيتَامِينَات مف/ج

vocabulary /vəˈkæbjələri/ *n* pl -ries مُفْرَدَات

voice /vɔɪs/ *n* صَوْت

volatile /ˈvɒlətaɪl/ *adj* مُتَقَلِّب

voltage /ˈvəʊltɪʤ/ *n* مِقْيَاس الفُولْط

volume /ˈvɒljuːm/ *n* (of a container, etc) حَجْم/أَحْجَام مف/ج (book) مُجَلَّد/ مُجَلَّدَات مف/ج

voluntary /ˈvɒləntri/ *adj* طَوْعِيّ

volunteer /vɒlənˈtɪə(r)/ *n* مُتَطَوِّع

vote /vəʊt/ *n* صَوْت انْتِخَابِيّ
♦ *v* يُصَوِّت

voter /ˈvəʊtə(r)/ *n* نَاخِب

voucher /ˈvaʊtʃə(r)/ *n* إِيصَال/ إِيصَالاَت مف/ج

voyage /ˈvɔɪɪʤ/ *n* رِحْلَة بَحْرِيَّة أَو فَضَائِيَّة

W

waist /weɪst/ *n* خَصْر

wait /weɪt/ *v* يَنْتَظِر

waiter /ˈweɪtə(r)/ *n* نَادِل/نُدَلَاءُ مف/ج

waiting /ˈweɪtɪŋ/ *n* انْتِظَار

waitress /ˈweɪtrəs/ *n* نَادِلَة

wake /weɪk/ *v* **woke, woken** يُوقِظ
♦ *n* مَرَاسِم تَوْدِيع المَيِّت

Wales /weɪlz/ *n* مُقَاطَعَة وِيلْز

walk /wɔːk/ *n* مَشْي
♦ *v* يَمْشِي

walker /ˈwɔːkə(r)/ *n* مَاشٍ

wall /wɔːl/ *n* (external) سُور/أَسْوَار
(internal) جِدَار/جُدْرَان مف/ج

wallet /ˈwɒlɪt/ *n* مِحْفَظَة

walnut /ˈwɔːlnʌt/ *n* جَوْز

want /wɒnt/ *v* (bread, a new car) يُرِيد (sb to do sth) يَرْغَب

war /wɔː(r)/ *n* حَرْب/حُرُوب (م) مف/ج

ward /wɔːd/ *n* جَنَاح/أَجْنِحَة مف/ج

wardrobe /ˈwɔːdrəʊb/ *n* خِزَانَة مَلَابِس/خَزَائِن مف/ج

warehouse /ˈweəhaʊs/ *n* مُسْتَوْدَع/مُسْتَوْدَعَات مف/ج

warm /wɔːm/ *adj* دَافِئ
a warm day يَوْم دَافِئ
a warm winter شِتَاء دَافِئ
It's warm today. اليَوْم دَافِئ
♦ *v* (water) يُدَفِّئ

warmth /wɔːmθ/ *n* دِفْء

warn /wɔːn/ *v* يُحَذِّر

warning /ˈwɔːnɪŋ/ *n* تَحْذِير/تَحْذِيرَات مف/ج

wash /wɒʃ/ *v* يَغْسِل

Washington /ˈwɒʃɪŋtən/ *n* وَاشِنْطُون

wasn't /ˈwɒznt/ *contr* (= was not: see be)

wasp /wɒsp/ *n* دَبُّور/دَبَابِيرُ مف/ج

waste /weɪst/ *n* تَبْدِيد
♦ *v* يُسْرِف

watch /wɒtʃ/ *n* سَاعَة
♦ *v* يُشَاهِد

water /ˈwɔːtə(r)/ *n* مَاء
♦ *v* يُسْقِي

watermelon /ˈwɔːtəmelən/ *n* بَطِّيخ

wave /weɪv/ *n* (gesture) تَلْوِيحَة (in the sea) مَوْجَة
♦ *v* يُلَوِّح

W

wavelength /'weɪvleŋθ/ *n* طُول المَوْجَة

way /weɪ/ *n* (method) طَرِيقَة/طُرُق (route) طَرِيق/طُرُق وَطُرُقَات مف/ج مف/ج

we /wi:/ *pron* نَحْنُ

We live in Tripoli. نَعيش فِي طَرَابُلُس

weak /wi:k/ *adj* (person) ضَعيف/ ضُعَفَاء مف/ج (tea) خَفِيف

weaken /'wi:kən/ *v* يُضْعِف

weakness /'wi:knəs/ *n* ضَعْف

wealth /welθ/ *n* ثَرْوَة

wealthy /'welθi/ *adj* ثَرِيّ/أَثْرِيَاء مف/ج

weapon /'wepən/ *n* سِلَاح/أَسْلِحَة مَف/ج

wear /weə(r)/ *n* اهْتِرَاء

♦ *v* **wore, worn** يَلْبَس

wear out *phv* (a person) يُرْهِق

weather /'weðə(r)/ *n* طَقْس

weave /wi:v/ *v* **wove, woven** يُحيك

web /web/ *n* (spider's) نَسْج العَنْكَبُوت (Internet) شَبَكَة

web page *n* صَفْحَة إِلِكْتْرُونِيَّة

website /'websaɪt/ *n* مَوْقِع شَبَكَة

we'd /wi:d/ *contr* (= we had, we would: see have, would)

wedding /'wedɪŋ/ *n* عُرْس

Wednesday /'wenzdeɪ/ *n* يَوْم الأَرْبِعَاء

on Wednesday فِي يَوْم الأَرْبِعَاء

every Wednesday كُلّ يَوْم أَرْبِعَاء

last Wednesday يَوْم الأَرْبِعَاء المَاضِي

next Wednesday يَوْم الأَرْبِعَاء القَادِم

weed /wi:d/ *n* عُشْبَة ضَارَّة

week /wi:k/ *n* أُسْبُوع/أَسَابِيعُ مف/ج

weekend /wi:k'end/ *n* عُطْلَة نِهَايَة الأُسْبُوع

weekly /'wi:kli/ *adj* أُسْبُوعِيّ

weigh /weɪ/ *v* يُوَزِّن

weight /weɪt/ *n* وَزْن/أَوْزَان مف/ج

welcome /'welkəm/ *adj* أَهْلاً وَسَهْلاً

You're welcome! عَفْواً

You are welcome! أَهْلاً بِكَ

♦ *n* تَرْحِيب

♦ *v* يُرَحِّب

welfare /'welfeə(r)/ *n* رَفَاه

well /wel/ *adj* بِصِحَّة جَيِّدَة

♦ *adv* جَيِّد

♦ *n* بِئْر/آبَار مف/ج

we'll /wi:l/ *contr* (= we will: see will)

Welsh /welʃ/ *adj* وِيلْزِيّ

♦ *n* (language) اللُغَة الوِيلْزِيَّة (people) وِيلْزِيُّون

we're /wɪə(r)/ *contr* (= we are: see be)

weren't /wɜ:nt/ *contr* (= were not: see be)

west /west/ *adj* غَرْبِيّ

♦ *adv* نَحْوَ الغَرْب

♦ *n* (point of the compass) غَرْب

The sun sets in the west.
تَغْرُبُ الشَمْسُ فِي الغَرْب (of a country)
to live in the west
يَعِيش فِي غَرْبِيّ البِلاَد
the West الغَرْب

western /'westən/ *adj* غَرْبِيّ
♦ *n* غَرْبِيّ

wet /wet/ *adj* (clothes, grass) رَطْب
(weather) مَاطِر

we've /wi:v/ *contr* (= we have: see have)

whale /weɪl/ *n* حُوت/حِيتَان مف/ج

what /wɒt/ *pron* (in questions) مَاذَا
What do you mean? مَاذَا تَعْنِي؟
What? مَاذَا؟
(with surprise) *What!* مَاذَا!
What a goal! مَا هَذَا الهَدَف الجَمِيل!
(relative) مَا
Show me what you bought.
أَرِنِي مَا اشْتَرَيْتَ

whatever /wɒt'evə(r)/ *pron* أَيّ شَيْء

wheat /wi:t/ *n* قَمْح

wheel /wi:l/ *n* عَجَلَة

wheelchair /'wi:ltʃeə(r)/ *n* كُرْسِيّ المُقْعَدِين

when /wen/ *adv* مَتَى
When is your birthday?
مَتَى عِيد مِيلاَدك؟
♦ *conj* عِنْدَمَا
Call me when he arrives.
هَاتِفْنِي عِنْدَمَا يَصِل
She called when I was out.
هَاتَفَت عِنْدَمَا كُنْتُ فِي الخَارِج

whenever /wen'evə(r)/ *conj* كُلَّمَا

where /weə(r)/ *adv* أَيْنَ
Where are you going? أَيْنَ أَنْتَ ذَاهِب؟
Where are the plates? أَيْنَ الصُحُون؟
I'll tell you where to go.
سَوْفَ أُخْبِرُكَ إِلَى أَيْنَ تَذْهَب

whether /'weðə(r)/ *conj* إِذَا مَا
I don't know whether it will be finished on time.
لاَ أَدْرِي إِذَا مَا سَوْفَ تَنْتَهِي فِي مَوْعِدِهَا

which /wɪtʃ/ *adj, pron* أَيّ
Which of these is yours? أَيّ هَؤُلاَء لَكَ؟
I don't know which is better.
لاَ أَعْلَم أَيُّهُم أَفْضَل
Which CD do you prefer?
أَيّ الأُسْطُوَانَات تُفَضِّل؟
I've lost the key which was on the table.
فَقَدْتُ المِفْتَاح الَّذِي كَانَ عَلَى الطَاوِلَة

while /waɪl/ *n* بُرْهَة
in a while بَعْدَ بُرْهَة
a little while بُرْهَة قَصِيرَة
♦ *conj* (during) بَيْنَمَا

whip /wɪp/ *n* سَوْط/سِيَاط مف/ج

whiskers /'wɪskəz/ *n pl* شَارِب الحَيَوَان

whisper /'wɪspə(r)/ *v* يَهْمِس

whistle /'wɪsl/ *n* صُفَّارَة
♦ *v* يَصْفِر

W

white /waɪt/ *adj* أَبْيَض/بَيْضَاء/بِيض مذ/م/ج

the white community العِرْق الأَبْيَض

to turn white يُصْبِح أَبْيَض/يَبْيَض

♦ *n* اللَوْن الأَبْيَض

to wear white يَلْبَس الأَبْيَض

who /hu:/ *pron* مَن

Who's that man? مَن ذَلِكَ الرَجُل؟

Who do you want to speak to? مَن تُرِيد أَن تُحَادِث؟

Who is it? مَن هَذَا؟

I know who did it. أَعْلَم مَن فَعَلَهَا

whoever /hu:'evə(r)/ *pron* كُلّ مَن

whole /həʊl/ *adj* كَامِل

the whole time الوَقْت كَامِلاً

the whole family كُلّ العَائِلَة

wholly /'həʊlli/ *adv* بِالكَامِل

whom /hu:m/ *pron* (object) الَّذِي

The man, whom the police arrested, was innocent. الرَجُل الَّذِي اعْتَقَلَتْهُ الشُرْطَة كَانَ بَرِيئاً

(with prep) مَن

To whom was it addressed? لِمَنْ كَانَت مُرْسَلَة؟

whose /hu:z/ *pron* لِمَن

Whose is it? لِمَن هِي؟

Whose is this purse? لِمَن حَقِيبَة اليَد هَذِه؟

I know whose it is. أَعْلَم لِمَن هِي

why /waɪ/ *adv* (in questions) لِمَاذَا

Why are you late? لِمَاذَا تَأَخَّرْت؟ (in explanations) سَبَب

That's why he left. ذَلِكَ هُوَ سَبَب مُغَادَرَتِه

wide /waɪd/ *adj* وَاسِع

widen /'waɪdn/ *v* (to become wider) يَتَّسِع (to make wider) يُوَسِّع

widow /'wɪdəʊ/ *n* أَرْمَلَة/أَرَامِلُ مف/ج

width /wɪdθ/ *n* عَرْض

wife /waɪf/ *n* pl **wives** زَوْجَة

wild /waɪld/ *adj* (animal) وَحْشِيّ (plant) بَرِّيّ (attack) هَائِج

wildlife /'waɪldlaɪf/ *n* الحَيَاة البَرِّيَّة

will /wɪl/ *modal v* (in future tenses) سَوْفَ

I will / I'll see you tomorrow. سَوْفَ أَرَاكَ غَداً

Will he arrive today? هَل سَيَأْتِي اليَوْم؟

She won't talk to me. لَن تَتَحَدَّث إِلَيَّ

♦ *n* وَصِيَّة/وَصَايَا مف/ج

willing /'wɪlɪŋ/ *adj* مُسْتَعِدّ

win /wɪn/ *v* **won** يَفُوز

♦ *n* انْتِصَار

wind *n* /wɪnd/ رِيح/رِيَاح (م) مف/ج

♦ *v* /waɪnd/ (roads, paths) يَلْتَفّ (a clock, rope) يَلُفّ

wind farm *n* مِنْطَقَة مَرَاوِح هَوَائِيَّة

window /'wɪndəʊ/ *n* نَافِذَة/نَوَافِذ مف/ج

wine /waɪn/ *n* خَمْرَة/خُمُور مف/ج

wing /wɪŋ/ *n* (bird's) جَنَاح/أَجْنِحَة (in sport) لاَعِب الجَنَاح

winner /'wɪnə(r)/ *n* فَائِز

winning /'wɪnɪŋ/ *adj* فَائِز

winter /'wɪntə(r)/ *n* شِتَاء

wipe /waɪp/ *v* يَمْسَح

wire /'waɪə(r)/ *n* سِلْك/أَسْلاَك مف/ج

wireless /'waɪələs/ *adj* لاَسِلْكِيّ

wisdom /'wɪzdəm/ *n* حِكْمَة/حِكَم مف/ج

wise /waɪz/ *adj* حَكِيم/حُكَمَاء مف/ج

wish /wɪʃ/ *n* أُمْنِيَّة
♦ *v* يَتَمَنَّى

wit /wɪt/ *n* ظَرَافَة

witch /wɪtʃ/ *n* سَاحِرَة

with /wɪð/ *prep* (accompanying) مَعَ (using) بِـ

withdraw /wɪð'drɔː/ *v* **-drew, -drawn** يَسْحَب

withdrawal /wɪð'drɔːəl/ *n* سَحْب

within /wɪ'ðɪn/ *prep* دَاخِل

without /wɪ'ðaʊt/ *prep* بِدُون

witness /'wɪtnəs/ *n* شَاهِد/شُهُود وَشُهَّاد مف/ج
♦ *v* يَشْهَد

W

wolf /wʊlf/ *n* pl **wolves** ذِئْب/ذِئَاب مف/ج

woman /'wʊmən/ *n* pl **-men** امْرَأَة/نِسَاء مف/ج

wonder /'wʌndə(r)/ *v* يَتَسَائِل

wonderful /'wʌndəfl/ *adj* (day) رَائِع (selection) مُدْهِش

won't /wəʊnt/ *contr* (= will not: see will)

wood /wʊd/ *n* (material) خَشَب/حُرْش/أَحْرَاش (trees) أَخْشَاب مف/ج مف/ج

wooden /'wʊdn/ *adj* خَشَبِيّ

wool /wʊl/ *n* صُوف

word /wɜːd/ *n* كَلِمَة

word processing *n* مُعَالِج النُصُوص

work /wɜːk/ *n* (activity) عَمَل/أَعْمَال مف/ج (place) عَمَل
♦ *v* (do one's duty) يَعْمَل (be effective) يَنْجَح

worker /'wɜːkə(r)/ *n* عَامِل/عُمَّال مف/ج

workshop /'wɜːkʃɒp/ *n* وَرْشَة/وِرَش مف/ج

world /wɜːld/ *n* عَالَم

worldwide /'wɜːldwaɪd/ *adj* عَالَمِيّ

worm /wɜːm/ *n* دُودَة/دِيدَان مف/ج

worry /'wʌri/ *n* pl **-ries** هَمّ/هُمُوم مف/ج
♦ *v* يَقْلَق

worse /wɜːs/ *adj* أَسْوَأُ
The film was worse than expected. كَانَ الفِيلْم أَسْوَأ مِمَّا تَوَقَّعْتُ
My leg is worse. سَاقِي أَسْوَأ حَالاً
♦ *adv* أَسْوَأ مِن

He played worse than ever.
لَعِبَ أَسْوَأَ مِن أَيِّ وَقْت مَضَى

worsen /ˈwɜːsn/ *v* يَسُوء

worship /ˈwɜːʃɪp/ *n* عِبَادَة
♦ *v* يَعْبُد

worst /wɜːst/ *adj* الأَسْوَأ
my worst mistake خَطَأي الأَسْوَأ
♦ *adv* أَسْوَأ
Who played worst? مَن لَعِبَ أَسْوَأ؟

worth /wɜːθ/ *n* قِيمَة/قِيَم مف/ج

worthwhile /wɜːθˈwaɪl/ *adj* مُجْدٍ

would /wʊd/ *modal v* (conditional) سَوْفَ
That would be good.
سَوْفَ يَكُون ذَلِكَ جَيِّداً
They said it wouldn't rain.
قَالُوا إِنَّهَا لَن تُمْطِر (polite requests) هَلاَّ
Would you answer the phone?
هَلاَّ أَجَبْتَ عَلَى الهَاتِف؟ (habitual past)
كَانَ مِن عَادَتِه أَن
He would come every day at six.
كَانَ مِن عَادَتِه أَن يَأْتِي كُلّ يَوْم فِي السَاعَة السَادِسَة

wouldn't /ˈwʊdnt/ *contr* (= would not: see would)

wound /wuːnd/ *n* جُرْح/جُرُوح وَجِرَاح مف/ج
♦ *v* يَجْرَح

wrap /ræp/ *v* يَلُفّ

wreck /rek/ *n* سَفِينَة غَارِقَة

wrestle /ˈresl/ *v* يُصَارِع

wrist /rɪst/ *n* رُسْغ/أَرْسَاغ مف/ج

write /raɪt/ *v* **wrote, written** يَكْتُب
write off *phv* يَشْطُب

writer /ˈraɪtə(r)/ *n* كَاتِب

written /ˈrɪtn/ *adj* مَكْتُوب

wrong /rɒŋ/ *adj* (incorrect) خَاطِئ
the wrong key المِفْتَاح الخَاطِئ (morally) لاَ أَخْلاَقِيّ
What you did was wrong.
مَا فَعَلْتَهُ كَانَ غَيْر أَخْلاَقِيّ
♦ *adv* بِشَكْل خَاطِئ
I did it wrong. عَمِلْتُهُ بِشَكْل خَاطِئ
♦ *n* بَاطِل
to tell right from wrong
يَقُول الحَقّ مِن البَاطِل

W

x-ray /'eksreɪ/ *n* صُورَة أَشعَّة
♦ *v* يُصَوِّر بِالأَشِعَّة

yam /jæm/ *n* يَام: نَوْع من البَطَاطَا كَبِيرَة الحَجْم

yard /jɑːd/ *n* (of house) فِنَاء/أَفْنِيَة (measure) يَارْدَة مف/ج

yawn /jɔːn/ *v* يَتَثَاءَب

year /jɪə(r)/ *n* عَام/أَعْوَام مف/ج

yeast /jiːst/ *n* خَمِيرَة/خَمَائِرُ مف/ج

yellow /'jeləʊ/ *adj* أَصْفَر/صَفْرَاءُ/صُفْر مذ/م/ج
to turn yellow يُصْبِح أَصْفَر/يَصْفَرّ
♦ *n* اللَّوْن الأَصْفَر

Yemen /'jɛmən/ *n* اليَمَن

Yemeni /'jɛməni/ *adj, n* يَمَنِيّ

yes /jɛs/ *interj* نَعَم
I said yes. قُلْتُ نَعَم
Yes, please. نَعَم إِذَا سَمَحْتَ

yesterday /'jestədeɪ/ *adv* أَمْس
We met yesterday. اجْتَمَعْنَا أَمْس
♦ *n* أَمْس
yesterday's newspaper جَرِيدَة الأَمْس

yet /jet/ *adv* بَعْد
It isn't ready yet. لَيْسَت جَاهِزَة بَعْد

yield /jiːld/ *v* يَسْتَسْلِم
♦ *n* مَحْصُول/مَحَاصِيلُ مف/ج

yoghurt /'jɒgət/ *n* **-gurt** زَبَادِيّ

you /juː/ *pron* (sing: subject) أَنْتَ/أَنْتِ ض/مذ/م
Are you happy? هَل أَنْتَ سَعِيد؟ (pl: subject) أَنْتُم/أَنْتُنَّ ض/مذ/م

You could ride your bikes. تَسْتَطِيعُون قِيادَة دَرّاجَاتِكُم (sing: direct object) كَ/كِ ض/مذ/م *Did it hit you?* هَل صَدَمَتْكَ؟ (plural: direct object) كُم/كُنَّ ض/مذ/م *Am I interrupting you?* هَل أُقَاطِعُكُم؟ (sing: indirect object) كَ/كِ ض/مذ/م *I sent you a letter.* أَرْسَلْتُ لَكَ رِسَالَة *He gave it to you.* أَعْطَاهَا لَكَ (pl: indirect object) كُم/كُنَّ ض/مذ/م *I'll give you the leaflets.* سَوْفَ أُعْطِيكُم النَشَرَات *I'll post the cheque to you.* سَوْفَ أُرْسِلُ الشيك لَكُنَّ بِالبَرِيد (sing: after prep) كَ/كِ ض/مذ/م *I'm older than you.* أَنَا أَكْبَر مِنْكَ سِنّاً (plural: after prep) كُم/كُنَّ ض/مذ/م *I'll go with you.* سَوْفَ أَذْهَب مَعَكُم

you'd /ju:d/ *contr* (= you had, you would: see have, would)

you'll /ju:l/ *contr* (= you will: see will)

young /jʌŋ/ *adj* شَاب/شُبَاب مف/ج
a young woman امْرَأَة شَابَّة
♦ *n* الشَبَاب

your /jɔ:(r)/ *adj* (of you, sing) كَ/كِ ض/مذ/م
your flat شِقَّتُكَ
your brothers إِخْوَانُكِ (of you, pl) كُم/كُنَّ ض/مذ/م
your money أَمْوَالُكُم
your parents أَبَوَاكُنَّ

you're /jʊə(r)/ *contr* (= you are: see be)

yours /jɔ:z/ *poss pron* (sing) لَكَ/لَكِ أ م/مذ/م
Is she a friend of yours? هَل هِيَ صَدِيقَة لَكَ؟ (pl) لَكُم/لَكُنَّ أ م/مذ/م
Our house is smaller than yours. بَيْتُنَا أَصْغَر مِن بَيْتِكُم

yourself /jɔ:'self/ *pron* (reflexive) نَفْسَكَ/نَفْسَكِ ض/مذ/م
You've hurt yourself. لَقَد جَرَحْتَ نَفْسَكَ (for emphasis) بِنَفْسِكَ/بِنَفْسِكِ ض/مذ/م
You can do it yourself! تَسْتَطِيعِين عَمَلَهَا بِنَفْسِكِ
Are you by yourself? هَل أَنْتَ بِمُفْرَدِكَ؟

yourselves /jɔ:'selvz/ *pron* (reflexive) أَنْفُسَكُم/أَنْفُسَكُنَّ ض/مذ/م
You are hurting yourselves. أَنْتُم تُؤْذُون أَنْفُسَكُم (for emphasis) بِأَنْفُسِكُم/بِأَنْفُسِكُنَّ ض/مذ/م
You said it yourselves. قُلْتُمُوهَا أَنْفُسُكُم

youth /ju:θ/ *n* شَبَاب

you've /ju:v/ *contr* (= you have: see have)

Z

zebra /ˈzebrə/ *n* حِمَار الوَحْش

zebra crossing *n* مَمَرّ المُشَاة

zero /ˈzɪərəʊ/ *num* صِفْر/أَصْفَار مف/ج

zone /zəʊn/ *n* مِنْطَقَة/مَنَاطِقُ مف/ج

zoo /zuː/ *n* حَدِيقَة الحَيَوَانَات

zucchini /zuˈkiːni/ *n* كُوسَا

Zurich /ˈzjʊərɪk/ *n* زْيُورِخ

Centrematter

Arabic numbers

There are two categories of number in Arabic, *cardinal* (i.e. 1, 2, 3 etc.) and *ordinal* (i.e. 1st, 2nd, 3rd etc.):

Cardinal numbers

Arabic cardinals can be divided into separate groupings.

1 to 10

These numbers are gender specific in Arabic. However, while the gender of the numbers 1 and 2 matches the gender of the objects numbered, the gender of the numbers 3 to 10 does not. So, if the object is masculine, the number must be feminine and vice versa. The object numbered by the numbers 3 to 10 is always given in the indefinite genitive plural when preceded by them, as in

أَرْبَعَةُ رِجَالٍ *four men*

ثَلَاثُ نِسَاءٍ *three women*

Note that numbers 1 and 2 are often omitted as they are understood from the usage of the singular or dual form in the object noun. When they are used they function as adjectives and are placed after the object numbered, as in

رَجُلٌ وَاحِدٌ *one man*

اِمْرَأَتَانِ اِثْنَتَانِ *two women*

The word for zero, صِفْرٌ, and the two words for one, أَحَدٌ and إِحْدَى, are only ever used as nouns.

		masc. Object	*fem.* Object	
0	Zero	صِفْرٌ		٠
1	One	أَحَدٌ وَاحِدٌ	إِحْدَى وَاحِدَةٌ	١
2	Two	اثْنَانِ	اثْنَتَانِ	٢
3	Three	ثَلَاثَةٌ	ثَلَاثٌ	٣
4	Four	أَرْبَعَةٌ	أَرْبَعٌ	٤
5	Five	خَمْسَةٌ	خَمْسٌ	٥
6	Six	سِتَّةٌ	سِتٌّ	٦
7	Seven	سَبْعَةٌ	سَبْعٌ	٧
8	Eight	ثَمَانِيَةٌ	ثَمَانِي	٨
9	Nine	تِسْعَةٌ	تِسْعٌ	٩
10	Ten	عَشَرَةٌ	عَشْرٌ	١٠

11 to 19

These numbers are also gender specific and are a compound of the word for ten, عَشَرٌ, and one of the numbers one to nine listed about. Hence, eleven is literally one-ten. The 'ten' part of the number always matches the gender of the object numbered while the other part follows the rules for the numbers 1 to 10 mentioned above. The object numbered by the numbers 11 to 19 always comes after them in the indefinite accusative singular, as in

خَمْسَةَ عَشَرَ رَجُلًا *fifteen men.*

		masc. Object	*fem.* Object	
11	Eleven	أَحَدَ عَشَرَ	إِحْدَى عَشْرَةَ	١١
12	Twelve	اِثْنَا عَشَرَ	اِثْنَتَا عَشْرَةَ	١٢
13	Thirteen	ثَلَاثَةَ عَشَرَ	ثَلَاثَ عَشْرَةَ	١٣
14	Fourteen	أَرْبَعَةَ عَشَرَ	أَرْبَعَ عَشْرَةَ	١٤
15	Fifteen	خَمْسَةَ عَشَرَ	خَمْسَ عَشْرَةَ	١٥
16	Sixteen	سِتَّةَ عَشَرَ	سِتَّ عَشْرَةَ	١٦
17	Seventeen	سَبْعَةَ عَشَرَ	سَبْعَ عَشْرَةَ	١٧
18	Eighteen	ثَمَانِيَةَ عَشَرَ	ثَمَانِيَ عَشْرَةَ	١٨
19	Nineteen	تِسْعَةَ عَشَرَ	تِسْعَ عَشْرَةَ	١٩

20 to 90

With the numbers *twenty, thirty, forty, fifty* etc., the numbered object is placed after them in the indefinite accusative singular in the same way as with the numbers 11 to 19. However, unlike numbers 11 to 19, they are always non-gender specific, or invariable. For example:

> عِشْرُونَ رَجُلاً *twenty men*
>
> عِشْرُونَ اِمْرَأَةً *twenty women*

But, if you want to say, for example, *twenty-one, forty-two* or *ninety-seven,* then you must say *one-and-twenty, two-and-forty* and *seven-and-ninety* with the numbers 1 to 9 following their rules mentioned above with respect to their gender. The object numbered, however, remains in the indefinite accusative singular, as in ثَلَاثٌ وَعِشْرُونَ امْرَأَةً *twenty-three women.*

20	Twenty	عِشْرُونَ	٢٠
21	Twenty-one	أَحَدٌ وَعِشْرُونَ إِحْدَى وَعِشْرُونَ	٢١
30	Thirty	ثَلَاثُونَ	٣٠
40	Forty	أَرْبَعُونَ	٤٠
50	Fifty	خَمْسُونَ	٥٠
60	Sixty	سِتُّونَ	٦٠
70	Seventy	سَبْعُونَ	٧٠
80	Eighty	ثَمَانُونَ	٨٠
90	Ninety	تِسْعُونَ	٩٠

100 and above

Large numbers, such as 100 or 1000, are also non-gender specific. However, unlike with numbers 20 to 90, the numbered object is placed after them in the indefinite genitive singular, as in

ثَلَاثُمِائَةِ رَجُلٍ *three hundred men*

اِثْنَا عَشَرَ أَلْفَ امْرَأَةٍ *twelve thousand women*

Thousand: Note that the word for a thousand is treated as if it were an numbered object in terms of its grammar when multiple units of a thousand are numbered, so it appears in the indefinite genitive plural when preceded by 3 to 10, in the indefinite accusative singular when preceded by 11 to 19 and so forth.

Hundred: The word for a hundred, however, is slightly different as it appears in the indefinite genitive singular after 3 to 9 and is often joined to them to make a single word.

100	One Hundred	مِائَةٌ	١٠٠
200	Two Hundred	مِائَتَانِ	٢٠٠
300	Three Hundred	ثَلَاثُمِائَةٍ	٣٠٠
400	Four Hundred	أَرْبَعُمِائَةٍ	٤٠٠
500	Five Hundred	خَمْسُمِائَةٍ	٥٠٠
600	Six Hundred	سِتُّمِائَةٍ	٦٠٠
700	Seven Hundred	سَبْعُمِائَةٍ	٧٠٠
800	Eight Hundred	ثَمَانِمِائَةٍ	٨٠٠
900	Nine Hundred	تِسْعُمِائَةٍ	٩٠٠
1000	One Thousand	أَلْفٌ	١٠٠٠
2000	Two Thousand	أَلْفَانِ	٢٠٠٠
3000	Three Thousand	ثَلَاثَةُ آلَافٍ	٣٠٠٠
11,000	Eleven Thousand	أَحَدَ عَشَرَ أَلْفًا	١١٠٠٠
12,000	Twelve Thousand	اِثْنَا عَشَرَ أَلْفًا	١٢٠٠٠
13,000	Thirteen Thousand	ثَلَاثَةَ عَشَرَ أَلْفًا	١٣٠٠٠
100,000	One Hundred Thousand	مِائَةُ أَلْفٍ	١٠٠٠٠
200,000	Two Hundred Thousand	مِائَتَا أَلْفٍ	٢٠٠٠٠
300,000	Three Hundred Thousand	ثَلَاثُمِائَةِ أَلْفٍ	٣٠٠٠٠
1,000,000	One Million	أَلْفُ أَلْفٍ	١٠٠٠٠٠٠
2,000,000	Two Million	أَلْفَا أَلْفٍ	٢٠٠٠٠٠٠
3,000,000	Three Million	ثَلَاثَةُ آلَافِ أَلْفٍ	٣٠٠٠٠٠٠

There are two ways of writing large numbers made up of units, tens, hundreds and thousands, such as, for example, 3985: You may either start with the thousands, followed by the hundreds, units and tens, as

ثَلَاثَةُ آلَافٍ وَتِسْعُمِائَةٍ وَخَمْسٌ وَثَمَانُونَ

or you may reverse the order and start with the units and tens, as

خَمْسٌ وَثَمَانُونَ وَتِسْعُمائَةٍ وَثَلَاثَةُ آلافٍ

However, the grammar of the numbered object depends on the number that is written last, so if the thousands are last, the object goes into the indefinite genitive singular; if the tens are last, the object goes into the indefinite accusative singular; and if the units are last, the object goes into the indefinite genitive plural.

Ordinal Numbers

As in English, ordinal numbers in Arabic are adjectival — they describe the object and as such they agree with it in terms of gender and grammar, so you say

الرَّجُلُ الْأَوَّلُ *the first man*

الْمَرْأَةُ الرَّابِعَةَ عَشْرَةَ the fourteenth woman

For ordinals such as *twentieth, thirtieth, one-hundredth* and *one-thousandth,* simply take the cardinal number and use it as an adjective after the object being described. Cardinals used in this way are non-gender specific, with the same word being used for masculine and feminine objects, as in

الرَّجُلُ الْعِشْرُونَ *the twentieth man*

الْمَرْأَةُ الْعِشْرُونَ *the twentieth woman*

		masc.	*masc. & fem.*	*fem.*
1st	First	الأَوّلُ		الأُولَى
2nd	Second	ثَانٍ		ثَانِيَةٌ
3rd	Third	ثَالِثٌ		ثَالِثَةٌ
4th	Fourth	رَابِعٌ		رَابِعَةٌ
5th	Fifth	خَامِسٌ		خَامِسَةٌ
6th	Sixth	سَادِسٌ		سَادِسَةٌ
7th	Seventh	سَابِعٌ		سَابِعَةٌ
8th	Eighth	ثَامِنٌ		ثَامِنَةٌ
9th	Ninth	تَاسِعٌ		تَاسِعَةٌ
10th	Tenth	عَاشِرٌ		عَاشِرَةٌ
11th	Eleventh	حَادِيَ عَشَرَ		حَادِيَةَ عَشْرَةَ
12th	Twelth	ثَانِيَ عَشَرَ		ثَانِيَةَ عَشْرَةَ
13th	Thirteenth	ثَالِثَ عَشَرَ		ثَالِثَةَ عَشْرَةَ
20th	Twentieth		عِشْرُونَ	
21st	Twenty-first	حَادٍ وَعِشْرُونَ		حَادِيَةٌ وَعِشْرُونَ
30th	Thirtieth		ثَلَاثُونَ	
100th	One-hundredth		مِائَةٌ	
1000th	One-thousandth		أَلْفٌ	

Arabic verbs

There are two categories of verb in the Arabic language: **ground-form** verbs, which are usually made up of three root letters but sometimes have four; and **derived** form verbs. There are fourteen of these derived forms, although the last five are extremely rare. These forms are listed in the table below (form I is the three letter **ground-form**). All the verb forms are listed in the 3rd person singular masculine simple past, as it is the simplest form of the verb and so tends to be used as its infinitive:

اِفْعَالَّ		XI	تَفَاعَلَ		VI	فَعَلَ		I
to redden	اِحْمَارَّ		to retire	تَقَاعَدَ		to hear	سَمِعَ	
اِفْعَوْعَلَ		XII	اِنْفَعَلَ		VII	فَعَّلَ		II
to be green	اِخْضَوْضَرَ		to break	اِنْكَسَرَ		to teach	عَلَّمَ	
اِفْعَوَّلَ		XIII	اِفْتَعَلَ		VIII	فَاعَلَ		III
to last long	اِجْلَوَّذَ		to be probable	اِحْتَمَلَ		to help	سَاعَدَ	
اِفْعَنْلَلَ		XIV	اِفْعَلَّ		IX	أَفْعَلَ		IV
to be dark	اِسْحَنْكَكَ		to be black	أَسْوَدَّ		to insert	أَدْخَلَ	
اِفْعَنْلَى		XV	اِسْتَفْعَلَ		X	تَفَعَّلَ		V
to be stout	اِعْلَنْدَى		to receive	اِسْتَقْبَلَ		to graduate	تَخَرَّجَ	

In the table above, ف refers to the first root letter in the verb, ع to the second and ل to the third. Therefore, when the ع or ل is mentioned twice, that means that that root letter appears twice in the verb.

There are two main tenses in the Arabic language, the *simple past* and the *simple present*, although it would be more correct to refer to them as the *perfect* and *imperfect*. The *future* is formed by prefixing the present tense with the letter سَ, or by placing the word سَوْفَ in front of it. Arabic grammar books often refer to the *imperative* form as the future tense since when you command someone to do an action, that action takes place in the future. The imperative is included in the verb paradigms below.

Arabic verbs are not defined as being regular or irregular, but rather as being *strong* or *weak*. A strong verb is one which retains its original letters throughout all its inflexions, whereas a weak verb is one which does not because of the presence of one or more of the letters و ,ا and ي, in its infinitive form. In the tables that follow, tables 1-4 give the paradigms of the different forms of strong verb, while the remainder give the paradigms of the different types of weak verbs.

Strong verbs

The first table gives a paradigm for a typical triliteral verb (one made up of three root letters), the second for a typical quadrilateral verb, the third for a typical verb that has a derived form, and the fourth for a form of triliteral verb in which the last two root letters are the same. This latter type of verb is called a doubled verb.

1) Typical triliteral Strong Verb:

To study		دَرَسَ			
Imperative	Simple Present	Simple Past	Gender	Person	Number
———	أَدْرُسُ	دَرَسْتُ	m/f	1st	Singular
أُدْرُسْ	تَدْرُسُ	دَرَسْتَ	m	2nd	
أُدْرُسِي	تَدْرُسِينَ	دَرَسْتِ	f		
———	يَدْرُسُ	دَرَسَ	m	3rd	
———	تَدْرُسُ	دَرَسَتْ	f		
———	نَدْرُسُ	دَرَسْنَا	m/f	1st	Dual
أُدْرُسَا	تَدْرُسَانِ	دَرَسْتُمَا	m/f	2nd	
———	يَدْرُسَانِ	دَرَسَا	m	3rd	
———	تَدْرُسَانِ	دَرَسَتَا	f		
———	نَدْرُسُ	دَرَسْنَا	m/f	1st	Plural
أُدْرُسُوا	تَدْرُسُونَ	دَرَسْتُمْ	m	2nd	
أُدْرُسْنَ	تَدْرُسْنَ	دَرَسْتُنَّ	f		
———	يَدْرُسُونَ	دَرَسُوا	m	3rd	
———	يَدْرُسْنَ	دَرَسْنَ	f		

2) Typical Strong quadrilateral verb:

To roll		دَحْرَجَ			
Imperative	Simple Present	Simple Past	Gender	Person	Number
———	أُدَحْرِجُ	دَحْرَجْتُ	m/f	1st	Singular
دَحْرِجْ	تُدَحْرِجُ	دَحْرَجْتَ	m	2nd	
دَحْرِجِي	تُدَحْرِجِينَ	دَحْرَجْتِ	f		
———	يُدَحْرِجُ	دَحْرَجَ	m	3rd	
———	تُدَحْرِجُ	دَحْرَجَتْ	f		

Typical Strong quadrilateral verb (cont):

To roll		دَحْرَجَ			
Imperative	Simple Present	Simple Past	Gender	Person	Number
———	نُدَحْرِجُ	دَحْرَجْنَا	m/f	1st	Dual
دَحْرِجَا	تُدَحْرِجَانِ	دَحْرَجْتُمَا	m/f	2nd	
———	يُدَحْرِجَانِ	دَحْرَجَا	m	3rd	
———	تُدَحْرِجَانِ	دَحْرَجَتَا	f		
———	نُدَحْرِجُ	دَحْرَجْنَا	m/f	1st	Plural
دَحْرِجُوا	تُدَحْرِجُونَ	دَحْرَجْتُمْ	m	2nd	
دَحْرِجْنَ	تُدَحْرِجْنَ	دَحْرَجْتُنَّ	f		
———	يُدَحْرِجُونَ	دَحْرَجُوا	m	3rd	
———	يُدَحْرِجْنَ	دَحْرَجْنَ	f		

3) Typical derived verb:

To use		اِسْتَعْمَلَ			
Imperative	Simple Present	Simple Past	Gender	Person	Number
———	أَسْتَعْمِلُ	اِسْتَعْمَلْتُ	m/f	1st	Singular
اِسْتَعْمِلْ	تَسْتَعْمِلُ	اِسْتَعْمَلْتَ	m	2nd	
اِسْتَعْمِلِي	تَسْتَعْمِلِينَ	اِسْتَعْمَلْتِ	f		
———	يَسْتَعْمِلُ	اِسْتَعْمَلَ	m	3rd	
———	تَسْتَعْمِلُ	اِسْتَعْمَلَتْ	f		
———	نَسْتَعْمِلُ	اِسْتَعْمَلْنَا	m/f	1st	Dual
اِسْتَعْمِلَا	تَسْتَعْمِلَانِ	اِسْتَعْمَلْتُمَا	m/f	2nd	
———	يَسْتَعْمِلَانِ	اِسْتَعْمَلَا	m	3rd	
———	تَسْتَعْمِلَانِ	اِسْتَعْمَلَتَا	f		

To use		اِسْتَعْمَلَ			
Imperative	Simple Present	Simple Past	Gender	Person	Number
———	نَسْتَعْمِلُ	اِسْتَعْمَلْنَا	m/f	1st	Plural
اِسْتَعْمِلُوا	تَسْتَعْمِلُونَ	اِسْتَعْمَلْتُمْ	m	2nd	
اِسْتَعْمِلْنَ	تَسْتَعْمِلْنَ	اِسْتَعْمَلْتُنَّ	f		
———	يَسْتَعْمِلُونَ	اِسْتَعْمَلُوا	m	3rd	
———	يَسْتَعْمِلْنَ	اِسْتَعْمَلْنَ	f		

4) Typical strong doubled verb:

To run away		فَرَّ			
Imperative	Simple Present	Simple Past	Gender	Person	Number
———	أَفِرُّ	فَرَرْتُ	m/f	1st	Singular
فِرَّ	تَفِرُّ	فَرَرْتَ	m	2nd	
فِرِّي	تَفِرِّينَ	فَرَرْتِ	f		
———	يَفِرُّ	فَرَّ	m	3rd	
———	تَفِرُّ	فَرَّتْ	f		
———	نَفِرُّ	فَرَرْنَا	m/f	1st	Dual
فِرَّا	تَفِرَّانِ	فَرَرْتُمَا	m/f	2nd	
———	يَفِرَّانِ	فَرَّا	m	3rd	
———	تَفِرَّانِ	فَرَّتَا	f		
———	نَفِرُّ	فَرَرْنَا	m/f	1st	Plural
فِرُّوا	تَفِرُّونَ	فَرَرْتُمْ	m	2nd	
اِفْرِرْنَ	تَفْرِرْنَ	فَرَرْتُنَّ	f		
———	يَفِرُّونَ	فَرُّوا	m	3rd	
———	يَفْرِرْنَ	فَرَرْنَ	f		

Weak verbs

A verb in Arabic is called weak when its infinitive form contains a و, ا or ي. These weak verbs are commonly divided up according to where in the word the weak letter occurs, and how many weak letters it contains. Examples are given for each type in the tables below. Multiple examples are given in some categories because the paradigm varies according to which weak letter occurs in the verb — a verb whose weak letter is و will often decline differently from one whose weak letter is ي and so on:

5) Verbs whose initial letter is weak:

To arrive		وَصَلَ			
Imperative	Simple Present	Simple Past	Gender	Person	Number
-----	أَصِلُ	وَصَلْتُ	m/f	1st	Singular
صِلْ	تَصِلُ	وَصَلْتَ	m	2nd	
صِلِي	تَصِلِينَ	وَصَلْتِ	f		
-----	يَصِلُ	وَصَلَ	m	3rd	
-----	تَصِلُ	وَصَلَتْ	f		
-----	نَصِلُ	وَصَلْنَا	m/f	1st	Dual
صِلَا	تَصِلَانِ	وَصَلْتُمَا	m/f	2nd	
-----	يَصِلَانِ	وَصَلَا	m	3rd	
-----	تَصِلَانِ	وَصَلَتَا	f		
-----	نَصِلُ	وَصَلْنَا	m/f	1st	Plural
صِلُوا	تَصِلُونَ	وَصَلْتُمْ	m	2nd	
صِلْنَ	تَصِلْنَ	وَصَلْتُنَّ	f		
-----	يَصِلُونَ	وَصَلُوا	m	3rd	
-----	يَصِلْنَ	وَصَلْنَ	f		

To eat		أَكَلَ			
Imperative	Simple Present	Simple Past	Gender	Person	Number
———	آكُلُ	أَكَلْتُ	m/f	1st	Singular
كُلْ	تَأْكُلُ	أَكَلْتَ	m	2nd	
كُلِي	تَأْكُلِينَ	أَكَلْتِ	f		
———	يَأْكُلُ	أَكَلَ	m	3rd	
———	تَأْكُلُ	أَكَلَتْ	f		
———	نَأْكُلُ	أَكَلْنَا	m/f	1st	Dual
كُلَا	تَأْكُلَانِ	أَكَلْتُمَا	m/f	2nd	
———	يَأْكُلَانِ	أَكَلَا	m	3rd	
———	تَأْكُلَانِ	أَكَلَتَا	f		
———	نَأْكُلُ	أَكَلْنَا	m/f	1st	Plural
كُلُوا	تَأْكُلُونَ	أَكَلْتُمْ	m	2nd	
كُلْنَ	تَأْكُلْنَ	أَكَلْتُنَّ	f		
———	يَأْكُلُونَ	أَكَلُوا	m	3rd	
———	يَأْكُلْنَ	أَكَلْنَ	f		

6) Verbs whose middle letter is weak. These are usually called hollow verbs:

To say		قَالَ			
Imperative	Simple Present	Simple Past	Gender	Person	Number
———	أَقُولُ	قُلْتُ	m/f	1st	Singular
قُلْ	تَقُولُ	قُلْتَ	m	2nd	
قُولِي	تَقُولِينَ	قُلْتِ	f		
———	يَقُولُ	قَالَ	m	3rd	
———	تَقُولُ	قَالَتْ	f		

To say		قَالَ			
Imperative	Simple Present	Simple Past	Gender	Person	Number
———	نَقُولُ	قُلْنَا	m/f	1st	Dual
قُولَا	تَقُولَانِ	قُلْتُمَا	m/f	2nd	
———	يَقُولَانِ	قَالَا	m	3rd	
———	تَقُولَانِ	قَالَتَا	f		
———	نَقُولُ	قُلْنَا	m/f	1st	Plural
قُولُوا	تَقُولُونَ	قُلْتُمْ	m	2nd	
قُلْنَ	تَقُلْنَ	قُلْتُنَّ	f		
———	يَقُولُونَ	قَالُوا	m	3rd	
———	يَقُلْنَ	قُلْنَ	f		

To sleep		نَامَ			
Imperative	Simple Present	Simple Past	Gender	Person	Number
———	أَنَامُ	نِمْتُ	m/f	1st	Singular
نَمْ	تَنَامُ	نِمْتَ	m	2nd	
نَامِي	تَنَامِينَ	نِمْتِ	f		
———	يَنَامُ	نَامَ	m	3rd	
———	تَنَامُ	نَامَت	f		
———	نَنَامُ	نِمْنَا	m/f	1st	Dual
نَامَا	تَنَامَانِ	نِمْتُمَا	m/f	2nd	
———	يَنَامَانِ	نَامَا	m	3rd	
———	تَنَامَانِ	نَامَتَا	f		
———	نَنَامُ	نِمْنَا	m/f	1st	Plural
نَامُوا	تَنَامُونَ	نِمْتُمْ	m	2nd	
نَمْنَ	تَنَمْنَ	نِمْتُنَّ	f		
———	يَنَامُونَ	نَامُوا	m	3rd	
———	يَنَمْنَ	نِمْنَ	f		

To sell		بَاعَ			
Imperative	Simple Present	Simple Past	Gender	Person	Number
———	أَبِيعُ	بِعْتُ	m/f	1st	Singular
بِعْ	تَبِيعُ	بِعْتَ	m	2nd	
بِيعِي	تَبِيعِينَ	بِعْتِ	f		
———	يَبِيعُ	بَاعَ	m	3rd	
———	تَبِيعُ	بَاعَتْ	f		
———	نَبِيعُ	بِعْنَا	m/f	1st	Dual
بِيعَا	تَبِيعَانِ	بِعْتُمَا	m/f	2nd	
———	يَبِيعَانِ	بَاعَا	m	3rd	
———	تَبِيعَانِ	بَاعَتَا	f		
———	نَبِيعُ	بِعْنَا	m/f	1st	Plural
بِيعُوا	تَبِيعُونَ	بِعْتُمْ	m	2nd	
بِعْنَ	تَبِعْنَ	بِعْتُنَّ	f		
———	يَبِيعُونَ	بَاعُوا	m	3rd	
———	يَبِعْنَ	بِعْنَ	f		

7) Verbs whose final letter is weak. These are usually called defective verbs:

To hope		رَجَا			
Imperative	Simple Present	Simple Past	Gender	Person	Number
———	أَرْجُو	رَجَوْتُ	m/f	1st	Singular
أُرْجُ	تَرْجُو	رَجَوْتَ	m	2nd	
أُرْجِي	تَرْجِينَ	رَجَوْتِ	f		
———	يَرْجُو	رَجَا	m	3rd	
———	تَرْجُو	رَجَتْ	f		

To hope			رَجَا		
Imperative	Simple Present	Simple Past	Gender	Person	Number
———	نَرْجُو	رَجَوْنَا	m/f	1st	Dual
أُرْجُوَا	تَرْجُوانِ	رَجَوْتُمَا	m/f	2nd	
———	يَرْجُوانِ	رَجَوَا	m	3rd	
———	تَرْجُوانِ	رَجَتَا	f		
———	نَرْجُو	رَجَوْنَا	m/f	1st	Plural
أُرْجُوا	تَرْجُونَ	رَجَوْتُمْ	m	2nd	
أُرْجُونَ	تَرْجُونَ	رَجَوْتُنَّ	f		
———	يَرْجُونَ	رَجَوْا	m	3rd	
———	يَرْجُونَ	رَجَوْنَ	f		

To meet			لَقِيَ		
Imperative	Simple Present	Simple Past	Gender	Person	Number
———	أَلْقَى	لَقِيتُ	m/f	1st	Singular
اِلْقَ	تَلْقَى	لَقِيتَ	m	2nd	
اِلْقَيْ	تَلْقَيْنَ	لَقِيتِ	f		
———	يَلْقَى	لَقِيَ	m	3rd	
———	تَلْقَى	لَقِيَتْ	f		
———	نَلْقَى	لَقِينَا	m/f	1st	Dual
اِلْقَيَا	تَلْقَيَانِ	لَقِيتُمَا	m/f	2nd	
———	يَلْقَيَانِ	لَقِيَا	m	3rd	
———	تَلْقَيَانِ	لَقِيَتَا	f		
———	نَلْقَى	لَقِينَا	m/f	1st	Plural
اِلْقَوْا	تَلْقَوْنَ	لَقِيتُمْ	m	2nd	
اِلْقَيْنَ	تَلْقَيْنَ	لَقِيتُنَّ	f		
———	يَلْقَوْنَ	لَقُوا	m	3rd	
———	يَلْقَيْنَ	لَقِينَ	f		

To throw		رَمَى			
Imperative	Simple Present	Simple Past	Gender	Person	Number
———	أَرْمِي	رَمَيْتُ	m/f	1st	Singular
اِرْمِ	تَرْمِي	رَمَيْتَ	m	2nd	
اِرْمِي	تَرْمِينَ	رَمَيْتِ	f		
———	يَرْمِي	رَمَى	m	3rd	
———	تَرْمِي	رَمَتْ	f		
———	نَرْمِي	رَمَيْنَا	m/f	1st	Dual
اِرْمِيَا	تَرْمِيَانِ	رَمَيْتُمَا	m/f	2nd	
———	يَرْمِيَانِ	رَمَيَا	m	3rd	
———	تَرْمِيَانِ	رَمَتَا	f		
———	نَرْمِي	رَمَيْنَا	m/f	1st	Plural
اِرْمُوا	تَرْمُونَ	رَمَيْتُمْ	m	2nd	
اِرْمِينَ	تَرْمِينَ	رَمَيْتُنَّ	f		
———	يَرْمُونَ	رَمَوْا	m	3rd	
———	يَرْمِينَ	رَمَيْنَ	f		

8) Verbs that have two weak letters. These are called doubly weak verbs:

To see		رَأَى			
Imperative	Simple Present	Simple Past	Gender	Person	Number
———	أَرَى	رَأَيْتُ	m/f	1st	Singular
رَ	تَرَى	رَأَيْتَ	m	2nd	
رَيْ	تَرَيْنَ	رَأَيْتِ	f		
———	يَرَى	رَأَى	m	3rd	
———	تَرَى	رَأَتْ	f		

To see		رَأَى			
Imperative	Simple Present	Simple Past	Gender	Person	Number
———	نَرَى	رَأَيْنَا	m/f	1st	Dual
رَيَا	تَرَيَانِ	رَأَيْتُمَا	m/f	2nd	
———	يَرَيَانِ	رَأَيَا	m	3rd	
———	تَرَيَانِ	رَأَتَا	f		
———	نَرَى	رَأَيْنَا	m/f	1st	Plural
رَوْا	تَرَوْنَ	رَأَيْتُمْ	m	2nd	
رَيْنَ	تَرَيْنَ	رَأَيْتُنَّ	f		
———	يَرَوْنَ	رَأَوْا	m	3rd	
———	يَرَيْنَ	رَأَيْنَ	f		

To be faithful		وَفَى			
Imperative	Simple Present	Simple Past	Gender	Person	Number
———	أَفِي	وَفَيْتُ	m/f	1st	Singular
فِ	تَفِي	وَفَيْتَ	m	2nd	
فِي	تَفِينَ	وَفَيْتِ	f		
———	يَفِي	وَفَى	m	3rd	
———	تَفِي	وَفَتْ	f		
———	نَفِي	وَفَيْنَا	m/f	1st	Dual
فِيَا	تَفِيَانِ	وَفَيْتُمَا	m/f	2nd	
———	يَفِيَانِ	وَفَيَا	m	3rd	
———	تَفِيَانِ	وَفَتَا	f		
———	نَفِي	وَفَيْنَا	m/f	1st	Plural
فُوا	تَفُونَ	وَفَيْتُمْ	m	2nd	
فِينَ	تَفِينَ	وَفَيْتُنَّ	f		
———	يَفُونَ	وَفَوْا	m	3rd	
———	يَفِينَ	وَفَيْنَ	f		

To come		جَاءَ			
Imperative	Simple Present	Simple Past	Gender	Person	Number
–––––	أَجِيئُ	جِئْتُ	m/f	1st	Singular
جِئْ	تَجِيئُ	جِئْتَ	m	2nd	
جِيئِي	تَجِيئِينَ	جِئْتِ	f		
–––––	يَجِيئُ	جَاءَ	m	3rd	
–––––	تَجِيئُ	جَاءَتْ	f		
–––––	نَجِيئُ	جِئْنَا	m/f	1st	Dual
جِيئَا	تَجِيئَانِ	جِئْتُمَا	m/f	2nd	
–––––	يَجِيئَانِ	جَاءَا	m	3rd	
–––––	تَجِيئَانِ	جَاءَتَا	f		
–––––	نَجِيئُ	جِئْنَا	m/f	1st	Plural
جِيئُوا	تَجِيئُونَ	جِئْتُمْ	m	2nd	
جِئْنَ	تَجِئْنَ	جِئْتُنَّ	f		
–––––	يَجِيئُونَ	جَاءُوا	m	3rd	
–––––	يَجِئْنَ	جِئْنَ	f		

9) Verbs that have three weak letters. These are called trebly weak verbs:

To seek shelter		أَوَى			
Imperative	Simple Present	Simple Past	Gender	Person	Number
–––––	آوِي	أَوَيْتُ	m/f	1st	Singular
اِيوِ	تَأْوِي	أَوَيْتَ	m	2nd	
اِيوِي	تَأْوِينَ	أَوَيْتِ	f		
–––––	يَأْوِي	أَوَى	m	3rd	
–––––	تَأْوِي	أَوَتْ	f		

To seek shelter		أَوَى			
Imperative	Simple Present	Simple Past	Gender	Person	Number
———	نَأْوِي	أَوَيْنَا	m/f	1st	Dual
اِيوِيَا	تَأْوِيَانِ	أَوَيْتُمَا	m/f	2nd	
———	يَأْوِيَانِ	أَوَيَا	m	3rd	
———	تَأْوِيَانِ	أَوَتَا	f		
———	نَأْوِي	أَوَيْنَا	m/f	1st	Plural
اِيوُوا	تَأْوُونَ	أَوَيْتُمْ	m	2nd	
اِيوِينَ	تَأْوِينَ	أَوَيْتُنَّ	f		
———	يَأْوُونَ	أَوَوْا	m	3rd	
———	يَأْوِينَ	أَوَيْنَ	f		

To promise		وَأَى			
Imperative	Simple Present	Simple Past	Gender	Person	Number
———	أَءِي	وَأَيْتُ	m/f	1st	Singular
إِ	تَإِي	وَأَيْتَ	m	2nd	
إِي	تَإِينَ	وَأَيْتِ	f		
———	يَإِي	وَأَى	m	3rd	
———	تَإِي	وَأَتْ	f		
———	نَإِي	وَأَيْنَا	m/f	1st	Dual
إِيَا	تَإِيَانِ	وَأَيْتُمَا	m/f	2nd	
———	يَإِيَانِ	وَأَيَا	m	3rd	
———	تَإِيَانِ	وَأَتَا	f		
———	نَإِي	وَأَيْنَا	m/f	1st	Plural
أُوا	تَأُونَ	وَأَيْتُمْ	m	2nd	
إِينَ	تَإِينَ	وَأَيْتُنَّ	f		
———	يَأُونَ	وَأَوْا	m	3rd	
———	يَإِينَ	وَأَيْنَ	f		

Numbers

Cardinals		Ordinals	
العدد الأصلي		اسم العدد	
0	zero, nought (GB) أُنظُر الى المُلاحظة حول استِخدام الصِفر		
1	one	1st	first
2	two	2nd	second
3	three	3rd	third
4	four	4th	fourth
5	five	5th	fifth
6	six	6th	sixth
7	seven	7th	seventh
8	eight	8th	eighth
9	nine	9th	ninth
10	ten	10th	tenth
11	eleven	11th	eleventh
12	twelve	12th	twelfth
13	thirteen	13th	thirteenth
14	fourteen	14th	fourteenth
15	fifteen	15th	fifteenth
16	sixteen	16th	sixteenth
17	seventeen	17th	seventeenth
18	eighteen	18th	eighteenth
19	nineteen	19th	nineteenth
20	twenty	20th	twentieth
21	twenty-one	21st	twenty-first
22	twenty-two	22nd	twenty-second

القائِمة التالية تُظهر أسماء الأعداد من ثَلاثون الى تِسعون

30	thirty
40	forty*
50	fifty
60	sixty

70 seventy
80 eighty
90 ninety

القائِمة التالِية تُظهِر أسماء الأعداد من 100 الى 999

100 a hundred, one hundred
101 a hundred and one, a hundred one (US)
200 two hundred
210 two hundred and ten, two hundred ten (US)
999 nine hundred and ninety-nine, nine hundred ninety-nine (US)

القائمة التالية تُظهر بَقِية أسماء الأعداد

1,000 a thousand, one thousand
1,001 one thousand and one, one thousand one (US)
1,050 one thousand and fifty, one thousand fifty (US)
2,000 two thousand
2,015 two thousand and fifteen, two thousand fifteen (US)
100,000 one hundred thousand
1,000,000 one million
1,490,070 one million, four hundred and ninety thousand and seventy
1,000,000,000 one billion

ملاحظة: الحرف u يُحذف في forty لكن لا يُحذف في fourteen

Miscellaneous: In Britain it is common to say oh for zero, especially when saying telephone numbers and years, e.g. 7-oh-4-7-5-0h for 704750. In the USA 'zero' is usually used. In scores in sport *nil, nothing* and *zip* are also used when saying the score: a score of 5-0 could be said: 5-nil (GB), 5-nothing, 5-zip (US)

استخدامات بَديلة: من المُعتاد استخدام oh بَدلاً من zero في الإنجليزية البَريطانِية خاصةً عند استِخدامِها في أرقام الهاتِف وعدد السنوات مثل

7-oh-4-7-5-oh بدلاً من 704750. أما في الإنجليزية الأمريكية فَيتم استِخدام zero في جَميع الحالات. في حالات الحَديث عن النقاط المُحرَزة يُمكن استِخدام nil و nothing و zip بَدلاً من zero. النَتيجة 5-0 يُمكنَ التَعبير عنهاَ بـ 5-nil (GB)، 5-nothing، 5-zip (US).

English irregular verbs الأفعال الإنجليزية الشاذة

الفعل المجرد *Infinitive*	صيغة الماضي *Preterite*	اسم المفعول *Past participle*
be	was	been
bear	bore	borne
beat	beat	beaten
become	became	become
begin	began	begun
bend	bent	bent
bet	bet, betted	bet, betted
bite	bit	bitten
bleed	bled	bled
blow	blew	blown
break	broke	broken
breed	bred	bred
bring	brought	brought
build	built	built
burn	burnt, burned	burnt, burned
burst	burst	burst
buy	bought	bought
catch	caught	caught
choose	chose	chosen
come	came	come
cost	cost, costed	cost, costed
cut	cut	cut
deal	dealt	dealt
dig	dug	dug

do	did	done
draw	drew	drawn
dream	dreamt, dreamed	dreamt, dreamed
drink	drank	drunk
drive	drove	driven
eat	ate	eaten
fall	fell	fallen
feed	fed	fed
feel	felt	felt
fight	fought	fought
find	found	found
flee	fled	fled
fly	flew	flown
forecast	forecast, -casted	forecast, -casted
forget	forgot	forgotten
freeze	froze	frozen
get	got	got, gotten *US*
give	gave	given
go	went	gone
grow	grew	grown
hang	hung	hung
have	had	had
hear	heard	heard
hide	hid	hidden
hit	hit	hit
hold	held	held
hurt	hurt	hurt
keep	kept	kept
kneel	knelt	knelt
know	knew	known
lay	laid	laid
lead	led	led
lean	leaned, leant	leaned, leant
leap	leaped, leapt	leaped, leapt
learn	learnt, learned	learnt, learned

leave	left	left
lend	lent	lent
let	let	let
lie	lay	lain
lose	lost	lost
make	made	made
mean	meant	meant
meet	met	met
pay	paid	paid
put	put	put
quit	quit, quitted	quit, quitted
read	read	read
ride	rode	ridden
ring	rang	rung
rise	rose	risen
run	ran	run
say	said	said
see	saw	seen
sell	sold	sold
send	sent	sent
set	set	set
sew	sewed	sewn, sewed
shake	shook	shaken
shine	shone	shone
shoot	shot	shot
show	showed	shown
shut	shut	shut
sing	sang	sung
sink	sank	sunk
sit	sat	sat
sleep	slept	slept
smell	smelt, smelled	smelt, smelled
speak	spoke	spoken
spell	spelled, spelt	spelled, spelt
spend	spent	spent

spit	spat	spat
split	split	split
spoil	spoilt, spoiled	spoilt, spoiled
spread	spread	spread
stand	stood	stood
steal	stole	stolen
stick	stuck	stuck
sting	stung	stung
strike	struck	struck
swear	swore	sworn
sweep	swept	swept
swell	swelled	swollen, swelled
swim	swam	swum
swing	swung	swung
take	took	taken
teach	taught	taught
tear	tore	torn
tell	told	told
think	thought	thought
throw	threw	thrown
understand	understood	understood
wake	woke	woken
wear	wore	worn
win	won	won
write	wrote	written

يَهوديّ س ج /يَهود/ (شَخْص يُؤْمِنُ بِاليَهوديَّة) Jew

يَهوديَّة س Judaism

يود س iodine

يورو س euro

يولِيو س (الشَهْر السابِع بِالتَقْويم المِصْريّ) July

يَوْم س ج /أيّام/ day

يَوْميّ ص daily

يَوْميّات س diary

يونان س (اليونان) Greece

يُونانيّ ص ج /يونان/ Greek

يونِيو س (الشَهْر السادِس بِالتَقْويم المِصْريّ) June

ي

يَئِسَ ف to despair

يا س vocative particle

أَيْنَ كُنْتَ يا سام؟ Where were you, Sam?

يائِس hopeless

يابان س (اليابان) Japan

يابانيّ ص، س Japanese

يابِس ص dry

يابِسَة س land

يارْدَة س yard

يَأْس س despair

ياسَمين س jasmine

يافِطَة س signboard

ياقوت س ruby

يانْسون س anise

يَتَّمَ ف to orphan

يَتيم س ج /أَيْتام/يَتامى/ orphan

يَد (م) س ج /أَيْدٍ/أَيادٍ/ (كَفّ اليَد) hand

(الذِراع) arm

(مِقْبَض) handle

يَدَويّ ص manual

يَسار س left

يَساريّ ص left-wing

يَسَّرَ ف to facilitate

يُسْر س easiness

يَسوع س Jesus Christ

يَسير ص (سَهْل) easy

(قَليل) little

يَقْطينَة س ج /يَقْطين/ pumpkin

يَقِظ ص (حَذِر) alert

(مُسْتَيْقِظ) awake

يَقَظَة س (حَذَر) alertness

(صَحْو) wakefulness

يَقين س certainty

يَمَن س (اليَمَن) Yemen

يَمَنيّ ص، س Yemeni

يَمين (م) س ج /أَيْمُن/ right

ج /أَيْمان/ oath

يَمينيّ ص right-wing

يَنّ س (عُمْلَة اليابان) yen

يَنايِر س (الشَهْر الأَوَّل بِالتَقْويم المِصْريّ) January

يَنْبوع س ج /يَنابيع/ spring

يَهوديّ ص (مُتَعَلِّق بِاليَهوديَّة) Jewish

وَقاحَة س rudeness

وِقايَة س precaution

وَقَّتَ ف to time

وَقْت س ج /أَوْقات/ time

كَم الوَقْت؟ What time is it?

وَقْت بَدَل الضائِع injury time

وَقِح ص rude

وَقَّعَ ف to sign

وَقَعَ ف (سَقَطَ) to fall

(حَدَثَ) to happen

وَقَفَ ف to stand

وَقود س fuel

وُقوع س (سُقوط) fall

وُقوف س (حالَة الوُقوف عَلى الأَرْجُل) standing up

(التَحَوُّل مِن حالَة الحَرَكَة إلى حالَة السُكون) stopping

وَقى ف to shield

وِكالَة س agency

وَكْر س ج /أَوْكار/ den

وَكَزَ ف to nudge

وَكَّلَ ف to authorize

وَكيل س ج /وُكَلاء/ representative

وَلاء س allegiance

وِلادَة س birth

وِلايَة س state

وَلَد س ج /أَوْلاد/ boy

وَلَّدَ ف (أَنْتَجَ) to generate

(ساعَدَ امْرَأَة عَلى الوِلادَة) to deliver

وَلَدَ/ت ف to give birth

وَلَع س obsession

وَلِيّ س ج /أَوْلِياء/ guardian

وَلِيَ ف to follow

وَليمَة س ج /وَلائِم/ feast

وَميض س ج /أَوْمِضَة/ flash

وَهْم س ج /أَوْهام/ (تَخَيُّل) fantasy

(شَيْء يَبْدو أَنَّهُ مَوْجود لَكِنَّهُ غَيْر مَوْجود) illusion

ويلْز س Wales

ويلْزِيّ ص، س Welsh

وَسَّعَ ف (كَبَّرَ أو زادَ في المَساحَة) to widen
(طَوَّرَ وَزادَ في الاِنْتِشار) to expand

وَسيلَة س ج /وَسائِل/ means
وَسيلَة الرِزْق livelihood

وَسيم ص handsome

وِشاح س ج /أَوْشِحَة/ scarf

وَشيك ص imminent

وِصايَة س custody

وَصْف س ج /أَوْصاف/ description

وَصَفَ ف to describe

وَصْفَة س recipe
وَصْفَة طِبِّيَّة prescription

وَصَّلَ ف (سَلَّمَ سِلْعَة لِصاحِبِها) to deliver
(شَبَكَ شَيْئَيْن بِبَعْضِهِما البَعْض) to connect

وَصَلَ ف to arrive

وَصْلَة س (نُقْطَة رَبْط) connection
(أَداة تُسْتَخْدَمُ في شَبْك جِسْمَيْن خاصَّة في السَمْكَرَة) joint
(تَمْديدَة كَهْرَبائيَّة أو لِلهاتِف) extension

وُصول س arrival

وَصِيّ س ج /وُصاة/ guardian

وَصِيَّة س ج /وَصايا/ (إرادَة الشَخْص الَّتي يَكْتُبُها قَبْلَ وَفاتِه) will
(نَصيحَة ضَروريَّة) commandment

وَضَّحَ ف to clarify

وَضْع س ج /أَوْضاع/ (الظَرْف) condition
(حالَة الجِسْم في الجُلوس أو الوُقوف) posture

وَضَعَ ف to put

وُضوح س clarity

وَطَن س ج /أَوْطان/ homeland

وَطَنِيّ ص (مُتَعَلِّق بِالوَطَن) national
(شَخْص لَدَيْه نَزْعَة قَويَّة نَحْوَ وَطَنِه) patriotic

وَظَّفَ ف to employ

وَظيفَة س ج /وَظائِف/ job
وَظيفَة شاغِرَة vacancy

وَظيفِيّ ص functional

وِعاء س ج /أَوْعِيَة/ vessel

وَعْد س ج /وُعود/ promise

وَعَدَ ف to promise

وَعِر ص rugged

وَعَظَ ف to preach

وَعْكَة س bout

وَعْي س awareness

وَفاء س faithfulness

وَفاة س death

وَفْد س ج /وُفود/ delegation

وَفَّرَ ف to spare

وَفْرَة س plenty

وِفْقَ ظ according to

وَفِيّ ص faithful

وَفير ص plentiful

وِقائِيّ ص preventive

وِجْهَة س direction
وِجْهَة نَظَر viewpoint

وَجْهِيّ ص facial

وُجوب س necessity

وُجود س existence

وَجيز ص brief

وَحَّدَ ف to unite

وَحْدَة س (اتِّحاد) unity
(جُزْء) unit

وَحْدَوِيّ ص unionist

وَحْش س ج /وُحوش/ monster

وَحْشِيّ ص brutal

وَحْشِيَّة س cruelty

وَحْل س mud

وَحْي س inspiration

وَحيد ص (يَعيشُ بِمُفْرَدِهِ) alone
(لا يوجَدُ غَيْرُهُ) only

وَخَزَ ف to prick

وَدَّ ف to like

وُدّ س cordiality

وَداع س farewell

وَداعاً ظ goodbye

وَدَّعَ ف to say goodbye

وَدود ص friendly

وُدِّيّ ص friendly

وَراءَ ظ (ما وَراءَ) beyond
(خَلْفَ) behind

وَرِثَ ف to inherit

وَرَّدَ ف to export

وَرْدَة س ج /وُرود/ rose

وَرْشَة س ج /وِرَش/ workshop

وَرَّطَ ف (أَشْرَكَ شَخْصاً في عَمَل سَيِّئ) to involve
(أَوْقَعَ شَخْصاً في مُشْكِلَة) to trap

وَرَقَة س ج /وَرَق/ (وَرَقَة النَبات) leaf
(وَرَقَة لِلكِتابَة) paper

وِرْك (م) س ج /أَوْراك/ hip

وَرَم س ج /أَوْرام/ (انْتِفاخ تَحْتَ الجِلْد) lump
(تَضَخُّم في الخَلايا) tumour

وَريث س ج /وَرَثَة/ heir

وَريد س ج /أَوْرِدَة/ vein

وِزارَة س ministry

وَزَّة س ج /وَزّ/ goose

وَزَّعَ ف to distribute

وَزْن س ج /أَوْزان/ weight

وَزَنَ ف to weigh

وَزير س ج /وُزَراء/ minister

وِسادَة س pillow

وِساطَة س (التَدَخُّل بَيْنَ فَريقَيْن) mediation
(تَوْظيف الأَقارِب وَالمَعارِف) nepotism

وَسَط س ج/أَوْساط/ middle

وَسْطَ ظ among

و

وَ حج (تُسْتَخْدَمُ لِلإضافَة) and
ذَهَبْنا إلى مِصْر وَفِلَسْطين We went to Egypt and Palestine.
(تُسْتَخْدَمُ لِلقَسَم) by
وَالله لَأَقولُ الحَقيقَةَ By God, I will tell the truth.

واثِق ص confident

واجِب س ج /واجِبات/ duty

واجِب ص due

واجَهَ ف (عانى) to encounter
(تَعامَلَ مَعَ أَو قابَلَ وَجْهاً لِوَجْه) to face

واحِد عد one

وادٍ س ج /وِدْيان/ valley

وارِث س ج /وَرَثَة/ heir

وارِدَة س import

واسِطَة س means

واسِع ص extensive

واسى ف to comfort

واصَلَ ف to continue

واضِح ص obvious

واعٍ ص conscious

وافِد ص incoming

وافَقَ ف to agree

وافٍ ص (يُؤَدّي الغَرَض) adequate
(كافٍ) enough

واقِع س reality

واقِعيّ ص realistic

واقٍ ص protective

والٍ س ج /وُلاة/ governor

وَباء س ج /أَوْبِئَة/ epidemic

وَثائِقيّ ص documentary

وَثَبَ ف to hop

وَثْبَة س hop

وَثِقَ ب ف to trust

وَثيق ص firm

وَثيقَة س ج /وَثائِق/ document

وَجَبَ ف ought to

وَجْبَة س meal
وَجْبَة خَفيفَة snack

وَجَدَ ف to find

وُجْدان س sentiment

وَجْه س ج /وُجوه/ face

وَجَّهَ ف to direct

هُوَ ض (ضَمير الغائب لِلمُذَكَّر المُفْرَد) he
هُوَ صاحِب عَمَل كَريم He is a generous employer.
(ضَمير الغائب لِلحَيَوان وَالجَماد المُفْرَد) it
هُوَ قَصْر عَظيم. It's a grand palace.

هَواء س air

هَوائيّ س antenna

هِوايَة س hobby

هَوَس س (مَشاعِر عارِمَة أَو خَوْف خارِج عَن السَيْطَرَة) frenzy
(فِكْرَة تُسَيْطِرُ عَلى تَفْكير الشَخْص) obsession

هوكي س hockey
هوكي الجَليد ice hockey

هَؤُلاءِ إ إش (اسْم إِشارَة لِلجَمْع القَريب) these
هَؤُلاءِ الطُلّاب جَيِّدون These students are good.

هولَنْدا س Netherlands

هولَنْديّ ص Dutch

هولَنْديّ س Netherlander

هَوى ف to like

هُوِيَّة س identity

هِيَ ض (ضَمير الغائِب لِلمُؤَنَّث المُفْرَد) she
هِيَ طَبيبَة أَسْنان. She's a dentist.

هَيْئَة س (مَجْموعَة) agency
(شَكْل) appearance

هَيَّأَ ف (كَيَّفَ) to adjust
(أَعَدَّ) to prepare

هَيّا let's
هَيّا نَذْهَبْ! Let's go!

هَيَّجَ ف to irritate

هَيْدْروجين س hydrogen

هَيْكَل س ج /هَياكِل/ (البِناء) frame
(أُسُس وَأَنْظِمَة مُخَطَّط أَو مَشْروع) framework
هَيْكَل عَظْميّ skeleton

هيل س cardamom

هَيْمَنَ عَلى ف to dominate

هَيْمَنَة س domination

This is a beautiful car. هٰذِهِ سَيّارَةٌ جَميلَةٌ

هٰذَيْنِ إ إش (اسْم إشارَة لِلمُذَكَّر المُثَنّى القَريب) these (two)

I have got bored with these two books. سَئِمْتُ مِن هٰذَيْنِ الكِتابَيْنِ

هُراء س nonsense

هِراوَة س club

هَرَبَ ف to escape

هَرَّبَ ف to smuggle

هُروب س escape

هَزَّ ف to shake

هَزَل س comedy

هَزَمَ ف to defeat

هَزيل ص (سَيِّئ) poor

a poor solution حَلّ هَزيل

(عَديم القُوَّة) frail

a frail stem. غُصْن هَزيل

هَزيمَة س ج /هَزائِم/ defeat

هَشّ ص fragile

هَضَمَ ف to digest

هٰكَذا in this manner

هِلال س ج /أَهِلَّة/ crescent

هَلَع س panic

هِلْيَوْن س asparagus

هَمّ س ج /هُموم/ worry

هَمَّ ف to bother

هُمْ ض (ضَمير الغائِب لِلمُذَكَّر الجَمْع) they

They are men of the future. هُم رِجال المُسْتَقْبَل

هُما ض (ضَمير الغائِب لِلمُثَنّى) they

They are two true friends. هُما صَديقان مُخْلِصان

هَمَرَ ف to growl

هَمَسَ ف to whisper

هَمْسَة س whisper

هَمْهَمَ ف to hum

هُنَّ ض (ضَمير الغائِب لِلمُؤَنَّث الجَمْع) they

They work at a bank. هُنَّ يَعْمَلْنَ في بَنْك

هُنا أ إش here

هَنَّأَ ف to congratulate

هُناكَ أ إش (في ذلك المَكان) there

(يوجَدُ) there is/are

(أداة إشارة لِلبَعيد) over there

هُنالِكَ أ إش therein

هِنْد س (الهِنْد) India

هِنْدِباء س endive

هَنْدَسَة س engineering

هَنْدَسيّ ص technical

هِنْدوسيّ ص Hindu

هِنْدوسيّ س ج /هِنْدوس/ Hindu

هِنْدوسيَّة س Hinduism

هِنْديّ ص، س ج /هُنود/ Indian

ه

هـ

هائِج ص wild

هائِل ص massive

هابِط ص low

هاتان إ إش (اسْم إشارَة لِلمُؤَنَّث المُثَنّى القَريب) these

هاتان الفَتاتان طالِبَتان These two girls are students.

هاتِف س ج /هَواتِف/ telephone

هاتَفَ ف to phone

هاجَرَ ف to emigrate

هاجَمَ ف to attack

هادِئ ص calm

هامّ ص significant

هامِش س ج /هَوامِش/ margin

هامِشيّ ص marginal

هاوٍ س ج /هُواة/ amateur

هَبَّ ف to blow

هَبَطَ ف (نَزَلَ) to descend
(حطَّ عَلى الأرْض) to land
(انْخَفَضَ) to drop

هُبوط س descent

هَجَرَ ف to abandon

هِجْرَة س emigration

هِجْريّ ص Hegira

هَجْمَة س offensive

هُجوم س attack

هُجوميّ ص offensive

هَجّى ف to spell

هَدَّدَ ف to threaten

هَدَف س ج /أهْداف/ (غايَة تُريدُ تَحْقيقَها) aim
(غايَة أو هَدَف في المَرْمى) goal
(نُقْطَة التَسْديد) target

هَدَمَ ف to demolish

هُدْنَة س ج /هُدَن/ ceasefire

هُدوء س calm

هَديَّة س ج /هَدايا/ gift

هَذا إ إش (اسْم إشارَة لِلمُذَكَّر المُفْرَد القَريب) this

هَذا الكِتاب لي. This book is mine.

هَذان إ إش (اسْم إشارَة لِلمُذَكَّر المُثَنّى القَريب) these

هَذان طِفْلايَ These are my (two) children.

هَذِهِ إ إش (اسْم إشارَة لِلمُؤَنَّث المُفْرَد القَريب) this

(مَصْدَر الإنْتاج) make

نَوْعيّ ص qualitative

نَوْعيّة س quality

نوفِمْبِر س (الشَهْر الحادي عَشَر بِالتَقْويم المِصْريّ) November

نَوْم س sleep

نَوَويّ ص nuclear

نَوى ف to intend

نيء ص raw

نِيابَة س deputyship

نِيابيّ ص parliamentary

نِيَّة س intention

نَيْتْروجين س nitrogen

نيسان س April

نَيِّف س something

عِشْرون وَنَيِّف. twenty something

نَيْل س obtaining

نَقَّبَ ف to mine

نَقَّحَ ف to revise

نَقْد س (انْتِقاد) criticism
(مال) cash

نَقَدَ ف to criticize

نَقْديّ ص monetary

نَقَرَ ف to click

نَقْرَة س tap

نَقَشَ ف to carve

نَقْش س ج /نُقوش/ (شَيْء مَنْقوش أو عَمَلِيَّة النَقْش)
carving

نَقْص س shortage

نَقَّصَ ف to reduce

نَقَصَ ف to decrease

نَقَّطَ ف to drip

نُقْطَة س ج /نُقَط/ (عَلامَة دائِرِيَّة صَغيرَة في الكِتابَة أو الطِباعَة) dot
ج /نِقاط/(فِكْرَة) point
نُقْطَة تَقاطُع crossing

نَقَعَ ف to soak

نَقْل س transport

نَقَلَ ف (حَرَّكَ من مَكان إلى آخَر) to move
(رَحَّلَ) to transfer
(نَقَلَ عُضْواً أو نَبْتَة وَزَرَعَها في مَكان آخَر)
to transplant

نَقْلَة س move

نَقيّ س purc

نَقيب س ج /نُقَباء/ (رُتْبَة عَسْكَرِيَّة) captain

نُكْتَة س ج /نُكَت/ joke

نَكْسَة س reverse

نَما ف to grow

نَمِر س ج /نُمور/ tiger

نِمْسا س (النِمْسا) Austria

نِمْساويّ ص، س Austrian

نَمَط س ج /أَنْماط/ pattern

نَمْلَة س ج /نَمْل/ ant

نُموّ س growth

نَموذَج س ج /نَماذِج/ (شَكْل) form
(مِثال يُحْتَذى بِهِ) model

نَميمَة س malicious gossip

نِهائيّ ص eventual

نَهار س day

نِهايَة س (الخاتِمَة) conclusion
(آخِر الشَيْء) end

نَهْج س approach

نَهْر س ج /أَنْهار/ river

نَهَضَ ف to rise

نَواة س ج /نَوى/ (الجُزْء الرَئيسيّ في الذَرَّة)
nucleus
(بِزْرَة بَعْض النَباتات) stone

نوبَة س fit

نور س ج /أَنْوار/ light

نَوْع س ج /أَنْواع/ (صِفَة) type

ن

نِصْف عد ج /أنْصاف/ half

نَصْل س ج /أنْصال/ blade

نَصيب س lot

نَصيحَة س ج /نَصائِحُ/ advice

نَصير س ج /نُصَراءُ/ proponent

نِضال س struggle

نُضْج س maturity

نَضَحَ ف to drain

نِطاق س scope

نَطَقَ ف to pronounce

نَظافَة س cleanliness

نِظام س ج /نُظُم/ system
ج /أنْظِمَة/ regime

نَظَرَ ف to look

نَظَراً in view of

نَظْرَة س look

نَظَرِيّ ص theoretical

نَظَرِيَّة س theory

نَظَّفَ ف to clean

نَظَّمَ ف to organize

نَظير س ج /نُظَراءُ/ counterpart

نَظيف ص clean

نَعَم yes

نِعْمَة س ج /نِعَم/ blessing

نَعْناع س mint

نَغَمَة س tone

نِفاق س hypocrisy

نِفايَة س waste

نَفَخَ ف to blow

نَفَّذَ ف (أجْرى) to execute
(طَبَّقَ) to implement

نَفَر س ج /أنْفار/ individual

نَفَّرَ ف to irritate

نَفَس س ج /أنْفاس/ breath

نَفْس (م) س ج /نُفوس/أنْفُس/ soul

نَفْس ظ same

نَفْسِيّ ص (مُتَعَلِّق بِدِراسَة النَفْس)
psychological
(مُتَعَلِّق بِالحالَة النَفْسِيَّة وَطِباعِها) mental

نَفْط س oil

نَفَق س ج /أنْفاق/ tunnel
نَفَق مُشاة subway

نَفَقَة س maintenance

نُفوذ س influence

نَفى ف to deny

نَقاء س purity

نِقاب س niqab

نِقابَة س trade-union

نِقابِيّ ص trade-unionist

نَقّال ص mobile

نَقانِقُ س sausage

ن

نَزَلَ ف to go down

نُزْهَة س ج /نُزَه/ outing

نَزيف س ج /أَنْزِفَة/ haemorrhage

نَزيل س ج /نُزَلاء/ guest

نَزيه ص honest

نِساء س (جَمْع امْرَأة) women

نِسائيّ ص (مُتَعَلِّق بِالمَرْأة) women's

نِسْبَة س ج /نِسَب/ (جُزْء مِن كُلّ) proportion

(مُعَدَّل مِقْياس) rate

نِسْبَة مِئَوِيَّة percentage

نَسَخَ ف to copy

نُسْخَة س ج /نُسَخ/ (صورَة عَن أَصْل) copy

(طَبْعَة مِن كِتاب أَو غَيْر ذلك) version

نَسْر س ج /نُسور/ eagle

نَسَفَ ف to blow up

نَسَّقَ ف (رَتَّب) to arrange

(أَعَدَّ الشَكْل النِهائيّ لِمَطْبوعَة) to format

نَسْل س ج /أَنْسال/ offspring

نَسَمَة س inhabitants

نَسِيَ ف to forget

نَسيج س ج /أَنْسِجَة/ (مَجْموعَة مِن عِدَّة خَلايا في الجِسْم) tissue

(صِناعَة المَلابِس) textile

نَسيم س breeze

نَشَأَ ف (عاشَ أَو تَرَبّى) to be brought up

(ظَهَرَ أَو حَدَث) to arise

نَشْأَة س rise

نَشاط س ج /أَنْشِطَة/ activity

نَشَبَ ف to break out

نَشْر س publication

نَشَرَ ف (وَزَّعَ القوّات أَو أَشْياء في أَماكِن مُخْتَلِفَة) to deploy

(وَزَّعَ عَمَلاً مَطْبوعاً أَو أَعْلَنَ خَبَراً) to publish

نَشْرَة س (مَطْبوعَة صَغيرَة تَحْتَوي عَلى تَعْليمات) leaflet

(مَطْبوعَة تُفَصِّلُ المَهامّ لِلعامِلين) brief

نَشِط ص ج /نُشَطاء/ active

نَشَّطَ ف to activate

نُشوء س development

نُشوب س outbreak

نَشْوَة س climax

نَشيط ص ج /نُشَطاء/ active

نَصّ س ج /نُصوص/ text

نَصَّ عَلى ف to stipulate

نَصَبَ ف to erect

نُصُب تِذْكاريّ س statue

نَصَحَ ف to advise

نَصْر س victory

نَصْرانيّ ص (مُتَعَلِّق بِالمَسيحيَّة) Christian

نَصْرانيّ س ج /نَصارى/ (شَخْص يُؤْمِنُ بِالمَسيحيَّة) Christian

نَصْرانيَّة س Christianity

نَباتات س vegetation

نَبَحَ ف to bark

نَبَذَ ف to renounce

نَبْرَة س accent

نَبْض س pulse

نَبْع س ج /نُبوع/ spring

نَبَعَ ف to spring

نَبَّهَ على ف to call attention to

نَبيّ س ج /أَنْبِياء/ prophet

نَبيل ص ج /نُبَلاء/ noble

نَتَجَ عَن ف to result

نُتوء س ج /نُتوءات/ lump

نَتيجَة س ج /نَتائِج/ result from

نَثَرَ ف to scatter

نَجا ف (تَخَلَّصَ مِن ظَرْف سَيِّئ) to escape
(خَرَجَ مِن خَطَر المَوْت) to survive

نَجاة س survival

نَجاح س success

نَجّار س carpenter

نَجَحَ ف (اجْتازَ امْتِحاناً) to pass
(حَقَّقَ إِنْجازاً) to succeed

نَجَدَ ف to rescue

نَجْدَة س rescue

نَجْم س ج /نُجوم/ star

نَجْمَة س ج /نُجوم/ star

نُحاس س copper

نَحَتَ ف to carve

نَحْت س carving

نَحْلَة س ج /نَحْل/ bee

نَحْنُ ض (ضَمير المُتَكَلِّم لِلمُثَنّى وَالجَمْع المُذَكَّر وَالمُؤَنَّث) we

نَحْنُ طُلّاب في الجامِعَة We are students at the university.

نَحْو س grammar

نَحْوَ ظ towards

نَحيف ص slim

نَخْلَة س ج /نَخيل/ palm tree

نِداء س call

نَدَبَ ف to delegate

نَدَّدَ ف to denounce

نَدَم س regret

نَدِمَ ف to regret

نَدْوَة س symposium

نِزاع س dispute

نَزاهَة ف integrity

نَزَعَ ف (انْتَزَعَ) to tug
(أَزالَ أَو خَلَعَ مَلابِسَهُ) to take off

نَزْع س removal

نَزْع السِلاح disarmament

نَزْعَة س tendency

نَزَفَ ف to bleed

ن

ناءٍ ص remote

نائِب س ج /نُوّاب/ (شَخْص تَكونُ وَظيفَتُهُ بَعْدَ المُدير) deputy
(عُضْو بَرْلَمَان) member of parliament

نائِم س sleeper

نائِم ص sleeping

نابَ ف to replace

ناب س ج /أَنْياب/ canine

ناجٍ س survivor

ناجِح س successful

ناحَ ف to whine

ناحِيَة س ج /نَواحٍ/ (اتِّجاه) direction
(مِنْطَقَة) area

ناخِب س voter

نادِر ص rare

نادِل س waiter

نادِلَة س waitress

نادى ف to call

نادٍ س ج /نَوادٍ/ club

ناسَبَ ف to suit

ناشَدَ ف to beseech

ناشِر س publisher

ناشِط س activist

ناصَرَ ف to champion

ناضِج ص (كَبير وَمَسْؤول) mature
(جاهِز لِلقَطْف) ripe

ناطِق س spokesperson

ناعِم ص soft

نافِذَة س ج /نَوافِذ/ window

نافَسَ ف to compete

نافِع ص beneficial

نافورَة س ج /نَوافير/ fountain

ناقِد س ج /نُقّاد/ critic

ناقَشَ ف to discuss

ناقِص ص ج /نَواقِص/ incomplete

ناقِص س minus

نالَ ف to obtain

نامَ ف to sleep

ناهِض ص up

نَبَأ س ج /أَنْباء/ piece of news

نَبات س plant

مَيَّزَ ف to distinguish

ميزان س ج /مَوازين/ scales
ميزان المُسْتَوى level

ميزانيَّة س budget

ميزَة س advantage

مُيَسَّر ص comfortable

ميعاد س ج /مَواعيد/ appointment

ميكانيكيّ ص mechanical

ميكانيكيّ س mechanic

مَيْكْروويف س microwave

ميل س ج /أَمْيال/ mile

مَيْل س tendency

ميناء س ج /مَوانِئ/ harbour

مَوْرِد س income

مُوَرِّد س exporter

مُوَزِّع س distributor

مُؤَسَّسَة س institution

مُوَسَّع ص extended

مُؤْسِف ص sad

مَوْسِم س season

مَوْسِمِيّ ص seasonal

موسيقى س music

مُؤَشِّر س (نَشاط لِإظْهار ما سَيَحْدُثُ) indicator
(دَلالَة) sign

موضَة س fashion

مَوْضِع س ج /مَواضِع/ place

مَوْضِعِيّ ص local

مَوْضوع س ج /مَواضيع/ subject

مَوْضوعِيّ ص objective

مُوَظَّف س employee
مُوَظَّف اسْتِقْبال receptionist
مُوَظَّف كاش cashier

مَوْعِد س ج /مَواعيد/ appointment

مُوَفَّق ص successful

مُؤَقَّت ص temporary

مَوْقِع س ج /مَواقِع/ (مَكان) location
(مَكانَة) position

مَوْقِف س ج /مَواقِف/ (رَأْي) attitude
(مَكانَة حِيالَ القَضِيَّة) position

(مَكان وُقوف مُؤَقَّت لِمَرْكَبَة) stop

مَوْكِب س ج /مَواكِب/ procession

مُؤَكَّد ص certain

مَوَّلَ ف to fund

مُوَلِّد س ج /مُوَلِّدات/ (مُوَلِّد كَهْرَبائِيّ) generator
(شَخْص مُدَرَّب لِتَوْليد النِساء) midwife

مَوْلِد س birthday

مُؤَلِّف س author
مُؤَلِّف موسيقِيّ composer

مُؤْلِم ص painful

مَوْلود س ج /مَواليد/ born

مُؤْمِن believer

مُؤَمَّن ص insured

مُؤَمِّن س insurer

مُؤَنَّث ص female

مَوْهِبَة س ج /مَواهِب/ talent

مُؤَهِّل س qualification

مُؤَهَّل ص qualified

مَوْهوب ص talented

مَيِّت س ج /أَمْوات/ dead

ميثاق س ج /مَواثيق/ charter

ميدالْيَة س medal

مَيْدان س ج /مَيادين/ (ساحَة يُعَدُّ فيها نَشاط) arena
(ساحَة عامَّة) square

ميراث س ج /مَواريث/ legacy

مُهَرِّج س clown

مَهْرَجان س rally

مُهِمّ ص important

مَهْما ظ whatever

مُهِمَّة س duty

مُهْمِل ص careless

مِهْنَة س ج /مِهَن/ career

مُهَنْدِس س engineer

مُهَنْدِس مِعْماريّ architect

مِهَنيّ ص professional

مَهْووس ص mad

مُهَيْمِن ص dominant

مُهين ص demeaning

مُواجَهَة س confrontation

مُواساة س consolation

مُواصَفَة س specification

مُواصَلات س communications

مُواصَلَة س connection

مُواطِن س citizen

مُواطَنَة س citizenship

مُوافِق ص agreeing

مُوافَقَة س approval

مُوالٍ ص pro-

مُؤامَرَة س ج /مُؤامَرات/ conspiracy

مُؤَبَّد س eternal

سِجْن مُؤَبَّد life imprisonment

مَوْت س death

مُؤْتَمَر س ج /مُؤْتَمَرات/ conference

مُؤَثِّر ص (لَهُ فاعلِيَّة) effective

(يَجْلِبُ الانْتِباه) impressive

مَوْثوق بِهِ reliable

مَوْج س ج /أَمْواج/ wave

موجِب ص necessary

مَوْجَة س wave

مُؤَجِّر س landlord

موجَز س summary

مَوْجود ص available

مُوَحَّد ص (مُتَماثِل) uniform

أَسْعارُنا مُوَحَّدَة. Our prices are uniform.

(مُتَّحِد) united

موحِش ص lonely

مُؤَخَّراً ح recently

مُؤَخِّرَة س rear

مُؤَدٍّ س performer

مُؤَدَّب ص polite

مَوَدَّة س intimacy

مودِم س modem

مُؤْذٍ ص harmful

مُؤَذِّن س the caller for prayers

مُؤَرِّخ س historian

مَنَحَ ف to grant

مِنْحَة س ج /مِنَح/ grant

مِنْحَة دِراسِيَّة scholarship

مُنْحَدَر س slope

مُنْحَنى س ج /مُنْحَنَيات/ curve

مُنْخَفِض ص low

مُنْخَفَض س ج /مُنْخَفَضات/ low ground

مَنْدَرين س tangerine

مَنْدوب س delegate

مُنْذُ حج (تَدُلُّ عَلى بِدايَة فَتْرَة زَمَنِيَّة) since

إنَّنا نَعيشُ هُنا مُنْذُ We have lived here since 1970.

مَنْزِل س ج /مَنازِل/ house

مَنْسَف س ج /مَناسِف/ (وَجْبَة تُصْنَعُ مِن اللَحْم وَالأَرُزّ وَاللَبَن) mansaf

مُنْشَأَة س facility

مِنْشار س ج /مَناشير/ saw

مَنْصِب س ج /مَناصِب/ office

مُنْصَرِم ص past

مَنْصوص ص mentioned

مَنْطِق س logic

مِنْطَقَة س ج /مَناطِق/ area

مَنْطِقِيّ ص logical

مُنْطَلَق س starting point

مَنْظَر س ج /مَناظِر/ view

مُنَظِّف س cleaner

مُنَظَّمَة س organization

مَنْع س prohibition

مَنَعَ ف to prevent

مُنْعَطَف س bend

مُنْفَرِد ص alone

مُنْفَصِل ص separate

مَنْفَعَة س ج /مَنافِع/ (خِدْمَة عامَّة) utility
(فائِدَة) benefit

مَنْفى س ج /مَنافٍ/ exile

إنَّهُ يَعيشُ في المَنْفى. He lives in exile.

مَنْفِيّ س exile

مَنْفِيّ سِياسِيّاً political exile

مُنَقِّب س miner

مِنْهاج س ج /مَناهِج/ curriculum

مَنْهَج س ج /مَناهِج/ method

مُنير ص (مُضيء) luminous
(مُوَضِّح) illuminating

مَنيع ص immune

مُهاجِر س emigrant

مُهاجَمَة س attack

مَهارَة س skill

مَهْبِل س vagina

مُهْتَمّ ص interested

مَهْد س ج /مِهاد/ cradle

مُهَذَّب ص polite

مَهْر س ج /مُهور/ dowry

مَمْلَكَة س ج /مَمْلَكات/مَمالِك/ kingdom

مَمْنوع ص forbidden

مُميت ص fatal

مُمَيَّز ص distinctive

مِن حج (تَدُلُّ على نُقْطَة البِدايَة) from
مَشَيْتُ مِن البَيْت إلى السوق I walked from my house to the market.
(تَدُلُّ عَلى بِدايَة فَتْرَة زَمَنيَّة)
عَمِلْتُ مِن الصَباح حَتّى المَساء I worked from morning till evening.
(تَدُلُّ عَلى البَعْض مِن الكُلّ) of, from
سُرِقَ مِائَة دينار مِن المال A hundred dinars of the money was stolen.
(تَدُلُّ عَلى المَصْدَر) from
شَرِبْتُ مِن الحَنَفيَّة. I drank from the tap.
(تَدُلُّ عَلى المُكَوِّنات) of, from
يُصْنَعُ الخُبْزُ مِن الطَحين Bread is made from flour.

مَنْ أ إس (تُسْتَخْدَمُ لِلسُؤال عَن شَخْص) who
مَنْ زارَكُم في الأَمْس؟ Who visited you yesterday?

مَناخ س climate

مُناسِب ص appropriate

مُناسَبَة س occasion

مُناصِر س champion

مُناضِل س fighter

مُناظَرَة س argument

مَناعَة س immunity

مُنافِس س competitor

مُنافَسَة س competition

مُنافِق ص hypocrite

مُناقَشَة س discussion

مُناقَصَة س bid

مُناقِض ص contrary

مُناوَبَة س shift

مُناوَرَة س manoeuvre

مِنْبَر س ج /مَنابِر/ pulpit

مُنْبَسِط س level

مُنْتِج س producer

مُنْتِج ص productive

مُنْتَج س product

مُنْتَخَب ص elected

مُنْتَخَب وَطَنيّ national team

مُنْتَدى س ج /مُنْتَدَيات/ forum

مُنْتَشِر ص common

مُنْتَصِر س victor

مُنْتَصَف ظ middle

مُنْتَصَف س half

مُنْتَظَم ص regular

مُنْتَقى ص select

مُنْتَه ص over

مُنْجَز ص finished

مَنْجَم س ج /مَناجِم/ mine

مِلْح س ج /أَمْلاح/ salt

مُلْحِد س atheist

مُلْحَق س ج /مَلاحِق/ extension

مَلْحَمَة س ج /مَلاحِم/ epic

مُلَحِّن س composer

مُلَخَّص س summary

مُلْزِم ص binding

مَلَّسَ ف to pat

مُلْصَق س (يُلْصَقُ عَلى المُنْتَج) label
(صورَة تُلْصَقُ بِهَدَف الدِعايَة) poster

مَلْعَب س ج /مَلاعِب/ playground

مِلْعَقَة س ج /مَلاعِق/ spoon

مُلْغى ص cancelled

مِلَفّ س file

مَلَك س ج /مَلائِكَة/ angel

مَلِك س ج /مُلوك/ king

مَلَكَ ف to possess

مَلِكَة س queen

مِلْكِيّ mine

مَلَكِيّ س royal

مِلْكِيَّة س property

مَلَكِيَّة س monarchy

مَلْمَس س ج /مَلامِس/ texture

مَلْموس ص tangible

مَلْهى س ج /مَلاهٍ/ a place of amusement

مَلْهى لَيْلِيّ nightclub

مُلوخِيَّة س mloukheya

مُلَوَّن ص coloured

مَليء ص full

مِلْيار عد ج /مِلْيارات/ billion

مَلْيون عد ج /مَلايين/ million

مُماثِل ص similar

مُمارَسَة س practice

مُماطَلَة س delay

مُمْتاز س excellent

مُمْتَدّ ص extended

مُمْتِع ص enjoyable

مُمْتَلِئ ص full

مُمْتَلَكات س possessions

مُمَثِّل س (يَعْمَلُ في السينَما أو المَسْرَح) actor
(يُمَثِّلُ جَماعَة) representative

مُمَثِّلَة س actress

مِمْحاة س rubber

مَمَرّ س passage

مُمَرِّض س nurse

مَمْزوج ص mixed

مَمْشوق ص slender

مُمْكِن ص possible

مُمِلّ ص boring

مَقْعَد س ج /مَقاعِد/ seat

مَقْلوب ص turned over

مَقْلوبَة س (طَبْخَة تُصْنَعُ مِن اللَحْم وَالأَرُزّ وَالزَهْرَة) maqloobah

مُقْنِع ص convincing

مَقْهى س ج /مَقاهٍ/ café

مِقْياس س ج /مَقاييس/ measurement

مُقيم س resident

مُكافَأَة س reward

مُكافَحَة س fighting

مُكالَمَة س call

مَكان س ج /أَمْكِنَة/ place

مَكانَة س position

مِكْبَح س ج /مَكابِح/ brake

مُكْتَئِب ص depressed

مَكْتَب س ج /مَكاتِب/ (مِنْضَدَة لِلكِتابَة) desk

(مَقَرّ العَمَل) office

مَكْتَبَة س library

مُكْتَمِل ص complete

مَكْتوب ص written

مَكَثَ ف to stay

مُكَثَّف ص intensive

مُكْرَه ص reluctant

مَكْسَب س ج /مَكاسِب/ gain

مَكْسور ص broken

مَكْسيك س (المَكْسيك) Mexico

مَكْسيكيّ ص، س Mexican

مَكْشوف ص unveiled

مُكَعَّب س cubic

مُكَلِّف ص expensive

مُكَمِّل ص complementary

مَكَّنَ ف to enable

مِكْواة س ج /مَكاوٍ/ iron

مُكَوِّن س ج /مُكَوِّنات/ component

مَلَّ ف to be bored

مِلاءَة س sheet

مُلائِم ص appropriate

مُلاءَمَة س convenience

مَلابِس س clothes

مِلاحَة س navigation

مُلاحَظَة س (مَعْلومَة تُكْتَبُ مِن أَجْل التَذْكير بِشَيْء) note

(تَعْليق عَلى أَمْر) observation

مَلارْيا س malaria

مُلازِم س (رُتْبَة عَسْكَرِيَّة) second lieutenant

مُلازِم أَوَّل (رُتْبَة عَسْكَرِيَّة) lieutenant

مُلاكَمَة س boxing

مَلَأَ ف to fill

مُلْتَزِم ص committed

مَلْجَأ س ج /مَلاجِئ/ refuge

مُفَكِّرَة يَوْمِيَّة diary

مُفْلِس ص (أَفْلَسَ بَعْدَ غِنى) bankrupt
(لا نُقود لَدَيْهِ) penniless

مَفْهوم س ج /مَفاهيم/ concept

مَفْهوم ص understandable

مُفيد ص useful

مُقابِلَ ظ in return for
opposite

مُقابَلَة س interview

مُقاتِل س fighter

مُقارَن ص comparative

مُقارَنَة س comparison

مَقاس س size

مُقاضاة س prosecution

مُقاطَعَة س (مِنْطَقَة) province
(حالَة عَدَم التَعامُل مَعَ جِهَة مُعَيَّنَة بِهَدَف العِقاب) boycott

مَقال س article

مَقام س ج /مَقامات/ (مَكان يَزورُهُ الناس حَيْثُ يَرْمُزُ لِشَيْء هامّ) shrine
(مَكان) place

مُقاوِل س contractor

مُقاوَلَة س contract

مُقاوَمَة س resistance

مُقايَضَة س swap

مَقْبَرَة س ج /مَقابِر/ cemetery

مِقْبَض س ج /مَقابِض/ handle

مُقْبِل ص (يَأْتي في المُسْتَقْبَل) coming
(التالي) next

مَقْبول ص acceptable

مَقَتَ ف to detest

مَقْت س abhorrence

مُقْتَرَح ص proposed

مُقْتَرَح س proposition

مُقْتَضى س ج /مُقْتَضَيات/ requirement

مُقْتَطَف س extract

مُقْتَنى ص acquired

مِقْدار س ج /مَقادير/ amount

مُقَدَّس ص holy

مُقَدَّم س (رُتْبَة عَسْكَرِيَّة) lieutenant colonel

مُقَدَّماً ح in advance

مُقَدِّمَة س (واجِهَة الشَيْء) front
(شَرْح مُخْتَصَر لِعَمَل) introduction

مَقَرّ س seat

مُقَرَّر س decided

مُقْرِض س lender

مُقْرِف ص disgusting

مَقْصَف س ج /مَقاصِف/ cafeteria

مَقْطَع س ج /مَقاطِع/ passage
مَقْطَع شِعْرِيّ verse

مَقْطورَة س trailer

مَعْهَد س ج /مَعاهِد/ institute

مُعَوِّق س setback

مُعَوَّق ص disabled

مَعونَة س relief

مِعْيار س ج /مَعايير/ standard

مَعيشَة س life

مُعَيَّن ص determined

مُغادَرَة س departure

مُغامَرَة س adventure

مُغَبَّر ص dusty

مُغْتَرِب س migrant

مَغْرِب س (المَغْرِب) Morocco
ج /مَغارِبُ/ (لَحْظَة غُروب الشَمْس) sunset
(فَتْرَة زَمَنيَّة) a period of two hours after sunset
(مَكان غُروب الشَمْس) place of sunset

مَغْرِبيّ ص، س ج /مَغارِبَة/ Moroccan

مَغْرور ص arrogant

مَغْسَلَة س ج /مَغاسِل/ laundry

مُغْضِب ص infuriating

مُغَفَّل ص naive

مُغْلَق ص closed

مَغْمور ص obscure

مُغَنٍّ س singer

مِغْناطيسيّ ص magnetic

مُفاجِئ ص (حَدَثَ بِسُرْعَة وَعَلى غَفْلَة) sudden
(جاءَ بِمُفاجَأَة) surprising

مُفاجَأَة س surprise

مُفاوَضَة س negotiation

مِفْتاح س ج /مَفاتيح/ key
مِفْتاح الحَلّ clue
مِفْتاح الكَهْرَباء switch

مُفْتَرَض ص (مَوْعِد حُدوثُهُ) due
(واجِب حُدوثُهُ) supposed

مُفَتِّش س inspector

مَفْتوح ص open

مُفْجِع ص tragic

مُفْرَد ص singular

مُفْرَدات س vocabulary

مُفْرِط ص excessive

مَفْرَق س ج /مَفارِق/ junction

مَفْروض ص (أَمْر مُجْبَر) imposed
(شَيْء مِن الأَفْضَل عَمَلُهُ) supposed

مُفْزِع ص terrifying

مُفَصَّل ص detailed

مَفْصِل س ج /مَفاصِل/ joint

مَفْصول ص (غَيْر مَوْصول) detached
(مَطْرود مِن العَمَل) dismissed

مُفَضَّل ص favourite

مَفْقود ص missing

مُفَكِّر س thinker

مُفَكِّرَة س notebook

م

مُعاوَنَة س assistance

مَعْبَد س ج /مَعابِد/ temple

مَعْبود س deity

مُعْتاد ص usual

مُعْتَدٍ س offender

مُعْتَدِل ص moderate

مُعْتَقَد س ج /مُعْتَقَدات/ belief

مُعْتِم ص dim

مُعْتَنِق س convert

مُعْجِزَة س miracle

مُعَجَّنات س pastry

مَعْجون س ج /مَعاجين/ paste

مُعْدٍ ص infectious

مُعَدّات س equipment

مَعِدَة س stomach

مُعَدَّل ص modified

مُعَدَّل س average

مَعْدِن س ج /مَعادِن/ metal

مَعْدِنيّ ص mineral

مَعْرَض س ج /مَعارِض/ exhibition
مَعْرَض فُنون gallery

مَعْرِفَة س ج /مَعارِف/ (شَخْص تَعْرِفُهُ دونَ أَنْ يَكونَ صَديقاً) acquaintance
(المَعْلومات أو العُلوم) knowledge

مَعْرَكَة س ج /مَعارِك/ battle

مَعْروف س favour

مَعْروف ص known

مَعْزِل عَن س isolation from

مَعْزول ص isolated

مُعَسْكَر س camp

مُعْضِلَة س dilemma

مِعْطَف س ج /مَعاطِف/ coat
مِعْطَف للمَطَر waterproof
مِعْطَف نِسائيّ dolman

مُعَطَّل ص broken

مُعْظَم ظ most

مُعَقَّد ص complicated

مُعَقِّم س sterile

مَعْقول ص reasonable

مَعْكَرونَة س pasta

مُعَلِّق س commentator

مُعَلَّق ص hung

مُعَلِّم س instructor

مَعْلَم س ج /مَعالِم/ landmark

مَعْلومَة س piece of information

مِعْماريّ ص architectural

مَعْمَل س ج /مَعامِل/ factory

مَعْنَويّات س morale

مَعْنى س ج /مَعانٍ/ meaning

مَعْنيّ ص concerned

م

مَضَغَ ف to chew

مِضْمار س ج /مَضامير/ (مَوْضوع) domain
(ساحَة) arena

مَضْمون س connotation

مَضْمون ص guaranteed

مُضيف س host
مُضيف جَوّيّ/ مُضيفَة جَوّيَّة flight attendant

مَطار س ج /مَطارات/ airport

مُطارَدَة س chase

مَطّاط س rubber

مُطالَبَة س claim

مَطْبَخ س ج /مَطابِخ/ kitchen

مَطْبَعَة س ج /مَطابِع/ print shop

مَطْحَنَة س ج /مَطاحِن/ mill

مَطَر س ج /أَمْطار/ rain

مُطْرِب س singer

مِطْرَقة س ج /مَطارِق/ hammer

مَطْروح ص raised

مَطْعَم س ج /مَطاعِم/ restaurant

مُطْفَأ ص off

مَطْلَب س ج /مَطالِب/ demand

مُطَّلِع ص informed

مَطْلَع س ج /مَطالِع/ beginning

مُطْلَق ص absolute

مَطْلوب ص (يوجَدُ حاجَة لَهُ) needed
(مُطارَد مِن قِبَل الشُرْطَة) wanted

مُطَوَّل ص lengthy

مُظاهَرَة س demonstration

مِظَلَّة س umbrella

مُظْلِم ص dark

مَظْلَمَة س grievance

مَظْلوم ص wronged

مَظْهَر س ج /مَظاهِر/ appearance

مَعَ ظ with
مَعَ أَنَّ although

مَعاً together

مُعادٍ ص hostile to

مُعارَضَة س opposition

مَعاش س salary
مَعاش التَقاعُد pension

مُعاصِر ص contemporary

مُعافى ص م مُعافاة healthy

مُعاق ص، س disabled

مُعاكِس ص opposite

مُعالِج س therapist

مُعالَجَة س treatment

مُعامَلَة س (تَعامُل) treatment
(إِجْراء بَنْكيّ) transaction

مُعاناة س suffering

مُعاهَدَة س treaty

م

مُشير س (رُتْبَة عَسْكَرِيَّة) field marshal

مُشَيِّق ص interesting

مَصّ ف to suck

مُصاب س wounded

مُصادَرَة س confiscation

مُصادَفَة س coincidence

مُصارَعَة س wrestling

مَصّاصَة س straw

مُصالَحَة س reconciliation

مَصَبّ س ج /مَصَبّات/ mouth

مِصْباح س ج /مَصابيح/ lamp

مِصْبَغَة س ج /مَصابِغ/ laundry

مَصْدَر س ج /مَصادِر/ source

مِصْر س Egypt

مُصْران س ج /مَصارين/ bowel

مَصْرِف س ج /مَصارِف/ bank

مَصْرَف س ج /مَصارِف/ drain

مَصْرِفيّ س banker

مَصْروف س ج /مَصاريف/ expenditure

مِصْريّ ص، س Egyptian

مَصْطَبَة س ج /مَصاطِب/ terrace

مُصْطَلَح س term

مِصْعَد س ج /مَصاعِد/ lift

مِصْفاة س ج /مَصافٍ/ (غِرْبال) filter
(تُسْتَخْدَمُ في المَطْبَخ) sieve

مَصْل س ج /أَمْصال/ serum
مَصْل اللَّبَن whey

مُصَلٍّ س one who is praying

مَصْلَحَة س ج /مَصالِح/ interest

مُصَمِّم ص determined

مُصَمِّم س designer

مُصَنِّع س manufacturer

مَصْنَع س ج /مَصانِع/ factory

مَصْنوعات س manufactured products

مُصَوِّر س photographer

مِصْيَدَة س ج /مَصائِد/ trap

مَصير س ج /مَصائِر/ destiny

مُضادّ س ج /مُضادّات/ anti-
مُضادّ حَيَويّ antibiotic

مُضارِب س speculative

مُضارَبَة س speculation

مُضارِع س present tense

مُضايَقَة س harassment

مَضْبوط س controlled

مُضْحِك ص funny

مِضَخَّة س pump

مُضِرّ ص harmful

مَضْرَب س ج /مَضارِب/ (في أَلْعاب البيسْبول وَالكْريكيت وَتِنِس الطاوِلَة) bat
(في التِنِس الأَرْضيّ) racket

مُضْطَرِب ص nervous

م

مِسْمار س ج /مَسامير/ nail

مِسْمار قَدَم corn

مَسْموح ص allowed

مُسِنّ ص elderly

مُسَوَّدَة س draft

مَسْؤوليَّة س responsibility

مُسيء ص abusive

مَسيحيّ ص (مُتَعَلِّق بِالمَسيحيَّة) Christian

مَسيحيّ س (شَخْص يُؤْمِنُ بِالمَسيحيَّة) Christian

مَسيحيَّة س Christianity

مَسيرَة س march

مَشْئوم ص unfortunate

مُشاة س pedestrians

سِلاح المُشاة infantry

مُشادَّة س row

مُشارِك س participant

مُشارَكَة س participation

مَشاعِر س feelings

مُشاوَرَة س consultation

مَشْبوه ص suspicious

مُشْتَبَه بِهِ س suspect

مُشْتَرٍ س buyer

مُشْتَرَك ص joint

مُشْتَرِك س (شارِك في عَمَل نَشاط) involved (ذو عُضْويَّة في مُؤَسَّسَة) subscriber

مُشْتَرَيات س shopping

مَشْتَل س ج /مَشاتِل/ nursery

مُشَجِّع ص encouraging

مُشَجِّع س fan

مَشْحون ص loaded

مَشْدود ص tight

مُشَرِّع س legislator

مُشْرِف س supervisor

مَشْرِق س ج /مَشارِق/ east

مُشْرِك س polytheist

مَشْروب س ج /مَشاريب/مَشْروبات/ drink

مَشْروع س ج /مَشاريع/ project

مِشْط س ج /أَمْشِطَة/ comb

مُشْعَل ص on

مَشْغول ص busy

مُشْكِلَة س ج /مَشاكِل/ problem

مُشْمِس ص sunny

مِشْمِش س apricot

مَشْمول ص included

مَشْهَد س ج /مَشاهِد/ sight

مَشْهور ص famous

مَشورَة س counsel

مَشى ف to walk

مَشْي س walk

م

مُسْتَخْدَم س employee

مُسْتَدِير ص circular

مُسْتَشار س adviser

مُسْتَشْفى س ج /مُسْتَشْفَيات/ hospital

مُسْتَعِدّ ص (لَدَيْهِ الاسْتِعْداد) willing
(جاهِز) ready

مُسْتَعْمِر س colonizer

مُسْتَعْمَرَة س colony

مُسْتَقْبَل س future

مُسْتَقْبَلِيّ ص future

مُسْتَقِرّ ص stable

مُسْتَقِلّ ص independent

مُسْتَقِيم ص straight

مُسْتَمِرّ ص continuing

مُسْتَمِع س listener

مُسْتَنَد س document

مُسْتَنْقَع س ج /مُسْتَنْقَعات/ pond

مُسْتَهْلِك س consumer

مُسْتَهْلَك ص spent

مُسْتَوْدَع س store

مُسْتَوْصَف س clinic

مُسْتَوْطِن س settler

مُسْتَوْطَنَة س settlement

مُسْتَوْقَد س fireplace

مُسْتَوًى س level

مُسْتَوٍ ص flat

مُسْتَيْقِظ ص awake

مَسْجِد س ج /مَساجِد/ mosque

مَسَحَ ف to wipe

مَسْحوق س ج /مَساحيق/ powder

مَسَّدَ ف to stroke

مُسَدَّس س ج /مُسَدَّسات/ pistol

مَسْرَب س ج /مَسارِب/ lane

مَسْرَح س ج /مَسارِح/ theatre

مَسْرَحِيَّة س play

مَسْروق ص stolen

مَسْطَرَة س ج /مَساطِر/ ruler

مُسْعِف س paramedic

مَسْعور ص frantic

مَسَكَ ب ف to hold

مَسْكَة س grip

مَسْكَن س ج /مَساكِن/ accommodation

مِسْكِين س ج /مَساكِين/ needy

مُسَلٍّ ص entertaining

مُسَلَّح ص armed

مُسَلَّح س militant

مَسْلَك س ج /مَسالِك/ route

مُسْلِم س (شَخْص يُؤْمِنُ بِالإسْلام) Muslim

مُسْلِم ص (مُتَعَلِّق بِالإسْلام) Muslim

مَزَاج س ج /مَزَاجات/ mood

مَزَاد س ج /مَزادات/ auction

مُزارِع س farmer

مُزايَدَة س auction

مَزْبَلَة س ج /مَزابِل/ dump

مَزَجَ ف to mix

مَزْحَة س joke

مُزْدَحِم ص packed

مُزْدَوَج ص double

مَزْرَعَة س ج /مَزارِع/ farm

مُزْعِج ص annoying

مَزَّقَ ف to tear

مِزْلَجَة س skate

مُزْمِن ص chronic

مَزيج س ج /أَمْزِجَة/ mixture

مَزيد س supplement of

مُزَيَّف ص fake

مَسَّ ف to touch

مَسئول س responsible

مَسئوليَّة س responsibility

مَساء س ج /أَمْسِيَة/ evening

مُسابَقَة س competition

مِساحَة س (مِنْطَقَة) area
(مُتَّسَع) space

مَسار س track

مِساس س touching

مُساعِد س (مُعاوِن) assistant
(رُتْبَة عَسْكَرِيَّة) sergeant
مُساعِد أَوَّل master sergeant

مُساعَدَة س assistance

مَسافَة س distance

مُسافِر س traveller

مَسْأَلَة س ج /مَسائِل/ (سُؤال) question
(مُشْكِلَة) problem

مُسانَدَة س support

مُساهِم س (مُشارِك) contributor
(يَمْلُكُ أَسْهُماً) shareholder

مُساهَمَة س (الاشْتِراك
وَالتَعاوُن) contribution
(شِراء أَسْهُم) sharing

مُساوٍ ص equivalent

مُساواة س equality

مُسْبَقاً ح in advance

مُسْتَأْجِر س tenant

مُسْتَبِدّ ص tyrant

مُسْتَبْعَد ص (غَيْر مُحْتَمَل) unlikely

مُسْتَثْمِر س investor

مُسْتَحَقّ ص due

مُسْتَحِقّ ص deserving

مُسْتَحيل ص impossible

مُسْتَخْدِم س user

م

مَرَح س fun

مِرْحاض س ج /مَراحيض/ toilet

مَرْحَباً hello

مَرْحَلَة س ج /مَراحِل/ stage

مَرْحوم ص deceased

مَرَّرَ ف to pass

مِرْساة س ج /مَراسٍ/ anchor

مُرْسِل س (مَن أَرْسَلَ خِطاباً إلخ) sender
(مُراسِل شَبَكَة الإنْتِرْنِت) poster

مَراسِمُ س ritual

مَرْسى س ج /مَراسٍ/ harbour

مُرَشَّح س (شَخْص يَقْتَرِحُ نَفْسَهُ لِمُنافَسَة) candidate
(شَخْص مُقْتَرَح لِمُنافَسَة) nominee

مُرْشِد س (دَليل) guide
(مُرْشِد أكاديميّ) tutor

مَرَض س disease
مَرَض السَرَطان cancer

مُرْضٍ ص satisfactory

مَرْطَبان س jar

مُرْعِب ص dreadful

مَرْغَرين س margarine

مَرْغوب فيهِ ص desirable

مَرْفَأ س ج /مَرافِئ/ harbour

مِرْفَق س ج /مَرافِق/ elbow

مَرْفوض ص unacceptable

مَرْكَب س ج /مَراكِب/ boat

مَرْكَبَة س vehicle

مَرْكَز س ج /مَراكِز/ (وَسَط أو مَكان) centre
(مَنْصِب) position
مَرْكَز لِياقَة gym

مُرَكَّز ص concentrated

مَرْكَزِيّ ص central

مَرْموق ص prestigious

مَرْمى س (ما تَصوبُ إلَيْهِ الكُرَة) goal
(مَدى التَهْديف) range

مَرِن ص flexible

مُرْهَف ص delicate

مُرْهِق ص stressful

مَرْهَم س ointment

مُرَوِّج س promoter

مِرْوَحَة س ج /مَراوِح/ fan

مُرور س passage

مُرَوِّع ص horrible

مُريب ص dubious

مُريح ص comfortable

مَريض س ج /مَرْضى/ patient

مَريض ص ج /مَرْضى/ ill

مُريع ص dreadful

مَرْيَلَة س ج /مَرايِل/ apron

مَرْيَمِيَّة س sage

م

مَذْبَحَة س ج /مَذابِح/ massacre

مُذَكَّر ص male

مُذَكِّرات س memoirs
diary

مُذَكِّرَة س memorandum

مُذْنِب س culprit

مُذْنِب ص guilty

مَذْهَب س ج /مَذاهِب/ doctrine

مُذْهِل ص astonishing

مِذْياع س radio

مُذيع س presenter

مُرّ ص bitter

مَرَّ ب ف to pass

مَرَّ عَن to go past

مَرْئِيّ ص visible

مِرْآة س ج /مَرايا/ mirror

مَرْأَب س ج /مَرائِب/ garage

مُراجَعَة س revision

مُرادِف س synonym

مِراراً ح often

مَرارَة س bitterness

مُراسِل س correspondent

مُراسَلَة س correspondence

مُراعاة س regard

مَرافِقُ س amenities

مُرافِق س attendant

مُراقِب س (شَخْص يَعْمَل عَلى خِدْمَة الزَبائِن في مَكان عامّ) attendant
(شَخْص يَعْمَلُ عَلى مُتابَعَة الأَحْداث) observer
مُراقِب التَذاكِر conductor

مُراقَبَة س observation

مُراهِق س teenager

مُراهَقَة س adolescence

مُراوَغَة س dribbling

مَرْأى س sight

مُرْبِح س profitable

مُرَبَّع س square

مُرَبّى س jam

مَرَّة س once

مُرْتاح ص comfortable

مَرَّتَيْن س twice

مُرَتَّب ص neat

مُرَتَّب س salary

مَرْتَبَة س (مُسْتَوى) level
(رُتْبَة) rank

مُرْتَبِط ص related

مُرْتَبِك ص confused

مُرْتَعِش ص shaky

مُرْتَفِع ص high

مَرْجان س coral

مَرْجِع س ج /مَراجِع/ reference

مُخَمَّن ص estimated

مُخيف ص frightening

مُخَيَّم س ج /مُخَيَّمات/ camp

مَدّ: مَدّ وَجَزْر س tide

مُداعِب ص playful

مُدان ص convicted

مُدَّة س ج /مُدَد/ period

مِدَّة س ج /مِدَد/ pus

مَدَحَ ف to praise

مُدَّخَرات س supplies

مَدْخَل س ج /مَداخِل/ (مَكان الدُخول) entrance
(إمْكانيَّة اسْتِخْدام شَيْء) access

مُدَخِّن س smoker

مِدْخَنَة س ج /مَداخِن/ chimney

مَدَّدَ ف to extend

مَدَد س support

مُدَرِّب س (مُدَرِّب لِلسلوك) trainer
(مُدَرِّب رِياضيّ) coach
(مُدَرِّب عَلى أداء المَهارات) instructor

مَدْرَج س ج /مَدارِج/ runway

مُدَرَّج س ج /مُدَرَّجات/ stand

مُدَرِّس س teacher

مَدْرَسَة س ج /مَدارِس/ school

مُدَرَّعَة س armoured vehicle

مُدْرِك ص aware

مُدَّعٍ س plaintiff
مُدَّعٍ عامّ prosecutor
مُدَّعًى عَلَيْه defendant

مِدْفَأَة س heater

مَدْفَع س ج /مَدافِع/ canon
مَدْفَع رَشّاش automatic weapon

مَدْفَن س ج /مَدافِن/ cemetery

مُدَلَّل ص spoilt

مُدَمِّر ص devastating

مُدْمِن ص addict
مُدْمِن الكُحول alcoholic

مَدَّنَ ف to civilize

مَدَنيّ ص civic

مَدَنيّ س civilian

مُدْهِش ص astonishing

مُدْهِن ص fatty

مَدى س extent

مُدير س ج /مُدَراء/ manager
مُدير مَدْرَسَة head teacher

مُديريَّة س province

مَدينَة س ج /مُدُن/ city
مَدينَة مَلاهٍ theme park

مَدْيونيَّة س indebtedness

مَذاق س (طَعْم) flavour
(ذَوْق) taste

مَذْبَح س ج /مَذابِح/ slaughter-house

ج /مُحيطات/ (مُسَطَّح مائيّ) ocean

المُحيط المُتَجَمِّد الشَمالِيّ the Arctic Ocean

المُحيط الهِنْدِيّ the Indian Ocean

المُحيط المُتَجَمِّد الجَنوبِيّ the Antarctic Ocean

المُحيط الهادئ the Pacific Ocean

المُحيط الأَطْلَسِيّ the Atlantic Ocean

مُخّ س ج /أَمْخاخ/مِخاخ/ brain

مُخابَرات س intelligence

مَخاض س labour

مُخاط س ج /أَمْخِطَة/ mucus

مُخاطَرَة س ج /مَخاطِر/ risk

مُخالِف ل ص contradictory with

مُخالَفَة س (مال تَدْفَعُهُ لاِخْتِراق قانون السَيْر) fine (كَسْر القانون) breach

مَخْبَأ س ج /مَخابِئ/ hiding place

مُخْبِر س reporter

مَخْبَز س ج /مَخابِز/ bakery

مَخْبول ص ج /مَخابيل/ crazy

مُخْتار ص selected

مُخْتار س ج /مَخاتير/ head of a tribe

مُخْتَبَر س ج /مُخْتَبَرات/ laboratory

مُخْتَرِع س inventor

مُخْتَصّ ص specialized

مُخْتَصَر س brief

مُخْتَلِس س embezzler

مُخْتَلَط ص mixed

مُخْتَلِف ص different

مُخْجِل ص shameful

مِخَدَّة س pillow

مُخَدِّر س ج /مُخَدِّرات/ (مَوادّ إِدْمانِيّة ضارّة) drug (موادّ تُسْتَعْمَلُ لأَغْراض طِبِّيّة) narcotic

مُخْرِج س director

مَخْرَج س ج /مَخارِج/ (مَكان الخُروج) exit (فَتْحَة في الحاسوب حَيْثُ يُوَصَّلُ مِن خِلالِها جِهاز آخر) port

مَخْزَن س ج /مَخازِن/ store

مَخْزون س stock

مُخَصَّص س ج /مُخَصَّصات/ (مَصْروف) allowance

مُخَطَّط س (مُخَطَّط بَيانيّ لِمَشْروع) blueprint (خِطّة لِتَنْفيذ هَدَف) plan (مُخَطَّط بَيانيّ لإِظْهار نَتائِج) diagram

مَخْطوب ص engaged

مَخْطوطَة س manuscript

مَخْفِيّ ص hidden

مُخَفَّض ص reduced

مِخْلَب س ج /مَخالِب/ claw

مُخْلِص ص faithful

مُخَلَّل س pickle

مَخْلوق س ج /مَخْلوقات/ creature

م

مُحِبّ ص loving

مَحَبَّة س affection

مُحْبَط ص frustrated

مَحْبوب ص beloved

مُحْتال س fraud

مُحْتَرَم ص respected

مُحْتَفِل ص festive

مُحْتَلّ س occupier

مُحْتَلّ ص occupied

مُحْتَمَل ص likely

مُحْتَوى س content

مَحْجَر س ج /مَحاجِر/ quarry

مُحَدَّد ص particular

مَحْدود ص limited

مُحْرِج ص embarrassing

مُحَرِّر س (مَسْؤول المَجَلَّة أو الجَريدَة) editor
(المُخَلِّص مِن الاِحْتِلال أو الأَسْر) liberator

مُحْرِق ص burning

مُحَرِّك س engine

مُحَرَّم س (الشَهْر الأَوَّل بِالتَقْويم الإِسْلاميّ) Muharram

مُحْزِن ص saddening

مَحْشيّ س ج /مَحاشٍ/ (أَيّ نَوْع خُضار مَحْشيّ بِالأَرُزّ وَاللَحْم) stuffed vegetable

مُحَصِّلَة س result

مَحْصول س ج /مَحاصيل/ crop

مَحْض ص pure

مَحَطَّة س station

مَحْظوظ ص fortunate

مُحَفِّز س ج /مُحَفِّزات/ incentive

مِحْفَظَة س (مِحْفَظَة النِساء) purse
(مِحْفَظَة الرِجال) wallet

مَحْفوظات س archives

مُحَقِّق س detective

مُحَكِّم س arbitrator

مَحْكَمَة س ج /مَحاكِم/ court

مُحَلٍّ س sweetener

مُحَلِّل س analyst

مَحْلول س ج /مَحاليل/ solution

مَحْلول ص loose

مَحَلّيّ ص local

مُحَمَّص ص roasted

مُحَمَّل ص loaded

مَحْمول ص portable

مِحْنَة س ج /مِحَن/ ordeal

مُحَنَّط ص mummified

مَحْو س rubbing out

مِحْوَر س ج /مَحاوِر/ hub

مُحيط س (الظُروف المُحيطَة) environment

مُجَدِّد س renewer

مُجَدَّد ص renewed

مُجَدَّرَة س (طَبْخَة تُصْنَعُ مِن الأَرُزّ وَالعَدَس) mujaddarah

مَجَرَّة س galaxy

مُجَرَّد ظ(فَقَط) merely

مُجَرَّد ص (عارٍ) naked
(غَيْر مُغَطّى) bare
(نَظَرِيّ) abstract

مُجْرِم س criminal

مَجْرى س ج /مَجارٍ/ (أُنْبوب مَجارٍ) sewer
(قَناة ماء) watercourse

مَجْزَرَة س ج /مَجازِر/ massacre

مَجَلَّة س magazine

مُجَلَّد س (جُزْء مِن كِتاب) volume

مُجَلَّد ص (مَكْسوّ بِالجِلْد) bound

مَجْلِس س ج /مَجالِس/ council
مَجْلِس الإدارَة board
مَجْلِس النوّاب parliament

مُجَمِّع س collector

مُجَمَّع س compound

مَجْمَع س assembly
مَجْمَع عِلْميّ / أَدَبيّ academy

مَجْموع س total

مَجْموعَة س (عَدَد مِن الأَشْياء) collection
(عَدَد مِن الأَشْخاص) group

مُجَنَّد س recruit

مَجْنون ص ج /مَجانين/ mad

مِجْهَر س ج /مَجاهِر/ microscope

مَجْهود س effort

مَجْهول ص anonymous

مُجَوْهَرات س jewellery

مَجيء س coming

مَجيد ص glorious

مَحا ف to erase

مُحادَثَة س conversation

مَحار س oyster

مُحارِب س warrior

مُحاسِب س accountant

مُحاسَبَة س accounting

مُحاضِر س lecturer

مُحاضَرَة س lecture

مُحافِظ ص conservative

مُحافِظ س governor

مُحافَظَة س (الإبْقاء عَلى الأَشْياء السَليمَة) conservation
(حِفْظ الأَشْياء) preservation

مُحاكَمَة س trial

مُحامٍ س lawyer

مُحاوَرَة س dialogue

مُحاوَلَة س attempt

مُحايِد ص neutral

مُتَواجِد ص available

مُتَوازٍ ص parallel

مُتَوازِن ص balanced

مُتَواصِل ص endless

مُتَواضِع ص modest

مُتَوافِق ص compatible

مُتَوالٍ ص progressive

مُتَوَتِّر ص nervous

مُتَوَرِّط ص involved

مُتَوَسِّط ص (بَيْنَ الأَعْلى وَالأَدْنى) average
(في الوَسَط) intermediate

مُتَوَفِّر ص available

مُتَوَقَّع ص prospective

مُتَوَقِّف على ص dependent on

مَتى أ إس (تُسْتَخْدَمُ لِلسُّؤال عَن الزَمَن) when
مَتى رَأَيْتَهُ آخِر مَرَّة؟ When did you see him last?

مُتَيَسِّر ص accessible

مَتين ص tough

مُثابِر ص persistent

مُثابَرَة س persistence

مِثال س ج /أَمْثِلَة/ example

مِثاليّ ص ideal

مَثانَة س bladder

مُثْبَت ص established

مُثَقَّف ص educated

مِثْلَ أ تش as
like

مَثَل س ج /أَمْثال/ saying

مَثَّلَ ف (أَدّى دَوْراً في عَمَل سينَمائيّ أَو مَسْرَحيّ)
to act
(نابَ عَن شَخْص أَو مَجْموعَة) to represent

مُثَلَّث س triangle

مِثْلَما أ تش as

مُثْمِر ص (مُرْبِح) profitable
(يُعْطي ثِماراً) fruitful

مُثَنّى ص dual

مَثْنيّ ص folded

مُثول س appearance

مُثير ص exciting
مُثير لِلجَدَل controversial

مُجادَلَة س argument

مُجازَفَة س risk

مَجال س ج /مَجالات/ field

مُجامَلَة س compliment

مَجّانٍ ص free

مُجاوِر ص adjacent

مُجْتَمَع س ج /مُجْتَمَعات/ community

مَجْد س ج /أَمْجاد/ glory

مَجَّدَ ف to glorify

مُجْدٍ ص worthwhile

م

مُتْعَب ص tired

مُتْعِب ص troublesome

مُتْعَة س ج /مُتَع/ pleasure

مُتَعَدِّد ص (كَثير) numerous

(مُخْتَلِف) manifold

مُتَعَصِّب س fanatic

مُتَعَلِّق ب ص concerning

مُتَعَلِّم ص (شَخْص في مَرْحَلَة الدِراسَة) learner

(حاصِل عَلى شَهادَة جامِعيَّة) educated

مُتَعَمَّد ص deliberate

مُتَعَهِّد س contractor

مُتَعَوِّد على ص accustomed to

مُتَغَطْرِس ص arrogant

مُتَغَيِّب ص absent

مُتَغَيِّر ص variable

مُتَفائِل ص optimistic

مُتَفاوِت ص disparate

مُتَفَجِّر ص explosive

مُتَفَجِّر س ج /مُتَفَجِّرات/ explosive

مُتَفَرِّج س spectator

مُتَفَرِّق ص (مُنْفَصِل) separated

(مُتَشَتِّت) dispersed

مُتَفَشٍّ ص rampant

مُتَقاعِد س retired

مُتَقَدِّم ص advanced

مُتَقَشِّف ص austere

مُتَقَلِّب ص volatile

مُتَكافِئ ص equal

مُتَكامِل ص complete

مُتَكَبِّر ص arrogant

مُتَكَرِّر ص frequent

مُتَلَهِّف ص eager

مُتَماسِك ص coherent

مُتَمَثِّل في ص represented in

مُتَمَدِّن ص civilized

مُتَمَكِّن ص able

مُتَمَلِّص ص elusive

مُتَمَيِّز ص distinctive

مُتَناثِر ص scattered

مُتَناسِب ص proportionate

مُتَنافِس س contestant

مُتَناقِض ص contradictory

مُتَناوِب ص alternate

مُتَناوَل س reach

مُتَنَزَّه س park

مُتَنَقِّل ص mobile

مُتَنَوِّع ص various

مُتَّهَم ص accused

مُتَهَوِّر ص impulsive

م

مُتَحَمِّس ص keen

مُتَحَيِّز ص biased

مُتَخَصِّص ص specialist

مُتَخَلِّف ص backward

مُتَداخِل ص overlapping

مُتَداوَل ص circulating

مُتَدَرِّب ص trainee

مُتَدَنٍّ ص down

مُتَدَهْوِر ص deteriorated

مُتَدَيِّن ص religious

مُتَذَمِّر ص complaining

مِتْر س ج /أَمْتار/ metre

مُتَرابِط ص coherent

مُتَرْجِم س translator
مُتَرْجِم فَوْرِيّ interpreter

مُتَرَدِّد ص hesitant

مَتْروك ص abandoned

مُتَزامِن ص simultaneous

مُتَزايِد ص increasing

مُتَزَوِّج ص married

مُتَسابِق س (في مُنافَسَة غَيْر السباق) contestant
(في سِباق) racer

مُتَسامِح ص tolerant

مُتَساهِل ص lenient

مُتَساوٍ ص equal

مُتَّسِخ ص dirty

مُتَسَرِّع ص hasty

مُتَّسَع س room

مُتَسَلِّط ص dominating

مُتَسَوِّق س shopper

مُتَسَوِّل س beggar

مُتَشائِم ص pessimistic

مُتَشابِه ص identical

مُتَشَدِّد ص strict

مُتَشَرِّد ص homeless

مُتَشَكِّك ص dubious

مُتَّصِل ص online

مُتَطابِق ص identical

مُتَطَرِّف ص extreme

مُتَطَرِّف س extremist

مُتَطَلَّب س requirement

مُتَطَوِّر ص developed

مُتَطَوِّع ص volunteer

مُتَظاهِر س (قائِم بِمُظاهَرَة) demonstrator
ص (مُدَّعٍ) pretender

مُتَعارِض ص contradicting

مُتَعاطِف ص sympathetic

مُتَعاقِب ص consecutive

مُتَعاوِن ص cooperative

م

مُبَعْثَر ص scattered
مُبْعَد س deportee
مَبْعوث س envoy
مُبَكِّر ص early
مَبْلَغ س ج /مَبالِغ/ amount
مُبَلِّغ س reporter
مُبَلَّل ص wet
مَبْنى س ج /مَبانٍ/ building
مَبْنيّ ص built
مَبْنيّ لِلمَجْهول passive
مُبْهِج ص delightful
مُبْهَم ص ambiguous
مُبيد ص ج /مُبيدات/ annihilative
مُبيد للحَشائش herbicide
مُبيد الحَشَرات insecticide
مُبيد المَيكْروبات microbiocide
مُتابَعَة س continuation
مُتَأَثِّر ب ص affected by
مُتاجَرَة س trade
مُتاح ص accessible
مُتَأَخِّر ص late
مُتَأَسِّف ص sorry
مُتَأَصِّل ص deep-rooted
مَتاعِب س troubles
مُتَأَكِّد ص certain
مُتَآلِف ص integrated
مُتَأَلِّق ص bright
مُتَأَلِّم ص in pain
مُتَآمِر س conspirator
مُتَأَهِّب ص ready
مُتَبادَل ص mutual
مُتَبَرِّع س donor
مُتَبَقٍّ ص remaining
مُتَتابِع ص successive
مُتَتالٍ ص successive
مُتَجانِس ص homogeneous
مُتَجَدِّد ص renewed
مَتْجَر س ج /مَتاجِر/ shop
مَتْجَر كَبير supermarket
مُتَجَعِّد ص (المَلْبَس وَالوَجْه) creased
(الشَعْر) curly
مُتَجَمِّد ص frozen
مُتَحَدٍّ س challenger
مُتَّحِد ص united
مُتَحَدِّث س speaker
مُتَحَدِّث بِلِسان spokesman
مُتَحَرِّر ص liberal
مُتَحَرِّك ص mobile
مُتَحَسِّن ح better
مُتَحَضِّر ص civilized
مَتْحَف س ج /مَتاحِف/ museum

ماطَلَ ف to procrastinate

ماعِز س goat

ماكِر ص cunning

مَأْكَل س food

ماكْياج س make up

ماكينَة س machine

مالَ ف to incline

مال س ج /أَمْوال/ money

مالِح ص ج /مَوالِح/ salty

مالك س ج /مُلاّك/ owner

مالك الأَرْض landlord

مالِكَةالأَرْض landlady

مَأْلوف ص familiar

ماليّ ص financial

ماليَّة س finances

مَأْمَن س ج /مَآمِن/ safe place

مانْجو س mango

مانِح س donor

مانَعَ ف to object to

ماهِر ص skilful

مَأْوى س ج /مَآوٍ/ shelter

مايو س (الشَهْر الخامِس بِالتَقْويم المِصْريّ) May

مايوه س swimming suit

مُباح ص permitted

مُباحَثات س talks

مُباحَثَة س negotiation

مُبادَرَة س initiative

مُبادَلَة س exchange

مُباراة س ج /مُبارَيات/ match

مُبارَزَة س duel

مُبارَزَة بِالسُيوف fencing

مُبارَك ص blessed

مُباشِر ص direct

مُباشَرَةً ح directly

مُبالَغَة س exaggeration

مُبْتَدِئ ص beginner

مُبْتَسِم ص smiling

مُبْتَكِر ص creator

مُبْتَهِج ص cheerful

مَبْدَأ س ج /مَبادِئ/ (قاعِدَة) principle (عَقيدَة) dogma

مُبْدِع ص creative

مُبَذِّر ص wasteful

مِبْراة س pencil sharpener

مِبْرَد س file

مُبَرِّر س ج /مُبَرِّرات/ justification

مُبَرْمِج س programmer

مَبْروك س congratulations

مُبَسَّط ص simplified

مُبَشِّر س preacher

مِئذَنَة س ج /مَآذِن/ minaret

مِئَوِيّ ص in percentage

ما أ إس (تُستَخْدَمُ لِلسُّؤال عَن مَعْلومات) what

ما هَذا؟ What is this?

ما أ ن (تُستَخْدَمُ لِلنَفْي الماضي) did not

ما سافَرْتُ إلى عُمان I did not travel to Oman.

ما عَدا أداة استِثناء except

ما لَم unless

ماء س ج /مِياه/ water

مِائَة عد ج /مِئات/ hundred

مائِدَة س ج /مَوائِد/ table

ماتَ ف to die

ماجِسْتير س master's degree

مَأْخَذ س ج /مَآخِذ/ shortcoming

مَأْدُبَة س banquet

مادَّة س ج /مَوادّ/ (شَيْء مَحْسوس) material

(نَوْع) item

(شَيْء صُلْب أَو سائِل أَو غازِيّ ذو خَواص) substance

(بَنْد) article

(مَوْضوع) subject

مادَّة حافِظَة preservative

مادَّة خام raw material

مَوادّ غِذائِيَّة foodstuff

مادِّيّ ص material

ماذا أ إس (تُستَخْدَمُ لِلسُّؤال عَن مَعْلومات) what

ماذا سَوْفَ تَعْمَلُ؟ What will you do?

مارِد س giant

مارَسَ ف to practice

مارِس س (الشَهْر الثالِث بِالتَقْويم المِصْرِيّ) March

مارْكَة س brand

مارونِيّ س ج /مَوارِنَة/ Maronite

مازَحَ ف to kid

مَأْزَق س ج /مَآزِق/ (وَضع سَيِّئ صَعْب الخُروج مِنْهُ) deadlock

مَأْساة س ج /مَآسٍ/ (تَجْرُبَة مَريرَة وَمُحْزِنَة) tragedy

ماسَة س ج /ماس/ diamond

ماسورَة س ج /مَواسير/ pipe

ماشٍ ص ج /مُشاة/ pedestrian

ماشِيَة س ج /مَواشٍ/ cattle

ماضٍ ص، س past

ماطِر ص rainy

Hani not come to school?

لَمَحَ ف to glance

لَمَّحَ إلى ف to hint

لَمْحَة س glimpse

لَمْس س touch

لَمَسَ ف to touch

لَمَعَ ف to shine

لِمَن أ إس (تُسْتَخْدَمُ لِلسُّؤال عَن صاحِبِ المُلْكيَّة) whose

لِمَن هذا الكِتاب؟ Whose book is this?

لَن أ ن (أداة نَفْي لِلمُسْتَقْبَل) will not

لَن أَخْرُجَ اليَوْم. I will not go out today.

لَهُ أ م (تَدُلُّ على المُلْكيَّة لِلغائِب المُفْرَد المُذَكَّر) his

لَها أ م (تَدُلُّ عَلى المُلْكيَّة لِلغائِب المُفْرَد المُؤَنَّث) her, hers

لَهَب س flame

لَهَثَ ف to pant

لَهْجَة س accent

لَهُم أ م (تَدُلُّ عَلى المُلْكيَّة لِلغائِب الجَمْع المُذَكَّر وَالمُؤَنَّث) their, theirs

لَهُما أ م (تَدُلُّ عَلى المُلْكيَّة لِلغائِب المُثَنّى) their, theirs

لَهُنَّ أ م (تَدُلُّ عَلى المُلْكيَّة لِلغائِب الجَمْع المُؤَنَّث) their, theirs

لَو أداة تمَنّي if

لِواء س ج /أَلْوِيَة/ (رُتْبَة عَسْكَرِيَّة) major general

(مَجْموعَة كَبيرَة مِن الجُنود) brigade

لَوَّثَ ف to pollute

لَوْح س ج /أَلْواح/ board

لَوَّحَ ف to wave

لَوْحَة س painting

لَوْحَة مَفاتيح keyboard

لُؤْلُؤَة س ج /لآلِئ/ pearl

لَوْم س blame

لَوْن س ج /أَلْوان/ colour

لَوْن مائيّ watercolours

لَوَّنَ ف to colour

لَوى ف to twist

لِياقَة س (صِحَّة البَدَن) fitness

(حُسْن التَعامُل) politeness

ليبيّ ص، س Libyan

ليبيا س Libya

لَيْتَ حج it would be good if

ليتْشي س (نَوْع نَبات) lychee

لَيْسَ أ ن (أَداة نَفْي في حالَة المُذَكَّر المُفْرَد) is not

هذا لَيْسَ سَبَباً مُقْنِعاً This is not a valid reason.

لَيْسَت أ ن (أداة نَفْي في حالَة المُؤَنَّث المُفْرَد) is not

ماري لَيْسَت لُبْنانيَّة. Mary isn't Lebanese.

لَيِّق ص (قَويّ البُنْيَة) fit

(حَسَن الخُلُق) polite

لَيْل س night time

لَيْلَة س ج /لَيالٍ/ night

ليموناضَة س lemonade

لَيْمونَة س ج /لَيْمون/ lemon

ل

لُعْبَة الهوكي hockey
لُعْبَة كُرَة القَدَم soccer/football

لَعِقَ ف to lick

لَعَلَّ ف perhaps

لَعَنَ ف to curse

لَعْنَة س curse

لُغَة س language

لُغْز س ج /ألْغاز/ puzzle

لُغْم س ج /ألْغام/ mine

لَغَّمَ ف to mine

لُغَوِيّ ص linguistic

لُغَوِيّ س linguist

لَفَّ ف (لَفَّ حَبْلاً أو نَحْوَهُ حَوْلَ جِسْم) to wind
(دارَ) to turn
(غَلَّفَ) to wrap
(تَجَوَّلَ) to walk around

لَفَّة س roll

لِفْت س turnip

لَفَظَ ف to pronounce

لَفْظ س pronunciation

لَفَّفَ ف to wrap tightly

لِقاء س (اجْتِماع) meeting
(مُقابَلَة) interview

لِقاح س vaccine

لَقَب س ج /ألْقاب/ nickname

لَقْطَة س snapshot

لَقِيَ ف (وَجَدَ بالصُدْفَة) to come across
(قابَلَ) to meet

لُقيَّة س find

لَكَ أ م (تَدُلُّ عَلى المُلْكيَّة لِلمُخاطَب المُفْرَد المُذَكَّر) your, yours
هَل هذه السَيّارَة لَكَ؟ Is this car yours?
(تَدُلُّ عَلى المُلْكيَّة لِلمُخاطَب المُفْرَد المُؤَنَّث) your, yours
هَل هذا الطِفْل لَكِ؟ Is this child yours?

لَكَزَ ف to poke

لَكَمَ ف to punch

لَكُم أ م (تَدُلُّ عَلى المُلْكيَّة لِلمُخاطَب الجَمْع المُذَكَّر والمُؤَنَّث) your, yours

لَكُما أ م (تَدُلُّ عَلى المُلْكيَّة لِلمُخاطَب المُثَنّى) your, yours

لَكْمَة س punch

لكِن but

لَكُنَّ أ م (تَدُلُّ عَلى المُلْكيَّة لِلمُخاطَب الجَمْع المُؤَنَّث) your, yours

لِكَي in order to

لِمَ أ إس (تُسْتَخْدَمُ لِلسُؤال عَن السَبَب) why
لِمَ فَعَلْتَ ذلك؟ Why did you do that?

لَم أ ن (أداة نَفْي لِلماضي) did not, didn't
لَم أَحْصُل عَلى الوَظيفَة. I did not get the job.
has not, hasn't
إنَّهُ لَم يَصِل بَعْد. He has not arrived yet.

لَمّا ظ when

لِماذا أ إس (تُسْتَخْدَمُ لِلسُؤال عَن السَبَب) why
لِماذا لَم يَأْتِ هاني إلى المَدْرَسَة؟ Why did

ل

لَبَّسَ ف to clothe

لُبْس س ambiguity

لَبِق ص tactful

لَبَن س ج /أَلْبان/ milk

لَبَن زَباديّ yogurt

لُبْنان س Lebanon

لُبْنانيّ ص، س Lebanese

لَبِنَة س brick

لَبَنَة س yogurt

لَبُؤَة س lioness

لِتْر س litre

لِثَة الفَم س gum

لَجَأَ إلى ف (اتَّخَذَ مَلْجَأً) to take refuge in

(اتَّخَذَ أو عَمِلَ شَيْئاً كَحَلٍّ أخير) to resort to

لَجْنَة س ج /لِجان/ committee

لُجوء س (حِمايَة تَمْنَحُها دَوْلَة لِلهارِبين مِن دُوَلِهِم) asylum

(الاِضْطِرار إلى أَمْر) taking refuge

لَحْس س lick

لَحَسَ ف to lick

لَحْظَة س moment

لَحِقَ ف to catch up

لَحْم س ج /لُحوم/ (لَحْم الإنْسان) flesh

(لَحْم الحَيَوان أو الطَيْر) meat

لَحْم البَقَر beef

لَحْم الحَمَل lamb

لَحْم الخِنْزير pork

لَحْم الضَأْن mutton

لَحَمَ س to weld

لَحَّنَ ف to compose

لَحْن س ج /أَلْحان/ melody

لِحْيَة س ج /لِحى/ beard

لَخَّصَ ف to summarize

لَدْغَة س bite

لَدى ظ to have

لَذيذ ص delicious

لَزِمَ ف to necessitate

لُزوم س necessity

لِسان س ج /أَلْسِنَة/ tongue

لَسَعَ ف to sting

لَسْنَ أ ن (أَداة نَفْي في حالَة الجَمْع المُؤَنَّث) are not

هُنَّ لَسْنَ غائِبات .They are not absent

لِصّ س ج /لُصوص/ thief

لَطافَة س courtesy

لَطَّخَ ف to stain

لُطْف س kindness

لَطيف ص ج /لُطَفاء/ kind

لُعْب س play

لَعِبَ ف to play

لُعْبَة س ج /أَلْعاب/ game

لُعْبَة أَطْفال toy

لُعْبَة الجولْف golf

لُعْبَة الرَغْبي rugby

ل

لِ حج (تَدُلُّ عَلى المُلْكيَّة) belongs to
السَيّارَة لِمُحَمَّد The car belongs to Muhammad.
(تَدُلُّ عَلى الانْتِهاء لِمَكان أَو حال) to
ذَهَبَ لِقَطَر. He went to Qatar.
جاءَ لِجَمْع التَبَرُّعات He came to collect donations.
(بِمَعْنى مِن أَجْل) for
ادَّخَرْتُ مالاً لِلمُسْتَقْبَل I have set aside money for the future.
هذه الرِسالَة لَكَ. This letter is for you.

لا أن no
(أَداة نَفْي لِلحاضِر) do not, don't
لا تَنْظُر إلى الوَراء. Do not look back.

لاءَمَ ف to suit

لائِحَة س ج /لَوائِح/ list
لائِحَة اتِّهام indictment

لائِق ص appropriate

لاجِئ ص refugee

لاحَظَ ف to notice

لاحِق ص forthcoming

لاذِع ص bitter

لازَمَ ف to be with

لازِم ص necessary

لاسِلْكِيّ ص wireless

لاعِب س (مَن يَلْعَبُ عَلى آلات إلِكْترونيَّة) gamer
(مَن يُشارِكُ في أَلْعاب رِياضيَّة) player
لاعِب الجَناح winger
لاعِب خَطّ الوَسَط midfielder
لاعِب الهُجوم striker
لاعِب الدِفاع defence

لافِتَة س sign

لامَ ف to blame

لامْبَة س bulb

لامِع ص (مَشْهور) prominent
(بَرّاق) shiny

لانَ ف to relent

لأَنَّ سَبَبيَّة because

لُبّ س ج /أَلْباب/ (قَلْب الشَيْء) core
(عَقْل) mind

لِباس س ج /أَلْبِسَة/ clothing
لِباس داخِلِيّ underwear

لَباقَة س tact

لَبِثَ ف to stay
ما لَبِثَ أَنْ not long before

لِبْد س felt

لَبِسَ ف to wear

كُوَيْتي ص، س Kuwaiti

كَي in order to

كَيّ س (شَفْط الدَم بِواسِطَة كوب) cupping
(مَلا بِس) ironing

كِياسَة س grace

كِيان س entity

كيس س ج /أَكْياس/ (كيس صَغير) bag
(كيس كَبير) sack

كَيَّفَ ف to adapt

كَيْفَ أ إس (تُسْتَخْدَمُ لِلسُؤال عَن الطَريقَة أو الحال) how
كَيْفَ جِئْتَ إلى هُنا؟ How did you get here?

كَيْفَما ظ however

كَيْفيَّة س manner

كيلومِتْر س kilometre

كيماويّ ص chemical

كيمْياء س chemistry

كيمْيائيّ س chemist

كيوي س kiwi fruit

كَم طالِباً في الصفّ؟ How many students are there in the class?
كَم مِن المال تَمْلُكُ؟ How much money do you have?
(تُسْتَخْدَمُ لِلسُؤال عَن فَتْرَة زَمَنيَّة) how long
كَم اسْتَغْرَقَ الطَريق؟ How long did the trip take?
(تُسْتَخْدَمُ لِلسُؤال عَن عَدَد المَرَّات) how often
كَم مَرَّة تَزورُ والِدَيْكَ خِلالَ الأُسْبوع؟ How often do you visit your parents in the course of a week?
(تُسْتَخْدَمُ لِلسُؤال عَن المَسافَة) how far
كَم يَبْعُدُ السوق مِن هُنا؟ How far is the market from here?

كَما ح as

كَمال س perfection

كَمان س violin

كَمّون س cumin

كِمْياء س chemistry

كَمِّيَّة س quantity

كَنَدا س Canada

كَنَديّ ص، س Canadian

كَنْز س ج /كُنوز/ treasure

كَنْزَة س (مَلْبَس) sweater
(كَنْزَة مَفْتوحَة مَعَ أَزْرار) cardigan
(كَنْزَة بِقَبَّة عالِيَة) polo neck
كَنْزَة صوف pullover

كَنَّسَ ف to sweep

كَنيس س ج /كُنُس/ synagogue

كَنيسَة س ج /كَنائِس/ church
كَنيسَة المَهْد nativity church
كَنيسَة القِيامَة Church of the Holy Sepulchre

كَهْرَباء س electricity

كَهْرَبائيّ ص electric/al

كَهْف س ج /كُهوف/ cave

كوب س /أَكْواب/ (وِعاء لِشُرْب الشاي وَالقَهْوَة) cup
(كَأس بِيَد) mug

كوخ س ج /أَكْواخ/ cottage

كوسا س marrow

كوسى س marrow

كوع س ج /أَكْواع/ knee

كوكايين س cocaine

كَوْكَب س ج /كَواكِب/ planet
كَوْكَب الأَرْض Earth
كَوْكَب المَرّيخ Mars
كَوْكَب الزَهْرَة Venus
كَوْكَب عُطارِد Mercury

كوكْتيل س cocktail

كولِسْتْرول س cholesterol

كوم س ج /أَكْوام/ heap

كَوَّمَ ف to pile

كَوْمَة س pile

كَوْن س universe

كَوى ف to iron

كُوَيْت س (الكُوَيْت) Kuwait

ك

كَساد س recession

كَسَبَ ف to gain

كَسْتَناء س chestnut

كَسْر س (عَمَلِيَّة التَكْسير) breaking
ج /كُسور/ (جُزْء مِن عَدَد) fraction
(كَسْر في العَظْم أو جِسْم صلْب) fracture

كَسَرَ ف to break

كُسْكُس س couscous

كَسول ص ج /كَسْلى/كُسالى/ lazy

كَسى ف to cover

كَسيح ص cripple

كَشّافَة س girl scout

كَشَطَ ف to scrape off

كَشْف س disclosure

كَشَفَ ف to reveal
كَشَفَ النِقاب عَن to unveil

كُشْك س ج /أكْشاك/ kiosk

كَعْب س ج /أكْعاب/ heel

كَعْكَة س ج /كَعْك/ cake

كَفّ (م) س ج /كُفوف/ palm

كَفَّ عَن ف to stop

كُفُؤ ص competent

كَفاءَة س competence

كِفاح س struggle

كَفالَة س bail

كِفايَة س sufficiency

كُفْر س infidelity

كَفِلَ ف (دَفَعَ مالاً لإخْراج شَخْص مِن السِجْن) to bail
(ضَمِنَ) to guarantee

كَفى ف to suffice

كُلّ ظ (لِلجَميع) all
(لِلمُفْرَد) each

كِلا ظ both

كَلام س talking

كَلْب س ج /كِلاب/ dog

كَلْبَة س bitch

كَلْسون س ج /كَلاسين/ briefs
كَلْسون نِسائيّ knickers

كَلَّفَ ف (تَطلَّبَ) to cost
(أَسْنَدَ إلَيْهِ مَهَمَّة) to entrust with

كُلَّما ظ whenever

كَلِمَة س word
كَلِمَة المُحَرِّر editorial

كِلَمَنْتينا س clementine

كُلّيّ ص total

كُلّيَّة س college

كُلْيَة س ج /كُلى/ kidney

كُمّ س ج /أكْمام/ sleeve

كَم أ إس (تُسْتَخْدَمُ لِلسُؤال عَن كَمِّيَّة سَواء مَعْدودَة أو غَيْر مَعْدودَة) how many, how much

ك

كَبير ص ج /كِبار/ (عَجوز) old
(ضَخْم الحَجْم) big

كِتاب س ج /كُتُب/ book

كِتابَة س writing

كَتَبَ ف to write

كَتِف (م) س ج /أَكْتاف/ shoulder

كُتْلَة س ج /كُتَل/ (كَمِّيَّة مِن شَيْء) block
(تَضَخُّم خَلِيَّة في الجَسَد) lump

كَتَمَ ف to hide

كُتَيِّب س brochure

كَثافَة س density

كَثْرَة س abundance

كَثَّفَ ف to intensify

كَثير ص (تُسْتَخْدَمُ لِلمَعْدود) many
(تُسْتَخْدَمُ لِغَيْر المَعْدود) much

كَثيف ص (مُكْتَظّ) dense
(شَديد اللُزوجَة) thick

كُحْلِيّ ص dark blue

كُحول س alcohol

كَدَّسَ ف to accumulate

كَذا so and so

كَذّاب س liar

كَذَبَ ف to lie

كِذبَة س lie

كَذَلِكَ أد ر also

كَرامَة س dignity

كَراهِيَّة س hatred

كَرْب س agony

كُرْبَة س ج /كُرَب/ tribulation

كَرْبون س carbon

كُرَة س ball
الكُرَة الأَرْضِيَّة globe
كُرَة السلَّة basketball
كُرَة الطائِرَة volleyball
كُرَة القَدَم football
كُرَة اليَد handball

كَرْتون س cardboard

كَرَّرَ ف (صَفّى المَوادّ) to refine
(أَعادَ) to repeat

كَرَز س cherry

كَرَّسَ ف to devote

كُرْسِيّ س ج /كَراسِيّ/ chair

كَرَفْس س celery

كَرَم س generosity

كُرُنْب س cabbage
كُرُنْب بْروكْسِل س Brussels sprout

كُرْه س hate

كَرِهَ ف to hate

كْريكِت س cricket

كَريم ص ج /كُرَماء/ generous

كَريه ص (غَيْر مَحْبوب) unpleasant
(مُتَعَفِّن) foul

كُزْبَرَة س coriander

ك

كَ حج (تُسْتَعْمَلُ لِلتَشْبيه) like
يَبْكي كَطِفْل صَغير. He cries like a baby.

كَئيب ص gloomy

كابوس س ج /كَوابيس/ nightmare

كاتِب س ج /كَتَبَة/ (مُوَظَّف في مُؤَسَّسَة) clerk
ج /كُتّاب/ (مُؤَلِّف) writer
كاتِب آلَة typist

كاثِدْرائيَّة س cathedral

كاجو س cashew

كاحِل س ج /كَواحِل/ ankle

كادَ ف almost

كاذِب ص lying

كارْبوهَيْدْرات س carbohydrate

كارَّة س cart

كارِثَة س ج /كَوارِث/ disaster

كارِثيّ ص disastrous

كاز س kerosene

كَأْس (م) س ج /كُؤوس/ (وِعاء لِلشُرْب) glass
(وِعاء لِلشُرْب مَعَ يَد) cup
(جائِزَة الفائِز في المُنافَسات) cup

كاف ص enough

كافَأَ ف to reward

كافَّة ح totality

كافَحَ ف to struggle

كافِر س ج /كُفّار/كَفَرَة/ unbeliever

كاكاو س cocoa

كالْسيوم س calcium

كامِل ص (تامّ) complete
(كُلُّه) whole
(مِثاليّ) perfect

كاميرا س camera

كانَ ف to be

كَأَنَّ أ تش as if

كانون الأَوَّل س December

كانون الثاني س January

كاهِن س ج /كَهَنَة/ priest

كَبْت س inhibition

كُبَّة س (عَجينَة بُرْغُل مَحْشيَّة بِاللَحْم وَالبَصَل) kubbah

كَبِد (م) س ج /أَكْباد/ liver

كَبَّرَ ف to enlarge

كَبُرَ ف to grow

كِبَر س (زِيادَة الحَجْم) bigness
(قِدَم السِنّ) old age

ك

standard (الأمور)
record (الأَفْضَل أو الأسْرَع)

قِيام س (النُهوض) rise
(تَنْفيذ) undertaking

قيثارَة س guitar

قَيْد س ج /قُيود/ constraint

قَيَّدَ ف (حَدَّدَ) to limit
(رَبَطَ) to tie

قَيْلولَة س nap, siesta

قَيِّم ص invaluable

قَيَّمَ ف to assess

قيمَة س ج /قِيَم/ value

قَلِق ص (مُتَخَوِّف مِن أَمْر) anxious
(يُفَكِّرُ بِاهْتِمام زائِد) concerned

قَلِقَ ف to worry

قَلَّلَ ف to minimize

قَلَم س ج /أَقْلام/ pen
قَلَم رَصاص pencil

قَلَّمَ ف to trim

قَلَّما ظ rarely

قَلى ف to fry

قَليل ص (تُسْتَخْدَمُ لِلمَعْدود) few
(تُسْتَخْدَمُ لِغَيْر المَعْدود) little

قُماش س ج /أَقْمِشَة/ fabric

قُمامَة س litter

قِمَّة س ج /قِمَم/ (أَعْلى الشَيْء أَو اجْتِماع لِلرُؤَساء) summit
(ذِرْوَة الشَيْء) top

قَمْح س wheat

قَمَر س ج /أَقْمار/ moon
قَمَر صِناعِيّ satellite

قُمْرَة س (غُرْفَة السائِق/القُبْطان) cabin
(غُرْفَة صَغيرَة) room

قَمَعَ ف to suppress

قَمْع س suppression

قَميص س ج /قُمْصان/ shirt
قَميص نِسائِيّ blouse

قَناة س ج /قَنَوات/ (مَمَرّ مائِيّ) canal
(مَحَطَّة تِلفِزْيونِيَّة) channel

قَنّاص س sniper

قِناع س ج /أَقْنِعَة/ mask

قَناعَة س satisfaction

قِنَّب س canvas

قُنْبُلَة س ج /قَنابِل/ bomb
قُنْبُلَة حارِقَة Molotov cocktail
قُنْبُلَة ذَرِّيَّة atomic bomb
قُنْبُلَة نَوَوِيَّة nuclear bomb
قُنْبُلَة عُنْقودِيَّة cluster bomb

قَهْقَهَ ف to giggle

قَهْوَة س coffee

قُوَّة س (مَجْموعَة مُدَرَّبَة لِغايات الدِفاع) force
(الطاقَة) power
(مَدى التَحَمُّل) strength

قَوْس س ج /أَقْواس/ (بِناء مَعْقوف) arch
(سِلاح يُسْتَخْدَمُ لِإِطْلاق النَشّاب) bow
قَوْس قُزَح rainbow
قَوْس مَعْقوف bracket

قَوْل س ج /أَقْوال/ saying

قَوْمِيّ ص national

قَوْمِيَّة س nationalism

قَوّى ف to strengthen

قَوِيّ ص ج /أَقْوِياء/ strong

قِيادَة س leadership

قِيادِيّ ص leading

قِياس س ج /أَقْيِسَة/ measurement

قِياسِيّ ص (مُسْتَوى أَو مُواصَفَة تُقاسُ بِهِ

ق

palace (بَيْت المَلِك أو المَلِكَة)

قَصَّرَ ف to shorten

قَصَفَ ف to bombard

قَصْف س bombardment

قَصيدَة س ج /قَصائِد/ poem

قَصير ص ج /قِصار/ short

قَضاء س (جِهاز المَحْكَمَة) justice

(إنْجاز وَتَحْقيق الهَدَف) fulfilment

(نَصيبُكَ في الحَياة) fate

قَضائيّ ص judicial

قَضَمَ ف to bite

قَضْمَة س bite

قَضى ف to spend

قَضيب س ج /قُضْبان/ (قَضيب حَديد) bar

(ذَكَر الرَجُل) penis

قَضيَّة س ج /قَضايا/ (أَمْر يُدْرَسُ مِن قِبَل المَحْكَمَة) case

(مَوْضوع) matter

(مَسْأَلَة صِراع) cause

قِطّ س ج /قِطَط/ cat

قَط أد ن never

قِطار س train

قَطّارَة س drip

قِطاع س ج /قِطاعات/ sector

قُطْر س ج /أَقْطار/ country

قَطَر س Qatar

قَطَريّ ص، س Qatari

قَطَّعَ ف to chop

قَطَعَ ف to cut

قَطْع س cutting

قِطْعَة س ج /قِطَع/ piece

قَطَفَ ف to pick

قُطْن س cotton

قَطيع س /قُطْعان/ herd

قُفّاز س glove

قَفَزَ ف to jump

قَفْزَة س jump

قَفَص س ج /أَقْفاص/ cage

قَفَص صَدْريّ thorax

قُفْل س ج /أَقْفال/ lock

قَفَلَ ف to lock

قَلَّ ف to be few

قِلادَة س ج /قَلائِد/ necklace

قَلْب س ج /قُلوب/ (عُضْو) heart

(وَسَط) inside

قَلَبَ ف to overturn

قِلَّة س shortage

قَلَّدَ ف (عَمِلَ شَيْئاً مَثيلاً لِشَيْء آخَر) to copy

(قَلَّدَ حَرَكات شَخْص) to mimic

قَلْعَة س ج /قِلاع/ (بِناء مُحَصَّن) citadel

(صَخْرَة كَبيرَة) rock

قَلَق س anxiety

ق

قِراءَة س reading

قَرار س ج /قَرارات/ decision

قُرْآن س the Qur'an

قَرَأَ ف to read

قُرْب س closeness

قُرْبَ ظ near

قُرْحَة س ulcer

قِرْد س ج /قُرود/ monkey

قَرَّرَ ف to decide

قَرَصَ ف (شَخْص يَلْسَعُ آخَر أَو يَفْلِقُ شَيْئاً بِإصْبَعَيْه) to pinch
(لَسَعَ) to bite

قُرْص س ج /أَقْراص/ (أَداة تَخْزين إلِكْترونيّ) disc
(حَبَّة دَواء) tablet
قُرْص العَسَل honeycomb

قُرْصان س ج /قَراصِنَة/ pirate

قَرْض س ج /قُروض/ loan

قَرَعَ ف (قَرَعَ الباب أَو نَحْوَ ذلك) to knock
(قَرَعَ الجَرَس) to ring

قَرْع س squash

قِرْفَة س cinnamon

قِرْميدَة س ج /قَراميد/ tile

قَرْن س ج /قُرون/ (فَتْرَة مِائَة عام) century
(عَلى رَأْس الحَيَوان) horn

قَرْنَبيطَة س ج /قَرْنَبيط/ cauliflower

قَرْنِيَّة س cornea

قَريب س ج /أَقْرِباء/ relative

قَريب ص close

قَريباً ظ shortly

قَرْيَة س ج /قُرى/ village

قُرَيْدِس س prawn

قِسْط س ج /أَقْساط/ premium

قِسْم س ج /أَقْسام/ section

قَسَم س oath

قَسَّمَ ف to divide

قِسْمَة س division

قَسْوَة س hardness

قَشّاش س (لاعِب دِفاع مُتَأَخِّر) sweeper

قَشَّة س ج /قَشّ/ straw

قِشْدَة س cream

قَشَّرَ ف to peel

قِشْرَة س ج /قُشور/ (الغِشاء الخارِجيّ لِبَعْض الفَواكِه وَالخُضار) skin
(غِشاء خارِجيّ خَشِن عَلى بَعْض الفَواكِه كَالحَمْضِيّات) peel

قَصَب س reed

قِصَّة س ج /قِصَص/ story

قَصَدَ ف (عَنى) to mean
(اسْتَهْدَفَ) to aim at

قَصْدير س tin

قَصْر س ج /قُصور/ (بَيْت كَبير مُحاط بِحَدائِق) mansion

قامَ ف (وَقَفَ) to stand up
(أدّى) to undertake

قامَرَ ف to gamble

قاموس س ج /قَواميس/ dictionary

قانون س ج /قَوانين/ law

قانونيّ ص legal

قاوَمَ ف to resist

قايَضَ ف to swap

قَبْر س ج /قُبور/ tomb

قَبَضَ على ف to catch

قَبْضَة س fist

قُبْطان س ج /قَباطِنَة/ pilot (air, sea)

قُبَّعَة س hat

قَبِلَ ف to accept

قَبَّلَ ف to kiss

قَبْلَ ظ before

قُبْلَة س ج /قُبَل/ kiss

قَبَليّ ص tribal

قُبَّة س ج /قُبَب/ dome

قَبَّة س collar

قَبو س basement

قُبول س admission

قَبيح ص ugly

قَبيلَة س ج /قَبائِل/ tribe

قِتال س fight

قَتَلَ ف to kill

قَتيل ص ج /قَتْلى/ dead

قَد ف (رُبَّما) may
(تَدُلُّ عَلى حَداثَة وُقوع فِعْل) has, have-pp

قَدَّ ف to rip

قُدّامَ ظ (أمامَ) in front of

قَدِرَ ف to be able to

قَدَر س ج /أقْدار/ fate

قِدْر س ج /قُدور/ pot

قَدَّرَ ف (شَكَرَ واحْتَرَمَ) to appreciate
(خَمَّنَ) to estimate

قُدْرَة س ability

قَدَم (م) س ج /أقْدام/ foot

قِدَم س oldness

قَدَّمَ ف to present

قَدِمَ ف to come

قُدُماً ظ straight ahead

قِدّيس س saint

قَديم ص old

قَذِر ص filthy

قَذَفَ ف (رَمى) to throw
(أخْرَجَ الرَجُل أو الحَيَوان ماءَهُ) to ejaculate
(قَصَفَ) to shell

قَذْف س (رَمْي) throw
(إخْراج الرَجُل أو الحَيَوان ماءَهُ) ejaculation

قَذيفَة س ج /قَذائِف/ rocket

ق

قائِد س ج /قادَة/ (ضابِط عَسْكَريّ) commander
(مَسْؤول) leader

قائِل س advocate

قائِم ص (مُتَوَقِّف عَلى أَرْجُلِه) standing
(الحاليّ) existing

قائِمَة س ج /قَوائِم/ list
قائِمَة الطَعام menu

قابِس س ج /قَوابيس/ plug

قابِض س ج /قَوابِض/ clutch

قابَلَ ف to interview
to meet

قابِلَة س midwife

قاتِل س ج /قَتَلَة/ killer

قاتَلَ ف to fight

قاتِم ص bleak

قادَ ف (قادَ مَرْكَبَة) to drive
(قادَ دابَّة أو دَرّاجَة) to ride

قادِر ص able

قادِم ص coming

قاذِفَة س launcher

قارِئ س ج /قُرّاء/ reader

قارِب س ج /قَوارِب/ boat

قارَّة س ج /قارّات/ continent

قارَنَ ف to compare

قارّيّ ص continental

قاسَ ف to measure

قاسٍ ص harsh

قاصِر س minor

قاضٍ س ج /قُضاة/ judge

قاضى ف (يَرْفَعُ عَلَيْهِ قَضيَّة في المَحْكَمَة) to sue

قاطِرَة س ج /قَواطِر/ engine

قاطَعَ ف to interrupt

قاطِع ص (لا شَكَّ فيهِ) definite
(قادِر عَلى قَطْع الأَشْياء) cutting

قاطِع س ج /قَواطِع/ partition

قاع س ج /قيعان/ bottom

قاعَة س hall
قاعَة المَحْكَمَة courtroom

قاعِدَة س ج /قَواعِد/ (مَرْكَز عَسْكَريّ) base
(أَساس) principle
قاعِدَة بَيانات database

قالَ ف to say

فُنْدُق س ج /فَنادِق/ hotel

فَنّي ص artistic

فَنّي س technician

فِهْرِسْت س ج /فَهارِس/ index

فَهْم س understanding

فَهِمَ ف to understand

فَواكِهُ س fruits

فَوَّتَ ف to skip

فَوْرَ ظ immediately after

فَوْراً ح immediately

فَوْريّ ص immediate

فَوْز س (النَصْر) victory
(النَيْل) winning
(النَجاح) success

فوشيّ ص magenta

فَوَّضَ ف to authorize

فَوْضَويّ ص (الأحْوال) chaotic
(الأشْخاص) messy

فَوْضى س (الأحْوال) chaos
(أماكِن) mess

فوطَة س ج /فُوَط/ towel

فَوْقَ ظ (أعْلى مِن) above
(عَلى) on

فولاذ س steel

فولَة س ج /فول/ bean
kidney bean

فول الصويا soybean

فول سودانيّ peanut

فولْطيَّة س voltage

في حج (تَدُلُّ عَلى المَكان) at
كُنْتُ في البَيْت. I was at home.
(تُسْتَخْدَمُ للدَلالَة عَلى الوَقْت)
سَيُعْقَدُ الامْتِحان في الساعَة العاشِرَة The exam will be held at ten o'clock.
(تَدُلُّ عَلى مَكان وُجود شَخْص أو شَيْء) in
الساعَة في الخَزانَة The watch is in the safe.
الطُلاّب في الصَفّ The students are in class.
(تُسْتَخْدَمُ لِتَحْديد فَتْرَة زَمَنيَّة) within
عَمِلَ كُلّ ذَلِكَ في سَنَة واحِدَة He did all of that within a single year.

فيتامين س vitamin

فَيْروس س ج /فَيْروسات/ virus

فَيْروسيّ ص viral

فيزْياء س physics

فيزْيائيّ ص physicist

فَيَضان س ج /فَيَضانات/ flood

فيل س ج /فِيَلَة/ elephant

فيلاّ س ج /فيلاّت/ villa

فَيْلَسوف س ج /فَلاسِفَة/ philosopher

فيلْم س ج /أفْلام/ (شَريط تَخْزين الصُوَر أو فيلْم مُصَوَّر) film
(فيلْم مُصَوَّر) movie

فيلْم كَرْتون cartoon

ف

فَطيرَة س ج /فَطائِر/ pie

فَظّ ص gross

فَظيع ص horrible

فَعّال ص efficient

فَعّالِيَّة س efficiency

فَعَلَ ف to do

فِعْل س ج /أَفْعال/ (عَمَل) deed
(كَلِمَة تُسْتَخْدَمُ في القَواعِد تُعَبِّرُ عَن أَداء) verb
(حَدَث) action

فِعْلاً indeed

فِعْلِيّ ص actual

فُقّاعَة س ج /فَقاقيع/ bubble

فَقَدَ ف (أَضاعَ) to lose
(اشْتاقَ) to miss

فُقْدان س loss

فَقْر س poverty

فَقْرَة س ج /فَقَرات/ (جُزْء مِن نَصّ) paragraph
(جُزْء مِن فِلْم) chapter
(فَقْرَة في العامود الفَقْرِيّ) vertebra

فَقَسَ ف to hatch

فَقَط only

فُقْمَة س ج /فُقَم/ seal

فَقيد س ج /فُقَداء/ deceased

فَقير ص ج /فُقَراء/ poor

فَكّ س ج /فُكوك/ jaw

فَكَّ ف to undo

فَكَّة س (فَكَّة النُقود) change

فَكَّرَ ف to think

فِكْر س thought

فِكْرَة س ج /أَفْكار/ idea
فِكْرَة خاطِئَة stereotype

فِكْرِيّ ص intellectual

فَكَّكَ ف to dismantle

فَلاّح س peasant

فِلاحَة س agriculture

فَلافِل س falafel

فِلِسْطين س Palestine

فِلِسْطينِيّ ص، س Palestinian

فَلْسَفَة س philosophy

فِلْفِل س pepper
فَلْفِل أَخْضَر green pepper
فِلْفِل حارّ chilli

فَلَك س orbit

فِلْم س ج /أَفْلام/ film

فِلّينَة س cork

فَم س ج /أَفْواه/ mouth

فَنّ س ج /فُنون/ art

فِناء س yard

فَنائِيَّة س mortality

فَنّان س artist

فِنْجان س ج /فَناجين/ cup

فَرْعِيّ ص sub divisional

فَرَّقَ ف to part

فَرْق س difference

فِرْقاطَة س frigate

فِرْقَة س ج /فِرَق/ team
فِرْقَة موسيقيَّة band

فَرَكَ ف to rub

فَرْمَة س (فَرْمَة لَحْمَة) mince

فُرْن س ج /أَفْران/ oven

فَرَنْسا س France

فَرَنْسِيّ ص French

فَرَنْسِيّ س Frenchman

فَرْو س fur

فَريد ص unique

فَريضَة س ج /فَرائِض/ religious obligation

فَريق س ج /فِرَق/ (فِرْقَة رِياضيَّة) team
(رُتْبَة عَسْكَريَّة) lieutenant general
فَريق أَوَّل(رُتْبَة عَسْكَريَّة) general

فَساد س corruption

فُسْتان س ج /فَساتين/ dress

فُسْتُق س peanut
فُسْتُق حَلَبِيّ pistachio

فَسَّرَ ف to interpret

فَسيح ص vast

فُشار س popcorn

فَشَخَ ف to stride

فَشَل س failure

فَشِلَ ف to fail

فَصَلَ ف (طَرَدَ) to dismiss
(فَرَّقَ الأَشْياء) to separate

فَصْل س ج /فُصول/ (فَتْرَة أَرْبَعَة أَشْهُر) season
(تَفْريق الأَشْياء) separation
(في كِتاب) chapter
فَصْل دِراسِيّ semester

فَصيل س ج /فَصائِل/ group

فَضَّ ف to dissolve

فَضاء س space

فِضَّة س silver

فَضَحَ ف to divulge

فَضْل س ج /أَفْضال/ merit

فَضَّلَ ف (اسْتَقْبَلَ شَخْصاً) to welcome
(قَدَّمَ الطَعام أَو الشَراب لِضَيْف) to offer
(اخْتارَ شَيْئاً لأَنَّهُ أَفْضَل مِن غَيْرِهِ) to prefer

فَضْلَة س residue

فُضول س curiosity

فُضوليّ ص curious

فَضيحَة س ج /فَضائِح/ scandal

فَضيلَة س virtue

فُطْر س (نَبات يَعيشُ عَلى نَباتات أُخْرى أَو مَرَض جِلْدِيّ) fungus
(نَوْع نَبات) mushroom

فِطْنَة س discretion

فَتْح س (احْتِلال بَلَد) conquest
(فَتْح شَيْء مِن غَيْر أَداة) opening
(فَتْح شَيْء بِأَداة) unlocking

فَتْحَة س (فَراغ) opening
(شَقّ في جِسْم لإِدْخال أَشْياء مِن خِلاله) slot

فَتْرَة س period

فَتَّشَ ف to inspect

فَتَقَ ف to rip

فَتَنَ ف to fascinate

فَجّ ص crude

فَجْأَةً ح suddenly

فَجْر س dawn

فَجَّرَ ف to explode

فِجْل س radish
فِجْل الجِرْجار horseradish

فَجْوَة س gap

فَحَسْب only

فَحْص س ج /فُحوص/ (اخْتِبار لا يَشْمَلُ المَهارات)
examination
(تَفَقُّد) check
(اخْتِبار مَهارات) test

فَحَصَ ف (تَفَقَّدَ) to check
(اخْتَبَرَ) to examine
(فَحَصَ عَن طَريق الأَشِعَّة) to scan
(اخْتَبَرَ المَهارات) to test

فَحْم س coal

فَخّ س ج /فِخاخ/ trap

فُخّار س pottery

فَخْذ (م) س ج /أَفْخاذ/ thigh
فَخْذ الخِنْزير ham

فَخْر س pride

فَخور ص proud

فِدائيّ س resistance fighter

فِدْراليّ ص federal

فَراشَة س butterfly

فَراغ س emptiness
فَراغ هَوائيّ vacuum

فَراوْلَة س strawberry

فَرْد س ج /أَفْراد/ individual

فَرْديّ ص single

فَرَزَ ف to sort

فَرَس س ج /أَفْراس/ mare

فُرْشاة س ج /فُرَش/ brush
فُرْشاة شَعَر س hairbrush

فَرْشى ف to brush

فُرْصَة س ج /فُرَص/ chance

فَرَضَ ف to impose

فَرْض س ج /فُروض/ (واجِب) obligation
(الإِجْبار بِالقوَّة) imposing

فَرْضيَّة س hypothesis

فَرْع س ج /فُروع/ (قِسْم مِن شَرِكَة يَعْمَلُ في مَكان مُخْتَلِف) branch
(قِسْم داخِل مُؤَسَّسَة) section

ف

ف

فِئَة س (نَوْع) category
class
(مَجْموعَة) group

فائِدَة س ج /فَوائِدُ/ (مَنْفَعَة) benefit
(رِبا) interest

فائِز س winner

فائِز ص winning

فائِض س surplus

فاتَ ف to pass

فاتِح ص ج /فَواتِح/ (خَفيف اللَّوْن) light
(مَفْتوح) open

فاتِن ص fascinating

فاتورَة س ج /فَواتير/ bill

فاجَأَ ف to surprise

فاجِع ص traumatic

فاجِعَة س ج /فَواجِع/ trauma

فاخِر ص classic

فادِح ص serious

فَأْر س ج /فِئْران/ mouse

فارِس س ج /فُرْسان/ knight

فارِغ ص empty

فارِق س ج /فَوارِق/ difference

فازَ ف to win

فَأْس (م) س ج /فُؤوس/ axe

فاسِد ص (ذو سُلوك سَيِّئ) corrupt
(غَيْر صالِح لِلاِسْتِعْمال) rotten

فاسِق س ج /فَسَقَة/ immoral

فاشِل ص failing

فاشِيّ ص fascist

فاصِل س ج /فَواصِل/ interval

فاصولِياء س bean
فاصولِياء مُجَفَّفَة haricot

فاقَ ف to exceed

فاكْس س fax

فاكِهَة س ج /فَواكِه/ fruit

فاوَضَ ف to negotiate

فِبْرايِر س (الشَهْر الثاني بِالتَقْويم المِصْريّ)
February

فَتاة س ج /فَتَيات/ young woman

فِتامين س vitamin

فَتَحَ ف (فَتَحَ شَيْئاً مِن غَيْر أَداة) to open
(فَتَحَ شَيْئاً بِأَداة) to unlock
(احْتَلَّ بَلَداً) to conquer

ف

غَوّاصَة س submarine

غِياب س absence

غِيار س change

غَيْب س unseen

غَيْبوبَة س (فُقْدان الوَعْي نَتيجَة إصابَة دِماغيَّة) coma

(فُقْدان الوَعْي المُؤَقَّت) unconsciousness

غَيْث س rain

غَيَّرَ ف to change

غَيْر أد ن un-, non-

تَفاصيل غَيْر مُهِمَّة unimportant details

مَوادّ غَيْر أساسيَّة non-essential materials

غَيْرَة س jealousy

غَيْمَة س ج /غُيوم/ cloud

غَيور ص jealous

western
westerly (باتِّجاه الغَرْب)
غَرْبيّ س (شَخْص يَعيش في الغَرْب) westerner
غَرَض س ج /أغْراض/ (هَدَف) aim
(شَيْء أو مادَّة) stuff
غَرَفَ ف to scoop
غُرْفَة س ج /غُرَف/ room
غُرْفَة النَوْم bedroom
غَرِقَ ف to drown
غُرَّة س ج /غُرَر/ fringe
غُروب س sunset
غُرور س vanity
غَريب ص ج /غُرَباء/ strange
غَريزَة س ج /غَرائِز/ instinct
غَزَلَ ف to spin
غَزْو س conquest
غَزا ف to invade
غَسّالَة س washing machine
غَسَلَ ف to wash
غَسَّلَ ف to wash
غَسيل س (المَلابِس المَغْسولَة) laundry
غَشَّ ف to cheat
غِشّ س cheating
غِشاء س ج /أغْشِيَة/ membrane
غُصْن س ج /أغْصان/ branch

غَضَّ ف to turn a blind eye
غَضَب س anger
غَضَب شَديد fury
غَضِبَ ف to be angry
غَطَّ ف to dip
غِطاء س ج /أغْطِيَة/ (غِطاء لأيّ شَيْء) cover
(غِطاء وِعاء) lid
غَطَسَ ف to dive
غَطّى ف to cover
غِلاف س ج /أغْلِفَة/ cover
غِلاف جَوّيّ atmosphere
غَلَط س ج /أغْلاط/ mistake
غَلَّطَ ف to make sb make a mistake
غَلْطَة س mistake
غَلَّقَ ف to seal
غَلَقَ ف to shut
غَلى ف to boil
غَلَيان س boiling
غَلْيون س ج /غَلايين/ pipe
غَمَرَ ف (غَطّى) to flood
(أفاضَ بِالمَشاعِر) overwhelm
غَمَزَ ف to wink
غُموض س mystery
غَنّى ف to sing
غَنيّ ص ج /أغْنِياء/ rich
غَوّاص س diver

غ

غ

غائِب ص absent

غائِم ص dull

غاب س jungle

غابَ ف (لَم يَحْضُر) to be absent
(اخْتَفى) to disappear
(أفَلَ) to set

غابَة س forest

غادِر ص treacherous

غادَرَ ف to leave

غار س cave

غارَ ف (هاجَمَ فَجْأة) to raid
(شَعَرَ بِالغَيْرَة) to feel jealous

غارَة س raid

غاز س gas

غازَلَ ف to flirt with

غاصَ ف to dive

غاضِب ص angry

غالِب ص dominant

غالِباً generally

غالٍ ص expensive

غامِض ص ambiguous

غامِق ص ج /غَوامِق/ dark

غايَة س aim

غُبار س ج /أغْبِرَة/ dust

غَبَّشَ ف to blur

غَبَش س blur

غَبيّ ص ج /أغْبِياء/ stupid

غَداً ظ tomorrow

غَداء س lunch

غَدّار ص treacherous

غُدَّة س ج /غُدَد/ gland

غِذاء س ج /أغْذِيَة/ diet

غِذائيّ ص nutritious

غُراب س ج /غِرْبان/ raven

غْرام س gram

غَرام س love

غَرامَة س fine

غَراميّ ص romantic

غَرَبَ ف to set

غَرْب س west

غَرْبيّ ص (مُتَعَلِّق بِالغَرْب كَطَعام، مَلْبَس، إلخ)

عُنْصُرِيّ ص racist

عُنْصُرِيَّة س racism

عُنْف س violence

عُنُق س ج /أَعْناق/ neck

عَنْكَبوت س ج /عَناكِب/ spider

عُنْوان س ج /عَناوين/ (مَكان الإقامَة) address
(الخَطّ الرَئيسيّ أَعْلى المَقال) headline
(اسْم الكِتاب أَو المَجَلَّة) title

عَنْوَنَ ف to address

عَنى ف to mean

عَنيد ص stubborn

عَنيف ص violent

عَهْد س ج /عُهود/ (فَتْرَة مُحَدَّدَة مِن الزَمان) era
(وَعْد) promise
(ميثاق) convention

عود س ج /عيدان/ (قَضيب خَشَبيّ) rod
(آلَة موسيقيَّة شَبيهَة بِالجيتارَة) lute
عود ثِقاب match

عَوَّدَ على ف to accustom to

عَوْدَة س return

عَوَّضَ ف to compensate

عِوَض س compensation

عِوَضاً عَن in replacement for

عَوْلَمَة س globalization

عِيادَة س clinic

عَيْب س ج /عُيوب/ (خَلَل) fault
(شَيْء مُخْجِل) shame

عيد س ج /أَعْياد/ holiday
عيد الفِصْح Easter
عيد الأَضْحى Eid al-Adha
عيد الفِطْر Eid al-Fitr
عيد الميلاد المَجيد Christmas
عيد الميلاد birthday

عَيْش س living

عَيْن (م) س ج /عُيون/ (وَسيلَة الرُؤْيا) eye
(نَبْع مِياه) spring

عَيَّنَ ف (وَظَّفَ) to appoint
(حَدَّدَ مَكاناً) pinpoint

عَيِّنَة س sample

ع

عُمانيّ ص، س Omani

عَمَّة س paternal aunt

عَمَدَ ف to resort to

عَمْداً ح deliberately

عُمْدَة س ج /عُمَد/ mayor

عُمْر س ج /أعْمار/ age

عَمَّرَ ف (بَنى وَطَوَّرَ) to build
(عاشَ لِفَتْرَة طَويلَة) to live long

عُمْق س ج /أعْماق/ depth

عَمَّقَ ف to deepen

عَمَل س ج /أعْمال/ (أعْمال التِجارَة) business
(فِعْل) deed
(مُمارَسَة نَشاط) function
(وَظيفَة) job

عَمِلَ ف (أدّى نَشاطاً) to do
(صَنَعَ) to make
(اشْتَغَلَ) to work

عُمْلَة س currency
عُمْلَة مَعْدِنيَّة coin

عَمَلِيّ ص practical

عَمَلِيَّة س (نَشاط أو أداء) operation
(سِلْسِلَة أحْداث) process

عَمود س ج /عِمْدان/ (جِسْم مُدَوَّر طَويل أو خَطّ عَاموديّ عَريض) column
(رَكيزَة وَدَعامَة لِبِناء) pillar
العَمود الفَقَرِيّ backbone

عَموديّ ص vertical

عُمولَة س commission

عُموم س generality

عُموماً generally

عُموميّ ص (شامِل لِلجَميع) general
(عامّ) public

عَميد س ج /عُمَداء/ brigadier

عَميق ص deep

عَميل س ج /عُمَلاء/ agent

عَن حج (تَدُلُّ عَلى المُجاوَزَة وَالانْتِقال) away from
ابْتَعَدْتُ عَن الخَطَر I went away from the danger.
(تَدُلُّ عَلى المَصْدَر) from
نُقِلَ عَن الرَئيس تَصْريحات announcements have been conveyed from the president
(تَدُلُّ عَلى مَوْضوع مُعَيَّن) about
تَحَدَّثوا عَن الاحْتِلال they spoke about the occupation
(تَدُلُّ عَلى تَمْثيل شَخْص مُعَيَّن) on behalf
حَضَرْتُ الاجْتِماع عَن المُدير I attended the meeting on behalf of the director.

عَناء س trouble

عِناق س hug

عِنايَة س care

عِنَب س grape

عِنْدَ ظ (بِالقُرْب مِن) by
(في مَكان) at

عُنْصُر س ج /عَناصِر/ element

ع

عِلاجيّ ص clinical

عَلاقَة س relation

عَلاّقَة س hanger

عَلاّقَة مَفاتيح key holder

عَلامَة س (عَلامَة مَدْرَسيَّة أَو إِشارَة) mark

(دَليل) sign

عَلانيَّة ح openly

عِلاوَة س (زِيادَة عَلى المَعاش) increment

عِلاوَةً moreover

عِلاوَةً على in addition to

عُلْبَة س ج /عُلَب/ packet

عِلَّة س ج /عِلَل/ (خَلَل) defect

(مَرَض) disease

عَلَّقَ ف (قالَ رَأْيَهُ حَوْلَ مَوْضوع) to comment

(رَبَطَ شَيْئاً مِن أَعْلاهُ أَو ثَبَّتَ شَيْئاً بِالحائِط) to hang

(أَوْقَفَ أَمْراً مُؤَقَّتاً) to suspend

عِلْكَة س ج /عِلَك/ gum

عَلَّلَ ف to explain

عَلَم س ج /أَعْلام/ (رايَة) flag

(إِنْسان مَشْهور) celebrity

عَلَّمَ ف (دَرَّس) to teach

(وَضَعَ عَلامَة) to mark

عَلِمَ ف to know

عِلْم س ج /عُلوم/ science

عِلْم الاقْتِصاد economics

عِلْم الأَدْيان theology

عِلْم البيئَة ecology

عِلْم النَفْس psychology

عِلْم الهَنْدَسَة geometry

عِلْم الأَحْياء biology

عِلْم الصناعَة technology

عِلْم النَحْو وَالصَرْف grammar

عَلْمانيّ ص secular

عَلْمانيَّة س secularism

عِلْميّ ص (مُتَعَلِّق بِالعُلوم الأَدَبيَّة) scholarly

(مُتَعَلِّق بِالعُلوم الطَبيعيَّة) scientific

عَلَنيّ ص public

عُلوّ س highness

عُلْويّ ص upper

عَلّى ف to raise

عَلى حج (تَدُلُّ عَلى مُلامَسَة أَعْلى الشَيْء) on

الكِتاب عَلى الطاوِلَة The book is on the table.

(تَدُلُّ عَلى مُلامَسَة جِسْم الشَيْء)

كَتَبَ عَلى اللَوْح He wrote on the board.

عَلَّقَ الصورَة عَلى الحائِط He hung the picture on the wall.

عَمّ س ج /أَعْمام/ paternal uncle

عَمَّ ف to prevail in

عِمارَة س (تَشْييد) architecture

(مَبْنى) building

عِمالَة س employment

عُمّاليّ ص labour

عِمامَة س ج /عَمائِم/ turban

عُمان س Oman

ع

عُضْو س ج /أَعْضاء/ (شَخْص أَو دَوْلَة إلخ)
member
(أَحَد أَجْهِزَة الجِسْم) organ
(ذَكَر الرَّجُل) penis
عُضْو مَجْلِس councillor

عُضْوِيّ ص organic

عُضْوِيَّة س membership

عَطاء س (عَرْض لِتَقْديم خِدْمَة مُقابِلَ مَبْلَغ مُعَيَّن) bid
(التَبَرُّع) donation

عِطْر س ج /عُطور/ scent

عَطَسَ ف to sneeze

عَطْشانُ ص ج /عِطاش/ thirsty

عَطْف س sympathy

عَطَّلَ ف to disrupt

عُطْلَة س ج /عُطَل/ holiday

عَظْمَة س ج /عِظام/ bone

عَظيم ص ج /عُظَماء/ great

عَفا عَن ف to pardon

عَفاف س chastity

عِفَّة س chastity

عِفْريت س ج /عَفاريت/ afreet

عَفْو س pardon

عَفَوِيّ ص spontaneous

عِقاب س punishment

عَقِبَ ظ after

عَقَبَة س obstacle

عَقْد س ج /عُقود/ (وَثيقَة) contract
(فَتْرَة عَشْر سَنَوات) decade
عَقْد إيجار lease
عِقْد necklace

عَقَّدَ ف to complicate

عَقَدَ ف (رَبَطَ) to tie
(أَجْرى اجْتِماعاً) to hold

عُقْدَة س ج / عُقَد/ (جِسْم صُلْب مُدَوَّر في عِرْق الشَجَرَة أَو رَبْطَة حَبْل) knot
(مُشْكِلَة عَقْلِيَّة) complex

عَقْل س ج /عُقول/ mind

عَقْلانِيّ ص rational

عَقْلِيّ ص intellectual

عَقْلِيَّة س mentality

عُقْم س infertility

عُقوبَة س penalty

عَقيد س ج /عُقَداء/ colonel

عَقيدَة س ج /عَقائِد/ creed

عُكّازَة س walking stick

عِكِر ص impure

عَكْس س reverse

عَكَسَ ف (عَكَسَ رَأْياً أَو صورَة) to reflect
(عَكَسَ اتِّجاه) to reverse

عَكْسِيّ ص reverse

عَلا ف to ascend

عِلاج س ج /عِلاجات/ (دَواء) remedy
(مُعالَجَة) treatment

عَرين س den

عَزا إلى ف to attribute to

عَزاء س condolence

عِزْبَة س ج /عِزَب/ estate

عَزَّزَ ف to enhance

عَزَفَ ف (أدّى مَعْزوفَة عَلى آلَة موسيقيَّة) to play
(هَجَر) to give up

عَزْف س playing music

عَزَلَ ف (أبْعَدَ) to isolate
(أقالَ) to dismiss

عَزْل س (إبْعاد) separation
(إقالَة) dismissal

عُزْلَة س isolation

عَزَمَ ف to resolve

عَزْم س resolution

عَزّى ف to condole

عَزيز ص ج /أعِزّاءُ/ dear

عَزيمَة س ج /عَزائِمُ/ firm will

عَسْكَريّ ص military

عَسْكَريّ س ج /عَساكِرُ/ military man

عَسَل س honey

عَسى ف may

عَسير ص challenging

عُشّ س ج /أعْشاش/ nest

عَشاء س dinner
العَشاء الأخير the last supper

عِشاء س night from two hours after sunset till midnight

عُشْب س ج /أعْشاب/ (عُشْب ضارّ) grass
(نَبات يُسْتَخْدَمُ كَدَواء) herb

عُشْر عد ج /أعْشار/ one tenth

عِشْرَة س companionship

عَشْرَة عد ج /عَشَرات/ ten

عِشْرون عد twenty

عِشْق س adoration

عَشِقَ ف to adore

عَشْوائيّ ص random

عَشيق س ج /عُشّاق/ lover

عَصا (م) س ج /عِصيّ/ stick

عِصابَة س gang

عَصَب س ج /أعْصاب/ nerve

عَصَبيّ ص nervous

عَصَرَ ف to squeeze

عَصْر س late afternoon
ج /عُصور/ age

عَصْريّ ص modern

عَصى ف to disobey

عَصيدَة س ج /عَصائِدُ/ porridge

عَصير س ج /عَصائِرُ/ juice
عَصير تُفّاح apple juice

عَضَلَة س muscle

عَضَليّ ص muscular

ع

عَديم ص lacking

عَذاب س torture

عَذَّبَ ف to torture

عَذْب ص sweet

عُذْر س ج /أعْذار/ excuse

عَذَرَ ف to excuse

عَذْراء ص virgin

عُذْرِيَّة س virginity

عِراق س (العِراق) Iraq

عِراقيّ ص، س Iraqi

عَرَّبَ ف to Arabize

عَرَبَة س carriage

عَرْبَدَ ف to bully

عَرْبون س deposit

عَرَبيّ ص، س ج /عَرَب/ Arab

عَرَبيَّة س (اللُغَة العَرَبيَّة) Arabic

عُرْس س ج /أعْراس/ wedding

عَرْض س (تَقْديم أو مَنْح شَيْء) offer
(إظْهار) show
(عَكْس طول) width

عَرَضَ ف (أظْهَرَ) to show
(قَدَّمَ أو مَنَحَ شَيْئاً) to offer

عَرَّضَ ف to widen

عَرَّفَ ف (قَدَّمَ شَخْصاً لِشَخْص آخَر) to introduce
(حَدَّدَ) to identify

عُرْف س ج /أعْراف/ custom
عُرْف الديك crest

عَرَفَ ف to know

عِرْفان بِالجَميل gratitude

عِرْق س ج /أعْراق/ (نَوْع مِن البَشَر) race
ج /عُروق/ (غُصْن) branch
(وِعاء دَمَويّ) vein
عِرْق النَسا sciatica

عَرَق س sweat

عَرِقَ ف to sweat

عَرْقَلَ ف (عَطَّلَ) to hinder
(قامَ بِعَمَل ضِدَّ القانون خِلالَ مُباراة) to foul

عَرْقَلَة س ج /عَراقيل/ (تَعْطيل) obstacle
(كَسْر القانون في مُباراة) foul

عِرْقيّ ص ethnic

عُروبَة س Arabism

عُرْوَة س ج /عُرى/ buttonhole

عَروس س ج /عَرائِس/ bride

عَروض س (ميزان الشِعْر) prosody

عُرْيان ص ج /عُراة/ naked

عَريس س ج /عِرْسان/ bridegroom

عَريض ص broad

عَريضَة س ج /عَرائِض/ petition

عَريف س ج /عُرَفاء/ (طالِب يَقومُ بِإدارَة الصَفّ في حال خُروج المُدَرِّس مِنْهُ) prefect
(رُتْبَة عَسْكَرِيَّة أعْلى مِن جُنْديّ) commissioned officer

ع

عَبَسَ ف to frown

عَبْقَرِيّ ص genius

عَبْقَرِيَّة س genius

عُبودِيَّة س slavery

عُبور س crossing

عَتّال س porter

عَتَبَة س threshold

عَتيق ص ج /عُتُق/ ancient

عَجَب س wonder

عَجَزَ ف to fail

عَجْز س (إعاقَة جَسَدِيَّة أو عَقْلِيَّة) disability
(عَدَم القُدْرَة عَلى فِعْل شَيْء) incapacity
عَجْز مالِيّ deficit

عِجْل س ج /عُجول/ calf

عَجَّلَ ف to accelerate

عَجَلَة س (سُرْعَة) hurry
(دولاب) wheel

عَجوز ص ج /عَجائِز/ old

عَجيب ص ج /عَجائِب/ wonderful

عَجين س ج /عَجائِن/ dough

عَدّ س count

عَدَّ ف to count

عَدا أ اس except

عَداء س hostility

عَدّاء س runner

عَدائِيّ ص hostile

عَدّاد س meter

عَدالَة س justice

عُدَّة س gear

عِدَّة س several

عَدَد س ج /أَعْداد/ digit

عَدَّدَ ف to enumerate

عَدَس س lentil

عَدَسَة س lens

عَدَّلَ ف (حَسَّنَ) to improve
(جَعَلَ مَعْدِناً أو أيّ جِسْم بِشَكْل مُسْتَوٍ) to straighten
(أَدْخَلَ تَعْديلات عَلى نَصّ) to amend
(بَدَّلَ لِلأَفْضَل) to change

عَدْل س justice

عَدَلَ ف to be fair

عَدَم non-, un-, in-
عَدَم الوَعْي unconsciousness
عَدَم الدِقَّة inaccuracy
عَدَم الحُضور non-attendance

عَدوّ س ج /أَعْداء/ enemy

عَدْو س running

عُدْوان س aggression

عُدْوانِيّ ص aggressive

عَدْوى س infection

عَديد ص numerous

عاقِل ص ج /عُقَلاء/ rational

عال ص (تُسْتَخْدَمُ لِعُلُوّ الأشْياء) high
(تُسْتَخْدَمُ لِحَجْم الصَوْت) loud

عالَجَ ف (تَخَلَّصَ مِن مُشْكِلَة) to handle
(داوى مَريضاً) to treat

عالَم س world

عالِم س ج /عُلَماء/ (عالِم في العُلوم الأدَبيَّة) scholar
(عالِم في العُلوم الطَبيعيَّة) scientist

عالَمِيّ ص global

عامّ ص (مَعْلوم لَدى العامَّة) general
(مُسْتَخْدَم مِن قِبَل العامَّة) public

عام س ج /أعْوام/ year

عامَ ف to float

عامِل س ج /عَوامِل/ (مَبْدأ) factor
ج /عُمّال/ (شَغّيل) labourer
عامِل مَنْجَم miner

عامَلَ ف (عالَجَ) to treat
(تَعامَلَ) to deal with

عامود س ج /أعْمِدَة/ (عامود الرُخام أو الحَجَر) column
(عامود الكَهْرَباء) post
(عامود رَكيزَة) pillar
(مَقال دائِم في جَريدَة أو مَجَلَّة) column

عاموديّ ص vertical

عامِّيَّة س slang

عانِس ص ج /عَوانِس/ spinster

عانَقَ ف to hug

عانى ف to suffer

عاهَة س infirmity

عاهَدَ ف to pledge

عاهِر س ج /عُهَّر/ adulterer

عاهِرَة س adulteress

عاهِل س ج /عَواهِل/ king

عاوَنَ ف to assist

عايَنَ ف to view

عِبْء س ج /أعْباء/ burden

عَباءَة س (قِطْعَة لِباس طَويلَة يَرْتَديها القُضاة أو النِساء في المُناسَبات) gown
ج /عَباءات/(قِطْعَة لِباس طَويلَة يَرْتَديها الرِجال والنِساء العَرَب) abaya

عِبادَة س worship

عِبارَة س phrase

عَبّارَة س ferry

عَبَّأَ ف to fill

عَبَثاً ح in vain

عَبْد س ج /عَبيد/ slave

عَبَدَ ف to worship

عَبَّدَ ف (رَصَفَ) to pave

عَبْرَ ظ (عَلى طول) across
(بِواسِطَة أو مِن خِلال) via

عَبَرَ ف to cross

عَبَّرَ عَن ف to express

عِبْرِيَّة س (العِبْرِيَّة) Hebrew

ع

ع

عائِد ص return

عائِد س ج /عَوائِد/ income

عائِق س ج /عَوائِق/ obstacle

عائِلَة س family

عابِد ص worshipper

عابِر ص passing

عابِر لِلقارّات intercontinental

عاتَبَ ف to reprimand

عاتِق س ج /عَواتِق/ shoulder

عاجِز ص ج /عَجَزَة/ (مُقْعَد) disabled

ج /عَواجِز/ (غَيْر قادِر) incapable

عاجِل ص urgent

عادَ ف to return

عادَة س (سُلوك مُعْتاد بَيْنَ الناس) custom

(سُلوك يُمارِسُهُ شَخْص بِاسْتِمْرار) habit

عادِل ص fair

عادَلَ ف (ساوى) to equal

(أَحْرَزَ نَفْس نِقاط الخَصْم في مُباراة) to draw

عادِيّ ص (طَبيعِيّ) normal

(كَالمُعْتاد) ordinary

عارٍ ص bare

عار س shame

عارِض ص accidental

عارَضَ ف to oppose

عارِضَة س ج /عَوارِض/ (قِطْعَة خَشَبِيَّة أَو حَديدِيَّة طَويلَة) bar

ج /عارِضات/ (عارِضَة أَزْياء) model

عارِضَة الهَدَف crossbar

عارَكَ ف to fight

عارِم ص violent

عازِب ص ج /عُزّاب/ single

عاشَ ف to live

عاشَرَ ف to associate with

عاشِق ص ج /عُشّاق/ in love

عاصِفَة س ج /عَواصِف/ storm

عاصِمَة س ج /عَواصِم/ capital

عاطِفَة س ج /عَواطِف/ emotion

عاطِل ص (سَيِّئ) bad

عاطِل عَن العَمَل unemployed

عاقَبَ ف to punish

عاقِبَة س ج /عَواقِب/ consequence

عاقِر ص ج /عُقَّر/ ج م/عَواقِر/ barren

ظ

ظالِم ص unfair

ظاهِر س apparent

ظاهِرَة س ج /ظَواهِر/ (حَقيقَة أَو حَدَث في مُجْتَمَع خاصَّة أَنَّها غَيْر مَفْهومَة جَيِّداً) phenomenon
(دَلالَة عَلى تَغَيُّر في شَيْء ما) symptom

ظَرافَة س wit

ظَرْف س ج /ظُروف/ (عَبْوَة رِسالَة أَو غِلاف) envelope
(وَضْع مُعَيَّن) circumstance

ظَريف ص ج /ظُرَفاء/ (لَطيف المُعامَلَة) kind
(ذو حِسّ دُعابَة) witty

ظُفْر س ج /أَظافِر/ nail

ظِلّ س ج /ظِلال/ shade

ظَلَّ ف to remain

ظَلام س darkness

ظُلْم س injustice

ظَلَمَ ف to wrong

ظُلْمَة س darkness

ظَمْآن ص thirsty

ظَنَّ ف (تَوَقَّع) to guess
(اعْتَقَد) to think

ظَنّ س ج /ظُنون/ doubt

ظُهْر س noon

ظَهْر س ج /ظُهور/ back

ظَهَرَ ف to appear

طُفولَة س childhood

طَفيف ص slight

طَقْس س ج /طُقوس/ (حالَة الجَوّ) weather
(شَعيرَة) ritual

طَقْطَقَ ف to crack

طَقْطَقَة crack

طَقْم س ج /أَطْقِمَة/ kit

طِلاء س paint

طَلاق س divorce

طَلَب س demand
تَقَدُّم بِطَلَب application

طَلَبَ ف to ask for

طَلَبِيَّة س order

طَلَّقَ ف to divorce

طَلْقَة س (إطْلاق رَصاصَة أو صَوْتُهُ) shot
(رَصاصَة) bullet

طَليعَة س ج /طَلائِع/ forefront

طَليق ص ج /طُلَقاء/ loose

طَمْأَنَ ف to reassure

طُمَأْنينَة س serenity

طَمَحَ إلى ف to aspire to

طُموح س ambition

طَموح ص ambitious

طُنّ س ج /أَطْنان/ ton

طَهى ف to cook

طَوارِئ س emergency

طِوالَ ظ all during

طَوَّرَ ف to develop

طَوْعِيّ ص voluntary

طَوْق س ج /أَطْواق/ collar
طَوْق شَعَر hair band

طَوَّقَ ف to surround

طول س (ارْتِفاع الشَخْص) height
(مَدى بُعْد المَسافَة) length

طَوَّلَ ف to prolong

طولَ ظ all during

طونا س tuna

طَوى ف to fold

طَوِيَّة س fold

طَويل ص (ذو مَسافَة طَويلَة) long
(ذو ارْتِفاع عالٍ) tall

طَيّار س pilot

طَيِّب ص good

طَيْر س ج /طُيور/ bird

طَيَّرَ ف to fly

طَيَران س aviation

طين س clay

طَبْعَة س (نُسْخَة من كِتاب أو مَجَلَّة) edition
(كَلام أو رَسْمَة مَطْبوعَة) stamp

طَبَق س ج /أَطْباق/ dish

طَبَّقَ ف to apply

طِبْقاً ل in accordance with

طَبَقَة س layer

طَبْلَة س drum

طِبِّي ص medical

طَبيب س ج /أَطِبّاء/ doctor
طَبيب اسْتِشارِيّ consultant
طَبيب أَسْنان dentist
طَبيب عامّ general practitioner
طَبيب نَفْسانِيّ psychiatrist
طَبيب أَطْفال paediatrician
طَبيب بَيْطَرِيّ vet

طَبيخ س ج /طَبائِخ/ broth

طَبيعَة س nature

طَبيعِيّ ص natural

طَحّان س miller

طَحَنَ ف to grind

طَحين س flour

طَحينَة س tahini

طِراز س type

طَرْبوش س ج /طَرابيش/ tarbush

طَرَحَ ف (أَنْزَلَ بِضاعَةَ في الأَسْواق أو نَحْوَهُ) to launch
(قَدَّمَ) to introduce

طَرْح س ج /طُروح/ offer

طَرْد س ج /طُرود/ (مادَّة مُرْسَلَة بِالبَريد) package
(إِنْهاء وَظيفَة أَو عَلاقَة شَخْص بِمُؤَسَّسَة) dismissal

طَرَدَ ف (أَنْهى عَمَل شَخْص) to dismiss
(أَخْرَجَ شَخْصاً إلى الخارِج) to kick out

طَرَّزَ ف to embroider

طَرَف س ج /أَطْراف/ (أَحَد أَطْراف الجِسْم) limb
(فَريق) party
(جانِب) side

طَرَفَ ف to blink

طَرَقَ ف to knock

طَرْق س knocking

طَرْقَة س knock

طَرّى ف to soften

طَرِيّ ص tender

طَريق س ج /طُرُق/ road

طَريقَة س ج /طُرُق/ way

طَعام س ج /أَطْعِمَة/ food

طُعْم س ج /طُعومات/ (قِطْعَة طَعام تُسْتَخْدَمُ لِجَذْب الفَريسَة) bait
(مادَّة تُعْطى لِلإِنْسان لِحِمايَتِه مِن الأَمْراض) vaccine

طَعَنَ ف to stab

طَعْنَة س stab

طَفا ف to float

طَفِقَ ف to begin

طِفْل س ج /أَطْفال/ child

ط

طائِر س ج /طُيور/ bird

طائِر ص (قادِر عَلى الطَيَران) flying

طائِرَة س plane

طائِرَة عَموديَّة helicopter

طائِرَة نَفّاثَة jet plane

طائِرَة شِراعيَّة glider

طائِرَة مَدَنيَّة civil plane

طائِرَة مُقاتِلَة warplane

طائِفَة س ج /طَوائِف/ sect

طابِع س ج /طَوابِع/ (مُلْصَق) stamp

ج /طِباع/ (صِفَة في الإنْسان) character

طابِعَة س printer

طابِق س ج /طَوابِق/ floor

طابِق سُفْليّ downstairs

طابِق عُلْويّ upstairs

طابور س ج /طَوابير/ queue

طارَ ف to fly

طارِئ ص urgent

طارَدَ ف to chase

طازِج ص fresh

طاشَ ف to float

طاعون س plague

طاقَة س (حَيَويَّة) energy

(قوَّة) power

طاقِم س ج /طَواقِم/ crew

طالِب س ج /طُلاّب, طَلَبَة/ student

طالَبَ ف (طَلَبَ إعادَة حَقّ لَهُ) to claim

(طَلَبَ تَنْفيذ أَمْر بِحَزْم) to demand

طالَما ظ (ما دامَ) as long as

(مُنْذُ وَقْت طَويل) for a long time

طاهٍ س ج /طُهاة/ cook

طاهِر ص pure

طاوِلَة س table

طاووس س ج /طَواويس/ peacock

طاويّ ص، س Taoist

طاويَّة س Taoism

طِبّ س medicine

طِباعَة س printing

طَبّال س drummer

طَبَعَ ف (اسْتَخْدَمَ لَوْحَة مَفاتيح الحاسوب لِلكِتابَة) to type

(أَعْطى أَمْراً لِلآلَة بِالطَبْع أَو أَنْتَجَ مَطْبوعَة) to print

طَبْع س (إِنْتاج أَعْمال مَطْبوعَة) printing

ج /طِباع/ (صِفَة في الشَخْصيَّة) trait

طَبْعاً of course

ضَعُفَ ف to weaken

ضَعَّفَ ف to intensify

ضَعيف ص ج /ضُعَفاء/ weak

ضَغْط س ج /ضُغوط/ pressure

ضَغَطَ ف to press

ضَفَّة س ج /ضِفاف/ bank

ضِفْدَع س ج /ضَفادِع/ frog

ضِلْع س ج /أَضْلاع/ (إِحْدى عِظام القَفَص الصَدْرِيّ)
rib
(فَرْع شَجَرَة) branch

ضَلَّلَ ف to mislead

ضَمَّ ف to include

ضِمادَة س pad

ضَمان س guarantee

ضَمَّدَ ف to dress

ضَمِنَ ف to guarantee

ضِمْنَ ظ within

ضَمير س ج /ضَمائِر/ conscience

ضَوْء س ج /أَضْواء/ light
ضَوْء النَهار daylight
ضَوْء الشَمْس sunlight
ضَوْء خافت dim
ضَوْء ساطِع glare
ضَوْء كَشّاف spotlight

ضَوْضاء س noise

ضِيافَة س hospitality

ضَيَّعَ ف (أَنْفَقَ مِن غَيْر فائِدَة) to waste
(فَقَدَ) to lose

ضَيْعَة س ج /ضِياع/ village

ضَيْف س ج /ضُيوف/ guest

ضَيِّق ص (رَفيع المَسافَة) narrow
(مَشْدود) tight

ضَيَّقَ ف to tighten

ض

ضَئيل ص small

ضائِقَة س hardship

ضابِط س ج /ضُبّاط/ officer

ضاجّ ص noisy

ضاحِيَة س ج /ضَواحٍ/ suburb

ضارّ ص harmful

ضارَبَ ف to undercut

ضاعَ ف to be lost

ضاعَفَ ف to multiply

ضاهى ف to match

ضايَقَ ف to annoy

ضَبَّ ف (أعادَ الشَيْء إلى مَكانِهِ) to take back to

(خَبَّأَ) to hide

ضَباب س fog

ضَبَطَ ف (سَيْطَرَ عَلى) to restrain

(مَسَكَ) to catch

(جَعَلَ شَيْئاً يَعْمَلُ بِشَكْل مُنْتَظِم) to adjust

ضَبْط س (السَيْطَرَة عَلى الأُمور) restraint

(جَعْل شَيْء يَعْمَلُ بِشَكْل مُنْتَظِم) adjustment

(الإمْساك) catch

ضَبُع س ج /ضِباع/ hyena

ضَجيج س noise

ضَحِكَ ف to laugh

ضَحِك س laugh

ضَحْل ص shallow

ضَحّى ف to sacrifice

ضَحِيَّة س ج /ضَحايا/ victim

ضَخَّ ف to pump

ضَخْم ص ج /ضِخام/ huge

ضَخَّمَ ف to amplify

ضِدَّ against

ضَرَبَ ف to beat

ضَرْبَة س ج /ضَرَبات/ blow

ضَرْبَة جَزاء penalty kick

ضَرْبَة تَماسّ throw-in

ضَرْبَة حُرَّة free kick

ضَرْبَة رَأْس header

ضَرْبَة مَرْمى goal kick

ضَرَبات تَرْجيحيَّة penalty shoot-out

ضَرَر س ج /أضْرار/ damage

ضَرورَة س necessity

ضَروريّ ص necessary

ضَريبَة س ج /ضَرائِب/ tax

ضُعْف س weakness

ض

صَمْغ س ج /أَصْماغ/ gum

صَمَّمَ ف (رَسَمَ أو أَعَدَّ شَكْلاً) to design
(أَقَرَّ بِحَزْم على عَمَل شَيْء) to insist

صُمود س steadfastness

صِناعَة س industry

صِناعِيّ ص industrial

صُنْدوق س ج /صَناديق/ box
صُنْدوق اسْتِثْمار unit trust
صُنْدوق السَيّارَة boot

صَنَعَ ف to make

صُنْع س (اخْتِلاق وَتَدْبير أَمْر) fabrication
(إِنْتاج مُنْتَج) production

صِنْف س ج /أَصْناف/ brand

صَنَّفَ ف to classify

صَنَم س ج /أَصْنام/ idol

صَنَوْبَر س pine

صِهْر س son-in-law

صَهْيونِيّ ص Zionist

صَهْيونِيَّة س Zionism

صَوْت س ج /أَصْوات/ (صَوْت مُزْعِج) noise
(أَيّ صَوْت صادِر مِن غَيْر الإِنْسان) sound
(صَوْت الإِنْسان) voice
(صَوْت انْتِخابِيّ) vote

صَوَّتَ ف to vote

صَوْتِيّ ص vocal

صَوَّرَ ف (شَرَحَ أَمْراً بِاسْتِخْدام الصُوَر)
to portray
(سَجَّلَ مَقاطِع مِن فِلْم) to film
(الْتَقَطَ صُوَراً فوتوغْرافِيَّة) to photograph

صورَة س ج /صُوَر/ (تَصَوُّر) image
(صورَة مَطْبوعَة) picture

صوص س ج /صيصان/ chick

صوف س ج /أَصْواف/ wool

صَوْم س fast

صومال س (الصومال) Somalia

صومالِيّ ص، س Somali

صَيّاد س hunter
صَيّاد السَمَك fisherman

صِياغَة س formulation

صِيانَة س maintenance

صَيْحَة س shout

صَيْد س hunt

صَيْدَلانِيّ س ج /صَيادِلَة/ pharmacist

صَيْدَلِيَّة س pharmacy

صيغَة س ج /صِيَغ/ formula

صَيْف س summer

صَيَّفَ في ف to spend the summer in

صين س (الصين) China

صينِيّ ص، س Chinese

to spend (أَنْفَقَ)
to dismiss (طَرَدَ)
صَرَّفَ ف (بَدَّلَ عُمْلَة بِعُمْلَة أُخْرى) to exchange
to arrange (دَبَّرَ)
صَرِيح ص (يَقولُ رَأْيَهُ دونَ تَحَفُّظ) frank
clear (واضِح)
صَعْب ص difficult
صَعُبَ ف to become difficult
صَعَّبَ ف to harden
صَعَدَ ف to rise
صَعَّدَ ف to escalate
صُعوبَة س difficulty
صُعود س rise
صَعِيد س ج /أَصْعِدَة/ level
صَغِير ص ج /صِغار/ small
صَغِير س ج /صِغار/ child
صَفّ س ج /صُفوف/ row
غُرْفَة الصَفّ classroom
صَفاء س purity
صُفَّارَة س ج /صَفافير/ whistle
صِفَة س attribute
صَفْحَة س page
الصَفْحَة الرَئيسيَّة home page
صِفْر س ج /أَصْفار/ zero
صَفَر س (الشَهْر الثاني بِالتَقْويم الإِسْلاميّ) Safar
صَفَعَ ف to slap

صَفْعَة س slap
صَفَّقَ ف to clap
صَفْقَة س deal
صَفَّى ف (أَزالَ الشَوائِب) to filter
to close down (أَنْهى أَعْمالَهُ)
to end (أَنْهى)
صَقْر س ج /صُقور/ hawk
صَلاة س ج /صَلَوات/ prayer
صَلاة الجُمْعَة the Friday prayer
صَلاة الأَحَد Sunday service
صَلاحيَّة س (كَوْن الشَيْء صالِحاً) validity
(الحَقّ وَالقُدْرَة عَلى القِيام بِأَعْمال مُعَيَّنَة)
authority
صُلْب ص (شَيْء غَيْر قابِل لِلمُرونَة) hard
(شَخْص غَيْر مَرِن) inflexible
صَلْب س crucifixion
صَلَبَ ف crucify
صُلْب س steel
صِلَة س relevance
صَلَّحَ ف (أَزالَ خَراباً أَو عُطْلاً) to fix
(عَدَّلَ الأَخْطاء الكِتابيَّة وَالشَفَويَّة) to correct
صُلْح س reconciliation
صَلْصَة س sauce
صَلّى ف to perform the prayer
صَلِيب س ج /صُلْبان/ cross
صِمام س valve
صَمْت س silence

ص

صَحّ ف to be correct

صَحافَة س press

صَحِبَ ف to accompany

صُحْبَة س company

صِحَّة س health

صَحَّحَ ف (أزالَ الخَطَأ وَبَيَّنَ الصَواب) to correct
(فَحَصَ وَرَقَة امْتِحان وَقَدَّرَ العَلامَة) to mark

صَحْراء س ج /صَحارٍ/ desert

صُحُفِيّ س journalist

صَحْن س ج /صُحون/ dish

صَحيح ص (صائِب) correct
(كامِل) whole

صَحيفَة س ج /صُحُف/ newspaper

صَخْرَة س rock

صَخْرِيّ ص rocky

صَدارَة س top

صُداع س headache

صَداق س dowry

صَداقَة س friendship

صَدَأَ ف to corrode

صَدَأ س rust

صَدَد: في صَدَد ظ concerning

صَدْر س ج /صُدور/ (نَهْدَي المَرْأة) bust
(المِنْطَقَة أعْلى البَدَن) chest

صَدَرَ ف to be published

صَدَّرَ ف to export

صَدْرِيَّة س bra

صَدْع س fault

صُدْفَة س ج /صُدَف/ chance

صَدَفَة س shell

صِدْق س honesty

صَدَّقَ ف to believe

صَدَقَ ف to speak the truth

صَدَقَة س charity

صَدَمَ ف to collide
(رَطَمَ) to hit
(فاجَأ بِخَبَر غَيْر مُتَوَقَّع) to shock

صَدْمَة س shock

صُدور س (نَشْر) publication
(التَصْريح بِأمْر) coming out

صَدى س ج /أصْداء/ (ارْتِداد الصَوْت) echo
(التَأْثير) effect

صَديق س ج /أصْدِقاء/ friend

صَراحَة س frankness

صِراخ س scream

صِراع س conflict

صُرَّة س ج /صُرَر/ navel

صَرَّحَ ف to announce

صَرَخَ ف to scream

صَرْخَة س scream

صَرَفَ ف (بَدَّلَ شيكاً بِالمال) to cash

ص

ص

صائِب ص right

صائِم س one who is fasting

صابِر ص patient

صابونَة س ج /صَوابين/ soap

صاحَ ف to shout

صاحِب س companion

صاحَبَ ف to accompany

صاخِب ص noisy

صادَ ف to hunt

صادَرَ ف to confiscate

صادِر ص published

صادِرات س export

صادِق ص honest

صادَقَ ف (اتَّخَذَ صَديقاً) to befriend

صادَقَ على ف (اعْتَمَدَ أَو أَكَّدَ على صِحَّة أَمْر) to approve

صارَ ف to become

صارٍ س ج /صَوارٍ/ mast

صارَعَ ف (كافَحَ أَو واجَهَ ظُروفاً صَعْبَة لِلتَخَلُّص مِن ضيق) to struggle
(مارَسَ لُعْبَة المُصارَعَة) to wrestle

صارِم ص strict

صاروخ س ج /صَواريخ/ missile

صاغَ ف to formulate
صاغَ مُسْوَدَّةً to draft

صافٍ ص pure

صالَة س hall

صالَحَ ف to reconcile

صالِح ص suitable

صالون س salon

صامَ ف to fast

صامِت ص silent

صامِد ص steadfast

صانِع س ج /صُنّاع/ maker

صَبَّ ف to pour

صَباح س morning

صَبْر س patience

صَبَرَ ف to be patient

صِبْغَة س dye

صَبور ص patient

صَبِيّ س ج /صِبْيان/ boy

شَهيد س ج /شُهَداء/ martyr

شَهير ص famous

شَهيق س gasp

شَوّال س (الشَهْر العاشِر بِالتَقْويم الإسْلاميّ) Shawwal

شَوْط س ج /أَشْواط/ (أَحَد أَجْزاء مُباراة كُرَة القَدَم) half

(جُزْء مِن مُباراة أو لُعْبَة) round

شوفان س oats

شَوْكَة س ج /شِوَك/ (أداة تُسْتَخْدَمُ في الأَكْل) fork

ج /شَوْك/ (عُضْو حادّ وَصَغير جِدّاً يَكونُ عَلى أَغْصان بَعْض النَباتات) thorn

شوكولاتَة س chocolate

شَيْء س thing

شَيْخ س ج /شُيوخ/ (كَبير السِنّ) old man

(لَقَب يُطْلَقُ عَلى رَجُل مُتَدَيِّن أَو عَلى أَحَد أَعْضاء العائِلَة المالِكَة في بَعْض الدُوَل العَرَبِيَّة) sheikh

شَيَّدَ ف to erect

شَيْطان س ج /شَياطين/ the Devil

شَيَّعَ ف to accompany

شيعيّ س Shiite

شيك س cheque

شُيوعيّ ص communist

شُيوعِيَّة س communism

ش

شُغْل س ج /أشْغال/ work

شِفاء س recovery

شَفّاف ص transparent

شَفَة س ج /شِفاه/ lip

شَفَقَة س pity

شَفَهِيّ ص oral

شَفَوِيّ ص verbal

شَفَى ف to heal

شَقّ س ج /شُقوق/ crack

شَقَّ ف to split

شِقَّة س ج /شِقَق/ flat

شَقيق س ج /أشِقّاء/ half-brother

شَقيقَة س half-sister

شَكّ س ج /شُكوك/ doubt

شَكَّ ف to doubt

شَكَرَ ف to thank

شَكْل س ج /أشْكال/ figure

شَكَّلَ ف (مَثَّلَ أو كَوَّنَ) to constitute
(كَوَّنَ شَكْلاً مُعَيَّناً أو مَثَّلَ شَيْئاً) to form

شَكْلِيّ ص formal

شَكْوى س ج /شَكاوى/ complaint

شَلْحَة س slip

شَمَّ ف to smell

شِمال س ج /شَمائِل/ left

شَمال س north

شَماليّ ص (مُتَعَلِّق بِالشَمال كَطَعام، مَلْبَس، إلخ)
northern
(بِاتِّجاه الشَمال) northerly

شَماليّ س (شَخْص يَعيشُ في الشَمال)
northerner

شُمامَة س ج /شُمام/ melon

شَمْس (م) س ج /شُموس/ sun

شَمْعَة س ج /شَمَعات/ (تُسْتَخْدَمُ لِلإنارَة) candle
ج /شُمَع/ (عَمود) pillar

شَمْعَدان س ج /شَمْعَدانات/ (قاعِدَة لِعِدَّة شَمَعات)
manorah
(قاعِدَة لِشَمْعَة واحِدَة) candlestick

شَمِلَ ف to include

شَمَنْدَر س beetroot
شَمَنْدَر السُكَّر sugar beet

شَنَّ ف to launch

شَهادَة س (وَثيقَة رَسْميَّة) certificate
(الإدْلاء بِمَعْلومات أمامَ المَحْكَمَة) testimony
(المَوْت في سَبيل الله) martyrdom
شَهادَة التَأْمين policy

شَهِدَ ف (أدْلى بِما يَعْلَمُ عَن أَمْر أو حَدَث) to testify
(عاشَ الحَدَث) to be present at

شَهْر س ج /أَشْهُر/ month

شُهْرَة س fame

شَهِقَ ف to gasp

شَهْوَة س (الرَغْبَة بِمُمارَسَة الجِنْس أو امْتِلاك شَيْء)
desire

شَهيَّة س appetite

شَرَف س honour

شَرَّفَ ف to honour

شُرْفَة س ج /شُرَف/ balcony

شَرْق س east

الشَرْق الأَقْصى Far East

الشَرْق الأَوْسَط Middle East

شَرْقيّ ص (مُتَعَلِّق بِالشَرْق كَطَعام، مَلْبَس، إلخ) eastern

(بِاتِّجاه الشَرْق) easterly

شَرْقيّ س easterner

شِرْك س (خَديعَة أو مِصْيَدَة) trap

(الإيمان بِأَكْثَر مِن إله) polytheism

شَرِكَة س company

شَرِكَة طَيَران airline

شِرْيان س ج /شَرايين/ artery

شَريحَة س ج /شَرائِح/ (قِطْعَة رَقيقَة) slice

(كَرْت التَعْريف في الهاتِف الخَلَويّ) chip

(مَجْموعَة) group

(شَريحَة لَحْم) steak

شِرّير ص ج /أَشْرار/ evil

شَريط س ج /أَشْرِطَة/ (حَبْل لاصِق شَفّاف مِن القِماش أو البْلاسْتِك) Sellotape®, Scotch tape®

(قِطْعَة قِماش رَفيعَة وَطَويلَة تُسْتَخْدَمُ لِلرَبْط وَالزينَة) ribbon

(شَريط لِتَسْجيل الصَوْت) tape

شَريعَة س ج /شَرائِع/ law

شَريف ص ج /شُرَفاء/ noble

شَريك س ج /شُرَكاء/ partner

شَطْبَة س scar

شَطَرَ ف to split

شَطَرَنْج س chess

شَطيرَة س ج /شَطائِر/ sandwich

شِعار س (كَلام أو صورَة مَطْبوعَة تُمَثِّلُ مُؤَسَّسَة أو شَرِكَة) logo

(كَلِمَة أو جُمْلَة مَشْهورَة يُرَدِّدُها سِياسيّ) slogan

(كَلِمات تُمَثِّلُ سِياسَة مُؤَسَّسَة أو حِزْب) motto

شُعاع س ج /أَشِعَّة/ ray

شَعْب س ج /شُعوب/ people

شَعْبان س (الشَهْر الثامِن بِالتَقْويم الإِسْلاميّ) Shaban

شَعْبيّ ص popular

شِعْر س ج /أَشْعار/ poetry

شَعَرَ ف to feel

شَعْرَة س ج /شَعَر/ strand of hair

شُعْلَة س ج /شُعَل/ torch

شُعور س feeling

شَعير س barley

شَعيرَة س ج /شَعائِر/ rite

شَغَب س riot

شَغَف س love

شَغَّلَ ف (أَدارَ ماكينَة أو مَرْكَبَة) to operate

(اسْتَخْدَمَ عُمّالاً) to employ

شَغَلَ ف to occupy

ش

شَتَمَ ف to curse

شَتّى ص (مُخْتَلِف) different

(مُتَنَوِّع) various

شَتّى ف to spend the winter in

شِجار س fight

شُجاع ص ج /شُجْعان/ brave

شَجاعَة س bravery

شَجَبَ ف to denounce

شَجَرَة س ج /شَجَر/ tree

شَجَّعَ ف to encourage

شُجَيْرَة س bush

شَحَتَ ف to beg

شَحَنَ ف (عبَّأ جِهازاً كَهْرَبائيّاً بِالكَهْرَباء) to charge

(أَرْسَلَ بِضاعَة بِأَيَّة وَسيلَة نَقْل) to ship

شَحْن س (عَمَليَّة إرْسال البَضائِع) shipment

(عَمَليَّة تَعْبِئَة جِهاز بِالكَهْرَباء) charging

شُحْنَة س (البِضاعَة المُرْسَلَة) shipment

(الكَمّيَّة الَّتي تَمَّ تَخْزينُها في جِهاز كَهْرَبائيّ) charge

شَخْص س ج /أَشْخاص/ person

شَخَّصَ ف to diagnose

شَخْصيّ ص personal

شَخْصيَّة س character

شَدَّ ف (ضَيَّقَ) to tighten

(سَحَبَ فَجْأَة وبِقوَّة) to pull

شِدَّة س toughness

شَدَّة س playing cards

شَدَّدَ على ف to stress

شَديد ص (قاسٍ) acute

(صارِم) tough

شِراء س purchase

شَرارَة س ج /شَرار/ spark

شِراع س ج /أَشْرِعَة/ sail

شَراكَة س partnership

شَرِبَ ف to drink

شَرَحَ ف to explain

شَرْح س ج /شُروح/ explanation

شَرْط س ج /شُروط/ (شَيْء يَجِبُ أَنْ يَتَوَفَّرَ مِن أَجْل تَحْقيق شَيْء آخَر) condition

ج /أَشْراط/(جُرْح أَو قَطْع) slash

شَرَطَ ف to slash

شَرَّطَ ف to stipulate a condition

شَرْطَة س dash

شُرْطَة س police

شُرْطيّ س ج /رِجال شُرْطَة/ policeman

شُرْطيَّة س policewoman

شَرَعَ ف to start

شَرْع س (الشَرْع) law

شَرَّعَ ف to legislate

شَرْعيّ ص legal

ش

ش

شاءَ ف to wish

شائِع ص common

شابّ س ج /شُبّان/ young man

شابَهَ ف to resemble

شاحِب ص pale

شاحِنَة س lorry

شاحِنَة صَغيرَة van

شاذّ س ج /شَواذّ/ odd

شاذّ جِنْسيّاً homosexual

شارِب س ج /شَوارِب/ moustache

شارَة س badge

شارِع س ج /شَوارِع/ street

شارَكَ ف to participate

شاشَة س screen

شاطِئ س ج /شَواطِئ/ beach

شاعِر س ج /شُعَراء/ poet

شاغِر ص ج /شَواغِر/ vacant

شاقّ ص difficult

شاكِر ص thankful

شال س cloak

شامْبانْيا س champagne

شامِل ص inclusive

شَأْن س ج /شُؤون/ (عَمَل) business

(مَوْضوع) matter

شاهِد س ج /شُهّاد/ witness

شاهَدَ ف (تابَعَ رُؤْيَة شَيْء) to watch

(رَأى حُدوث شَيْء وَخاصَّة جَريمَة) to witness

شاوَرْما س kebab

شاي س tea

شَباب س youth

شُباط س February

شَبَح س ج /أَشْباح/ ghost

شِبْشِب س ج /شَباشِب/ slipper

شَبِعَ ف to be full up

شَبْعان ص full

شَبَكَة س ج /شِباك/ net

شِبْه ح -semi

شَبَه س resemblance

شَبَّهَ ف to liken

شُبْهَة س suspicion

شِتاء س winter

شَتات س diaspora

سِياحَة س tourism

سِيادَة س (القوَّة الكامِلَة في السَيْطَرَة على دَوْلَة)
sovereignty
(لَقَب يُسْتَعْمَلُ عِنْدَ مُخاطَبَة شَخْص ذي قيمَة عالِيَة)
Excellency

سَيّارَة س car
سَيّارَة الإسْعاف ambulance
سَيّارَة أُجْرَة taxi

سِياسَة س (نَهْج جَماعَة) policy
(عِلْم السِياسَة) politics

سِياسيّ ص political

سِياسيّ س politician

سِياق س context

سِياقَة س driving

سيجارَة س ج /سَجائِر/ cigarette

سَيِّد س ج /سادَة/ (المالِك أو القائِد) master
(لَقَب لِلمُخاطَب) mister (Mr)

سَيِّدَة س lady (لَقَب لِلمُخاطَبَة) madam (Mrs)

سَيَّرَ ف (حَرَّكَ أو قادَ شَيْئاً) to propel
(دارَ ودَبَّرَ) to conduct

سَيْر س (المَشْي) walk
(عَمَليَّة تَقَدُّم الشَيْء) progress
(حَرَكَة المُرور) traffic

سيرَة س ج /سِيَر/ biography
سيرَة ذاتيَّة autobiography

سيرْك س circus

سَيْطَرَ على ف to control

سَيْطَرَة س control

سَيْف س ج /سُيوف/ sword

سَيْل س ج /سُيول/ stream

سينَما س cinema

سينَمائيّ ص film producer

س

سُمْنَة س obesity

سُمُوّ س Highness

سَمّى ف (أَعْطى شَخْصاً اسْماً أَو عَدَّدَ أَسْماء أَو أَنْواعاً)
to name
(أَطْلَقَ لَقَباً على شَخْص) to call

سَميد س semolina

سَميك ص thick

سَمين ص fat

سِنّ س (أَحَد أَسْنان الفَم) tooth
(العُمْر) age

سَنَّ ف to establish
سَنَّ قانوناً to enact a law

سُنَّة س ج /سُنَن/ the prophet Muhammad's sayings and deeds

سَنَة س ج /سَنَوات/ year

سَنَد س ج /سَنَدات/ bond
سَنَدات تِجارِيَّة portfolio

سَنَوِيّ ص annual

سَنَوِيّاً ح annually

سَهْل ص easy

سَهْل س ج /سُهول/ plain

سَهَّلَ ف to ease

سَهْم س ج /سِهام/ (قَضيب خَشَبِيّ حادّ مِن أَحَد الأَطْراف يُسْتَعْمَلُ كَسِلاح) arrow
(وَحْدَة مِن قِيَم مالِيَّة مُتَساوِيَة في مُؤَسَّسَة) share

سَهْو س oversight

سُهولَة س ease

سوء س wickedness

سَواء ص (بِنَفْس المُسْتَوى) equal
(...إمّا) either

سُؤال س ج /أَسْئِلَة/ question

سودان س (السودان) Sudan

سودانِيّ ص، س Sudanese

سور س ج /أَسْوار/ wall

سورَة س ج /سُوَر/ chapter of the Quran

سورِيّ ص، س Syrian

سورِيا س Syria

سوسَة س ج /سوس/ pest

سَوْط س ج /سِياط/ whip

سَوْفَ ف will

سوق س ج /أَسْواق/ market

سَوَّقَ ف to market

سولار س diesel

سَوّى ف (جَعَلَهُ بِنَفْس المُسْتَوى) to level
(أَنْهى خِلافاً أَو مُشْكِلَة) to settle

سِوى أداة اسْتِثْناء except
but

سْوِيسْرِيّ ص، س Swiss

سَيِّئ ص bad
سَيِّئ السُمْعَة infamous

سَيِّئَة س (شَيْء يُؤَثِّرُ سَلْبِيّاً) disadvantage
(خَطيئَة) sin

سِياج س ج /أَسْيِجَة/ fence

س

سَلامَة س security

سَلْبيّ ص negative

سَلَّة س ج /سِلال/ (سَلَّة يوضَعُ بِها الحاجِيات) basket

سَلَّة المُهْمَلات(سَلَّة القِمامَة) bin

سَلَّحَ ف to arm

سُلَحْفاة س ج /سَلاحِف/ turtle

سِلْسِلَة س ج /سَلاسِل/ chain

سُلْطانيَّة س bowl

سُلْطَة س authority

سَلَطَة س salad

سِلْعَة س ج /سِلَع/ commodity

سَلَف س ancestor(s)

سَلَفاً ظ in advance

سَلَفيّ ص ancestral

سِلْك س ج /أَسْلاك/ (مَعْدِن رَقيق بِشَكْل خَيْط) wire
(مَجال) domain

سُلَّم س ج /سَلالِم/ ladder
سُلَّم موسيقيّ musical scale

سَلَّمَ ف to hand over

سِلْم س peace

سَلَمون س salmon
سَلَمون مُرَقَّط trout

سِلْميّ ص peaceful

سُلوك س behaviour
conduct

سَلّى ف to amuse

سَليم ص intact

سُمّ س poison

سَماء س ج /سَماوات/ (مَكان وُجود عَرْش الله وَالمَلائِكَة) heaven
(الفَراغ حَوْلَ الكُرَة الأَرْضيَّة) sky

سَماح س permission

سَماع س hearing

سَمّاعَة س loudspeaker
سَمّاعَة الهاتِف receiver

سَماكَة س thickness

سَماويّ ص divine

سِمَة س characteristic

سَمَحَ بِ ف to allow

سِمْسار س ج /سَماسِرَة/ broker

سُمْسُق س marjoram

سِمْسِم س sesame seed

سَمَع س hearing

سَمِعَ ف to hear

سُمْعَة س ج /سُمَع/ reputation

سَمَعيّ ص audio

سَمَكَة س ج /سَمَك/أَسْماك/ fish
سَمَكَة القِرْش shark
سَمَكَة القُدّ cod

سَمْكَريّ س ج /سَماكِرَة/ plumber

سَمَّمَ ف to poison

س

سَطْحيّ ص shallow

سَطْو س burglary

سَعادَة س (شُعور الفَرْحَة) happiness
(لَقَب يُقالُ لِشَخْص يَتَمَتَّعُ بِأَهَمِّيَّة عالِيَة جِدّاً) Excellency

سُعال س cough

سِعَة س capacity

سُعْر س calorie

سِعْر س price

سَعَّرَ ف to price

سَعَلَ ف to cough

سَعوديّ ص، س Saudi Arabian

سَعوديَّة س (السَعوديَّة) Saudi Arabia

سَعى ف to strive

سَعْي س effort

سَعيد ص ج /سُعَداء/ happy

سِفارَة س embassy

سَفَرْجَل س quince

سَفير س ج /سُفَراء/ ambassador

سَفينَة س ج /سُفُن/ ship
سَفينَة فَضاء spaceship

سَقَّطَ ف to drop

سَقَطَ ف to fall

سَقْف س ceiling

سُقوط س fall

سَقيفَة س shed

سُكّان س population

سَكَبَ ف to pour

سِكَّة س ج /سِكَك/ (مَسْلَك مُعَدّ مِن قُضْبان حَديديَّة) rail
(مَسار) way
سِكَّة حَديد railway

سَكَّتَ ف to silence

سَكَتَ ف to be quiet

سُكَّر س sugar

سُكْر س drunkenness

سَكْران ص ج /سُكارى/ drunk

سِكْرِتير س secretary

سَكَّرين س saccharine

سَكَنَ ف to dwell

سَكَّنَ ف (زَوَّدَ بِالسَكَن) to house
(خَفَّفَ وَهَدَّأَ) to soothe

سِكِّير س ج /سِكّيرَة/ alcoholic

سِكّين س ج /سَكاكين/ knife

سِلّ س tuberculosis

سِلاح س ج /أَسْلِحَة/ weapon
سِلاح البَحْرِيَّة navy
سِلاح المُشاة infantry
سِلاح يَدَويّ firearm

سُلالَة س breed

سَلام س peace
سَلام وَطَنيّ national anthem
السَلامُ عَلَيْكُم hello

س

سَحابَة س ج /سُحُب/ cloud

سَحْب س withdrawal

سَحَبَ ف to pull

سَحَبَ قُرْعَة to draw lots

سِحْر س (جاذِبيَّة النَفْس) charm

(مُمارَسَة الخِدَع) magic

سَحَقَ ف to overwhelm

سِحْلِيَّة س ج /سَحالٍ/ lizard

سَخَّرَ ف (هَيَّأَ أَمراً لِلاِسْتِخْدام) to make serviceable

سَخِرَ مِن ف to mock

سُخْرِيَّة س irony

سَخَّنَ ف to heat

سُخونَة س heat

سَخيف ص ج /سُخَفاء/ ridiculous

سَدّ س ج /سُدود/ dam

سَدَّ ف to block

سَدّادَة س plug

سَدَّدَ ف (دَفَعَ دَيْناً) to repay

(هَدَفاً) to score

سُدْس عد ج /أَسْداس/ one sixth

سِرّ س ج /أَسْرار/ secret

سَرَّ ف to please

سِرْب س ج /أَسْراب/ flock

سَرَّبَ ف to leak

سَرْج س ج /أَسْراج/ saddle

سَرَّحَ ف to discharge

سَرَطان س (مَرَض فتّاك) cancer

سَرَطان البَحْر (حَيَوان بَحْرِيّ) crab

سَرَّعَ ف to accelerate

سُرْعانَ ما ظ very soon

سُرْعَة س speed

سَرْعَة س fad

سَرَقَ ف to steal

سَرِقَة س theft

سُرور س pleasure

سِرّيّ ص confidential

سِرِّيَّة س secrecy

سَرِيَّة س battalion

سَرير س bed

سَريع ص (يَتَحَرَّكُ أَو قادِر عَلى الحَرَكَة بِسُرْعَة عالِيَة) fast

سَيّارَة سَريعَة a fast car

(شَيْء يَحْدُثُ بِسُرْعَة ثُمَّ يَتَوَقَّفُ) quick

هَل أَنْتَ مُتَأَكِّد أَن هذا أَسْرَع طَريق؟ Are you sure this is the quickest route?

سَريع الغَضَب quick-tempered

سَطا ف to burgle, to burglarize

سَطْح س (طَبَقَة مُسْتَوِيَة) surface

سَطْح الأَرْض the surface of the earth

ج /أَسْطِحَة/ (الغِطاء الَّذي يُغَطّي أَعْلى البِناء) roof

(مَساحَة مُسْتَوِيَة تَكونُ أَعْلى الشَيْء) top

سَطْح المَكْتَب the desk top

س

سافِر ص (فاضِح) blatant

سافَرَ ف to travel

ساق (م) س ج /سيقان/ (رِجْل) leg
(غُصْن) stem

ساقَ ف to drive

ساقٍ س barman

ساقِيَة س barmaid

ساكِن ص silent

ساكِن س ج /سُكّان/ inhabitant

سالَ ف to leak

سَأَلَ ف to ask

سامّ ص toxic

سامٍ ص supreme

سامَحَ ف to forgive

سانَدَ ف to support

ساهَمَ ف to contribute

ساوى ف to equal

سَبَّ ف to swear

سَبّاح س swimmer

سِباق س ج /سِباقات/ race
سِباق الدَرّاجات الهَوائِيَّة cycling race
سِباق القَوارِب الشِراعِيَّة sailing race
سِباق القَوارِب canoeing race

سَبانِخ س spinach

سَبَّبَ ف to cause

سَبَب س ج /أَسْباب/ reason

سَبْت س (السَبْت) Saturday

سِبْتِمْبِر س (الشَهْر التاسِع بِالتَقْويم المِصْرِيّ) September

سَبَحَ ف to swim

سُبْحان الله glory be to God

سُبْع عد ج /أَسْباع/ one seventh

سَبْعَة عد seven

سَبْعون عد seventy

سَبَقَ ف to precede

سَبّورَة س blackboard

سِتار س ج /سُتُر/ covering

سِتارَة س ج /سَتائِر/ curtain

سِتَّة عد six

سُتْرَة س ج /سُتَر/ jacket

سِتّون عد sixty

سَجّادَة س ج /سَجاجيد/ carpet

سِجِلّ س record

سَجَّلَ ف (حَفِظَ الصَوْت أَو مَعْلومات في مِلَفّ) to record
(حَفِظَ الأَسْماء في قائِمَة) to register

سِجْن س ج /سُجون/ prison

سَجَنَ ف to imprison

سَجين س ج /سُجَناء/ prisoner

سَحّاب س zip

س

س

سَئِمَ ف to feel bored

ساءَ ف to worsen

سائِح س ج /سوّاح/ tourist

سائِد ص prevalent

سائِر ص all

سائِق س driver

سائِل س ج /سَوائِل/ liquid

سابِق ص previous

سابِقاً ظ previously

ساحَة س square

ساحِر س ج /سَحَرَة/ magician

ساحِر ص fascinating

ساحِرَة س witch

ساحِق ص overwhelming

ساحِل س ج /سَواحِل/ coast

ساخِر ص ironic

ساخِط ص furious

ساخِن ص hot

سادَ ف (سَيْطَرَ وَحَكَمَ) to reign

(أَصْبَحَ أَكْثَر عَدَداً وكَمّيَّة) to predominate

ساذِج ص ج /سُذَّج/ silly

سارَ ف to walk

سارّ ص pleasing

سارٍ ص valid

سارْدين س sardine

سارَعَ ف to hasten

سارِيَة س ج /سَوارٍ/ mast

ساطِع ص bright

ساعٍ س ج /سُعاة/ postman

ساعِيَة البَريد postwoman

ساعَة س (ساعَة الحائِط) clock

(ساعَة اليَد) watch

(فَتْرَة ستّين دَقيقَة) hour

مُدَّة الدَرْس ساعَة واحِدَة The lesson lasts for one hour.

كَم الساعَة؟ What's the time?

الساعَة الرابِعَة وَالنِصْف half past four

الساعَة الخامِسَة وَالرُبْع quarter past five

الساعَة الواحِدَة وَعَشْر دَقائِق ten minutes past one

الساعَة العاشِرَة إلاّ الرُبْع quarter to ten

الساعَة الثانِيَة عَشْرَة إلاّ عِشْرين دَقيقَة twenty minutes to twelve

ساعَدَ ف to help

س

زَمان س /أَزْمِنَة/ time

زُنْبُرُك س spring

زَمَن س ج /أَزْمان/ time

زَمَنيّ ص temporal

زَميل س ج /زُمَلاء/ (رَفيق العَمَل) colleague

(رَفيق في غَيْر العَمَل) associate

زَميل الدِراسَة classmate

زِناد س ج /أَزْنِدَة/ trigger

زَنْبَق س lily

زُنْبور س ج /زَنابير/ wasp

زِنْزانَة س ج /زَنازين/ cell

زَهْرَة س ج /أَزْهار/ (بِدايَة تَفْتيح النَبْتَة) bloom

ج/زُهور/ (وَرْدَة) flower

(أَحَد أَنْواع الخُضار) cauliflower

زَهْرَة الآلام س passion fruit

زَهْريّ ص pink

زَواج س marriage

زَوال س demise

زَوْج س ج /أَزْواج/ (اِثْنان أَو رَجُل وَزَوْجَتُهُ)

couple

(الزَوْج) husband

(اِثْنان مِن نَفْس النَوْع) pair

زَوْج الأُمّ step-father

زَوْج الأُخْت brother-in-law

زَوْجَة س wife

زَوْجَة الأَب step-mother

زَوْجَة الأَخ / أُخْت الزَوْج / الزَوْجَة

sister-in-law

زَوَّدَ بِ ف to supply

زَوَّدَ بِالطاقَة to power

زَوَّرَ ف (قَلَّدَ شَيْئاً بِشَكْل غَيْر قانونيّ) to forge

(أَخَذَهُ في زِيارَة) to take on a visit to

زَوْرَق س ج /زَوارِق/ launch

زِيّ س costume

زِيّ مُوَحَّد uniform

زِيادَة س (اِزْدِياد) increase

(إضافَة) bonus

زِيارَة س visit

زَيْت س ج /زُيوت/ oil

زَيْت الزَيْتون olive oil

زَيْتون س olive

زَيْتونيّ ص olive green

زَيَّنَ ف to adorn

ز

زِئْبَق س mercury

زائِر س ج /زوّار/ visitor

زائِف ص false

زادَ ف to increase

زارَ ف to visit

زَأَرَ ف to roar

زالَ ف to remove

ما زالَ / لا يَزالُ ظ still

زامور س ج /زَوامير/ horn

زاوِيَة س ج /زَوايا/ (مُلْتَقى بُعْدَيْن في شَكْل هَنْدَسيّ) angle

(الجُزْء الَّذي يَلْتَقي فيهِ حَدَّيْن) corner

زَباديّ س yoghurt

زَبّال س dustman

زُبالَة س rubbish

زُبْدَة س butter

زَبون س ج /زَبائِن/ customer

زَبيب س raisin

زُجاج س glass

زُجاجَة س bottle

زَحَفَ ف to creep

زَحْف س advance

زَخَّة س shower

زَخْرَفَ ف to decorate

زِرّ س ج /أَزْرار/ button

زِراعَة س (عَمَليَّة زِراعَة النَبات) planting

(دِراسَة ومُمارَسَة الزِراعَة) agriculture

زِراعيّ ص agricultural

زَرَعَ ف to plant

زَعْتَر س (نَوْع نَبات) thyme

زَعْفَران س saffron

زَعَمَ ف to claim

زَعيم س ج /زُعَماء/ leader

زُقاق س ج /أَزِقَّة/ alley

زَكاة س (مال يَدْفَعُهُ الأَغْنِياء لِلفُقَراء) zakat

زُكام س cold

زَكّى ف (أَوْصى وَثَمَّنَ) to recommend

(دَفَعَ زَكاة) to pay zakat

زَكيّ ص clever

زَلّاجَة س ski

زَلَّة س slip

زِلْزال س ج /زَلازِل/ earthquake

رُواق س ج /أَرْوِقَة/ corridor

رِوايَة س (إفادَة) account
(قِصَّة أَدَبِيَّة مُطَوَّلَة) novel

روب س ج /أَرْواب/ dressing gown

روبِل س rouble

روح س ج /أَرْواح/ (سِرّ الحَياة) soul
(مَخْلوقات غَيْر مَرْئِيَّة) spirit

روحانِيّ ص spiritual

روسِيّ ص، س ج /روس/ Russian

روسِيا س Russia

رَوَّضَ ف to train

رَوْض س garden

رَوَّعَ ف to horrify

رَوْع س (خَوْف) dread

رَوْعَة س majesty

رَوى ف to relate

رُؤْيا س (خَيال) vision
(حُلْم) dream

رُؤْيَة س ج /رُؤى/ (فِكْرَة) vision
(القُدْرَة عَلى النَظَر) visibility

رَيّ س irrigation

رِياضَة س sport
رِياضَة الصَيْد shooting

رِياضِيّ س athlete

رِياضِيّ ص (مُتَعَلِّق بِالرِياضَة) athletic
(مُتَعَلِّق بِالرِياضِيّات) mathematical

رِيال س riyal

رَيْثَما ظ until

ريح (م) س ج /رِياح/ wind

ريشَة س ج /رِيَش/ feather

رَيْع س revenue

ريف س ج /أَرْياف/ countryside

ريفِيّ ص rural

رَقْص س dance

رَقَصَ ف to dance

رُقْعَة س ج /رِقاع/ (مَساحَة صَغيرَة) spot
(قِطْعَة صَغيرَة تُسْتَعْمَلُ لِتَغْطِيَة شَقّ أَو جُرْح) patch

رَقْم س ج /أَرْقام/ number
رَقْم قِياسيّ record

رَقَّمَ ف to number

رَقْميّ ص digital

رَقّى ف to promote

رُقِيّ س development

رَقيب س ج /رُقَباء/ warrant officer

رَقيب أَوَّل س ج /رُقَباءُ أوائِل/ staff sergeant

رَقيق ص delicate

رَكِبَ ف (رَكِبَ عَلى دابَّة) to mount
(رَكِبَ في وَسيلَة نَقْل) to get in/on

رُكْبَة س ج /رُكَب/ knee

رَكَّزَ ف to concentrate

رَكْض س (رَكْض سَريع) running
(رَكْض بَطيء) jogging

رَكَعَ ف to kneel

رَكَلَ ف to kick

رَكْلَة س kick

رُكْن س ج /أَرْكان/ (زاوِيَة) corner
(أَساس) pillar

رُكود س recession

رَماد س ash

رَماديّ ص grey

رُمّانَة س ج /رُمّان/ pomegranate

رِمايَة س archery

رَمْز س ج /رُموز/ (رَمْز رَقْميّ) code
(شِعار) symbol

رَمْزيّ ص symbolic

رِمْش س ج /رُموش/ eyelash

رَمَشَ ف to blink

رَمَضان س (الشَهْر التاسِع بِالتَقْويم الإِسْلاميّ الَّذي يَصومُهُ المُسْلِمون) Ramadan

رَمْل س ج /رِمال/ sand

رَمى ف to throw

رَمْي س throw

رَنَّ ف to ring

رِهان س bet

رَهْبَة س (خَليط مِن مَشاعِر الخَوْف وَالاِحْتِرام) awe
(الخَوْف) dread

رَهْن س pawn
(رَهْن عَقاريّ) mortgage

رَهَنَ ف to pawn
(رَهَنَ عَقار) to mortgage

رَهيب ص (سَيِّئ جِدّاً) terrible
(رائِع) wonderful

رَهينَة س ج /رَهائِن/ hostage

رِوائيّ س novelist

ر

رَسول س ج /رُسُل/ messenger

رَشّ ف to spray

رَشا ف to bribe

رَشَّحَ ف to nominate

رَشْح س cold

رَشْفَة س ج sip

رَشْوَة س ج /رُشى/ bribe

رَصاص س lead

رَصاصَة س ج /رَصاصات/رَصاص/ bullet

رَصَدَ ف to monitor

رَصَفَ ف to pave

رَصيد س ج /أَرْصِدَة/ balance

رَصيف س ج /أَرْصِفَة/ (مِنْطَقَة المُشاة عَلى جانِبَي الطَريق) pavement
(مِنْطَقَة يَقِفُ عَلَيْها الرُكّاب في مَحَطَّة قِطار لِلسَفَر فيهِ) platform
رَصيف الميناء dock

رَضَّة س bruise

رِضى س satisfaction

رَضِيَ ف to agree

رَضيع س ج /رُضَّع/ infant

رَطْب ص wet

رُطَب س dates

رَطَمَ ف to slam

رُطوبَة س (رُطوبَة المَكان أو الشَيْء) moisture
(رُطوبَة الجَوّ) humidity

رَعايا س congregation

رِعايَة س care

رُعْب س horror

رَعى ف (اعْتَنى بِشَخْص ضَعيف) to nurse
(اعْتَنى وَأَطْعَمَ الماشِيَة) to shepherd
(قَدَّمَ الدَعْم المالِيّ) to sponsor

رَغِبَ في ف to like

رَغْبَة س ج /رَغَبات/ desire

رَغْمَ in spite of

رَغيف س ج /أَرْغِفَة/ roll

رَفّ س ج /رُفوف/ shelf

رَفاة س remains

رَفاه س welfare

رَفاهِيَة س luxury

رَفْض س rejection

رَفَضَ ف to refuse

رَفَعَ ف to lift

رَفْع س lifting
رَفْع الأَثْقال weightlifting

رِفْقَة س company

رَفيع ص slender
first class

رَفيق س companion

رِقابَة س censorship

رُقاقَة س chip

رَقَبَة س ج /رِقاب/ neck

ر

رَجُل س ج /رِجال/ man
رَجُل نَظافَة dustman
رِجْل (م) س ج /أَرْجُل/ leg
رُجوع س return
رَحابَة س wideness
رَحَّبَ ب ف to welcome
رَحَلَ ف to leave
رِحْلَة س (رِحْلَة بَحْرِيَّة) voyage
(رِحْلَة جَوِّيَّة) flight
(رِحْلَة بَرِّيَّة) journey
(رِحْلَة قَصيرَة) trip
رَحِمَ ف to have mercy on
رَحِم س ج /أَرْحام/ womb
رَحْمَة س mercy
رَحيق س nectar
رَحيل س departure
رَحيم ص merciful
رَخاء س prosperity
رُخام س marble
رَخَّصَ ف to license
رُخْصَة س ج /رُخَص/ licence
رَخْو ص loose
رَخّى ف to loosen
رَخيص ص cheap
رَدّ س ج /رُدود/ reply
رَدَّ ف to reply

رِداء س clothes
رَداءَة س badness
رَدَّدَ ف to repeat
رَدَعَ ف to deter
رَدْع س deterrence
رِدْف س ج /أَرْداف/ bottom
رُدْهَة س ج /رُدَه/ hall
رَديء ص inferior
رَذاذ س spray
رَذيلَة س ج /رَذائِل/ vice
رِزْمَة س ج /رِزَم/ bundle
رُزْنامَة س calendar
رَزين ص serious
رِسالَة س ج /رَسائِل/ (مُلاحَظَة) message
(خِطاب مَكْتوب) letter
رِسالَة تَوْصِيَة reference
رَسّام س painter
رَسَبَ ف to fail
رُسْغ س ج /أَرْساغ/ wrist
رَسْم س (تَلْوين وَتَشْكيل رُسومات) drawing
(مال يُدْفَعُ مُقابِلَ خِدْمَة) fee
رَسْم بَيانيّ chart
رَسَمَ ف to draw
رَسْمَة س ج /رُسومات/ drawing
رَسْميّ ص formal
official

ر

راعي البَقَر cowboy

رافِع س jack

رافَقَ ف to escort

راقَبَ ف (تابَعَ وَحَلَّلَ نَتائِج) to observe
(شاهَدَ) to watch

راقِص س dancer

راقٍ ص advanced

راكِب س ج /رُكّاب/ passenger

راهِب س ج /رُهْبان/ monk

راهِبَة س nun

راهَنَ ف to bet

راهِن ص present

راوَغَ ف to dribble

رَأى ف to see

رَأْي س opinion

رايَة س banner

رُبَّ حج perhaps

رَبّ س ج /أَرْباب/ lord

رِباط س ج /أَرْبِطَة/ strap
lace

رُباعِيّ ص fourfold

رَبِحَ ف to gain

رِبْح س ج /أَرْباح/ profit

رَبَطَ ف (وَصَلَ الأَشْياء بِبَعْضِها) to link
(عَقَدَ) to tie

رَبْط س (تَوْصيل الأَشْياء بِبَعْضِها) connecting
(عَقْد الأَشْياء) tying

رَبْطَة س (عُقْدَة أَو رَبْطَة العُنُق) tie

رُبْع عد ج /أَرْباع/ one fourth

رُبَّما (لَعَلَّ) may
(مِن المُحْتَمَل) perhaps

رَبْو س asthma

رَبّى ف (كَبَّرَ وَسَمَّنَ الطُيور أَو الحَيَوانات) to breed
(أَنْشَأَ) to raise

رَبيع س spring

رَبيع الأَوَّل س (الشَهْر الثالِث بِالتَقْويم الإِسْلاميّ)
Rabi al-Awwal

رَبيع الثاني س (الشَهْر الرابِع بِالتَقْويم الإِسْلاميّ)
Rabi ath-Thani

رِتاج س bolt

رَتَّبَ ف to arrange

رُتْبَة س ج /رُتَب/ rank

رَتَّلَ ف to recite

رَجَّ ف to shake

رَجاء س (أَمَل) hope
(طَلَب) request

رَجَب س (الشَهْر السابِع بِالتَقْويم الإِسْلاميّ) Rajab

رَجَعَ ف to return

رَجَّعَ ف to give back

رَجْعِيّ ص reactionary

رَجَفَ ف to tremble

ر

رِئاسَة س presidency

رِئَة س lung

رَئيس ص (أساسيّ) principal

رَئيس س ج /رُؤَساء/ (رَئيس مُؤَسَّسَة) chairman
(رَئيس دَوْلَة أو مُؤَسَّسَة) president
رَئيس الوُزَراء prime minister

رَئيسيّ ص major

رائِحَة س ج /رَوائِح/ smell

رائِد ص leading

رائِد س (رُتْبَة عَسْكَرِيَّة) major

رائِع ص excellent

رابِط س ج /رَوابِط/ link

رابِطَة س ج /رَوابِط/ connection

رابِع س ج /رَوابِع/ fourth

راتِب س ج /رَواتِب/ salary

راجَعَ ف (دَقَّق) to revise
(تَقَيَّأ) to vomit

راحَ ف to go

راحَة س comfort
راحَة اليَد palm

راحِل ص (مَيِّت) late
(مُغادِر) departing

رادِع س deterrent

رادْيو س ج /رادْيوهات/ radio

رَأْس س ج /رُؤوس/ head
رَأْس حَرْبَة striker

راسِب س ج /رَواسِب/ (ما يَكونُ أَسْفَل السائِل) sediment
(فَشَل في النَجاح) failure

راسِب ص sedimentary

راسِخ ص deep-rooted

راسَلَ ف (زَوَّدَ بِمَعْلومات إخْبارِيَّة) to be a correspondent for
(أَرْسَلَ تَفاصيل) to report
(أَرْسَلَ رَسائِل) to correspond with

رَأْسْمال س capital

رَأْسْماليّ ص capitalist

رَأْسْمالِيَّة س capitalism

راشِد ص adult

راضٍ ص satisfied

راعٍ س ج /رُعاة/ (داعِم) sponsor
(حاضِر الأَغْنام) shepherd

ذَلَّ ف to humiliate

ذُلّ س humiliation

ذَلِكَ إ إش (اسْم إشارَة لِلمُذَكَّر المُفْرَد البَعيد) that
ذَلِكَ قَوْل حَكيم. That is a wise saying.

ذَلِكُما إ إش (اسْم إشارَة لِلمُذَكَّر المُثَنّى البَعيد) those
ذَلِكُما الطِفْلانِ ذَكيّانِ Those children are clever.

ذَنْب س ج /ذُنوب/ (خَطيئَة) sin
(خَطَأ) fault

ذَنَب س ج /أَذْناب/ tail

ذَهاب س (قَصْد مَكان) going
(مُغادَرَة) departure

ذَهَب س gold

ذَهَبَ ف to go

ذَهَبِيّ ص golden

ذِهْن س ج /أَذْهِنَة/ intellect

ذو الحِجَّة س (الشَهْر الثاني عَشَر بِالتَقْويم الإسْلاميّ الَّذي يَكونُ بِهِ الحَجّ) Dhulhijjah

ذو القَعْدَة س (الشَهْر الحادي عَشَر بِالتَقْويم الإسْلاميّ) Dhulqada

ذَوَّبَ ف to dissolve

ذَوْق س ج /أَذْواق/ taste

ذَيْل س ج /أَذْيال/ tail

ذ

ذ

ذِئْب س ج /ذِئاب/ wolf

ذابَ ف (انْصَهَرَ) to melt
(تَحَلَّلَ) to dissolve

ذات س (نَفْس) self
(تَدُلُّ عَلى امْتِلاك شَيْء أو صِفَة لِلمُؤَنَّث) with
المَرْأة ذات العُيون الزَرْقاء the woman with blue eyes
of
امْرَأة ذات أَخْلاق a woman of ethics

ذاتيّ ص (يَعْتَمِدُ عَلى الشَخْص في الحُكْم عَلى الأشْياء) subjective
(يَعْمَلُ بِمُفْرَدِه) automatic

ذاقَ ف to taste

ذاكَ أ إش (اسْم إشارَة لِلمُذَكَّر المُفْرَد البَعيد) that
ذاكَ الرَجُل صَديقي. That man is my friend.

ذاكِرَة س memory

ذُبابَة س ج /ذُباب/ fly

ذَبَحَ ف to slaughter

ذَبيحَة ج /ذَبائِح/ sacrifice

ذَخيرَة س ج /ذَخائِر/ ammunition

ذِراع س ج /أذْرِعَة/ arm

ذُرَة س corn, (US) maize
ذُرَة سُكَّرِيَّة sweetcorn

ذَرَّة س atom

ذُرْوَة س (النَشْوَة) climax
(أعْلى الشَيْء) peak

ذَرِّيّ ص atomic
القُنْبُلَة الذَرِّيَّة atomic bomb
الطاقَة الذَرِّيَّة atomic energy
المُفاعِل الذَرِّيّ atomic reactor

ذَريعَة س ج /ذَرائِع/ pretext

ذُعْر س panic

ذَقْن س ج /ذُقون/ chin

ذَكاء س intelligence

ذِكْر س mention

ذَكَرَ ف to mention

ذَكَر ص male

ذَكَر س (رَجُل أو حَيَوان) male
(العُضْو التَناسُلِيّ لَدى الذَكَر) penis

ذَكَّرَ ف to remind

ذِكْرى س memory
ذِكْرى سَنَوِيَّة anniversary
إحْياء ذِكْرى commemoration
أَحْيى ذِكْرى to commemorate

ذَكِيّ ص ج /أذْكِياء/ clever

دَوَّخَ to stun

دَوْخَة س dizziness

دودَة س ج /ديدان/ worm

دَوْر س ج /أَدْوار/ (جانِب مِن العَمَل) role
(دَوْر شَخْص في لُعْبَة أو أيّ نَشاط آخَر) turn
(طابِق) floor

دَوَران س revolving

دَوْرَة س (فَتْرَة تَعْليميَّة مِن عِدَّة دُروس) course
(دَوَران جِسْم دَوْرَة كامِلَة حَوْلَ نَفْسِه) cycle
الدَوْرَة الشَهْرِيَّة period
الدَوْرَة الدَمَوِيَّة blood circulation

دَوْرِيّ س league

دَوْرِيّ ص periodic

دَوْرِيَّة س patrol

دولاب س ج /دَواليبُ/ (عَجَلَة) wheel
(خِزانَة الثِياب) wardrobe

دولار س dollar

دَوْلَة س ج /دُوَل/ state

دُوَلِيّ ص international

دَوْماً ظ always

دَوَّنَ ف to record

دونَ ظ (مِن غَيْر) without
(أَقَلّ) less

دَوِيّ س (صَوْت خَبْطَة) bang
(صَوْت انْفِجار) boom

دِيانَة س religion

دَيْر س ج /أَدْيِرَة/ abbey

ديزِل س diesel

ديسِمْبِر س (الشَهْر الثاني عَشَر بِالتَقْويم المِصْرِيّ)
December

ديك س ج /دُيوك/ (ذَكَر الدَجاج) cock
(جِهاز في السِلاح يُطْلِقُ الرَصاص في حالَة الضَغْط عَلَيْه) trigger
ديك الحَبَش turkey

ديمُقْراطِيّ ص democratic

ديمُقْراطِيَّة س democracy

دَيْن س ج /دُيون/ debt

دين س ج /أَدْيان/ religion
يَوْم الدين day of judgement

دينار س ج /دَنانير/ dinar

دينِيّ ص religious

ديوان س ج /دَواوين/ (شِعْر) collection of poems
(مَجْلِس) council

د

دُفْعَة مُقَدَّمَة deposit

دَفْعَة س push

دَفْن س burial

دَفَنَ ف to bury

دَفيئَة س greenhouse

دَقَّ ف to knock

دِقَّة س accuracy

دَقيق س flour

دَقيق ص (لا خَطَأ فيه) accurate
(عالي التَقْنيَّة) sophisticated
(رَفيع جِداً) fine

دَقيقَة س ج /دَقائِق/ minute

دَكَّ ف (دَمَّرَ تَدْميراً كامِلاً) to level
(قَصَفَ) to shell

دِكْتاتور س dictator

دِكْتاتوريَّة س dictatorship

دُكْتور س ج /دَكاتِرَة/ doctor

دَلَّ عَلى ف (أشارَ إلى) to indicate
(أَرْشَدَ) to direct

دَلالَة س (إشارَة) indication
(مَعْنى) significance

دَلَقَ ف to spill

دَلَّكَ ف to massage

دَلْو س ج /أَدْلاء/ bucket

دَليل س ج /أَدِلَّة/ (مَعْلومَة تُثْبِتُ صِحَّة أَمْر ما)
evidence

(مُوَجِّه وَمُوَضِّح) guide
(دائِرَة تَعْمَلُ عَلى التَوْجيه وَالمُساعَدَة)
information

دَليل سِياحيّ tourist guide

دَم س ج /دِماء/ blood

دَمار س destruction

دِماغ س ج /أَدْمِغَة/ brain

دَمْج س merger

دَمَجَ ف to merge

دَمْدَمَ ف to mutter

دَمَّرَ ف to destroy

دَمْعَة س ج /دُموع/ tear

دَمَويّ ص bloody

دُمْيَة س ج /دُمى/ doll

دَناءَة س meanness

دَنَّسَ ف to profane

دَنيء ص mean

دُنْيا س world

دَهّان س painter

دِهان س paint

دَهْشَة س astonishment

دُهْن س fat

دَهَنَ ف to paint

دَواء س ج /أَدْوِيَة/ medicine

دَوام س permanence

ساعات الدَوام working hours

د

دُخول س entry

دَخيل ص ج /دُخَلاء/ exotic

دَرّاجَة هَوائِيَّة bicycle

دِراسَة س study

دِراسيّ ص academic

دَرْب س ج /دُروب/ trail

دَرَّبَ ف to train

دَرَبْزين س rail

دُرْج س ج /دُروج/ drawer
دُرْج النُقود till

دَرَج س ج /أَدْراج/ staircase

دَرَجَة س (وَحْدَة مِقْياس رِياضِيَّة أَو دَرَجَة الحَرارَة)
degree
(عَلامَة) grade
(إِحْدى دَرَجات المِصْعَد) step
دَرَجَة الحَرارَة temperature
دَرَجَة عِلْمِيَّة degree

دَرْدَشَ ف to chat

دَرَسَ ف to study

دَرَّسَ ف to teach

دَرْس س ج /دُروس/ lesson

دِرْهَم س ج /دَراهِم/ dirham

دَسْتَة س dozen

دُسْتور س ج /دَساتير/ constitution

دَسيسَة س ج /دَسائِس/ intrigue

دُشّ س ج /أَدْشاش/ shower

دَع ف let

دَعا ف (طَلَبَ مِن الله أَو تَوَسَّلَ لِمَن يَمْلِكُ قوَّة) to supplicate
(سَأَلَ) to ask
(طَلَبَ مِن شَخْص حُضور مُناسَبَة) to invite

دُعاء س ج /أَدْعِيَة/ supplication

دَعارَة س prostitution

دَعّامَة س support

دِعايَة س propaganda

دَعْم س (مال تَدْفَعُهُ حُكومَة أَو مُؤَسَّسَة لِلتَقْليل مِن تَكاليف مُنْتَج) subsidy
(مُساعَدَة) support

دَعَّمَ ف to reinforce

دَعَمَ ف to support

دَعْوَة س ج /دَعَوات/ invitation

دَعْوَى س ج /دَعاوٍ/ (دَعْوَى قَضائِيَّة) lawsuit

دَغَل س ج /أَدْغال/ jungle

دِفْء س warmth

دِفاع س defence
دِفاع مُتَأَخِّر centre back
دِفاع مُتَقَدِّم centre forward

دَفْتَر س ج /دَفاتِر/ notebook

دَفَعَ ف (سَدَّدَ) to pay
(أَزاحَ بِالقوَّة) to push

دَفَّعَ ف to force sb to pay
دَفَّعَ ضَريبَة to tax

دُفْعَة س payment

د

داء س disease

دائِرَة س ج /دَوائِر/ (فَرْع مِن مُؤَسَّسَة) department

(حَلَقَة) circle

دائِرَة الرَواتِب payroll

دائِرَة كَهْرَبيَّة circuit

دائِم ص permanent

دائِماً ظ always

دائِن س creditor

دابَّة س ج /دَواب/ beast

داخِلَ ظ inside

داخِل س interior

داخِلِيّ ص (مُتَعَلِّق بِالعائِلَة أو الدَوْلَة) domestic

(مُتَعَلِّق بِداخِل المَكان) internal

دار (م) س ج /دور/ house

دارَ ف to revolve

داسَ ف to step on

داعِرَة س prostitute

داعِيَة س ج /دُعاة/ propagandist

دافِئ ص warm

دافِع س ج /دَوافِعُ/ (مُحَفِّز) motive

(سَبَب) cause

دافَعَ عَن ف to defend

داكِن ص dark

دامَ ف to last

دانَ ف (أَثْبَتَ تُهْمَة عَلى شَخْص) to charge

(اسْتَنْكَرَ وَعَبَّرَ عَن سَخْطِه) to condemn

دُبّ س ج /دِبَبَة/ bear

دَبّابَة س tank

دَبَّرَ ف (خَطَّطَ) to plan

(أَعَدَّ لِمُؤامَرَة) to plot

to arrange

دَبِق ص sticky

دِبْلوماسِيّ ص diplomatic

دِبْلوماسِيَّة س diplomacy

دَبّوس س ج /دَبابيس/ pin

دَجاجَة س ج /دَجاج/ chicken

دَحْرَجَ ف to roll

دُخّان س smoke

دَخْل س income

دَخَلَ ف to enter

دَخَّلَ ف to insert

دَخَّنَ ف to smoke

خَيْبَة س disappointment

خَيْر س good

خَيْرِيّ ص charitable

خَيْشوم س ج /خَياشيم/ gill

خَيْط س ج /خُيوط/ thread

خَيَّطَ ف to sew

خَيَّمَ ف to camp

خَيْمَة س ج /خِيام/ tent

placenta (مَشيمَة)

خُلاصَة س abstract

خِلاف س disagreement

خِلافاً ل contrary to

خِلافيّ ص controversial

خَلّاق ص creative

خِلالَ ظ during

خَلَّصَ ف to rescue

خَلَطَ ف to mix

خَلَعَ ف to pull out

خَلَف س ج /أَخْلاف/ successor

خَلْفَ ظ behind

خَلَفَ ف to succeed

خَلْفيَّة س background

خَلَقَ ف to create

خَلْق س creation

خَلَل س defect

خَلَنْج س heather

خَليَّة س ج /خَلايا/ cell

خَليج س ج /خُلْجان/ gulf

خَليط س combination

خَليفَة س ج /خُلَفاء/ successor
caliph

خَليل س ج /أَخِلاّء/ friend

خِمار س ج /خُمُر/ veil

خَمْرَة س ج /خُمور/ wine

خَمْريّ ص dark red

خُمْس عد ج /أَخْماس/ one fifth

خَمْسَة عد five

خَمْسون عد fifty

خَمَّنَ ف to estimate

خَميرَة س ج /خَمائِر/ yeast

خَميس س (الخَميس) Thursday

خِنْجَر س ج /خَناجِر/ dagger

خَنْدَق س ج /خَنادِق/ trench

خِنْزير س ج /خَنازير/ pig

خَنَقَ ف to strangle

خَوْخ س peach

خوذَة س ج /خُوَذ/ helmet

خَوْف س fear

خِيار س choice

خِيارَة س ج /خِيار/ cucumber

خَيّاط س tailor

خَيّال س horseman

خَيال س (طَيْف) shadow
(غَيْر الواقِع أو القُدْرَة عَلى الإتْيان بِأَفْكار جَديدَة)
imagination

خَياليّ ص imaginary

خِيانَة س betrayal

خَيَّبَ ف to disappoint

خَشِن ص rough

خَشَّنَ ف to roughen

خُشونَة س roughness

خَشِيَ ف to fear

خَشْيَةَ for fear that

خَصَّ ف to concern

خِصْب ص fertile

خَصَّبَ ف (حَسَّنَ جَوْدَة شَيْء أو مادَّة) to enrich
(زَيَّدَ خُصوبَة الأَرْض) to fertilize
(لَقَّحَ) to inseminate

خَصْر س waist

خَصَّصَ ف (حَدَّدَ مَبْلَغاً أو مَكاناً إلخ) to allocate
(كَرَّسَ وَقْتاً أو جُهْداً) to dedicate

خَصْم س ج /خُصوم/ (تَقْليل في قيمَة المَبْلَغ المُسْتَحَقّ) discount
(نِدّ) opponent

خُصوصِيَّة س privacy

خَضَّ ف to shake

خُضْرَة س vegetable

خُضْرَوات س vegetables

خَضَعَ ل ف to submit to

خُضوع س submission

خَطّ س ج /خُطوط/ line

خِطاب س ج /خِطابات/ speech

خُطّاف س hook

خَطَأ س ج /أَخْطاء/ mistake

خِطْبَة س engagement

خُطْبَة س ج /خُطَب/ sermon
أَلْقى الإمام خُطْبَة جَيِّدَة The imam delivered a good sermon.

خِطَّة س ج /خِطَط/ plan

خَطَر س danger

خَطِر ص dangerous

خَطَّطَ ف to plan

خَطَفَ ف (أَخَذَ رَهينَة) to kidnap
(أَخَذَ شَيْئاً مِن شَخْص فَجْأَة أو سَرَقَ مِنْهُ شَيْئاً) to snatch

خَطْف س abduction

خُطْوَة س step

خُطورَة س seriousness

خَطى ف to step

خَطيئَة س ج /خَطايا/ sin

خَطير ص serious

خُفّاش س ج /خَفافيش/ bat

خَفَّضَ ف to reduce

خَفَّفَ ف (قَلَّلَ أَلَماً) to relieve
(قَلَّلَ وَزْناً أو لَوْناً إلخ) to lighten

خَفِيّ ص invisible

خَفيف ص light

خَلّ س vinegar

خَلا ف to be devoid of

خَلاص س (الخُروج مِن حالَة سَيِّئَة) salvation

خِتام س end

خَتّامَة س stamp

خِتان س circumcision

خِتْم س ج /أَخْتام/ seal

خَتَمَ ف (وَضَعَ خِتْماً) to stamp
(أَنْهى) to end

خِتْمَة س the Quran

خَتَنَ ف to circumcise

خَجول ص shy

خَدّ س ج /خُدود/ cheek

خِداع س deception

خَدْش س ج /خُدوش/ scratch

خَدَشَ ف to scratch

خَدَعَ ف to deceive

خُدْعَة س ج /خُدَع/ trick

خَدَمَ ف to serve

خِدْمَة س service

خَديج ص ج /خُدَّج/ premature

خَراب س destruction

خَرّامَة س punch

خَرَّبَ ف to ruin

خَرَجَ ف to go out

خُرْدَة س scrap metal

خَرْدَل س mustard

خَرَزَة س ج /خَرَز/ bead

خَرَس س dumbness

خُرْشوف س artichoke

خَرَّطَ ف to chop

خَرْطوشَة س ج /خَراطيش/ cartridge

خِرْقَة س ج /خِرَق/ cloth

خَرّوب س carob

خُروج س exit

خَروف س ج /خِرْفان/خِراف/ sheep

خِرّيج س graduate

خَريطَة س ج /خَرائِط/ map

خَريف س autumn

خَزّان س (خَزّان مِياه جَوْفيّ أَو اِصْطِناعيّ كَبير)
reservoir
(خَزّان مِياه صَغير داخِلَ البِنايَة) tank

خِزانَة س ج /خَزائِن/ (لِحِفْظ المَلابِس) wardrobe
(دائِرَة أَو وِزارَة الماليَّة) treasury

خَزَّنَ ف to store

خَزْنَة س safe

خَسّ س lettuce

خَسارَة س ج /خَسائِر/ loss

خَسِرَ ف to lose

خَسيس س ج /أَخِسّاء/ bastard

خَسيس ص mean

خَشَب س wood

خَشْخَشَ ف to rattle

خ

خ

خائف ص afraid

خائِن س ج /خَوَنَة/ traitor

خاتِم س ج /خَواتِم/ ring

خاتِمَة س ج /خَواتِم/ conclusion

خادِم س ج /خَدَم/ servant

خادِمَة س maid

خارِج ظ outside

خارِجيّ ص (خارِجَ المَكان) external
(مِن دَوْلَة أُخْرى) foreign

خارِطَة س ج /خَوارِط/ map

خاسِر ص losing

خاصّ ص private
special

خاصَّةً particularly

خاصِرَة س waist

خاصِّيَّة س characteristic

خاضَ في ف to pursue

خاطَ ف to sew

خاطِئ ص wrong

خاطَبَ ف to address

خاطَرَ ف to risk

خافَ ف to fear

خال س ج /أَخْوال/ (maternal) uncle

خالٍ ص empty

خالَة س (maternal) aunt

خالِد ص immortal

خالِص ص pure

خالَفَ ف to disagree

خام س (النَفْط في حالَتِهِ الطَبيعيَّة) crude
(تَعوزُهُ الخِبْرَة) inexperienced
(مادَّة في حالَتِها الطَبيعيَّة قَبْلَ تَصْنيعِها) raw

خانَ ف to betray

خَبَّأَ ف to hide

خَبّاز س baker

خِبْرَة س experience

خُبْز س bread

خَبَزَ ف to bake

خَبَطَ ف to slam

خَبْطَة س knock

خَبيث ص (سَريع النُموّ) malignant
(ذو حيلَة) crafty

خَبير س ج /خُبَراء/ expert

حَياة بَرِّيَّة wildlife

حِياد س neutrality

حَيْثُ ظ where

حَيْثُما ظ wherever

حَيَّرَ ف to confuse

حَيْرَة س confusion

حَيَّزَ ف to bias

حَيِّز س space

حيلَة س ج /حِيَل/ trick

حَيْلولَة دونَ س prevention of

حينَ ظ when

حين س ج /أَحْيان/ time

حينَما ظ when

حَيَوان س ج /حَيَوانات/ animal

حَيَوان أَليف pet

حَيَوِيّ ص (نَشيط) vigorous

(مُهِمّ وَفَعّال) vital

حَيّا ف to greet

حَماس س enthusiasm

حَماقَة س stupidity

حَمّالَة س (شَريط قِماشيّ لِرَفْع البَنْطَلون) brace
(عِدَّة رُفوف تُسْتَخْدَمُ لِلعَرْض) stand

حَمّام س bathroom

حَمامَة س ج /حَمام/ pigeon

حِمايَة س protection

حَمْد س praise

حَمَدَ ف to praise

حَمَّرَ ف to redden

حَمَّصَ ف to roast

حُمُّص س chickpea

حَمْض س ج /أَحْماض/ acid

حَمْضِيَّة س citrus

حِمْل س load

حَمْل س (رَفْع المَوادّ بِاليَد) carrying
(وُجود الجَنين في بَطْن أُمِّهِ) pregnancy

حَمَلَ ف to carry

حَمَل س lamb

حَمَّلَ ف (خَزَّنَ عَلى جِهاز الحاسوب) to download
(رَفَعَ مَوادّ عَلى ناقِلَة) to load

حَمَلَت ف to get pregnant

حَمْلَة س campaign

حُمولَة س load

حُمّى س fever

حَمى ف to protect

حَم س father-in-law

حِمْيَة س diet

حَميد ص benign

حَميم ص intimate

حَنْجَرَة س ج /حَناجِر/ larynx

حِنْطِيّ ص tan

حَنَفِيَّة س tap

حَنون ص affectionate

حِوار س dialogue

حَوارِيّ س disciple

حُوالَة س draft

حَوالَي ظ approximately

حوت س ج /حيتان/ whale

حَوْض س ج /أَحْواض/ (حَوْض المَغْسَلَة) basin
(وِعاء لِحِفْظ السَوائِل) tub
حَوْض اسْتِحْمام bath, (US) bathtub

حَوْلَ ظ around

حَوَل س squint

حَوَّلَ ف (غَيَّرَ أَو بَدَّلَ) to convert
(حَوَّلَ اتِّجاهَهُ) to divert

حَيّ ص alive
حَيّ وَمُباشِر live

حَيّ س neighbourhood

حَياء س shyness

حَياة س life

حَقيقَة س ج /حَقائِق/ (مَعْلومَة مُؤَكَّدَة) fact
(الصِدْق في القَوْل) truth

حَقيقيّ ص real

حَكَّ ف to scratch

حِكايَة س tale

حُكْم س ج /أَحْكام/ (عَمَلِيَّة إِصْدار الحُكْم)
judgment
(أَمْر يَجِبُ اتِّباعُهُ) rule
(قَرار في مَحْكَمَة أَو في خِلاف) sentence
(رَأْي اتَّفَقَ عَلَيْهِ عُلَماء أَو قُضاة) verdict

حَكَمَ ف (أَصْدَرَ الحُكْم) to sentence
(أَدارَ دَفَّة الحُكْم في) to rule

حَكَّمَ ف to appoint as arbitrator

حَكَم س ج /حُكّام/ (شَخْص يَحْكُمُ بَيْنَ فَريقَيْن
مُخْتَلِفَيْن) arbitrator
(حَكَم الرايَة) linesman
(حَكَم المُباراة) referee

حِكْمَة س ج /حِكَم/ wisdom

حُكومَة س government

حُكوميّ ص governmental

حَكى ف to tell

حَكيم ص ج /حُكَماء/ (عاقِل) wise

حَكيم س (طَبيب) doctor
(فَيْلَسوف) philosopher

حَلّ س ج /حُلول/ solution

حَلَّ ف (أَنْهى مُشْكِلَة أَو خَلَطَ مَسْحوقاً بِالماء)
to solve
(فَكَّ عُقْدَة أَو رَبْطَة) to untie
(مَكَث) to stay

حَلَّ مَحَلّ ف to take the place of

حَلّاق س hairdresser

حَلَبَ ف to milk

حَلَبَة س arena

حِلْف س ج /أَحْلاف/ (مُعاهَدَة) treatise
(تَعاهُد أَطْراف عَلى عَمَل مُشْتَرَك) alliance

حَلَفَ ف to swear an oath

حَلْق س ج /حُلوق/ throat

حَلَقَ ف to shave

حَلَّقَ ف to soar

حَلْقَة س (مَجْموعَة مِن الأَشْخاص) circle
(جِسْم دائِريّ) ring
(جُزْء مِن مُسَلْسَل) episode

حَلَّلَ ف to analyse

حُلْم س ج /أَحْلام/ dream

حَلِمَ ف to dream

حَلَمَة س nipple

حُلْو ص sweet

حَلْوَى س ج /حَلْوَيات/ (مُحَلَّوات لِلأَطْفال) candy
(فَطائِر مُحَلّاة) sweets

حَلّى ف to sweeten

حَليب س milk

حَليف س ج /حُلَفاء/ ally

حَماة س ج /حَمَوات/ mother-in-law

حِمار س ج /حَمير/ donkey

حَضانَة س nursery

حَضَّرَ ف to prepare

حَضَرَ ف to attend

حُضْن س lap

حُضور س (التَواجُد في مَكان) attendance

(المُشاهِدون) audience

حَطَّ ف to land

حُطام س (قِطَع مُحَطَّمَة مِن أَجْسام صَغيرَة)

debris

(مُخَلَّفات بِنايَة مُدَمَّرَة) ruins

حَطَب س firewood

حَطَّة س keffiyeh

حَطَّمَ ف to smash

حَظّ س ج /حُظوظ/ luck

حَظْر س ban

حَظَرَ ف to ban

حَظيرَة س barn

حِفاظ على س maintenance

حَفّاظَة أَطْفال س nappy

حَفَرَ ف to dig

حَفْر س excavation

حُفْرَة س ج /حُفَر/ pit

حَفَّزَ ف to motivate

حِفْظ س preservation

حَفِظَ ف (ادَّخَرَ) to save

(خَزَّنَ مُنْتَجاً لِحِفْظِهِ مِن الخَراب) to preserve

(حَمى) to protect

(حَفِظَ مَعْلومَة في ذاكِرَتِهِ بِحَيْثُ لا يَنْساها)

to memorize

حَفْلَة س party

حَفْلَة التَخَرُّج graduation ceremony

حَفْلَة الزِفاف wedding reception

حَفْلَة موسيقيَّة concert

حُفْنَة س ج /حُفَن/ handful

حَفيد س ج /أَحْفاد/ grandson

حَفيدَة س granddaughter

حَقّ س ج /حُقوق/ (شَيْء مِن حَقِّكَ امْتِلاكُهُ) right

(صِدْق) right

(قانون) law

حُقْبَة س epoch

حِقْد س malice

حَقَّقَ ف (أَنْجَزَ) to achieve

(اسْتَجْوَبَ) to investigate

حَقْل س ج /حُقول/ (أَرْض زِراعيَّة أَو مَوْضوع)

field

حَقْن س injection

حَقَنَ ف to inject

حُقْنَة س injection

حَقود ص malicious

حُقوق س (الحُقوق) law

حَقيبَة س ج /حَقائِب/ bag

حَقيبَة سَفَر suitcase

حَقير ص sordid

(عَمَلِيَّة إدارَة الأرْقام) calculation
حِساب التَوْفير savings account
حِساب دائِن credit account
حِساب جارٍ current account
حِساب مَدين debit account
حِساب مَصْرِفيّ bank account

حَسّاس ص sensitive

حَسّاسِيَّة س allergy

حَسَبَ ف to calculate

حَسِبَ ف to think

حَسَبَ ظ according to

حَسَدَ ف to envy

حَسْرَة س heartbreak

حَسَمَ ف to decide

حَسَّنَ ف to improve

حَسُنَ ف (وَجَبَ) ought to
حَسُنَ لَو أَنَّهُم اعْتَذَروا They ought to apologize.
(أَفْضَلَ) to improve

حَسَناً well

حَسْناء س ج /حَسْناوات/ beauty

حَسَنَة س charity

حَشا ف to stuff

حَشْد س ج /حُشود/ crowd

حَشَدَ ف to mobilize

حَشَرَة س insect

حَشْوَة س filling

حَشيش س (عُشْب) grass
(مُخَدِّر) hashish

حَصاد س harvest

حِصار س siege

حِصان س ج /حُصُن/ horse
حِصان أَصيل thoroughbred

حَصانَة س immunity

حِصَّة س ج /حِصَص/ lesson
portion

حَصَدَ ف to harvest

حَصَرَ ف (قَيَّدَ) to restrict
(جَمَعَ أَسْماء أَو أَرْقاماً في قائِمَة)
to enumerate

حَصْر س (تَقْييد) restriction

حَصْرِيّ ص exclusive

حَصَلَ (حَدَثَ) to happen

حَصَلَ على ف (نالَ) to obtain

حِصْن س fortress

حَصَّنَ ف to fortify

حَصْوَة س ج /حَصى/ pebble

حُصول س (حُدوث) happening
(نَيْل الشَيْء) obtainment

حَصى البان س rosemary

حَصيرَة س ج /حَصائِر/ mat

حَصيلَة س outcome

حَضارَة س civilization

ح

(مَدى سُخونَة الجَوّ) temperature

حِراسَة س guarding

حَرّاق ص burning hot

حَرام ص prohibited

حَرْب (م) س ج /حُروب/ war

حَرْبِيّ ص military

حَرَثَ ف to cultivate

حَرِج ص critical

حُرْج س ج /أَحْراج/ wood

حَرَّرَ ف (نَسَّقَ وَنَشَرَ عَمَلاً أَدَبِيّاً أَو سينَمائِيّاً) to edit
(أَخْرَجَ مِن الأَسْر) to free

حَرَسَ ف to guard

حَرْشَفَة س ج /حَراشِف/ scale

حِرْص س greed

حَرِصَ ف to take care

حَرَّضَ ف to incite

حَرْف س ج /حُروف/ letter

حَرَّفَ ف to distort

حِرْفَة س ج /حِرَف/ craft

حِرَفِيّ س craftsman

حِرَفِيّ ص professional

حَرْفِيّ ص literal

حَرْق س ج /حُروق/ burn

حَرَقَ ف to burn

حَرَّكَ ف to move

حَرَكَة س movement
حَرَكَة المُرور traffic
حَرَكَة عَكْسِيَّة reverse

حَرَم س wife

حَرَّمَ ف to prohibit

حَرَمَ ف to deprive of

حِرْمان س deprivation

حُرِّيَّة س freedom

حَرير س silk

حَريص ص (حَذِر) cautious
(لَدَيْهِ رَغْبَة قَوِيَّة) eager

حَريق س ج /حَرائِق/ fire

حِزام س ج /أَحْزِمَة/ belt

حِزْب س ج /أَحْزاب/ party

حَزَمَ ف to pack

حَزْم س resolve

حِزْمَة س ج /حِزَم/ bunch

حُزْن س ج /أَحْزان/ sadness

حَزِنَ ف to feel sad

حُزَيْران س June

حَزين ص sad

حِسّ س (حاسَّة) sense
(شُعور) feeling
حِسّ الدُّعابَة sense of humour

حِساء س soup

حِساب س (رَصيد في البَنْك) account

حَجّ ف to go on the hajj

حِجاب س hijab

حُجَّة س ج /حُجَج/ (وَثيقَة إِثْبات مِلْكيَّة) deed
(دَليل) proof
(عُذْر) pretext
(رَأْي مُوَثَّق) argument

حَجَر س ج /حِجارَة/ stone
حَجَر كَريم gem

حُجْرَة س room

حَجْز س (اشْتِراء بِطاقَة لِحَدَث قَبْلَ حُدوثِه)
booking
(التَوْقيف رَهْنَ التَحْقيق) custody

حَجَزَ ف (اشْتَرى بِطاقَة لِحَجْز مَكان) to book
(أَوْقَفَ رَهْنَ التَحْقيق) to detain

حَجْم س ج /أَحْجام/ size
حَجْم الصَوْت volume

حَدّ س ج /حُدود/ (خَطّ يُحَدِّدُ حُدود مَكان) border
(مَجال يُعَبِّرُ عَن نِطاق) limit
(عِقاب شَرْعيّ) punishment

حَدّ أَدْنى minimum

حَداثَة س novelty

حَدّاد س blacksmith

حِدَّة س sharpness

حَدَث س ج /أَحْداث/ incident

حَدَثَ ف to occur

حَدَّثَ ف (جَدَّدَ) to upgrade
(تَكَلَّمَ إِلى) to speak to

حَدَّدَ ف (قَرَّرَ) to determine
(قَيَّدَ) to restrict
(أَعْطى مُواصَفات أَو مَعْلومات مُحَدَّدَة)
to specify

حَدَّقَ ف to gaze

حُدوث س happening

حَديث ص (جَديد) contemporary

حَديث س (كَلام) speech
(أَقْوال أَو أَفْعال النَبيّ مُحَمَّد) prophetic tradition

حَديد س iron

حَديقَة س ج /حَدائِق/ (مَساحَة مُوَرَّدَة حَوْلَ المَنْزِل)
garden
(مُنْتَزَه) park
حَديقَة الحَيَوانات zoo

حِذاء س ج /أَحْذِيَة/ shoe
حِذاء رِياضَة trainers

حَذارِ ف beware

حَذِر ص careful

حَذِرَ ف to be careful

حَذَّرَ ف to warn

حَذْف س deletion

حَذَفَ ف to delete

حُرّ س ج /أَحْرار/ free

حَرّ س heat

حَرَّ ف to grieve

حَرارَة س (سُخونَة عالِيَة) heat

state (وَضْع)

حالَما ظ as soon as

حاليّ ص current

حامِض ص sour

حامِض س acid

حامِل ص ج /حَوامِل/ pregnant

حانَ ف to come (time)

حانَة س bar

حانوت س ج /حَوانيت/ shop

حاوَرَ ف to talk to

حاوَلَ ف to try

حَاوِيَة س container

حُبّ س love

حَبَّة س ج /حُبوب/ (نُواة بَعْض الأَغْذِيَة كالقَمْح وَالأَرُزّ)
grain
(نُتوء يَظْهَرُ عَلى الجِلْد) spot

حَبَّذَ ف to approve of

حَبَّذا how good

حِبْر س ink

حَبْر س (عالِم الدين المَسيحيّ) bishop
(عالِم الدين اليَهوديّ) rabbi
الحَبْر الأَعْظَم the Pope

حَبَسَ ف (وَضَعَ في السِجْن) to imprison
(قَيَّدَ في مَكان) to confine

حَبْكَة س plot

حَبْل س ج /حِبال/ rope

حَبْل الغَسيل clothesline

حَبِلَت ف to become pregnant

حُبْلى ص pregnant

حُبوب س (نَوْع طَعام مِن الحُبوب يُؤْكَلُ في الصَباح)
cereal
(أَنْواع المَحاصيل مِثْلَ الأَرُزّ وَالقَمْح) grain

حَبيب س ج /أَحْباب/ (مَن تُحِبُّ بِطَريقَة غَيْر جِنْسيَّة)
darling
(عَشيق) lover

حَتَّمَ ف to insist

حَتْماً surely

حَتْميّ ص inevitable

حَتّى حج (تَدُلُّ عَلى نِهايَة فَتْرَة زَمَنيَّة) until
انْتَظَرْتُهُ حَتّى المَساء I waited for him until evening.
(تَدُلُّ عَلى نِهايَة مَسافَة مُعَيَّنَة) up to
وَصَلَت المِياه حَتّى الرُكَب The water reached up to their knees.
(تُسْتَعْمَلُ لِلتَأْكيد) even
كانَ الطَقْس بارِداً حَتّى في الصَيْف The weather was cold even in summer.
(تَدُلُّ عَلى السَبَب) in order that
أَغْلَقَ الباب حَتّى لا يَدْخُلَ أَحَد He closed the door so that no one would enter.
أَطِع الله حَتّى يُدْخِلَكَ الجَنَّة Obey God in order that He admits you to Paradise.

حَثَّ ف to urge

حَجّ س ج /حِجَج/ hajj, pilgrimage to Mecca

ح

حائط س ج /حيطان/ wall

حاجّ س ج /حُجّاج/ pilgrim (لَقَب يُطْلَقُ عَلى مَن حَجَّ إلى مَكَّة مِن المُسْلِمين) hajji

حاجِب س ج /حَواجِب/ eyebrow

حاجَة س need

حاجِز س ج /حَواجِز/ barrier

حاخام س ج /حاخامات/ rabbi

حادّ ص (ماضٍ) sharp
(شَديد الانْحِدار) steep
(شَديد) acute

حادَثَ ف to speak to

حادِث س ج /حَوادِث/ accident

حادِثَة س ج /حَوادِث/ occurrence

حارّ ص (حَرّاق أو شَديد السُخونَة) hot

حارَبَ ف to fight

حارَة س neighbourhood

حارِس س ج /حُرّاس/ guard
حارِس المَرْمى goalkeeper
حارِس شَخْصيّ bodyguard

حازَ ف to obtain

حازِم ص determined

حاسَّة س ج /حَواسّ/ sense

حاسِم ص (جِدّيّ أو خَطير) crucial
(جِدّيّ في اتِّخاذ القَرار) decisive

حاسوب س ج /حَواسيب/ computer
حاسوب مَحْمول laptop

حاصَرَ ف to surround

حاضَرَ ف to lecture

حاضِر ص، س present

حافٍ ص ج /حُفاة/ barefooted

حافَّة س ج /حَوافّ/ (طَرَف أو حَدّ) edge
(نُقْطَة أو مَرْحَلَة قَريبَة) verge

حافِز س ج /حَوافِز/ motive

حافَظَ ف to preserve

حافِلَة س bus

حاكَ ف (أَنْتَجَ مَلْبَساً أو سَجّادَة) to weave
(دَبَّرَ في السِرّ) to plot

حاكِم س ج /حُكّام/ ruler

حال س ج /أَحْوال/ condition

حالَ دونَ ف to prevent

حالاً ظ immediately

حالَة س (قَضيَّة) case

جَوْز الطيب nutmeg

جوع س hunger

جَوَّعَ ف to starve

جَوْلَة س (جَوْلَة في مُباراة أَو التَمَشّي في مِنْطَقَة لِمَسافَة قَصيرَة) round

(جَوْلَة طَويلَة) tour

جَوْهَر س essence

جَوْهَرَة س ج /جَواهِر/ jewel

جَوْهَرِيّ ص essential

جَوِّيّ ص air

جَيْب س ج /جُيوب/ pocket

جيبوتي س Djibouti

جَيِّد ص good

جَيْش س ج /جُيوش/ army

جيل س ج /أَجْيال/ generation

جيلاتين س gelatine

جينيّ ص genetic

جِيولوجِيا س geology

جَنائِنيّ س ج /جَنائِنِيَّة/ gardener

جَنْب س ج /أَجْناب/ side

جَنْبَ ظ beside

جَنَّة س ج /جَنّات/ (مَكان الصالِحين في السَماء)
paradise
ج /جِنان/ (بُسْتان) garden

جِنْجَر س ginger

جَنَّدَ ف to recruit

جُنْدُب س ج /جَنادِب/ grasshopper

جُنْديّ س ج /جُنود/ soldier
جُنْديّ البَحْرِيَّة marine

جِنْس س (نَوْع الشَخْص) gender
(إجْماع) sex

جِنْسيّ ص sexual

جِنْسيَّة س nationality

جَنوب س south

جَنوبيّ ص (مُتَعَلِّق بالجَنوب كَطَعام، مَلْبَس، إلخ)
southern
(بِاتِّجاه الجَنوب) southerly

جَنوبيّ س (شَخْص يَعيشُ في الجَنوب)
southerner

جُنون س madness

جَنَى ف to earn

جِنّي س ج /جِنّ/ jinni

جُنَيْه س pound

جِهاد س jihad

جِهاز س ج /أَجْهِزَة/ (ماكينَة صَغيرَة) apparatus
(مُؤَسَّسَة خَدَماتيَّة عامَّة أَو تَتْبَعُ الحُكومَة) service

جِهَة س (وُجْهَة) direction
(جانِب) side

جُهْد س ج /جُهود/ effort

جَهَّزَ ف (زَوَّدَ بِالمُعَدّات) to equip
(أَعَدَّ) to prepare
(زَوَّدَ بِالاحْتِياجات) to provide with

جَهْل س ignorance

جَهِلَ ف to be unaware of

جَهَنَّم س hell

جَهير س bass

جَوّ س ج /أَجْواء/ (المَشاعِر وَالمَزاحيَّة) atmosphere
(الفَضاء المُحيط بِالأَرْض) air
(الطَقْس) weather

جَواب س ج /أَجْوِبَة/ answer

جَواد س ج /جِياد/ horse

جَوارِبُ س socks
(جَوارِب نِسائيَّة خَفيفَة وَضَيِّقَة) stockings

جَواز سَفَر س passport

جَوْدَة س quality

جودو س judo

جَوْرَب س ج /جَوارِبُ/ sock

جَوْز س walnut
nut
جَوْز الهِنْد coconut

ج

جِلْد س ج /جُلود/ leather
skin

جَلَدَ ف to whip

جَلَّدَ ف to bind (a book)

جَلَسَ ف to sit

جَلْسَة س session

جَلَطَ ف to graze

جَلْطَة س clot
جَلْطَة دِماغيَّة stroke

جَليد س ice

جُمادى الأولى س (الشَهْر الخامِس بِالتَقْويم الإسْلاميّ) Jumada al-Ula

جُمادى الثانِيَة س (الشَهْر السادِس بِالتَقْويم الإسْلاميّ) Jumada al-Thania

جِماع س sexual intercourse

جَماعَة س (مَجْموعَة كَبيرَة من الناس) community
(مَجْموعَة صَغيرَة) gang

جَماعيّ ص collective

جَمال س beauty

جَماهيريّ ص mass

جُمْباز س gymnastics

جُمْجُمَة س ج /جَماجِم/ skull

جَمَّدَ ف to freeze

جُمْرُك س ج /جَمارِك/ customs

جَمْع س (إضافَة الأَرْقام في الحِساب) addition
(تَجْميع) assembly
(أَكْثَر مِن اثْنَيْن) plural
جَمْع شَمْل س reunion

جَمَعَ ف (أَضافَ) to add (up)
(لَمْلَمَ) to collect

جُمْعَة س ج /جُمَع/ (الجُمْعَة) Friday

جَمْعِيَّة س society
جَمْعِيَّة خَيْرِيَّة charity

جُمْلَة س ج /جُمَل/ sentence
بَيْع جُمْلَة wholesale

جُمْهور س ج /جَماهير/ (مَجْموعَة مِن الناس تَتَجَمَّعُ في مَكان) crowd
(عامَّة الناس) public

جُمْهوريّ ص republican

جُمْهورِيَّة س republic

جُمود س (صَلابَة) rigidity
(غَلاظَة) thickness
(تَجَمُّد) frozen state

جَميع ظ all

جَميل ص beautiful

جَميل س ج /جَمائِل/ favour

جُنَّ ف to go mad

جَناح س ج /أَجْنِحَة/ (غُرْفَتان مَعَ حَمّام في فُنْدُق) suite
(غُرْفَة كَبيرَة لِلمَرْضى في مُسْتَشْفى) ward
(العُضْو الَّذي يُساعِدُ الطَيْر عَلى الطَيَران) wing

جَنازَة س funeral

جِنايَة س offence

جُرُف س ج /أَجْراف/ cliff

جَرَفَ ف to bulldoze

جَرْو س ج /جِراء/ puppy

جَرى ف (حَدَثَ) to happen
(رَكَضَ) to run

جَرِيء ص bold

جَرِيح ص ج /جَرْحى/ wounded

جَرِيدَة س ج /جَرائِد/ newspaper

جَرِيمَة س ج /جَرائِم/ (جَرِيمَة قَتْل) murder
(ارْتِكاب مُخالَفَة ضِدَّ القانون) crime

جُزْء س ج /أَجْزاء/ part

جَزاء س (عُقوبَة) penalty
(حَسَنَة) reward

جَزائِر س (الجَزائِر) Algeria

جَزائِرِيّ ص، س Algerian

جَزّار س butcher

جَزَرَة س ج /جَزَر/ carrot
جَزَر أَبْيَض parsnips

جَزْمَة س ج /جِزَم/ boots

جِزْيَة س poll tax

جَزِيرَة س ج /جُزُر/ island
شِبْه جَزِيرَة peninsula

جَزِيل س abundant

جَسَد س ج /أَجْساد/ body

جَسَّدَ ف to embody

جِسْر س ج /جُسور/ bridge

جِسْم س ج /أَجْسام/ body

جَسور ص bold

جُسَيْم س particle

جَسيم ص ج /جِسام/ vast

جَشَع س greed

جَشِع ص greedy

جَعَّدَ ف to curl

جَعَلَ ف to make

جُغْرافيا س geography

جَفَّ ف to dry

جَفاء س alienation

جَفاف س (الأَرْض) drought
(الإِنْسان) dehydration

جَفَّفَ ف (أَفْرَغَ السائِل مِن وِعاء أو مَكان) to drain
(نَشَّفَ) to dry

جَفَّلَ ف to startle

جَفَلَ ف to wince

جَفْن س ج /أَجْفان/ eyelid

جَلا ف to evacuate

جَلاء س evacuation

جَلاّبِيَّة س djellaba

جَلالَة س majesty

جَلَبَ ف to bring

جِلْباب س ج /جَلابيب/ garment worn by women

جُبْنَة س cheese

جَبْهَة س front

جَبى ف to collect

جَبيرَة س ج /جَبائِر/ cast

جَبين س forehead

جُثَّة س ج /جُثَث/ corpse

جُحْر س ج /جُحور/ hole

جَحْش س ج /جِحاش/ ass

جَدّ س ج /أَجْداد/ grandfather

جِداً ح very

جِدار س ج /جُدْران/ wall

جِدال س argument

جَدَّة س grandmother

جَدَّدَ ف to renew

جَدُرَ ب ف to be worthy of

جُدَرِيّ س smallpox

جَدْوَل س ج /جَداوِلُ/ (قائِمَة مَواعيد) schedule
(نَهْر صَغير) stream
جَدْوَل الأَعْمال agenda
جَدْوَل المُناوَبات roster
جَدْوَل زَمَنِيّ timetable

جَدْوى س benefit

جِدِّيّ ص serious

جِدِّيَّة س seriousness

جَديد ص ج /جُدُد/ new

جَدير ب ص worthy of

جَذّاب ص attractive

جَذْب س attraction

جَذَبَ ف to attract

جَذْر س ج /جُذور/ root

جِذْع س ج /جُذوع/ trunk

جَرَّ ف to drag

جَرُؤَ ف to dare

جِراب س socks

جُرْأَة س boldness

جَرّاح س surgeon
جَرّاح بَيْطَرِيّ veterinary surgeon

جِراحَة س surgery

جِراحِيّ ص surgical

جَرّار س ج /جَرّارات/ (آلَة زِراعيَّة) tractor
ج /جَوارير/ (جُزْء مِن المَكْتَب) drawer

جَرَّبَ ف to try out

جَرَب س mange

جُرْثومَة س ج /جَراثيم/ germ

جَرَحَ ف to injure
جَرَحَ شُعور to hurt the feelings of

جُرْح س ج /جُروح/ wound

جُرْذ س ج /جِرْذان/ rat

جُرْزايَة س ج /جَرازي/ jersey

جَرَس س ج /أَجْراس/ bell

جُرْعَة س ج /جُرَع/ dose

ج

جاءَ ف to come

جائِر ص unfair

جائِزَة س ج /جَوائِز/ prize

جائِع ص hungry

جابٍ س ج /جُباة/ collector

جادّ ص serious

جادَلَ ف to argue

جاذِبيَّة س (الجاذِبيَّة الأَرْضيَّة) gravity
(جَذْب الآخَرين) charm

جار س ج /جيران/ neighbour

جارٍ ص (في الوَقْت الحاضِر) present
(مُسْتَمِرّ) running

جازَ ف to allow

جازَفَ ف to risk

جاسوس س ج /جَواسيس/ spy

جاط س basin

جاعِد س ج /جَواعِد/ fleece

جافّ ص dry

جاكيت س jacket

جالِس ص sitting

جالِيَة س community

جامِد ص (صلْب) rigid
(غَليظ) thick

جامَعَ ف to have sex with

جامِع س ج /جَوامِع/ mosque

جامِعَة س university

جامِعيّ ص academic

جامَلَ ف to compliment

جانِب ص ج /جَوانِب/ side

جانِباً ح aside

جاهَدَ ف (قاتَلَ في سَبيل الله وَالوَطَن) to fight for one's faith
(بَذَلَ جُهْداً كَبيراً) to strive

جاهِز ص ready

جاهِل ص ج /جُهّال/ ignorant

جاهِلِيَّة س era of ignorance (before Islam)

جاوَزَ ف to exceed

جَبان ص ج /جُبَناء/ coward

جِبَّة س ج /جِبَب/ jibbah

جِبْس س gypsum

جَبَل س ج /جِبال/ mountain

ثَمَر س fruit

ثَمَرَة س ج /ثِمار/ fruit

ثَمَن س ج /أَثْمان/ price

ثُمْن عد ج /أَثْمان/ one eighth

ثَمين ص valuable

ثُنائيّ ص (اثْنان) dual (يَحْتَوي عَلى عُنْصُرَيْن) twofold

ثَواب س reward

ثَوْر س ج /ثيران/ bull

ثَوْرَة س ج revolution

ثَوْريّ ص revolutionary

ثَوْم س garlic

ثائِر س ج /ثوّار/ rebel

ثابِت ص (لا يَتَغَيَّرُ) stable
(راسِخ) firm

ثابِت س ج /ثَوابِت/ base

ثارَ ف to rage

ثَأَرَ ف to avenge

ثَأْر س revenge

ثانَوِيّ ص (ذو قيمَة قَليلَة) minor
(التَعْليم غَيْر الإلْزاميّ) secondary

ثانَوِيَّة س (مَدْرَسَة ثانَوِيَّة) secondary school

ثانِيَة س ج /ثَوانٍ/ second

ثَبات س firmness

ثَبَّتَ ف to fix

ثَبَّطَ ف to discourage

ثَدْي س (نَهْد المَرْأَة) breast

ثَدْيِيّ س ج /ثَدْيِيّات/ (فَصيلَة الحَيَوانات الَّتي تَتَكاثَرُ بِالوِلادَة) mammal

ثَرْثَرَ ف to chatter

ثَرْثَرَة س chat

ثَرْوَة س wealth

ثَرِيّ ص ج /أَثْرِياء/ wealthy

ثُعْبان س ج /ثَعابين/ snake

ثَعْلَب س ج /ثَعالِب/ fox

ثَقافَة س culture

ثُقْب س ج /ثُقوب/ hole

ثَقَبَ ف to drill

ثِقَة س confidence

ثَقَّفَ ف to educate

ثِقْل س ج /أَثْقال/ weight

ثَقيل ص ج /ثِقال/ heavy

ثُلاثاء س (الثُلاثاء) Tuesday

ثَلاثَة عد three

ثَلاثون عد thirty

ثَلّاجَة س fridge

ثُلْث عد ج /أَثْلاث/ one third

ثَلْج س ج /ثُلوج/ snow

ثَلَجَ ف to snow

ثُمَّ then

ثَمانون عد eighty

ثَمانِيَة عد eight

ثَمَّة there is

ت

تَوْثيق س documentation

تَوَجَّهَ إلى ف to turn to

تَوْجيه س (تَوْضيح مَسار) direction
(النَصْح وَالمُساعَدَة) guidance

تَوْحيد س unification

تَوْراة س the Torah

تَوَرُّط س involvement

تَوْريد س exportation

تَوْزيع س distribution

تَوَسَّطَ ف to mediate

تَوَسُّع س expansion

تَوَسَّلَ إلى ف to beg

تَوْسيع س (زِيادَة في الحَجْم أَو الكَمّيَّة أَو الأَهَمّيَّة) expansion
(زِيادَة مَساحَة الشَيْء) widening

تَوَصَّلَ ف to ascertain

تَوْصِيَة س recommendation

تَوْصيل س delivery

تَوْضيح س clarification

تَوْطيد س strengthening

تَوْطين س localization

تَوْعِيَة س enlightenment

تَوَفّى ف to die

تَوْفير س provision

تَوْفيق س (حُسْن الحَظّ) success
(جَعْل الأَشْياء مُتَوافِقَة) harmonizing

تَوَقُّع س expectation

تَوَقَّعَ ف to expect

تَوَقُّف س interruption
تَوَقُّف قَصير pause

تَوَقَّفَ ف to stop

تَوْقيت س ج /تَواقيت/ timing

تَوْقيع س signature

تَوَلّى ف to take over

تَوْليد س generating

تونِس س Tunisia

تونِسيّ ص، س Tunisian

تَوَهُّج س glow

تَوَهَّجَ ف to glow

تَيّار س current

تَيْسير س facilitation

تَيَّمَ ب ف to adore

تين س fig

تَفْصيل تَقاليد ج /تفاصيل/ detail

تَمْييز س discrimination

تَنازَعَ ف to clash

تَنازُل س concession

تَنازَلَ ف to concede

تَناسُبيّ ص proportional

تَناسَقَ ف to match

تَناسَلَ ف to breed

تَنافُس س competitiveness

تَنافُسيّ ص competitive

تَناقُض س contradiction

تَناقَضَ ف to contradict

تَناوَلَ ف (شَمِلَ) to include
(أَخَذَ) to take

تَنَبَّأَ ف to predict

تَنَبُّؤ س forecast

تنس س tennis
تِنِس الريشَة badminton
تِنِس الطاوِلَة table tennis

تَنْسيق س coordination

تَنَشَّقَ ف to sniff

تَنْشيط س activation

تَنَصَّرَ ف to convert to Christianity

تَنْظيف س cleaning

تَنْظيم س organization

تَنَغْنَفَ ف to sob

تَنَفُّس س breathing

تَنَفَّسَ ف to breathe

تَنْفيث س jet

تَنْفيذ س execution

تَنْفيذيّ ص executive

تَنْقِيَة س purification

تَنْقيح س revision

تَنَكَّرَ ف to disguise oneself

تَنَهَّدَ ف to sigh

تَنّورَة س ج /تَنانير/ skirt

تَنَوُّع س variety

تِنّين س dragon

تَهْديد س threat

تَهْريب س smuggling

تُهْمَة س ج /تُهَم/ charge

تَهْنِئَة س congratulations

تَهَوَّدَ ف to convert to Judaism

تَهْوِيَة س ventilation

تَواجُد س presence

تَوازُن س balance

تَوَافُق س agreement

تَوافَقَ ف to correspond

توت س berry
توت أَرْضيّ strawberry

تَوَتُّر س tension

تَكَوَّنَ ف to be formed

تَكْوين س (تَشْكيل وَبِناء جِسْم) forming
(خَلْق) creation

تَكَيُّف س adaptation

تَلاعُب س manipulation

تَلاعَبَ ب ف to manipulate

تَلْبِيَة س compliance

تِلْفاز س ج /تِلْفازات/ television

تِلِفون س ج /تِلِفونات/ telephone

تِلْقائيّ ص automatic

تَلَقّى ف to receive

تِلْكَ إ إش (اسْم إشارَة لِلمُؤَنَّث المُفْرَد البَعيد) that
تِلْكَ هِيَ المُشْكِلَة. That is the problem.

تَلْمود س the Talmud

تَلْميح س hint

تِلْميذ س ج /تَلاميذ/ pupil

تَلَّة س ج /تِلال/ hill

تَلَوُّث س pollution

تَلْويحَة س wave

تَمَّ ف to take place

تَماسُك س solidarity

تَماسَكَ ف to stick together

تَمام س perfection

تَماماً ح (بِشَكْل كامِل) completely
(بِشَكْل دَقيق) exactly

تَمايَلَ ف to sway

تَمَتَّعَ ب ف to enjoy

تَمْتَمَ ف to murmur

تَمَثَّلَ ف to assimilate

تَمْثيل س (القِيام بِنَشاط نِيابَة عَن مَجْموعَة لِلتَّعْبير عَن رَأْيِهِم) representation
(تَأْدِيَة أَدْوار في المَسْرَح أَو السينَما) acting

تَمْثيليّ ص representative

تَمْديد س extension

تَمَرَّدَ ف to rebel

تَمَرُّد س rebellion

تَمْريرَة س pass

تَمْرين س ج /تَمارين/ exercise

تَمَزُّق س tear

تَمَشّى ف (مَشى بِبُطْء مِن أَجْل المُتْعَة) to stroll
(وافَقَ شَخْصاً أَو جَماعَة في رَأْيِهِم) to agree with

تَمَكَّنَ مِن ف to be able to

تَمَنّى ف to wish

تَمْهيد س preparation

تَمْهيديّ ص preliminary

تَمَوُّج س wave

تَمّوز س July

تَمْويل س fund

تَمْوين س supply

تَمَيَّزَ ف to be differentiated

تَفْكير س thinking

تَفَهَّمَ ف to understand

تَفَوُّق س superiority

تَفَوَّقَ على ف to surpass

تَفْويض س mandate

تَقارُب س convergence

تَقاضٍ س litigation

تَقاطُع س intersection

تَقاعَدَ ف to retire

تَقاعُد س retirement

تَقاعُس س failure

تَقَدُّم س (الحالَة المُتَطَوِّرَة الَّتي تَمَّ التَوَصُّل إلَيْها) advance
(عَمَلِيَّة تَطْوير وَتَحْسين وَضْع) progress

تَقَدَّمَ ف (تَطَوَّرَ وَتَحَسَّنَ) to progress
(تَقَدَّمَ بِطَلَب) to apply for

تَقْدير س (الشُكْر وَالاِحْتِرام) appreciation
(تَخْمين) estimation

تَقْديم س (عَرْض) presentation
(تَسْليم) submission

تَقْريباً ظ almost

تَقْريبيّ ص approximate

تَقْرير س ج /تَقارير/ report

تَقْسيم س division

تَقَشُّف س austerity

تَقْليد س (عَمَلِيَّة اتِّباع السُلوك المَألوف) convention
(عَمَلِيَّة إنْتاج نُسْخَة لِعَمَل أَصْليّ) imitation
ج /تَقاليد/ tradition

ت

تَقْليديّ ص traditional

تَقْليمَة س stripe

تِقْنيّ ص technical

تِقْنيّ س technician

تَقَهْقَرَ ف to deteriorate

تَقْوِيَة س strengthening

تَقيّ ص God-fearing

تَقَيَّدَ ب ف to adhere to

تَقْييد س limitation

تَقْييم س assessment

تَكاثُر س (الإنْسان وَالحَيَوان) reproduction
(النَبات) propagation

تَكَبَّدَ ف to sustain

تَكَبُّر س arrogance

تَكْثيف س intensification

تَكَرَّرَ ف to be repeated

تَكْريم س honouring

تَكْلُفَة س ج /تَكاليف/ cost

تَكَلَّمَ ف to speak

تَكْليف س entrustment

تِكْنولوجيا س technology

تَكَوُّن س formation

تَعْقيد س complication

تَعَلُّم س learning

تَعَلَّمَ ف to learn

تَعْليق س (كَلام يُعَبِّرُ عَن رَأْي حَوْلَ مَوْضوع مُعَيَّن) comment

(رَبْط أَعْلى الشَيْء بِجِسْم ثابِت) hanging

(إيقاف مُؤَقَّت لِنَشاط) suspension

تَعْليم س (مَنْهَج الدِراسَة) education

(تَدْريس) teaching

تَعْليمات س instructions

تَعْميق س deepening

تَعْميم س generalization

تَعَهَّدَ ف to pledge

تَعَوَّدَ ف to be used to

تَعْويض س compensation

تَعيس ص unfortunate

تَعْيين س appointment

تَغاضى ف to overlook

تَغْذِيَة س nutrition

تَغْطِيَة س cover

تَغَلَّبَ على ف to overcome

تَغَيَّرَ ف to change

تَغَيُّر س change

تَغْيير س change

تَفاؤُل س optimism

تُفّاحَة س ج /تُفّاح/ apple

تَفادى ف to avert

تَفاعَلَ س react

تَفاعُل س (الاِشْتِراك وَالتَعاوُن مَعَ الآخَرين) interaction

(رَدّ الفِعْل) reaction

تَفاقَمَ ف to worsen

تَفاقُم س worsening

تَفاهُم س mutual understanding

تَفاوُت س variance

تَفاوُض س negotiation

تَفاؤُل س optimism

تَفَتَّتَ ف to crumble

تَفْتيش س inspection

تَفَجَّرَ ف to explode

تَفَجَّعَ ف to mourn

تَفَرُّع س branching out

تَفَرَّقَ ف to disperse

تَفْرِقَة س separation

تَفْسير س (تَوْضيح أَسْباب حُدوث أَو نَتائِج حَدَث) explanation

(تَوْضيح وَتَحْليل مَفْهومِك لِمَعْنى نَصّ أَو قَوْل) interpretation

تَفْصيل س ج /تَفاصيل/ detail

تَفَضَّلْ ف welcome

تَفْضيل س preference

تَفَكَّرَ ف to reflect

تَطْعيم س vaccination

تَطَفُّل س intrusion

تَطَلَّبَ ف to require

تَطْهير س (تَنْظيف وَإزالَة الشَوائِب) purification
(تَعْقيم) sterilizing

تَطَوُّر س development

تَطَوَّرَ ف to develop

تَطَوَّعَ ف to volunteer

تَطْوير س developing

تَطْويق س encirclement

تَظاهَرَ ف to demonstrate

تَعادُل س (الحُصول عَلى نَفْس النَتيجَة في مُباراة) draw
(حالَة وُجود أَمْرَيْن أَو أَكْثَر بِنَفْس المُواصَفات) equality

تَعارُض س discrepancy

تَعارُف س introduction

تَعاسَة س misery

تَعاطُف س sympathy

تَعاطى ف (أَخَذَ) to take
(تَعامَلَ) to deal with

تَعافى ف to recover

تَعاقُب س succession

تَعاقَدَ ف to contract

تَعامَلَ ف to deal (with)

تَعامُل س dealing

تَعاوُن س cooperation

تَعاوَنَ ف to cooperate

تَعاوُنيّ ص cooperative

تَعايُش س coexistence

تَعَب س tiredness

تَعِبَ ف to tire

تَعْبِئَة س (جَمْع الحُشود) mobilization
(رَزْم) packaging

تَعْبير س expression

تَعَثَّرَ ف to stumble

تَعْديل س adjustment

تَعَرُّض س exposure

تَعَرَّضَ ل ف to be exposed to

تَعْريف س (تَوْضيح مَعْنى) definition
(تِبْيان وَإظْهار مَعْلومات مُتَعَلِّقَة بِشَخْص أَو شَيْء) identification

تَعْزيز س enhancement

تَعَسُّف س arbitrariness

تَعَسُّفيّ ص arbitrary

تَعَشّى ف to dine

تَعَطُّل س breakdown

تَعَطَّلَ ف to fail

تَعْطيل س suspension

تَعْقيب س feedback

ت

تَشْريع س legislation

تِشْرين الأَوَّل س October

تِشْرين الثاني س November

تَشْغيل س operating

تَشْكيل س formation

تَشْكيلَة س range

تَشْويق س motivation

تَشْييع س accompanying

تَصاعَدَ ف to escalate

تَصْحيح س correction

تَصَدٍّ س confrontation

تَصَدَّرَ ف to lead

تَصَدَّعَ ف to crack

تَصَدَّقَ ف to pay charity

تَصَدّى ف to confront

تَصْديق س approval

تَصَرَّفَ ف to behave

تَصْريح س ج /تَصْريحات/ (الإعْلان عَن رَأْي) declaration
ج /تَصاريحُ/(رُخْصَة) permit

تَصْفِيَة س (عَمَلِيَّة التَخَلُّص مِن البِضاعَة المُخَزَّنَة) clearance
(عَمَلِيَّة بَيْع المُمْتَلَكات لِدَفْع دُيون) liquidation
(حَلّ مُشْكِلَة) settlement

تَصْفيق س applause

تَصَلُّب س rigidity

تَصْميم س ج /تَصاميمُ/ (رَسْم بَيانيّ لِمَشْروع) design
ج /تَصْميمات/(العَزْم عَلى تَنْفيذ أَمْر) determination

تَصْنيع س industrialization

تَصْنيف س classification

تَصَوُّر س imagination

تَصَوَّرَ ف to imagine

تَصْويت س voting

تَصْوير س (شَرْح أَمْر بِإعْطاء صُوَر) illustration

تَصْوير فوتوغْرافيّ photography

تَضاءَلَ ف to dwindle

تَضاريسُ س relief

تَضامُن س solidarity

تَضْحِيَة س sacrifice

تَضَخُّم س (حالَة ارْتِفاع الأَسْعار وَانْخِفاض العُمْلَة) inflation
(حالَة زِيادَة غَيْر طَبيعيَّة في الحَجْم) enlargement

تَضَمَّنَ ف (شَمِلَ) to comprise
(حَمَلَ في طَيّاتِهِ مَعْنى مُعَيَّناً) to imply

تَطابَقَ ف to conform

تَطْبيق س application

تَطَرُّف س extremism

تَطَرَّقَ إلى ف to arrive at

تَطْريز س embroidery

تَرْكيز س concentration

تَرْميم س renovation

تَرَنَّحَ ف to stagger

تَرْنيمَة س carol

تَرْويج س circulating

تَزامَنَ ف to coincide

تَزَلَّجَ ف (تَزَلَّجَ عَلى مِزْلاجَة) to skate
(تَزَلَّجَ عَلى الجَليد) to ski

تَزَلُّج س skating
skiing

تَزَوَّجَ ف to marry

تَزْويد س supply

تَزْوير س forgery

تَزْيين س decoration

تَساءَلَ ف to wonder

تَسَبَّبَ في ف to result in

تَسْجيل س (حِفْظ المَعْلومات في مِلَفّ أَو في شَريط صَوْتيّ) recording
(عَمَلِيّة سَرْد وَحِفْظ الأَسْماء) registration

تَسْديد س repayment

تَسَرُّب س leak

تَسَرَّبَ ف to leak

تَسْريب س leak

تُسْع عد ج /أَتْساع/ ninth

تِسْعَة عد nine

تِسْعون عد ninety

تَسَلَّحَ ف to arm os

تَسَلُّح س armament

تَسَلْسُل س (تَتابُع الأَحْداث) sequence
(تَسَلْسُل هَرَمِيّ) hierarchy

تَسَلُّق س climbing

تَسَلَّقَ ف to climb

تَسَلَّمَ ف to receive

تَسَلّى ف to have fun

تَسْلِيَة س amusement

تَسْليم س handing over

تَسْهيل س facilitation

تَسَوَّقَ ف to shop

تَسْوِيَة س compromise

تَسْويق س marketing

تَسْيير س management

تَشاؤُم س pessimism

تَشابُه س similarity

تَشاجَرَ ف to fight

تَشاوَرَ ف to consult

تَشاوُر س joint consultation

تَشْجيع س encouragement

تَشْخيص س (تَحْديد المَرَض) diagnosis
(تَحْديد كَيْفِيَّة حُدوث أَمْر) identification

تَشَرْدَقَ ف to choke

تَشَرَّفَ ف to have the honour of

ت

ت

تَدْشين س inauguration

تَدْعيم س support

تَدَفُّق س current

تَدَفَّقَ ف to flow

تَدْقيق س review

تَدْليك س massage

تَدْمير س destruction

تَدَهْوُر س decline

تَدَهْوَرَ ف to decline

تَذَكُّر س recollection

تَذَكَّرَ ف to remember

تَذْكَرَة س ج /تَذاكِر/ ticket

تَذَمَّرَ ف to complain

تَذَوَّقَ ف to taste

تُراب س ج /أَتْرِبَة/ earth

تُراث س heritage

تَراجُع س decline

تَرافَعَ ف to plead (in court)

تَراوَحَ ف to vary

تُرْبَة س ج /تُرَب/ soil

تَرْبِيَة س (إنْشاء الأطْفال) upbringing
(تَرْبِيَة الدَواجِن) breeding

تَرْبيع س squaring

تَرَتَّبَ ف to have to

تَرْتيب س arrangement

تَرْجَمَ ف to translate

تَرْجَمَة س translation
تَرْجَمَة شَفَوِيَّة interpreting

تَرَجّى ف to beg

تَرْحيب س welcome

تَرْخيص س ج /تَراخيص/ license

تَرَدُّد س (نِسْبَة اهْتِزاز الأَمْواج الكَهْرومَغْناطيسيَّة)
frequency
(عَدَم القُدْرَة عَلى اتِّخاذ قَرار صارِم)
hesitation

تَرَدَّدَ ف (احْتارَ) to hesitate
(زارَ بِاسْتِمْرار) to frequent

تِرْسانَة س arsenal

تَرَسُّب س deposit

تَرْشيح س nomination

تَرَف س luxury

تَرْفيه س entertainment

تَرْقِيَة س promotion

تَرْقيم س numbering

تَرَكَ ف (غادَرَ) to leave
(عَزَفَ عَن مُمارَسَة عادَة) to quit

تِرْكَة س heritage

تُرْكِيّ س ج /أَتْراك/ Turk

تُرْكِيّ ص ج /أَتْراك/ Turkish

تُرْكِيا س Turkey

تَرْكيب س (خَلْط وتَكْوين) composition
(تَجْميع) assembling

ت

تَحَطَّمَ ف to crash

تُحْفَة س ج /تُحَف/ masterpiece

تَحَقَّقَ ف (تأكَّدَ مِن صِحَّة شَيْء) to verify
(أُنْجِزَ) to happen

تَحْقيق س (اسْتِجْواب أو بَحْث في مَوْضوع) investigation
(إنْجاز) achievement

تَحَكُّم س control

تَحَكَّمَ في ف to control

تَحْكيم س arbitration

تَحَلَّلَ ف to degrade

تَحْليل س analysis

تَحَمَّلَ ف to bear

تَحَوَّلَ ف to turn into

تَحَوُّل س transition

تَحْويل س (التَغْيير مِن حال إلى آخَر)
conversion
(عَمَلِيَّة إرْسال شَخْص إلى مُسْتَشْفى) referral

تَحْويلَة س referral

تَحِيَّة س greeting

تَحَيُّز س prejudice

تَخَرَّجَ ف to graduate

تَخَرُّج س graduation

تَخْريب س sabotage

تَخْزين س storage

تَخَصُّص س specialization

تَخَصَّصَ ف to specialize

تَخْصيص س allocation

تَخْطيط س planning

تَخْفيض س reduction

تَخْفيف س diminution

تَخَلَّصَ مِن ف to get rid of

تَخَلَّفَ ف to be late

تَخَلُّف س backwardness

تَخَلَّلَ ف to follow

تَخَلّى ف to abandon

تَخْمين س guess

تَخْويف س intimidation

تَخَيُّل س imagination

تَخَيَّلَ ف to imagine

تَداخُل س interference

تَدَبَّرَ ف to manage

تَدْبير س management

تَدَخُّل س intervention

تَدَخَّلَ ف to intervene

تَدَرَّبَ ف to exercise

تَدْريب س training

تَدْريجيّ ص gradual

تَدْريجيّاً ح gradually

تَدْريس س (تَدْريس نَظَرِيّ) teaching
(تَدْريس عَمَلِيّ) instruction

تَجْديف س rowing

تَجَرَّأَ ف to dare

تَجْرُبَة س ج /تَجارِب/ (مُحاوَلَة عَمَل شَيْء) trial
(تَجْرُبَة عِلْميَّة) experiment

تَجْريبيّ ص experimental

تَجْريديّ ص abstract

تَجْزِئَة س dividing

تَجَزَّأَ ف to be divided

تَجَسَّسَ ف to spy

تَجَسُّس س espionage

تَجْسيد س materialization

تَجْعيدَة س ج /تَجاعيدُ/ (تَجْعيدَة شَعْر) curl
(تَجْعيدَة الوَجْه أَو المَلْبَس) wrinkle

تَجْفيف س (إزالَة البَلَل) drying
(نَضْح الماء مِن مَكان) drainage

تَجَلّى ف to become clear

تَجْليد س bookbinding

تَجَمَّدَ ف to freeze

تَجَمُّد س the state of being frozen

تَجَمُّع س assembly

تَجَمَّعَ ف to gather

تَجَمْهَرَ ف to gather

تَجْميع س collection

تَجْميل س beautification

تَجَنَّبَ ف to avoid

تَجْنيد س (تَوْظيف) recruitment
(جَمْع الجَيْش) mobilization

تَجَوَّلَ ف to wander

تَحالُف س alliance

تَحْتَ ظ under

تَحَجَّبَ ف to wear a headscarf

تَحَدَّثَ ف to speak

تَحَدٍّ س challenge

تَحَدّى ف to challenge

تَحْديد س restriction

تَحْذير س warning

تَحَرَّرَ ف to be liberated

تَحَرُّر س liberation

تَحَرُّريّ ص liberal

تَحَرُّريَّة س liberalism

تَحَرَّكَ ف to move

تَحَرُّك س ج /تَحَرُّكات/ move

تَحْرير س (إطْلاق سَراح) freeing
(إعْداد كِتاب أَو جَريدَة إلخ) editing

تَحْريض س incitement

تَحْريف س distortion

تَحَسَّنَ ف to improve

تَحَسُّن س improvement

تَحْسين س improvement

تَحْصيل س acquisition

(العَمَل عَلى جَعْل الشَيْء آمِناً) securing
(التَضْمين وَالتَأْكيد عَلى تَنْفيذ أَو تَوْفير أَمْر ما) assurance

تَأَهَّلَ ف to qualify

تايْكْوانْدو س taekwondo

تَأْييد س support

تَأْثير س ج /تَأْثيرات/ effect

تَأْجير س hire
تَأْجير سَيّارَة car rental

تَبادَلَ ف to exchange

تَبادُل س mutual exchange

تَباهى ف to boast

تَبايُن س contrast

تَبايَنَ ف to vary

تَبَخَّرَ ف to evaporate

تَبْديد س squandering

تَبْديل س change

تَبْذير س squandering

تَبَرَّعَ ف to donate

تَبَرُّع س ج /تَبَرُّعات/ donation

تَبْرير س justification

تَبَسَّمَ ف to smile

تَبْسيط س simplification

تَبِعَ ف to follow

تَبَعْثَرَ ف to be scattered about

تَبَعيَّة س dependency

تِبْغ س tobacco

تَبَقّى ف to remain

تَبَلْوَرَ س to crystallize

تِبْن س hay

تَبَنٍّ س adoption

تَبَنّى ف to adopt

تَبّولَة س tabbouleh

تَتابُع س succession

تَتَبَّعَ ف to track

تَتِمَّة س completion

تَثاءَبَ ف to yawn

تَثْبيت س stabilization

تَجاذُب س attraction

تِجارَة س trade
تِجارَة الجُمْلَة wholesale
تِجارَة المُفَرَّق retail

تِجاريّ ص commercial

تِجاهَ ظ towards

تَجاهَلَ ف to ignore

تَجاوَبَ ف to respond

تَجاوَزَ ف (زادَ عَن الطَبيعيّ أَو تَعَدّى التَعْليمات) to exceed
(اجْتازَ مَرْكَبَة) to overtake

تَجَدَّدَ ف to be renewed

تَجْديد س renewal

ت

تائِه ص lost

تابِع س ج /أتْباع/ follower

تابَعَ ف to continue

تابِل س ج /تَوابِل/ spice

تابوت س ج /تَوابيت/ coffin

تَأْثيث س furnishing

تَاج س ج /تيجان/ crown

تاجَرَ ف to trade

تاجِر س ج /تُجّار/ merchant

تَأْجيل س delay

تَأَخَّرَ ف (مَكَثَ في مَكان أكْثَر مِن اللازِم) to linger
(جاءَ بَعْدَ المَوْعِد المُعْتاد) to be late

تَأْخير س (حالَة عَدَم حُدوث أَمْر في مَوْعِده) lateness
(تَأْجيل أمْر إلى مَوْعِد آخر) delay

تَأْدِيَة س performance

تَأَرْجَحَ ف to swing

تاريخ س ج /تَواريخ/ (تَوْقيت يَدُلُّ عَلى الزَمَن) date
(قِصَص الماضي) history

تَأْريخ س writing history

تاريخيّ ص historic(al)

تَأْسيس س establishment

تَأْشيرَة س visa

تافِه ص trivial

تَأَكَّدَ ف to make sure

تَآكُل س erosion

تَآكَلَ ف to erode

تَأْكيد س (جَعْل الشَيْء أكيداً) confirmation
(التَرْكيز عَلى أَهَمِّيَّة أَو ضَرورَة شَيْء) emphasis

تالٍ ص following
next

تالِف ص damaged

تَأْليف س writing

تامّ ص complete

تَآمَرَ ف to plot

تَآمُر س conspiracy

تَأَمُّل س ج /تَأَمُّلات/ meditation

تَأَمَّلَ ف to meditate

تَأْميم س nationalization

تَأْمين س (مال يُدْفَعُ مِن أَجْل التَعْويض في حالَة حُصول ضَرَر) insurance

بُنْدُقِيَّة س ج /بَنادِق/ rifle

بَنَدورَة س tomato

بَنْزين س petrol

بَنْطَلون س ج /بَنْطَلونات/ trousers
بَنْطَلون جينْز jeans
بَنْطَلون قَصير shorts

بَنَفْسَجِيّ ص violet

بَنْك س ج /بُنوك/ bank

بَنى ف to build

بُنِّيّ ص brown

بَهْلَوان س clown

بَهيج ص delightful

بَوّاب س doorman

بَوّابَة س gate

بُؤْبُؤ س ج /بَآبيء/ pupil

بوذِيّ ص، س Buddhist

بوذِيَّة س Buddhism

بُؤْرَة س ج /بُؤَر/ focus

بورْصَة س stock exchange

بُؤْس س misery

بوق س ج /أَبْواق/ trumpet

بوكيه س bunch

بَوْل س urine

بَوَّلَ ف to urinate

بولَنْدا س Poland

بولَنْدِيّ س Pole

بولَنْدِيّ ص Polish

بولينْج س bowling

بيئَة س environment

بَيان س ج /بَيانات/ (تَعْبير بِالكَلام حَوْلَ أَمْر مُعَيَّن) statement
(مَنْشور يُوَزَّع لِإطْلاع الناس عَلى أَمْر مُعَيَّن) bulletin

بِيانو س piano

بَيْت س ج /بُيوت/ house
بَيْت الدَرَج staircase

بيتْزا س pizza

بيج ص beige

بيجاما س pyjamas, (US) pajamas

بيرَة س beer

بيروقْراطِيّ ص bureaucrat

بيروقْراطِيَّة س bureaucracy

بيسْبول س baseball

بَيْضَة س ج /بَيْض/ egg

بَيْطَرِيّ س ج /بَياطِرَة/ vet

بَيْع س sale

بَيْنَ ظ between

بَيَّنَ ف to clarify

بَيِّن ص obvious

بَيْنَما ظ while

ب

بَقِيَ ف to remain

بَقِيَّة س ج /بَقايا/ (كَمِّيَّة صَغيرَة تَتَبَقَّى مِن شَيْء) remnant
(الجُزْء المُتَبَقِّي) rest

بَكارَة س virginity

بِكْر ص ج /أَبْكار/ virgin

بَكَى ف to cry

بِكِّيني س bikini

بَل (تُسْتَعْمَلُ لِلتَأْكيد) but rather
بَل هُوَ مَن يُلامُ. Rather, he is to blame.

بَلَى yes

بِلا without

بَلاء س (لَعْنَة) curse
(مَرَض) disease

بِلاد س ج /بُلْدان/ country

بِلاسْتيك س plastic

بِلاسْتيكِيّ ص plastic

بَلاطَة س ج /بَلاط/ tile

بَلاغ س ج /بَلاغات/ communiqué

بَلاغَة س (عِلْم البَلاغَة) rhetoric
(فَصاحَة) eloquence

بَلَحَة س ج /بَلَح/ date
بَلَح البَحْر mussels

بَلَد س ج /بِلاد/بُلْدان/ country

بَلْدَة س town

بَلَدِيّ ص local

بَلَدِيَّة س municipality

بَلْطَة س axe

بَلَعَ ف to swallow

بَلَّغَ ف to report

بَلَغَ ف (وَصَلَ) to reach
(وَصَلَ سِنَّ الحُلُم) to become an adult

بَلّور س crystal

بْلوزَة س ج /بَلايِز/ sweater

بَلّوطَة س ج /بَلّوط/ oak

بُلوغ س (الانْتِقال لِمَرْحَلَة الرُجولَة) adulthood
وَصَلَ سِنَّ البُلوغ to reach adulthood
(الوُصول) reach

بَليد ص ج /بُلَداء/ stupid

بَليغ ص eloquent

بِما أَنَّ since

بِناء س (التَأْسيس وَالرَفْع) construction
(جِسْم ذو جُدْران وَسَقْف كَبَيْت أَو مَصْنَع) building

بَنّاء س builder

بِناءً عَلَى on the basis of

بِنايَة س building

بِنْت (م) س ج /بَنات/ (طِفْل أُنْثى) daughter
(أُنْثى لَم تَعُد امْرَأَة بَعْد) girl

بَنْجَر س beetroot

بَنْد س ج /بُنود/ clause

بُنْدُقَة س ج /بُنْدُق/ nut

بَطّارِيَّة س battery

بَطاطا س potato
بَطاطا حُلْوَة sweet potato
بَطاطِس س potato, potatoes

بِطاقَة س (كَرْت التَعْريف في الهاتِف الخَلَويّ) SIM card
(كَرْت مُزَوَّد بِمَعْلومات يَدُلُّ عَلى الشَخْصيَّة أَو أَصْل الشَيْء) card
(كَرْت يَكونُ عَلى سِلْعَة لِذِكْر المُواصَفات) tag
بِطاقَة إِلِكْترونيَّة e-card
بِطاقَة ائْتِمان credit card

بَطالَة س unemployment

بَطّانيَّة س blanket

بَطَّة س ج /بَط/ duck

بَطَل س ج /أَبْطال/ (شَخْص فازَ بِمُسابَقَة) champion
(شَخْص حَقَّقَ إِنْجازاً بُطولِيّاً عَظيماً) hero

بَطُلَ ف to be invalid

بَطَلَة س heroine

بَطْن س ج /بُطون/ belly

بُطولَة س (جُرْأَة أَو قوَّة كَبيرَة) heroism
(مُسابَقَة) championship
(الشَخْصيَّة الرَئيسيَّة في عَمَل فَنّيّ) starring

بُطوليّ ص heroic

بَطيء ص slow

بَطّيخ س watermelon
بَطّيخ أَصْفَر casaba

بُعْبُع س ج /بَعابيع/ bogey

بَعَثَ ف to send

بَعْث س resurrection

بِعْثَة س ج /بِعَث/ mission

بَعَجَ ف to dent

بُعْد س ج /أَبْعاد/ distance

بَعْدَ ظ after

بَعْض ظ (لِلمَعْدود) few
(لِغَيْر المَعْدود) some

بَعوضَة س ج /بَعوض/ mosquito

بَعيد ص far

بُغْض س hate

بَغَضَ ف to hate

بَغْضاء س hatred

بَغْل س ج /بِغال/ mule

بُغْيَةَ with the aim of

بَغيض ص unpleasant

بَقاء س (اسْتِمْراريَّة وُجود الشَيْء) remaining
(اسْتِمْراريَّة حُدوث الشَيْء) continuation

بَقّال س grocer

بَقْدونِس س parsley

بَقَرَة س ج /بَقَر/ cow

بَقْشيش س ج /بَقاشيش/ tip

بُقْعَة س ج /بُقَع/ spot

بُقوليّات س pulses

بَريء س ج /أبْرِياءُ/ (غَيْر مُتَوَرِّط بِجَريمَة) innocent
(ذو نَوايا حَسَنَة) innocent

بَرِّيَّة س ج /بَراريّ/ wilderness

بَريد س post
بَريد إلِكْتِرُونيّ email

بَريطانيّ ص British

بَريطانيّ س Briton

بَريطانِيا س Britain

بَريق س ج /أبْرِقَة/ glitter

بِزِلَّة س pea

بِساط س ج /بُسُط/ carpet

بَساطَة س simplicity

بُسْتان س ج /بَساتينُ/ (زَيْتون، نَخيل) grove
(تُفّاح، إجّاص) orchard

بَسَّطَ ف (سَهَّلَ وَوَضَّحَ أمْراً) to simplify
(جَعَلَ الشَيْء بِنَفْس المُسْتَوى) to even out

بَسَطَ ف to impose
بَسَطَ سُلْطَتَهُ بِالقوَّة He imposed his authority by force.

بَسْطَة س stall

بَسْكَويت س biscuit

بَسيط ص simple

بِشارَة س glad tidings

بَشاشَة س cheerfulness

بَشاعَة س ugliness

بِشَأْنِ regarding

بِشِدَّة ح intensely

بَشَّرَ ف to bring good news
بَشَّرَني عُمَر بِنَجاحي Omar brought me the good news of my success.

بَشَر س mankind

بَشَرَة س skin

بُشْرى س good news

بَشَرِيَّة س mankind

بَشِع ص ugly

بَشْكير س ج /بَشاكير/ towel

بَشوش ص pleasant

بَصَر س ج /أبْصار/ sight

بَصَرِيّ ص optical

بَصَقَ ف to spit

بَصْقَة س spit

بَصَلَة س ج /بَصَل/ (نَوْع مِن الخُضَر) onion
(بِدايَة الزَهْرَة) bulb

بَصَمَ ف to print

بَصْمَة س print

بَصير ص sighted

بِضاعَة س ج /بَضائِع/ goods

بِضْع ظ some

بَضَّعَ ف to supply with goods

بَطارِخ س roe

بَذَّرَ أَمْوالَهُ في القِمار He squandered his money on gambling.

بِذْرَة س ج /بُذور/ seed

بَذَلَ ف to spend

بَذَلَ جُهْداً to make an effort

بَذيء ص obscene

بَرّ س (اليابِسَة) land

بَرَّأَ ف to acquit

بَراءَة س (حالَة عَدَم التَوَرُّط بِجَريمَة) innocence

(سُلوك يَخْلو مِن الأذى أو العُنْف) innocence

بَراءَة اخْتِراع patent

بَرازيل س (البَرازيل) Brazil

بَرازيليّ ص، س Brazilian

بَراعَة س excelling

بَرّاق ص sparkling

بُرْتُغال س (البُرْتُغال) Portugal

بُرْتُغاليّ ص، س ج /بُرْتُغال/ Portuguese

بُرْتُقالَة س ج /بُرْتُقال/ orange

بُرْتُقاليّ ص orange

بُرْج س ج /أَبْراج/ tower

بَرَد س hail

بَرْد س cold

بَرُدَ ف to become cold

بَرَّدَ ف to cool

بُرْدايَة س curtain

بَرَّرَ ف (وَضَّحَ الأسْباب) to justify

بُرْعُم س ج /بَراعِم/ bud

بُرْغيّ س ج /بَراغي/ screw

بَرْق س lightening

بُرْقُع س ج /بَراقِع/ burka

بَرْقوق س plum

بَرْقيَّة س telegram

بَرَكَة س blessing

بِرْكَة س ج /بِرَك/ pool

بَرْمائيّ ص amphibious

بِرْميل س ج /بَراميل/ barrel

بَرْنامَج س ج /بَرامِج/ (عَرْض تلفزيونيّ يُناقِش مَوْضوعاً مُعَيَّناً) programme

(خِطَّة لِتَنْفيذ مَشْروع) programme

(قائمَة مِن مَعْلومات مُخَزَّنَة في الحاسوب لِتَنْفيذ أوامِر) programme

بُرْنُس الحَمّام س bathrobe

بُرْهان س ج /بَراهين/ proof

بَرْهَنَ ف to prove

بُرْهَة س ج /بُرَه/ while

بْروتين س protein

بُرودَة س coldness

بْروفَة س rehearsal

بْروكُليّ س broccoli

بَرى ف to sharpen

بَرّيّ ص wild

ب

بالون س balloon

باليه س ballet

بامْيا س okra

باهِت ص (قَليل وُضوح الرُؤْيَة) dim
(شاحِب) pale

باهِظ ص excessive

بِتْرول س oil

بَثّ س broadcast

بَثَّ ف to broadcast

بَثْرَة س spot

بَحّار س ج /بَحّارَة/ sailor

بَحْث س ج /بُحوث/أَبْحاث/ (تَحْقيق عِلْميّ) research
(تَفْتيش عَن أَمْر) search

بَحَثَ ف (دَرَسَ مَوْضوعاً عِلْمِيّاً مِن أَجْل الوُصول إلى نَتائِج جَديدَة) to do research
(فَتَّشَ عَن شَيْء) to look for

بَحْر س ج /بِحار/ sea
البَحْر المُتَوَسِّط Mediterranean

بَحْريّ س marine

بَحْريَّة س navy

بَحْرَيْن س (البَحْرَيْن) Bahrain

بَحْرَيْنيّ ص، س Bahraini

بِحَيْثُ in such a way that

بُحَيْرَة س lake

بُخار س ج /أَبْخِرَة/ steam

بَخْت س ج /بُخوت /أَبْخِتَة/ luck

بَخَّرَ ف to evaporate

بُخْل س miserliness

بَخور س incense

بَخيل ص ج /بُخَلاء/ miserly

بَدْء س starting

بَدا ف to seem

بَدَأَ ف to start

بَدانَة س obesity

بِدايَة س beginning

بَدْر س ج /بُدور/ full moon

بِدْعَة س ج /بِدَع/ heresy

بِدِقَّة س accurately

بَدَّلَ ف to change

بَدَل س swap
بَدَلاً مِن instead of
بَدَلاً مِن أَنْ يَدْرُسَ ذَهَبَ وَنامَ Instead of studying, he went and slept.

بَدْلَة س ج /بِدَل/ suit

بَدَن س ج /أَبْدان/ body

بَدَنيّ ص physical

بِدون ح without

بَديل س (خَيار) alternative
(شَخْص أَو شَيْء يَقومُ مَقام مَثيلِهِ) substitute

بَدين ص ج /بُدَناء/ fat

بَذَّرَ ف squander

بِ حج (تَدُلُّ عَلى المَكان) in

كانَ المِفْتاح بِيَدي The key was in my hand.

(تَدُلُّ عَلى الطَريقَة) with

كَسَرْتُ الزُجاج بِيَدي I broke the glass with my hand.

بِئْر س ج /آبار/ well

بائِس ص ج /بُؤَساء/ miserable

بائِع س seller

بائِع المُفَرَّق retailer

باب س ج /أَبْواب/ door

بابا س ج /باباوات/ pope

باتَ ف (مَكَثَ وَنامَ) to sleep over

(أَصْبَحَ) to become

باحِث س researcher

باخِرَة س ج /بَواخِر/ ship

بادِرَة س ج /بَوادِر/ sign

بادَلَ ف to exchange

باذِنْجان س aubergine

بارِجَة س ج /بَوارِج/ battleship

بارِد ص cold

بارِز ص (مُتَفَوِّق) outstanding

(ناتِئ) protruding

بارِع ص brilliant

بارَكَ ف (هَنَّأَ) to congratulate

(حَمى وَزادَ) to bless

باضَ ف to lay

باطِل ص (لاغٍ) futile

باطِل س (شَيْء سَيِّئ) evil

باطِنِيّ ص internal

باعَ ف to sell

باعَدَ ف to space out

باقٍ ص remaining

باقِلاءُ س broad bean

باكِر ص early

باكِسْتان س (الباكِسْتان) Pakistan

باكِستانيّ ص، س Pakistani

بالَ ف to urinate

بالٍ ص worn out

بالِغ ص (تَعَدّى مَرْحَلَة الطُفولَة) adult

(ذو أَهَمِيَّة كُبْرى) considerable

بالَغَ ف (صَوَّرَ شَيْئاً عَلى أَنَّهُ أَفْضَل أَو أَسْوَأ مِن حَقيقَتِه) to exaggerate

ا

إيلاج س penetration

أَيْلول س September

إيماءَة س gesture

إيمان س conviction
faith

أَيْمَنُ ظ (عَلى جِهَة اليَمين) right

أَيْنَ أ إس (تُسْتَخْدَمُ لِلسُؤال عَن المَكان) where
أَيْنَ وَضَعْتَ قَلَمي؟ Where did you put my pen?

أَيْنَما ظ ز (في أيِّ مَكان) wherever
سَأَجِدُكَ أَيْنَما ذَهَبْتَ I will find you wherever you go.

أَوْفَدَ ف to delegate

أَوْقَفَ ف to stop

أَوَّلُ ص م أولى ج /أوائِل/ ج م/أُوَل/ first

أولَئِكَ أ إش (اسْم إشارَة لِلجَمْع البَعيد) those

أولَئِكَ الناس غُرَباء Those people are strangers.

أَوْلَجَ ف to insert

أَوْلَوِيّة س priority

أَوَّلي ص (يَحْدُثُ في أوّل الأمْر) initial
(تَأْسيسيّ) primary

أَوْمَأَ ف to nod

أَوْهَمَ ف to bluff

أَيْ (بِمَعْنى...) that means

إيّا/أَنْ أ ن don't

أَيّار س May

إيّاكَ ض (ضَمير المُخاطَب لِلمُفْرَد المُذَكَّر) you

إيّاكِ ض (ضَمير المُخاطَب لِلمُفْرَد المُؤَنَّث) you

إيّاكُم ض (ضَمير المُخاطَب لِلجَمْع المُذَكَّر) you

إيّاكُما ض (ضَمير المُخاطَب لِلمُثَنّى) you

إيّاكُنَّ ض (ضَمير المُخاطَب لِلجَمْع المُؤَنَّث) you

إيّانا ض (ضَمير المُتَكَلِّم لِلجَمْع المُذَكَّر وَالمُؤَنَّث) us

إيّاهُ ض (ضَمير الغائِب لِلمُفْرَد المُذَكَّر) him
(ضَمير الغائِب لِلمُفْرَد لِلجَماد وَالحَيَوان) it

إيّاها ض (ضَمير الغائِب لِلمُفْرَد المُؤَنَّث) her

إيّاهُم ض (ضَمير الغائِب لِلجَمْع المُذَكَّر) them

إيّاهُما ض (ضَمير الغائِب لِلمُثَنّى) them

إيّاهُنَّ ض (ضَمير الغائِب لِلجَمْع المُؤَنَّث) them

إيّايَ ض (ضَمير المُتَكَلِّم لِلمُفْرَد المُذَكَّر وَالمُؤَنَّث) me

آيَة س (دَليل) sign
(مَقْطَع من القُرْآن) Quranic verse

إيجابيّ ص positive

إيجاد س creation

إيجار س rent

أَيَّدَ ف to support

إيران س Iran

إيرانيّ ص، س Iranian

إيرْلَنْدا س Ireland

إيرْلَنْديّ ص Irish

إيرْلَنْديّ س Irishman

أَيْسَرُ ظ (عَلى جِهَة اليَسار) left

إيصال س receipt

أَيْضاً ح also

إيضاح س clarification

إيطاليّ ص، س Italian

إيطاليا س Italy

إيقاع س rhythm

إيقاف س stopping

أَيْقَظَ ف to awaken

أَيْقونَة س icon

أَيْل س deer

ا

أَنْقَذَ ف to rescue

انْقِراض س extinction

انْقَضى ف to pass

انْقِلاب س overthrow

إنْكار س denial

أَنْكَرَ ف to deny

انْكَمَشَ ف to shrink

إنَّما (تُسْتَخْدَمُ لِلتَأْكيد) however

إنْهاء س termination

انْهارَ ف to collapse

أَنْهى ف to finish

انْهِيار س collapse
انْهِيار عَصَبيّ breakdown

أَنيق ص elegant

أَنين س moan

أَهانَ ف to insult

إهانَة س insult

اهْتِراء س decay

اهْتَرَأَ ف to wear

اهْتَزَّ ف to shake

اهْتَمَّ ب ف to be interested in

اهْتِمام س interest
care

اهْتِياج س excitement

أَهْدى ف to present a gift

أَهْل س ج /أَهالٍ/ (أَقْرِباء) relatives
(سُكّان) inhabitants

أَهْلاً وَسَهْلاً welcome

أَهْليّ ص national

أَهَمَّ ف to concern

أَهَمّ ح more important

إهْمال س neglect

أَهْمَلَ ف to neglect

أَهَمّيَّة س importance

أَو (أَداة تَخْيير) or
خُذ سَيّارَتي أَو سَيّارَة أَحْمَد Take my car or Ahmad's car.

أَواخِرُ ظ late

أَوان س ج /آوِنَة/ time

أوبِرا س opera

أَوْج س peak

أَوْجَدَ ف to bring into existence

أَوْجَزَ ف to outline

أَوْدَعَ ف to deposit

أورْجُن س organ

أوروبّا س Europe

أوروبّيّ ص، س European

أَوْشَكَ ف to be about to

أَوْصى ب ف to recommend

أَوْضَحَ ف to make clear

ا

انْدَفَعَ ف to rush

انْدِماج س integration

انْدَمَجَ ف to integrate

إنْذار س (صَوْت صادِر مِن جِهاز لِلتَحْذير) alarm
(تَحْذير خَطِّيّ أو شَفَوِيّ) warning

آنَذاك ظ then

انْزَلَقَ ف to slip

انْسابَ ف to flow

إنْسان س (البَشَر) human being
(شَخْص) person

إنْسانيّ ص (مُتَعَلِّق بِالإنْسان) human
(مُتَعَلِّق بِمُساعَدَة الآخَرين) humane
(مُظْهِر الرَحْمَة وَالإنْسانِيَّة) humanitarian

إنْسانيَّة س humanity

آنِسَة س miss

انْسِجام س harmony

انْسَجَمَ ف to be in harmony with

انْسَحَبَ ف to withdraw

إنْشاء س construction

أنْشَأَ ف (أسَّسَ) to establish
(خَلَقَ) to create

أنْشَدَ ف to chant

انْضِباط س discipline

انْضَمَّ إلى ف to join

انْضِمام س joining
entry

انْطِباع س impression

انْطَبَقَ على ف to apply to

انْطِلاق س starting

انْطَلَقَ ف to start off

انْعِدام س non-existence

انْعِزاليّ ص reclusive

أنْعَشَ ف to refresh

انْعِطاف س turn

انْعِقاد س convening

انْعَقَدَ ف to convene

انْعِكاس س (انْعِكاس صورَة أو تَأثير) reflection
(انْعِكاس في الاتِّجاه) reversal

انْغَمَرَ ف to be immersed

أنْف س ج /أنوف/ nose

آنِفاً ظ previously
تَمَّ ذِكْرُهُ آنِفاً It was mentioned previously.

إنْفاق س expenditure

انْفِجار س ج /انْفِجارات/ explosion

انْفَجَرَ ف to explode

انْفِراج س relaxation

انْفِراد س seclusion

أنْفَقَ ف to spend

إنْفِلْوَنْزا س flu

إنْقاذ س rescue

انْتِشار س spread

انْتَشَرَ ف to spread

انْتِصار س victory

انْتَصَرَ ف to prevail

انْتِظار س waiting

انْتَظَرَ ف to wait

انْتِفاضَة س uprising

انْتَفَخَ ف to swell up

انْتِقال س transfer

انْتِقاليّ ص transitional

انْتِقام س revenge

انْتَقَدَ ف to criticize

انْتَقَلَ ف to move

انْتَقَمَ ف to take revenge

أَنْتُم ض (ضَمير المُخاطَب لِلجَمْع المُذَكَّر) you
أَنْتُم طُلَّاب جَيِّدون You are good students.

أَنْتُما ض (ضَمير المُخاطَب للمُثَنَّى) you
أَنْتُما طِفْلان جَيِّدان You are (both) good children.

أَنْتُنَّ ض (ضَمير المُخاطَب لِلجَمْع المُؤَنَّث) you
أَنْتُنَّ مُدَرِّسات جَيِّدات You are good teachers.

انْتِهاك س violation

انْتَهَكَ ف to violate

انْتَهى ف to end

أُنْثَويّ ص feminine

أُنْثى س ج /أَناثى/ female

إنْجاز س achievement

أَنْجَزَ ف to achieve

إنْجِلْترا س England

إنْجِليزيّ ص ج/إنْجِليز/ English

إنْجِليزيّ س ج /إنْجِليز/ Englishman

إنْجيل س ج /أَناجيل/ (كِتاب السَيِّد المَسيح) gospel

انْحازَ إلى ف to be biased towards

انْحِدار س gradient

انْحَدَرَ ف (نَزَلَ إلى مِنْطَقَة مُنْخَفِضَة) to slope
(جاءَ أو كانَت أُصولُهُ) to descend

انْحِراف س deviation

انْحَرَفَ ف to deviate

انْحَرَقَ ف to burn

انْحَصَرَ ف to be restricted to

انْحَطَّ ف to deteriorate

انْحِطاط س (التَراجُع لِلأَسْوَأ) decline
(سوء الأَخْلاق) decadence

انْحَنى ف to bow

انْحِياز س bias

انْخِفاض س fall

انْخَفَضَ ف to decrease

انْدِفاع س impulse

أَمْكَنَ ف could

أَمَل س ج /آمال/ hope

أَمَلَ ف to hope

إمْلاء س dictation

أَمْلَأَ ف to fill

أَمْلَسُ ص smooth

أَمْلى ف to dictate

آمِن ص safe

أَمَّنَ ف to secure
to trust

آمَنَ ف to believe

أَمْن س security

أُمْنِيَّة س wish

أُمِّيّ ص illiterate

أُمِّيَّة س illiteracy

أَمير س ج /أُمَراء/ (أَحَد أفْراد العائِلَة المالِكَة)
prince
leader (قائِد)

أَمين ص trustworthy
أَمين سِرّ secretary
أَمين الصَنْدوق treasurer
الأَمين العامّ secretary general

آنَ ف to come (time)

أَنْ (حَرْف نَصْب) that

أَنَّ ف to moan

إِنْ أد ش if

أَنا ض (ضَمير المُتَكَلِّم للمُذَكَّر والمُؤَنَّث) I
أنا مِن بَريطانيا .I am from Britain

أَنارَ ف to illuminate

أَناقَة س elegance

أَناناس س pineapple

أَنانيّ ص selfish

أَنانيَّة س (حُبّ الذات) selfishness

انْبَعَثَ ف (صَدَرَ) to be sent out

انْبَغى ف (مِن المَفْروض) should

أُنْبوب س ج /أَنابيب/ (خُرْطوم) pipe
(ماسورَة تَعْبِئَة) tube

أَنْتَ ض (ضَمير المُخاطَب لِلمُفْرَد المُذَكَّر) you

أَنْتِ ض (ضَمير المُخاطَب للمُفْرَد المُؤَنَّث) you
هَل أنْتِ بَريطانيَّة ?Are you British

إنْتاج س production

إنْتاجيّ ص productive

انْتِباه س attention

أَنْتَجَ ف to produce

انْتِحار س suicide

انْتَحَرَ ف to commit suicide

انْتِخاب س election

انْتَخَبَ ف to elect

إنْتَرْنِت س Internet

انْتَزَعَ ف to pull out

انْتَسَبَ إلى ف to belong to

أَمان س safety

أَمانَة س (فَريق لإدارَة مُؤَسَّسَة) secretariat
(شَيْء يوضَعُ عِنْدَ شَخْص ما للاعْتِناء بِهِ وَحِفْظِهِ إلى حين) trust

إمْبِراطور س emperor

إمْبِراطوريّ ص imperial

إمْبِراطوريَّة س empire

إمْبِرِياليّ ص imperialist

إمْبِرِياليَّة س Imperialism

أُمَّة س ج /أُمَم/ nation

امْتِثال س compliance

امْتِحان س (امْتِحان قَصير) quiz
(اخْتِبار نَظَريّ) exam
(اخْتِبار عَمَليّ أو نَظَريّ) test

امْتَحَنَ ف to test

امْتَدَّ ف to stretch

امْتِداد س stretch

امْتَزَجَ ف to be mixed (with)

امْتَصَّ ف to absorb

امْتِصاص س absorption

امْتَطى ف to ride

أَمْتَعَ ف to make enjoy

أَمْتِعَة س luggage

امْتِلاك س possession

امْتَلَكَ ف to possess

امْتِياز س (تَفَوُّق) distinction
(تَرْخيص مِن مَصْلَحَة للعَمَل بِاسْمِها) franchise
(مِيزَة خاصَّة) privilege

أَمَدَّ ف to supply

إمْداد س supply

أَمْر س ج /أَوامِرُ/ (طَلَب يَجِبُ تَنْفيذُهُ) order
ج /أُمور/ (مَوْضوع) matter

أَمَرَ ف to order

امْرَأة س ج /نِساء/ woman

أَمْريكا س (قارّة أَمْريكا) the American continent
(الوِلايات المُتَّحِدَة) the United States of America

أَمْريكيّ ص، س American

أَمْس س yesterday

إمْساك س constipation

أَمْسَكَ ف to catch

أَمْسى ف (أَصْبَحَ) to become
ف (قَضى المَساء) to spend the evening

إمْضاء س (التَوْقيع) signature
(الاِسْتِمْرار) continuation

أَمْضى ف to spend

أَمْطَرَ ف to rain

أَمْعاء س guts

إمْعان س going too far

أَمْعَنَ ف to go too far

إمْكانيَّة س possibility

أَلِف س (الحَرْف الأوَّل في اللُغَة العَرَبيَّة) alif

أَلَّفَ ف (كَتَبَ عَمَلاً أَدبيّاً) to write
(جَمَعَ مَواضيع وَجَعَلَها في كِتاب) to compile

أَلْف عد ج /آلاف/ thousand

أُلْفَة س affinity

أَلْفيَّة س millennium

إلْقاء س (رَمْي) throw
(تَقْديم حَديث) presentation

أَلْقى ف (رَمى) to throw
(قَدَّمَ حَديثاً) to deliver

إلِكْتُرونيّ ص electronic (al)

الله س God

آلَمَ ف to hurt

أَلَم س pain

أَلْمانيّ ص، س ج /أَلْمان/ German

أَلْمانيا س Germany

إلَه س ج /آلِهَة/ god

إلْهام س inspiration

أَلْهَمَ ف to inspire

أَلْهى ف to distract

أَلو hello

إلى حج (تَدُلُّ عَلى الانْتِهاء لِمَكان) to
ذَهَبْتُ إلى فَرَنْسا. I went to France.
(تَدُلُّ على الانْتِهاء لِمَصْدَر)
أَرْسَلْتُ رِسالَةً إلى أخي I sent a letter to my brother.

آليّ ص (مُتَعَلِّق بِالآلَة) mechanical
(مُجَهَّز لِيَعْمَلَ ذاتياً) automatic

أَلْياف س fibres

آليَّة س (آليّات) machinery
(طَريقَة عَمَل الآلَة) mechanism

أَليف ص tame

أُمّ س ج /أُمَّهات/ mother

أَم (أَداة تَخْيير) or
هَل خَرَجْتَ اليَوْم أَم بَقَيْتَ في البَيْت؟ Have you gone out today or stayed in?

أَمَّ ف to lead the prayer

أَمّا (تُسْتَخْدَمُ للانْتِقال مِن نُقْطَة إلى أُخْرى في الحَديث أو الكِتابَة أَو للمُقارَنَة) ... as for
أَنا طَويل أَمّا أَخي فَهُوَ قَصير I am tall, but as for my brother, he is short.

إمّا ..وَإمّا / أو (تُسْتَخْدَمُ لِلتَخْيير بَيْنَ أَمْرَيْن)
either .. or
إمّا تُحْسِنُ العَمَل وإمّا تَذْهَبُ Either do your work well or go away.

إمارات العَرَبيّة المُتَّحِدَة س (الإمارات العَرَبية المُتَّحِدَة) United Arab Emirates

إماراتيّ ص، س Emirati

أَمالَ ف to tilt

أَمامَ ظ (مُقابِل) opposite
(في مُقَدِّمَة) in front of

إمام س ج /أَئِمَّة/ (أَيّ شَخْص يَقودُ المُسْلِمين خِلالَ الصَلاة) imam
(حاكِم المُسْلِمين) Muslim leader
(عالِم مُسْلِم وَخاصَّة أَحَد العُلَماء الأَوائِل)
famous Muslim scholar

اكْتَأَبَ ف to feel depressed

اكْتَسَبَ ف to acquire

اكْتِشاف س discovery

اكْتَشَفَ ف to discover

أُكْتوبِر س (الشَهْر العاشِر بِالتَقْويم المِصْريّ) October

أَكْثَرُ ح (رَقْم أَكْبَر) more
(الغالِبِيَّة) most

أَكَّدَ ف (شَدَّدَ عَلى حُدوث شَيْء) to confirm
(شَدَّدَ عَلى أَهَمِّيَّة شَيْء) to emphasize

أَكْر س (مِساحَة تُساوي ٤٠٥٠ مِتْراً مُرَبَّعاً) acre

أُكْسُجين س oxygen

أَكَلَ ف to eat

أَكَّلَ ف to feed

أَكْل س food

أَكْلَة س meal

إِكْمال س completion

أَكْمَلَ ف to complete

أَكيد ص certain

ال ال التَعْريف the

إلاّ أداة اسْتِثْناء (تُسْتَعْمَلُ لِلاسْتِثْناء) except
جاءَ جَميع أَصْدِقائي إلاّ سام All my friends came except Sam.

الآن ظ now

أَلْبُوم س ج /ألابيم/ album

آلَة س machine

آلَة تَصْوير camera

آلَة طابِعَة printer

الْتَحَقَ ب ف to join

الْتِزام س commitment

الْتَزَمَ ف to be committed

الْتَفَتَ ف to turn

الْتَقَطَ ف to catch

الْتَقى ف to meet

الْتَمَسَ ف to ask for

الْتِهاب س inflammation

الْتِهاب المَفاصِل arthritis

الْتِهاب رِئَوِيّ pneumonia

الْتِواء س twist

أَلَحَّ ف (طالَبَ بِضَرورَة أَمْر) to urge
(صَمَّمَ) to insist

إِلْحاح س (المُطالَبَة بِضَرورَة أَمْر) urgency
(التَصْميم) insistence

إِلْحاد س atheism

أَلْحَدَ ف to deny the existence of God

أَلْحَقَ ف (أَرْفَقَ) to attach
(أَضافَ) to add

إِلْزامِيّ ص compulsory

أَلْصَقَ ف to stick

أَلْعاب رِياضِيَّة athletics

إِلْغاء س cancellation

أَلْغى ف to cancel

ا

fast-breaking meal

أَفْطَرَ ف to have breakfast
to break one's fast

أُفُق س ج /آفاق/ (دائِرَة الْتِقاء الأَرْض بِالسَماء)
horizon
(مَدى خِبْرَة وَذَكاء الشَخْص)
range of experience

أُفُقِيّ ص horizontal

إِفْلاس س bankruptcy

أَفوكادو س avocado

أَقالَ ف to dismiss

إِقالَة س dismissal

أَقامَ ف (أَنْشَأَ أَو بَنى) to set up
(سَكَنَ) to dwell

إِقامَة س stay

اقْتِباس س quotation

اقْتَبَسَ ف to quote

اقْتِحام س invasion

اقْتَحَمَ ف to storm

اقْتِراح س proposal

اقْتِراع س ballot

اقْتَرَبَ مِن ف to approach

اقْتَرَحَ ف to suggest

اقْتَرَعَ ف to vote

اقْتِصاد س economy

اقْتِصادِيّ ص economic

اقْتَصَرَ عَلى ف to limit to

اقْتَضى ف to require

اقْتَلَعَ ف to pluck out

اقْتِناع س conviction

اقْتَنَعَ ف to be convinced

إِقْدام س venturing

أَقْدَمُ ظ more ancient

أَقْدَمَ عَلى ف to venture into

أَقَرَّ ف (اعْتَرَفَ) to admit
(أَكَّدَ) to confirm

إِقْرار س (قُبول) endorsement
(تَأْكيد) confirmation

أَقْرَضَ ف to lend

أَقْسَمَ ف to swear

أَقْصى ص extreme

أَقْعَدَ ف to seat

أَقْفَلَ ف to lock

أَقَلّ ح less

أَقْلَعَ عَن ف to give up

أَقَلِّيَّة س minority

إِقْليم س ج /أَقاليم/ region

أَقْنَعَ ف to persuade

أَكاديمِيّ ص academic

أَكاديمِيَّة س academy

اكْتِئاب س depression

إعْلام س (إخْبار) informing
(الصَحافَة) media

إعْلان س (التَرْويج لِمُنْتَج أو أَمْر ما)
advertisement
(جَعْل أَمْر ما مَعْروفاً لِلعامَّة) announcement

أَعْلَمَ ف to inform

أَعْلَنَ ف (نَشَرَ إعْلاناً) to advertise
(أَخْبَرَ العامَّة) to announce

أَعْلى ح higher

أَعْمى ص م عَمْياءُ ج /عُمْي/ blind

أَعْمى ف to blind

أَغاثَ ف to relieve

إغاثَة س relief

أَغارَ ف to raid

اغْتالَ ف to assassinate

اغْتَسَلَ ف to wash os

اغْتِصاب س rape

اغْتَصَبَ ف (امْرَأَة) to rape
(حَقّاً أَو مُلْكاً) to usurp

اغْتِيال س assassination

إغْراء س temptation

أَغْرى ف to tempt

أَغْضَبَ ف to anger

أَغْلَبِيَّة س majority

أَغْلَقَ ف to close

أُغْنِيَة س ج /أَغانيّ/ song

أُغوسْطوس س (الشَهْر الثامِن بِالتَقْويم المِصْريّ)
August

أَفادَ ف to benefit
to report

إفادَة س (تَقْرير مَعْلومات رَسْمِيَّة) statement
(شَيْء يَأْتي بِالمَنْفَعَة) benefit

آفَة س epidemic

افْتِتاح س opening

افْتِتان س fascination

افْتَتَحَ ف to open

افْتِراض س assumption

افْتَرَضَ ف to assume

افْتَقَدَ ف to miss

افْتَقَرَ إلى ف to lack

إفْراج س release

أَفْرَغَ ف to empty

أَفْرَهول س overalls

أَفْريقيّ ص، س ج /أَفارِقَة/
African

أَفْريقِيا س Africa

إفْساد س spoiling

أَفْسَدَ ف to spoil

إفْشاء س disclosure

أَفْشى ف to reveal

أَفْضَلُ ح better

إفْطار س breakfast

أَعانَ ف to help

إِعانَة س aid

إِعانَة مالِيَّة grant

اعْتِبار س consideration

اعْتِباراً مِن ظ starting from

اعْتَبَرَ ف (دَرَسَ أَمْراً) to consider

(نَظَرَ لِشَيْء بِشَكْل خاصّ) to regard

اعْتِداء س attack

اعْتَدَى على ف to assault

اعْتِذار س apology

اعْتَذَرَ ف to apologize

اعْتِراض س objection

اعْتِراف س (إِقْرار القِيام بِخَطَأ) confession

(إِقْرار بِالوُجود) recognition

(تَقْدير) acknowledgement

اعْتَرَضَ على ف to object to

اعْتَرَفَ ف (أَقَرَّ بِقِيام خَطَأ) to confess

(قَدَّرَ) to acknowledge

(اعْتَرَفَ بِوُجود) to recognize

اعْتِصام س sit-in

اعْتَصَمَ ف to hold a sit-in

اعْتِقاد س belief

اعْتِقال س arrest

اعْتَقَدَ ف to believe

اعْتَقَلَ ف to arrest

اعْتِلاء س accession

اعْتِماد س reliance

اعْتَمَدَ على ف to rely on

اعْتَنَقَ ف to embrace

اعْتَنَى ب ف to look after

اعْتِيادِيّ ص common

إِعْجاب س admiration

أَعْجَبَ ف to like

أُعْجِبَ ب to admire

أَعَدَّ ف to prepare

إِعْداد س preparation

إِعْدام س execution

أَعْدَمَ ف to execute

أَعْدَى ف to infect

أَعْرَبَ ف to express

أَعْرَجُ ص م عَرْجاءُ ج /عُرْج/ lame

أَعْزَبُ ص م عَزْباءُ ج /عُزّاب/ single

إِعْصار س hurricane

إِعْطاء س giving

أَعْطَى ف to give

إِعْفاء س (السَماح بِعَدَم دَفْع مَبْلَغ مُسْتَحَقّ أو تَأْدِيَة واجِب) exemption

(إِنْهاء مَهَمَّة) discharge

أَعْفَى ف (سَمَحَ بِعَدَم دَفْع مَبْلَغ مُسْتَحَقّ أَو تَأْدِيَة واجِب) to exempt

(أَنْهَى مَهَمَّة) to discharge

أَعْقاب: في أَعْقاب ظ following

(احْتِياطيّ) spare
(أكْثَر مِن اللازِم) extra
وَقْت إضافيّ (بَعْدَ الوَقْت المُحَدّد) overtime

أَضْحَكَ ف to make laugh

أَضْحى ف to become

أَضَرَّ ف to harm

إضْراب س strike

اضْطَجَعَ ف to lie down

أُضْطُرَّ ف to be compelled

اضْطِراب س (إخْلال) disturbance
(أَحْداث عُنْف) turmoil

اضْطِهاد س oppression

اضْطَهَدَ ف to oppress

إضْعاف ف weakening

أَضْعَفَ ف to weaken

إضْمامَة س pad

أَطاحَ ف to overthrow

إطار س ج /إطارات/ (دولاب السَيّارَة) tyre
ج /أُطُر/ (مادّة صُلْبَة تَكونُ حَوْلَ جِسْم أَو مِساحَة)
frame
(مَوْضوع) domain

أَطاعَ ف to obey

إطاعَة س obedience

إطْراء س praise

أَطْرَش ص م طَرْشاءُ ج /طُرْش/ deaf

أُطْروحَة س thesis

أَطْعَمَ ف to feed

أَطْفَأَ ف (أَخْمَدَ النار) to extinguish
(أَوْقَفَ تَشْغيل ماكينَة أَو ضَوْء) to turn off

إطْلاق س (بَدْء الشَيْء) launching
إطْلاق النار (فَتحَ النار مِن سِلاح)
opening fire

إطْلاق س launch

اطَّلَعَ ف to be informed

أَطْلَقَ ف (بَدَأَ) to launch
أَطْلَقَ النار (فتَحَ النار مِن سِلاح) to shoot

اطْمَأَنَّ ف to be reassured

أُظْفَر س ج /أَظافِر/ nail

إظْهار س display

أَظْهَرَ ف (أَبانَ وَوَضَّحَ) to demonstrate
(عَرَضَ) to display

أَعادَ ف (رَدَّدَ) to repeat
(أَرْجَعَ) to give back
أَعادَ النَظَر to reconsider
أَعادَ تَصْنيعاً to recycle

إعادَة س repetition
إعادَة تَأْهيل rehabilitation

أَعارَ ف to lend

إعارَة س lending

أَعاقَ ف to block
to hinder

إعاقَة س (عَجْز جَسَديّ) disability
(تَعْطيل) hindrance

إشْراك س giving a share

أَشْرَفَ ف to supervise

شُعاع س ج /أشِعَّة/ ray

أَشْعَلَ ف (أنارَ ضَوْئاً أو سيجارَة) to light
(أَحْرَقَ) to set fire

أَشْفى ف (أزالَ المَرَض) to heal

أَشْقَرُ ص م شَقْراءُ م /شُقْر/ blond

اشْمَأَزَّ ف to feel disgusted

اشْمِئْزاز س disgust

أَشْيَبُ ص م شَيْباءُ م /شُيَّاب/ white-headed

أَصابَ ف (جَرَحَ) to injure
(ضَرَبَ الهَدَف) to hit

إصابَة س (أذى) injury
(مُصاب) casualty
(رَمْيَة) score

أَصالَة س authenticity

أَصْبَحَ ف to become

إصْبَع س ج /أَصابِع/ finger
إصْبَع القَدَم toe
إصْبَع الإبْهام thumb

إصْدار س issue
version

أَصْدَرَ ف to issue

أَصَرَّ عَلى ف to insist on

إصْرار س insistence

اصْطادَ ف to hunt

إصْطَبْل س stable

اصْطَحَبَ ف to accompany

اصْطِدام س collision

اصْطَدَمَ ف to collide

اصْطِناعيّ ص artificial

أَصْغى ف to listen

أَصْفَرُ ص م صَفْراءُ ج /صُفْر/ yellow

اصْفَرَّ ف to turn yellow

أَصْل س ج /أُصول/ origin

إصْلاح س repair

أَصْلَحَ ف to repair

أَصْلَعُ ص م صَلْعاءُ ج /صُلْع/ bald

أَصْليّ ص original

أَصَمُّ ص م صَمَّاءُ ج /صُمّ/ deaf

أُصوليّ ص fundamentalist

أَصيل ص ج /أُصَلاء/ noble
حِصان أَصيل thoroughbred

أَضاءَ ف to light up

إضاءَة س light

أَضاعَ ف to lose

إضاعَة س (فُقْدان) loss
(تَبْديد) wasting

أَضافَ ف to add

إضافَة س addition

إضافيّ ص (زِيادَة) additional

أَسْلَمَ ف to convert to Islam

أُسْلوب س ج /أساليبُ/ (نَمَط) style
(مَنْهَج) manner

اسْم س ج /أَسْماء/ (اسْم عَلَم) name
(تُسْتَخْدَمُ للدَلالَة على اسْم غَيْر عَلَم في الإعْراب)
noun

أَسْمَرُ ص م سَمْراءُ ج /سُمْر/ brown

اسْمَرَّ ف to turn brown

إسْمَنْت س cement

أَسْنَدَ ف (كَلَّفَ) to entrust sth to
أَسْنَدَ المُهِمَّةَ إلى ابْنِهِ He entrusted the task to his son.
(اتَّكَأَ) to lean on

إسْهال س diarrhoea

إسْوارَة س ج /أَساوِر/ bracelet

أَسْوَأُ ح worse

أُسْوَة س role model

أَسْوَدُ ص م سَوْداءُ ج /سود/ black

اسْوَدَّ ف to blacken

آسِيا س Asia

أَسير س ج /أَسْرى/ prisoner

آسِيَوِيّ ص، س Asian

أَشادَ ب ف to commend

أَشارَ إلى ف (دَلَّلَ بِواسِطَة إصْبَعِهِ أو إيمائَة)
to point at
(ذَكَرَ) to refer to

إشارْب س head scarf

إشارَة س (دَلالَة) indication
(عَلامَة للإرْشاد) sign
(إشارَة الإرْسال) signal

أَشاعَ ف to divulge

إشاعَة س rumour

أَشْبَعَ ف to satisfy

اشْتاقَ ف to miss

اشْتِباك س clash

اشْتَبَهَ في ف to suspect

اشْتَدَّ ف to worsen

اشْتِراك س (دَفْع مَبْلَغ مُقابِلَ خِدْمَة)
subscription
(المُشارَكَة في نَشاط) involvement

اشْتِراكِيّ ص socialist

اشْتِراكِيَّة س socialism

اشْتَرَطَ ف to make a condition

اشْتَرَكَ ف (شارَكَ في عَمَل مُعَيَّن) to participate
(سَجَّلَ عُضْوِيَّة في مُؤَسَّسَة) to subscribe

اشْتَرى ف to buy

اشْتَعَلَ ف to burn
اشْتَعَلَ المَنْزِل بِالكامِل The house was completely burned out.

اشْتَغَلَ ف to work

اشْتَقَّ ف to derive

اشْتَكى ف to complain

إشْراف س supervision

اسْتِياء س resentment

اسْتيراد س import

اسْتيطان س settlement

اسْتيعاب س (اتِّساع) capacity
(فَهْم) comprehension

اسْتَيْقَظَ ف to wake up

اسْتيلاء س seizure

أَسَد س ج /أُسود/ lion

أَسْر س capture

أَسَرَ ف to capture

إسْرائيل س Israel

إسْرائيليّ ص، س Israeli

إسْراف س extravagance

أُسْرَة س ج /أُسَر/ family

أَسْرَعَ ف (اسْتَعْجَلَ) to hurry
(اجْتازَ السُرْعَة القانونيَّة في السِباقَة) to speed

أَسْرَفَ ف to be extravagant

أَسَّسَ ف to establish

إسْطَبْل س stable

أُسْطُوانَة س cylinder

أُسْطورَة س ج /أساطير/ myth

أُسْطوريّ ص legendary

أُسْطول س ج /أساطيل/ fleet

إسْعاف س medical service
إسْعاف أَوَّليّ first aid
سَيَّارَة الإسْعاف ambulance

أَسْعَدَ ف to make happy

أَسْعَفَ ف to relieve

آسِف ص sorry

أَسِفَ ف to feel sorry

أَسَف س (إحْساس بِالأَلَم) sorrow
(نَدَم) regret

أَسْفَرَ عَن ف to result in

أَسْفَل ص (تَحْتيّ) bottom

أَسْفَل ظ (تَحْتَ) under

إسْفِنْج س sponge

إسْقاط س (الإطاحَة) overthrow
(إيقاع الشَيْء) dropping
(وَفاة الجَنين) miscarriage

أَسْقَطَ to drop

أُسْقُف س ج /أَساقِفَة/ bishop

إسْكان س (تَوْفير المَسْكَن) housing
(تَهْدِئَة أو تَخْفيف حالَة) relief

إسْكُتْلَنْدا س Scotland

إسْكُتْلَنْديّ س Scot

إسْكُتْلَنْديّ ص Scottish

أَسْكَنَ ف (وَفَّرَ السَكَن) to house
(هَدَّأَ أو خَفَّفَ حالَة) to relieve

إسْكَنْدينافيّ ص، س Scandinavian

إسْكَنْدينافِيا س Scandinavia

إسْلام س (الإسْلام) Islam

إسْلاميّ ص Islamic

اسْتِفْسار س inquiry

اسْتَفْسَرَ ف to inquire

اسْتَقالَ ف to resign

اسْتِقالَة س resignation

اسْتِقْبال س reception

اسْتَقْبَلَ ف to receive

اسْتَقَرَّ ف to settle down

اسْتِقْرار س stability

اسْتِقْراض س borrowing

اسْتَقْرَضَ ف to borrow

اسْتَقَلَّ ف (حَصَلَ عَلى السِيادَة التامَّة) to gain independence

(قادَ وَسيلَة سَفَر) to drive

اسْتِقْلال س (الحُصول عَلى السِيادَة التامَّة) independence

(الذَهاب) departure

اسْتِكْشاف س exploration

اسْتِكْمال س completing

اسْتَكمَلَ ف to complete

اسْتَلَفَ ف to borrow

اسْتَلَمَ ف to receive

اسْتِماع س listening

اسْتَمَرَّ ف to continue

اسْتِمْرار س continuation

اسْتِمْرارِيَّة س continuity

اسْتَمَعَ ف to listen

اسْتِنْباط س inference

اسْتَنْبَطَ ف to infer

اسْتِنْتاج س inference

اسْتَنْتَجَ ف to infer

اسْتَنَدَ ف to depend

اسْتَنْشَقَ ف to inhale

اسْتَنْفَذَ ف to exhaust

اسْتِنْكار س condemnation

اسْتَنْكَرَ ف to condemn

اسْتَهانَ ف to disdain

اسْتَهْدَفَ ف to target

اسْتِهْزاء س mockery

اسْتَهْزَأَ ف to mock

اسْتَهَلَّ ف to begin

اسْتِهْلاك س consumption

اسْتِهْلاكيّ ص consumer

اسْتَهْلَكَ ف to consume

اسْتِواء س evenness

اسْتِوائيّ ص tropical

اسْتَوْرَدَ ف to import

اسْتَوْعَبَ ف (اتَّسَعَ) to contain

(فَهِمَ) to grasp

اسْتَوْلى عَلى ف to seize

اسْتَوى ف (انْبَسَطَ) to even out

(نَضَجَ) to ripen

ا

اسْتَرْخَى ف to relax

اسْتَرَدَّ ف to retrieve

اسْتِرْداد س recovery

اسْتِسْلام س surrender

اسْتَسْلَمَ ف to surrender

اسْتَشارَ ف to consult

اسْتِشارَة س consultation

اسْتَشْهَدَ ف (قُتِلَ في سَبيل الله أو الوَطَن) to die for one's faith
to cite (اسْتَدَلَّ)

اسْتِصْلاح س reclamation

اسْتَصْلَحَ ف (أَرْضاً) to reclaim

اسْتَضافَ ف to entertain

اسْتِضافَة س entertainment

اسْتَطاعَ ف can, to be able to

اسْتَطْعَمَ ف to taste

اسْتَعادَ ف to recover

اسْتِعادَة س recovery

اسْتَعارَ ف to borrow

اسْتِعارَة س (أَخْذ شَيْء لاِسْتِعْمال مُؤَقَّت) borrowing
(التَشْبيه في العَمَل الأَدَبيّ) metaphor

اسْتَعْبَدَ ف to enslave

اسْتِعْجال س urgency

اسْتَعْجَلَ ف to hurry

اسْتَعَدَّ ف to prepare

اسْتِعْداد س (قابِليَّة) willingness
(التَحْضير لأَمْر) readiness

اسْتِعْراض س (تَقْديم عَرْض) parade
(مُراجَعَة) review

اسْتَعْرَضَ ف (قَدَّمَ عَرْضاً) to parade
(نَظَرَ في) to review

اسْتِعْلامات س information

اسْتِعْمار س colonialism

اسْتِعْمال س usage

اسْتَعْمَرَ ف to colonize

اسْتَعْمَلَ ف to use

اسْتَغْرَقَ ف to last

اسْتَغْفَلَ ف to make a fool of

اسْتَغَلَّ ف (اسْتَخْرَجَ مَصادِر مِن الأَرْض) to exploit
(اسْتَفادَ مِن شَخْص أو عَمَل) to take advantage of

اسْتِغْلال س (اسْتِخْراج مَصادِر مِن الأَرْض) exploitation
(الاِسْتِفادَة مِن شَخْص أو عَمَل) taking advantage of

اسْتَغْنَى عَن ف to do without

اسْتَفادَ ف to profit

اسْتِفادَة س gain

اسْتَفَزَّ ف to provoke

اسْتِفْزاز س provocation

اسْتِفْزازيّ ص provocative

اسْتَأْجَرَ ف to rent

إسْتاد س stadium

أُسْتاذ س ج /أَساتِذَة/ (شَخْص يُعَلِّمُ في مَدْرَسَة) teacher
(مُدَرِّس جامِعيّ بِرُتْبَة أكاديميَّة عالِيَة) professor

اسْتَأْصَلَ ف to uproot

اسْتَأْنَفَ ف (بَدَأَ بِالعَمَل بَعْدَ تَوَقُّف زَمَنيّ) to resume
(طَلَبَ رَسْمِيّاً مِن سُلْطَة مُعَيَّنَة لِتَغْيير قَرار) to appeal

اسْتِباق س anticipation

اسْتَبَدَّ ب ف to be despotic

اسْتِبْداد س despotism

اسْتِبْدال س replacement

اسْتَبْدَلَ ف to replace

اسْتَبَقَ ف to anticipate

اسْتِبْيان س (لأغْراض أكاديميَّة) questionnaire
(لِجَمْع مَعْلومات) survey

اسْتِثْمار س investment

اسْتَثْمَرَ ف to invest

اسْتِثْناء س exclusion

اسْتِثْنائيّ ص exceptional

اسْتَثْنَى ف to exclude

اسْتَجابَ ف to respond

اسْتِجابَة س response

اسْتِجْمام س recreation

اسْتِجْماميّ ص recreational

اسْتِجْواب س interrogation

اسْتَجْوَبَ ف to interrogate

اسْتِحْضار س evocation

اسْتَحْضَرَ ف to evoke

اسْتَحَقَّ ف to deserve

اسْتَحَمَّ ف to bathe

اسْتَحَى ف to feel embarrassed

اسْتِخْدام س use

اسْتَخْدَمَ ف to employ
to use

اسْتِخْراج س extraction

اسْتَخَفَّ ب ف to undervalue

اسْتَخْلَصَ ف (اسْتَخْرَجَ) to extract
(اسْتَنْتَجَ) infer

اسْتَدْعى ف to summon

إسْتِراتيجيّ ص strategic

إسْتِراتيجيّ س strategist

إسْتِراتيجيَّة س strategy

اسْتِراحَة س break

أُسْتُراليّ ص، س Australian

أُسْتُراليا س Australia

اسْتِرْجاع س recovery

اسْتَرْجَعَ ف to recover

اسْتِرْخاء س relaxation

ا

ج أَراضٍ (مِساحَة لِلزراعَة) land

أَرْضَعَ/ت ف (عَن طَريق الصَدْر) to breastfeed
to bottle-feed (بِواسِطَة قِنينَة)

أَرْضى ف to satisfy

أَرْضِيّ ص ground

أَرْضِيَّة س floor

أَرْعَبَ ف to scare

أَرْغَمَ على ف to force

أَرْفَقَ ف to attach

أَرْكَنَ ف (أَوْقَفَ) to park
to trust (وَثِقَ)

أَرْمَلَة س ج /أَرامِل/ widow

أَرْنَب س ج /أَرانِب/ rabbit

إِرْهاب س terrorism

إِرْهابِيّ ص، س terrorist

أَرْهَقَ ف to exhaust

أَريكَة س ج /أَرائِك/ couch

أَزالَ ف to remove

إِزالَة س removal

ازْدادَ ف to increase

ازْدِحام س congestion

ازْدَحَمَ ف to be crowded

ازْدِراء س contempt

ازْدَرى ف to disdain

ازْدِهار س prosperity

ازْدَهَرَ ف to flourish

آزَرَ ف to support

أَزْرَق ص م زَرْقاءُ ج /زُرْق/ blue

ازْرَقَّ ف to turn blue

إِزْعاج س annoyance

أَزْعَجَ ف to annoy

أَزَل س eternity

أَزَّمَ ف to worsen

أَزْمَة س ج /أَزَمات/ crisis

أَزْمَعَ ف to decide to

أَساءَ ف to wrong
to do badly
أَساءَ الفَهْمَ to misunderstand

إِساءَة س offence

أَساس س ج /أُسُس/ basis

أَساسِيّ ص essential
basic

إِسْبانِيّ س ج /إِسْبان/ Spaniard

إِسْبانِيّ ص ج /إِسْبان/ Spanish

إِسْبانِيا س Spain

أُسْبوع س ج /أَسابيع/ week

اسْتِئْناف س (إِعادَة البَدْء في عَمَل من جَديد)
resumption
appeal (طَلَب إِعادَة النَظَر في قَرار)

اسْتاءَ ف to resent

ا

إذْلال س humiliation

أُذُن (م) س ج /آذان/ ear

إذْن س ج /أُذونات/ permit

أَذِنَ ف to allow

أذَّنَ ف to call to prayer

أذى س harm

أذى ف to harm

أرادَ ف to want

إرادَة س will

أراقَ ف to shed

أرْباح س dividend

أرْبِعاء س (الأربِعاء) Wednesday

أرْبَعَة عد four

أرْبَعون عد forty

أرْبَكَ ف to confuse

ارْتاحَ ف to rest

ارْتِباط س connection

ارْتَبَطَ ب ف (تَعَلَّقَ بِأمْر) to relate to

(تَواصَلَ) to be connected to

ارْتَدَّ ف (ارْتَطَمَ ورَجِعَ) to bounce back

(خَرَجَ عَن دينِهِ) to apostatize

ارْتَدى ف to wear

ارْتَعَبَ ف to be frightened

ارْتَعَشَ ف to shiver

ارْتِفاع س (عُلوّ) height

(حالَة الصُعود) rise

ارْتَفَعَ ف to rise

ارْتِقاء س ascension

ارْتَكَبَ ف to commit

ارْتِياح س satisfaction

إرْث س inheritance

أُرِجانو س (نَوْع تابِل) oregano

أرْجَعَ ف to return

أرْجَنْتين س (الأرْجَنْتين) Argentina

أَرْجَنْتينيّ ص، س Argentinean

أُرْجُوانيّ ص purple

أُرْجوحَة س ج /أراجيح/ swing

أرَّخَ ف to date

أرْخَصُ ح cheaper

أُرْدُنّ س (الأُرْدُنّ) Jordan

أُرْدُنّيّ ص، س Jordanian

أُرُزّ س rice

إرْسال س (بَثّ) transmission

(بَعْث) sending

أرِسطو س Aristotle

أرْسَلَ ف to send

أرْسَلَ بِالبَريد to post

أرْشَدَ ف (نَصَحَ) to advise

(وَجَّهَ) to guide

أرْض (م) س (كَوْكَب الكُرَة الأرْضيَّة) earth

إدارَة س management

إداريّ ص administrative

أَدانَ ف (نَدَّدَ) to condemn

(أعارَ) to lend

(أَثْبَتَ تَوَرُّطَهُ في جَريمَةٍ) to convict

إدانَة س (إثْبات التَوَرُّط في جَريمَة) conviction

(تَنْديد) condemnation

(إعارَة مال) lending

أَدَب س ج /آداب/ (أَعْمال مَكْتوبَة ذات قيمَة مِثْل القِصَّة أو الشِعْر) literature

(السُلوك الحَسَن) good manners

أَدَب خَياليّ fiction

أَدَب مَسْرَحيّ theatre

أَدَّبَ ف (عَلَّمَ الأَدَبَ وَالأَخْلاق) to edify

(عاقَبَ) to discipline

أَدَبيّ ص (مُتَعَلِّق بِالأَدَب) literary

ادَّخَرَ ف to save

أَدْخَلَ ف (قَبِلَهُ في مُؤَسَّسَة) to let in

(عَبَّرَ) to insert

(أَوْجَدَ) to introduce

إدْراج س registration

إدْراك س (فَهْم) perception

(وُصول) arrival

إدْراكيّ ص cognitive

أَدْرَجَ ف to register

أَدْرَكَ ف (فَهِمَ) to perceive

(تَحَقَّقَ) to realize

ادِّعاء س (المُطالَبَة بِشَيْء) claim

(ادِّعاء المَحْكَمَة) allegation

ادَّعى ف (في المَحْكَمَة) to allege

(طالَبَ) to claim

أَدْفَأَ ف to warm

أَدْلى ب ف to give

آدَم س Adam

إدْمان س addiction

أَدْمَنَ ف to be addicted

أَدْنى ظ (مُنْخَفِض أَكْثَر) lower

(أَقَلّ) less

أَدْهَشَ ف to astonish

أَدّى ف (قامَ بِتَنْفيذ شَيْء) to perform

أَدّى صَلاة الصُبْح في المَسْجِد to perform the Dawn prayer in the mosque

(وَصَّلَ لِنَتيجَة) to lead to

التَدْخين يُؤَدّي إلى مَشاكِل صِحّيَّة Smoking leads to health problems.

أَديب س ج /أُدَباء/ author

أَديب ص ج /أُدَباء/ polite

إذا ش if

إذاً ظ so

آذار س March

أَذاعَ ف (أَعْلَنَ عَلى المِذْياع) to broadcast

(نَشَرَ خَبَراً) to spread

إذاعَة س radio station

أَذان س the call to prayer

أَذَلَّ ف to humiliate

اختِلال س (حُدوث فَوْضى) disorder
(زِيادَة الشَيْء سوءاً) deterioration

اخْتَلَسَ ف to embezzle

اخْتَلَطَ ف to mix with

اخْتَلَفَ ف to differ

اخْتَلَقَ ف to make up

اختِناق س suffocation

اخْتَنَقَ ف to suffocate

اخْتِيار س choice

اخْتِيارِيّ ص optional

أَخَذَ ف to take

آخِر ص last

آخَر ص م أُخْرى ج م /أُخْرَيات/ another

أَخَّرَ ف to delay

إخْراج س (عَمَل فِلْم) (film) directing
(تَسْريح أو تَخَلُّص) discharging

آخِرَة: الآخِرَة س Hereafter

أَخْرَجَ ف (صَوَّرَ فِلْماً) to direct
(سَرَّحَ أو تَخَلَّصَ) to discharge

أَخْرَسُ ص م خَرْساءُ ج /خُرْس/ dumb

أَخْرَقُ ص م خَرْقاءُ ج /خُرْق/ stupid

أَخِصّائِيّ س specialist

أَخْضَرُ ص م خَضْراءُ ج /خُضْر/ green

اخْضَرَّ ف to turn green

أَخْضَعَ ف to subjugate

إخْطار س notice

أَخْطَأَ ف (قامَ بِعَمَل ضِدَّ التَعاليم الدينيَّة) to commit a sin
(عَمِلَ شَيْئاً بِغَيْر شَكْلِهِ الصَحيح) to make a mistake

أَخْفَقَ ف to fail

أَخْفى ف to conceal

أَخَلَّ ف to violate

إخْلاء س evacuation

إخْلاص س sincerity

أَخْلاق س morality

أَخْلاقِيّ ص moral

أَخْلى ف to evacuate

أَخْمَدَ ف (أَنْهى بِالقوَّة) to suppress
(أَطْفَأَ) to extinguish

أُخُوَّة س brotherhood

آخى ف to treat sb like a brother

أَخير ح final

أَداء س performance

آداب س arts

أَداة س ج /أَدَوات/ (قِطْعَة عُدَّة تُسْتَخْدَمُ في الأَعْمال المِهَنِيَّة) tool
(وَسيلَة) means
أَداة التَعْريف definite article
أَدَوات التَجْميل make up

أَدارَ ف (دَبَّرَ) to manage
(وَجَّهَ) to turn

إحْصائيّ ص statistical

إحْصائيّات س statistics

أحْصى ف to enumerate

إحْضار س bringing

أحْضَرَ ف to bring

أحْمَرُ ص م حَمْراءُ ج /حُمْر/ red

احْمَرَّ ف to turn red

أحْمَقُ س م حَمْقاءُ ج /حَمْقى/ fool

أحْمَقُ ص م حَمْقاءُ ج /حَمْقى/ foolish

أحْوَلُ ص م حَوْلاءُ ج /حول/ cross-eyed

إحْياء س revival

أحْياء س biology

أحْياناً ظ ز sometimes

أحْيى ف (نَشَّطَ) to revive
(أعْطى الحَياة) to bring to life
أحْيى ذِكْرى to commemorate

أَخ س ج /إخْوَة/ إخْوان/ brother

أخافَ ف to frighten

أخْبار س news

أخْبَرَ ف to tell

أُخْت س ج /أخَوات/ sister

آخَتَ ف to treat another woman as a sister

اخْتارَ ف to choose

اخْتِبار س test

اخْتَبأَ ف to hide

اخْتَبَرَ ف to test

اخْتِتام س conclusion

اخْتِتان س circumcision

اخْتَتَمَ ف to conclude

اخْتَتَنَ ف to be circumcised

اخْتِراع س invention

اخْتِراق س penetration

اخْتَرَعَ ف to invent

اخْتَرَقَ ف to penetrate

اخْتَصَّ ف to specialize in

اخْتِصار س (تَقْليل نَصّ) abridgment
(الحَرْف الأوَّل مِن الكَلِمَة) abbreviation

اخْتِصاص س specialization

اخْتِصاصيّ س specialist

اخْتَصَرَ ف to abridge

اخْتِطاف س abduction

اخْتَطَفَ ف (أخَذَ شَخْصاً) to abduct
(انْتَزَعَ فَجْأة) to snatch
(أخَذَ طائِرَة) to hijack

اخْتِفاء س disappearance

اخْتَفى ف to disappear

اخْتِلاس س embezzlement

اخْتِلاط س intermingling

اخْتِلاف س difference

احْتِشاد س assemblage

احْتَشَدَ ف to congregate

احْتَضَنَ ف to hug

احْتِفال س (نَشاط لِلتَعْبير عَن الفَرْحَة) celebration
(مَوْقِع إقامَة الحَفْلَة) festival

احْتِفاليّ ص festive

احْتَفَظَ ب ف to keep

احْتَفَلَ ف to celebrate

احْتِقار س disdain

احْتِقان س congestion

احْتَقَرَ ف to disdain

احْتَقَنَ ف to clog up

احْتِكار س monopoly

احْتِكاك س friction

احْتَكَرَ ف to monopolize

احْتَلَّ ف to occupy

احْتِلال س occupation

احْتِمال س ج /احْتِمالات/ (إمْكان حُدوثِه) probability
(تَحَمُّل) tolerance

احْتِماليَّة س likelihood

احْتَمَلَ ف (تَحَمَّلَ) to tolerate
(تَوَقَّعَ) to expect

احْتَوَى ف to contain

احْتِياج س need

احْتِياط س (إجْراء لِتَدارُك خَطَر) precaution
(مَخْزون) reserve

احْتِياطيّ ص reserve

احْتِيال س fraud

أُحْجِيَة س puzzle

أَحَد س one
يَوْم الأَحَد Sunday

أَحْدَبُ س م حَدْباءُ ج /حُدْب/ hunch-back

أَحْدَثَ ف to cause

إحْراج س embarrassment

أَحْرَجَ ف to embarrass

أَحْرَزَ ف (سَجَّلَ نِقاطاً في مُباراة) to score
(حَقَّقَ) to achieve
(رَبِحَ) to win

أَحْرَى more appropriate
بِالأَحْرَى rather

أَحْزَنَ ف to grieve

أَحَسَّ ف to feel

إحْساس س ج /أحاسيس/ (شُعور) feeling
(إدْراك) sensation

أَحْسَنُ ح (أَفْضَل) better

أَحْسَنَ ف (تَصَدَّقَ) to give charity
(أَتْقَنَ) to be proficient in
(أَجادَ) to do well
(فَعَلَ خَيْراً) to do good

إحْصاء س enumeration
عِلْم الإحْصاء statistics

إجْراء شَكْلِيّ formality

إجْرام س crime

إجْرامِيّ ص criminal

أَجْرَبُ ص م جَرْباءُ ج /جُرْب/ mangy

أُجْرَة س (مال يُدْفَعُ مُقابِلَ اسْتِخْدام عَقار) rent

(مال يُدْفَعُ مُقابِلَ اسْتِخْدام شَيْءٍ أو جُهْد) charge

(مَعاش) salary

(وَسيلَة تُؤَجَّرُ مُقابِلَ مال) hire

أَجْرَدُ ص م جَرْداءُ ج /جُرْد/ hairless

أَجْرَمَ ف to commit a crime

أَجْرى ف to carry out

أَجْعَدُ ص م جَعْداءُ (المَلْبَس والوَجْه) creased

(الشَعْر) curly

أَجْفى ف to alienate

أَجَّلَ ف to postpone

أَجَل س ج /آجال/ (مَوْعِد مُحَدَّد في المُسْتَقْبَل) appointed time

(نَعَم) yes

أَجْل: مِنْ أَجْلِ؛ لِأَجْلِ for the sake of

إجْلاء س evacuation

إجْماع س consensus

إجْمالِيّ ص total

أَجْمَلُ ح more beautiful

أَجْنَبِيّ ص ج /أَجانِب/ foreign

أَجْنَبِيّ س ج /أَجانِب/ foreigner

إجْهاض س abortion

أَجْهَدَ ف to overexert

أَجير س ج /أُجَراء/ labourer

أَحاطَ ف (طَوَّقَ) to surround

(أَدْرَكَ) to understand fully

أَحَبَّ ف (أُعْجِبَ ب) to like

(عَشِقَ) to love

إحْباط س frustration

أَحْبَطَ ف (أَثارَ شُعور اليَأْس وَخَيْبَة الأَمَل) to frustrate

(عَطَّلَ شَيْئاً قَبْلَ حُدوثِه) to foil

احْتاجَ ف to need

احْتاطَ ف to take precautions

احْتالَ ف to cheat

احْتَجَّ ف to protest

احْتِجاج س protest

احْتِجاز س detention

احْتَجَزَ ف to detain

احْتِراس س caution

احْتِراف س professionalism

احْتِراق س burning

احْتِرام س ج /احْتِرامات/ respect

احْتَرَسَ ف to be wary of

احْتَرَفَ ف to take on as a profession

احْتَرَقَ ف to burn

احْتَرَمَ ف to respect

ا

أَتْقَنَ ف to be proficient in

اتَّقى ف to be God-fearing

أَتْلَفَ ف to damage

أَتَمَّ ف to accomplish

إتْمام س accomplishment

اتِّهام س accusation

اتَّهَمَ ف to accuse

أَتى ف to come

أَثاث س furniture

أَثارَ ف (ضايَقَ) to annoy
(أَفْرَحَ) to excite

إثارَة س (إبْهاج) excitation
(إغْضاب) irritation

أَثْبَتَ ف to prove

أَثَّثَ ف to furnish

أَثَّرَ ف (كانَ لَهُ فاعِليَّة) to affect

أَثَر س ج /آثار/ (عَلامَة) mark
(شَيْء يُدَلِّلُ عَلى شَخْص أو حَدَث) trace
(شَيْء مِن الماضي البَعيد) antiquity

أَثْلَجَ ف to snow

إثْم س ج /آثام/ sin

أَثِمَ ف to commit a sin

آثِم ص sinful

أَثْمَرَ ف (يُعْطي نَتيجَة) to yield
(يُعْطي ثِماراً) to bear fruit

أَثْناءَ ظ ز during

اثْنان عد two

اثْنَيْن س (الاثْنَيْن) Monday

أَجابَ ف to answer

إجابَة س answer

أَجادَ ف (أَتْقَنَ) to be proficient in
(أَحْسَنَ) to do well

أَجازَ ف to permit

إجازَة س holiday
إجازَة سَنَوِيَّة annual leave
إجازَة مَرَضِيَّة sick leave
إجازَة وِلادَة maternity leave

إجّاص س pear

إجْباريّ ص compulsory

أَجْبَرَ عَلى ف to force to

اجْتاحَ ف to invade

اجْتازَ ف (نَجَحَ) to pass
(مَرَّ مِن خِلال) to pass through

اجْتِماع س meeting

اجْتِماعيّ ص social
sociable

اجْتَمَعَ ف to meet

اجْتَهَدَ ف to work hard

أَجَّرَ ف to hire

أَجْر س ج /أُجور/ (مال تَأْخُذُهُ مُقابِلَ جُهْد فَعَلْتَه)
wage
(ثَواب تَأْخُذُهُ عَلى عَمَل الخَيْر) reward

إجْراء س procedure

ا

أَبْطَلَ ف to invalidate

إِبْعاد س deportation

أَبْعَدَ ف (رَحَّلَ) to deport
ف (جَنَّبَ) to eliminate
ف (نَقَلَ لِمَسافَة أَبْعَد) to move away

أَبْعَدُ ظ farther

أَبْقى ف (حافَظَ على اسْتِمْرارِيَّة شَيْء)
to maintain
(احْتَفَظَ ب) to keep

أَبْكَمُ ص م بَكْماءُ ج /بُكْم/ dumb

أَبْلَغَ ف to inform of

إِبْليس س ج /أَباليس/ Beelzebub

ابْن س ج /أَبْناء/ son
ابْن الأَخ أَو الأُخْت nephew
ابْن الزَوْج أَو الزَوْجَة step-son
ابْن العَمّ أَو الخال cousin
ابْن زِناء bastard

ابْنَة س ج /بَنات/ daughter
ابْنَة الأَخ أَو الأُخْت niece
ابْنَة الزَوْج أَو الزَوْجَة step-daughter
ابْنَة العَمّ أَو الخال cousin

إِبْهام س ج /أَباهيم/ (إِصْبَع اليَد الكَبير) thumb
(إِصْبَع القَدَم الكَبير) big toe

أَبْهَجَ ف to make sb happy

أَبْهَرَ ف to dazzle

أَبى ف to refuse

أَبْيَضُ ص م بَيْضاءُ ج /بيض/ white

ابْيَضَّ ف to turn white

آتٍ ص coming

أَتاحَ ف to grant

اتِّباع س following

اتَّبَعَ ف to follow

اتِّجاه س direction

اتَّجَهَ ف to turn towards

اتِّحاد س (تَوْحيد) unification
(الانْدِماج في جِسْم واحِد) union
(مُؤَسَّسَة تَخْدِمُ هَدَفاً) association
(اتِّحاد دَوْلَتَيْن) federation

اتِّحاديّ ص federal

اتَّحَدَ ف to unify

اتِّخاذ س taking

اتَّخَذَ ف to take

اتِّساع س broadness

اتَّسَعَ ف (زادَت سِعَتُهُ) to expand
(وَسِعَ) to accommodate

اتَّسَمَ ب ف to be marked by

اتِّصال س ج /اتِّصالات/ communication

اتَّصَلَ ب ف (خابَرَهُ عَن طَريق وَسيلَة اتِّصال) to contact
(هاتَفَ) to ring up

اتَّضَحَ ف to clear up

اتِّفاق س ج /اتِّفاقات/ agreement

اتِّفاقيَّة س ج /اتِّفاقيّات/ agreement

اتَّفَقَ عَلى ف to agree with

ا

ائْتِلاف س coalition

ائْتِمان س credit

أَب س ج /آباء/ father

آب س August

أَباحَ ف to allow

إباحيَّة س permissiveness

أَبادَ ف to annihilate

إبادَة س annihilation

إبادَة جَماعيَّة genocide

إبّانَ ظ ز during

ابْتِكار س invention

ابْتَكَرَ ف to invent

ابْتَلَعَ ف to swallow

ابْتِهاج س joy

ابْتَهَجَ ف to feel happy

أَبْجَدِيّ ص alphabetical

إبْحار س navigation

أَبْحَرَ ف to sail

أَبَّدَ ف to perpetuate

أَبَداً never

إبْداء س manifestation

إبْداع س creation

إبْداعيّ ص creative

أَبْدى ف (أَظْهَرَ) to make manifest

(عَبَّرَ وَوَضَّحَ) to express

أَبَدِيّ ص eternal

أَبَدِيَّة س eternity

إبْراز س bringing out

إبْرام س ratification

إبْرَة س ج /إبَر/ needle

أَبْرَزَ ف (بَيَّنَ) to bring out

(عَرَضَ) to show

أَبْرَشيَّة س parish

أَبْرَصُ ص م بَرْصاءُ ج/ بُرْص/ leprous

أَبْرَمَ ف to ratify

إبْريق س ج /أباريق/ jug, pitcher (US)

إبْريل س (الشَهْر الرابع بِالتَّقْويم المِصْريّ) April

إبْزيم س ج /أبازيم/ buckle

أَبْشَعُ ح uglier

إبْط س armpit

أَبْطَأَ ف to slow down

قاموس أُكسفورد الأساسي
إنجليزي عربي - عربي إنجليزي